Twelve
Doors
to Japan

By JOHN WHITNEY HALL, *Yale University*
and RICHARD K. BEARDSLEY, *University of Michigan*

With chapters by:
Joseph K. Yamagiwa, *University of Michigan*
B. James George, Jr., *University of Michigan*

MCGRAW-HILL BOOK COMPANY
New York, St. Louis, San Francisco
Toronto, London, Sydney

Twelve Doors to Japan

TWELVE DOORS TO JAPAN

25610

56789–MP–9

Preface

As an introduction to the study of Japanese culture and society, this book derives its individuality from its distinctive history. It has grown directly out of the graduate course taught for a decade and a half at the University of Michigan as a basic segment of the training program of the Center for Japanese Studies. Graduate students with special interest in Japan are introduced to the subject as seen from various academic points of view in this one-year course, known to staff and students as the Central Integrated Course (its catalog listing is "Anthropology 583–584: Peoples and Culture of Japan"). The book, like the course, has two simultaneous and equal aims: first, to provide introductory information to those who know relatively little about Japan beforehand; and, second, to acquaint students with the aims, materials, and methods of disciplines other than the one they have been best trained for by their undergraduate work.

The chapters of this work, consequently, have a purposely academic flavor. It is hoped that this will add to their interest rather than detract from it. The authors are convinced, at any rate, that academic disciplines serve to give meaning and direction to otherwise haphazard information, not to drain away the vital juices. Hence, they present the book in this form with the expectation that its value will be enhanced by its academicism. At the same time, two explicit disclaimers are made. First, the book does not attempt to offer *all* introductory information on Japan. It is not encyclopedic, and the Select Bibliographies that follow the text must be considered necessary to supplement the factual data pertinent to any field, as well as to provide a wider range of interpretations of viewpoints. Second, the book is not intended as a handy cram course in each of the social science and humanistic disciplines that appear in the chapter titles. It is not a substitute for introductory textbooks in these disciplines.

Further elaboration of this last point may prevent any prospective reader from taking hasty alarm at the academic intention avowed above.

Our writing is not directed to specialists. Persons already trained in the various fields, from geography to economics, who acquire a research interest in Japan naturally are pushing at the frontiers of their disciplines; the problems and situations that most intrigue them and their colleagues may be only vaguely intelligible to outsiders who do not share their background. Conversely, they may take for granted, as beneath discussion, points which are "old hat" to anyone with their training but which may be novel and vastly enlightening to specialists in other fields. Our aim, as already stated, is to show "outsiders" what insights and explanations each discipline furnishes for the study of Japanese culture; so each chapter is more apt to contain old-hat material than frontier material as seen by specialists in that field.

It may be difficult to defend certain chapters as fair representations of an entire discipline. Personality psychology is only one branch of a much larger field and is drawn upon only in limited degree in Chapter 8, as dictated by the aim of offering a succinct introduction to the psychological aspects of Japanese culture. Again, one might complain that philosophy has been shortchanged in Chapter 7, "Religion and Philosophy," for there is little of the speculative and metaphysical content normally taken as philosophical subject matter by comparison with the historical and sociological content. In reply, we must reiterate that the selection and emphasis were governed by our judgment of what is most valuable to nonphilosophers rather than to specialists in philosophy. The same standard has guided our treatment of every field. Each discipline has been asked to explain itself, not in the abstract, but for what it can contribute to a fuller understanding of the Japanese people and their culture.

Even though our focus is elsewhere than on current and urgent research issues, we have not hesitated to mention unsolved problems in each field. Indeed, we have sought the occasion to do so. All too often we find that students emerge from their sessions with textbooks feeling that all the answers are already in, that there are no more problems to solve. This illusion is fostered, of course, by the cunning and dexterity of scholars in hiding their loose ends and camouflaging vital issues under restrictive assumptions whenever they write a textbook. Yet the fact is that we are just becoming aware of how little we know and how poor our conceptual tools are in any of the fields—or, more deferentially, let us say *almost* any of the fields—represented here. Problems that cannot yet be explained adequately are abundant, indeed. Perhaps we have pointed to too few, but our purpose is served if the reader, on putting the book down, retains some lurking curiosity about certain of the issues dealt with.

A further problem which the authors have faced is created by the fact that conditions in Japan (social, economic, and political in particular) have been changing so drastically and rapidly in the last few years that interpretive statements, particularly as they apply to "the present situation" or to "future prospects," are subject to obsolescence at an alarming rate. Changes of viewpoint regarding the state of affairs in Japan or prognosis for the future can be reduced in essence to the question of whether one is optimistic or pessimistic, whether one paints with rosy colors or mixes in the more somber tones of skepticism. The authors in revising their work have discovered that it was first set down when the direction of Japan's postwar recovery and growth was not by any means certain. Few writers had the confidence then to predict that Japan would achieve the degree of economic prosperity, the amount of political stability, or the stature in world affairs which the 1960s have brought to it. To deny the present state of optimism would be to ignore the evidence of our eyes, yet to retain a sense of skepticism is only prudent.

Several notes should be provided here in explanation of the "interdisciplinary" framework of this book and its parent classroom course, if only because this word has acquired so many connotations. In the world of professional scholars, the term *interdisciplinary study* sometimes connotes a threat to the integrity of respectable, well-established disciplines. This fear is aroused especially by enthusiasts who wish to "unify all knowledge," canceling out its branches or somehow erasing the differences between branches. Alternatively, some claim that the humanities —art, literature, philosophy, and perhaps history—possess inviolate sovereignty, each over its own domain of thought or feeling, that cannot brook limitations or be harnessed to serve other purposes than its own, whereas the social sciences can join together, because each applies analysis to only one segment of human experience. These rather a priori and metaphysical arguments may or may not be satisfactorily answered in the body of this book; likewise, this volume must furnish its own answer, as far as possible, to the utilitarian argument that the space of one book (or the span of one course) is too brief to do justice to so many disciplines, that it can be no better than a sort of short-order counter that offers morsels and scraps torn from various richer menus.

In our view, each discipline properly should have its own integrity respected in adding to the sum of human knowledge. Being only human, we are biased more in favor of certain disciplines than of others, but we intend each viewpoint to have a fair hearing for whatever it may offer to neighboring specialists. For this reason, each chapter includes either a definitional statement of the field's characteristic methods or viewpoint or an outline of its typical subject matter, in addition to presenting a selection of representative information about Japan. Disciplines differ as much by viewpoint as by subject matter; agriculture, government, the imperial tradition, and so on may each be examined by several disciplines, each for its own uses. To avoid needless duplication, major subjects treated in one chapter have been avoided or alluded to only briefly in other chapters. As a result, we have perhaps not stressed as much as we might that overlapping among fields which is one of the most obvious avenues of interdisciplinary cooperation. Nevertheless, the effect of interdisciplinary work will probably appear to the watchful reader in any given chapter, where he will find materials or viewpoints that are not standard fare in the discipline but have been brought in from another social science or humanity field to enrich insight. In other words, while disciplinary integrity has been respected, interdisciplinary transfusions have been permitted or encouraged.

Problem areas are what must determine and define interdisciplinary cooperation. Academic fields of research cannot be forced together: they must come together for reasons of mutual interest. Art and anthropology may be combined on quite different problems than anthropology and political science; and political science, in turn, will find itself teamed with economics on issues that perhaps are of slight interest to anthropologists. In each case, the mutual support each offers the other for its research problems dictates their association, not any arbitrary decision that interdisciplinary study is a good thing. Nevertheless, profitable associations are hardly apt to develop among strangers. Therefore, we urge students to get acquainted with each other's disciplines before immersing themselves in their own special field in order to know what may eventually help them to resolve their own problems. This does not imply any amalgamation of disciplines or the creation of a new universal discipline with a single, unified presentation or viewpoint. To avoid any such misapprehension, we tend to prefer the word "multidisciplinary" over the more familiar "interdisciplinary."

Chapter order is more or less arbitrary in this book. The authors do not presume to rank disciplines as either more or less primary and immediate. Various other arrangements might be equally satisfactory. It may be said of the present arrangement, however, that it has a practical logic derived from experiment over years of teaching. It commences with subjects that have fairly concrete, visible subject matter (geography, anthropology) or a familiar scheme of coordinates (history). It then proceeds into more abstract, value-laden aspects of traditional Japanese culture (literature, art, philosophy). How this distinctive culture affects the individual and is taught to him is next considered (via personality psychology and education). Finally, the stage is held by disciplines that deal most explicitly with contemporary Japan (political science, law. economics).

But no matter what order is given to the twelve discrete and necessarily partial treatments of Japan which comprise the chapters of this book, there is still the problem of how one is to gain a conception of the "whole Japan" and of the interdependence among the disciplines into which the whole has been separated. The process by which any individual builds up his knowledge of a foreign country, if broken down analytically, will undoubtedly show a considerable movement of the mind back and forth from the general to the particular and from the parts to the whole. Ideally, therefore, a study of Japan which emphasizes its several disciplinary subparts, as we do in this book, should be backed by some prior acquaintance with the subject in its undifferentiated form. It would be hard to imagine a subject of comparable scope relating to Europe or the United States for which a minimum acquaintance would not be part of the American reader's background. With Japan the situation is quite different. While there may have been a time after 1945 when most Americans who expressed serious interest in Japanese studies were inspired by some intimate acquaintance with Japan, perhaps having lived in the country as Occupation personnel or as servicemen, today any prior exposure comes at most from a single college course or a casual and hasty tourist visit. For such readers there is much to be gained from the schedule of general reading which has become a prerequisite for students taking the Central Integrated Course at Michigan. The list of titles which appears in the General Bibliography is designed for those who might take up the study of Japan without prior acquaintance. It also includes a number of standard references which contain descriptive details which we of necessity have had to omit in the various chapters.

The authors are greatly indebted to their many colleagues and to others—not least of all to their students in the Japanese studies program—for direct and indirect assistance in the preparation of this book. In ways that will be familiar to all teachers, we have been enriched by association with our staff colleagues and visiting specialists who have contributed to the Central Integrated Course and, equally, by the perceptive response of students in the course. We wish to thank by name colleagues who in various years past prepared, revised, or constructively reviewed syllabus materials for some of the fields represented in the course: Ronald S. Anderson (University of Hawaii), George DeVos (University of California), B. James George, Jr. (University of Michigan),

L. A. Peter Gosling (University of Michigan), Charles F. Remer (East-West Center, Honolulu), Robert E. Ward (University of Michigan), Joseph K. Yamagiwa (University of Michigan), and the late James Plumer (University of Michigan). Also to be mentioned individually are former graduate students who assisted staff members in compiling these syllabus materials: Mrs. Karen Brazell, Noah Brannen, Janet S. Cowie, Harry Harootunian, Yoshio Iwamoto, Chaote Lin, Irwin Scheiner, Bernard Silberman, Robert Spaulding, and Rosita Valdez. At Yale University the assistance of William Hauser and William Massey was gratefully received. Although the present chapters for each field have been freshly written in a scope and style designed expressly for this book, certain of them may justly claim lineal or collateral descent from earlier syllabus materials. It must be emphasized, moreover, that the experience gained from using the syllabus materials as teaching aids greatly assisted the planning of all chapters included here. Finally, the chapters of this book were individually scrutinized by colleagues outside the Michigan family, and to them we owe a considerable measure of gratitude for suggestions for improvement or amplification. They are Kenneth Butler (Yale University), Otis Cary (Amherst College), James Crowley (Yale University), Douglas Eyre (University of North Carolina), Dan Henderson (University of Washington), Marius Jansen (Princeton University), Donald Keene (Columbia University), George Lee (Yale University), Herbert Passin (Columbia University), and Hugh Patrick (Yale University).

Acknowledgment by individual name is hardly possible in the case of visiting Japanese scholars who have been called on at various times for review and criticism of syllabus materials that are among the sources of the present book. Nevertheless, the tolerant yet conscientious assistance of each of these numerous associates is warmly remembered even if not separately acknowledged here.

Collaborators in joint work such as ours run the hazard of sharing collective guilt for shortcomings along with collective honor for accomplishments. We, therefore, emphasize that responsibility for the scope and content of each chapter lies with its accredited writer, not with any of those to whom our collective indebtedness has been expressed above. Chapters 4, "Language as an Expression of Japanese Culture," and 11, "Law in Modern Japan," appear here *de novo*, there being no ancestral syllabus materials in either field. The two authors bear ultimate responsibility for the overall plan of the work in addition to the chapters which they have written.

A final word of sincere thanks goes to the unsung heroines of scholarship: to Mrs. Donna Botero and Mrs. Judith Hopkins of the Michigan

Center for Japanese Studies office and to Mrs. Patricia Connor, Mrs. Bonnie Knight, Mrs. Marilyn Mulholland, Mrs. Nancy Watson, and Miss Arlene Zuckerman at Yale for preparing the manuscript at various stages under the usual urgent deadlines.

John Whitney Hall
Richard K. Beardsley

Acknowledgments

This work was originally prepared under a contract between the University of Michigan and the United States Office of Education, Department of Health, Education, and Welfare. It has since been thoroughly rewritten. The authors are grateful to both the University of Michigan and the Office of Education for their support and for permission to publish the work in its present form. Particularly warm acknowledgment is due to the Carnegie Corporation of New York; this book's genesis lies in the academic environment of the Center for Japanese Studies research and training activities, begun in 1947 and maintained since then in large part through generous grants from the Carnegie Corporation. The authors also wish to thank the following publishers and writers for permission to reprint short passages from the works listed: *The Journal of Asian Studies* for Robert Brower and Earl Miner, "Formative Elements in the Japanese Poetic Tradition"; Dorsey Press for Edward Norbeck and George DeVos, "Japan," in Frances L. Hsu (ed.), *Psychological Anthropology: Approaches to Culture and Personality;* Alfred A. Knopf, Inc., for Kenneth Yasuda, *A Pepper Pod; Language* for Edward Sapir "The Status of Linguistics as a Science"; Kenneth L. Pike for *Language in Relation to a Unified Theory of the Structure of Human Behavior;* Prentice-Hall, Inc. for Robert E. Ward and Roy C. Macridis, *Modern Political Systems: Asia;* and Princeton University Press for Robert E. Ward and Dankwart A. Rustow, *The Political Modernization of Japan and Turkey.*

Note on romanization

Japanese words are romanized according to the Hepburn system. The macron has been omitted in words, including proper names, that have passed into common American usage and are found in standard English-language dictionaries. Except in the case of nisei, personal names are given in the customary Japanese order, with the family name first.

J.W.H.
R.K.B.

Contents

3 THE HISTORICAL DIMENSION

John Whitney Hall *122*

4 LANGUAGE AS AN EXPRESSION OF JAPANESE CULTURE

Joseph K. Yamagiwa   186

5 LITERATURE AND JAPANESE CULTURE

Joseph K. Yamagiwa   224

10 JAPAN'S POLITICAL SYSTEM

Richard K. Beardsley   *428*

11 LAW IN MODERN JAPAN

B. James George, Jr.   *484*

12 ASPECTS OF JAPANESE ECONOMIC DEVELOPMENT

John Whitney Hall   538

RICHARD K. BEARDSLEY

JOHN WHITNEY HALL

A Geographic Profile of Japan[*]

INTRODUCTION

The Japanese archipelago, celebrated for its scenic charm among the lands of the earth, rather bears out the wry maxim that men may live picturesquely or live well but not both together. The land has imposed great difficulties on the Japanese, as will appear in the following pages, and it would certainly lose many of its pictorial qualities were it easier to inhabit. Yet from earliest times the Japanese have looked upon their islands as good and beautiful, accepting storm and earthquake as the unavoidable companions of a mild climate and lush vegetation. Although the aesthetic qualities of the landscape are hardly the proper concern of the geographer, a word of tribute may be permitted, in introduction, to the scenic virtues of Japan's four mountainous islands set in their temperate sea. Photography has made the Japanese scene too familiar to need depiction in words here. Let it simply be said that beauty is one widely recognized geographical feature of Japan.

Introductions to Japan usually start with the words of the geographer, for it is he who "places" the country for us and sketches in the first outlines of the nation's personality. To many of us in the United States our first knowledge of Japan comes from elementary school geography lessons. There is something rocky and basic about the elements of distance, size, shape, climate, and material life on which the geographer reports. But the geographer is not limited to statements about the physical environment. All sciences are rooted in the attempt to interpret the relations, if such exist, between two or more phenomena; relations in space are the particular province of the geographer. Various social and natural sciences may choose to comment on the same phenomena as the geographer; but geography, above all, interests itself in location or distribution as an attribute of the factors which they seek to interpret. Its subject matter may overlap those of geology and meteorology on the one side and history and the various social sciences, particularly

---

[*] Lectures by Robert B. Hall and L. A. Peter Gosling and a critical reading of the manuscript during revision by John D. Eyre have contributed to this chapter.

economics, on the other. In borrowing viewpoints from natural science at one stage and social science at another and asking their sort of questions about this subject matter, the field becomes interdisciplinary in appearance. Yet it consistently emphasizes the influence of location or of relationships that include the element of space or location.

The work of the modern geographer on Japan has passed through several phases. Physical geography and climatology early held his attention, to be followed by studies in topography and the morphology of land use and human settlement. Later on his attention turned to what he calls historical and cultural geography, and more recently to political geography and current problems in industrial location, transportation, and resource supply. Human or cultural geography has undoubtedly informed the nongeographer most richly. Its strong ecological element, interpreting the relation of society or persons or cultural phenomena to the natural environment, goes to the core of the questions which the student of culture so often puts to the geographer. It may, in fact, concern itself with purely social or cultural subjects, insofar as their locational attributes are of interest: a study of the distribution network for books published in Japan, for example, is germane to geography. In all of this, cultural geography has acquired a sophistication that goes beyond the simple environmental determinism once attributed, with some reason, to the field. Special note of this advance is needed in introducing a geographical discussion of Japan, where not a few observers seem determined to seize on some feature or other of natural environment as the key to Japanese culture or temperament.

The folklore of geographical determinism has a deep and persistent vitality. The ever-present threat of earthquakes, tidal waves, typhoons, and other natural dangers is supposed to make the Japanese fatalistic, violent, or poignantly aware of nature and its precarious beauty. The ever-visible mountains or fields are said to induce serenity; or else, depending on the theorizer, the small-scale fields and villages create an obsession with miniatures or develop a sensitivity to social nuances. Whether any modicum of truth is to be found in these popular myths about Japanese society and personality is beside the point. The geographer need only point out that the heterogeneity of natural environment in any part of Japan gives ground for a wide range of contradictory generalizations. Geography draws no simple key to insight into culture from any given natural phenomenon; but as long as people must live in some specific location, geographical study calls attention to the relation between their natural and social environment and their patterns of life.

Increasingly, however, the geographer finds himself less concerned with relations between man and his natural environment than with relationships inside human society itself. As the works of man and the web of his habitats to a growing degree overlay the natural environment and reduce his dependence upon his physical setting, the geographer must grapple with problems of human ecology, urban planning, transportation, and economic development and of their social and political consequences. Along with the economist and the sociologist, he enters the realm of social engineering as a solver of problems, not simply as a describer. In what follows we shall first review some of the older and more descriptive observations which comprise the "geographical dimension" of Japan, after which we shall inquire into the problems which stand on the frontiers of the geographer's interest in the country.

LOCATION AND AREA

The four major islands and several groups of smaller islands (totaling about one thousand) which make up Japan extend in an arc, running from the northeast to the southwest, that lies off the eastern coast of Asia. The Japanese archipelago covers a considerable range of latitude: the northern tip of Hokkaido lies north of the 45th parallel, at the level of northern Maine, and southern Kyushu touches the 31st parallel and corresponds in latitude to Georgia. This range in latitude, most of it within the warmer part of the temperate zone, provides a variety of climates but with a long and warm growing season predominant in all but the extreme north. Japan is separated from the continent by the East China Sea, Korea Strait, and the Sea of Japan and is bounded on the east by the Pacific Ocean. To the north are the island of Sakhalin and the Kuril group, now in Soviet hands. To the south lie the Ryukyu Islands, of which Okinawa is the most important. Although considered

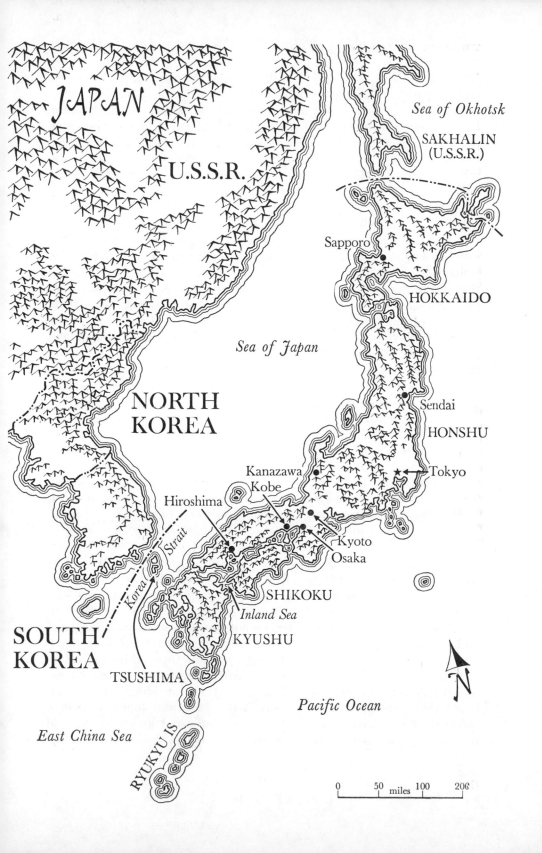

Japanese territory, Okinawa is still occupied by the United States as an aftermath of World War II.

Japan's total area is approximately 142,700 square miles. Honshu is the largest island (88,968 square miles) and the center of Japanese population and cultural development, both historical and modern. Honshu, Kyushu (15,756 square miles), and Shikoku (7,280 square miles) constitute "Old" Japan. Hokkaido (30,334 square miles) has only within the last half-century become an important area of settlement and economic development.

What do these bare facts about Japan's location and size signify? Although they constitute the hardest and most irreducible of the geographer's data, their meaning is not absolute but relative to the changing conditions of human society in Japan and in the world at large. *Today* these facts describe a medium-sized country: larger than Britain but smaller than France, slightly smaller, as is so often pointed out, than the state of California. Japan's location off the coast of Asia is strategic either for playing continental politics or for maintaining a pose of isolation. Above all it is a good location from which to develop as a maritime nation. Yet no more than 100 years ago Japan would have been described as a large country by Asian standards and the most remotely and poorly situated of all. The paucity of her natural resources was then hardly noticeable, since for the technology of the day her greatest resources, man and land, were comparatively abundant. Historically, then, "isolation" and "an amply productive land base" were the most significant aspects of Japan's location and topography. Japan was distinctly marginal with regard to Asia both culturally and geographically. Yet the land was of sufficient size so that the Japanese could support an advanced civilization despite long periods of almost complete isolation from the continent.

Today the Japanese islands have not moved or altered in size, yet the meaning of the "unchanged facts" of location has been remarkably transformed. As modern transportation has shrunk the world, isolation has been less and less a reality. Once at the end of European trade routes, Japan appeared to the nineteenth-century American traders as the "front door to China." Japan herself, once oriented toward Korea and China, has turned eastward and southward. Her Pacific-side ports and cities today have grown in size and significance, while the more western areas of the country, whose earlier prosperity reflected the western orientation of Old Japan, have lagged behind. The island homeland, once idealized for its productive land, was found so inadequate in the resources needed for modern industrial and trade expansion that Japan undertook aggressive colonial expansion. Yet today in a world of electronics and plastics it is the human resource as much as the material which has given Japan her great competitive advantage. The loss of Japan's colonies is given less thought today than was ever expected at the end of World War II.

POPULATION

Japan's population, which has risen steadily during the modern period from about 30 million in 1868, passed beyond 97 million in 1965 and is still climbing. According to current estimates, her population will cross the 100 million mark by about 1971 and rise more slowly until about 1990, when it should level off at around 108 million, if present projections hold. The density of population for Japan as a whole is today about 653 persons per square mile. Population growth before the war was concentrated in urban areas, particularly a metropolitan belt extending southwestward from central Honshu. By 1940, nearly one-fifth of Japan's population lived in her six major cities. Rural population had remained fairly stable since 1868. (In some areas it had declined, while in others, notably northern Honshu and Hokkaido, it had increased somewhat.) During the economic collapse which followed defeat in 1945, many urban dwellers moved or returned to rural areas, but this condition quickly reversed itself, and today Japan's cities are swollen far above their prewar size. Nearly two-thirds of the Japanese live within city limits today. Japan's population places her seventh in a list of the most populous nations of the modern world, behind mainland China, India, the U.S.S.R., the United States, Pakistan, and Indonesia. The density of population per square mile is higher than that of any of these nations, and Japan ranks perhaps fourth in such a list, behind Belgium, the Netherlands, and Great Britain. In density of population per square mile of *arable* land, she leads all other nations.

Population pressure has long been considered one of Japan's greatest problems. Yet we may well ask whether the country has really been overpopulated. Long habits of referring to "overpopulation" in areas of low economic development have perhaps unduly influenced our thinking about crowded Asian nations, none more than Japan. If dense peopling were a cause of economic lag, Japan's should be hindmost, not foremost, among Asian economies. Were Japan dependent upon agriculture alone, she would be in serious straits, but she is not. Industry and the services attending a highly urbanized and organized society have expanded to provide the needed employment opportunities. As it stands, employment problems loom ahead because of the youth of her population, but certainly the ratio of services to population is still low compared with that of the United States or countries of Europe. And it should not be overlooked that people are an important and positive economic resource, especially in proportion to their skills, their outlook, and the tools provided by their culture. Historically, Japan's population has been a major asset. Japan today is densely populated, not necessarily overpopulated.

TOPOGRAPHY AND CLIMATE

If, as we have observed, location and population are apt to vary in significance depending on their relations to other factors rather than being just inert "givens" in any calculation, so with the natural environment. The value of any one factor is conditional, not constant, depending on other variables. More concretely, for instance, "climate" represents not just rainfall or temperature but their proportional relation through the year (we ignore still other ingredients here, for the sake of simplicity); moreover, the significance of climate can be assessed only in conjunction with the vegetation and landforms it impinges upon. Finally, the joint significance of climate, topography, and resources in human geography depends on the cultural equipment and activities of people in the location being considered. The significance of these factors is in large part a function of the technology of the culture upon which they exert their influence.

Another problem with respect to such elements of the environment as climate is that generalizations seldom do justice to diverse actualities. To illustrate, Japan's span of latitude and intricate surface patterns create great climatic variety. A chart of the broad regional pattern of climate can hardly satisfy anyone concerned with "sensible" climate (as subjectively experienced by a person in any given location) or with crops and other things immediately responsive to climate. One reason is that every region shows considerable differences between plain, valley, and ridge or between north and south slope—enough to occasion local, microclimate contrasts as great within a few hundred yards as may be found over several degrees of latitude. Major regions differ according to their proportion of various microclimates and physiographic features rather than according to absolute or uniform contrasts. A human consequence is that ecological problems common to most or all regions— flood control, typhoon protection, erosion, expansion of farmland—get the region's or the nation's attention, whereas more nearly unique problems, such as the lack of adequate modern communication between Shikoku and the rest of Japan, tend to be submerged in the welter of otherwise pan-Japanese environmental problems. With these qualifications in mind and having called attention to the interlinked impact of climate, topography, and culture, we now turn to each separate component as the geographer sees it.

Physical Setting

The arc, roughly parallel to the eastern coast of Asia, which is formed by the Japanese islands is one part of an extensive series of such arcuate island groups known as the *circum-Pacific Ring of Fire,* the elements of which also include the archipelagoes to the north and south of Japan, the Aleutian chain, and so on around to the coasts of California and Chile. The Japanese islands are the crests of submarine mountains upthrust from the bottom of the Pacific Ocean when orogenic pressures in the area were released beneath the relatively unstable ocean floor (rather than the highly stable Asiatic landmass) in a process of vulcanism and complex patterns of faulting. The geological history of the entire Ring of Fire is roughly equivalent to that of Japan. In all its segments instability is now expressed in continued volcanic action and in constant rearrangement of rock masses, causing frequent earthquakes and tidal waves. When one element in the Ring of Fire is disturbed by earth movements, the entire series of arcs may respond to the changed tensions, with widespread earthquakes throughout the area. Japan alone experiences about fifteen hundred shocks each year; and in Japan proper there are 192 volcanoes, of which 52 have been active within historic times.

Not only the original weakness of the materials from which the Japanese islands are formed, but the present range of elevation from sea bottom to mountain peaks—about 7 or 8 miles—contributes to their great instability. Just off the eastern coast of Japan lies one of the deepest submarine trenches known, the Tuscarora Deep, where ocean depths reach 32,644 feet. Even on the west coast the Sea of Japan reaches depths of more than 10,000 feet, although the East China Sea is much shallower (only 125 to 150 feet deep in most places) and is actually a submerged portion of the continent.

Japan's arcuate form is typical of many mountain ranges throughout the world, in which curving chains of peaks intersect at points known as nodes, where there is often a complex knot of highland and mountain country. In the case of Japan, the following arcs and nodes may be distinguished: at the northern end is the Hokkaido node, at which the Karafuto (Sakhalin) and Kuril arcs from the northwest and northeast intersect with the Honshu arc; the latter runs southward from this point through most of the island of Honshu and intersects at the Gifu

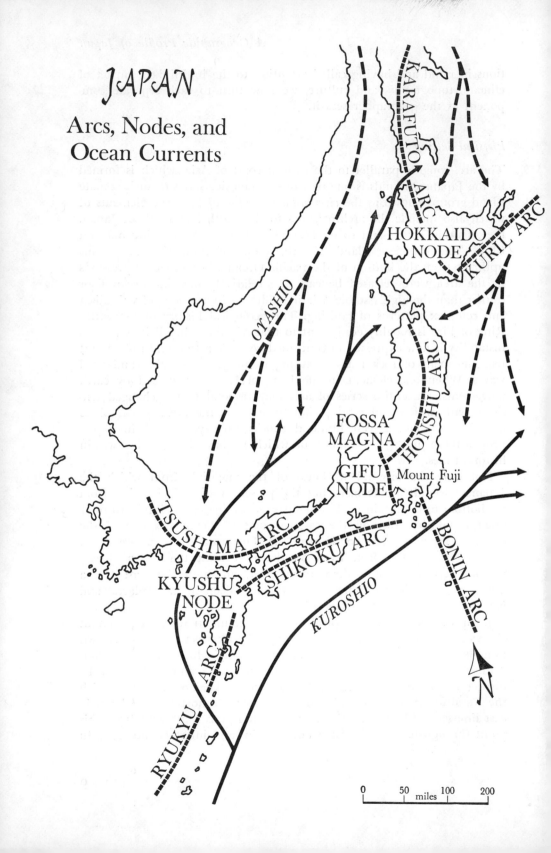

JAPAN
Arcs, Nodes, and
Ocean Currents

KARAFUTO ARC

HOKKAIDO NODE

KURIL ARC

OYASHIO

FOSSA MAGNA

HONSHU ARC

GIFU NODE

Mount Fuji

TSUSHIMA ARC

SHIKOKU ARC

BONIN ARC

KYUSHU NODE

KUROSHIO

ARC

RYUKYU

N

0   50   100   200
    miles

delta fans laid down by mountain streams as they approach the sea. Especially along the Japan Sea coast, the outer edges of the plains, consisting of finer sands, are frequently blown into dunes and ridges which parallel the coastline. Riverbeds often lie higher than the surrounding plains and are held to their courses by natural and man-made levees. Behind many of these alluvial lowlands along the coast are diluvial terraces composed of older sediments deposited by the same rivers when the terraces were at sea level and now lying some distance above the present shoreline because of subsequent uplift. The rivers have now cut shallow canyons into the surfaces of these terraces and carried much of their alluvium down to the newer delta fans on the shoreline. Among the major plains of Japan are the Kanto Plain at the head of Tokyo Bay, in which Tokyo and Yokohama are situated, the Nobi Plain at the head of Ise Bay, where Nagoya lies, and the Kinai or Settsu Plain at the head of Osaka Bay, where Osaka and Kobe are clustered. Inland plains, as mentioned above, are the result of river deposition in interior mountain basins. Many of them occur in lines of basins lying in zones of subsidence or fracture within the mountain core.

Japan has a long and complex coastline of 16,241 miles and many bays and harbors. The western coast, facing Asia, is more regular than the eastern (Pacific) coast, presumably because uplift on the west has caused the emergence of wave-eroded weak-rock formations, while subsidence on the east coast has submerged more resistant and rugged formations. The chief exception is the irregular coastline of western Kyushu, where the deep harbor of Nagasaki is located. The Inland Sea coast is quite irregular and has a number of good harbors. The southeastern coast, facing the Pacific and extending north to Tokyo, is highly irregular, but the best harbors do not occur adjacent to the most productive river-mouth plains, for the erosional load of the rivers has been dumped in sediment-filled bays in which channels must be dredged (as in the cases of Tokyo, Ise, and Osaka Bays), or else, where the coast has been depressed (on the west coast), the plains are fronted with dunes and shallow bays.

mate

rall climate in Japan is influenced greatly by major wind and her patterns, accounted for partly by latitude and partly by the pelago's relation to the Asian continent and the Pacific Ocean. untry's narrow separation from the great Asian landmass makes articipant to a considerable degree in the climates of the conr of its eastern fringe, but with softened extremes. Because node with three arcs which run southward. These are the Tsushima arc, which forms most of southwestern Honshu; the Shikoku arc, which forms the island of Shikoku and parts of southern Honshu; and the Bonin arc, which is largely a submarine ridge but emerges in the Bonin Islands southeast of Japan. Between the Tsushima and Shikoku arcs lies the Inland Sea, dividing Honshu from Shikoku and Kyushu. The Tsushima and Shikoku arcs converge at their southern ends in the Kyushu node, where they intersect with the Ryukyu arc, which forms the islands of the same name.

There is, in addition to the arcs and nodes, a further morphological feature of importance, the Fossa Magna, which cuts across the Honshu arc north of the Gifu node, from the Japan Sea to the Pacific Coast. This is a wide depressed zone caused by a fracture of the Honshu arc and now partially filled by the Fuji volcanic chain, including the famous Mount Fuji.

The above are the major features of the geological skeleton of the Japanese islands. At a level of somewhat greater detail we note, of course, a great diversity of land forms and topography, caused by subsequent folding and faulting, volcanic action, and erosion. Reflecting the orogenic origin of the Japanese islands is the high percentage of mountainous topography. About 74 per cent of the total land area has a slope of more than 15 degrees and is consequently unfit for agriculture; less than 15 per cent of the land is flat. The most mountainous terrain is in the area of the complex Gifu node, where peaʼ reach elevations of more than 10,000 feet, but a large share of interior of Japan is characterized by angular mountain country, a few upland plains. Volcanic cones and lava plateaus are also coʼ and many of them are still active, while others are now unʼ erosion. Volcanoes are most frequent in the area of nodes whe arcs intersect.

Japan's rivers, fed by plentiful rainfall, rise in the moun bone of the country and follow short courses down naʼ both coasts. The Shinano River, in central Honshu, whiʼ reaches only 229 miles. The rivers are rarely navigabʼ ness makes them good sources of hydroelectric poweʼ midcourse mountain valleys are narrow, they broaʼ limited floodplains which are the chief centersʼ interior.

Most of Japan's plains are the result of riʼ level and in mountain basins. They areʼ Plain, which forms the hinterland of theʼ and has an area of only 2,500 square ɪ bodies of land heat and cool more rapidly than bodies of water, the continent develops an immense high-pressure zone in the winter; its cold dry air streams outward toward low-pressure regions farther south and over the ocean. In the summer, the process is reversed as the land warms rapidly and warm moist winds blow toward the continent, cooling as they move north or are forced to rise over mountain barriers and dropping plentiful rain during the growing season. This simple basic pattern of rain and winds, called the *monsoon,* affects Japan along with other parts of South and East Asia. But Japan's situation, in midlatitudes and separated from the continent by the oceanic pocket called the Sea of Japan, modifies the monsoon pattern. Prevailing winter winds do come from the northwest, out of Siberia. But these cold and dry air masses, after crossing 200 to 600 miles of warm ocean surface to reach Japan, have warmed and sucked up moisture by the time they rise up the mountain slopes; accordingly, winter temperatures are milder than on the continent, although winter snows are deep on the Japan Sea coast. Snow falls in all of Japan in winter, but no entire region has heavy snowfall except the Japan Sea coast. Conversely, this region, though foggy, has less summer rainfall, owing to the reversal of the prevailing wind direction. The summer monsoon winds provide all of southern Japan with ample rainfall during the growing season and are supplemented with cyclonic storms in the early summer, which produce the *baiu,* or plum-blossom rains, and with typhoon rains in the late summer and early fall. Precipitation is heavier in the summer than in the winter in most of Japan, with the exception of the Japan Sea coast. The Inland Sea area, screened by mountains both toward the continent and toward the Pacific, escapes extremes of either the winter or the summer wind and rainfall described above; the main disturbance of its climatic serenity is fear of drought.

Temperatures in Japan, as well as rainfall patterns, are conditioned by the location of the country leeward of the huge Asiatic landmass but separated from it by moderating bodies of water. Winter temperatures are less severe than those of the eastern coast of Asia but colder than the average temperature for the latitude. The coasts, with lower elevations as well as nearness to ameliorating seas, have generally warmer winters, but the Japan Sea coast is more humid and windy than the Pacific Coast. Summer temperatures in most of Japan are quite warm (July averages in central and southern Japan are from 77 to 81 degrees F), and humidity is commonly high. The northeastern coast, on the Pacific, is cooler, thanks to the influence of the cold Oyashio (Okhotsk or Kuril Current) on the onshore winds. Japan's frost-free season ranges from 120 to 130 days in central Hokkaido to about 240 or 250 days in the south and is lengthened by the influence of the warm Kuroshio (Japan Current).

GEOGRAPHICAL REGIONS OR ZONES

Time and space are constant dimensions of human experience. Historians, by second nature, try to gain for themselves or convey to others historical insights into events and processes by dividing time into periods. Geographers, out of equally ingrained habit, mark off space into regions or zones to demonstrate relationships among particular phenomena. Neither space divisions nor time periods are ordained in nature, as are the data we have discussed to this point. They are conceptual images imposed on the space-time continuum by persons who seek thereby to capture segments that are significant units in terms of their interests and that answer their questions.

There are better and worse classifications for Japanese geography, as for any other subject matter, in respect to the subject matter itself: one classification distorts less or includes more of the whole in its scope than others, and so on. But there are also alternative classifications, each suitable for conveying insight into a different group of problems. One asks what regions exist in Japan in terms of this or that viewpoint, not merely what regions exist. No set of categories rests inherent in the subject for all time and all purposes. The best typology is one that is fruitful over a wide range of problems, yet any typology may have biases of internal logic, for it is a human product; let the user first identify such biases, then use whichever system is best suited to his questions.

One observes with interest that, in describing the regions of Japan, geography stands with one foot planted firmly in the natural sciences, the other wedged as tightly among the social sciences. A selection may be made from these two quite different approaches to classification, and an example of each is given below. The first deals with the geological structure and physiography of the land, relating it with insight to the land-building and erosional forces of nature; its outlines would be unchanged if Japan were uninhabited. The second deals with land use and ecological relations; it is a classification of human activities almost as much as of regions in Japan and stresses the social science orientation of geography.

Physiographic Regions

One method of dividing Japan by regions is to follow the gross physical morphology of the Japanese islands, using two clearly visible topographical lines. A line drawn along the central core of Honshu divides "inner" and "outer" Japan (on the west and east, respectively). A second line crossing the first and running along the Fossa Magna, an almost uninterrupted cleft across mountainous central Honshu, divides "northern" from "southwestern" Japan. The two crossed axes may be thought of as creating four physical regions. Outer Japan, in both its northern and southwestern sectors, is characterized by folded geological formations in quite regular arrangements. The rock is largely sedimentary. Inner Japan is more irregular, and faulting of its formations is more common than folding. Igneous rock and volcanic activity are more common here. The dividing line is recognized from a series of downfaulted depressions and fault scarps. The physical features of these four regions reduce to the following characteristics:

SOUTHWESTERN OUTER JAPAN. Mountains are rugged and high, with few sizable plains. Predominant rocks are crystalline schists and older sedimentaries, greatly folded; granites and younger volcanics are rare. The region includes the Akaishi Mountains of central Honshu and the slightly lower mountains of Kii Peninsula and southern Shikoku and Kyushu, ending in volcanic formations at the Kyushu node.

SOUTHWESTERN INNER JAPAN. Rugged hill country, including a series of dissected block plateaus, prevails in this region. Granite is abundant, eroding into rounded forms and slopes. Fault-block structures have associated valleys and basins. Widespread volcanic activity occurs. The highest elevations are in Hida Range (Japanese Alps), on the northern end. The Inland Sea, in a depressed area, forms the Inner-Outer border between Shikoku and Honshu.

NORTHERN OUTER JAPAN. This region embraces five segments of highland. These are the Kanto and Ashio blocks on the south, the Abukuma and Kitakami farther north in Honshu, and the Hidaka Mountains of central Hokkaido. All are uplifted, tilted, dissected peneplains, commonly of gneiss, crystalline schists, older sedimentaries, and intrusive rocks. Volcanic piles are prominent in central Hokkaido, where the Outer Zone is intersected by the Kuril arc.

NORTHERN INNER JAPAN. This region comprises two parallel ranges of hills and mountains separated by a series of fault basins. The more eastern range, which forms the watershed of northern Japan, is composed of recent sedimentary strata over a core of gneiss and granite, capped by volcanic cones. The more western range is similar but more varied in altitude.

Although major physiographic zones give insight into the geological structure of Japan, thus laying a basis for understanding soils and to some extent the "sensible" physical environment, they do not take into account important physiographic and cultural variations contained within them. All the zones are primarily mountainous or hilly, and all contain scattered plains and centers of population. But the topography within each is extremely diverse, with numerous local variations. Numberless subzones exist in each prime zone, comprising types that are repeated all over the country, giving a kind of homogeneity through the repetition of the same variations. This is also true of climatic varieties. Topography and climate undoubtedly limit to some extent the ways of life possible within a given locality, but relatively few patterns of life come clear on the basis of purely geological or physiographic considerations.

Cultural Regions

The regional terminology most commonly used by Japanese reflects, instead of this extremely technical base, human and cultural factors more closely linked to historical traditions of land use, settlement, and even political organization. The prime territorial units of Japan until modern times have been the sixty-six provinces, known as *kuni*. Established as political divisions in the eighth century, they continued to hold some semblance of administrative significance until the sixteenth century, though the provincial system which brought them into existence had all but disappeared several centuries earlier. As administrative entities and as units of folk custom and folk grouping, the *kuni* tended to acquire separate personalities based on their geographical features and the regional peculiarities of their settlement. Many *kuni* were in fact distinct regions based on one or more agricultural plains and separated from adjoining provinces by rings of hills or mountains. For many centuries, therefore, the *kuni* held definite regional meaning for the Japanese. Today, of course, they have been merged into the larger prefectures (to, dō, fu, and ken, of which there are forty-six) and have lost much of their contemporary meaning.

Still widely used today, however, is another set of terms which also had its origin in the eighth century. These are the larger regional combinations of provinces known as circuits (dō), of which, if the central provinces were excluded, there were traditionally seven. The conception of these larger units has undergone some change, particularly after the fifteenth century. Today the standard nomenclature, beginning in the north, is as follows: Hokkaido, Tōhoku, Kanto, Chūbu (including Tōkai, Hokuriku, and Tōsan), Kinki, Chūgoku (sometimes divided into San'in and San'yō), Shikoku, and Kyushu. In the popular mind these regions have acquired distinctive characteristics which stem from a composite of physical environment, climate, and cultural history. Usages

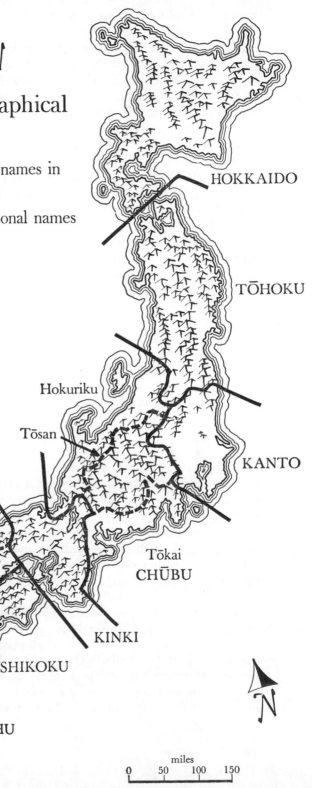

JAPAN
Cultural-Geographical Regions

CHŪBU — Regional names in modern usage

Tōkai — Premodern regional names

HOKKAIDO

TŌHOKU

Hokuriku

Tōsan

KANTO

CHŪGOKU
San'in

Tōkai
CHŪBU

San'yō

KINKI

SHIKOKU

KYUSHU

N

miles
0   50   100   150

for this reason tend to be imprecise: for instance, one tends to read into the term *Kinki* much of the history of the old home provinces as well as its geographic characteristics; Kanto (the region around Tokyo), though now the growth center of Japan, still carries the aura of being a frontier area where the samurai first came into prominence.

The present prefectures created after 1871 have been in use long enough to have acquired a certain amount of individual identity too, about in the way the states of the United States have built up personalities derived from their major cities or the chief features of their topography. One can easily imagine the day when automobile license plates in Japan will carry such phrases as "Akita—land of heavy snows," "Nagano—mountain vacationland," "Okayama—peach prefecture," and the like. Again we should reiterate the observation that these popularly assigned regional tags are true only in a limited sense and are worthy of our attention chiefly because they are so common in the modern Japanese vocabulary. Regions, if they are to be meaningful to the geographer, must have more measurable criteria upon which they are based. And since regions emerge as the geographer scans the Japanese geographical scene with some particular criterion in mind, he is most apt today to think in terms of land use and industrial-urban development; in other words, in terms of the interplay between human activity and natural resources. We now must turn to these two areas of the geographer's analysis of Japan.

RESOURCES AND THEIR UTILIZATION

As we have stated, it was not until the nineteenth century that the Japanese became acutely aware of the meager resources with which nature had endowed their homeland. The narrowness of the land base was probably not felt until perhaps the eighteenth century. Japan today holds a low-middle position among modern nations in area and a high-middle rank in population and has a favorable location in the temperate zone, but her rugged topography limits her arable land to a little more than 15 million acres, or 16 per cent of her total area. As a result, the pressure of her modern population on such restricted land resources is very great, and Japan's man to arable-land ratio of about forty-two hundred persons per square mile is the highest in the world. Arable land is pocketed in the small coastal plains and upland basins which are the centers of agricultural production and population for their regions. Virtually all arable land is under cultivation, and current efforts to create new fields in the mountains or on the sea borders are not expected to pay their cost. Though soil is seldom of top quality,

Japanese crop yields are among the highest in the world, owing to a favorable climate with ample rain in the summer growing season, the abundant use of natural and chemical fertilizers, and the intensive use of labor. But despite all efforts to increase arable acreage and its productivity, Japan has had since just before World War I a food deficit, and since that time from one-fifth to one-fourth of her imports from overseas and from her former colonial possessions have consisted of foodstuffs.

The paucity of arable land is somewhat compensated for by the resources of the sea. Parallel to the eastern coast of Japan, the warm Kuroshio flows northward, creating a suitable environment for sardines, mackerel, tuna, and other warmwater fish. Off the coast of northeastern Honshu the Kuroshio meets the cold, southward-flowing Oyashio, so that salmon, herring, cod, and crab abound. Particularly from this area off northeastern Honshu and from other coastal waters come the seafood resources which are so important in the Japanese diet and also make up a share of Japan's exports.

More recently the Japanese have discovered that the mountainous character of their islands can bring certain advantages. The steep mountain slopes with their numerous swift and short rivers provide a reasonably high hydroelectric potential, which the Japanese are now exploiting to the full. Lack of large storage basins rather than lack of water created a perennial dry-season electric power crisis prior to World War II, but today the active building of dams and more particularly the expansion of thermoelectric plants have remedied this weakness. Although the per capita generation of electricity is less than one-third of that of the United States, it is greater than that of any other Asian nation.

Resources capable of contributing to Japan's development as an industrial nation were probably the most critical shortages which Japan faced after 1868. Domestic minerals and other industrial raw materials are almost all in short supply. Coal is not plentiful and is of poor quality; the main producing area is northern Kyushu, but reserves in Hokkaido are now being exploited. High-grade coking coals for heavy industry must all be imported and were formerly acquired from China, Manchuria, Korea, and Indochina. Japan is now dependent primarily upon the United States. Petroleum resources are extremely limited, and today Japan must import 98 per cent of her oil and petroleum products, much of them from the United States. The two major domestic sources, neither very rich, are in western Hokkaido and northwestern Honshu, in a strip along the Japan Sea coast. Iron resources can supply only 5 per cent of Japan's needs today. The major deposits are in Hokkaido, and a few are scattered in northeastern Honshu. Manchuria and Korea were important sources of iron ore; Japan now looks to the United States, Malaysia, India, and the Philippines. Among the other major minerals, Japan is adequately supplied only with copper, limestone, and sulfur. Lead, zinc, and phosphate and potassium materials for fertilizers must all be imported, along with most of the minor industrial raw materials.

Japan's forest resources are also inadequate to meet modern needs, although over half of the country (55 million acres) is forested. The forests fall in three major zones: (1) boreal forests, spreading over northern and eastern Hokkaido and parts of Honshu, contain spruce, fir, larch, and birch; (2) mixed forests cover most of Honshu south to the Tokyo region with both deciduous and coniferous trees; and (3) southern forests of pine, broad-leaved evergreens, and deciduous trees (mostly oaks) cover the rest of the country. About 60 per cent of the mixed forests consist of brush or fuel woods, unsuitable for building purposes. Wood is needed in Japan for domestic building, for utensils and fuel, and for pulp used in paper and rayon production. Before the war Japan obtained both timber and wood pulp from Sakhalin and also imported about 30 per cent of her pulp from North America and Scandinavia. Fiber resources, for the textile industries, are also deficient. Wood fiber must be imported in large part, and other textile fibers (e.g., cotton, hemp, flax, and jute) once grown to some extent are now imported almost in their entirety. Virtually no wool or leather is produced in Japan, and production of silk fiber, a mainstay of economic growth during the early period and an important supplementary crop on Japanese farms, has lost much of its importance as the world market has diminished.

These are the resources with which Japan has had to develop her economy and support a culture of growing complexity. The pattern of resource utilization, to which we now turn, has both its dimension in time and its dimension in space. This concept can best be understood by tracing a series of zones of increasing intensity of utilization without reference to the geographic regions we have described above.

LAND-USE ZONES

Suppose that, instead of viewing Japan as so many sculptured islands bounded by uninhabitable and featureless water, one pictures the archipelago as a field for receiving televisionlike pulsations from "transmitters" lined along the Inland Sea. Depending on the height and orientation of mountains and other barriers to reception as well as on distance, one might then draw in a Core Zone of excellent reception, a Periphery of fair reception, and a Frontier Zone reached only intermittently by the Inland Sea pulsations. This fanciful image approximates the actual roughly concentric zones surrounding a Core area which appear when we focus attention on land use. The Core Zone is a belt roughly west to east in orientation which takes in all shores of the Inland Sea with their hinterlands and loops farther east to include eastern Honshu as far as Tokyo. This belt was the center of the earliest agricultural settlement of Japan and the region of fullest cultural and economic development throughout history; from it, people and ideas and modes of organization filtered out to more isolated regions. Our review will show that it has been the area of greatest rural population density and of most intensive agriculture; agricultural developments elsewhere in Japan are just beginning to challenge this traditional preeminence. The Core Zone, meanwhile, maintains its integrity when we shift our attention from traditional to recent conditions of resource utilization: it contains nearly all the metropolitan centers of Japan with populations of more than 400,000 (the exceptions since 1960 are Sapporo and Sendai in the north); it has the most highly developed communication and transport facilities and the bulk of the complex industrial installations and is the center of intellectual and artistic activity. The zone is not a region of uniform topography or climate or of concentration of natural resources. Its unity is derived historically from the relative ease of internal intercourse and trade, coupled with close access to continental stimuli, but it preserves much of its integrity today.

Surrounding the Core Zone is what can be termed a Periphery; and farther out toward the fringes, both south and north, is a Frontier Zone composed of southern Kyushu and northern Honshu. Hokkaido, a hinterland of trade with non-Japanese aborigines (the Ainu) until the late nineteenth century, has only recently been developed with agriculture, lumbering, fishing, and industry. Each successive zone, outward from the Core, shows a decreasing intensity of land use.

Agricultural Land Use

Agricultural land use may be considered first, drawing on the study of Ogasawara Yoshikatsu, deviser of this concentric-zone classification. The Core Zone is characterized by highly developed irrigation systems; the use of unlikely lands for paddy rice, even those high on mountain slopes; rice grown for cash as well as for subsistence; high yields per acre; extensive double-cropping; specialized production of various cash crops, particularly near urban centers; considerable reforestation; and land reclamation, which was largely completed by 1600. Correlated with these features are the long history of this area, its importance as the political and cultural center of the nation, and currently its position as the industrial and commercial heart of the country.

Surrounding the Core region and somewhat isolated from it by mountain barriers and poor transportation facilities, the Peripheral Zone includes the Japan Sea side of southwestern Honshu, the Kii Peninsula, southern Shikoku, and a belt across central Kyushu. This is a region of relatively long occupation but historical isolation. Where transportation facilities have improved, patterns of land use tend to develop toward those of the Core region. Elsewhere this zone generally has fewer large irrigation systems and more recently built ones; lower yields per acre; less extensive double-cropping (despite the fact that parts of the Periphery are farther south and have a longer growing season than parts of the Core); a lower percentage of land devoted to irrigated paddies; later and incomplete reclamation, especially of less desirable lands; and a greater development of subsistence crops, such as millet, as opposed to diversified cash crops,

Still further isolated from the Core is the Frontier Zone of Old Japan, where intensiveness in agriculture is even less marked. This region includes both far northern Honshu and the southern part of Kyushu. The inclusion of the latter area is significant in that it indicates the limited effect of latitude and growing season alone as the prime determinants in the regionality of Japan. In southern Kyushu double- and even triple-cropping are practiced; but agricultural techniques have not been perfected, and yields per acre are quite low largely because of the infertile soils. On the northern frontier, there is almost no double-cropping in some sections. Other features of both parts of this Frontier Zone are the limited extent of reclamation, the high ratio of dry fields to paddies, the extent of natural forests and pastureland, and the concentration of subsistence crops to the almost total exclusion of cash crops.

Partial but striking alterations to this pattern have begun to appear in Tōhoku in post-World War II decades. Today agricultural yields in northern Japan are among the highest in the country. Multiple causes are responsible, including scientific research on cold-resistant and quick-ripening rice strains, a new spirit rising from the farmland reform of 1947, and a commercial demand for specialty dry-field crops emanating from cities in the south. Less highly developed agricultural lands are also in some instances more responsive to new mechanized techniques of cultivation which have been gaining ground in Japan.

Hokkaido's northern position outside the range of the typical subtropical climates of Japan sets some limits on agriculture: only one crop can be grown per year, and some crops do not thrive in the climate, while others produce lower yields than farther south. The recency of the island's development also has its effects: Hokkaido is not so crowded as the rest of Japan; its farms are larger and rely less on the reclamation of poor land; and there is still extensive grassland and pasturage, especially in the most recently settled eastern part, where some ranching is actually practiced, along with subsistence agriculture. The more accessible and longer-settled (also warmer) western half of Hokkaido is more nearly similar to Old Japan, with smaller farms, diversified cash-crop production, and considerable land reclamation.

Agricultural Practices

Having recognized that Japanese farmers differ from one region to another in what they or their ancestors have done to the land to make it more or less useful, we should turn to consider the cumulative significance of agriculture in Japanese life and economy. Under the regional variations is one common pattern, that of "intensive agriculture," comprising parallel scales of landholding and methods of getting out crops, the most universal of which is rice. The pattern of intensive agriculture extends the length and breadth of Japan, excluding only the segments of Hokkaido noted above.

Agriculture may still be Japan's leading industry in capital investment and net value of product, though its share of the national income is considerably below that of manufacturing. Though deeply rooted in traditional ways, it has nonetheless successfully kept pace with the demands of modernization. Despite the scarcity of arable land, Japan's 15 million cultivated acres produce between 70 and 80 per cent of her domestic food supply and employ about one-third of her population. There are close to 6 million farm households in Japan, with an average farmholding of only 2.5 acres. Japan's arable land could not possibly go so far toward supporting her people as it does were it not for ameliorating factors of plentiful rainfall in the primary spring and summer growing seasons, a temperate or subtropical climate with a long growing season, and abundant fish resources; to which we must add innumerable ponds and canals to store and manage water (whatever the rainfall), the development of productive crops (whatever the climate), the utilization of soybeans and other protein substitutes (whatever the catch of fish), and finally, abundant human labor. Japanese farming has applied great inventiveness and effort to make the most of its natural potentialities.

Even large landowners in Japan seldom own much land. Whereas American methods can hardly support a family normally with as little as 125 acres of good land, holdings above 125 acres are rare indeed in Japan. In fact, the present land laws restrict the total holding which a farmer may own to about 7.5 acres in all areas but Hokkaido. There is variation in the average size of farms: in Hokkaido, where the land is not yet overcrowded and climatic conditions make intensive rice cultivation uncommon, the average farm covers 12.5 acres; but in the heart of southwestern Japan, holdings in some areas average only 1.5 acres. Farms consisting only of unirrigated land, often referred to as upland fields, are more common in the north and are less productive, since they lack the highest yielding crop of all, rice; they are consequently somewhat larger even in the central southwest.

The small Japanese farm is usually made up of still smaller plots, some of them irrigated and others dry, lying scattered around a rural village of clustered houses and outbuildings. These small plots, generally marked off from each other by a raised margin even in absolutely level land and having to be tended more like gardens than like farm fields, cover from one-tenth to one-fourth of an acre each. A typical farmer has from ten to twenty of these fields.

Scarcity of land is reflected in the size of farmholdings, in crops planted, and in intensive techniques of cultivation. Lowland paddy fields are carefully leveled and surrounded by mud-lined earth margins or dikes, with intricate networks of narrow irrigation canals threading between the fields. The lower slopes of diluvial uplands are sometimes leveled in the same way and terraced, either for dry crops or for rice where irrigation is feasible. Fields are planted carefully and neatly, and land between fields or surrounding farmhouses is used for odd crops or for fruit trees. Multiple-cropping is practiced wherever possible and particularly in the south. One-third of Japanese farmland is double-cropped. Paddy land is replanted wherever the growing season is long enough, as it is in the south, and where fields can be successfully drained. From 30 to 40 per cent of paddy land is planted in winter crops of wheat, barley, rape, beans, or legumes. Upland fields vary more in the extent of double-cropping possible, again according to climatic conditions, but also according to the crop planted—mulberry and tea as upland crops in central Honshu and fruit orchards farther southwest permit only one crop each year. Where upland double-cropping is practiced, a summer crop of various vegetables, often planted in alternating rows, is usually followed by a winter crop of wheat, barley, or legumes. In the suburbs of major cities, there is intensive vegetable gardening in unirrigated fields, and the ratio of land harvested to land cultivated is between 2.4 and 2.7 to 1; that is, each acre produces an average of about two and one-half crops yearly.

The intensive use of fertilizer, especially in upland soils, further increases the productivity of the land. Chemical fertilizers are now almost universally used in greater quantity than stable straw, woodlot scrapings, and such organic fertilizers. Farmers store night soil (human excrement), animal manures, compost, and chemical fertilizers in varying proportions in cement cisterns, with water, and after decomposition pour the liquid around the growing crops; only the soil supporting each plant is nourished. Fertilizer accounts for about 20 per cent of the cost of agriculture and about 35 per cent of the cash expenditures of the average farm family.

Perhaps more important than any of these other techniques as a means of increasing yields is the intensive use of human labor. There is about one agricultural worker to each acre of cultivated land, and the hours of labor arc long and arduous. Only recently has the entire national economic situation begun to make extensive mechanization practical, and even animal power has only limited use. Small gasoline and electric motors, however, are now available and are used on more than half of the farms to run irrigation pumps, small threshing machines, and other equipment. About one-sixth of the farm families now use motorized cultivators. Additional machinery, generally in forms devised in Japan, is making headway not only in cultivating and processing crops but in easing household chores. Even so, this reduces only by fractions the labor-intensive patterns of crop growing.

Though Japan is only at the edge of "Monsoonia," center of the world's rice production, rice dominates her agriculture. Its high yield per acre is an attractive feature where land is scarce and climatic conditions are so favorable. In 1960 rice covered about 56 per cent of the cultivated land, and other cereals 21 per cent; rice made up 45 per cent of total farm income. Rice is grown in irrigated fields in all parts of Japan except northern and eastern Hokkaido. It has long been supposed that by the beginning of the twentieth century the Japanese had reached the limit of efficiency in the production of rice. Yet in the last two decades numerous advances have improved production often in considerable ways. For instance, recently developed quick-ripening strains, first used in the north, have begun to make double crops of rice feasible where they had once been impossible.

Probably no form of agriculture is more intensive than that which grows two crops of rice on a single field. When double-cropping is practiced on rice-paddy land, seedbeds are prepared and flooded in April; rice shoots are nurtured there for forty days, to the point of harvest of winter crops in June. Then the shoots are transplanted in perfectly straight rows in the flooded fields and carefully weeded, fertilized, and cared for until the harvest in late October or November. Threshing and polishing go on for the next month, but not before the fields are replanted as they were in June. Where crops other than a second planting of rice follow the first, the paddy fields are kept dry and hoed up into ridges and furrows. On the ridges a fast-maturing plant, such as radishes, may be planted immediately and harvested when the major winter crop, usually wheat or barley, is planted along the ridges. In the furrows another crop, such as eggplant, may be growing. After its harvest, while the grain is still maturing, a further crop, perhaps cucumbers, can be put in its place, so that in the winter alone the paddy produces four crops—radish, eggplant, grain, and cucumbers—each occupying about half of its area for part of the period. This kind of combined interculture and multiple-cropping is practiced primarily in the Core region, where land use is most intensive and urban markets are available for such vegetables.

The several techniques mentioned above for intensifying land use and the judicious choice of the most productive crops for each type of land have combined to give Japan yields per acre for several of her major crops which are among the highest in the world. Japanese rice yields are two to four times as large as those of Indochina, another rice producer, because of improved varieties and intensive techniques. Wheat and barley yields were from two to three times as great as those of the United States before the very recent boom of agricultural technology in the latter country.

Japan has specialized in food crops, mostly for domestic consumption and principally in rice. More than four-fifths of the cultivated land is under various foods. Scarcity of productive land and a large and expanding population require that the land produce as many calories per unit as possible. For this reason, industrial crops are not an important part of the pattern, and industrial raw materials which might be grown at home are imported. Tobacco is the chief domestically produced crop of this variety; it is grown everywhere but in Hokkaido. Rape, hemp, flax, reeds, rushes, peppermint, sugarcane, fibers for native paper, and other similar crops are grown to a lesser extent. The mulberry bush, used to feed silkworms, occupies 9 per cent of the total cultivated area, and its product is second in value only to rice. It is grown everywhere south of the 39th parallel but is concentrated in central Honshu, where it occupies foothills, diluvial terraces, sandy beach ridges, and levees, areas which could not easily support other crops. Tea is grown in small patches on uplands and slopes, primarily in central Japan.

The livestock and dairying industry in Japan is still limited, though rapidly growing. Much of the countryside is too steep for pasturage, and wild grasses are unnourishing, while the moist climate is not suitable for better varieties of planted grass. Moreover, land planted in food crops yields six or seven times as many calories as would be produced by cattle fed on grass planted in the same unit, and the high land values prevent most farmers from entering the livestock industry. But it is no longer true that milk and milk products are distasteful, and demand is growing as it did earlier to transform the one-time aversion to meat, backed by Buddhist tradition though it was, into a regular market demand. The number of milk cows has increased fourfold in the last ten years and now stands at roughly one million. Most protein for the Japanese diet, however, still comes from certain vegetables, especially soy in a variety of preparations, and from fish. Cattle and horses are kept primarily as draft animals and manure producers, and the typical farm family has no more than one such animal. Dairying is most plentiful in Hokkaido, where beef cattle are also raised in limited numbers, but very many farmers in Old Japan as well are now fattening beef cattle or keeping a milk cow as a cash venture. There are few hogs, sheep, or goats but rather large numbers of poultry.

One of the most significant products of the Japanese farm has been raw silk. The process is of course partially industrial, but it starts on the farm with the raising of silkworms by feeding them the leaves of specially cultivated mulberry bushes. The cocoons produced by the worms are sold to factories, which reel them into raw silk. Sericulture is also an intensive occupation, requiring not only the careful cultivation of mulberry bushes but the picking of leaves and the routine of feeding them to the silkworms. Raw silk is historically important as having saved the balance of trade and having added to farm incomes at critical times in Japan's early economic modernization. In the 1930s, when world demand for silk was high, more than 30 per cent of Japanese farm households engaged in sericulture as a subsidiary occupation. In postwar years, partly as a result of shifting markets but principally because of the development of synthetic fibers, raw-silk production has fallen below half of the 1930 index, and only about one-ninth of the farms are engaged in sericulture. A most recent surge in silk production reflects the capacity of the Japanese themselves to purchase clothing and other articles made of silk, since silk retains its prestige in Japan as a luxury fabric. As subsidiary cash crops, fruits, vegetables, and milk have largely taken the place of mulberry.

Fishing has traditionally been of major importance to the Japanese, and in modern times the fishing industry has become a big business.

27

Fish is the second most important element in the Japanese diet and one of the country's primary exports. Japan takes from the sea more fish than any other country, or about 18 per cent of the world's haul. All told, something under 700,000 persons are involved in fishing; 90 per cent of them are engaged in small-scale coastal fishing, with traditional boats and equipment, operating out of fishing villages. These small coastal fishermen account for only 20 per cent of the annual catch, however, while deep-sea fishermen, with large boats and modern equipment, fish in the politically troubled waters toward Korea or in the North Pacific and have developed rich tuna fisheries in the South Central Pacific. Sardines and herring are the most important fish in value and quantity and are used in oils, meals, and fertilizers, but many food fish are caught for domestic consumption and for export.

Chapter 12, "Aspects of Japanese Economic Development," will have some more general remarks to make about the role of agriculture in the overall growth of the Japanese economy. Specific attention should be given at this point, however, to the pattern of agricultural development over the last 100 years, for while Japan shares with the rest of East Asia an intensity of farming based on a large input of manpower, elaborate irrigation, and heavy fertilization, the Japanese farmer has been able to modernize this intensive technology to an extent still unknown in neighboring countries. The fact that agricultural production increased by nearly 40 per cent during the 1950s at the same time that farm population dropped by more than 10 per cent is perhaps the most startling indication of what the Japanese farmer has achieved.

It is probably safe to assume that traditional agricultural technology had reached a level of production as high as that of any area in East Asia during the Tokugawa period (1600–1868). While regional distribution of the highest levels of production was not uniform, the country had achieved a number of areas of peak complexity in integration between agricultural and commercial economies. The Japanese of the nineteenth century, moreover, shared a remarkable receptiveness to new methods and an ability to adjust themselves to new conditions. After 1868 a series of revolutionary changes hit the agricultural sector. Reforms of the land laws and the tax system put landownership in the hands of cultivators, created a free market in land, and levied in place of the old produce tax a uniform monetary tax. Simultaneously the government took the lead in establishing agricultural research stations and directing the latest scientific insights into improvement of farm technology, toward understanding soils, crops, fertilizers, and pesticides, and toward bettering hygienic conditions. For these and other reasons agriculture underwent a remarkable improvement from the

1880s to the 1910s, including, for instance, a near doubling of rice production per unit of area and the startling development of sericulture. Agricultural surplus, as is well known, carried government finances and the early phase of industrial growth through the first decades of Japan's economic modernization.

As Japan acquired a colonial empire and the new industrial sector of the economy expanded, agriculture decreased its contribution to the growing income. Several factors also began to affect adversely the health of the agricultural community: the importation of rice from Korea, the growing tenancy among cultivators, and the stagnation of farm incomes while industrial wages rose. The collapse of the silk market in the late 1920s was a serious blow to the independent farms. By 1940 nearly 70 per cent of Japanese farmers were full or part-time tenants, and nearly 30 per cent owned no land. Rents were in the neighborhood of 50 to 60 per cent of the crop. Agrarian unrest leading to tenant strikes or protests had been a problem since the 1920s.

Wartime food shortages in urban areas and the consequent rise in farm prices aided the Japanese farmer, but in 1945 his situation was still poor. In 1946 the Occupation sponsored a land reform law to relieve the pressure on farmers who were tenants or part tenants. The law, which went into effect in 1947, required absentee landlords to sell all, and resident landlords all but 17.6 acres, of their agricultural land to the government for redistribution to former tenants, who would pay the state in small installments over a number of years. To protect those who would remain tenants, the law required that rental contracts, formerly mostly oral and based on the crop itself as payment, should be in writing, for a stipulated period, and payable in cash. The cash rental was put at a lower ceiling, approximately 25 per cent of crop value in rice and 15 per cent in other crops. By 1951, 3 million part or whole tenants had purchased 4.5 million acres from their former landlords, and only 1.6 million acres were still tenant-operated, under improved conditions. In recent years, farm tenancy has run 10 per cent, which is considered a rate necessary for turnover in most countries. This redistribution of land gave independence but preserved a farm population on barely viable holdings. It was assumed by many that these conditions were better for the health of the village communities but that little improvement could be expected in farm income, production, or the man-land ratio. The forecast was unduly pessimistic.

The last twenty years have seen changes in Japanese agriculture which some observers have described as revolutionary. Improved pesticides and cheaper commercial fertilizers, mechanization (perhaps 1 million rototillers were in use by 1961), the steady improvement of water-control techniques and the use of new lands for orchards and pasture, a greatly expanded market for agricultural products, and a steady drift of the farming population into new occupations have begun to change the complexion of the Japanese farm. While there seems to be no likelihood that there will be a wholesale integration of farmlands into large highly capitalized and mechanized holdings, as happened in Europe, a propensity toward amalgamation of fields and the easing of the intensity of human labor through small-scale mechanization have made Japanese farms more productive per individual worker. Meanwhile, the drift into the village of new consumer equipment (electric rice cookers, television sets, refrigerators, motor bicycles, solar water heaters, etc.) has given a new look to rural life.

A feature of Japanese farm life which should never be lost sight of is that few farm families are entirely dependent upon farming for their income. In premodern times cottage industries occupied the hands of villagers in the off-seasons. In modern times industry has frequently gone more than halfway to put itself within commuting distance of village sources of labor. Moreover, with the development of modern means of transportation, few villagers can claim to be beyond walking distance to a bus or train line which can lead to factory or office work. In the community of Niiike in Okayama Prefecture studied a decade ago, 90 per cent of the households reported members engaged in non-agricultural work, while 50 per cent received income from city jobs as store clerks, mill hands, office workers, or teachers. The life of the villager in Japan today, except perhaps in remote Frontier areas, has become increasingly involved with the expanding urban way of life not only through the interdependence of income sources but through the universalizing influence of state education, the popular press, radio, and television.

INDUSTRIAL DISTRIBUTION

The scarcity of industrial raw materials has presented Japan with many critical problems in modern times but not to the point of crippling her capacity for industrial growth. In fact, Japan has a great variety of mineral and energy resources, so that minor needs have been met from time to time or in terms of purely local dimensions. But the great industries subsist in large part on imported raw materials.

Of the major metallic resources, Japan's copper output most nearly meets her overall needs. Today about half of the active mines in the country are copper mines. They produce some 88,000 tons of ore, or about two-thirds of Japan's needs. In addition, sulfur, zinc, clay, and lime are mined in sufficient quantities to meet national requirements. The Matsuo mine in Tōhoku and the Yanahara mine in Chūgoku are well known for their production of high-quality sulfur.

Japan produced only slightly more than 1 million tons of iron ore in 1961, or about one-twentieth of her needs. The best mines are in northern Honshu and Hokkaido, but the quality of the ore is poor. The search for iron was one of Japan's main incentives for continental expansion. Today she is actively involved in locating and developing mining operations in Malaysia, the Philippines, Latin America, and India. In the latter country Japan is actually providing technical assistance and equipment for the development of new mines along with capital contributions from the United States. This new variety of overseas venture contrasts markedly with the prewar effort to seek Chinese sources of iron by political and military means.

Japan's annual coal production of about fifty million tons ranks her eighth in world production but meets only half of the needs of her industry. The coal is generally of poor quality, and the deposits are hard to get at, so that heavy mechanization is impractical. Japan is almost entirely lacking in important supplies of coking coal and anthracite. A further difficulty is that the major mines in Kyushu and Hokkaido are far from the major industrial centers. Recent attempts to locate and exploit oil and natural gas reserves have yielded some results, but oil production fills hardly more than 1 per cent of Japan's needs. The transportation of crude oil is one of the main items in Japan's marine transport, and it is the availability of plentiful sources of oil in the United States and the Near East which has converted petroleum into the principal source of industrial energy used in Japan today. Massive new harbor facilities for giant tankers combined with storage and refining facilities now dot the Inland Sea coast, making this one of the most spectacular industrial developments of the 1960s. The availability of oil has also had a profound effect upon the production of electrical energy. Today nearly half of Japan's electrical capacity is produced thermally, much of it by burning petroleum.

The distribution of Japanese industry, as can be imagined, depends not so much on the location of domestic sources of raw materials or power as on the availability of workers and deepwater ports. While there is some variation for individual industries, most industry is concentrated along what has been called the *urban-industrial axis,* in almost the same area which is included in the Core region of most intensive agricultural land use. This industrial belt runs along the Inland Sea and extends from northern Kyushu eastward and northward to Tokyo. It is characterized by the highest value of industrial production, the greatest variety of industry, and the greatest degree of urbanization in Japan. Within it are 53 per cent of the cities with populations greater than 25,000, and before the war from 75 to 80 per cent of Japanese industrial employees worked in this zone. There is no single internal reason for its preeminence in the industrial structure. A chief factor in its advantage is its accessibility to coastal ports and hence to the overseas trade routes that have so markedly colored Japan's modern development. But the region had also been the long-time center of premodern Japanese culture, which gave it well-developed agricultural hinterlands and nearby supplies of surplus rural labor, as well as better land communications systems than are found in the rest of the country. It was within this area that the new government established itself in 1868 at Tokyo, and from it radiates not only the older highways established during the Tokugawa era but the best of the modern roads and railways. The area has no special accessibility to power resources, although some of the nation's best coalfields are found at the western end of the belt, and the eastern end is relatively close to the hydroelectric power resources of central Honshu. Because Japan must import most of her industrial raw materials, the industries tended to congregate near good ports rather than in the regions in which limited raw-material supplies are found.

Within the urban-industrial belt are four areas of special concentration:

1. The Kanto Complex, coincident with the Tokyo-Yokohama (Keihin [1]) conurbation, includes Tokyo, Yokohama, Kawasaki, and twenty-four lesser cities. It contributes about 25 per cent of the nation's industrial output. The complex is close to good hydroelectric sources and to the Jōban coalfield. Yokohama is its port, the largest in imports in Japan. The Kanto Plain is also Japan's largest. This great complex is a center for a variety of industries, especially heavy manufacturing industries (metal, automotive, electrical appliance, machinery, chemical) and the publication industry.

2. The Nagoya (Chūkyo) Complex, at the head of Ise Bay, includes Nagoya and eighteen or more lesser cities. Its share of the national industrial output is about 10 per cent. The complex is situated on a large plain, with no local coal resources but with access to the hydroelectric power of central Honshu; its harbor has recently been improved and is strategically located on the Tōkaidō Railway. Most of its indus-

---

[1] A common practice of the Japanese is to combine the first characters of two place names to form an abbreviation standing for a double urban complex. The characters are pronounced in their "Chinese" form; hence the abbreviation is not recognizable to one unfamiliar with written Japanese.

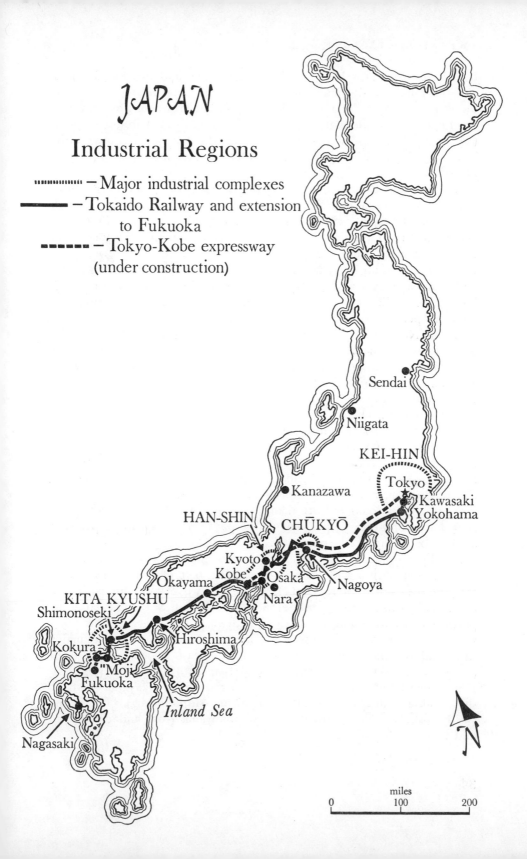

JAPAN

Industrial Regions

.... — Major industrial complexes
——— — Tokaido Railway and extension
    to Fukuoka
- - - - — Tokyo-Kobe expressway
    (under construction)

Sendai

Niigata

KEI-HIN

Kanazawa

Tokyo

Kawasaki
Yokohama

HAN-SHIN   CHŪKYŌ

Kyoto

Kobe

Okayama   Osaka   Nagoya

Nara

KITA KYUSHU

Shimonoseki

Kokura   Hiroshima

"Moji
Fukuoka

Inland Sea

Nagasaki

N

miles
0   100   200

tries have up to now been on the smallish side, and textiles, ceramics, and other light industries dominated the scene even during the prewar buildup of heavy industries. Today Nagoya has grown in both size and the importance of its manufactures. A major integrated iron-steel plant (Tōkai Steel) is under construction near the port of Nagoya, while in nearby Toyota is Japan's leading automobile-assembly plant (Toyota Motors).

3. The Kinki Complex, covering the Osaka-Kobe (Han-shin) conurbation, is on Osaka Bay. It includes Osaka and Kobe, which are both ports, and Kyoto, as well as ten or eleven smaller cities. Both its rail and its water shipping facilities are good, and its plains are good-sized. Formerly textiles were the leading industry, but in the prewar years this area became an important center of production for metals, machines and tools, and iron and steel. Kyoto is primarily a craft center, carrying on the traditional industries of Old Japan. This complex produces about 20 per cent of Japan's industrial output.

4. The Northern Kyushu Complex, near the primary coalfields, is the one area which in prewar years was more industrial than urban in its prime function. In 1963 five northern Kyushu cities (including Yawata, Kokura, and Moji) were merged into a single large city, Kita Kyushu, which ranks seventh in population in Japan, with more than 1 million inhabitants. The government steel mills of Yawata have long dominated this industrial complex, and in prewar Japan accessibility to Manchurian iron resources and to continental colonial commerce gave this particular location special importance. Coal mines, iron and steel industries, and shipyards continue to predominate. There is little textile production, and most factories are large and modern. The area's share of the national industrial output has now fallen to about 4 per cent, but it produces 33 per cent of the pig iron and 40 to 50 per cent of the steel domestically processed.

Not by any means as congested as these major centers but highly concentrated over a wide area is the entire belt of Core Japan from the Kanto to northern Kyushu. It comprises two prime regions: Tōkai (from Tokyo to Nagoya) and Setouchi (the Inland Sea). The latter in particular is undergoing dramatic growth in recent years as new ports are created and industrial lands reclaimed from the sea. The major industrial centers along this Core belt from east to west are Hitachi (copper and electrical appliances), Fuji (paper), Hamamatsu (textiles), Himeji (electrical equipment), Hirohata (iron mills), Okayama (textiles, shipbuilding, and petroleum), Onomichi (shipbuilding), Hiroshima (shipyards), Iwakuni (petrochemicals), Tokuyama (coal and chemicals), and Niihama (metals and chemicals).

Some industries should be mentioned as not being concentrated in any particular fashion or even restricted to the industrial belt. The primary example of a scattered industry is silk reeling, which is found wherever mulberries and cocoons are produced. The filatures are generally small, hiring only 120 persons on the average, and are situated in rural towns. There are few north of the Kanto, since little sericulture is found north of the 40th parallel. Some concentration is found in Gumma and Nagano Prefectures. Silk weaving, now largely for the domestic market, is also found in small family workshops in many small towns and is rarely much modernized. Cotton spinning and weaving are more often concentrated in the industrial belt, where the work is done in larger establishments with more modern equipment, but cloth for the domestic market is frequently woven in small plants located in the lesser cities of the industrial belt. Some new industries, such as those making chemicals and plastics, are placed where they have ample soft water rather than out of concern for the raw-material supply or labor. Many traditional Japanese craft industries are similarly scattered or are concentrated in the regions where they have traditionally been located.

The heavy industries, as we have seen, are located almost entirely in the industrial belt, within which they have tended to concentrate in certain areas, though this pattern is now breaking down. Pig iron production was formerly found primarily in northern Kyushu, but with expansion of the industry it has spread to Osaka, Yokohama, Nagoya, Chiba, and Muroran, which is near important coalfields in Hokkaido. Steel production itself remains heavily concentrated in the northern Kyushu area, but the machine and tool industries operate in large modern plants in the Kinki and Kanto regions. Shipyards are located in all the four major complexes; and some of the world's largest ships are being built between centers in the Inland Sea yards, enlarged in postwar years. Economic planners look with considerable favor on the spread of industry outside the congested urban complexes, and today government encouragement is widely given to voluntary attempts to disperse industries and move factories into less highly built-up regions.

URBAN DEVELOPMENT

Today industrial location and the structure of its growth are heavily interrelated with the pattern of urban development. Urbanization had a considerable start in Japan before 1868. Probably more than 10 per cent of the Japanese at that time lived in cities of 10,000 inhabitants or more. Edo, the capital of the shoguns, may once have had 1 million inhabitants; Osaka and Kyoto were cities of 300,000 or more; and Kanazawa and Nagoya had populations of about 100,000.

The most important preindustrial towns grew up around the administrative offices and castle strongholds of feudal lords. They served as political and cultural centers of considerable agricultural hinterlands. Their populations were large because of bodies of armed retainers and groups of servants and artisans which were assembled in them. Many such castle towns (jōkamachi) were to continue as administrative centers of present-day prefectures, and some have survived as production centers of local specialities. Other preindustrial towns of some note were post towns, along the routes between Edo and the outlying castle towns; and temple towns, tourist centers around important religious establishments. Temple towns have persisted with unchanged functions, though they have tended to shrink in comparative size. Most post towns declined with the introduction of railroads.

In any event, it was only with the overlay of modern economic functions (industrial, commercial, or financial) that the older cities were transformed into modern metropolises. The largest of the modern cities are no longer purely administrative or service centers but serve a variety of functions. Multifunction cities which emphasize industrial, financial, service, and cultural activity are most common in the Core Zone. In the Peripheral Zone, the multiplicity of functions is more limited, and emphasis is more apt to be placed on general service and transportation coordination for a given local region. Mining and similar extractive functions have given rise to sizable cities in the Frontier Zone, and the frequent tendency is for regional administrative functions to settle in the same location.

The 1960 census indicated that six cities had populations of more than 1,000,000; these were Tokyo (8,300,000), Osaka (3,000,000), Nagoya (1,600,000), Yokohama (1,400,000), Kyoto (1,300,000), and Kobe (1,100,000). Kita Kyushu, created in 1963, has a population of roughly 1,000,000. There are an additional forty-six cities with populations of more than 200,000. All the main cities have distinct personalities. Tokyo, the capital of Japan, is a metropolis of about the same size as London. Centered upon the remains of old Edo Castle (now the Imperial Palace), it contains the greatest concentration of government buildings; is the headquarters of financial, insurance, industrial, and commercial firms; and serves as the center of mass communication, education, art, and entertainment. Yokohama is a port city serving Tokyo. Osaka is considered a businessman's city, and though its life and functions are extremely varied, its mood is to a large extent set by the textile industry. Kobe, the foremost port in central Japan, has something of a cosmopolitan aura by virtue of its having once been a treaty port. Nagoya, once the castle town of an important *daimyō,* has developed so recently as to have a reputation of being particularly "modern." Kyoto, the old court capital, retains its status as a cultural center and major tourist attraction to the Japanese. Of the newer cities, Sapporo, capital of Hokkaido, is unusual for having been built to a regular plan. The city has something of the frontier atmosphere about it.

The Japanese are the most highly urbanized people in Asia. As we have noted, more than two-thirds of the Japanese live within city limits (a Japanese city is by definition a community of 30,000 or more persons). The ratio is constantly growing, and the press of population upon the already highly urbanized area continually increases. Tokyo is growing at a rate of 300,000 annually (half of the nation's annual population increase), and Core Japan continues to attract greater numbers of individuals at the expense of other parts of the country. Many areas are losing population to the already built-up Core, and northern Japan (Tōhoku and Hokkaido) remains far below its potential development. The so-called "densely inhabited districts" of Japan, defined by a concentration of 10,000 or more persons to the square mile, find 44 per cent of the Japanese in an area so small that it covers just 1 per cent of the total land surface.

The Japanese cities tend as yet to be poorly organized and to sprawl over large areas. Substantial multistory buildings are found only in the centers of cities, and the skyscraper is avoided for fear of earthquakes. Transportation, supply, and distribution of services constitute the major problems of the new cities. Yet there is a dynamism about cities like Tokyo, Osaka, and Nagoya that stems from their constant evidence of growth and construction, which forever gives the appearance of incompleteness. One recent writer has called Tokyo the "Purest of All the Great Cities" on the ground that it most intimately responds to "the zest, the excitement and the personality created by its people. . . . Tokyo is the only great city in the world that has escaped the dread dullness of metropolitan zoning and economic segregation. . . ." [2]

Despite their modern façades Japanese cities have a capacity for looking exotic to the American visitor. Unlike the great (and old) cities of Europe, Tokyo and Osaka retain very little evidence of their historic pasts. In Tokyo only fragments of Edo Castle remain. In Osaka the great castle of Hideyoshi has been rebuilt of ferroconcrete as a tourist

[2] A. M. Rosenthal, " 'Purest of All Great Cities,' " *New York Times Magazine,* May 5, 1963.

attraction. Traces of history, except in places like Kyoto and Nara, have been erased by numerous fires, earthquakes, and the devastating bombings of World War II. On the other hand, the contrast between modern (or Western) and traditional is everywhere visible. While there is no "old" and "new" city dichotomy, as in so many Asian cities (especially those in areas once colonized), there tends to be a much more heterogeneous mixture of land use and contrast between styles of architecture. Behind the modern department stores of Tokyo or Osaka are alleys of wooden structures housing restaurants, bars, and specialty shops.

The great cities in Japan have passed through many cycles of growth and dislocation. Urban problems early in the twentieth century were primarily those of squalor, poor sanitation, inconvenience, and fire hazard. Today the chief problems are those of overcrowding, congestion, smog, and poor transportation. Of these, the transportation problem is apparent to all who have visited Tokyo. The sudden postwar increase in automotive traffic in itself has created a problem of major dimensions. Small wonder that Tokyo's urban planners are now frantically attempting to devise a rational long-range plan for regional development of the metropolitan area.

TRANSPORTATION AND COMMUNICATION

Japan's roads and railroads, air and shipping lines, telephone and radio broadcasting systems are an increasingly important part of her "social overhead." Most observers agree that this side of Japan's economic development has not kept up with the production sectors. Roads, railroads, and shipping routes were developed at a rapid rate by both state and private investment in the early phase of Japanese modernization, the railroads serving the more modern sector and the roads the more traditional sector of the economy. Then came years of heavy military budgets up through World War II, followed by budgets slanted to reconstruction (in decreasing amounts) and to social welfare (in growing amounts). In the wake of these new trends of public expenditure, transportation was somewhat shortchanged, and Japan now is at the brink of having to decide how far to stretch the old network, with its weak links, and how much to renew and modernize.

Japanese roads, first systematically developed by the Tokugawa government, are far from up to date by modern standards because of the ruggedness of the topography as well as of the early modern emphasis on railways as the chief means of land transport. They are probably the weakest link in the system of transportation. In premodern times the Japanese relied chiefly on coastal shipping for bulk transport, so that roads were limited to foot and packhorse travel. The Tokugawa rulers built a network of post roads to connect their capital (Edo, now Tokyo) with the territories of the *daimyō*. These domains were scattered along the coasts on the various agricultural plains, and the road system for the most part also paralleled the coast. The major elements in the system were the Tōkaidō, from Tokyo to Kyoto along the coast; the Nakasendō, from Tokyo to Kyoto through the interior; the Nikkōkaidō, connecting Tokyo with Nikko in Tochigi Prefecture; the Ōshūkaidō, from Tokyo to Utsunomiya; and the Kōshūkaidō, connecting Tokyo with Shimosuwa in Nagano Prefecture. Under the new regime after 1868, intensive railway development, often along routes much the same as these Tokugawa trunk roads, overshadowed highway development.

By 1939 there were only 5,340 miles of nationally maintained roads, very little more than there had been fifty years before. Paving proceeded very slowly. Highways deteriorated during the war, and some were destroyed. In the early years of the Occupation, a five-year program of highway improvement was undertaken under the Ministry of Construction, a new organ of the postwar government. In 1947, at the beginning of this program, there were only 6,000 miles of national roads and a total of 621,400 miles of roads of all types, with most of the mileage in cities and towns. Only 1 per cent of the mileage was paved, and motor transport was still of minor importance. Most of the roads were narrow, winding, and steep; they served for horse carts and three-wheeled motorcycle delivery trucks but badly for larger vehicles. Beginning with huge freight trucks and ostentatious passenger buses, however, vehicular traffic has grown to crisis proportions. By 1962 there were 2 million automobiles in use in Japan. In response to national needs, at present writing, one wide modern highway is linking Nagoya with Osaka, and planning has proceeded on an expressway southward from Tokyo, deterred mainly by the cost of thrusting through one mountain range after another. Tokyo and other major cities are developing circumferential highways and through arteries.

Whereas the early modern government of Japan neglected highway development, the building of railways with Western equipment and technical advice began almost immediately after 1868. In 1869, a loan was floated in England to finance the first stretch of railroad from Tokyo to Yokohama, which was completed in 1872. By 1889, the government, following the route of the old Tokugawa highway, had constructed the Tōkaidō line connecting Tokyo and Kobe. Privately capitalized spur lines and loops were built in various regions. In 1892, legislation was passed to finance a greatly expanded government program of railway construction, and in 1907 the main railway system was nationalized. By 1947, there were 15,904 miles of railroad in Japan, 14,000 of them state-owned. This gave Japan more miles of track per unit-area than the United States.

Japan's railways, like her roads, reflect the ruggedness of her interior topography, and most lines parallel the lower coastlines, while secondary lines cross the mountains to connect the Pacific and Japan Sea coasts. Grades are frequently steep, there are a great many tunnels, and the tracks are rarely straight for any great distance. The tracks are narrow-gauge, and the rolling stock therefore is small and lightweight.

Railway transportation is critical for passenger movement, leaving much cargo transport to coastal shipping, although freight cargoes increased during the war as coastal steamers were impressed into military duty. There was a good deal of damage and deterioration of railway facilities and rolling stock during the war, but by 1950 rehabilitation was under way. Electrification has been a major postwar improvement on certain central lines. The first major broad-gauge electrified railroad was begun in 1961, and now a line which hurtles express trains at the rate of 120 miles per hour connects Tokyo and Osaka, cutting the time between these two cities to slightly more than three hours.

Japan, an insular country with its population primarily littoral and with some 758 seaports, makes much use of coastal shipping. On the other hand, there is little transport on her short swift rivers. On the quiet Inland Sea, even small boats can carry freight between the various ports. After World War I, there was a steady expansion of the merchant marine until in the 1930s Japan ranked behind only Britain and the United States in this field. About 15 to 20 per cent of its shipping tonnage was engaged in coastal trade. After 1937, much of the civilian shipping was placed under government control. During the war many coastal ships were diverted to ocean shipping, and domestic freight shifted to the railways; since that time coastal ships have been unable to regain their former lion's share of freight carriage. But Japan's merchant fleet ranks fifth in the world, and in 1956 Japan became the foremost shipbuilding nation.

Commercial air transportation began in Japan in 1922. In 1929 the important Japan Air Transportation Company was established, and by 1938 it had 9,575 miles of air routes and dominated the industry. In 1938 the government fostered the merger of existing air companies into a semigovernmental organization monopolizing commercial air transport, domestic and international. In 1941 civil aviation was put under government control, and many civilian aircraft took part in the war.

In 1945 the Occupation banned all flying by Japanese, and until 1950 there was no domestic civil air transportation. Now Japan Air Lines carries passengers between Japan and the United States or Southeast Asia and is competing for passengers with Pan American through the lure of Japanese hostesses en route.

TRADE AND EXTERNAL RELATIONS

With the mention of transportation we return to the subject of foreign trade and Japan's economic relationship with the outside world. It is well known that the most significant element in Japan's ability to attain a high level of economic development on the meagerest of resource bases is her voluminous import-export trade. Trade today accounts for 20 per cent of the country's gross national product and is of even greater significance to individual industries. Japan's pattern of trade relations with foreign countries and the relationship of trade to her domestic industrial structure have gained in complexity since 1858, when the first commercial treaties were signed with Western powers.

In keeping with the trend in other developing countries, this pattern has passed through several phases. During the early decades the import of finished goods (cotton, thread, and cloth) and the export of raw materials (raw silk and copper) and foodstuffs (tea) predominated. From the 1890s to World War I, imports of raw cotton, iron ore, petroleum, and machinery increased, while Japan began to export cotton, textiles, and yarns. After World War I, cotton-textile exports came to exceed those of raw silk. By the 1930s, Japan began to export chemicals and machinery. The great change in the structure of foreign trade came after 1950, by which time Japan was exporting greater quantities of iron and steel products, machinery, appliances, and chemicals than of cotton fabrics. Imports were by then predominantly oil, raw cotton, iron ore, and foodstuffs. During the same period of roughly a century, Japan went through a complete cycle in her relations with foreign countries: from isolation (before 1854) to the creation of a colonial empire in East Asia (by 1910), to the attempted creation of a bloc economy (during the 1930s and 1940s) heavily reliant on China as a major producer of cotton and iron ore and as a major market, and finally to the post-World War II situation, in which Japan has become increasingly interrelated with the United States and other nations outside the Communist bloc.

Today the structure of Japan's trade is typified by the fact that among her imports only 15 per cent consist of goods wholly manufactured, whereas 90 per cent of her exports are finished or semifinished goods. To the United States Japan exports pottery, porcelain, stain-less-steel ware, sewing machines, cameras, radios, television sets, and ready-made clothing. To Southeast Asia Japan no longer sends primarily cheap cotton and rayon goods but rather factory equipment and machinery. In such other areas as Europe and Latin America, Japan finds herself competing for the same markets as other industrialized countries, chiefly Britain, Germany, and the United States. It is a triumph of Japanese industrial and engineering advance that Japanese manufacturers are now being called upon to deliver ships, rolling stock, and precision tools and instruments in competition with European manufacturers. Most recently Italian industry paid Japanese electronics the supreme compliment of imitating Japanese products.

CONCLUSION

At the outset of this chapter we made some impressionistic comments on the scenic beauty of the Japanese islands. We conclude on yet another subjective note which takes us beyond the verifiable observations of the geographer. One cannot escape the sense of dynamic change, of movement, growth, and congestion, which everywhere characterizes the human scene in Japan today. Even in rural areas where once bucolic villages seemed unaware of the city bustle, new highways are being cut through the countryside and television antennas bristle on thatched rooftops. In the cities or in the new areas of industrial development new construction is so much in evidence that preparation for the future seems everywhere to crowd out the possibility of satisfaction in the present. As we shall note in Chapter 12, the statistical evidence of Japan's modernization is startling enough, for Japan has expanded her economy during the last century literally at the fastest rate of any major world power. But it is the evidence of cultural change, of the great social and political upheaval, and of the new intellectual ferment which everywhere impresses one in his travels through Japan. Modernization is not a new phenomenon either in Europe or the United States, and for this matter the process has been at work for over a century in Japan as well. Yet one senses that the Japanese along with the rest of the people of Asia have been confronted by a revolution in culture as well as in technology, and we are startled to discover how well the Japanese have met both of these challenges.

Prior to World War II, books on the geography, economy, or the contemporary scene of countries such as Japan or China made a considerable point of describing the contrasts between the "Oriental" or "traditional" aspects and the "Western" or "modern." Frequently the modern was talked of as being a veneer, a thin overlay, the durability of which was not at all apparent. The question of whether any "Asian" society could successfully or permanently modernize itself was left open, and many a skeptic claimed that the evidence, even with respect to Japan, was not sufficient. The vigor of Japan's modern sectors was not questioned. What was in doubt was whether the social and particularly the political institutions which have supported modern economies in the West could also be created in Japan.

Since World War II, more particularly since 1952, when it began to appear that Japan had successfully pulled herself out of the wreckage of the war, most observers have been willing to state with some confidence that Japan has in fact "become modern" to the point of irreversibility. Beginning with economists and geographers (but yet to be followed by political scientists), scholars have expressed confidence that a major (and permanent) breakthrough has been achieved. Perhaps the economists have been the first to postulate a tangible and measurable set of criteria which can mark the difference between a state of cultural traditionalism and that of modernity. And indeed it does appear that the difference between a society bounded by a static conception of social or economic organization and limited by its natural environment and a modern economy in which the growth power of capital and industrial surplus is able to nourish its own further expansion is one of kind, not degree. Has Japan then achieved that state of economic growth which is self-generating and hence vaulted over the limitations of inadequate resources and seemingly uncontainable population pressures? Are now the only limitations those found within the minds and desires of the Japanese which could come from a failure of nerve or the subsidence of the will to excel? The geographer who witnesses the creation of great petrochemical works and steel mills along the Inland Sea on land reclaimed from the sea as giant dredges scoop up the ocean floor to make the solid earth upon which new factories are to be built and to deepen the channels through which the largest ships in the world will pass, can hardly think otherwise.

Today there are two aspects of the way of life of the majority of the Japanese people which strike us as significant. One is that the standard of living has reached such a level that there is no longer any question of whether there will be enough food, clothing, or shelter. The Japanese have now come to expect almost as necessities items which were once considered luxuries. The Japanese diet has begun to absorb more meat and milk. In the kitchen electric and gas appliances predominate. There are now washing machines, rice cookers, and refrigerators. Three-quarters of the urban families own television sets, and nearly everyone has a radio. Leisure and cultural pastimes are now as much the expectation of the urban intellectual in Japan as in the West.

The second aspect is that whereas a generation ago one had the feeling that the old and traditional (the native) was accommodating itself to modern ways, today one feels that it is the modern which has begun to find a place for the old and the characteristically Japanese. The boom in tourism as Japanese flock to their own historical sites, the fantastic prices paid for Japanese works of art, original or in reproduction, and the development of the modern novel and movie based upon traditional themes are all evidence that the contemporary resident of Tokyo can think of himself as a citizen of the world and yet remain proudly Japanese.

Whether Japan can continue to move in the direction in which it is going seems now to be the major concern of the geographer rather than whether the contemporary scene is real or not. And here the geographer must share his concerns and thoughts for the future with the urban planner, the transport engineer, the social worker, the specialist in finance and foreign trade, and particularly the student of Japan's politics and international relations. Japan's continued success as the foremost industrial nation in Asia, the only truly modern Asian nation, depends on both the health of her society at home and her relations with the rest of the world.

Whether one ends a discussion of Japan's prospects for the future on an optimistic or a pessimistic note depends these days in large part on one's assessment of world conditions as a whole. Growth and prosperity are everywhere visible in Japan, yet it is worth noting that the Japanese writers tend to be more suspicious of the future than the American. This is in some measure the result of a long habit of the Japanese intellectual to question whether anything good can come out of a capitalistic organization and to distrust government, big business, and the intentions of the great powers. His remembrance of the wartime disaster is still fresh, and before that there were periods of depression and labor unrest. It may be well to ask some of the questions which can arise in the minds of the geographer in this less optimistic mood as he looks upon the present prosperity in "new Japan."

Rapid economic growth, industrialization, and urbanization, while bringing to more Japanese the results of an economy of plenty, also create new and complicated problems. Today the older generation complains of urban congestion, a whole generation of Japanese brought up to scorn the values of their parents (to expect a life of material ease, for instance, rather than to take pride in a virtuous and frugal life), and new social and personal tensions arising from the obsolescence of old patterns of behavior, from the changing balance between urban and rural life, or from the gap in generations. What happens as the structure of the family is still further destroyed, or if the hold of the conservative political parties gives way to a Socialist victory? Growth and prosperity are creating political, social-structural, and value problems in an ever-compounding fashion at home, while abroad Japan is becoming enmeshed in world affairs in an ever more complex and sensitive fashion. In sum, only through the continued ability to solve social, political, and international problems of great complexity can Japan hope to avoid future difficulties.

RICHARD K. BEARDSLEY

Cultural Anthropology:
Prehistoric and Contemporary Aspects*

INTRODUCTION

The prime function of the cultural anthropologist in the study of
Japanese culture is to draw attention to relationships among its various
segments. Few if any other disciplines make as great a point of discovering how the grand facets of a culture fit together or how they are
related to the smaller, more intimate parts. The subjects discussed in
this chapter therefore range between extremes and yet are hopefully
drawn together under the unified concept of *culture*. At some times
we take a quite general view, for instance, when discussing cultural
origins or the overall style of Japanese life and thought. Elsewhere we
examine the organization of households or daily community activities
as small segments of the total society or, more correctly, the total
culture.

The concept of culture which is central to the anthropologist's approach has been treated and defined in multitudinous ways during the
last century: a list of 257 definitions, for example, was once compiled by
Alfred L. Kroeber and Clyde Kluckhohn. Running through most definitions, however, is the sense of interrelation among the parts of a culture, particularly the recognition that change at any one point has
many-sided consequences. The effort to grasp the "whole culture" of a
people has led anthropologists into narrative descriptions especially of
primitive societies or isolated peoples throughout the world; the effort
to explore processes of change has stimulated the tracing of actual
instances of change or the analysis of how some initial change has led
to altered structure and function in particular cultures. General propositions that emerge have been usually of the conditional sort: "if A,
then B."

Sociologists share an interest in similar subjects, but anthropologists,
because of their tradition of studying many unrelated cultures, have
been prone to use crosscultural comparison to elucidate similarities and
differences that enhance understanding of any one culture; whereas
sociologists lay more stress on our own multinational society and its

* This chapter has benefited from critical comment by Herbert Passin on an earlier
manuscript.

antecedents to analyze its diverse elements of social structure. The differences narrow and blur when both fields deal with Japan as their subject matter; for instance, anthropologists have been learning to use quantitative data and sampling theory to cope with the complexities of Japanese culture, while sociologists have given attention to qualitative or stylistic peculiarities of family, community, class, and other groups. If this chapter remains more anthropological than sociological, it does so on two counts. It does not seek "social problems" with a prescriptive or curative goal, as do some branches of sociological research, on the ground that definition and analysis of Japanese culture in its own terms constitute a first task which should precede the search for disorder or pathology. Second, it puts rather less emphasis on quantified data and more on impressionistic observations than is common in sociological work, an unavoidable consequence of the large number of cultural variables which concern the anthropologist. Within every anthropologist, so to speak, there is a tension between the drive toward increasing scientific precision of terminology, hypotheses, and objective field methods, on the one hand, and the disinclination to forgo qualitative and aesthetic discriminations and propositions he considers equally essential to explaining the major premises of a culture in its entirety, on the other. For better or worse, a blend of these two approaches tends to characterize anthropological research.

To comprehend the purposes of this chapter, just as with the field of anthropology itself, it is more important to anticipate the interplay between the two varieties of analysis than to be concerned with the separate domains of different disciplines. Matters treated in other chapters will be touched on here as well, though often lightly and incidentally, because our eyes are on the cultural whole. The anthropologist is grateful, in fact, to have each division of culture treated by a specialist, especially in the case of a complex, diversified society such as Japan. By analogy with the field of medicine, in which the general practitioner needs the findings and skills of a number of specialists to comprehend the whole person but himself bears chief responsibility for neglecting no part that may affect others, anthropological examination of the whole culture needs the findings and methods applied by other fields.

Out of their experience among primitive cultures, anthropologists have developed at least one area of technical specialty, namely, the analysis of kinship, community, and other small-scale social phenomena (corresponding to the principal units of primitive societies); and out of their concern for human culture from its beginnings they have developed an area of historical specialty, namely, the analysis of archaeological data. In this chapter these two modes of analysis will be brought out, but be it understood that both aim toward the same goal of understanding. Both seek to answer the general question: what does it mean to be Japanese? Both look for answers within culture, not by merely listing isolated traits, but rather with the conviction that the Japanese culture type has a distinctive and discoverable style. Japanese culture we believe had its origin in prehistory and has retained a discernible continuity to modern times. Whatever its content at a given time, the basic elements of this tradition, be they accented or muted, nonetheless have persistently related to each other in particular, pervasive ways that constitute a special style. The first section of this chapter, therefore, traces the continuity of such style upward from its earliest identifiable origins to modern times, taking account of modulation or displacement along the way. The second section cuts across various aspects of contemporary Japanese culture, applying in the main a structural-functional method of analysis. The aim of the second section is to clarify diverse institutions or social units to determine how they operate or alter under changing pressures. An especially useful conception for this purpose is the *ideal type,* an institution or set of organizations conceived of in ideal form as it would exist under consistent and uniform conditions.

The use of ideal types, it may be noted, furnishes an illustration of the tensions within the anthropological approach to culture. Types are of the utmost use in anthropological research. They are "discovered" and then verified or refined and polished through subsequent research, much as any scientist tests the classes or types in his field of study. As types are validated, they must be taken into account in further research, and so research becomes cumulative. This is certainly one of the fondest expectations of the social scientific side of the anthropologist. Nevertheless, certain features of cultural style suggested below are less subject to classification, testing, and verification than others; they are metaphorical or analogic assertions which, however apt, must be accepted as figurative approximations to a complex reality that may equally well be presented in different terms for different purposes. These figurative statements illustrate the leaning toward the humanities that is found in the work of many anthropologists.

THE JAPANESE CULTURE STYLE

Membership in any great collectivity of persons such as a minority or majority ethnic group is partly a subjective assessment—what Harold Isaacs calls the possession of a group self-image. Japanese, like others, have numerous self-images; they perceive themselves as farmers, as students, or in other occupational roles; as members of a particular family, interest group, or class; as Tokyoites, as Asians, and as Japanese. Among these self-images, their perception of themselves as Japanese is especially important because it is intimately linked with another subjective question: what do we stand for? It is based not merely on what they are but what they have behind them, for history recounts mainly the events that affected Japanese as a people or lesser groups as segments of this entity. Group identity is only partly subjective, however, especially when ethnic identity is concerned: most people can by observation determine whether other persons are members of their own or of other groups, with fairly high precision. Interestingly enough, such objective facts as place of birth or residence and national citizenship, which provide most of the labels we use for ethnic groups, are *not* among the immediately observable features by which we assess ethnic membership. It is easy to find, for example, persons born or naturalized in Japan and now living there whom we nonetheless immediately categorize as German or Chinese, conceivably in contradiction to their own self-image. The criteria we use are subsumed in anthropological terminology under the word "culture." Thus, objectively, a person who speaks Japanese as his sole or primary language, is a member of Japanese social units, practices Japanese customs, and shares Japanese views is objectively categorized as Japanese, wherever he may live or whatever his physical characteristics may be. Cultural characteristics expressed in a particular style furnish his ethnic identity.

Of course the vast majority of Japanese are restricted in their residence to the Japanese islands. Here they form an unusually homogeneous population. In 1960, there were 22,262 Euro-Americans (including 10,673 United States citizens) residing in Japan; Chinese numbered 45,255, and Koreans 619,096. Roughly eighteen thousand persons were classed as Ainu, an ethnic group with a distinctive language. (Parenthetically, it should be noted that very few Ainu retain the practices of their hunting and gathering ancestors in Hokkaido and Sakhalin, and only some live in modified tribal conditions comparable to those of the American Indians on reservations, for most are assimilated in the dominant Japanese society.) An even more tenuous category is that of the Eta, probably numbering 1,000,000 or 1,500,000, who were legal outcasts, not considered as being Japanese or even as being fully human, until the late nineteenth century. Today, even with equal legal rights, they are distinctly a minority under the handicap of social discrimination, still concentrated in the Inland Sea and Kinki regions, mostly in segregated villages and city wards, though colonies exist elsewhere and considerable numbers are moving to metropolitan areas. Their history suggests that their status as a single despised group developed after the mid-fifteenth century. Eta are essentially Japanese in language, culture, and general appearance. As against these small minorities, ordinary Japanese are by far preponderant, numbering more than 93 million in 1963.

The Japanese are more clearly distinguishable culturally than physically. The popularly used term *Japanese race* implies a genetic homogeneity which cannot clearly be shown to exist. Geneticists investigating physical or generic affiliation prefer to avoid most visible features, such as hair and skin color or stature and proportions, all of which alter readily under varying environmental conditions or blend confusingly in cross-mating. Such purely genetic features as the ABO blood groups occur in varying frequencies among separate populations; regional populations of Japan show similar frequencies of the ABO types everywhere, except for a rising frequency of type B northward from Kyushu toward Hokkaido. Yet these frequencies are in the general range of frequencies measured among the Chinese, Koreans, Ainu and northeastern Siberians, and Micronesians; it is clear that, in general terms, the Japanese form part of a large genetic pool covering East Asia. Biological features do not set them apart.

With respect to culture, there would seem to be none of the ambiguities noted in the other criteria for identifying Japanese, until we reflect on what a high proportion of the elements of Japanese life, taken separately and individually, are shared by non-Japanese. Telephones, automobiles, and the thousand and one modern features are found all around the world; a preponderance of what we would consider "traditional" features occurs also in Korea and China. A few specific social institutions, many food dishes and clothing styles, certain elements of architecture, and so on are distinctly Japanese, but these by no means make up the great bulk of Japanese culture today. It is not easy to define Japanese culture in terms of "lists of traits" then, for many traits are shared with other cultures and the few which seem unique (except perhaps language) are not central to the Japanese way of life. Yet no one would deny that Japanese culture provides its bearers with a distinctive design for living, a style that attaches to a broad constellation of traits, some unique, others shared, but in a particular combination that makes it Japanese. As we have noted, we can approach this particular Japanese style of life both vertically and cross-sectionally, that is, through the insight of history or by use of a social-scientific analysis of contemporary Japanese society. We shall begin our analysis with the vertical approach.

ORIGINS AND CONTINUITY

A 1963 Tokyo magazine article under the title "Where do the Japanese come from?" presented recently discovered stone tools dating from perhaps 200,000 years ago and made an effort to reconstruct a crude life of what were presumably the earliest "inhabitants" of the Japanese islands based on the hunting of large animals of the Pleistocene period. If it is accepted that all people who exist in Japan are not necessarily Japanese, there arises a serious question as to whether such ancient inhabitants can be regarded as ancestral Japanese. If not, then at what point did the successive occupants of the islands become Japanese? An excursion into prehistory is clearly necessary to find an answer, for there is an irrefutable continuity of Japanese culture from very early times to the present revealed by history. By A.D. 700 a Japanese language was distinguishable from that of neighboring cultural groups, and so were the style and content of the way of life of the speakers of this language. How far back this date may be pushed requires a more careful survey of the prehistoric culture sequence.

Early Prehistoric Periods (Preceramic Cultures)

The known time span of the occupation of the islands has been moved far back by a series of discoveries since 1948. Tools of flaked stone are the only surviving evidence; no skeletal remains have been found. Dating of the oldest known tools, discovered in 1962 and later at scattered sites in western Japan, notably at Niu in northern Kyushu, awaits fuller confirmation. The tools occurred in buried gravels of streams which may date from the third interglacial period; similarities are fairly close to the roughly flaked, large stone tools known as *chopper-chopping tools* found through China, Southeast Asia, and India. The continental finds, being better known, permit the conjecture that their probable makers were premodern hominids who lived at a date estimated to be between 150,000 and 200,000 years ago. A time gap intervenes between these earliest implements and the next known series of stone implements, supposedly in use about thirteen thousand years ago. The culture that produced these later tools has not revealed its human type either, but enough sites have been found to present a sequence of stone tool styles, first smaller versions of the chopper-chopping tools, followed by blades, projectile points, and tiny, sharp-edged stone flakes (microliths). The makers of these later tools also were hunters and gatherers, and we surmise that they were of modern physical type.

Middle Prehistoric Period (Jōmon)

Pottery was introduced into Japan and made in a succession of styles by people who continued to live from wild resources: deer and acorns in the hills, fish and shellfish along the seacoast. Their settlements have occasionally been found and excavated, revealing small, one-room huts, often semisubterranean. The dead were buried with offerings of red ocher, rarely with any other grave goods. There were tools of some variety made from stone and bone, along with pottery fashioned by hand, all showing successive changes over a long period of time. The pottery was of a simple basic shape but was provided with increasingly elaborate external ornamentation, often made by cord impressions (from which comes the type name, Jōmon, meaning "rope-marked"). There is no good evidence of the practice of any agriculture or of the use of animals other than the dog. It is clear that Jōmon pottery and its associated culture lingered in the north perhaps some centuries after the entrance of a new culture, the Yayoi, into western Japan. The initial date of Jōmon pottery is moot; dates obtained from radioactive carbon from the sites are still technically dubious but would suggest, if confirmed, the unlikely proposition that Japan, about 7000 B.C., was the site where the earliest pottery in the world was invented. Considering the trends of culture growth all over Asia, an initial date of about 4500 B.C. or later is more likely for the introduction of pottery to Japan. It is not apt to have been separately invented there. The usual terminal date, for Jōmon pottery in western Japan, is 250 B.C.

High regional variation within the simple limits of Jōmon culture strongly indicates that there were many separate tribes, perhaps speaking a variety of languages. In the far north, it is possible to trace some continuity with what is probably early Ainu culture, yet nothing justifies the older view that all Jōmon cultures were of Ainu stock.

Late Prehistoric Period (Yayoi)

In the third century B.C., profound cultural changes occurred in Japan, as agriculturists bearing the Yayoi culture entered the country from the west. The Yayoi people's physical type, though poorly known, falls in the Mongoloid range; they brought the method of growing rice in flooded fields and lived in settlements on stream bottoms and coastal plains, in what became and still remain highly productive regions for agriculture. They spread through southwestern Japan, but until late very few sites occur in the north, where Jōmon ways of life lingered until perhaps the ninth century A.D. Yayoi houses, built of wooden posts and beams with external thatching, were larger and more permanent than those of the Jōmon people and generally had the inside floor at ground level. The horse and the cow were known but uncommon. Yayoi pottery was wheel-made, and containers were varied in shape and function. Decoration was limited, perhaps, to brush squiggles in horizontal bands, but a more varied repertory of jars, bowls, and plate shapes existed than in the Jōmon style.

Among the tools preserved in the low, swampy sites of the Yayoi period are wooden farm implements, including hoes, rakes, and spades. Stone tools included the celt, the chisel, and a semilunar harvesting knife; stone arrow points were still made, as well as stone fishing weights, indicating that agriculture alone did not meet all the subsistence needs of these people. Even the early Yayoi people had the skill to smelt iron and forge simple tools. The dead were not buried within the village itself, as the Jōmon dead had been buried at their campsite, but the mode of their disposal is known only for Kyushu, where two large jars set mouth to mouth served as a coffin, or (in the same cemetery) pits were lined with rock slabs and capped with low mounds of earth, presaging the custom of the dolmen building.

Protohistoric Period (Later Yayoi)

In later Yayoi sites are found Chinese coins and bronze mirrors of the Former (Earlier) Han dynasty (202 B.C. to A.D. 9), imported from the mainland. The Japanese had no native records until the sixth or seventh century A.D., but such datable materials in Japanese sites, along with sporadic reference to the Japanese in contemporary Chinese histories, remove the later Yayoi people from the purely prehistoric context and make this a protohistoric period.

Within 200 years, during the second century A.D., the Yayoi people had begun to cast bronze objects themselves, many of them in forms unknown on the continent. Among these were large bronze bells and purely ceremonial weapons (swords, spears, and halberds). Bells were cast in the Inland Sea region and northern Kyushu; weapon forms characterized the eastern Inland Sea and the area eastward to the Chūbu region. These two regions formed the center of Yayoi agricultural and population growth. Similarities are so strong throughout this area as to suggest that if these were not all one people, they at any rate had regular connection with each other. As to the rapid disappearance of Jōmon culture, acculturation and absorption among the newcomers seem more likely than violent extinction.

Semihistoric Period (Tomb Culture)

About A.D. 250, in the eastern sector of the Inland Sea, an elite who had come to rule the Yayoi agricultural people began to build huge earth-mound tombs for their burials. By A.D. 300, the practice had spread westward to northern Kyushu, in a reversal of the customary (west to east) direction taken by cultural influences of the protohistoric period. The imposing mounds which were the prerogative of a powerful ruling group have given a name, *Tomb period,* to the era bridging the gap between the all but historic Yayoi and the fully historic Buddhist period. Tombs were built in several forms, including a giant keyhole shape which has no parallel among other mound-building cultures. Others were round or square, with sloping or terraced sides. They were located at first on small hilltops and later in the middle of agricultural plains. Throughout the period megalithic chambers and passage graves were also hollowed into the hill slopes. Near the top of the mound was placed the body of a leader and with him perhaps one or two other bodies. There was no mass retainer burial. Outside the mound, however, pottery cylinders were set up in rows around the slopes to prevent soil erosion. Atop some of them were placed pottery figurines, called *haniwa,* of armed warriors, animals, houses, and other objects. Perhaps these represented retainers and goods for the deceased; in any case, they are a valuable source of information on the culture of the semihistoric period. As revealed by material remains and *haniwa* representations, the people who were buried in the mounds rode on horseback, wore tailored quilted clothing or slat armor, were painted or tattooed, and carried long iron swords, lances, battle axes, and bows, some of them recurved. Their pottery was a bluish gray, highly fired ware, and they used complex forges and furnaces to make iron weapons and tools, including, at last, the plow. Tomb finds speak unmistakably of a ruling class dominating groups of almost unaltered Yayoi villagers, whose agriculture supported them.

Whether the inspiration for building tombs of the unique size and shape found in Japan came from abroad is unclear. Most types of grave goods of tombs during the first two centuries appeared *de novo,* though

research focused on this point is beginning to find some Yayoi antecedents. It may well be the case that high chieftainship grew from
within Yayoi culture; it was not clearly an import. What keeps the
image of foreign conquest alive is evidence from the late, not the early,
Tomb period, when there appeared the first long swords, elaborate
horse trappings, and ornament types that clearly were derived from the
continent. Conquistadores from adventurer bands such as then ranged
along the nomad-beset northern fringe of China and north Korea very
likely came fortune hunting and stayed, bringing traits ultimately
derived from the equestrian cultures of Inner Asia. Probably they wedged
themselves in among the elite that already existed in Japan. A mass ethnic
invasion of the islands at this point seems unlikely.

Recension of Archaeological Findings

Let us return to the question raised in the magazine article cited at the
head of this section: "Where do the Japanese come from?" The odds
are high indeed against there being any significant ancestral Japanese
quality in the hunters and shellfish gatherers of the early and middle
prehistoric periods. These people did inhabit all areas of Japan, to be
sure, but the primitive preceramic and Jōmon cultures, though leaving
often picturesque remains, disappeared without any vital continuity
among later inhabitants. They may, however, have made partial contributions at two points, in the language and in the genetic constitution
of the Japanese. In recent Japanese speech, certain items of vocabulary
which have a Malayo-Polynesian affinity have been identified through
current linguistic studies. These items may have been picked up from
Jōmon speech by the Yayoi successors—among them, for instance, local
names for plants, animals, and environmental features. Acculturated
Jōmon people, moreover, need not have died out as a physical stock.
But these two open possibilities of continuity by no means provide a
core of Japanese culture.

The case for Yayoi ancestry, on the contrary, has a lot in its favor.
For one thing, the Yayoi people subsisted through the same economic
pattern of rice growing as did later people. Peoples all over the Far
East grow rice, to be sure, but certain surviving Yayoi implements
closely resemble the forms of later ones used down to this day: the
hoe, pestle, geta (foot clogs) for the soft mud of the swampy fields,
and so on. Moreover, the Yayoi culture type still predominated with
little modification in villages of the semihistoric period.

As to language, reconstructed guess dates of the origin of Japanese suggest that Japanese and Okinawan began their separate development about eighteen or nineteen hundred years ago, say, within two hundred years on either side of the first century A.D. The dating techniques do not tell us how the Japanese single-speech community separated and began distinct courses of development; but the date of roughly A.D. 1 to 100 fits the supposition that the joint ancestors of the Japanese and the Okinawans were Yayoi migrants to Japan who moved respectively toward different islands, those in the Ryukyu chain losing contact with the main body.

There are further types of evidence, among them the signs of a distinctive ideological orientation. Late Yayoi data offer an unusual and intriguing problem of interpretation connected with the bronze objects mentioned above: so-called "bells" and "weapons." Careful examination shows very few of them were suited to actual use. The weapon blades are of exaggerated breadth and thinness in this soft metal, and holes purposely cast in the bells would have destroyed their capacity to ring well. Only mirrors were usable as such, and they, too, were much ornamented. By and large, these were ceremonial objects, and almost all have been discovered in exceptional locations, on hill slopes or in caves (rather than in the settlements) and buried in nests, and not infrequently disfigured. Why? Perhaps they were important symbols of community solidarity, enshrined in sanctuaries but hidden for safe-keeping in time of trouble, or else damaged and cast away by conquerors of the community who substituted their own symbols. Such a conjecture is supported better by analogy to recent Japanese shrine practices than in any other way: various objects, such as mirrors, weapons, and jewelry, often are the articles of essential sanctity that justify the existence of a shrine today, and shrines of this type are the ultimate focus or central expression of community solidarity. We may at least suggest continuity, from the Yayoi era to recent times, in the practice of attributing sanctity to quasi-utilitarian objects, and as additional evidence is gathered, we may eventually be able to trace the essential system of Shinto from Yayoi times. Granted, nothing is yet known of shrines as such in the Yayoi culture or in the succeeding period when tombs were being built; mirrors and jewels in tomb burials, however, are found under circumstances which suggest that special sanctity or power was attributed to them.

If the foregoing conjecture is accepted, it leads to other significant implications as to the association of ritual with control of government. Any further suppositions may be hazardous at this point, yet they may be stated as a set of assumptions which extend logically from the fragmentary actual evidence of the Yayoi period. First, as already stated, let us assume that certain objects (e.g., bronze bells, mirrors, and weapons) symbolized communal solidarity; that is, actual possession of them validated whatever control the shrine keepers exerted over community affairs. Next, let us assume that, as certain historians suggest for early Shinto, shrine keepers held mainly a peacemaking, dispute-reducing authority. Finally, let us assume that the concrete symbols held for a succession of generations came to be regarded as hereditary possessions of particular houses. At this point, we possess a theory that a priestly-judicial aristocracy arose indigenously. Should invaders have arrived from abroad in, say, the mid-Tomb period, armor-clad, mounted, and sword-girded, their force-of-arms legitimacy would differ from that of the local aristocracy. But the two bases for rule could be reconciled, to their mutual benefit, and we should then expect the indigenous ritual symbols, representing religious legitimacy, to be found together with weaponry of exotic origin, representing the authority of arms, as actually happens to some extent in the great tombs of Japan. Such combinations would result through the formation of confederations or through conquest, the results of which would be clothed in the morality of peace keeping. That is, instead of bald aggression by power-hungry clans sweeping all before them and exterminating all opponents, we should expect wars of alliances or pacification to take place, in the name of priestly-judicial aristocrats.

Such a hypothesis, however conjectural, strongly recommends itself as the most plausible explanation for certain key aspects of the early Japanese state and society and particularly those features of the Emperor institution that have made it so durable right to the present day. To be sure, we do not know the point at which the Imperial House transcended its status as a chief clan and gained supremacy, but we have many studies to show that its rule is legitimatized through ritual symbols (sword, mirror, and jewels) kept in shrines; that this priestly character has been a paramount feature; that the house has provided no examples of strong men or conquerors since the time of the legendary founder, Jimmu, but has employed generals and surrogates (some of them imperial princes, to be sure) to do the necessary fighting; and that this is how it has survived the buffets and blows of regencies, aristocratic coups, and exile without ever having suffered usurpation or losing its essentially sacred legitimacy.

Finally, when we turn to historians to check their support for the conjectures made here, we find only minor obstacles, although the myth quality of such early records as the *Kojiki* or the *Nihongi (Nihon Shoki)* gives them disappointing insubstantiality. (For example, what is to be done with the *Nihongi*'s full account of the Emperor who prohibited the burial of retainers in the tombs of masters and in their place commanded that figures be substituted? Archaeology has not yet found a tomb with enough bodies to support the actual existence of retainer burial, and we are bound to suppose that the myth really was an attempt to account for the many *haniwa* figures still rising out of the earth of the tombs.) There is no reason, however, to doubt the historicity of tombs, especially in the old Yamato area (embracing Nara and Kyoto), that are named as the resting places of specific emperors, their consorts, and other more or less authentic historic figures. Archaeologists have even verified a few attributions, though they have been restrained from intensive probing, which is costly and also is still considered sacrilegious in some quarters. Meanwhile, certain historians have looked critically at Japan's long list of emperors and reigns, shortening the entire chronology and rejecting, as mythical, most or all of the first ten emperors, so that their independent historical conclusions tend to place the beginning of the Yamato dynasty squarely in the mid-Yayoi period of archaeology. In general, then, historians and their materials lend substantial support to the linguistic and archaeological interpretation that the bearers of Yayoi culture were the first Japanese and that the long-lived Japanese cultural style began to crystallize in that period.

Ancient and Medieval Periods

By the sixth to seventh centuries A.D., the Japanese were turning to face Chinese civilization, more and more intensely aware of and awed by its cultural riches. Their awareness quickly turned into a high tide of borrowing, which ebbed and rose in two or more cycles over a long span, lasting until near the end of the eighteenth century. Particularly in the early phase of intensive borrowing, roughly from A.D. 600 to 850, Chinese institutions augmented Japanese culture in almost every dimension. We can readily picture the ardent court-linked enthusiasts who read, spoke, and wrote in Chinese (for lack of script for their own language), studied Buddhism and the marvelous complexity of the Confucian apparatus of state, and admired continental architecture. Most of this was beyond the reach of common people out in the fields or on their fishing boats. Yet everyday culture, too, was enriched by methods of transplanting and double-cropping, raising silkworms, glazing ceramics, and other skills.

Each new wave of cultural adaptation from China gave a spurt of advancement to Japanese culture. But let us reiterate what is obvious and undisputed: Japanese culture remained Japanese. The Japanese were captivated but not captured by the awesome Chinese. This fact is recognized and underscored by every historian dealing with Sino-Japanese cultural relations; substantiating details appear in other parts of this volume and need not be repeated here. It need only be added that several centuries passed before, for instance, the new writing system was painfully adapted, by the evolution of kana syllabaries, to the local language, or before Buddhism became virtually centered in ancestor veneration (as it had not been in China); whereas in other cases a Japanese quality adhered to newly acquired institutions from the beginning, as in the Imperial Court, where, although they utilized T'ang court rank titles, the Japanese never compromised their principle of hereditary investiture in office in favor of the Chinese appointive system.

In apprehending that Chinese borrowings were reshaped, quickly or gradually, to conform with the Japanese cultural style, we should not mistakenly look on this design as fixed, narrow, or inadaptable, for the cumulative effect of a multitude of choices for or against innovation was a somewhat new and richer configuration: an aristocratic state, for instance, in the place of aristocratic confederations. There was, then, an interplay between the overall pattern and the constellation of elements in which it was expressed, in the course of which, however, Japanese culture retained its individuality.

Intercourse with China in the medieval period produced less spectacular changes in Japanese culture. Most simply put, after making her initial contributions China had less to offer that was clearly lacking in Japan. Innovations supplemented or were alternatives to things supplied within Japanese culture. And as before, the Japanese style marked these innovations before long: porcelain, schools of art, the Ch'an (Zen) school of Buddhist philosophy. In small or large ways, many innovations advanced Japanese culture; that is, their increments enabled the Japanese to cope more effectively than before with the problems of living, in the broadest sense.

Modern Period

For the first time, about 1800, certain Japanese articulated their strong doubt that China had any more to offer the Japanese than could be found at home: this movement of nationalistic scholars (*kokugakusha*) can be interpreted in various ways, yet it epitomizes rather aptly the evident fact that, except in terms of size and national power, Japan was about on a par with China in cultural development. Before long, the Japanese figuratively turned their backs on China, faced about toward the Pacific, now coming alive with the sailing vessels of European nations, and embarked again on a course of intensive culture change. This change usually goes under the name *westernization.*

Japan in a brief century has been conspicuously successful in adopting traits and patterns that were first developed in Western Europe and have become central features of civilization there. At the close of the Tokugawa period of seclusion, Japan lacked modern systems of communication, modern machinery, modern institutions of commerce and finance, and the apparatus of a modern state and its military capacity. She now has the world's fourth most productive industrial complex, based on "guided capitalism." Her metropolitan centers rank with those anywhere in size and in the sociological characteristics of urbanism. She has a highly bureaucratized government and well-developed ranks of scholars, scientists, engineers, artists, intelligentsia, and juvenile delinquents. This seems adequate proof, at first glance, of her westernization.

An immediate question is whether the new stance facing toward the non-Asian world, adopting non-Asian inventions, and developing non-Asian institutions is making Japan more Western than Japanese in cultural style, creating an unprecedented discontinuity. If, indeed, Japan has been or is being westernized, the eventual result should be just this. The problem may be clarified here by brief reference to theory. Westernization implies, literally, partial or total dissemination of culture from one geographic area, Western Europe, to another geographic area, Japan. In anthropological terminology, this process is diffusion; most anthropological thinking about culture change was couched in diffusion studies or in studies of acculturation, the first tracing the dissemination of traits to new areas and the second tracing alterations in a single culture through dissemination. Both approaches conceive of change occurring along a horizontal axis, as it were. Another point of view, however, perceives a vertical axis of culture change, termed cultural development, or evolution. From this viewpoint (which more nearly coincides with the Japanese view of themselves as "catching up"), the Japanese for the past century have been adding increments to their culture in order to rise to a new evolutionary level. They have been "modernizing," in other words, not just westernizing. This viewpoint, largely harmonizing with the economists' view of economic development, considers various internal adjustments to be features of the growth process itself rather than parts of either a European or a Japanese tradition. It also opens issues that remain closed or obscure under purely diffusional interpretation: identifying a main stimulant to change, understanding selective change, and accounting for change that emerges out of the background of Japanese culture, not out of European culture. Subsequent chapters of this volume deal in some detail with each of these matters in respect to particular sectors of modern Japanese culture; hence, we need touch only on how evolution affects cultural style. If Japanese culture is evolving toward a higher level of efficiency and capacity through the process which we call *modernization,* it does not become less Japanese simply for having banks and factories and trains. The continuity of the Japanese cultural style does not depend on the geographic point of origin of elements of culture, but simply on whether the commitment to particular premises is flexible enough for evolution to go on within it or whether these premises will be abandoned if development continues beyond a certain limit.

We see these points illustrated most clearly in the latest period of culture contact. The Allied Occupation of Japan from 1945 to 1952 was a period of intense pressure on Japanese culture. The large-scale, directed culture change, over which the Occupation presided, was aimed to a greater degree at revamping the Japanese cultural style than at changing its content. Thus it required the remodeling of a wide range of institutions to establish a basis for democracy. High policy was to democratize, not Americanize, but many elements of this policy pressed the Japanese to accept specifically American stylistic premises in the place of long-standing Japanese viewpoints, even where militarism was not at issue. Long-run consequences of the double impact of technological revolution and American-styled democratization are yet to be measured. Certain modes of organization and behavior that seem, on the whole, discontinuous with the Japanese and are particularly American are embedded in major institutions developed in modern times as products of Japan's own socioeconomic revolution. Here the Occupation directives seem to have taken well. Yet, at the same time, these very institutions exhibit features that are quite consistent with Japanese tradition and differ more or less sharply from parallel institutions of the United States or the societies of Western Europe. Americans, even after remodeling these institutions during the Occupation, found that some of their assumptions about what was vital to their effective functioning were unpalatable to the Japanese.

In effect, what it means to be Japanese today is not by any means congruent with Western practices and premises. The incongruities, to be sure, are not especially apparent in the structure of most institutions that qualify Japan as a modern society but come more clearly into view in the way these institutions are made to function, in the behavioral patterns of people participating in them. We see the Japanese as becoming modern but remaining Japanese. By way of illustration, we may select several prominent categories, such as government, law, and business. As to structure, Japan has a diversified bureaucratic state, with legislative and executive bodies at national, prefectural, and municipal or village levels; in jurisprudence, she has a uniform system of courts rendering judgments under codified bodies of law; her businessmen, acting in an apparatus of companies and corporations, operate in a context of contractual agreements and market-controlled prices; and these businesses employ a wide range of occupationally diversified wage workers and salary earners, many of them members of well-developed unions. Comparing each category, say, with parallel American or British institutions, we would find differences; but the differences in structure impress most observers rather less than the differences in function.

Patterns of Japanese behavior that catch the eye as accounting for differences in function often are derived from the tradition of commitment to collectivities, to group solidarity, to particular ways of maintaining or restoring harmony. The collectivities are often hierarchical and authoritarian, with gradations of privilege, but they are not necessarily so. Their members are bound by indefinitely enduring attachments. Conformity and efficiency on the part of members are valued for group solidarity and welfare; initiative is more often the prerogative of leaders. The individual is expected to give precedence to group welfare over his own interests; it is the group that acts, while its members seek anonymity. Should a member lapse from propriety in some way, his punishment need not be in proportion to the crime or wrong itself so much as in proportion to his willingness to return to good standing. All such groups may seek power, but they also seek harmony, internally and externally, rather than abstract justice. Their main methods to maintain or restore harmony are consensus, conciliation, compromise, and the intervention of a higher authority.

Little of this pattern is completely unfamiliar outside Japan, and it may appear at first that if Japan differs even from American or English society, it is in degree rather than in kind. In the United States as in Japan, for example, there are common-knowledge instances of tight, enduring cliques in local and national government, and committee consensus or compromise on the part of legislators or administrators is a familiar way of moving government along. In the United States, again, much attention has been given to the "organization man," anonymous in a great collectivity and exhibiting all the symptoms mentioned above; equally, Americans know something of the role of common college ties or kin connections in constituting business cliques or interlocking directorates. Not only Japanese but Americans, also, often are ready to suffer in silence for the sake of harmony rather than seek justice in litigation.

There is a significant difference between American and Japanese societies in this matter, however. While it is not difficult for Americans to recognize these phenomena as part of the reality of life, it is more difficult for them to justify them or honor them; that is, common American value orientations point away from rather than toward these phenomena. American society inherits from its own tradition certain premises or presuppositions that provide for different modes of behavior; if they are not regularly practiced, they are nonetheless comprehended and anticipated in others. It is these very premises which are so uncongenial, unpalatable, and awkward for the many Japanese who accept or feel at home with patterns of collective solidarity.

A major premise on which the functioning of many American institutions is based is the supposition that the common welfare may be attained through adversary relationships, which might equally well be styled "antagonistic cooperation." This supposition runs through government, law, and business in ways that need be mentioned only briefly to be recognized. It is implicit in the confrontation between political parties before elections and in the legislative debates that follow them. In law, litigation presupposes adversary action to such an extent that it is difficult to substitute conciliation, compromise, or other procedures even when their merit is recognized, as in divorces and other family cases. In business, classical theory, at least, assumes adversaryship between competitors as the basic force behind the free market. Again, the acceptance of collective bargaining between management and labor as a means of advancing the general social welfare is an application of the premise of antagonistic cooperation.

Modern Japanese are not unaware of these methods as applied to government, law, and business. There are now, in fact, various legal and procedural provisions intended to promote adversary confrontation or to preserve a setting in which it is appropriate. Most such provisions date from the Allied Occupation period, to be sure, but government and business have provided an arena for their practice for a much longer period of time. Notwithstanding the fact that this pattern is recognized and advocated, it is by no means yet easily applied even in the major areas we have discussed—government, law, and business—not to mention other areas of life. Adversaryship conflicts with presuppositions of self-effacement and harmony. In politics, an important corollary of adversaryship, the acceptance of minority dissent, is difficult to apply because it brings into the open a disharmony which should be covered over by the technique of consensus. In sum, antagonistic cooperation is not an established premise in Japanese culture.

Must the Japanese inevitably accommodate themselves to adversary patterns as their society moves farther from its premodern antecedents? It seems hazardous to assume so. Even in the Occident, where this pattern or something like it has been ingrained since premodern times and has helped to mold modern social institutions, there is reason to wonder about its future. One's view of its chances of blossoming in Japan rather depends on one's view of the as yet undisclosed future—whether, for example, as modern societies grow and diversify, they may require increasingly free and mobile individuals, or, as David Riesman, William Whyte, and others suggest, members will increasingly conform to the regimenting demands of organization. The future Japanese society must be assessed using past experience in the West as a guiding standard, perhaps, but in relation to the future of all modern societies.

Let it be clearly understood that the process of modernization in Japan carries dynamic implications that are not echoed in societies split, for example, into dual divisions of aristocrat and peasant. Japan once knew only the latter sort of division, and there are more than slight traces of it today. But these are far overshadowed by what can best be conceived of as a modern versus traditional duality, in which neither aspect is static and in which all aspects of the culture are involved. Both, in other words, are moving along paths of change, interconnecting and gradually converging. "Moderns" are often less than a generation away from "traditionals": their grandparents or parents or they themselves lived under traditional conditions. On the other hand, those who live close to tradition, for one reason or another, nevertheless are in contact with modern life both in the material, concrete sense and in the conceptual sense. The mental horizons of a farmer may be just as wide as those of a factory worker, and in recent decades this has come to mean horizons not significantly more limited than those of people in any modern society. His ambitions are predicated as much on what exists in Japanese culture as a whole as on the elements of his immediate surroundings.

To glimpse more concretely what exists in Japanese culture as a whole as it might appear to an ordinary Japanese person, one need only pick a magazine off the rack. (Japan is a nation with a prodigious publication industry, and its people tend to be conscientious readers; the magazine one selects may be addressed mainly to city women, but it will be accessible also in remarkably remote localities.) Here is a skimming of contents from a pictorial woman's magazine at the luxury price of ¥290 (80 cents), published in the summer of 1962 and carrying 124 pages of articles and a great many pages of advertisement. It has feature articles on the Eskimo and the Tirol, on early man in Japan and a Japanese fishing village. It suggests vacation spots for the family and pictures a Japanese girl swimming star training for the 1964 Olympics. Its family section carries articles on pregnancy and the first year of infancy, on child rearing, and on a school for deaf and dumb children in England and also offers a simple story for children. Its home section shows a housing-development area near Tokyo, discusses rooftop gardens and garden furniture, gives recipes for refrigerator dishes for the summer, and shows a series of foreign homes in Los Angeles, Paris, and Ceylon. In colorplate style pages it shows men's and women's shirts and ancient Egyptian jewelry. It reproduces paintings by Pablo Picasso and Joan Miró in full-page color (and a portrait of Miró in Japanese kimono). It offers several short stories; its departments include columns on records and photography. Advertisements are presented by firms offering services (banking, insurance, and northeastern apples), as well as by manufacturers of automobiles and bicycles, home appliances (television sets, radios, refrigerators, washing machines, sewing machines), household goods (kitchen equipment, bedding), drugs, and food.

We should not take too literally the images of financial affluence, leisure, and sophistication such a magazine conjures in our minds. It doubtless flatters and idealizes its feminine readers, playing up to their dreams and fantasies. But the most ordinary reader does know that somewhere in Japan there actually are women who prepare delectable cold confections in homes with roof gardens, who can converse intelligently about the Eskimo and child psychology, and who travel to see the Tirol. Whether any high proportion of readers currently has all these capacities or not, they are what Japanese culture makes possible for women today. It is closer to being within the grasp of those who have reached the "new life" but is neither incomprehensible nor beyond conceivable attainment for those whose life and outlook are still to a large extent traditional or "old."

Nor should we exaggerate the prevalence of the modern features of Japanese life as depicted in such a magazine, for although its kind of life is the aim of most aspiring Japanese, there are still a number of persons who through preference or necessity live in ways much closer to those which prevailed before the influx of modern ways in Japan. In broad, comparative terms, Japan is still a transition culture, one which began its modernization both later than the pioneering modernizers of Europe and from a vastly different historical background. The modern in Japan today may not be strictly Western, but neither is it in all instances a natural evolution from the traditional. Today in Japan there is still a considerable coexistence, even confrontation, between two modes of life. It is this which gives the country its charm to the American tourist. It is this which gives a novelist like Tanizaki Jun'ichirō his themes of conflict between cultural styles and values. And it is this which the anthropologist must balance in his assessment of the whole culture of Japan today.

COMMUNITIES

Since at least well back in the Tokugawa era, townsmen in Japan have looked at countrymen across a subjective chasm as if the two were of different races or species. Townsmen frankly considered peasants to be brutish, dull, and not a little grotesque, a sentiment echoed perhaps more truly in European attitudes than in the relatively weak American dichotomy between city slicker and country rube. One still comes across this attitude in Japan, though it has had to outlast a series of sociocultural transformations on both sides, the former towns having grown into cities that are the centers of industrial capitalism while countrymen have turned from peasants into today's farmers. Considering how many denominators of experience link city and country folk—common schooling, common networks of the mass media of communication, the drawing of a majority of the new city population from rural areas—one may well wonder how discriminatory attitudes can continue to be nourished. Whether differences are appropriately phrased or not, however, it is incontestably true that a city creates an environment for its residents that is very different from anything experienced in the country.

In the review of features of Japanese society which follows, it is necessary to speak of two subpatterns within each area. In each section of the review, accordingly, part of the description pertains to Japanese of the modern type, and part to Japanese of the traditional type. An attempt is made to show their interrelationships and overlapping, insofar as space permits, but the reader is asked to recognize that so brief an account, in terms of comparison, separates into extremes or makes unduly explicit contrasts which are often less definite. We begin with an account of where the Japanese live, for example, distinguishing city from country as major categories, yet there are also many who live in intermediate communities of a mixed character.

Japanese cities have passed through several phases of development, each creating different conditions of life from one generation to the next; for instance, the consumer-oriented period since about 1955, when the economic boom began to solidify the base for middle-class living patterns, stands in contrast to the prewar period, when production went into war materials and regimentation prevailed. Certain constant features, however, have distinguished urban from rural life at whatever phase of city development. Two obvious features are the great size and the wide diversity of the city as a sociocultural entity. The city must have unified administration but is too large to be administered directly by its residents. City dwellers manage only a fraction of their own affairs by themselves at home or in local neighborhoods; they depend on professionals and official organizations for transportation, police and fire protection, public sanitation, entertainment, and a host of other facilities and services. They buy provisions rather than producing them and get them from widely dispersed sources. Friends and associates also are dispersed; the groups or cliques of intimates of a husband, wife, grandparent, and child overlap only partly, so that interests and activities of members of a single household tend to be diffused in different directions. Near neighbors, of varying occupational and social characteristics, often have few links other than part-time proximity to draw them together.

Thus, cities by their very nature as large, heterogeneous entities tend to imprint urban characteristics on the lives of their residents, all the more strongly in the case of metropolitan agglomerations such as Tokyo, Osaka, or Nagoya. Japanese urban communities, however, preserve a duality that requires attention. In general, the social duality corresponds with economic duality. The urban imprint (in the characteristics just cited) is strongest on the lives of persons who are the executives and employees of large firms or who are skilled permanent laborers in factories—the white-collar and lunch-box employees who live on salaries and wages. As Tokyo itself has become crammed to the bursting point with an added 3 or 400,000 new residents each year, "bedroom suburbs" have been growing on the perimeter of the metropolitan area. Here one finds concentrations of the "new middle-class" urbanites, in apartments and small homes, their living attuned to scattered occupations and recreations and their main interests—in home, job, school, union, and recreation—bypassing the community where they reside.

Both the metropolis and the smaller city, however, have also a large contingent of residents who own or work in small stores or workshops or are occupied in other self-employed enterprises: carpenters, plumbers, barbers, dentists, truckers, machinists, and so on. The owner of a small restaurant or furniture shop often works where he lives, his shop and quarters perhaps having been established by his father or grandfather. His family help with the work, and a handful of employees may live nearby or even be quartered in his home. Districts where such small enterprises are plentiful have marked qualities of neighborliness; inhabitants are punctilious about sharing services and exchanging gifts with their immediate neighbors on both sides of the street (in the standard phrase, "the three houses opposite and the one on either side"), they accord some importance to meetings of the block or ward unit (*chōnai-kai*), and they act as a more or less coherent unit in services at the local shrine as well as in donations to the Red Cross or the Community Chest. Their community organization, thus, exhibits a good deal of the corporate character of the rural community described below, although diversity, mobility, and dependence on the resources of the city as a whole dilute communal cohesiveness.

In the last two decades, changes in rural society have been particularly striking. Long-range socioeconomic trends coincided with specific postwar circumstances to accelerate these changes and spread them to areas of the nation that previously were almost isolated from major influences. Crop production has long been high and rising, for example, but new fertilizers, techniques, and plant strains have recently boosted the total to still higher levels, while specialist farming has also increased to take advantage of postwar market conditions. The postwar land reform dissolved tenancy and gave independence to thousands of rural households, but on so small a landholding that increasing numbers of small farmers have looked for and found secondary occupations. In 1962, according to figures of the Ministry of Agriculture and Forestry quoted by Nakano Takashi, in a full 47 per cent of farm households nonagricultural income was earned by those still living in the households. Increased use of farm machinery facilitates this doubling of occupations; in the current phrase, day-to-day farm work is done by the *sanchan* (the three women of the family: grandmother, mother, and daughter), while the men commute to work in town or factory and use tractors to do the heavy farm work on weekends. For the first time, total farm population has been declining, at a rate of about 400,000 annually since 1960, as youths in a position to inherit farms prefer to leave their villages. More ready access to higher education in the colleges created in each prefecture after World War II has, of course, increased their employability off the farm. Meanwhile, those who stay on the farm are disinclined to leave conditions in their traditional state; some 70 per cent now have television to reinforce their awareness of alternatives to local practices, and all have greatly increased incomes from the prosperous postwar years to finance changes in their ways of living.

These developments have considerable impact on the local community. This is not to say that revolution overnight is to be expected, but rather that the local community, which has adapted itself to a great deal of change during the past century, now faces a new and possibly sharper set of adjustments. Certain basic conditions of agricultural life which gave shape to the stable traditional community still exist, however, and are likely to continue, counterpoised against the forces for change. An examination of traditional community forms will reveal the conditions that tend to stabilize them.

The primary rural community in Japan is the *buraku,* a unit within which residents expect to provide most of their own public services and many of their own goods. Its residents may colloquially refer to it by the traditional and historically accurate term *mura,* though the expanded official or administrative mura now incorporates from several to thirty or more *buraku.* In appearance, a *buraku* is apt to be a tight or loose cluster of houses and auxiliary small buildings; some large clusters are split into two or more *buraku,* and some *buraku* are composed of scattered houses. They range in size from two to sixty or so houses, though most range between twenty and thirty. Seldom are the houses all of one family line. Nonetheless, a strong tradition of solidarity unites all member houses of this elemental community. Prime rice land, it is true, has been household-owned for centuries, but unirrigated fields, pastures, and woodlots once were managed and redistributed by the community as its collective property; some pastures and groves still are so owned. In any case, the community has such joint property as an assembly hall, a cemetery, fire-fighting gear, and perhaps crop-spraying or food-processing equipment.

Households form small groups within the *buraku* for limited purposes, a few banding together for the purchase of machinery or for economic or social cooperation. Some groups are interrelated, comprising a kindred or a lineage (two distinct forms, as explained in the following section); others, unrelated, are referred to as a *kumi* (team). Since ancient times outside government was apt to utilize for its own purposes the mutual responsibility felt by such groups, holding them jointly responsible for tax paying and keeping public order; dissolved as official units after World War II, such groups have only spasmodically re-formed for reciprocal aid in cities but are practically as vital as ever in the village communities. They thus illustrate how pervasive are patterns of collective assistance; illustration is offered also by cooperative groups comprising two or more *buraku,* perhaps for woodlot management, shrine maintenance, or irrigation. But cooperation above and below the *buraku* level is intermittent and for limited purposes, whereas the *buraku* collectivity has extremely broad scope.

The traditional *buraku* often is the prime agency taking collective responsibility to manage irrigation, maintain informal self-government under a headman and other officers, give assistance to member households at funerals and other crises, sponsor joint recreation managed by its young people as a subgroup, handle mutual insurance or moneylending, and perform joint religious rituals at its collective shrine (the *ujigami*). These functions that are internal to the community are managed by the *buraku* households organized as a *kō* or *kōjū;* each household is represented, and all decisions are binding on every household. The same solidarity is shown in dealing with the outside world, this time as a *buraku* or political entity. The head represents his households to the administrative officers of the encompassing mura. Again, decisions and actions are considered binding on every household; the sum of rice quotas (in postwar years), personal taxes, or Community Chest contributions that are due outside is thought of as a collective responsibility and paid in full even if certain households are delinquent.

Solidarity works because people are lifetime associates. A newcomer might gain title to a house or fields without being recognized as a member of the collective community. Solidarity can be mobilized also against a would-be individualist within the community, by ostracizing (*hachibu*) his household from some or all collective functions. And solidarity may paralyze decision on moot issues, for a matter must be decided by unanimous consensus or not at all; there is no provision for a dissenting minority. In restricting membership (members are often spoken of as "having shares" in the community) and in imposing the collective will on its members, the *buraku* shows itself to be designed as a corporate body.

This solidary, corporate, traditional community is not necessarily a community of equals. On the contrary, social equality is difficult to observe except where economic and political power is more or less uniform. Acreage differentials, kin ties, power vis-à-vis other associated *buraku,* and other considerations affect the internal structure. Just as individual persons in traditional households are minutely stratified into hierarchical statuses, so are most traditional communities. Seemingly insignificant differences in property holding and seniority can be the basis for considerable differences in power and influence. For example, a household with just insufficient land, renting from another with a little to spare, is in a poor position to oppose its landlord on community issues; if, moreover, the renting house is junior kin to the landowning house and if its resources are not quite enough to tide it over a crisis, this junior, part-tenant house will tend to be in perennial subservience to the senior house even if the crisis never arrives. Not one but several houses, sometimes a majority, can be in similarly dependent status vis-à-vis one or two houses. Such relations may arise on the basis of no more than a 2- to 3-acre difference in landholdings. Other factors, such as outside social or business connections, also tend to put privilege and leadership into the hands of certain influential houses or persons (*yūryokusha*) who exercise that power with all-pervading scope in a pattern that may have continued for generations. Most houses that manage to wield power or influence are fortified by their kinship connections; junior houses of a lineage may have to do the bidding of a senior because of economic dependence, as just noted, or they may offer support in the hope of eventual benefit from the senior's position of power. The entire local community then may either fall under the domination of a single lineage or be the arena of long-drawn-out contests for power among several lineages. It is not surprising, judging from this instance, that Japanese look on the kinship group as an instrument to organize long-term manipulations in search of power on the one hand and security on the other. They have extended its patterns outside kinship proper over a wide range of their society. Such extensions are examined below (see "*Dōzoku* and *Oyabun-Kobun*").

The corporate, collective, often hierarchical elemental community we have been considering here is best regarded as the base from which modern communities are emerging. Among modern Japanese, communities of this type are in poor repute as being remnants of a "feudal" tradition. Strong new forces noted above have, in fact, diluted the self-contained collective community everywhere, especially in the decades since 1945. The agricultural land reform of 1947 greatly alleviated economic inequalities that promoted hierarchical subservience among tenant households. Agricultural cooperatives have been able to provide savings and loan services on an impersonal, contractual basis, have found markets for differentiated and specialized crops, and have helped to promote higher crop yields, while lower taxes and continued market demand at good prices have reduced the poverty which was so readily exploited for power by more well-to-do houses. Particularly striking has been the capacity of farmers, especially those just entering community life as young adults, to find outside jobs or side work at home, get machinery, and break away from unconditioned dependence on their land and on communal assistance. Nevertheless, the tight discipline of the *buraku* remains an important consideration. Landlordism continues in forests, pastures, and other lands exempted from the land reform program, and even where landholdings are equalized, irrigation and other matters continue to impose collectivity on farmers. Politically, also, *buraku* solidarity overrides diverse interests. Even though men from many *buraku* are apt to be members of one or another voluntary interest association (for agricultural improvement, technical activities, hobbies and recreation, etc.), such associations rarely try to exert any political influence on issues that might cut across *buraku* interests, which are those defined by the influential members of the *buraku*. Members tend to vote en bloc for a candidate for local office, hoping to win favors for their hamlet, whereas their vote might be split widely were each person to vote his respective economic, occupational, or other interests. Should inter-*buraku* interest groups become active rather than latent in political channels, their crosscutting organization would provide genuine alternative choices to *buraku* residents both as voters and as candidates for election. Maneuvering for political support would open up fields of political action and inject a dynamic function into politics, which tends to be strongly suppressed under the joint traditions of *buraku* solidarity and unanimous consensus within each collectivity.

HOUSEHOLD, LINEAGE, AND KINDRED

Households tend to take shape differently when they have different ways of making a living. The members of a wage or salary earner's family have no direct part in his work and add no increment to his pay, though all must live on his wages or salary. They comprise a consumption unit but not a production unit and fare better when they are few. The wage or salary earner's family, other things being equal, tends to shrink to the smallest possible size: a *nuclear* or *conjugal family* (a married couple and their children). The case of a craftsman or an owner of a small store may well be different (likewise, that of a farmer dependent on family labor), since a wife or child or parent or sibling often may help in the work; the enterprise may in fact be able to absorb the part- or full-time labor of a number of persons. Being both a production and a consumption unit, such a family tends to be larger than the salary earner's family.

Japan has not one but several family patterns, each adapted to different economic circumstances. Small families are most typical where there are the greatest numbers of salaried employees of large firms or the government. Laborers' families are less uniformly small, apparently because, though money in wages is their source of support, there are situations of low pay in which two or more working members are needed to keep a single household going. As wage levels rise, laborers' families can be expected to become smaller. Larger families, then, are more characteristic of persons in self-employed occupations, particularly when the home is used as a workshop or the family helps run a store. Farm areas, also, traditionally have had larger families.

Size difference is not, however, the crucial index feature of different family types in Japan. In fact, the average difference between "large" and "small" is not startling. The nation's highest averages in family size in 1960 reached 5.8 members in the rural northeastern prefectures; small cities averaged 4.5 members; and the metropolitan areas, with an average membership of 4.3, still did not match the United States average of 3.4 persons per family in the same year. Family membership figures throughout Japan have been dropping gradually over the years, indicating a long-term trend toward smaller families even in nonsalaried occupations, but very large families were not typical of most of Japan even three and four generations ago, being found only in localities such as the famous Shirakawa village near Kyoto, where special conditions favored expansion toward fifteen, twenty, or more persons. Occupational conditions, however, not only control size; they also lead toward very different conceptions and expectations about the family on the part of family members. Our attention, thus, will be directed to these expectations about the role of the family.

To avoid confusion, we shall abandon the term *family,* which has a variable meaning in English usage. The term *household* will serve for persons living together and acting as a consumption unit, that is, operating on a common budget. Larger groups will be referred to by such terms as *lineage* and *kindred,* as explained below. The term *corporate group* will also be used, referring to any group (whether composed of kin or not) that controls property of any sort, preserves its structure without essential change through the addition or loss of members, and endures beyond the lifetime of its current members. The members of a corporate group have the role of representatives or trustees, whose personal wants and rights tend to be subordinated to the needs and rights of the group entity.

Households of the new middle class supported by salaries, as described by Ezra Vogel in a suburb near Tokyo and by Ronald P. Dore in a Tokyo ward, are nuclear households, consisting of a married couple and their children. They do not function as corporate entities. In composition and the roles of their members, they resemble typical American households. Many are apartment dwellers or live in rented houses. While husbands go off to work, their wives do the shopping, clean the house, tend preschool children, and, in their spare time, may go out for lessons in flower arranging, etc., or meet at home with a group of friends who have formed a reading club or have other common interests. The husband is home only at night and for part of the weekend; as Vogel puts it, he manages employment and recreation, while his wife manages home and children. The wife actually controls the greater part of spending and income management. Except in new-built areas, such families are mingled among others, including some of traditional organization. Of 297 households counted by Dore in a ward of Tokyo, 254 consisted of single persons or couples with or without young children; 43 consisted of parents with married children. Many households of the more numerous group were immature households of young persons, a majority of whom had moved to the city from rural areas; in time, they may become three-generation households. More than half of these surveyed by Dore rather expected in old age to be supported by their children; only 10 per cent explicitly hoped to stay independent. These 10 per cent are significant because they evince the conception of a family that lasts only for one lifetime; for a good many of the rest, however, this is far too casual a view of what a family should be.

The more traditional household, once established, is expected to endure without a foreseeable end. This expectation tends to give it an individuality transcending the personal rights of its members, making it a corporate household. It is a property-holding unit, though modern law puts the property in the name of one or more of its members. The household clusters around a descent line of males (father and one son, as well as grandfather or grandson, if alive). The position of the descent line is that of trustee of the household's welfare and its patrimony, which passes from the head to his chosen successor, ideally the eldest son. Other members, who join the household by birth or marriage or leave it through marriage or migration, move in and out without altering this continuity; but their full loyalty to the household is expected while they are members, and they abide by household decisions, generally issued by the male head, who is thus in a position of strong authority. Within the household, each member occupies a unique status. Certain tasks and prerogatives are assigned to each status position by relative age, sex, and birth order rather than by individual talents or tastes; allocation of household functions, thus, is almost identical from house to house, since all have the same roster of hierarchical status positions (whether each is occupied or not). This system, providing statuses clustered around and focused on a unilateral descent line, is known as the *stem family*. The stem family system was clearly prescribed and upheld by prewar law, which fostered it as "the Japanese family system." Occasionally in strict or "ideal" form but more often in modified form, it continues to be common where the household business or property is small and not in a suitable form to be broken up among, say, a widow and several children as heirs. The average farm in Japan covers 2 acres, too small an area to be viable if divided, and so it goes as a unit to a single heir. It is not hard, then, to see why the stem family is a common rural form and why the term *family* means a succession of generations, not a cluster of persons who temporarily live together for part of one generation.

The stem family differs from an *extended family* (the classic ideal in China, for example), which treats all children as heirs and so fans out in succeeding generations if possible. The stem family excludes brothers and sisters of the single heir and tries to find other means for their survival. It must have one heir, however, and if no children or only girl children are born, it preserves the patrilineal ideal by adopting a son, called a *yōshi*, who becomes the daughter's husband if girl children have been born. Literally, in this case the descent line is continued not through males but through a daughter, but in Japanese thinking the stem family pattern is not broken so long as a male (the *yōshi*, in this case) occupies the status of "house head."

The failure to divide land or property among several survivors is a matter of necessity, not choice, for the household resources are simply not ample enough to support more than one household. One might ask: why not have more than one child? If we go back not so very far into the past, high mortality if nothing else dictated having several children, so that one, at least, would survive to inherit. Even in a small community, things would tend to balance out, since girls would leave home at marriage and a noninheriting son might enter a house with no natural son, wed to a daughter as a *yōshi*. But some sons found no place to go and, instead, spent dreary lives as bachelor "uncles." Industrialization rather changed this pattern on the farms, at least, because propertyless male youths were siphoned away into the urban labor force or off to the United States or some other foreign land. There is evidence to show that unitary inheritance first became common among ordinary people, in contrast to the elite, who had long practiced it, when cities began to grow and increase demands for labor.

Over the course of several generations, however, the household resources of a farmer or a small craftsman or businessman might well grow large enough to be viable after division. In such a case, a second son would receive enough to live, with luck, as head of a household of his own. Nevertheless, his branch house (*bunke*) would continue to recognize kinship with the main house (*honke*) and often have to depend on it, especially in a crisis. Thus, the hierarchy already established within each household (by closeness to the stem descent line, in terms of sex and relative age) appeared also between main and branch houses, tending to be preserved down through generations. Main and branch house connections tend to be important in the thinking of a large proportion of Japanese today, including those who live ostensibly as conjugal-family households, because these are in effect new-formed branch houses.

The Japanese term *ie* (house) may apply to only one household, but the *ie* included all branch houses under prewar law and tends on the whole to apply to the main and branch cluster today if the households live in close enough proximity to maintain relations. Thus the *ie* is a *patrilineage,* a network of households related through their respective heads, comprising main houses, branch houses, and branches of branch houses traced down through generations. In traditional Japanese thinking, households rather than individual persons are the essential units of a lineage, and this thinking extends to census counts and membership in various organizations. It is the household, as a collectivity, that is enumerated or has membership rather than certain individual persons within it.

The patrilineage in Japan, then, is the system within which are handled corporate ownership, property inheritance, and perpetuation of the kin group. Various other functions, however, may be handled within a different system, called the *bilateral kindred.* Persons included in a network of bilateral kindred are relatives, connected through the wife, sister, or mother (affinal and matrilineal relatives) as much as through males. The network is not identical for any two persons, by definition and also because people trace connections in different directions and to varying degrees of remoteness, depending on circumstances. Hence these networks are not corporate entities. Bilateral kindred do not own property collectively but may assist each other regularly or occasionally in work that needs larger than household groups (house building, rice transplanting, etc.), in money matters, in ceremonial or social activities, and on life-crisis occasions. They comprise a reciprocally cooperative, nonhierarchical group, seen in action perhaps most clearly when the death of a kinsman brings them together for his funeral. Some attendants at a funeral are lineage members, and some are community members, for death hurts these two groups as well, of course; but kinsmen attend whose links are by marriage or through females and who may live some distance away. These are neither part of the lineage nor part of the community but are the bilateral kindred. This kindred group consists of more than just "leftover" relatives, for, as Harumi Befu notes in reviewing studies of the two groups, a given household may count maternal relatives close within its circle of intimacy while omitting certain patrilineally linked households (which belong to the main and branch house cluster that comprise the lineage). Thus, a person's bilateral kindred crosscuts his lineage.

To some extent, lineage and kindred are complementary, having separate functions. Yet a dual loyalty may engender conflict or tension between the two groups, depending on the situation. The bilateral kindred flourishes where economic opportunities are varied, but kinsmen still live fairly close together, e.g., in villages that have a diversified and market-oriented agriculture and are within commuting range of cities. In such cases, nonkin associations (agricultural cooperatives, local government, etc.) serve a good many functions; so kindreds do not become all-pervasive as a basis for social life. By contrast, a situation of relatively deficient economic opportunity, whether due to isolation, land scarcity, low technical capacity, or other factors sufficiently acute to keep some households at the very margin of existence and unable to cope alone even with predictable crises—in short, a situation of economic dependency—promotes patron-client relationships. The hierarchical, corporate lineage provides a framework for such relationships, and it tends to have greater importance than the bilateral insurance to the weaker branch households in return for their subservience.

Yanagida Kunio presents evidence to show that lineage organization, that is, the *ie*, gained strength as a nationwide rather than merely an elite family pattern when industrial urbanization of the nineteenth and twentieth centuries drew younger sons and daughters out of Japan's villages. As he points out, village and kindred cooperative patterns could not help migrants in the city, support them there temporarily, or give them refuge at home in times of crisis. A more widely extended system, the *ie*, served these functions better. Moreover, the corporate *ie* served to concentrate capital for entrepreneurial ventures. By the present day, however, the high-risk aspect of emigration to the city has been reduced; education meriting permanent skilled jobs rather than unskilled labor brings many newcomers to the city, and households that are already stabilized in the city can do without lineage support. Since urban living tends to center in the nonkin relations of job, neighborhood, public services, and commercial purchasing and entertainment, the lineage and the bilateral kindred, as well, fade into relative unimportance for city dwellers. City people are conscious of both but not keenly concerned about either.

Present-day Japanese conceptions of kinship are obviously varied, this being a period of transition. Conjugal families have formed among the urbanized salaried or wage-paid groups in the society; we cannot yet foresee how many of these families will mature into stem families that aim at indefinite perpetuation in keeping with tradition, but a good many aim neither at large size nor at indefinite continuance. Among most other segments of society, the household is still regarded as one link in a perpetual line of descent. Its main and branch ties with other households are traced through male house heads, where possible. Simultaneously, it is part of a bilateral kindred, which crosscuts several distinct lineages. The kindred may remain latent or undeveloped under circumstances that give functional advantage to a corporate lineage structure. It is rather rare in Japan to have the emphasis completely reversed, with stress on kindred and unconcern about lineage, since the patrilineal transmission of name, property, and status keeps people conscious of their paternal descent line. The individual person or household whose resources are scanty can find security within a strong corporate kin group but at the price of submission to discipline and loss of personal freedom. Conversely, the more flexible bilateral kindred offers broader freedom but no assurance of limitless support for its core members, there being no structural core to a kindred. Most studies of Japanese kinship structure have been made in rural areas; they show clearly that structure follows function: kinship structures respond sensitively to the pressure of economic, political, and social conditions. In former times, persons had to rely largely on kin and near neighbors —on lineage or kindred plus community but seldom on both equally— for many indispensable functions. Their concern for kinship was strong, for good reasons. But kinship has been of decreasing prominence in recent years, as impersonal nonkin types of association usurp many of its functions. Moreover, prosperity, increased economic opportunity, and mobility throughout rural Japan since its recovery after World War II have created situations in which kinship is no longer significant and the traditional forms face decay. As in the case of the *buraku* community, the traditional kinship and household patterns are held in disrepute by the modern Japanese, and the corporate holding of property is even illegal in certain instances. Yet the claim of the "emancipated" urban intellectual that old patterns no longer hold for him is often wishful thinking rather than actuality.

DŌZOKU AND *OYABUN-KOBUN*

Societies of considerable size and complexity cannot be organized solely as genealogically integrated groups, but kinship as a prime principle of association can be extended to incorporate persons outside an actual descent group. Holding the premise that the most sure, enduring bonds are those among relatives, people formalize associations which they wish to make certain and lasting by treating them as if they had a genealogical basis. Traditional Japanese society is certainly to be numbered among the societies in which parakinship devices have been used with great frequency. Parakinship in Japan has brought together not only individual persons but entire households as units. This procedure, of course, follows easily and naturally from the practice of viewing genealogical links as existing among households, not among individual persons. The *honke-bunke* grouping described above is just such a house-based way of dealing with kinsmen, and its extension is the *dōzoku*.

The constituent units of a *dōzoku* are households, not persons, just as the members of an ordinary lineage are households, not persons. *Dōzoku* is the scholar's term applied to a lineage in which (1) non-related households are "adopted" into the cluster and designated as kindred; and (2) hierarchical relationships do not remain latent but are strongly emphasized to ensure tightly disciplined, authoritarian control of the entire group. These days, *dōzoku* are becoming rare except in vestigial form. They flourished in economically handicapped or stagnant rural regions; most isolated and mountainous localities had *dōzoku* or retain them still, and northeastern Japan until recently was especially known as a region of general emphasis on lineage and of frequent appearances of *dōzoku*. *Dōzoku* also existed in cities; an outstanding study by Nakano Takashi deals with drug firms in Kyoto that, in times before codified law offered safeguards to corporations, established and controlled chains of branch stores by putting them under sons and servants who were branches of *dōzoku*.

How does a *dōzoku* take form and carry out its functions? As treated by scholars, a *dōzoku* is a hierarchically differentiated group of households bonded together for common support; it comprises mostly members of a lineage but is apt to include the household of onetime servants, tenants, or other recipients of patronage; all member households are addressed or referred to by terms implying kinship with their patron and, consequently, with other members of the group. At the highest social level in premodern Japan the Tokugawa house used the *dōzoku* pattern of organization to tie the various lords of regional domains into a single organization under its leadership. We tend to describe this procedure by the special term *vassalage*, calling attention to an equivalent relation in premodern Europe; and vassalage it was, but the political bond of vassalage was both symbolized and reinforced by kinship ties of descent, marriage, adoption, and the gift giving of surnames. The Tokugawa house could thus conceive of itself as a *honke*, controlling all the lands of Japan. It gave fiefs to junior houses of its own lineage but also created parakinship ties with lordly houses that had no initial kin relation by arranging marriages or other ritual links that would both symbolize and reinforce their membership in and loyalty to the corporate group. This was the common pattern by which the "ruling families" in Japan habitually reinforced the power structure through which they exerted their influence.

Ordinary people did not have great military power or titles to consolidate and protect or to use in recruiting new supporters. A growing owner of land, craft shops, or a business, however, could enlarge his support group not merely by creating branch houses for one or more sons when he retired or died, but by awarding fields, a homestead, or a branch of the shop or business to a deserving servant or protégé, either as an outright grant or in tenancy. A formal ritual of adoption often accompanied the bestowal, but the servant's status was inferior to that of a member of a genealogical branch, just as his subsistence stake was lower. Kinship status thus tended to match land or share holdings in a *dōzoku*, in a hierarchical series based both on closeness of kinship to the main house and on seniority of the branch as counted by generations: the lowest members (known by such terms as *nago, bekke,* and so on) were simply serfs, tenants, or hired hands newly incorporated into the group; genealogical *bunke* owned part of their land (or a small branch shop, etc.), while the *honke* retained control of the main resources. All were joint but unequal participants in the enterprise, be it farming plus lacquerwork, as described in the outstanding monograph on *dōzoku* by Ariga Kizaemon, rental rights to land granted to the keeper of a shrine, or a chain of inns or stores.

The economic basis of *dōzoku* affiliation has been stressed in this brief description. It is significant that *dōzoku* organization has faded into the background where both increased opportunities for livelihood and greater occupational diversity have appeared; the *dōzoku* exists to combat scarcity, it would seem, and thrives best where the many houses must draw their livelihood from a small range of monopolizable resources. Yet even where economic foundations weaken or decay, the kin ties long continue to be echoed in political, social, and ceremonial affairs. All marriages, for instance, may continue to be performed at the main house, where branch and parakin houses also gather for ceremonies honoring the group's protective deity. Branch members may continue to seek guidance from the stem house on financial matters or voting, education of their children, and many other matters, while the head of this *honke* depends on them to vote himself or his candidates into office or to give other loyal support.

There are various other instances of houses linked into solidary groups in the style of *honke* and *bunke*, though less firmly bound to a single economic enterprise. People acting as if linked by kinship follow the *dōzoku* paradigm, as demonstrated by such conditions as these: priests and abbots of head and branch Buddhist temples (most explicitly those of the Shin sect, as studied by Morioka Kiyomi), the chiefs of head and branch offices of various firms (such as the Kyoto drug firms mentioned above), the keepers of chains of inns or places of entertainment, and so on. Often enough, members of such groups do share actual descent, but it is not necessary. Such explicit linking of kinship with business or religious affairs has a decidedly old-fashioned flavor today, and new examples rise only rarely. Yet the established instances often have much vitality. Perhaps the most vital single trait in this pattern is that of adoption. It is by adoption of his most talented apprentice that the master (*iemoto*) of a school of Kabuki acting, flower arranging, the sport of sumo, or other occupations stressing skill establishes authority over the novice's career while ensuring that his own *ie* name (or even his given name, conferred on the discipline) will carry its luster into the next generation. A considerably looser pattern of kin linkage, involving descent and intermarriage, was employed by numerous great and near great houses of finance and commerce to knit together their enterprises in a family-centered empire; here, again, adoption recruited talented successors. A good many, though not all, of the big-business *zaibatsu* comprised such family empires, but today their continued strength is maintained through agreements, understandings, and financial links without necessarily being reinforced by kinship.

But here we verge on another distinct pattern, though similarly hierarchical and phrased in kin terminology. In this pattern, individual persons rather than households assume or virtually create parakin relationships with each other. Such kin ties have a rich basis in traditional culture, corresponding in general form and function to the European folk custom of godparenthood: a ritual tie phrased in terms of kinship and established at an age-grade transition of one partner. Thus, a maturing boy selects a man as his ritual parent, a girl selects a woman, and a bridal couple have their go-betweens. By no means does everyone in Japan now have even one such partner, but many have one or two. From such a prototype relation comes the *oyabun-kobun* (quasi-parent–quasi-child) relation.

The *oyabun* is a ritual father who protects or stands as a patron to *kobun* or ritual sons in return for their loyalty or service. He is also their boss and is often referred to by this term, *bosu*, in Japan today; his gang or team of subordinates work under his orders on the job and also must clear with him any significant actions off the job or between jobs. This hierarchical relationship frequently appears in industries requiring quantities of unskilled labor at intervals, in which the man who is an *oyabun* (his social role) holding a foreman position (his occupational role) signs on his own *kobun* when he finds work or tides them over between jobs. As John Bennett and Ishino Iwao have shown in a study of forestry organization, the pattern is flexible enough to admit degrees of semiskilled and skilled labor as well. When bosses of small scale become formally attached to a larger boss, *oyabun-kobun* teams several generations deep (including grandchild, child, parent, or uncle relations) emerge. Mining and other occupations involving considerable risk while requiring skill also have such *oyabun-kobun* groups; one function is to ensure care for one's family in the event of injury or death. Be it noted that everyone gets some sort of reward for submitting to an *oyabun*; consequently, followers remain faithful to their leader when times are hard, as they never would for a man who has used sheer power to subordinate others.

Japanese use the terms *oyabun* and *bosu* rather loosely today for a wide range of situations: among gamblers and gangsters, longshoremen, and shoeshiners; in labor unions; within political machines; and in the academic world. Some cases so labeled were never initiated with the formal, weddinglike ritual that is traditional to the pattern. Instead, they are merely tacit hierarchical systems of patronage from above and loyalty from below; even a student-professor relation, if close, may be given the label, though it is not apt to be self-acknowledged. Nevertheless, even the informally linked pairs or groups preserve kin-patterned qualities: long-term or lifelong associations, superior-inferior differentiation, and recognition of mutual obligation outside the primary functional relationship (e.g., when the senior provides medicine for an ill subordinate or smooths things out after a spat with his wife). The superior and inferior are not on impersonal terms; quite the reverse. They must take the other person's feelings continually into account, and they share affection along with a working relationship.

The disrepute which such personalizing of political and economic relations has now gained in Japan is apt to undervalue the positive aspects of the traditional social patterns in a transition society. In situations approaching the ideal types, *oyabun-kobun* or *dōzoku* and *honke-bunke* thrived while modern institutions of social welfare were rudimentary in Japan. They offered economic security to underpaid proletarian workers in the city as well as to dependent farmers in the country, along with a measure of companionship wanted, for example, by persons displaced from their ancestral homes to the cities or other places of work. The need to rely on such relations has dropped as wage and salary income has risen above the minimum level for existence, yet their functions are not at all obsolete in present-day Japan. Granted that ritual affirmation is rare, nevertheless observers see such patterns binding together cliques in the Diet or local legislatures, that is, among the most modern Japanese institutions.

SOCIAL STRATIFICATION

For all its diversity, Japanese society can also be regarded as a single entity or system. Taking the society as a whole, it can be thought of as a system having functionally diverse parts and, at the same time, assorted levels, expressed as differences in control of power, prestige, and wealth, which cut across the functional diversities. In studies of the class system, or system of social stratification, students of society attempt to form a consistent, empirical image of the whole society. This attempt requires two operations: (1) constructing an image that represents different levels within the society and (2) finding suitable criteria for locating real persons accurately within the image. Classes in a complex society, and all the more in a changing society, may not be arranged as simply as layers in an old-fashioned cake. If we look at the pattern of social stratification through the so-called "elites," for instance, we can see that no simple drawing of horizontal lines will tell the whole story. There are apt to be functionally differentiated elites in a modern, changing society, who may not enjoy equal amounts of wealth, power, and prestige. People of high prestige may be impoverished, and vice versa. Few have equal shares of all three criteria of eminence. Moreover, elites of different functions qualify as "the people who matter" only in limited contexts in which their respective functions are important. Thus it is necessary to distinguish two broad patterns of social order, the one committed to clear-cut grades and ranks in which the criterion of power is at the same time nearly identical with the criteria of wealth and prestige, the other adhering to an ideal of fluid movement that tolerates or strives to maintain open or blurred boundary zones between its various levels.

We may start with the assertion that in premodern Japan it was considered essential for all three criteria to converge on the same group, a unique elite, who were identified with their high status from birth onward. Today, the three criteria are separate enough so that each can be used as a path upward; hence a person's status may fluctuate during his lifetime.

Japanese tradition inherited a Chinese image of social structure that was applied to Japan as the official view during the Tokugawa period. From top to bottom, it contained four fixed levels or strata: the samurai or warrior aristocracy, the farmers, the artisans, and the merchants. In Chinese theory, the upper class was that of the scholar-bureaucrat, with the implication that social order was chaotic when warriors seized power; but this theory did not fit the fact in Japan, inasmuch as warriors as such monopolized the administrative eliteship. The Japanese therefore fitted theory to fact, treating warriors as the topmost class. (They were able to point out, to their delight, that the society in which Confucius lived was more nearly like that of Tokugawa Japan than the supposed Confucian ideal.) At the other end of the scale, in the case of merchants, the Tokugawa regime attempted to preserve theory. As an "unproductive" group, merchants should rank below all producers of goods—farmers and artisans—and discriminatory edicts throughout the Tokugawa era vainly reiterated this logic while in fact merchant status ceaselessly rose. The Tokugawa theory of clear, fixed, and stable class divisions requisite to an orderly society could be maintained best if criteria of power, prestige, and affluence coincided, that is, if the groups that had the most prestige truly exercised the most power and controlled the most wealth. Over the 2½ centuries of Tokugawa rule, society fell away from this principle through several developments. Feudal lords withdrew samurai from the land into their administrative headquarters and, in lieu of their previous revenue rights to specific fields, paid them stipends from the general treasury. Farmers who had been made the representatives of their communities consequently bore increased responsibility for managing internal village affairs; they became, in effect, landlord-administrators over their fellow villagers. Meanwhile, trade demands gave increasing wealth and a measure of power to merchants. These alterations blurred the divisions between classes, weakened the theoretical four-class system, and eventually transformed it.

Even before changing conditions undermined the system, moreover, there were qualifications and exceptions to its ostensible fixity. Ascribed statuses were supposed to match ascribed functions and, as in any theoretically frozen-status society, "residue" categories existed for persons or groups that did not fit the functions called for by their birth. To some extent, the Buddhist orders absorbed warrior sons or daughters who did not fulfill expectations, peasants who were crowded off the land, widows, and others and so provided such a residue category. Even more noteworthy were the provisions for achievement and mobility. For instance, adoption was a frequent device whereby families of high status recruited talented persons of lower status. A merchant, in rising to power, might never gain commensurate prestige himself but could improve his son's status by remitting debts of a samurai family that would adopt the son. This example illustrates the wider principle of achievement in behalf of a collective group rather than for personal gain alone, of which many examples could be noted. Such devices as adoption and achievement for the group were distinctive Japanese embellishments of their system, which gave it resilience to survive in more recent times rather than having to be shattered completely to make mobility possible.

Before concluding this summary analysis of traditional Japanese society, we should consider an alternative view of its classic or ideal form not as a four-class system but as a two-class system. A basic premise of the Tokugawa economy was that the control of land and its products should be the major criterion of power, prerogative, and wealth; that is, those persons who administered agriculture and distributed its proceeds should at the same time monopolize government, maintain armed capacity to control and defend society, and enjoy the privileges of wealth. This class, consisting of lords and their samurai retainers, was the class of privilege; the balance of society, diverse in occupations but alike in being excluded from these functions, comprised the second, the nonprivileged class. Any agrarian society, counting on tilled fields and pastures as its only resource, tends to separate into two such classes. To Karl Marx, this fateful division into two classes appeared inevitable not in agrarian societies alone but in industrial societies as well, on the premise that capital could be monopolized as fully as land, and the Marxist analysis has seemed persuasive to many thoughtful Japanese as an explanation of the persistent gulf between privileged and nonprivileged groups in recent times as well as in the past. For our purposes, it is most significant that the Marxist interpretation treats merchants not merely as an additional or third class of the Tokugawa system but as harbingers of a two-class system based on capital that eventually superseded the former system based on the products of agriculture. The Marxist analysis fits the past better than the present, a fact that is increasingly apparent to formerly convinced Marxists.

The traditional basis of social stratification has been significantly leavened in the past century of economic and social transformation. Capitalistic enterprise, occupational diversification, and education have served as driving forces for extensive mobility. Surveys requesting information on paternal occupation show that, outside such traditional sectors as agriculture, more than half of the persons responding are employed in fields different from their fathers' occupations. Occupational mobility is not limited to lateral movement; there is considerable vertical fluidity also, apart from the overall improvement in standards of living. A middle class, presaged for half a century in shadowy form, has now clearly emerged. Perhaps the most telling change of all is the widespread expectation, evidenced in children of school age and up, that they may achieve higher social status in their lifetime. In short, mobility that was, so to speak, smuggled into the hierarchical system of rigid classes of the Tokugawa era has become an openly emphasized feature of modern social structure. Not, however, that hierarchy, ascription of status at birth, and status by group affiliation have been left in the past; far from it. On the national scale, despite the general relaxation of boundaries, contemporary Japanese society is class-structured and status conscious.

Nationwide uniformity of class divisions has disappeared, however, and society has moved far toward pluralism. It is necessary to take into account plural and often competing elite groups. A simple illustration may be given at the level of local communities, such as a small town or rural village where, in the phrase of Fukutake Tadashi, leadership is split between members of an "old middle class" and a "new middle class" (members of the national elites rarely have their homes outside metropolitan centers, and the middle classes on a national scale function locally as the upper stratum). Persons of the old middle class derive status mainly from traditional sources: inherited land, money, business, ancestral eminence or former warrior rank, family connections with shrines, temples, or local enterprises, and so on. Members of the new middle class may have more modest economic standing and often depend on a salary or professional income but wield influence or power that comes from non-traditional sources: technical skill or knowledge, bureaucratic experience, former military rank, or entrepreneurial success. Members of the new middle class are apt to be such persons as doctors, engineers, and heads of departments of local government, whereas typical members of the old middle class may be owners of sake breweries or grain-processing mills, operators of handicrafts or inns, owners of forest land, and the like, who usually retain an interest in farmland and farm products. The new middle class may play second fiddle in local political and social affairs; but its power and prestige come to the fore when the community or its members must deal, say, with big business or the prefectural and central government, for its members have ties with the metropolis or capital through university friendships, company contracts, or acquaintances among outside government offices. Pluralism at the local level, thus, is in no small measure a consequence of each community's growing involvement in national affairs and, reciprocally, the central government's widening role in matters ranging from road and dam building to health insurance and wage setting.

A new way of life has been crystallizing around the new middle class, of which we have just examined a local sample. It is not easy to specify the limits of this class precisely. Some 8 million salaried or white-collar workers, in addition to self-employed professionals, form its core; but its fringes include a much larger proportion of the total society. Let us for the moment accept the premise that middle-class status is in part a subjective attitude or state of mind: a perception of oneself as belonging to a group possessing a measure of economic, political, and social independence, capacity to set and achieve personal goals, and responsibility to plan and exercise foresight in progressing toward those goals, together with a realization that influence over national affairs rests with others. No given level of income guarantees that this self-perception will exist, but income is clearly one prerequisite. Hence we can say that the middle class, though broader than the core of salaried and professional groups, falls somewhere within the limits of those who, in surveys, declare themselves as belonging to a middle-income group, as did 76 per cent of the respondents to a 1961 survey.

This middle class deserves special attention here, both to indicate what novel ingredients it adds to Japanese society and to caution the reader against a too easy equation with the middle class of American or Western European society. Family patterns in this class, described above, reflect its mobility, its dependence on individual drive and achievement, and its partial divorce from particularistic principles of social intercourse. New middle-class families have scarcely more than enough children to maintain their numbers in the next generation; but this rapidly growing class recruits new members not only from among yellow-collar (independent services) and blue-collar (labor) workers, but also directly from the countryside, thanks to a national school system so evenly developed that farm-bred migrants to town do not have to drift into factories before rising upward but flow in even greater numbers directly into salaried positions in banks, company offices, and government bureaus. Consumer-oriented manufacturers and businessmen direct much of their selling effort to this class, which has income beyond daily needs to pay for university education, automobiles and television sets, vacations, and new houses and to invest in the stock market.

As yet, however, this new middle class is far from being a focal area or center of gravity of power and prestige. Its members do in fact share many interests, goals, and problems, but they have not managed to articulate them in a united voice that commands attention from others. If they have across-the-board cohesion, it is most apparent in its negative aspects. Politically, they are among the neglected little people represented by no strong political organization, who are negatively resigned to various patterns of protest voting against the *status quo*. The Liberal Democratic Party appeals to big business or the rural voter, while the Socialist parties seem to be captured by labor; neither side consistently shapes issues to gather support from the new middle class. Economic structure, too, militates against positive sentiments of horizontal solidarity, especially among the salaried members of the class. The young salaryman enters a company as the young scholar joins a university, with every expectation of staying for life, not so much out of choice as because these organizations do not yet cross-bid competitively or encourage the transfer of employees. It does him little practical good to be concerned about how other companies treat employees in his position; his own company tends to become his sole unit of reference. Even in his own organization, efficiency is apt to be much more highly valued than initiative; he has little opportunity to influence the organization that will occupy so much of his life. To the educated young man, Japan's economy offers many different routes to a higher station in life; but each is difficult of ascent for any great distance, and his entry into one virtually seals off his access to another. Restricted mobility is acknowledged to be a major problem in Japanese economic organization; as we have noted, the structure seems to permit intergenerational mobility as an incentive to achievement (along a pattern we were able to identify even in the Tokugawa period, in which the father's efforts might be rewarded in the son), but less frequently to facilitate mobility within a man's own career span.

An employee with little chance to change jobs or occupations understandably develops only a marginal interest in parallel occupations. The consequence is a pattern of vertical solidarity (commitment to his own company and occupational group), with a sharp cleavage between groups; it is a pattern analogous to the one already discerned in summarizing kinship and community organization. Bureaucrat, industrial technician or engineer, office worker, doctor, jurist, artist, journalist, and scholar comprise, as it were, parallel columns; few channels of communication, movement, or solidarity cut across these columns to bring to people at roughly equivalent levels in the separate columns a lively sense of common purpose or common cause which might counterbalance their solidarity with groups above and below them in the same column. An office worker identifies himself positively as part of his office or department clique, his company, and his occupation or profession; he has little to share with all office workers, let alone with all the three-quarters of the population who claim to be in the same middle-income category. The Japanese new middle class clearly covers a narrower range than similar classes in the United States or Western Europe. Even more significantly, it still lacks and may not for a long time acquire the comprehensive and pluralistic solidarity that makes the American middle class, particularly, an entity with economic, political, and social power.

Below the middle class are skilled laborers whose rising wage structure gives them a toehold on many of the material amenities that are now commonplace in salarymen's lives, but whose prestige level suffers from the fact that their work soils their hands. Wages in Japan's multitude of small enterprises formerly lagged well behind those of employees in large companies, but small-business workers now are on a nearly equal basis of pay. These skilled workers, together with salary earners, partly fill the formerly void gap between the impoverished masses and the wealthy economic elite of Japanese society. Continued postwar agricultural prosperity has lifted the incomes of a large proportion of farm households also out of the category of depressed groups. Nevertheless, there remain stark instances of economic inequality. A substantial segment of the labor force classed as "temporary workers" is ineligible to gain union membership, wage increments, job security, and other benefits and so falls among the depressed groups, along with workers in small service establishments, unskilled laborers, miners, and people in isolated mountain and fishing communities. Discriminatory sentiments also keep the urban segments of the subsociety of outcasts—the *"buraku* people," or Eta—in poverty. Such groups comprise "the masses" in Japan, a still large number who have been almost bypassed by prosperity but suffer from price inflation, who out of economic necessity rarely can forsake whatever traditional collective social arrangements they possess. Traditional patterns of Japanese society continue to characterize this social stratum.

Members of the upper strata of contemporary society—financiers, great industrialists and merchants, publishers, statesmen, big-name politicians, writers, and performing artists—gather in metropolitan areas. To a considerable degree, these upper-class Japanese, like Japanese of the middle class, comprise compartmented occupational cliques. They are the elite upper levels of the distinct columns depicted at the middle level of society. Each category is cohesive within its own occupational compartment; for instance, networks of marriage, kinship, and parakinship of the *oyabun-kobun* type that link certain elite business families to others are often cited as the substructural basis for close cooperation among large companies even after the dissolution of the formal corporate combines which held these companies together until the end of World War II. More or less similar cohesiveness characterizes elite members within other compartments as well, whereas bonds that span several compartments are relatively rare. An example or two of crosscutting bonds must, however, be cited. The university-classmate bond is one; graduates of Tokyo University Law School once constituted the chief recruitment pool for certain government departments and business firms; even though this school's monopoly on such jobs is now diminished, former graduates furnish a channel of communication between these businesses and branches of the bureaucracy. Moreover, large firms doing business with particular government agencies find posts in their own organizations for higher officials retiring from these agencies. Up to now, business-government connections have attracted close scrutiny, perhaps more so than possible connections among other elites. Further study may yet reveal stronger cross-elite solidarity than is now suspected, but at present it would be rash to consider the columns that comprise the top strata of Japanese society to be linked together in an "Establishment," to use the British term.

PATTERNS OF INTERPERSONAL RELATIONS

Having outlined the basic social institutions of Japan, noting particularly its dual structures, we may now inquire more closely into the behavioral patterns of contemporary Japanese. Institutional structures of society, from one viewpoint, are no more than generalized patterns of attitude and behavior; yet they do have a distinct existence, from the opposite viewpoint, in that they enforce these patterns on the people who participate in them. Thus we may say that dual institutions in Japan require dual patterns of behavior. To deal with these contrasting patterns, convenient though rather specialized terminology may be borrowed from the sociological analytic system developed by Talcott Parsons. In his view, relationships between particular persons can be categorized along several axes of variation. Four such axes are (1) affectivity-affective neutrality, (2) diffuseness-specificity, (3) ascription-achievement, and (4) particularism-universalism. Were we to illustrate each axis in American society, we would find that the relations among members of a single family or another similarly intimate group cluster toward the first-named pole of each axis, whereas typical business transactions congregate toward the opposite pole. That is to say, we expect that parents' relations with their children will be colored by affection (affectivity), that parents will maintain their parental role in a variety of situations (diffuseness), that the status of parent as parent and of child as offspring is permanent, once initiated (ascription); and that other persons cannot be substituted in either status without altering it (particularism). Familial relations can, indeed, be businesslike on occasion but not constantly so. By contrast, persons dealing with each other in a typical business transaction need invest no personal feelings in the matter (affective neutrality), need not extend their relation beyond the business of the moment (specificity), expect each other to meet certain standards of performance (achievement), and may deal with any number of other persons similarly (universalism).

Patterns of relationship at the neutral, specific, achieved, and universalistic poles of these several axes are conveniently adapted to a large, mobile, and diversified society. In such societies in modern times the business corporation and the business contract have become prevalent as effective devices for bringing persons together to mobilize effort without challenging or diluting these qualities of relationship. Accordingly, for shorthand reference, some refer to such societies as *contractual*. Japan's newer social institutions of large scale—the government, law courts, big business, and industry—bring contractual relations into play; the sheer size of her great cities requires that certain relationships be governed by impersonal, specific, and universalistic patterns.

On the other hand, even a casual examination of both formal and informal institutions of traditional Japanese society shows a clustering of relationships in modes that to modern Americans would seem appropriate only for intimate and familial situations. Particularism even stronger than is normal in American families characterized relations in the household and *ie,* creating differences in privilege among each sibling according to sex and order of birth or among each branch house of the *ie* according to its relative age of establishment. Parakinship institutions such as the *dōzoku, oyabun-kobun,* and *iemoto,* being based on a kinship prototype of interaction, extended such intimate patterns into areas of economic, political, religious, and other activity far outside the household. The resident of a corporate community, where his neighbors were also his companions in work, leisure, prayer, mourning, and collective welfare or disaster, had affective, diffuse, ascribed, and particularistic qualities that dominated his relations with them.

To say that relationships of a personal and particularistic nature were widely prevalent is not to deny the existence of other qualities altogether. Even the seventeenth and eighteenth centuries provided examples of young samurai who strove to rise to eminence, commoners who sought an education, and shopkeepers who labored to enlarge their market. These clear instances of achievement orientation were applauded rather than discredited in their time. Evidence for such an orientation is all the more interesting, however, precisely because its performance in traditional Japanese society appears to have stemmed from institutions and values quite different from those that have reinforced the drive for achievement in recent Euro-American societies. As we have noted, efforts at achievement in Japan gained the highest praise when they were exerted for the gain of a collective group or for reward in the next generation rather than for immediate self-benefit. That is to say, achievement somehow was reconciled with diffuse and particularistic relationships.

Since that time, as we have noted, elements of a contractual society have emerged in Japan. But duality is as evident in interpersonal relationships as in institutional forms; tradition-based patterns are by no means obsolescent, as is clearly brought out in studies of how people act when concerned about expectations or obligations that others place upon them. Particularly notable analyses of traditional obligation have been made by Ruth Benedict in *The Chrysanthemum and the Sword* and Ronald P. Dore in *City Life in Japan.* Professor Dore also provides analysis and clear examples of modern patterns intermingled with relations based on traditional assumptions. Miss Benedict's endeavor is to demonstrate how unique the Japanese tradition is; Dore, however, accepts the reasoning advanced earlier in this chapter that Japanese society differs not in its categories or species of behavior but in extending to more public situations the attitudes and actions that Euro-American societies, for example, reserve for their narrowest, most intimate relations. Certain Japanese terms specifically denote such attitudes and actions: they are *on* (and its reciprocal, *ongaeshi*) and *giri.*

On is a beneficence handed down from one's superior. It institutes an obligation (*ongaeshi*) to the superior on the part of the person who receives it or enjoys its benefits. By its very nature, *on* always connotes a hierarchical relation between two specific actors; the obligations that rise from *on* therefore are not part of an abstract code or principle but have at least shades of difference, inasmuch as the specific participants in one relation differ from another. The superior may be of four sorts: (1) a class superior, such as a master who gives employment to a servant, a lord who supports his retainer, or a shogun who grants a fief to a lord; (2) a kin superior, such as one's father or elder brother; (3) an age-status superior, such as one's teacher: or (4) a superior in a limited situation, such as the go-between who arranges one's marriage. Whatever his degree of superiority, a person in one of these four classes becomes permanently important to another person by having conferred *on*. The size or durability of the gift has some importance, but more essential is the implicit superior-inferior relationship that colors interaction between giver and receiver from that time onward.

The word *on* has altered its character somewhat through time. As used in the *Kojiki,* it covered both an obligation and the expected return (here called *ongaeshi*); next, under Buddhism, it came to be used for the insight or exaltation conferred on a believer. In the thirteenth century, as feudal practices arose, it concretely denoted a fief. Later it was extended to cover a number of less specific beneficences, especially the care and protection a parent gives to his child or a teacher to his pupil.

How may one make *ongaeshi,* or reciprocate for an *on*? An inferior obviously cannot repay his superior in the same coin. Indeed, the repayment is not spelled out and may well depend on the whim of the superior, which puts the recipient of *on* in an awkward and sometimes painful position (at least as viewed by moderns). By late Tokugawa times, two particular sorts of *ongaeshi* came to be singled out which thereafter were stressed by the Meiji government's rule makers as important features of discipline. One was *kō,* or filial devotion; the other was *chū,* or personal loyalty to one's lord. Repayment to parents or kin superiors through *kō* was a well-nigh universal obligation on elite and commoner alike. While feudal ranks lasted, everyone of samurai class was bound by *chū* to his lord. Loyalty to lord, of course, was hierarchical, and in the late Tokugawa and Meiji periods *kō,* as well, was on the whole an obligation of unilateral devotion upward toward the autarchical head of one's *ie,* although it earlier had carried a connotation of mutual concern between parent and child.

The implications of *giri* are closely similar to those of *on* and *ongaeshi.* To some Japanese today, *giri* is the blanket term for obligations between specific persons in concrete, actual situations, as contrasted with a universalist ethic of duty, and *on* or *ongaeshi* are merely special forms of *giri*. Others draw the following distinction: two individual persons are always hierarchically linked through *on,* whereas *giri* relations include obligations toward groups and do not necessarily establish superiority on one side and inferiority on the other. In either case, *giri* connotes obligation and as such sets the tone of relationship toward specified or specifiable other persons. *Giri* is lucid enough if considered in the matrix of collectivity-oriented behavior. It is in this matrix that one can perceive how dramas and stories written in the Tokugawa era drew their essential dramatic tension from the conflict between *giri* and *ninjō. Ninjō* refers to what one would like to do as a human being and equally to what one finds distasteful or abhorrent out of personal sentiment; *giri* pertains to what one must do or avoid doing because of status and group membership. As a human being one might revel in indolence or dissipation or abandon oneself to passionate love of one person and impassioned detestation of another, but such releases of feeling cannot be condoned if they go against collective solidarity or welfare. *Giri* implies the self-discipline that must be used to repress or channel such emotions; hence it often carries a cold or even painful connotation.

A parakinship relation, for example, is a *giri* relation establishing obligations that may conflict with personal disposition or *ninjō*. Put in other words, the Japanese, like others, do not always love their in-laws; but in-laws are *giri* parents and *giri* siblings, toward whom one must pretend affection even if one does not feel it inwardly. *Giri* requires the adopted son to take even greater pains then a natural son to show consideration and affection toward the family that incorporates him, simply because nobody can ever quite take for granted that he feels the warmth of attachment a natural son would have. It is a mistake to consider *giri* to be necessarily and inevitably painful, however; quite to the contrary, one may find happily congenial, warm affection linking one to one's *giri* partners: *ninjō* and *giri* then coincide.

Giri obligations often are mutual and reciprocal, especially within a collectivity: one offers a gift to a neighbor for his newborn child or his son's wedding or assists at a funeral, anticipating reciprocation at one's own life-crisis occasions or emergencies. *Giri* works well in a society of lifelong neighbors and associates. It is measured not from a single incident or transaction but from its coloring of an association that is expected to extend indefinitely through time. It sustains horizontal mutuality and interdependence, whether among neighbors or friends or business acquaintances. Accordingly, since such mutual support often extends to a network of persons, *giri* relations may link not just two but a whole row of participants. If *X*, who wants to buy a motor scooter, gets it cheaply from a friend of his neighbor's son, he should reciprocate by a gift or favor to two persons, in terms of *giri*.

Giri inevitably loses its effect in an environment of impersonal transactions among strangers and incidental acquaintances. One might question, therefore, whether it survives in the present-day metropolitan environment of Japan. Professor Dore shows that it indeed remains important in the midst of Tokyo at present, having functions which he specifies: it supports some economic activities, such as those of local storekeepers; it expresses one's nonrejection of neighbors and sets a clear framework of intimacy into which newly arriving residents may find their way; it offers security to all in an underdeveloped state of public welfare services; and it strengthens influence and prestige in political and business affairs.[1] It may weaken, he adds, as private savings grow, social services expand, industry rationalizes its processes further in the search for profits, civil service principles become more strictly enforced, and greater numbers of voters base their choices on issues rather than on persons.

Some persons actively cultivate enduring personal attachments within the small, close neighborhoods that nestle in the heart of every Japanese metropolis, for the reasons Professor Dore suggests. Others accept such attachments more reluctantly. And there are increasing numbers of Japanese who elect every opportunity to escape or slough off *giri* relations, regarding them as old-fashioned or feudal. The special quality of a city is that it offers a gamut of alternative ways from which its residents can make certain choices. It must be recognized, of course, that choice is not unrestricted. On the one hand, the very nature of a city imposes on all its residents a certain amount of impersonality: one uses city utilities and the transportation system, pays taxes, and buys movie tickets while having only momentary contact, at most, with clerks and ticket takers whom one may never see twice; and one moves daily among great numbers of strangers who are heterogeneous in origin, occupation, tastes, and aspirations. Those who prefer traditional relationships may develop them in their local neighborhoods but are inescapably involved in nontraditional dealings as well. Conversely, those who welcome the anonymity of city life as a release from traditional bonds must nonetheless deal often with others in a particularistic context, using personal introductions, family connections, or mutual friends to expedite their affairs or, indeed, to get them done at all. The urbanite of Japan today must be able to cope with particularistic expectations on the part of others

---

[1] Ronald P. Dore, *City Life in Japan: A Study of a Tokyo Ward*, Berkeley, Calif., 1958, p. 258.

even though he may choose to model much of his life on other patterns.

Government and business, as we have noted, are carried on in a mixture of universalistic and particularistic relationships. The proportion of universalism has gradually increased—or, not so gradually, but rather has risen, broadened, or been beaten down at different phases of transition. For example, in creating a nation-state after 1868, leaders of the Meiji era made adroit use of particularistic patterns to bind popular sentiment to the new nation, even though they also introduced new concepts as circumstances altered. *Chū* and *kō* were favorite watchwords of nationalism. As Kawashima Takeyoshi has shown, the strategy was to proclaim samurai standards to be open now to the lower classes as well and to enlarge the samurai's loyalty to lord (*chū*) from provincial to national scope by abolishing the lords as a class and presenting the Emperor as every man's lord. Reiterating the doctrine that all Japanese, being a special race, comprised a kindred under the Emperor, a father above fathers, the leaders also buttressed *chū* with *kō*, filial loyalty, to the Emperor. Thus they taught not an abstract loyalty to the state or its principles so much as a personal loyalty in terms of *ongaeshi* to the person of the Emperor. It was not long, however, before the newly codified laws, drawing on European prototypes, introduced a modern concept of "duty" and its counterpart, "rights," that had no precise antecedent in premodern Japanese culture and, in fact, required new terminology. Previously, persons of a given status might possess obligations or prerogatives with respect to other statuses. Now the codes established certain roles—ownership, citizenship, house headship—with specific functions or duties (*gimu*) that required certain power or rights (*kenri*) for their performance. Thus, a person in the role of a house head was entitled to powers over subordinate members in order to fulfill his managerial responsibility over the *ie*. In this role, he held specified *kenri* in order to fulfill specified *gimu*; in other roles, his rights and duties differed. Rights and duties pertained to roles rather than to persons and were standard for whoever performed the function of the role, a functionally specific concept that was a far cry from the more diffuse privilege held by particular persons under the premodern status system. The new concept began to establish a new order within the nation. Vis-à-vis the nation itself, the duties of subjects were spelled out in considerably greater detail than their rights, however, until the close of World War II brought a second Constitution and new codes of laws. Under the Occupation, from 1945 to 1952, the people of Japan, now citizens rather than subjects, were declared to hold specific rights, including the supreme right of government. In a dramatic swing away from personalism, a legal basis was established for a more impersonal, universalistic governmental and legal system. Critics have not failed to point out and lament continuing particularistic practices, which are part of the accepted machinery of government even though not in the spirit of the law; but their earnest complaints, made from a far more universalistic standpoint than would have been possible before the war, testify clearly how universalistic expectations in public affairs have grown in recent decades.

In the business world, the most unequivocal particularism is found in crafts practiced by families which cherish craft secrets, train apprentices living with the family, and expand by founding *dōzoku,* though a dwindling proportion of Japanese business is carried on in such trades. Until very recently, however, workers in small enterprises received low wages and worked under conditions of employment much more like those of family members in a family-based craft than like those prevailing in large industries and businesses, and the diffuse relationships between employers and workers are not apt to disappear quickly even though wages have now risen to a level competitive with that of large firms. Such small enterprises are very common in Japan; in 1955, two of every five industrial workers were in firms employing less than thirty persons. Middle-scale enterprises, with up to 200 workers, are comparatively scarce; so the business scene presents a contrast between extremes of small and large scale. Even the giant corporations tend to have labor policies of a familistic nature that would be regarded as incompatible with profit-measured efficiency in Euro-American counterpart firms. As studies by James Abegglen, Solomon Levine, and others show, pay scales take into account the worker's age and seniority, family size, and other factors apart from the job itself; workers who are in the category of permanent employees fear no layoffs when business falls away, being long-range members of the "company family"; and should they quarrel with their wives, drink, or have trouble outside their jobs, the chances are that their foreman will be around to try to help straighten things out. The company, having contracted for labor, feels obliged to act in noncontracted matters as well. Japanese business has set an almost unmatched record of productive growth even without strict adherence to the impersonality of contract relations, fixed pay for specified performance, and other businesslike practices. But successful new companies in emerging fields of industry tend more toward organization along Western lines and so increase the pressures toward rationalization of older firms.

It is not surprising, in this environment that mixes such radically different patterns of organization and interpersonal behavior, that tensions and conflict exist. A wide gulf separating the values of elders and youngsters of the present generation is an openly recognized fact. Young workers and technicians, often more highly educated and specialized than senior employees in the same company, rise over the latter to positions of decision and responsibility but may receive less pay than elder persons under them who have greater seniority and larger families; this inconsistency, from the universalistic viewpoint, puts a bitter taste in the mouth. Parents whose reflexes were attuned for most of their lives to solidarity and authority are nonplussed by youngsters who want to go their own way in marriage and work even at the cost of breaking with family tradition and advice or who strike out peevishly at a constraining society through organizations of a left-wing political color. Exacerbating the tension is the lack of clear-cut directions and goals for young people in their lifetime, the war and subsequent changes have smashed old values without showing them precisely how to reach new ones under Japanese socioeconomic conditions. On the other hand, however, the older and younger generations do have something in common to ease tensions, for the elders themselves grew up in a changing society and share respect for hard work and ambition which at least have improved material living conditions when much else has remained shifting and insecure.

DAILY AND ANNUAL CYCLES; THE LIFE CYCLE

The discovery that human life runs in repeated cycles must have been made almost as soon as human beings possessed enough speech to think about themselves. Anthropologists certainly were not the first to become aware of this phenomenon, but they were the first social scientists to seize on the fact of cyclic repetition as a way to edge closer to their elusive goal of viewing a culture whole and entire but in segments small enough to be comprehensible. Especially useful for this purpose are the cycles that will be briefly sketched here: the daily cycle, the annual cycle, and the individual life cycle.

As one of these cycles moves through its course, it gives the observer an opportunity to note the interaction among the basic aspects—technological, sociological, ideological—of a given culture, as well as the interaction of this whole culture with the physical environment and with the individual. In a cycle, particular aspects do not stand isolated as systems (e.g., the social system) but present themselves as parts of an integrated whole, alive and in action. Yet one can view any cycle as being particularly revealing of a culture's technological or material aspect, the ideological aspect, or the way in which the whole culture impinges on its individual members. Accordingly, the following review will stress technological-material features of the daily cycle, ceremonial-ideological features of the annual cycle, and the individual's relation to his social system in his life cycle.

Daily Cycle

The ordinary Japanese family eats three meals a day at hours approximating Euro-American mealtimes; in seasons of heavy work, the farm family eats four meals while working longer hours. The central feature of each meal, *gohan,* or plain boiled rice, was and still is rarer in many farmhouses than a cheaper grain, such as barley or millet; and a notable urban trend toward wheat, consumed in baked goods, has helped make Japan recently almost self-sufficient in domestic rice production, without imports. Still, rice is most typical, served either hot or cold with various vegetables and, as proteins, soybean products, fish, or occasional bits of meat. Social ritual at the time of eating has now become much more relaxed than formerly. Women's places around the table or hearth, in rural tradition, were "lower" than those of men. More and more, however, convenience dictates positions at the table in farms as well as in city households, though on any special occasion men may eat first and separately from women and take seats punctiliously according to the protocol of rank or seniority.

In the traditional Japanese home, with more space per person than in most Asian countries, the family's sleeping arrangements are not confined to only one of the three or four rooms in the house, for thick mats called tatami, in frames of standard size of 3 by 6 feet, furnish complete flooring for all rooms except the kitchen, bath, and workrooms. Thick quilts *(futon)* laid out on any tatami constitute a bed at night; when the housewife folds the quilts into a wall cupboard in the morning, the room is available for other uses. Light sliding doors (fusuma) dividing the rooms can be opened or removed to make the space flexible for various uses. In keeping with this flexibility, many furnishings and decorations are easily moved: flat pillows *(zabuton)* for sitting, low tables, decorative roll-up scrolls.

In a multigeneration farm home, the first person to rise each morning is usually a young married woman, who builds a fire and starts breakfast. Self-timing electric rice cookers, however, have taken most of the edge off this undesired chore. When others leave the house for work and the children are sent off to school, household tasks occupy her and her mother-in-law or any other woman relative who may be in the household. The household domain, if a traditional country house, is a rectangular structure of unpainted wood roofed with grass thatch or tile. The living space, with tatami floor covering, is raised well above the ground, while the cooking and work space is at ground level; the latter is almost windowless and dark, whereas much wall space around the tatami rooms is open to the outside except for light sliding doors covered with translucent paper (shoji). In the city, living space may be more cramped in structures built for several families, floor plans differ, and gas or electricity is used for cooking in place of raised fire pits for wood and straw or braziers for charcoal; but tatami-mat flooring is as conventional in the city as in the countryside, and people regularly walk shoeless inside the house. City apartments and houses are just beginning to introduce central heating. One Tokyo builder, not entirely in jest, claimed that in fitting modern doors with locks into his new small-family apartment houses he had revolutionized family life by enabling the whole family to go out together, leaving their home unattended for the first time in history.

On farms, the wife cuts housework short to go out to the fields. Though irrigable rice fields are the most prized and costly, some dry fields and a woodlot are indispensable for household food needs, and vegetable cultivation and grass gathering are apt to be mostly women's work. In towns and cities, daily shopping is time consuming even for women not employed at outside jobs or doing piecework at home, for each open-front shop sells only a limited range of goods and a housewife must go through numerous transactions to collect each day's necessities. Supermarkets appearing here and there and the growing use of refrigerators to store several days' food tend to reduce shopping tasks, and housewives in town do have time free to read, sew, or arrange gatherings at each other's homes.

In the fields, farmers still use mostly hand tools. Today's farmers have better materials, thanks to research, and much greater knowledge and skill than their grandparents. Lack of land and capital are the present impediments to greater production. Manpower in prodigious amounts is substituted, for with their hand tools the Japanese invest an estimated 900 man-hours per acre for a slightly higher rice yield than a United States grower gets with 50 man-hours per acre. The most important farm tools are wooden steel-bladed plows, hoes, harrows, weeding devices, and sickles. Wide adoption of a portable kerosine engine or an electric motor has mechanized irrigation, threshing, and some other tasks. Tractor-cultivators made in Japan in small models accommodated to tiny fields have come rather widely into use since the war, often being jointly owned by several households. Household groups or small villages also are apt to own more complex crop-processing equipment, such as hullers, polishers, or barley mills. The tractor-cultivators, not always worth their cost to full-time farmers, have greatly facilitated off-farm jobholding by small-scale cultivators, who save their weekends to do heavy work in their fields but could not fit the work in without such machinery.

The diffusion of machinery to farms is greatly changing the overall picture of the rural economy, though equal credit must go to the ubiquitous motor bicycles, buses, and trains and to schools that have qualified farmers for away-from-home jobs. The traditional labor-intensive system required all available hands at certain busy seasons but left a worrisome amount of spare time at other periods. This so-called "concealed unemployment" has been greatly eased. Some farm dwellers find a product to make at home, often using farm materials. In other cases, young people leave each day to work in town or at local industries. As we have noted, roughly half of all farmers have some such nonagricultural income. Now, increasingly, young people are abandoning farming. As fewer people stay on the land, the prospect emerges, for the first time, of throwing together the traditional small fields into units large enough for more powerful machinery; until this can occur, there is a growing shortage of farm labor.

The long-continued contrast between town folk and country folk is becoming blurred. Farm-bred boys and girls hold jobs in town; they and their families may still produce about four-fifths of their food, but for clothing, furnishing, and tools they are dependent on the same factories and stores that supply townspeople. A glance at the daily cycle, however, restores perspective. Particularly in metropolitan areas that encompass millions of Japanese, the urban pattern of life differs immensely from the rural pattern, what with one or two hours of bus or train riding to and from work, a box lunch and perhaps a glass of beer at midday, and an office or factory milieu throughout the day, for a livelihood totally dependent on monetary earnings. Farmers do not yet habitually schedule their work, let alone compress it into an eight-hour day or take off Sundays and Saturday half-days. Their rhythms remain traditional and quite different from those of wage- and salary-paid workers.

Among people at work in the city, one sees suits or shirts and trousers among men, skirts and blouses or dresses among women, all as in Euro-American cities except for details. Older persons frequently go visiting in the traditional costume of kimono; young people on special occasions or when attending a traditional Japanese function may also wear kimono (girls more readily and frequently on account of the attractiveness of this colorful costume), and after-hours use of the light, figured-cotton robe, called *yukata*, is common for both sexes at all ages. For casual wear, in any costume, people are apt to use the wooden clogs called geta or variations of the straw *zōri* sandal (a molded-rubber version of it has become familiar as women's wear in the United States, Europe, and South Asia). Country folk relatively rarely wear shoes except in town; they work barefoot or wear rubberized "socks" (*jikatabi*) in the fields and don geta or *zōri* elsewhere. At least half of the time, the rest of the country work costume is the "contemporary international" shirt and trousers for men and one-piece dress or blouse and skirt for women at their housework. Farm women for work in the field tuck skirts into baggy trousers called *mompe*, and in cold weather both sexes rely to a greater degree on Japanese traditional garments, of padded cotton, supplemented by abundant sweaters and long, machine-knit underwear.

As the family gathers in the evening, almost invariably enjoying electric light and radio, school-age children are busy with homework until bedtime, and women reseam traditional clothing that must be ripped apart for washing or do mending. Men on the farm, in leisure seasons, pass quiet evenings; workingmen in town may go out for a drink or a game. Many city businessmen spend a good many evenings outside the home combining business with entertainment (with or without geisha dancing) and habitually think of outside recreation in the company of other men rather than with their wives as companions. Town wives, thus, tend to be much more available than their husbands for children's needs; it is they who manage household affairs as well as cooking, sewing, shopping, and decorating the living-room niche, or tokonoma. In stem-family homes, theoretically centered on male members, it is regularly a woman who makes the usual daily offerings to the husband's ancestors enshrined in the *butsudan* or to the household spirit enshrined in the *kamidana;* there is no *butsudan* in most nuclear-family households in the city, for they are branches which have no ancestors apart from those shared with their main house and worshiped at the latter.

Two features of the division of labor between the sexes stand out from the daily cycle. First, traditional tasks are clearly assigned to one or the other sex, so that little trading off according to convenience is tolerated. Mutual interchange in work and recreation is being introduced into the lives of the postwar urban generation, but still with hesitancy. Second, women's heavy share of work outside the home is not an assertion of equality with men but a response to economic want. Some 60 per cent of the women who work are unpaid, usually farm wives; to be released to devote themselves to household chores would be a step upward to the level enjoyed by most urban wives. Still higher upward is the "release" from housework being rather tentatively worked out by some women in each community, who emerge from domesticity to take part in public activities or work for a salary. Upper-class families often depended upon "living-in" servants to take care of a variety of chores, but such households complain of the difficulty of acquiring servants today. A married woman at work, unless she displays special talents or skills, is apt to be regarded as not quite dignified, and a similar handicap cools the ordinary woman's zeal for civic activity; so the second step upward waits upon further change in the climate of opinion before it becomes a widespread phenomenon.

Annual Cycle

Duality is strikingly evidenced in the way people's activities are organized through the year in Japan. The official and business year follows the Gregorian calendar in all main features, with its division into twelve months and seven-day weeks (years officially still are numbered from the accession of each Emperor, but the Christian year count is tending to overshadow this mode of numeration). Company employees consequently live in terms of a week turning on the Sunday holiday (without religious connotations except for Christians) and of months that match those of the West except in name. The farm year, however, took shape around the growth cycle of major crops—especially rice, which is in the fields from early June to early November—and follows an organic rhythm of work and slack, harvest and planting and around to another harvest. Time for a farmer does not stretch out in a linear sequence of matched units but circles upon itself in a seasonal cycle of variable units. Various subtle differences in habits of thought and outlook flow from these contrasting annual schedules; only a few can be suggested here.

For town-living company workers, there are two sorts of accents to the year other than the weekend break. One is the scattered series of national holidays; the other is the schedule of school vacations. Many national holidays were renamed or shifted after World War II and have few compelling roots in custom. In fact, labor spokesmen have suggested shifting the holidays again to rearrange them in groups to provide suitable three-day vacations. The New Year, however, offers a three-day break that is strongly entrenched in custom; in addition, people have taken up the gift aspect of Christmas, and the intervening week has become a pause period on a nationwide scale. Of next importance, though secondary, is the Bon ancestral observance in August inherited from Buddhist tradition, for which a worker can get three to six days off to visit his home village, usually without pay. For a great many people (especially the self-employed) the city work year is punctuated merely by weekends and the midwinter pause near the New Year. But many more persons are taking vacations, chiefly in the summer, when school is closed from July to October and the entire family can travel away from home. Thus the pulsations of the year for modern Japanese, spaced by the convenience of school, the firm, and the government, closely resemble those of Western nations.

Farm life, however, is still responsive to seasonal changes. Though new crops and new techniques change the work-year schedule gradually but persistently, a similar rhythm of seasonal adjustment to work and slack still closely linked to ancient tradition pulses in all parts of the country-side. The main calendar of ceremonies is adjusted to this work schedule, with ceremony-packed intervals coming when work slacks off. The ceremonies once reflected cultivation needs in their purpose as well as their timing; changes in their focus that took place in the cities have now affected rural attitudes as well, making ceremonial content similar in city and country but blurring the agricultural significance of the ceremonial calendar. A good many widespread ceremonies, observed in towns and cities, still make urbanites conscious of the rhythm of farm life even if they treat such occasions merely as extra holidays. Gradual secularization of religious occasions, a phenomenon almost worldwide in modern times, brings it to pass that every religious festival varies in its religious intensity from person to person and from place to place; hence it cannot be said that the traditional ceremonial calendar is devoutly observed even in the country. Yet the religious overtones to various festive occasions are not entirely ignored, inasmuch as Shinto, which gives rise to a large number of seasonal festivals for crop welfare, and Buddhism, which has its nationwide festivals of remembrance of saints or family ancestors, still characterize religious life in city and country alike. These two religions, in fact, occasion the majority of the ceremonial days. A third group of festivals set as strategic seasonal turning points is of Chinese derivation, each such day symbolized by a flower or a plant. The official national holidays, previously noted, which comprise a fourth group, seldom receive much attention in rural areas. It is this, then, that most sets the calendar of holidays in rural and urban areas. The twenty or more local, traditional ceremonies of Shinto, Buddhist, or Chinese derivation set rural rest days, comprising a holiday calendar largely unrelated to the urban holiday schedule based mainly on national days of observance. But the traditional festivals are also celebrated in the city, if only because they furnish occasions for a nostalgic return to customary practices. Official holidays are celebrated with official functions; the ordinary person can only participate as a spectator, at best, for instance, by attending a program of speeches and performances scheduled on Culture Day or Thanks for Labor Day. To the contrary in the case of traditional festivals, it is celebrations in each home and community that make the heart of the occasion, as in the case of the American Halloween or, possibly, Thanksgiving.

To give a sample of their content, we list below certain traditional festive occasions that are prominent in most localities of Japan, condensed to their major features, proceeding in general from the beginning to the end of the year. Dates of celebration vary slightly from one locality to the next in the countryside but are regularly scheduled, originally exclusively by the lunar calendar, which makes them a month or more later and variable from year to year on the solar calendar. More than a few country localities, however, follow the lead set long ago by towns and use a solar-calendar date. To allow for both lunar and solar dating, we list both the usual month and day by number.

1. New Year (lunar 1/1–3, 4–6, 9, 11, 15): Shinto and Buddhist.
   Purpose: to welcome the new year and renew community ties (Shinto); to venerate ancestors (Buddhist).
   Persons: everyone.
   Preparation: all debts cleared, house cleaned; straw ornaments (*shime-kazari*) or pine branches (*kadomatsu*) put at entrance of house by last day of old year (*ō-misoka*); bright clothing made ready; glutinous rice (*mochi*) pounded to make cakes or balls.
   Activities: 1–3—feasting at home and visiting nearby to pay "best wishes"; visit to shrine of community; 4–6—return home of wives and relatives who may be living away from home; ancestors venerated at home and at graves (Buddhist); 9, 11, 15—rest days; 15—community bonfire of ornaments (*tondo*).
   Foods: *mochi* balls as decoration and as foods; a soup (*zōni*); tangerines.
2. Doll Day (lunar or solar 3/3): Shinto and secular.
   Purpose: amusement; fertility in former times.
   Persons: girls below teen age, in general, with boys joining in.
   Preparation: dolls representing an ancient Imperial Court and belonging to the household are set up on a tiered stand; varicolored rice cakes in stepped tiers of diamond shape (*hishimochi*) are displayed.
   Activities: food served to children's party; various games played.
   Foods: *hishimochi;* "red rice" (red beans scattered through rice); "sweet" (nonalcoholic) sake; cakes.
   Remarks: popularized in the nineteenth century, replacing old fertility ceremonies (e.g., mountain climb [*yama-agari*] to bring mountain spirit [*yama-no-kami*] down to fields).
3. Higan (equinoctial period; solar 3/18–25; also, solar 9/21–28): Buddhist.
   Purpose: to venerate ancestors.
   Persons: household members, with or without priest.
   Preparation: ancestral tablets (*ihai*) are set in the tokonoma; family graves are cleaned and decorated with *shikimi* leaves.
   Activities: prayers and food (rice and water) are offered before ancestral tablets and also before gravestones at sunset.
   Foods: meals served without salt, fish, flesh, eggs, or sake (*shōjin ryōri*, ascetic fare).
   Remarks: essentially same ceremony duplicated at New Year, spring equinox, Bon (see below), and fall equinox.

4. Boys' Day (lunar or solar 5/5): Shinto or secular.
   Purpose: amusement stressing male virtues; prophylaxis in former times.
   Persons: boys below teen age, in general.
   Preparation: large wind-sock banners in carp shape are flown above house; vertical banners picturing a mounted warrior are raised; in the tokonoma are set a warrior helmet or doll, a bobbing-head tiger doll, and *kintoki* (strong-boy) dolls.
   Activities: a party meal for boys.
   Foods: *mochi* wrapped in oak leaves; red-rice balls; cakes.
   Remarks: popularized in the nineteenth century, replacing ceremonies of prophylaxis for health of community; names of the latter (*tango no sekku, shōbu no sekku*) still used.

5. Tanabata (lunar or solar 7/7): secular, borrowed early from China.
   Purpose: honor to stars, especially Vega (Weaving Girl).
   Persons: children in general (taken up by schools).
   Preparation: using ink supposedly made with morning dew, children write poems (if able) or characters on colored cards and tie them to twigs of a long bamboo stalk to be set up in house yard; cut eggplant, etc., is hung on branches; vegetable animals are carved for display.
   Activities: bamboo stalks are set up and then are cast into stream or pond in the evening.
   Foods: red rice.

6. Bon (lunar or solar 7/13-15, varying with locality): Buddhist.
   Purpose: to welcome ancestral spirits for three-day visit.
   Persons: household (for the dance, community).
   Preparation: practice for dance; set offerings (seasonal vegetables, fruits, rice, water) before ancestral tablets, which are placed in the tokonoma; graves are cleaned.
   Activities: prayers for ancestors (as at Higan and New Year); a community folk dance. Additionally, pine roots are burned in small fires in the cemetery each day to please ancestral spirits with the "incense" and at approaches to village on first and last evenings to welcome and send off the spirits.

7. Spring, Summer, and Fall Festivals (lunar or solar 5/14, 6/14, 10/12-13, with local variation): Shinto.
   Purpose: to renew well-being of community through its shrine.
   Persons: household representatives of community under one shrine (usually several *buraku*).
   Preparation: make ready pairs of vertical banners, an arch, and a litter with ark (if shrine spirit is paraded).
   Activities: banners and arch on community roads or streets for duration. Pray at shrine, and parade ark through community (or to place of worship or not at all). Visiting and feasting, with sake, and homecoming for relatives. Fall being most important, Spring and Summer Festivals may be abbreviated to visiting only.
   Foods: fish and sake in plenty. The object of achieving communion with the

shrine spirit is assisted both by sharing food in the vicinity of the shrine and, for young men, by becoming ecstatically drunk.

Remarks: Fall Festival usually is biggest. This set of ceremonies resembles a different set (*gokitō,* prayers), except that the latter lacks festivities.

8. Shichigosan (lunar 11/15): Shinto.

Purpose: to introduce children of community to shrine at end of infancy.

Persons: three-year-olds; also, five- and seven-year-olds, as the name of the festival implies.

Preparation: mother's parents and others send child's dress costume.

Activities: shrine visit in best clothes; simple meal with relatives.

Foods: red rice at meal.

Remarks: modernized version of older age-grade ceremonies at which a child changed elements of his costume.

9. Kurisumasu (solar 12/25): Christian or secular.

Remarks: In Japan today it is impossible to leave the subject of special celebrations without mention of Christmas. Though still seldom observed in rural areas, Kurisumasu has become such a popular celebration in the large cities that it has actually been suggested for designation as a national holiday (under the euphemistic name of International Goodwill Day). Christian sentiments are almost entirely absent, but decorated trees, Santa Clauses, angels, and the like are common in downtown shopwindows and in the houses of moderns. Gift giving is relished both by department stores and by family members. Few better examples exist of the easy assimilation of certain aspects of Western culture into Japanese urban life and of the shifts in emphasis which inevitably take place when such assimilation succeeds.

Individual Life Cycle

Biological patterns of maturation and aging are much alike for all mankind. What makes them seem remarkably different is the idiosyncratic interpretation each society imposes on them. The life cycle of the Japanese has its own distinct coloration or, rather, several sorts of coloration, since, of course, besides the usual differences according to sex or class of occupation we must take into account the contrasts imposed on individual lives by the dual social styles to which we have repeatedly drawn attention. Today, in fact, it is rather hard to conceive of a single pattern to which all Japanese must somehow conform or else be considered "different." Rather than attempt to coalesce variant patterns or link all acceptable events in any single pattern, we shall find it easier to consider first the highlights of the more traditional order of things and then fit in separately the notable changes imposed on either sex by modern conditions.

AGE-GRADES. Let us first consider the existence and nature of age-grades. In any society, although persons are scattered randomly through all ages, custom groups them into grades that are assigned particular stigmata or signs, status, and functions. The particular categories vary from one society to another, and so does the emphasis that is placed on certain grades or on the grading system as a whole. Under traditional conditions, the status of a Japanese individual has depended on many circumstances over which he has had no control: his household reputation and class rating, his sex, his age relative to other persons, and so on. Age-grades also classified him and tended strongly to dictate standards of conduct as he moved through life. In a country of mobility and stress on achievement, such as the modern United States, conduct tends to be standardized less by age itself than by other criteria. An important exception is the teen-age period, which is a grade of great importance, typically characterized by special sorts of problems and adjustments and distinctive speech forms, clothing, interests, and behavioral patterns. For reasons we shall investigate presently, the traditional Japanese order of things had no specific teen-age period. A person under such an order stayed in the category of childhood until sometime between the ages of fifteen and seventeen, whereupon he assumed the functions and status of a youth (*seinen*) or young adult without passing through any clear-cut intervening status. It should be noted here that this state of affairs, so clearly in contrast with the contemporary American pattern, is altering year by year even in quite remote localities as socioeconomic changes penetrate them, but many localities still lack signs of special teen-age behavior among adolescent youngsters, who are considered part of a group of grown-ups as soon as they stop being children.

Age-grades were, of course, important in traditional Japanese culture, and the transition from one to another was marked by specific ceremonies that made the identification of each an easy matter. Though ceremonies differed locally, they established basically similar divisions everywhere. The list of the main "rites of passage" which follows thus sets off the principal traditional age-grades:

1. Naming ceremony: about three days after birth. The child is named and introduced to its close relatives.

2. Shrine visit (*miya-mairi*): thirty-one or thirty-three days after birth. The child is taken by its mother or another close relative to the local shrine, an offering is made there, and the child is introduced to the protecting spirits of the community and, in effect, to the community itself as a new member. The child wears a new kimono sent to it by its mother's family for this occasion. This ritual also terminates the ritual impurity of the mother after childbirth.

3. First birthday: a full year after birth. A meal is prepared for close

relatives, and prayers are offered by a Shinto priest for the good health of the infant during childhood. Personal birthdays subsequent to the first had no celebration in the past, and everyone's age was considered constant from New Year to New Year; birthday parties are now becoming regularized.

4. *Gempuku* or *kanetsuke:* the former a ceremonial for boys of seventeen; the latter, for girls of fifteen. At the *gempuku* (also called *hanko* and other names), the boy is given his first adult clothing or Western-style suit at a feast. The *kanetsuke*, at which women related to the girl once applied black stain to the teeth as an adult cosmetic, now involves only new clothes and limited feasting or is ignored altogether. On the present official calendar, Adult Day, January 15, has the purpose of honoring youths who are reaching adulthood, as a mass substitute for individual family ceremonies that are now often neglected.

5. Marriage (*kekkon*): preferably by the time men are twenty-five and women twenty-three but now more variable, especially among urbanites, with whom the age of marriage tends to be delayed. The wedding ceremony marks the transition from young-adult to full adult status. For a girl who marries an inheriting son, it marks her introduction to his close relatives.

6. Succession (*sōzoku*) or retirement (*inkyo*): ceremoniously observed when the successor's father reaches the age of sixty or when the successor's first son is born, at least in northern Japan, but becoming a gradual process there as elsewhere without the performance of ritual. The eldest (or chosen) son succeeds to leadership and, traditionally, supreme status in the household (*sōzoku*), while the former house head attains the status of grandfather (*ojii-san*) or retired person (*inkyo-san*), relieved of major responsibility. Inheritance of property, an event distinct from succession to the head position, takes place only at the death of the retired person.

7. Funeral (*sōshiki*): at death, the family member does not simply cease to exist but enters the new status category of ancestor, honored at specified intervals by his household for at least the next generation and, each day, recognized by a simple obeisance before the ancestral tablet bearing his name, which rests in the ceremonial Buddhist cabinet (*butsudan*).

Traditionally certain organizations to which only members of a particular age-grade belonged existed to accentuate certain age-grades. But these have now mostly fallen into disuse. A few survive or have changed their character to fit new functions and new age-grade organizations. An instance of the latter sort is the organization for young people; once a *wakamono-gumi* (young people's group) independent in each local community, it is now the Seinendan (Youth Association), part of a national organization. It was and still is essentially an adult group; so many young people put off joining it while they are in school, and city dwellers are apt never to join at all. Where an active branch exists, it still performs traditional functions (labor service for the community and entertainment of its members), and it may have both male and female divisions. But such a branch operates sometimes as a sort of auxiliary of the schools in organizing athletic contests and sometimes as an aid to an agricultural cooperative, and it must compete for participants against Boy Scouts, Four-H clubs, and informal friendship groups. Thus, its age-grade connotations have been watered down.

Modern life brings new conceptions of age-grades and introduces new instruments of change in the life-cycle patterns of the Japanese. For sub-adults, for instance, school has become a central feature of life rather than an activity interrupted, as in the old-time village, by harvests and transplanting and eventually by full-time farm work. Infants old enough to toddle outside the yard become preschool children; thereafter they tend to be grouped by elementary (six years), middle (three years), and high school (three years) levels, subdivided by school grades. School thus sets a new series of age-grade categories. Diversification also affects sub-adults, for while some remain "students" through college, others become "young adults" at work after high school or even after middle school. Modern circumstances prevent youngsters from having a specific, solidary young people's organization in towns and cities. Teen-agers of urban areas and even in the country are clearly developing a group identity, less marked than in, say, the United States, but of the same nature. The sense of belonging to an age-grade is now a phenomenon on a different, broader scale than that which gave rise to the organized associations in which previous generations participated. At more advanced age levels, adults are still more thoroughly diversified by occupation, residence, and other features. Accordingly, age-grades are much less clear-cut and specific among the Japanese whose lives have departed far from traditional patterns, and groups specifically organized on the basis of age are missing. Grades may be identified in rather general and overlapping terms, which are quite parallel with those found throughout modern societies: infancy; preschool; school age and teen age; adulthood, job holding or house-keeping, and parenthood; mature years; and old age. People in each of these rather arbitrarily labeled modern categories have much in common with their counterparts in similar age groups in the West, but the categories are still influenced by the Japanese tradition from which they have emerged. And it is this which gives the life of the modern Japanese its particular quality. We turn now to an examination of the new categories into which the life cycles of the modern Japanese tend to fall.

CHILDHOOD SOCIALIZATION. Socialization may be considered

to have two rather distinct facets. First, children in their formative years work out what has graphically been termed a *cognitive map* of their culture; they use this map to locate themselves and determine their identity. Second, each acquires motivation toward becoming a particular sort of person. The second facet of socialization, the preparation of an individual career plan, logically should be a function of the first. It is no surprise to find that in modern Japanese culture, where growth and change offer pathways for the ambitious, children show themselves strongly motivated by ambition to launch careers and improve their lives despite obvious obstacles and threats of frustration. We do not understand in detail how things may have differed in the traditional culture. One would suppose that a child in, say, late Tokugawa times would have formed a cognitive map of fixed, hierarchical units offering few clear pathways to a different life. Contemplating this map, he might well be impelled to perform efficiently in his ascribed position but could hardly expect to benefit from ambition for a different life. Nevertheless, a good many persons did in fact exhibit strong motivations toward achievement, if only to make small increments of advance. In the economist's parlance, Japan at that time had no lack of willing entrepreneurs, and the record is similar in political, scholarly, and artistic fields.

Several suggestions have been made to account for this strong Japanese drive for achievement in the midst of institutions so firmly based on ascription. One is that achievement was and still is viewed not in terms of self-betterment so much as in terms of the benefit of some collective group. A second suggestion takes note of parakinship mechanisms such as adoption that have provided a pathway to achievement. A third suggests that it is a mistake to assume uniform socialization of children in a society of fixed positions; specifically, the potential heir of an established household (presumptively, the first son) may have been motivated merely to perform his privileged and predetermined role well and to cherish the system that guaranteed it to him, whereas other sons whose future was more undefined and open could have been imbued with entrepreneurial characterstics and the practice of initiative. Some evidence supports each of these suggestions; but the question could bear further examination and fuller, systematic explanation, analyzing, for example, the socialization of girls as well as of boys at various social levels.

People in a country community today still do assume that the first boy in a family will have the happiest fortune; parents then show a determination to compensate noninheriting boys in other ways. Additional schooling is one such compensation. Education, however, is perceived not just as a second-best thing but as a good affair for everyone, including even girls, and far more youngsters go on than stop with the present compulsory nine years. This sentiment is buttressed by the tradition of respect for scholars in Japan and, more practically, by awareness that the educated man in the modern world possesses advantages not for himself alone but for his family line as well. Thus, schools are popular even in exceedingly tradition-oriented localities, while in towns and cities parents struggle with their children not just to get through school but to gain admission to the most prestigious school available, even drilling preschool children to excel in the aptitude tests by which schools of top repute select their kindergartners.

It is fair to say that many parents, modern and traditional alike, have a disproportionately exaggerated respect for formal education, expressed in a way which betrays their own authoritarian outlook. To them and their children the teacher is a person of authority. The role of authority is diffuse, not specific; accordingly the teacher is conceived as responsible not only for imparting certain information and developing specified skills but also for forming character. When worried, then, over their children's supposedly low level of etiquette, unsettled outlook, or uncertain moral values, these parents tend to lay the blame most particularly on the school, not on their own failures at home or on the unsettled world about them. One senses that they are not merely choosing a convenient scapegoat. In the logic of a society polarized toward authoritarianism and diffuse relationships, they see it as correct to abdicate responsibility broadly to whoever is in a status of authority. Their only proper function is to urge their children to study hard and heed what the teacher says; it is up to the teacher to form the children's mind.

TEEN-AGE PHENOMENA. Primarily in cities but increasingly in towns and villages also, Japanese parents are experiencing the bafflement and wonder common to parents wherever the teen-age syndrome has emerged. Some features of adolescence are common to all mankind, but most phenomena that go under the teen-age label are specific to countries of rapid change accompanying industrialization and technical diversification. Some reasons for their blossoming in Japan may be seen if we compare the traditional village with modern Japanese urban culture.

By the time the Japanese farm boy or girl reached the age of fifteen or sixteen a generation or more ago, he or she was ready to assume most of the functions of an adult. Most needed skills had been learned at home or in the fields, working in close company with adults, from whom adult manners could simultaneously be picked up. A person of sixteen is biologically mature enough to perform a day's work and consummate a marriage. Admitted as a member to low status in the adult hierarchy, the midadolescent could expect to continue a submissive role not greatly contrasting with his childhood role until, with increased experience, he would rise to a position of greater responsibility as house head or, for girls, housewife. If the family occupation were a craft or a small business, its demands would not impose psychological or social dislocations of a much more marked degree than farming, thanks to apprenticeship.

Modern adulthood by contrast imposes numerous dislocating demands, set against a much less stable background. Children spend much time with each other at school and little time with adults in the serious business of making a living. Parental experience, in any event, may give little precedent for many decisions and choices the adult of the next generation must make. In an increasingly diverse society, there are occupational and other choices to be made by each person for himself; the scope of this society just begins to become comprehensible to a child who is entering the teens. We may conceive of the teen-age period, when a person is no longer a child and yet not fully an adult, as a period to practice making choices and decisions, to practice adult behavior before having to bear the consequences that come with full economic and social adulthood. It is a difficult period, for the temptation is to reach for privileges but postpone accepting corresponding responsibilities, whereas one's parents and others tend to stress responsibilities before privileges. One takes comfort from others of one's age who are uniformly experiencing this transition and identifies oneself with them by cultivating activities, dress, speech, and mannerisms peculiar to teen-agers or peculiar even to one's own limited "gang."

Japanese society does not yet present most of its teen-agers with all the challenges toward individuation that, say, American teen-agers experience. Relatively seldom is the Japanese adolescent put on an allowance or urged to get a paper route or some other source of money to be managed by him alone; seldom does he have the frightening privilege of finding his own date, if a boy, or of attracting dating invitations, if a girl. Japanese parents still disburse money and arrange most social occasions according to their own best judgment, at least until a relatively advanced period. Dating is known but by no means standardized or practiced throughout the teens. On the other hand, formidable school entrance examinations face those who opt for higher education and whose family resources permit; family circumstances narrow the range of occupational choices more often than in the United States, also, and those who are free to make a first choice of a job are acutely aware that there is not likely to be a chance to second-guess. For all these contrasts, however, Japan's cities now exhibit the external signs of the teen-age pattern: clothing, haircuts, slang, magazines, nonmusic and nondance crazes, teen-age hangouts—the whole bit. In subdued measure, these signs seep into villages, where the assumptions and circumstances of tradition are losing force for adolescents who may not even stay long in the villages. An upsurge of juvenile delinquency—a symptom of dislocation, not merely of social change—is a source of great distress to the Japanese, though insofar as rates of this phenomenon can be assessed, the incidence is still low for an industrially advanced nation.

WEDDINGS. Yanagida Kunio reminds us that some of what we now consider traditional Japanese culture actually took form in the early phase of modernization (Meiji era), using marriage as an example. He asserts that rural marriage once was arranged mainly by the individual choice of the young people concerned, who had mutual contact and formed attachments in the course of youth-group activities within the village. As he interprets the situation, the village rather than its families was then the prime unit of society, and its integrity suffered no jeopardy from such freedom in the choice of a marriage partner; whether married or not, the young people would be working on land whose fruits were in some sense at the disposal of the community. As village collectivity melted away under new economic conditions and with more diffuse social intercourse, however, young people began to find spouses outside the village, and the family as prime property holder became the basically important unit and protected its interests in marriage by treating the choice of a spouse as a concern of the family or of its head. This, of course, was the chief concern of families in the samurai class, in which the added elements of political or social influence entered into the arrangement of marriages. Thus, collective welfare prevailed over individual desires both before the Meiji era and during that era, and a filial youngster was expected to let his family arrange his marriage.

Marriage in traditional localities is still seen as more than a pairing of individuals. For the boy's family, it is a means of perpetuating a household by producing offspring or of enlarging the *ie* by creating a new branch. His family looks for a strong and healthy girl who is a willing worker, while the girl's family wants her to marry into the best possible situation, one in which she will not suffer poverty or maltreatment from in-laws. In an established house, the girl will join the groom's family and have to adapt herself to its household ways *(kafū)*. Because of these considerations, marriage arrangements require careful investigation of each family by the other. In this delicate situation each family asks a go-between (often a couple who are elderly, diplomatic, and experienced) to provide a suitable list, sorts out the best prospects, and then has the go-between make a detailed inquiry into each household's economic status and reputation, any history of disease that might affect the proposed spouse or offspring, and the household's attitude toward a proposed marriage. If these preliminaries make the match look promising, the go-betweens arrange an elaborately casual meeting (*miai*) of the young people, sometimes alone but more often accompanied by their parents. If either party takes exception to the proposal at this point, the meeting can be passed off as a chance encounter in a park or department store, but if all signs are favorable they proceed to a betrothal with appropriate attention to a dowry of goods from the girl's side and a compensatory gift of money from the boy's side. Finally, they perform the wedding.

Perhaps only one-third to one-half of all Japanese proceed exactly as indicated, for today's young people do have enough unsupervised contacts to form their own attachments. These may even lead to *ren'ai* (love marriage) or *jiyū kekkon* (free marriage) without any apparatus of a go-between or negotiation over dowry and bride price. But this modern alternative has not yet become a general form, because it bears the connotation of defiance of parents or, at the very least, implies impetuous and immature haste. Hence, even when the boy and girl have reached their own understanding, they are apt to inform their parents and follow some or all of the forms of the arranged marriage, thus joining, in form, the many young people who still let their parents take the initiative. Or else, these days, when the detailed investigation undertaken by a go-between seems unnecessary and repugnant, they substitute a "witness" or two, that is, a friend of established status whose presence testifies to the deliberation and dignity of their marriage. A 1957 survey of young married couples living in a set of Tokyo apartments (as modern a sample as might be found) revealed that the majority by far had followed the forms of an arranged marriage, a not unwise precaution considering that, on the average, there had been no more than three meetings between a pair before their marriage!

MARRIED LIFE. Early married life sets quite different problems for persons in a stem family and those in a modern nuclear family. It should be stressed that the problems are not simply a function of household size but rise out of the different social environments in which these family types exist. A young farm couple may live in a home of their own, but because the new wife goes to live in her husband's community where he has land or other means of livelihood, she must adjust herself to his relatives and friends more than he must to hers. Her problems are more like those of the bride in a stem family than the bride living alone with her salaried husband in a town or city. The odds are about 2 to 1, in any case, that the country girl will marry a stem-family heir and live in his parental home. Here adjustment to her in-laws is quite apt to be her major concern for a year or more. The pivotal personality in this situation is not her husband but his mother. As house mistress, this older woman is primarily responsible for molding the new bride to the ways of the household and must be the first to mark her faults and correct them, though the entire household and, indeed, the whole community sits in judgment of what is in truth a trial marriage: legalization by registry at the village office may be postponed for months and is done almost as an afterthought unless a baby is quickly on the way. So the girl is in an initial position of social weakness, which she overcomes by hard work, modest demeanor, and submissive obedience. As if this were not enough, she is at a disadvantage psychologically as well, for her mother-in-law is the person whose own deep emotional commitments are most severely threatened by the marriage. Whether either one is conscious of the fact or not, the new girl is the mother's rival for the son-husband's affections. The child-raising mechanisms described in Chapter 8 tend to create a strong dependency relationship between son and mother, so that the son wants from his bride mainly the same maternal solicitude he gets from his mother. It is difficult for the mother to cede her position to the bride; jealousy complicates her supervision of the bride's training, and the son may be emotionally disposed as well as sociologically required to support his mother in the event of a clash. Enough women fall victim to this tension to make the mother-in-law problem one of notorious prominence in stem-family tradition.

Newly married couples living in their own homes on a salary escape the full weight of the in-law problem but may run into others. The wife competes at a potential disadvantage against the office or shop, the office gang, and various girls who work in the office or in bars and cafés where her husband goes with his clique after hours. Her husband and his friends get together for a convivial hour or two (or more) after work and may not their wives until well along in the evening. The office clique provides the husband's main social outlet, and his wife, being unlikely ever to meet them or enter his office and see his after-hours haunts, remains a stranger to a good part of his life, as he does to hers. Not a lot of time or money is left for the pair to pay social visits to friends or have parties at home. The wife makes her own social life mainly among woman friends while the children are at school. Upon her devolves almost all the management of children and the household budget. However welcome the husband may be at home, communication tends to run short and domestic schedules are upset if he is around very long. In sum, husband and wife face a gradually increasing danger of estrangement after the early days of getting used to each other, in contrast to the couple in a traditional setting where the critical period is apt to arrive at the beginning and bears most heavily on the new wife as she makes adjustments to her husband's relatives.

SUCCESSION, OLD AGE, AND DEATH. By postwar law, each married couple comprises a household regardless of where the pair lives; in social fact, sons who live in their parental homes after marriage comprise merely a segment of the larger households. Household property is joint, however it may be registered, and it tends to be inherited as a unit by one person even though the law entitles each offspring to an equal share. Inheritance customarily comes with the death of the older house head; succession may come ten or more years earlier. Succession is important, at present, only in traditional stem families; it once was a clear-cut, ceremonious affair at which the retiring house head formally handed over his responsibilities and prerogatives to his chosen successor, the presumptive inheritor. For a long time in some parts of the country, though quite recently in others, people have omitted formalities and transferred house-head functions gradually. One house-head function was to represent the house at local meetings, whether for business or ceremony or both purposes mixed together, but now someone else is apt to be sent, at first occasionally and then more often, until the old man ceases going altogether. The successor gradually substitutes for his predecessor more often in community tasks, such as street or road cleaning, for which one representative from each house is expected to appear. Moreover, since income taxes, market crops, and machinery have become standard features of country life and are better understood, on the whole, by young people, the successor has been increasingly involved in managing affairs from an early age. The role of house mistress, as well, once transferred as a unit on an occasion symbolized by handing over the household rice ladle to the successor's wife at the time of the ceremony of succession, now tends to be taken over gradually and as dictated by convenience.

The progressive dissipation of the ceremony of succession testifies to gradual relaxation of the authoritarian structure of traditional society. It also testifies to the lengthening life-span throughout Japan. In the early 1960s, crude life expectancy (not excluding deaths in infancy) stood at over sixty-four years for males and over seventy-two years for females. By this token, parents are still able and healthy for some years after their children have reached adulthood, with physical and mental capacity to represent the household in the community.

The stem family can take care of its own elderly men and women. Social and economic problems of old age have now become matters of concern in Japan, however, as in other nations where the life-span has lengthened and nuclear families have simultaneously become prevalent. Apart from the well-to-do, not many persons in Japan have earned enough in their working years to provide against old age with bank accounts or insurance policies. Retirement programs instituted by business firms are admittedly inadequate for the most part, and the government's social security measures need to be made more ample and given broader coverage to fill the gap. The economic problem is now evident and is expected to grow rapidly, for at the same time that the proportion of elderly people is increasing in the nation as a whole, business companies under pressure to rationalize their operation are trying to institute compulsory retirement ages rather than continue workers indefinitely on their payrolls. The social problem of providing humane alternatives to lonely declining years is still less acute than in societies that have been longer committed to nuclear family organization; so community or national planning is still in its beginning phases.

Death calls forth a substantial show of sympathy and solidarity in all parts of Japanese society. In the city, the condolence of friends, business associates, and even relatively casual acquaintances is expressed at least in formal notes containing a small amount of money toward expenses, but also more elaborately in the sending of elaborate floral wreaths, to be displayed in a row along the funeral route. In the country, death is still a major occasion for the community as a whole to spring into self-sufficient action. Each household of a *buraku* (in larger communities, each household of a *kumi*) sends one representative to perform the essential functions: the digging of the grave or collecting of firewood for the pyre, the preparation of the coffin, and the cooking of food for the bereaved family and the funeral helpers. Some members are sent to notify the kindred by bicycle, telephone, or telegraph. The kindred and friends arrive, while close relatives prepare the corpse for burial and cremation. Apart from *kumi* or *buraku* helpers, those who come deposit formal notes with money enclosed and receive a hastily printed, black-bordered card as well as a card of gratitude at a later date. All are offered food in the house, though they may leave gracefully before the funeral procession of relatives, followed by close mourners, starts to the cemetery. All these functions among bereaved families in a city environment have to be performed by grieving relatives or by paid professionals; so they tend to be abbreviated, not in order to economize but because the hiring of such service, while preserving the instrumental functions, sucks out their expressive content and leaves the ritual emotionally empty. Following death, the deceased is honored by members of the family at seven-day intervals for seven occasions and then by anniversary services at increasing intervals for up to twenty-five years at least and possibly for up to forty-nine years. Ancestors belong to the family, but death as an occasion belongs to the community in traditional Japan, and the effective way in which the community takes care of its members in this time of pain and crisis, with warmth and solicitude, graphically illustrates the endearing aspect of collective solidarity that makes many Japanese submit willingly and gladly to its discipline.

JOHN WHITNEY HALL

The Historical Dimension

THE MEANING OF JAPANESE HISTORY

In a completely literal sense, "the history of Japan" would consist of a record of everything that has ever happened in Japan up to the present moment. Obviously such an immensity of events cannot be recollected, much less comprehended, by the human mind. History as remembered or as recorded is inevitably a selection out of the infinitude of the past. The selection is both accidental, since the past leaves its traces in uncertain ways, and contrived, since these traces must be reported through the mind of the historian. We do not often stop to think how, out of the jumble of historical data available to the historian, the coherent narrative which we call the history of Japan comes into being. Nor do we often question why, though the writers of history may differ in style and manner of emphasis, they show such a remarkable uniformity in the subjects which they consider worthy of their attention. History, one of the oldest branches of scholarship, has developed its own professional conventions and objectives. At least until very recent times, historians have tended to recall the past in a set and stylized fashion, and it is essential that we learn to recognize the difference between history as it happened and history as it is written.

The past, of course, is not by any means the exclusive preserve of the professional historian. Each discipline takes up some segment of Japan's past as a dimension of its study. The purpose of these backward glances is clear. Fields such as sociology or political science are interested in history because of the conviction that patterns of past social or political behavior or past value systems have relevance in setting the boundaries of the possible or the probable in the present or for the future. They use the past, in other words, as a means of understanding the present and predicting the future. The discipline of history may also regard the past in this way, but most historical writing is not explicitly dedicated to the illumination of the future or even the present. It is devoted primarily to an attempt to "explain" the past.

Efforts of historical explanation, though they may differ in methodology or in certain important premises about the causes of change, are essentially attempts to group clusters of events into sequences which appear to contain reasonable elements of coherence. Historians speak of "causal" or "necessary" relationships between events. And in narrating a sequential episode, they are interested in showing how some set of past events is joined to other sets so as to account for the appearance or disappearance of institutions or for the occurrence of particular happenings. What distinguishes the historical approach to culture from that of other disciplines is not necessarily some special ingredient, some purportedly unique form of "historical explanation," for historians tend to borrow ideas about significant social relationships from other disciplines. Rather, the historical approach is distinguished by its exclusive concern with the past and the attempt to give it meaning.

The history of Japan has been set down in many different styles and from many varying points of view. This does not mean, of course, that each historian's effort is equally valid or, on the contrary, that each is equally the impressionistic result of a capricious imagination. Written history differs from chronology or the collection of archival materials in its search for coherence in the past. Events are explained; that is, the historian purports to demonstrate the relevant antecedents to events. Different interpretations may stem from different assumptions which can be made about important causal motives in human society and hence about what is relevant to any given historical event. Such assumptions may be crude or sophisticated; they may exhibit honest idiosyncrasies of opinion or conscious biases. They are not equally valid. And the historian is not without ways of evaluating the conceptual validity of his predecessors' work and of correcting for ignorance or distortion.

The earliest "histories" of Japan consisted of legends and oral stories relating the genealogies of aristocratic Japanese families and the exploits of their chieftains in an age when the "divine" origin of such ruling families was taken for granted. These stories, brought together in the

Kojiki (compiled in 712), began a tradition of historical writing in which the development of the Japanese people was mirrored in the actions of the Imperial House. Histories which consider the Emperor as the prime moving force in Japanese history have been written as late as the 1940s (for example, Akiyama Kenzō's *History of Nippon*). But while there is good reason to emphasize the role of the Emperor in Japan, we are well aware today that the existence of an "imperial grace" is not by any means the ultimate key to Japanese history.

Other early historical writings showed the influence of Confucian and Buddhist philosophical attitudes toward human affairs. The *Nihon shoki* (completed in 720) was largely a restatement of early myths and house records in the light of what were then considered the more "scientific" ideas of retribution for good and evil derived from Confucian historiography. Histories written during Japan's feudal age often carried the dominant Buddhist themes of the insignificance of man and the impermanence of life. Contemporary historians, though they may be interested in these semireligious views of causation as evidences of the way of thinking of the early Japanese people, would never consider adopting such views for their own explanations of historical change.

Yet the historian, even today, must be alert constantly to avoid biases and preconceptions which can distort the story he tells as surely as do these older and obviously anachronistic concepts. One of his most persistent problems is to overcome his own cultural bias. All premodern histories written by Japanese naturally put Japan at the center of their narrative. The Emperor-centered histories, in particular, were written from a Japan-centered viewpoint. But has the treatment given Japan in the writings of the West been any less biased? To the Western historian the center of human history (at least until recently) has been the Greco-Christian tradition. For many centuries, only those areas of Asia which impinged upon the West reached our history books and then only as "foreign relations." Even in 1951 it was still possible for the French historian René Sédillot to write *The History of the World* in which over 90 per cent of the subject matter dealt with the West. Only in the last century have historians made a serious effort to form a balanced picture of world history which would avoid the bias of any one national or cultural tradition. Yet few narratives, whether by Japanese or by Western historians, have avoided the pull of ethnocentricism altogether.

Modern historians no longer subscribe to the idea of supernatural intervention in human events, yet every history written rests on certain basic assumptions regarding causal relationships in human life. There is a propensity among historians who write extended cultural histories to cling to some overall scheme which helps to account for the great sweeps of human development. Some historians have even claimed to discover "laws of history." Yet the best of these are hardly more than hypotheses of uncertain validity, while the most grandiose are often mere statements of faith. Most modern historians do not consciously rely on such systems, though they are often unconsciously influenced by them. For this reason there is some value in identifying the more prominent of the contemporary "systems of history," since the ideas exemplified in them often are elaborations of some of the common but less explicit assumptions with which modern historians write.

Arnold Toynbee, whose cult in Japan was heightened by a visit to Tokyo in 1957, having identified a pattern in Greco-Roman history, has purported to see its parallel in other historical sequences. In his study of civilizations, Toynbee applied the analogy of the living organism which goes through a cycle of birth, life, and decay. At the time of its birth each civilization, he believes, is faced with its own particular challenges. If the challenges are met and overcome, the civilization grows; if the responses are inadequate, the civilization dies. Response is determined by the inner energy and spirit of the civilization. Once established, a civilization appears to pass through certain stages of development: a time of growth, when leadership is held by a "creative minority"; a time of troubles; and then an attempted resurgence under a "universal state," when it is forcibly ruled by a "dominant minority." Thereafter the civilization declines. But it has been possible for old civilizations to give birth to new ones through the revitalizing spiritual force of new and more universal religious beliefs.

In East Asia, Toynbee concludes that there have been two civilizations. The first, which he calls *Sinic*, had its classic period in Shang times, its time of troubles in the Chou, and its universal state during the Han (202 B.C. to A.D. 220). Its rebirth into a new Far Eastern civilization under the Sui and T'ang dynasties (589–907) was made possible through the spiritual force of Buddhism. Toynbee treats Japan as an offshoot of Far Eastern civilization.

In Toynbee's view, although Japan was but a fragment of Far Eastern civilization, the great challenge presented by the sea gap between Japan and the continent gave to Japanese civilization a semiautonomous character. Japan's classical period, when it accepted Buddhism and the Chinese style of government, coincided with the Nara and Heian periods; its time of troubles, marked by the rise of the military aristocracy, occupied the Kamakura and Ashikaga periods; and its universal state was fashioned under the Tokugawa hegemony. Thus to Toynbee the Western impact in the nineteenth century fell upon a mortally wounded Japan. No historian has tried to apply Toynbee's ideas to a full-scale history of Japan, and the results would be most awkward indeed. But the analogy between a culture and a living organism, the emphasis on inner spiritual vitality, and the pattern of rout and rally which Toynbee identifies in the decaying stages of a culture are all ideas which have had frequent, if perhaps unconscious, advocates among contemporary historians.

Karl Jaspers, the German existentialist historian, has given shape to another common attitude toward human history. Man, he says, has one origin and one goal. Between origin and goal, history is a process of continuous growth from (1) the primitive state, during which man existed in isolated social pockets; to (2) the early regional civilizations, such as Greece, Egypt, and China; to (3) the great cultures which developed through the unifying ideas of universal religions; and finally into (4) "one world," yet to be achieved through the spread of science.

Central to Jaspers' theory is his concept of the "axial period." Jaspers is fascinated by the fact that within one period of man's history (800–200 B.C.) a number of similar-minded great men arose: Confucius and Lao-tse in China, Buddha and the writers of the Upanishads in India, Zarathustra in Persia, the prophets in Israel, and the philosophers from Homer to Plato in Greece. At that time man first became conscious of himself and his cosmic limitations. He experimented with and developed the categories of thought and reasoning that are still used today. With these ideas and the beginning of world religion, man took his step into "civilization." For Jaspers, Japan remained in a primitive, prehistorical condition until it was brought under Chinese influence. Once it became part of the Chinese world, Japan entered the stream of world events. Japan gave rise to a history and a civilization which have continued into the scientific era. While Jaspers places limited emphasis upon the future unity through science which he foresees, nonetheless it is the idea of ultimate perfectibility that links him to the faith in progress so common among Western historians.

One of the most influential interpretations of what it is that drives a civilization along the course of progress from the primitive to the modern is the Marxist conception of economic determinism and class struggle. Marxist historians have disputed whether all civilizations should be conceived of as following a single pattern of development from barbarism through slavery, feudalism, and capitalism to socialism, or whether there is a distinct "Asiatic" developmental type. They agree, however, on a basic methodology and on the theory of dialectic or historical materialism as the explanation of historical causation. According to this theory, the character of a society is determined by its modes of production and by the struggle for their control. As new productive

techniques develop, a class struggle results. New stages of social development are reached as new classes succeed to the control of the state. The
nature of each new stage of development is determined not only by the
mode of production, however, but also by the "superstructure," the
political and religious mores, of the former society. The new society,
then, is a synthesis of the new and the old.

The social units with which the Marxist historians deal are states.
Japan thus qualifies as such a unit. Japanese history, to the Marxist historian, has gone through four stages. In the first stage Japan had a
subsistence economy and a communal society. Because of technological
change, the spread of rice culture, and the use of iron, however, an
economic surplus was produced. Classes came into existence, and a ruling aristocratic class emerged after the fourth century. In the second
stage (seventh through twelfth centuries) this aristocratic class created
an absolute state resting on slave labor. Further technological advances
brought new changes in the class structure. Slaves became free, and the
third stage, feudalism (from the twelfth century to 1868), evolved under
the domination of a military aristocracy. Finally, after 1868, Japan
entered the fourth and present stage of capitalistic society, in which the
bourgeois class occupies the dominant position.

Marxism has strongly influenced Japanese professional historical circles, especially since World War II. And although Western historians
have generally rejected the determinist approach as a whole, many elements of Marxist vocabulary have entered their writings, and many
basic tenets, such as the assumed relationship between wealth and
power, have found very general acceptance.

The views of Toynbee, Jaspers, and Marx, though based on widely
different conceptions of what the essential moving forces of history might
be, have in common a belief that human society, whether in the East or
in the West, can be explained by a uniform theory of development. Not
all writers have stressed the oneness of the human condition, and it is
interesting to note that Toynbee in his latest writings has begun to
dissent from his early insistence on this point. Many writers have
insisted upon the existence of certain fundamental differences between
"Eastern" and "Western" ways of life and thought. Typical of these is
F. S. C. Northrop, who sees East and West deeply divided by contrasting philosophical approaches to life. Actually Northrop is elaborating
the common opinion that Easterners are intuitive and spiritual and
Westerners are rational and practical. To Northrop the Eastern artist,
philosopher, or common man draws no distinction between the perceiving subject and the object being perceived. Thus the observer is a part
of the observed. Westerners, on the other hand, draw distinctions in

thinking. The West uses logic, analysis, categories (i.e., the "theoretic component"); the East uses intuition and direct apperception (i.e., the "non-differentiated aesthetic continuum").

Northrop places Japan among the nations of the East with a common heritage in Confucianism, Taoism, and Buddhism, but he sees a distinction between Japan and the others because of the speed with which it was industrialized after 1868. He believes that Shinto supplied the Japanese with a theistic religion and a "chosen-nation" sentiment similar to that of Western nations. This helped engender a feeling of nationalism and distinctiveness which supplied the material to build a strong nation. Thus Japan's success in modernizing was due to her rejection of Asia's nonexclusive beliefs. To this extent Japan is a meeting place of East and West. And while not many writers have accepted the whole of Northrop's argument, most will agree that Japan does occupy a special position in the interplay of Europe and Asia in modern times.

Max Weber, the German sociologist, began the study of Asia to test methods he had used to trace the interplay between the economic ethic of religion and the form of social life in Europe. He believed that if all institutional forms—state, church, joint-stock companies, etc.—were reduced to their essentials, they would be found to center in social activities. Weber's conclusion that a strong link existed between Protestantism and the rise of capitalism led him to study similar situations in the East. In studying China, he noted that different social norms gave rise to different economic and political institutions. Confucianism placed its greatest emphasis on "proper" human relations. In Confucian society "charismatic leadership" and "sib-loyalties" became the basis of a leading bureaucratic class. This class set an ideological norm for China which was basically anticapitalist.

In a brief allusion to Japan, Weber noted how the samurai became the dominant status group in Japan. The education of a samurai aimed at making him a dedicated fighter and minimized both the bureaucratic and the commercial goals. These distinctions in the aims, desires, and obligations of the Western entrepreneur, Chinese literatus, and Japanese samurai serve to identify marks of cultural individuality which Weber believed basic to historical interpretation of these societies.

The systems of historical explanation which we have just reviewed are representative of some of the more speculative lines of inquiry into the past. Not many writers, of course, have been tempted to write the history of Japan on the basis of any such "unified theories" of historical causation. (The Marxists are the chief exception.) The significance of these systems is mainly that they illustrate and systematize a variety of popular ideas about historical causation. Historians as a whole tend not to rely on any single theory but to pick up their concepts as they need them from a variety of sources. A given historian will tell his tale in terms of the actions of "great men," the influence of ideas, the existence of "key institutions," or perhaps the psychological composition of individual or group behavior. Historians (in fact, whole generations of historians) have differed in the particular mixture of causal principles to which they subscribe. Thus the work of each generation of writers of history tends to differ from that of its predecessors and can be thought of as the result of rethinking the past in terms of new interests or of new concepts about human causation. While it is commonly assumed that it is the discovery of new data (documents or records) which changes the course of historical interpretation, it is more frequently the reverse that accounts for these shifts. New concepts lead to the discovery of new materials or to the new use of old ones. Thus as historians learn of new interpretations of human behavior from the sociologist, psychologist, or political scientist, as they discover ways of handling complex phenomena, such as nationalism or modernization, they find new meaning in old histories.

For the student of contemporary Japan, history has a primarily utilitarian interest. He may be excited by the grandeur of ancient monuments or the narratives of heroic deeds, but his main concern is with the past as it has affected the present, as it provides a matrix from which he can logically evolve the Japan of today. For those who look at history in this fashion the past can be said to exist in the present in two ways. First, it exists in the unconscious heritage of cultural behavior —in the structure of social and political institutions and in particular value systems—in all those aspects of Japanese life which cannot be explained purely as the result of recent mutation or external influence. Second, it exists in the conscious effort of the society to "remember" its past. The history of Japan as taught in the schools or as perpetuated in the folk consciousness of the people may differ greatly from "history as reality." Yet it is nonetheless real; it constitutes an important element of the heritage of ideas which shape the minds and social mores of the Japanese. History as inheritance and history as remembrance are both significant dimensions of Japanese culture today. And to this extent we may look to the past as a "mirror for the present."

HISTORICAL PERIODS AND THEIR SIGNIFICANCE

The historian's first step in approaching the history of a nation like Japan is to divide his narrative into a number of manageable units or periods. Surveys of Japanese history abound in periodizing names, the most common being those attached to major eras known as *jidai*, i.e., Yamato, Nara, Heian, Kamakura, Muromachi, and Edo (refer to the table on page 131). But there are numerous other terms used to divide Japanese history. There are, first of all, alternative names for the standard periods: Muromachi is sometimes replaced by Ashikaga, and Edo by Tokugawa. Modern Japanese history, referred to sometimes as the Tokyo period, is more commonly separated into the reign eras of Meiji, Taishō, and Shōwa. Obviously there are many systems of periodization, and it is important to be aware of the origins of these systems and the reasons for their existence.

The chapters into which the historian divides his narrative do not appear ready-made or ready-named in the data of history. It is the historian who labels his own divisions. A given period is isolated by the historian because to him it comprises an entity containing some element of inner coherence, a coherence provided by the influence of some dominant institution, some personality, dynasty, or mood. Thus the act of periodization (if it is performed self-consciously) is in itself a form of historical interpretation, for it results from the historian's commitment to the significance of some particular theme or event over an extended passage of time. Different schools of historical interpretation and different fields of historical interest will consequently give rise to different systems of periodization.

Until modern times Japanese historians used the reigns of emperors and the names of year titles *(nen-gō)* as the means of dividing their history, thus revealing the common tendency of early historians to emphasize the actions of the sovereign or in fact to write as court historians. This practice has by now been largely abandoned. But a few remnants of imperial terminology are still to be found in the pages of Japanese history books. Since most of the "major" periods refer to segments of history which extend over more than a century, shorter, more manageable units are found useful. Imperial reign names or year titles are sometimes perpetuated to serve this purpose. Thus the art historian will refer to the Tempyō period (729–749) of the Nara age, or the literary historian will write of the Genroku period (1688–1704) of the Edo age. In each case, however, these names are used loosely to cover short but indefinite intervals during which some particular art form or artist may have flourished. Former year titles such as Tempyō or Genroku as used by contemporary historians are generally thought of symbolically; we talk of "Tempyō sculpture" or "Genroku literature." The dates to which the names originally referred are thus apt to lose their exact meaning.

The major period names which are now in standard use were made popular during the late nineteenth century by the first generation of Japan's modern political historians. These men based their periodization on two nearly identical sets of criteria, either the successive loci of political authority (Nara, Heian, Edo, etc.) or the succession of families which rose to political power (Fujiwara, Ashikaga, Tokugawa, etc.). This system of periodization, which is roughly comparable to the division of Chinese history by dynasties, has remained in general use, especially among Western writers on Japan. It is a convenient system despite the somewhat arbitrary lines which it draws through Japanese history.

One characteristic of historical periods of the above type is that they are defined by exact dates and specific occurrences. The traditional method of periodization therefore elevates a certain number of historical events to prominence as major turning points. The most important of these and the periods which they define are listed in the following table:

Date	Event	Period
ca. 300	— Conquest of Yamato	Yamato
592	— Accession of Empress Suiko	Asuka
710	— Completion of Heijō (Nara)	Nara
794	— Completion of Heian (Kyoto)	Heian
1167	— Victory of Taira-no-Kiyomori	Rokuhara
1185	— Victory of Minamoto-no-Yoritomo	Kamakura
1334	— Kemmu Restoration	Yoshino
1392	— Unification of northern and southern courts	Muromachi
1467	— Beginning of Ōnin War	Sengoku
1568	— Kyoto entered by Oda Nobunaga	Azuchi
1600	— Battle of Sekigahara	Edo
1868	— Meiji Restoration	Tokyo

There is no denying that the dates listed above identify some of the great moments in Japanese history, but the significance of these events as historical turning points is confined in the main to the political sphere and even then often only in a symbolic sense. For nearly every "great event" in the table there are others of equal or nearly equal significance close by. Historians will dispute, for instance, whether the Kamakura period should begin in 1185, or in 1180 (when the Minamoto began their attack on the Taira), or in 1192 (when Yoritomo obtained the title of Shogun). Modern historians therefore tend to read into whatever date is selected the other related events and hence think of one date as standing for a considerable range of activity. But however these dates are interpreted, they still relate to events which are primarily of interest to the old-style "political historian." The modern political historian, whose interest turns to the structure of government and the configuration of power relations, will find these events and the periods they demarcate of little importance even symbolically.

Modern political historians most commonly divide the history of Japan into five broad periods, each characterized by a distinct style of government. Beginning with the establishment of the first primitive state structure *(genshi kokka)*, Japanese government took on a succession of different forms to which historians have given the following names: *kodai kokka* (the ancient state), *bunkenteki hōkentai* (decentralized feudalism), *shūkenteki hōkentai* (centralized feudalism), and *kindai kokka* (the modern state). The periods defined by these types of political organization do not by any means coincide with the traditional divisions of the old-style political historian, and the events which serve as turning points between them are often quite different from those which have served as the "great dates" in Japanese history. Moreover, most structural changes, having taken place gradually over long stretches of time, cannot easily be tied to a single date. Thus the establishment of Sinified imperial government came in stages between the time of the Taika Reform in 645 and the promulgation of the Taihō Code in 702. Its decline, while unquestionable by 1185, had its origins as early as 743, when private ownership of rice land was made legally possible; it was hastened in 810 with the creation of an imperial chancellery (Kurōdo-dokoro), and again in 866, when Fujiwara-no-Yoshifusa was named imperial regent *(sesshō)*. The traditionally prominent dates of the twelfth through the fifteenth centuries are also of less significance to the modern political historian whose concern is with the fundamental political institutions of "feudal Japan." There is, for instance, no precise dating of the rise of the Ashikaga military governors *(shugo-daimyō)*, who came to power during the last half of the fourteenth century; nor is there an exact date at which the old civil proprietorships *(shōen)* were abandoned in favor of the practice of enfeoffment *(chigyō-chi)*. The Tokugawa system of administration matured from roughly 1600 to 1650, while many basic changes, such as the extension of the stipendiary *(hōroku)* system, were not complete until well into the eighteenth century.

For the historian whose interests are primarily social-structural, the standard political dates and periodization hold even less relevance. Social institutions change slowly and seldom absolutely. The historian of social classes and mores will necessarily divide Japanese history into lengthy segments with extended transition periods and overlaps. For instance, it is quite common to establish periods according to the changing nature of the dominant social class, i.e., the age of the patriarchal family elite *(ujizoku,* to the middle of the seventh century), the age of the nobility *(kuge,* sixth through thirteenth centuries), the era of military houses *(buke,* tenth through nineteenth centuries), and the age of the commoners *(heimin,* seventeenth century on).

The economic historian will also divide Japanese history into lengthy periods on the basis of certain fundamental economic practices. Moreover, the economic institutions which underlie his system of periodization never succeeded each other with clear breaks between them. The economic historian must consequently identify transition periods of considerable duration. Thus the familial *(uji)* system of economic organization was only gradually displaced by the practice of state control of rice lands *(handen-sei)* between 645 and 702. The replacement of state control by private proprietorships *(shōen)* began in 743 but was not complete until the fourteenth century. Nonetheless, the proprietary system had become common in most of Japan by the eleventh century. Meanwhile, another form of landholding, the fief *(chigyō-chi),* granted as part of the feudal bond between lord and vassal, had begun to appear in the twelfth century. By the fifteenth century practically all land in Japan was held in fief. It continued in this condition technically until 1871, but in actuality by the mid-seventeenth century the majority of fief holders had been withdrawn from the land and were supported by stipends *(hōroku)* paid out of the lord's treasury. Finally, to the economic historian the transition from an agriculturally based economy to one based primarily on commerce and industry is not a sudden occurrence which can be equated with the Meiji Restoration of 1868. Studies of the origins of capitalism *(shihon-shugi)* in Japan must embrace a broad transition period extending over the entire nineteenth century.

Marxist historiography, which has gained such a following in Japan since World War II, has popularized a style of periodization based on the stage theory of development. Surveys of Japanese history written by Marxists commonly identify four stages: primitive communalism *(genshi kyōsan-sei),* the ancient slave system *(kodai dorei-sei),* medieval feudal serfdom *(chūsei hōken nōdo-sei),* and modern capitalism *(kindai shihon-shugi-sei).*

More general than the Marxist system of periodization, and one which has had wide currency among modern Japanese historians, is the method derived from the Western historical practice of dividing history into the archaic, ancient, medieval, early modern, and modern periods. Japanese historians have borrowed these concepts and applied them to their own history, subsuming a number of the standard periods under them as follows: *genshi* (through Yamato), *kodai* (Nara, Heian), *chūsei*

(Kamakura, Muromachi), *kinsei* (Edo), and *kindai* (Tokyo). The fact that such terms referred originally to the major divisions of European history carries with it a vague assumption that Japanese history bears a basic structural similarity to that of Europe, though this is seldom openly acknowledged by those using these terms today.

It is obvious that many possible methods of periodization are available to the historian of Japan. Each has its particular reason for existence, and each is to some degree an arbitrary ordering of the narrative of Japanese history. Each may be adopted quite formalistically without giving thought to the implications of the particular divisions which it contains, yet each was derived at one time from the conscious play of the mind of the historian upon the data of history.

It remains therefore to select a method of periodization for our present study. Since our main interest in Japanese history is as a means of comprehending contemporary Japanese culture, it would be most appropriate if we could conceive of the past in terms of its bearing upon the present. One way in which the past impinges upon the present is through the traditional traits and values which have from time to time entered the mainstream of Japan's cultural inheritance. During the course of history, Japanese culture has appeared in a number of different manifestations, each characterized by certain distinct behavioral patterns and value systems. Each of these phases of historical development has contributed to the cumulative growth of Japanese culture and given rise to a body of tradition which has been accessible to later generations of Japanese as they have thought about themselves and their past. A periodization based upon what we might call *styles of cultural organization* holds meaning for us both as a method of organizing the past and as a method of explaining its relationship to the present.

The system of periodization adopted below is not particularly new as far as its divisions are concerned. (Actually it repeats the common five-fold system of classification derived from the West.) The names assigned to these five divisions, however, are selected so as to be more suggestive of the styles of the successive phases of Japanese cultural development and to bring out the fact that the periods have a real basis in Japanese historical experience. They are as follows:

1. Familial (coinciding roughly with the Yamato period in the standard periodization)
2. Aristocratic (extending over the Nara and Heian periods)
3. Feudal (covering the Kamakura and Ashikaga periods)
4. Military-bureaucratic (coinciding with the Tokugawa period)
5. Modern (following the Meiji Restoration)

The familiar fivefold division of Japanese history becomes a useful device if we employ it to show how during successive periods Japanese culture took on distinctive styles, each characterized by its own pattern of political organization, social and economic structure, system of values, and climate of thought. For each period, in other words, we can conceive of a special cultural model which in turn generated a distinctive historical tradition. Today Japan has inherited from its past elements from each of these historic traditions: from the familial age, for instance, it traces the origins of the Emperor system and certain ingrained attitudes toward religion and government; from the aristocratic phase, a memory of past literary glories, of aristocratic court life, of the continental system of bureaucratic government; from the feudal age, the mores of the warrior-aristocrat; and from the military-bureaucratic age, a habit of social and political regimentation. These and many other historically identifiable traits or their memories have carried over into the period of Japan's development as a modern society. The student of Japanese culture today will wish to inquire more fully into the nature of the major aspects of the country's cultural development as well as the interplay of tradition and innovation in the lives of the contemporary Japanese.

MAJOR PHASES OF JAPANESE CULTURAL HISTORY

The Familial Age

Prior to the seventh century, life in the Japanese islands had evolved through several stages of primitive culture into a state of civilization, despite relatively meager and indirect contact with the major center of civilization on the continent. The resulting style of early Japanese civilization, while not distinguished by any outstanding cultural achievements, was nonetheless of remarkable importance to Japan's subsequent historical development. For it was in these years that the Japanese people took on their distinctive homogeneous quality; the Japanese language acquired its basic structure; and a number of fundamental technological and institutional elements of the Japanese way of life became firmly established, among them irrigated rice cultivation and certain basic ways of handling the relationship between political power, social structure, and religious beliefs. By roughly the middle of the third century, Japanese culture had acquired a sufficiently uniform condition so that a model of what may be called the familial phase of Japanese development can be described.

In third-century Japan a strong line of demarcation divided the ruling families from the rest of society. Members of the elite were organized into a hierarchy of lineage groups called *uji* (sometimes, though rather unhappily, translated "clan"). *Uji* consisted of a number of kin-related (branch) families organized about the main family of the lineage. The head of the main family served as the patriarchal chief of the lineage (*uji-no-kami*). *Uji* chiefs rested their claims to authority within the *uji* upon their supposed descent from some mythically remembered, deified ancestor. They exerted both ritualistic and coercive power as patriarchal chiefs of their *uji*. Under the *uji*, the bulk of the Japanese people at this time were organized into functional communities of workers (known as *be*) who in one way or another served the superior *uji* families.

At some time from the middle of the third century to as late as the late fifth century the *uji* elite were brought under the political control of a powerful family based on the Yamato plain and claiming descent from Amaterasu Ōmikami (the Sun Goddess). This was the sun-line group which has maintained its continuous existence to the present as Japan's Imperial Family. Holding as their symbols of authority the "three sacred treasures" (sword, mirror, and jewels) and worshiping the Sun Goddess at their ancestral shrine of Ise, the chiefs of this lineage asserted temporal as well as religious sovereignty over the Japanese islands, assuming the title of *mikoto* (sovereign). The manner in which these chiefs translated their authority into a political system set a pattern which was to persist for many centuries and was not to die out completely until modern times. In familial Japan authority was exercised along kinship or pseudokinship lines of relationship. The sovereign *mikoto*, relying first of all upon his near relatives for support, exercised control over the several *uji*, demanding loyalty on the basis of whether their chiefs were distant relatives or unrelated houses subjugated at some earlier time. Intermarriage and the exaction of "tribute" males and females kept family ties fresh.

Ideas surrounding the position of sovereign as they were institutionalized at this time also had profound significance for Japan's political development. In familial Japan the power to exercise authority inhered in family status. The Japanese sovereign, as the direct descendant of the Sun Goddess, was himself considered an object of religious veneration. Or to turn this around, religious sanction adhered to political authority. This was true not only for the sovereign but to a lesser degree for other ruling families as well. The belief that government and religion were two sides of the same activity (*sai-sei itchi*) had a strong staying power in Japanese political practice and could even be revived in recent times as part of the ideology of ultranationalism during World War II.

Early religion in Japan was characterized by its lack of theoretical or metaphysical elements and its close association with the social community itself. Thus in religion, as in the social structure, there was a clear bifurcation of practices between the *uji* elite and the dependent populace. *Uji* religious ritual invoked the superior power of the deified first ancestor. The *be* engaged in the communal worship of a guardian deity of a locale. Both family and local deities were commonly referred to as *ujigami*, and both types of worship can be subsumed under the general category of religious beliefs and practices to which the name *Shinto* was later applied. Shinto concepts have served well into modern times to provide the religious basis for the identity of the Japanese to his community and his state. They seem also to have provided the essential rationale for the Japanese sense of uniqueness as a people. The nineteenth-century revival of interest in the myths and chronicles of the familial period was an important factor in the evolution of modern Japanese nationalism, giving support to the belief in Japan's special state structure (*kokutai*).

The Aristocratic Age

While the present Emperor of Japan is seldom seen in anything but Western-style clothes, it may be remembered that his enthronement, which took place in 1926, was held in the old court capital of Kyoto according to the ceremonial style of the tenth century. The now fading court ritual of Japan is part of the classical aristocratic tradition which typified the country from the seventh through the twelfth centuries.

By an aristocracy we refer to a comparatively closed elite stratum of families who claim hereditary rights to social privilege, political authority, and access to higher civilization. During the seventh century the familial elite of Yamato converted themselves into a tight group of families who by virtue of their superior social status and economic privileges maintained an opulent and sophisticated way of life high above the level of the common people who labored in the fields or engaged in crafts. Today the people of Japan resent the thought of a specially privileged aristocracy. In past ages, however, aristocrats were willingly respected and even venerated because of their breeding, courtly manners, and sophisticated accomplishments. The common people of the aristocratic age in Japan literally worshiped their nobility, the *kuge*.

Aristocratic culture in Japan was compounded of two basic ingredients: (1) an oligarchy made up of families drawn chiefly from the ruling lineages of the previous age and (2) a high material technology and advanced system of political and religious organization introduced from China. In other words, the rule of the aristocracy in Japan was based on special claims of noble descent and on the mastery of a superior culture derived from the continent. The emergence of an aristocracy was chiefly an indigenous development reflecting the growing political centralization of Japan during the sixth and seventh centuries, the rising economic and cultural standards of the Yamato Plain, and the concurrent rise in social prestige of a centrally located group of privileged families. These indigenous political and social changes were subsequently acted upon by the influence of Chinese civilization.

The seventh-century continental impact on Japan took three major forms. It flowed through the channels of Confucian political theory and practice, through the institutions and beliefs of organized Buddhism, and through the whole assemblage of Chinese cultural forms, such as the literature, art, and philosophy or the architecture, dress, and agricultural and transportation technology. Taken together, these influences created a new style of culture based upon a model radically different from that of the previous era. Although the power structure still took the form of an oligarchy of elite families, the affairs of state were now conducted through a bureaucracy. The sovereign assumed the guise of an absolute ruler, an Emperor in the Chinese image. The Japanese homeland was organized as a unified state ruled by the Emperor through a central and provincial bureaucracy. A systematic set of laws regulated private status, taxation, conditions of service to the state and many other activities. Religion, both Buddhist and Shinto, was brought to the support of the state and the aristocracy, and the resources of the state were channeled for the use of a conspicuous style of aristocratic life.

The age of the court aristocracy (*kuge*) falls into two major parts, to which two slightly different cultural models apply. The first half of this period, extending roughly to the middle of the ninth century, was marked by a strong and unselfconscious emulation of Chinese civilization. During this period the former *uji* chiefs successfully converted themselves into a civil nobility centered on the Imperial Court. Using political institutions modeled on those of imperial China, they consolidated their hold over a fairly unified country. They staffed a centralized bureaucratic officialdom with headquarters in the capital city of Heijō (or Nara, completed in 710) and later Heian (or Kyoto, completed in 794) and with branches established in each of the provinces. In 702 the Taihō Code (Taihō *ritsuryō*) was promulgated. This codification of Japanese law under the Chinese categories of *ritsu* (penal laws) and *ryō* (administrative practices) has given rise to the custom of referring to this first half of the aristocratic age as the age of the *ritsuryō* institutions.

Another far-reaching reform of the early aristocratic period was the adoption of the concept of state control over rice land and the rationalization of the system of agricultural landholding and taxation. Under what was known as the *jōri* system the former communities which had served the *uji* (primarily the *be*) were abolished. The cultivators of the land were made free tenants of the state and given uniform portions of land. (Remnants of the *jōri* system, whereby fields were divided into geometric patterns for distribution purposes, are still visible in Japan from the Kanto Plain in the east to southern Kyushu in the west.) Local government was systematized and administered as provinces (*kuni*), counties (*gun*), and villages (*ri*). Even the Buddhist temples were used to enhance central authority. The Great Roshana Buddha of Tōdaiji at Nara was built under imperial patronage to serve as the symbol of imperial grandeur and power. Provincial branch temples, known as *kokubunji,* carried the evidence of this superiority into the provinces.

The early aristocratic age (until about 838, the time of the last official mission to China) was one of the great dynamic eras in Japanese history. During this time the court aristocracy demonstrated unusual vigor in its statecraft and in its cultural pursuits. The magnificence and symmetry of Japan's public buildings, laws, and bureaucratic apparatus were truly reminiscent of T'ang China. This was the high era of Buddhist art, as demonstrated in the temple architecture of Hōryūji and Yakushiji and the iconographic sculpture of the Tempyō period. It was a time of young and heroic literature, as seen in the poetry of the *Man'yōshū* and the official national history, the *Nihon shoki.*

The second phase of aristocratic culture, which coincided roughly with the rise of the Fujiwara family to prominence in Kyoto, was distinguished by two notable modifications of the early model. First, the Emperor relinquished real political power to the Fujiwara family; and, second, the fiscal and administrative functions of the central government passed into the hands of the major aristocratic families and the central religious institutions. The Fujiwara family had long held a favored position at court as a result of its role in the Taika *coup d'état.* Having received the prerogative of supplying consorts to the Imperial Family, the Fujiwara eventually succeeded in dominating the Imperial House through marriage. When, in 866, the head of the Fujiwara house was named regent to the Emperor (a post heretofore restricted to imperial princes), the ascendancy of the family was complete. The titles of *sesshō* (regent) and *kampaku* (chancellor), held successively by heads of the

Fujiwara house, became the public indexes of Fujiwara dominance over the Emperor and court affairs.

With the rise of the Fujiwara, the Emperor lost for good his political authority but retained his hereditary right to serve as the ultimate symbol of national sovereignty. Henceforth the Emperor was to be the political puppet of such real power holders as the Fujiwara regents or the military hegemons of later centuries. But neither did these regimes see fit to displace the Imperial Family. The pattern of rule from behind the façade of legitimate delegation sanctioned by the Emperor became the typical form of national government in Japan.

From the middle of the ninth century, the gradual decline in power of the Emperor and the increasing Fujiwara monopoly of official posts seriously affected the operation of government at all levels. The central bureaucracy continued to exist as before but functioned less and less as an effective administrative organ. Offices tended to become hereditary and ceremonial, while the real business of government was carried on within the house organs of the great aristocratic families. The Fujiwara house maintained what amounted to its own private administration through which it dominated the country by controlling the Emperor on the one hand and extending its landholdings on the other.

These changes in aristocratic government and social structure cannot be understood without reference to the changing pattern of land tenure. By the ninth century the system of direct public control of land was increasingly giving way to practices of private proprietary holding. In the new proprietorships, known as *shōen*, cultivators and small land-holders no longer acknowledged the direct authority of the state but became linked in bonds of personal dependence to families of superior local influence and above these to the more powerful court houses and monastic institutions in the capital area. Ultimately, these court families and monasteries acquired complete rights of fiscal immunity and in-dependence of administration over their *shōen*. Thus by the eleventh century the great proprietors not only divided the powers of the central government among themselves but were able to extend their private influence over the land in the provinces and over the cultivators of the land. By administering their extensive territories, they were in effect carrying out the functions of local government.

The new distribution of power and wealth gave rise to a new style of aristocratic culture, distinguished by its conscious avoidance of undue reliance on Chinese precedents. There were many manifestations of a newly achieved sophistication in dress, food, architecture, and court ceremonial and of a reassertion of native tastes in the arts and letters. Cultural missions to China were officially abandoned in 894 (the last actual mission had returned in 838). A style of poetry uniquely suited to the mood of the society of the Kyoto Court was epitomized in the *Kokinshū* (905). The *Genji monogatari* (*The Tale of Genji*), written by a court lady in the early eleventh century, is still judged one of the great novels of world literature. The style of the late aristocratic age is well typified by this novel. Its hero, Hikaru Genji, is the model aristocrat of his day, a man of noble birth, handsome, accomplished in the arts, dance, and poetry. His life was dominated by the search for beauty and by a fine sense of the distinctions, both aesthetic and social, in the courtly life of the day.

The artistocratic tradition is today largely negated in Japan and remains only as a nostalgic dream for readers of *The Tale of Genji* or as a source of material for novelists and cinema producers. Yet as late as 1868 a conscious effort was made to return to the *ritsuryō* system of government. Japan's nobility persisted until 1945, and the awesome status of the Imperial Family was only more recently disavowed by the marriage of the Crown Prince to a commoner. The imperial tradition served the modern Japanese state until the end of World War II.

The Feudal Age

Japan's startling rise as a modern world power was made possible in large part by two factors: (1) the quality of national leadership which asserted itself after 1854 and (2) the remarkable mass effort of the Japanese people behind this leadership. Japan's early modernizers were notable for their militant self-dedication and their high degree of sensitivity to problems of national prestige and self-defense. But enlightened leadership could have achieved little without the disciplined following of the Japanese nation. Both these conditions reflected the values and the pattern of life of the centuries when the style of Japanese culture was essentially feudal.

The most characteristic feature of Japanese history at the end of the twelfth century was the rise to prominence of the military aristocracy (*bushi* or samurai) throughout Japan. As an elite type, the Japanese *bushi* contrasts sharply with other such types in East Asia, particularly with the Chinese scholar-official. Why it was that Japan developed a kind of military-agrarian society so similar to that of feudal Europe is still very much a matter of conjecture. Perhaps the period of civil imperial rule had never really wiped out the tradition of aristocratic arms bearing which had characterized early *uji* society. At any rate, during the Heian age there seems to have been a strong undercurrent toward the reappearance of an armed gentry, especially in local affairs.

The need for an elite military class in the Japanese provinces came gradually after the beginning of the tenth century and accompanied the decline in effectiveness of the police and military organs of the central government. It accompanied also the growth of the large immune proprietorships, which were required to provide their own enforcement services as a consequence of their immunity. As a result, local officials and provincial families of influence took up the bearing of arms as a social privilege and combined the functions of local administration or land management with those of enforcement and protection. By the eleventh century the *bushi* had begun to separate out as a definite functional type. By the twelfth century they had begun to emerge as a dominant social group. From this time to the 1870s the *bushi* constituted Japan's leading stratum of society (though the *kuge* retained the highest social prestige), providing the dominant way of life and key values for the entire culture. As frequently happens, it was not until near the end of the *bushi* age, after the beginning of the seventeenth century, that this warrior aristocracy became self-conscious of its social function and its common ideals, giving rise to the formulation of the principles of *bushidō* (the warrior's way).

Edwin O. Reischauer has pointed out that the type of society over which the *bushi* presided was more similar to that of feudal Europe than any other contemporaneous East Asian society. This fact, he believes, helps to account for the comparative ease with which Japan was later able to follow the Western lead in modernization. It is dangerous, of course, to carry this line of argument too far or to apply it too literally. But it is unquestionably true that the culture of the *bushi* gave rise in Japan to values and institutions which contrast most markedly with those of China, and, as Reischauer has aptly said, these very points of difference are most significant in providing an understanding of why Japan was able to modernize so much more rapidly than China.

We have called the *bushi*'s society feudal. The validity of such an assertion rests very much upon our conception of feudalism itself. Karl A. Wittfogel has provided a useful description of feudalism in contrast to the kind of bureaucratically organized state which typified China and had been tried in Japan during the early aristocratic age. He describes it as a "system of limited and conditional service (not unconditional subservience), vassalage (not bureaucracy), and fief (not office land)." [1] *Corvée* labor and serfdom, he claims, were characteristic of the economic base of both bureaucratic-agricultural and feudal societies, and so feudalism did not presuppose a change in the economy. If we stay within the bounds of some such generalized definition of feudalism as this, the "medieval" societies of both Europe and Japan can be con-

[1] Karl A. Wittfogel, *Oriental Despotism*, New Haven, Conn., 1957, p. 414.

sidered feudal, but it should be remembered that the feudal cultures of Japan and Europe differed in some significant and many less significant details. With respect to Japan the term *feudal* must be used with caution.

Perhaps the most tangible conception of what feudal culture in Japan was like can be had by studying the profile of the dominant figure of the feudal age, the *bushi*, for it was he who set the tone of the age and gave rise to the value system which so deeply permeated life in medieval Japan. The *bushi*, though an aristocrat, lived a life which had important differences from that of the court aristocracy. He was a provincial aristocrat professionally dedicated to the bearing of arms. His provincial origin and his cultivation of military skills necessitated a way of life quite different from that of the civil court aristocracy.

In contrast to the courtiers of the previous age, the *bushi* was preoccupied with problems of the sword and the land. He emphasized, in contrast to the genteel accomplishments of the *kuge*, such qualities as loyalty, honor, fearlessness, and frugality. The two most cherished symbols of the *bushi* class were the sword (the soul of the samurai) and the cherry blossom (the petals of which fall with the first breath of wind just as the samurai gives up his life without regret for his lord). The *bushi* often lived a life of harsh physical discipline (either by necessity or by choice), enduring extreme rigors in the belief that they were "building character." He was trained to scorn an easy life (which to him was a luxury) because of its softening influence. He even scorned an easy way of taking his life. (Suicide now gained respectability as an honorable way out.) The Japanese *bushi*, by resorting to the slashing of the bowels (*seppuku*) as his method of suicide, literally showed himself worthy of a class that prided itself on "having guts."

In time, as the *bushi* became the rulers, administrators, fighters, and guardians of the peace in Japan, they came to consider themselves the only competent leaders of Japanese society. Scorning the effete courtiers and the mercenary merchants, they expressed pride in a profession which, in theory at least, was dedicated to the general welfare. Self-righteousness has been a deep and exasperating quality of the military man not only in Japan. When linked to a belief in caste exclusiveness and social distinction, it made for a particular style of aggressiveness which was at once the strength and the weakness of the *bushi*. The warrior-aristocrat's belief that personal fortitude could overcome all obstacles accounts in part for the strength of Japan's leadership at the end of the nineteenth century, at the same time that it helps to account for the blunders of overconfidence and brutality which led to disaster in World War II.

As the members of the *bushi* class came to dominate more and more areas of Japanese life, they brought into being a new style of government in which the structure of authority was fundamentally feudal. In contrast to the bureaucratic system of the eighth century, in which the system recruited its personnel, in feudal government a preexisting network of military and social relationships provided the framework of government. *Bushi* government, in other words, functioned through an authority structure of personal allegiance, the superior (the lord) receiving loyal service from the inferior (the vassal) in return for the granting of a benefice (or fief).

The prototype of *bushi* government in Japan was created by Minamoto-no-Yoritomo at the end of the twelfth century. After an extended civil war, Yoritomo in 1185 emerged as the paramount military power in Japan at the head of a large band of *bushi* followers. When in 1192 he gained the title of Shogun, he acquired the legal authority to match his power. He now stood delegated by the Emperor as commander in chief of all armed forces. His headquarters, the shogunate (or *bakufu*), though not by any means possessed of full administrative powers over the country, became the locus of paramount military and police authority. From this time until 1868, all military and an increasingly large portion of civil powers were exercised through the shogunate or an equivalent form of military authority.

From 1185 to 1333 the seat of military authority in Japan was the town of Kamakura in the Kanto region, the center of Minamoto strength. During the Kamakura period the political powers of the shogunate were still limited by the continued existence of independent civil proprietorships and to some extent by the continuance of imperial governors in the provinces. In the thirteenth century, however, the political powers of the court constantly diminished. Especially in 1221, when the court raised arms against the Kamakura shogunate and was soundly defeated, military officials began to absorb civil administrative functions in the provinces and in the immune proprietorships.

The Kamakura "government" was primarily a system of control extended over the numerous and far-flung vassals of the shogun. These vassals, or house men (*gokenin*), ranged considerably in wealth and influence, from those who could command several hundred men to those who took the field alone, perhaps with but a single attendant. Around the shogun in the Kanto area was clustered a group of powerful vassals who served as the mainstay of the Minamoto band. Among these powerful supporters, the head of the Hōjō family acquired hereditary rights to the office of chief administrator (*shikken*) and served as head of the administrative board (Man-dokoro). Others of the shogun's vassals served as heads of a military board (Samurai-dokoro) and records office (Monchūjo). Outside Kamakura three important offices extended the shogun's authority. In Kyoto the shogun established a branch headquarters and placed in it his deputy to oversee the court. In the provinces he appointed from among his direct vassals military governors, or *shugo*, charged with recruiting provincial guards. In the several *shōen* and public lands, lesser vassals of the shogun functioned as military land stewards, or *jitō*, with the responsibility of maintaining order and facilitating tax collection. Thus through his house men the shogun touched local affairs in most of Japan.

The Kamakura shogunate was destroyed in 1333 in an uprising led by the Emperor Go-Daigo. An abortive attempt to revive imperial government led through a brief period of civil war to the establishment of a new military hegemony under the Ashikaga house in 1338. The Ashikaga shoguns selected Kyoto, the old court capital, as their headquarters, thereby completing the final ascendancy of the military houses over the court aristocracy. Under the Ashikaga shoguns the Imperial House and courtiers lost all power and wealth, retaining only their social prestige. Administrative authority, both civil and military, was now in the hands of the shogun and his chief vassals, the provincial *shugo*. In the provinces the *shugo* served both as military and as civil governors.

After the middle of the fifteenth century, however, the Ashikaga house lost its ability to control the great military houses. Political and military authority became almost totally decentralized. The frequent local wars of the sixteenth century hastened the division of Japan into a large number of independent domains, each governed by a powerful local lord (*daimyō*) and his vassals through the practice of enfeoffment. Feudal authority had become all-inclusive. All important functions of government now coincided with the feudal hierarchy. Under the *bushi* stratum, the peasantry, organized into villages, served as serfs, while merchant and craft functions were carried on through protected guilds. The Buddhist establishment, organized into temples and monasteries possessing extensive lands and armed forces, served as the refuge for arts and letters. The essential members of feudal society in Japan, the lord (*daimyō*), the knight (samurai), the priest, the villein, the merchant, and the artisan stood in much the same relationship to each other as the comparable groups under European feudalism. Perhaps for this reason Japan held few surprises for the European adventurers and missionaries when they began to arrive during the last half of the sixteenth century.

The Military-Bureaucratic Age

Whether the cultural history of Japan should be divided at the end of the sixteenth century or not is a matter of some dispute among historians. Many important features of feudalism continued into what we have termed Japan's *military-bureaucratic age,* so that most historians merely extend the limits of the feudal age to 1868. But the reasons for making a separate period of the 2½ centuries of Tokugawa rule should become apparent as we proceed.

Between 1568 and 1600 the *daimyō* fought among themselves for supremacy in Japan. A process of territorial consolidation had begun with the formation of regional *daimyō* confederations. By 1560 some ten or fifteen *daimyō* clusters had come into existence, and it is probably true that the leading *daimyō* of any one of these clusters held the capacity to attain national hegemony. Leadership was first grasped by Oda Nobunaga, who began the drive toward unification by capturing the imperial capital in 1568 and consolidating large portions of central Japan under his command. Assassinated in 1582, he was followed by Toyotomi Hideyoshi, who in 1590 succeeded in reducing all *daimyō* to a state of dependence. Hideyoshi's death in 1598 led to further warfare, but in 1600, at the great Battle of Sekigahara, Tokugawa Ieyasu seized the hegemony and went on to establish himself as head of a third shogunal dynasty.

Some historians have asserted that Japan during the sixteenth century was on the verge of becoming a centralized nation-state like those of western Europe. They claim that Japan's "failure" to destroy the decentralized feature of shogunal rule resulted from the conservative policies of Hideyoshi and Ieyasu, who combined to "refeudalize" Japan. It is doubtful, however, whether Japan in the seventeenth century was ready for national unification and the abolition of the *daimyō.* The political "unity" created by Hideyoshi and continued by Ieyasu was as dependent on the capacity of the *daimyō* to complete the consolidation of their local territories as upon the strength of the paramount national power wielded by the shogun.

The distinctive feature of Japan's political development between 1590 and 1650 was the ascendancy of the *daimyō* and the gradual perfection of an authoritarian, bureaucratic style of local government within the *daimyō* domains. Although most historians emphasize the national struggle for unification among the *daimyō,* it is important to realize that the *daimyō* were also fighting to gain control of their domains against the opposition of lesser military powers, Buddhist monasteries, and independent commercial towns. During these years Hideyoshi and Ieyasu are credited with restructuring the political and social institutions of Japan. Hideyoshi gained new imperial sanction for military rule. New legislation defined the social classes, confirming the status of the *bushi,* disarming the peasantry, and regulating commercial activity. A new land survey *(kenchi)* initiated by Hideyoshi laid the foundations for local government and systematic taxation. In its wake a strict line was drawn between samurai and peasant. The peasant village (mura) was systematically regulated as the new basis of rural society and administration. But while these changes were impressed upon the country by the national hegemons, the changes themselves reflected what the *daimyō* were already attempting to achieve in their separate domains. It is doubtful whether a national authority could have achieved these innovations and at the same time dispensed with the *daimyō*, who served to hold down the local areas in Japan.

By roughly 1650, through the efforts of the shogun and the *daimyō*, the foundations had been laid for a new political and social order which we have called *military-bureaucratic*. Its prime features were rule by the samurai (now a distinct military officer class) through bureaucratic organization. Between 1600 and 1650 the feudal method of rule through subinfeudation and serfdom was largely abandoned in favor of more impersonal, bureaucratic methods. The samurai were withdrawn from the land, collected in the castled administrative towns of the *daimyō*, paid salaries (*hōroku*) rather than being given fiefs, and organized into military and administrative corps. The villages were governed and taxed through a field administration staffed by the *daimyō* with their private retainers. Japan continued to be governed by a hereditary professional military class but increasingly through bureaucratic practices.

Characteristic of the late period of samurai rule was its rigid regimentation of the political, social, economic, and intellectual life of the country. The regime was first of all stabilized by the Tokugawa shogunate, which by 1650 was vastly more powerful than the hegemony created by Toyotomi Hideyoshi. Tokugawa Ieyasu secured the title of Shogun in 1603. Legally this made him an agent of the Emperor, but in actuality the Tokugawa only borrowed the legitimatizing prestige of the now politically powerless Emperor and his court. Through the office of shogun the Tokugawa leaders exacted the loyalty of all *daimyō* and proceeded to regulate their conduct through a strict code, the *Buke-sho-hatto*. A hostage system (*sankin-kōtai*) obliged all *daimyō* to reside for part of the year in the shogun's capital of Edo and leave wife and children behind when they traveled to their territories. But behind these control measures enforced by the shogun, the real basis of stability derived from the overwhelming military and economic might of the Tokugawa house. Nearly one-fourth of the entire country was held directly by the shogun, and this area contained the major cities of Osaka, Kyoto, Nagasaki, and Edo. In the remaining three-fourths of the country held by the *daimyō*, the Tokugawa worked out a careful balance of political interests among the closely allied *fudai daimyō* and the more independent *tozama daimyō* so as to preclude the formation of coalitions against the shogun.

The government of Japan during the Tokugawa period was carried out by the shogun and the various *daimyō* through an officialdom staffed exclusively by samurai. Since the *daimyō* domains had been created under conditions of strenuous civil warfare, the *daimyō* continued to administer their territories through a system of officials which was military in origin and organization. Though adapted to civil needs, government remained harsh and authoritarian. The ruling elite jealously guarded their political and social supremacy and protected their badge of identity, the wearing of two swords. The right to rule was theirs by virtue of this status.

In their social policy the shogun and the *daimyō* clarified and broadened the concepts of functional classes, applying laws and controls to large sectors of the population. Each class (and frequently subclass) was given its own regulations covering its political status and responsibilities; even the religious affiliations of the people were scrutinized. In theory every individual was registered and accounted for either on the samurai rolls, the village registers, or the occupational lists. Still recognized as a nobility were the *kuge*: members of the Imperial Family and the courtiers of Kyoto. The samurai formed a military aristocracy, the ruling class. Below them ranked the peasantry, the artisans, and the merchants. The latter two classes, since their members were generally found in cities and towns, were frequently referred to together as townsmen (*chōnin*). Priests were given a special status outside the hierarchy of classes but ranking somewhere between samurai and commoner.

In their economic policy the shogun and the *daimyō* were primarily concerned with the land and its taxable produce. Every effort was made to extend the productivity of the land by expansion of the cultivated area and by encouragement of the thrift and industry of the peasantry. Trade was carefully regulated. Merchant guilds (*nakama*) and monopolies (*za*) were officially sanctioned as means of controlling commerce and as agencies through which merchants could be taxed. The shogunate itself monopolized such key commodities as metallic currency and foreign imports.

The political and social order of Tokugawa Japan eventually received its ideological sanction from the principles of Confucianism, for after 1600 Japan became thoroughly saturated with the ideas of Confucianism, which replaced Buddhism as the dominant ethic of the country. Confucianism with its emphasis upon loyalty to the state, submission to authority, and maintenance of social order became the rationale for a highly stratified society. The important Confucian concept of *dō* (the path or the way) gave rise to rules of conduct for each social status. In particular, that combination of Confucian bureaucratic morality and feudal military values known as *bushidō* became the characteristic ethic of the Japanese samurai on the eve of Japan's modern encounter with the West. One of the prime legacies of the Tokugawa period to modern Japan was contained in concepts and practices of the well-regulated order presided over by the bureaucratically trained samurai class.

Of course, after 1854, when Japan was brought into closer contact with Western civilization, the country was obliged to draw upon all its historical resources to maintain its identity as a nation and as a distinctive culture. Out of its early history came the institution of the Emperor and the integrating beliefs of Shinto. Out of the aristocratic age the Japanese drew ideas of imperial grandeur and justified the existence of a modern nobility. From the feudal past were perpetuated the values of the fighting elite and the strong sense of personal loyalty which could unite the entire society. And, finally, from the Tokugawa age came the machinery of political, administrative, and social regulation which made the transition into a modern imperial state so orderly. To this extent our study of Japan's past should help in understanding the course of the country's rise as a modern power.

CAUSATION IN CULTURAL CHANGE

Before turning to Japan's modern history, however, we shall need to take up a number of interpretive problems that are raised by the survey which we have just completed. Ideas about periodization provide an essentially static way of looking at history. The system of periodization followed above has given us five cross-sectional views of Japanese history taken at different points of time. Each has revealed a different cultural style. But to discriminate periods in this way reveals nothing about how such periods are interrelated or how the style of one was transformed into that of another. We have yet to identify the stable and dynamic factors which made for continuity and change in Japanese history.

Obviously any attempt to deal with the causes of social change on a broad scale must be sensitive to a wide range of human conditions. The process of social change is compounded of many elements, some being derived from outside the system, others from within. We speak of traditional "institutions," which tend to retain their identity for extended periods of time; we speak of "forces" or "trends," of the "influence" of ideas or the "impact" of foreign culture as the sources of the dynamic factors in cultural change. Historical analysis, in other words, is apt to concern itself with two aspects of culture: "structures" and "processes," the one comprehending the stabilizing factors in society and the other the dynamic. The analysis of Japan's cultural history in terms of stable conditions and moving processes is the most common method of approaching the problem of general cultural change available to historians.

Some Enduring Structures:
Racial Characteristics and National Character

Many historians, in explaining the history and behavior of the Japanese, have simply claimed that "the Japanese are like that," that the Japanese are somehow distinguished by special "racial characteristics." Sir George B. Sansom, in his *Japan: A Short Cultural History*, came to the conclusion that the Japanese demonstrated throughout their history a "hard, non-absorbent core of individual character" which resisted and worked upon invading influences from outside Japan.[2] He did not attempt to define this character, and he was in fact careful not to elaborate his statement. The works of less cautious writers, however, abound in stereotyped statements and clichés about the Japanese people. Lafcadio Hearn, at the beginning of this century, popularized the "strangeness and charm" version of Japan, which depicted the Japanese as a primitive, naïve people, in many ways similar to the ancient Greeks. During World War II it was common to talk of the Japanese as a race of militarists and imitators. John M. Maki in his book *Japanese Militarism* presented a view of Japanese history in which the country's modern imperialism is linked to the long period of feudal military rule and to what he considered to be an ingrained oligarchic political tradition. Otto Tolischus, a wartime correspondent, devoted a number of books to the extreme view that the Japanese, being nothing but imitators, had mastered the machines of war but yet remained half civilized as a people.

Japanese writers have been equally prolific in their identification of certain special features in Japanese culture. They have claimed, as in Okakura Kakuzō's *Book of Tea* and Harada Jirō's *Glimpse of Japanese Ideals*, that the Japanese possess an unusual understanding of nature and an innate sense of beauty. The modern government textbook *Kokutai no hongi* expressed the extreme nationalistic version of the belief that Japan possessed a unique national structure (the idea of *kokutai*). The same book was one of many to embellish the Japanese claim that their culture has demonstrated a marked ability to absorb foreign cultural elements, to perfect these elements beyond the state in

[2] Sir George B. Sansom, *Japan: A Short Cultural History*, rev. ed., New York, 1943, p. 15.

which they were received, and then to add these to the indigenous culture without losing the essence of Japan's individuality. Historically they expected Japan to serve as the ultimate synthesizer of Eastern and Western civilizations. Most often, however, Japanese historians have stressed the inner qualities of uniqueness possessed by Japanese culture. Akiyama Kenzō, in his *History of Nippon*, and Hasegawa Nyozekan, in his *Educational and Cultural Background of the Japanese People,* both base their explanation of Japanese culture on certain inherent features, the one emphasizing the role of the Emperor, the other expounding Japan's "cultural democracy."

The whole question of the validity of concepts of national character is a matter of controversy. Historians have ranged in their thinking on the subject from the most naïve acceptance of geographical or racial determinism to outright rejection of the idea that differences in national character are real. Japan has in fact been very much in the center of recent efforts to redefine the concept of national character in more acceptable terms—a result of the fascination with which Western scholars observed the idiosyncracies of Japanese behavior during World War II. Ruth Benedict's efforts to describe a national behavioral profile, Douglas G. Haring's inquiry into the historical conditioning of Japanese behavior, and Geoffrey Gorer's variations on the theme of toilet training all emerged from this wartime stimulus. They have been followed most recently by studies of individual and group personality patterns. Such studies have done much to rehabilitate a concept of national character which avoids the old fallacies of racism or environmental determinism and penetrates the mystery of unexplained "uniquenesses." It helps to point up the necessary interplay between history, culture, and personality and has suggested lines of inquiry into the very real peculiarities of Japanese cultural life.

The weakness of the old concepts of Japanese character exemplified in some of the writings mentioned at the beginning of this section is that they looked upon national traits as being inborn and immutable and, furthermore, that they failed to distinguish between individual peculiarities and group characteristics. Recent scholars have been more conscious of the need for statistical sophistication in their statements at the same time that they have been less inclined to credit the existence of some innate "hard core" of special traits. Their interest has been drawn consequently to the measurable continuities in the Japanese historical environment, social as well as physical, and in the current social and psychological makeup of the Japanese people. Chapter 8 in this book, "Personality Psychology," attempts to summarize the findings of psychologists working with contemporary Japanese. One of the best summaries of the findings of cultural anthropologists is contained in Chapters 7 and 8 of Edwin O. Reischauer's *United States and Japan,* under such rubrics as emotionalism, conformity, shame and self-respect, competitiveness and acceptance of authority, hierarchy and self-discipline. These psychological and anthropological insights into the behavior of contemporary Japanese are of interest to the historian in that they identify the end products of a number of environmental factors which have exercised an influence over the Japanese people during their long history. The historian will wish to seek out the origins of such influences and the conditions which generated particular elements of Japanese character as they can be identified by contemporary observers. The subject of national character, therefore, is intimately related to the historian's search for continuities in Japanese cultural history, especially to his study of the public institutions and environmental circumstances which have channeled Japanese behavior through time. It is to these that we now turn.

Isolation and Cultural Homogeneity

No comparative historian can fail to be struck by Japan's relative isolation from foreign contacts and, until the last century, the almost total absence of foreign invasions or foreign wars. Japan's geographical position as a group of islands on the extreme fringe of the Old World is an environmental factor of quite obvious importance. The condition was substantially modified only after the Pacific was narrowed by the perfection of modern means of transportation. The obvious comparison between Japan and the British Isles has often been drawn, yet Japan differed from Britain in being both more isolated and, as a homeland, more capable of sustaining a vigorous self-sufficiency. Also from a fairly early time the Japanese islands were fused into a relatively homogeneous political and cultural entity. Consequently the history of Japan until well into the nineteenth century has shown a remarkable absence of sudden or violent change. (It is questionable, in fact, whether Japan ever experienced what we could call a real revolution.) Nor was Japan ever colonized or occupied until after World War II. Change has been slow and organic, and though the historian, as he takes his cross-sectional cuts of Japanese culture, can identify obvious dissimilarities between one period of Japanese history and another, the changes which lead from one period to another seem always to have been compounded of small increments of less than revolutionary scope.

The reason for this can only be surmised. The dissipation of foreign influence through distance and isolation is, of course, quite obvious.

Isolation and racial homogeneity may also help to explain why revolutionary social or political pressures failed to build up to the point of explosion and why the country, even during the period of extreme decentralization in the sixteenth century, did not break into subdivisions of sufficient independence so that civil war could become a struggle between separate states. There were no divisions in Japan equivalent to those between Scotland, England, Wales, and Ireland. Japan has in fact remained under a single sovereignty from its first origins as a primitive national unity to the very present. The implications of this condition are, in fact, of considerable importance.

The Emperor in Japanese History

One of the great continuities in Japanese political history has been provided by the Imperial House and the political and religious institutions which have supported the Japanese sovereign. Japanese historians, particularly before World War II, have tended to exaggerate the importance of the Emperor and the Shinto rituals over which he has presided, claiming that these have served as the central spiritual foundation upon which the Japanese nation was built and as the ultimately unifying force in Japanese history. On the other hand, Western writers and postwar Japanese historians have greatly discounted the importance of the Emperor. It is a matter of historical record, however, that the Imperial House as the repository of the powers of ultimate sovereignty, together with the native shrines to the ancestors of the house, has endured throughout Japanese history in one form or another.

The Imperial House has undergone many vicissitudes. In the early centuries of Japanese history the family wielded real political and even military power, establishing its claim to hegemony through conquest. During the aristocratic age the house lost its political power, but neither then nor at any later time was it deprived of its hereditary right to ultimate sovereignty. The Emperor, more as ritual head or sacred ark, retained the respect of the Japanese power elite as the fountainhead of political legitimacy. The continuity of the Emperor, whether as a real force or merely as a symbol of unchanging tradition, reveals as nothing else the enduring homogeneity of the Japanese political corpus. While there were civil wars in Japan, the political fabric was never torn so far that there was a contest of sovereignties. (The so-called "dynastic" wars from 1336 to 1392 represented only a momentary factionalism between claimants to the same throne.) Isolation protected Japan from the conquest by a foreign sovereignty, and the Japanese islands themselves never seemed to afford the space for a geographical base within which a rival dynasty might gain independent power with which to challenge the established order.

This continuity of dynasty in Japan explains (or, conversely, is explained by) a number of significant features of the historical behavior of the Japanese political elite. Until recent times the holders of power have persistently been organized into a social hierarchy presided over by the Imperial House. The structure of this aristocratic hierarchy showed certain characteristics from the time of its first appearance during the age of the patriarchal *uji*. As we have noted, the political system of the fifth century consisted of a group of aristocratic *uji* joined in a federation under a hegemon. There were certain distinctive features to this federation from the start. First, despite its early military successes, the sovereign family did not seem to have acquired commanding power over all parts of the Japanese islands. Second, the sovereign house constantly buttressed its temporal powers by claiming special religious sanctions. From the very beginning it appears that the head of the Imperial Family played the role of a sacred peacemaker, exercising hegemony over a closely integrated group of elite families. His position was gained through incomplete civil war in which compromise and conciliation had been extensively resorted to and in which the competitors were not eliminated but rather incorporated into a balance of power.

Once the Imperial Family was established as the sacred peacemaker, a symbol of elite unity, it continued to serve this function without serious lapses until modern times. It may well be that the loss of real power by the Emperor and his retention chiefly of ritual sovereignty served in the long run to protect the Imperial House from destruction. Perhaps also the strongly oligarchic nature of Japanese power politics, which served to make political authority and social position synonymous, had much to do with perpetuating a condition in which a peacemaker possessed of only residual sovereignty continued to be useful. Certainly struggles for national hegemony tended to take the form of intrigues or military action among the elite which repeated almost exactly the pattern of incomplete victory and compromise which had brought the Imperial House to its original position. And in these later struggles each leader of a winning coalition eventually acquired legitimacy for his *de facto* power by imperial delegation, just as the Emperor had justified his own position of sovereignty through his claims to sacerdotal legitimacy.

All of this helps to explain why, even after the decline of the court nobility, the whole set of attitudes toward court ranks, the traditionally "noble" genealogies, and certain ancestral or guardian Shinto shrines retained their importance. Despite the loss of power by the Emperor and later by the court nobility, the social hierarchy remained, so that in each age the politically ambitious families were obliged to climb the same ladder of social prestige as they gained political power. Even those leaders who came to the fore by military force were no exception. Since the power of each military hegemon rested upon a coalition rather than absolute force, legitimacy secured through the imperial system was always a necessity. One of the first acts of newly risen military leaders was to adjust their genealogies so as to place their families comfortably high in the social hierarchy. Along with military titles such as that of shogun went court ranks and honorary posts which gave their bearers the requisite social prestige to assume leadership over their sometimes reluctant followers.

This drama was reenacted in full as late as the seventeenth century, when the members of a new power elite led by the Tokugawa family built themselves into a status hierarchy capped by the nobility of the Kyoto Court. The Tokugawa family and its allies had gained at Sekigahara in 1600 a definite but nonetheless partial military victory over the country. The Tokugawa hegemony, despite its solidity, still rested upon a balance of power. The Tokugawa house therefore could not neglect the traditional symbols of legitimacy—a genealogy traced back to the Minamoto family, high court rank, and the imperial designation as shogun. Moreover, after the death of Ieyasu, his family capitalized on the feeling of reverence for departed ancestors by building a great shrine to the first Shogun at Nikko. This was the Tōshōgū, to which on frequent occasions the whole military aristocracy was obliged to pay homage in memory of Ieyasu. Eventually a cult of Ieyasu grew up around branch Tōshōgū, which were built in the territories of the several *daimyō*.

The Meiji Restoration brought an end to the landed aristocratic oligarchy which had dominated Japan up to that time. Yet the Emperor continued to play an important role. The restoration was itself rationalized as a movement to restore the Emperor to his prime function as head of state. And although the Emperor did not regain real power, the continuation of the throne as the symbol of national unity served as an ideological aid in overthrowing the Tokugawa regime and beyond that as a focus of patriotism for the new state. The eventual institutionalization of the Emperor in modern garb, the official sponsorship of shrine Shinto, and the establishment of a new peerage around the Emperor were important means of assuring a political and social continuity with the past in which fundamental inherited values were retained in the new state. In modern Japan the Emperor continued to play the role of peacemaker, the keystone in an edifice of national solidarity.

Land, Agriculture, and Local Authority

From a very early time the practice of growing rice in irrigated fields became the dominant form of agriculture in Japan. The chicken and egg question of whether the culture dictated the technology or whether the technology shaped the Japanese agrarian community need not trouble us. It is obvious that the forms of agriculture and rural society have been closely interrelated and that a whole range of continuities have flowed from the practices of wet rice cultivation, through the communal activities of agricultural villages, to touch the basic practices of land use, taxation, and local administration.

It is the nature of irrigated rice cultivation that it requires the expenditure of greater manpower per unit of cultivation than dry or "natural" agriculture. In compensation, paddy fields give a much higher yield per unit without the necessity of crop rotation and so can support the much denser population required for their cultivation. Irrigated rice production lends itself to labor-intensive concentration of effort upon small fields. By contrast, natural agriculture places a premium upon the working of large fields with the minimum amount of manpower. In Europe the use of draft animals and crop rotation was traditionally combined with animal husbandry, so that animals supplied power for cultivation at the same time that they produced manure to replenish the soil.

Intensive cultivation of rice has its own special requirements. It periodically demands large bodies of cultivators who can prepare the irrigation works and the flooded paddy fields, quickly make the laborious transfer of rice seedlings from nursery to field, and tend the rice plants during the growing season. Thus it fosters the existence of dense communities of cultivators disciplined to hard work and cooperative labor. Characteristically such communities have been comprised of large extended families organized into closely knit villages.

As Prof. Asakawa Kan'ichi has pointed out, these features had two prime effects upon conditions of land tenure. The cultivator himself, because of the laborious care with which he worked his parcels of land, tended to retain a strong sense of occupancy of the land, though his rights were seldom those of outright ownership. Above him the groups or individuals, private or government, possessing superior rights to the land, seldom obtained absolute rights of ownership and tended instead simply to acquire shares of profit from the land to which they held title. Thus from early times the relationship of the so-called "landowning class" in Japan to the land has tended to be proprietary or managerial. The aristocracy left the cultivators to their own communal devices, contesting among themselves for only the superior rights. This condition was most clearly exemplified in the *shōen* system, in which rights to the land (known as *shiki*) were considered separable at almost every level of detachment from the land (i.e., proprietor, superintendent, manager, cultivator, tenant, etc.). The most significant consequence of the comparative weakness of the concept of private ownership of land was seen at the end of the Tokugawa period, when the entire samurai class, traditionally defined as "landholders," was cut away from any residual rights they might have had over the land by the payment of stipends and, eventually, commutation bonds.

Because of the separation of rights of proprietorship and cultivation in Japan, the rural community was generally able to organize itself without regard to the exact contours of superior proprietary rights. There was no development of manors, for instance, in which lands were organized about the residence of a local landholder. There was an absence of home farms, and the individual cultivator seldom held compact holdings around his home. Instead the typical cultivating community was the village. Such a community, though cultivating fields which might owe dues to one or several proprietors, nonetheless had a sense of its own corporate identity which was derived from its own communal activity: work in the fields, ceremonial observances, and communal worship centering on a village deity. During much of Japanese history, therefore, local government consisted primarily of a system of controls thrown over a stratum of village communities, each managing its internal affairs under the supervision of its headmen. It is significant that probably at no time in Japanese history had the system of control over the village become more effective and impersonal than during the Tokugawa period, a factor which does much to account for the continuity of control which the Japanese government was able to exercise over the country after 1868.

Some Continuing Processes: Individual and Group Behavior

The search for continuities could be pushed much farther, but the two upon which we have focused our attention are both significant and typical. Let us turn, then, from continuities to processes of change. Japanese history is not readily explained in terms of dynastic cycles, foreign invasions, or great class or intellectual upheavals or even in terms of great individuals who have turned the course of Japanese history. Probably the only "theory of change" commonly acknowledged by historians of premodern Japan has been the view that China has been responsible for initiating the major innovations. But what of the internal sources of change?

For some reason the standard surveys of Japanese history depend much less upon the individual as the prime force in historical change than would the comparable histories of the countries of Europe. There are few great statesmen, generals, lawmakers, or thinkers who are made to stand out as the willful creators of their ages or as the originators of important institutions. Whether this relative lack of the great individual in Japanese history is due to the manner of Japanese historical writing or to the actual lack of heroes who can excite the imagination is difficult to determine. Of course Japanese history has its roster of prominent persons. Men like Shōtoku Taishi, the Emperors Kammu and Go-Daigo, Yoritomo, Hideyoshi, and Ieyasu are all worthy of standing in bold type in the chapter headings of Japanese history. Yet few of these men have been depicted as individuals whose personalities or ambitions have caused them to refashion a part of the Japanese tradition. The great hero in Japanese history is generally depicted as *illustrative* of his time and not as its creator, as a *consolidator* of existing powers and not as the fashioner of new ones.

One problem, of course, is that we know so little about the great men of Japanese history. Is this because such men have revealed less about themselves or that Japanese historians have been less interested in looking for evidence of their individuality? Perhaps the two questions are related. Japanese society has undoubtedly given less scope to the creative innovator. Family and institutional environments have always seemed to predominate over individual initiative. Combined with this is the tendency for ambitious individuals to hide behind institutional or family screens, so that most often the "great man" appears as a manipulator rather than a forceful autocrat. And so the Japanese historian has himself been less inclined to look for private motives for individual action. Once we move into the modern period of Japanese history, the individual appears as a prime activator of change. Yet again it is apt to be the Western historian who asks the question of what lay behind the actions of such men as Sakamoto Ryōma, Ōkuma Shigenobu, Yamagata Aritomo, or Hara Kei. For earlier periods, where the Western historian is dependent to a large extent upon the prior work of Japanese scholars, motivation tends to become dissipated into the group, the family, the class, or the faceless institution.

Here, perhaps, is one explanation of why Marxist historiography has appealed to so many writers on Japanese history. Certainly the historian is encouraged to look for his explanations of change in generalized concepts of the type we rehearsed at the beginning of this chapter, to lay across the warp of structure the woof of long-range process. And it must be admitted that Japanese history (perhaps because of its isolation) offers the most remarkable evidence of how the processes of institutional evolution make for cumulative changes of major proportions for the society as a whole. Two illustrations might be cited at this point: first, the obvious continuous line of technological innovation in Japanese culture; and, second, the equally continuous process of expansion in the volume of social participation in the higher culture.

By technology we should conceive not only of material objects, such as tools and artifacts, but also of the social achievements of government, communication, and education. The record of Japanese history gives undeniable evidence of a constant increase in the complexity of the technology of agriculture and commerce, of communication and urban life, and of administrative and military organization. Given even the inadequate tools of measurement we now have, it is nonetheless quite obvious that government in the Nara period was measurably less effective than government in the Tokugawa period, despite the fact that the former was on paper more symmetrically structured than the latter. To borrow the words of Prof. Karl Deutsch, the Tokugawa political organization represented a much greater potential of social transaction and served a community which was more sophisticated in its volume of social communication.

Paralleling the curve of technological change is another which shows what might be called an increase in social entropy, in other words, a process by which the elements of political power and cultural advantage become the property of an increasingly larger portion of the population as time goes on. Japanese history begins in the Yamato period with a handful of families in central Japan monopolizing the higher culture. During the seventh century an aristocracy of broadened membership was created and concentrated at the capital. With the growth of this aristocracy the higher culture was gradually disseminated into the provinces. The rise of the samurai class, though sometimes considered evidence of barbarization, more properly was a sign of the cultural advance of provincial families. This process was to continue until by the Tokugawa period fully 7 per cent of the population was included within the samurai aristocracy. Furthermore, whereas until the fifteenth century the higher culture of Japan had been limited to one or at most two urban centers, by the Tokugawa period the cultural elite had given rise to a dozen or more castle cities whose population surpassed 50,000. It was in these new cities that still other social elements were given access to an affluent way of life. For as the townsmen became part of a new urban culture, they added still another dimension to Japan's cultural development. The implications of these two long-range processes for the history of cultural change in Japan are enormous, for the conditions of Japan's political and social technology and social entropy at the middle of the nineteenth century must surely be rated favorably with the comparable features of Western civilization. Thus the encounter with the West, though traumatic, was not, as for some societies, immobilizing.

Foreign Influences on Japanese Culture

We are brought back again to the factor of foreign influence. The claim is often made that Japan has been essentially a land of imitators. And this judgment rests chiefly on the record of the country's heavy borrowing from China during the eighth century and from the most recent reception of Western civilization. But we need not involve ourselves in the quarrel over whether Japan has been unduly dependent upon foreign culture. No society has been completely self-sufficient, and only a very few centers of distinctive civilization have arisen on this earth. It is more common to find peoples such as the Japanese or those of Western Europe whose cultures are compounded from many sources. In the case of Japan it may well be, as Reischauer has suggested, that isolation has made the process of culture contact more obvious and the outside borrowings more easily identified, but it is not to Japan's discredit to admit a dependency upon wider cultural environments which were dominated first by China and then by Western Europe.

The Japanese nation came of age in the Chinese zone of civilization, and a rehearsal of the interaction between Japanese and Chinese culture will help in our understanding of the country's later involvement with the West. The relationship between Japan and the more dominant Chinese cultural tradition which formed the wider environment surrounding the country in premodern times was far from that of simple and constant absorption by the Japanese. The membrane of geographical distance and racial difference which has separated Japan from China at times permitted an easy flow of Chinese influence into Japan, while at other times it was practically impenetrable. On the one hand the pressure of Chinese influence was affected by the rise and fall of dynasties and by variations in China's cultural vitality, and on the other hand the absorptive capacity of the Japanese varied greatly according to circumstances within the country.

It should not be supposed that Japan was a particularly effective absorbent for Chinese culture. Many of the basic structural elements of Japanese society had been derived from a tradition quite different from that of the Chinese and had been set many centuries before Chinese influence touched Japan in any significant quantity. The political and social structure of the country during the *uji* period was more closely linked to the nomadic societies of Northeast Asia. The language was predominantly Altaic. As a consequence, China's first gifts to Japan were not the most easily assimilated. It is very probable, for instance, that the prestige of Chinese learning combined with the strangeness of the language in which it was introduced into Japan kept Japanese intellectuals constantly absorbed in the mechanics of an alien language, depressing their own capacity both for the understanding of Chinese ideas and for their own creative thinking.

Moreover, despite many overlays of Chinese influence, Japanese culture managed to retain unchanged its most fundamental institutions and beliefs. Japan's seventh-century experiment in adopting Confucian-style government, for instance, never seriously attempted to destroy the aristocratic structure of Japanese society. Again, the tradition of a warrior aristocracy predominated over the attempt to create a conscript army on the Chinese model. The Japanese culture hero remained the military aristocrat, the samurai, not the Chinese type of literatus. The same persistence is noticeable with respect to certain ethical concepts governing the relationship of the individual to the family and to the state. Despite the strong emphasis upon family in Japan, loyalty to a political superior ideally outranked family loyalties. The Chinese ideal placed family loyalties first. Does this explain, perhaps, the ready acceptance of the feudal pattern of loyalties in Japan and the quick florescence of modern state patriotism? Certainly the "political man" in China and in Japan were differently motivated. Even in material culture, the Japanese showed many surprising areas of resistance to China: for instance, clothing, domestic architecture, and food.

Yet, having said all this, there is little doubt that Japanese culture, like that of Korea or Annam, stands in the eyes of the comparative historian as simply a variant of the great East Asian tradition mothered by China. We have said that the Chinese impact on Japan was variable in terms of both intensity and quality. Matching the ebb and flow in Chinese influence was the cycle of Japan's own receptivity or lack thereof. The history of Chinese-Japanese cultural relations must be seen in terms of these variable factors.

Until the year 607 the Japanese people felt the influence of China mainly indirectly through the Korean Peninsula. It seems probable that the early rulers of Japan remained acutely conscious of their continental origins and their debt to continental civilization and that this explains why the Japanese were so eager to maintain a foothold on the continent through their Korean colony of Mimana. By the sixth century Japan had acquired some of the essentials of Chinese civilization: the writing system, the Confucian classics, the calendar, and crafts such as silk weaving and pottery making. Moreover, during the sixth century the introduction of Buddhism from Korea laid the foundation for a bridge of communication between the continent and Japan which was to prove of the greatest importance in the centuries to follow. Nonetheless, up to the seventh century Japanese culture remained fundamentally distinct from that of China in its political organization, social structure, and religious beliefs.

Beginning in the seventh century, several factors combined to bring Japan and China closer together. The many centuries of slow and indirect contact with the continent had laid a technological and intellectual base in Japan which now permitted the more rapid absorption of Chinese culture. Furthermore, conditions in Japan foreshadowed the breakdown of the Yamato social order and turned the interests of the Japanese elite to new techniques of government and religious organization. Meanwhile, China after several years of political disunity was being reunited by the Sui and T'ang emperors. From 607 to 838 the Japanese court sent twelve embassies to China in a conspicuous attempt to acquire the fruits of Chinese civilization. Social and political changes were intermixed with a flood of importations from China. The aristocracy in their push for new status and wealth drew upon the prestige of Chinese institutions and on the superior Chinese style of government. Buddhism was patronized as a means of extending the prestige and power of the aristocracy.

Several features of the eighth-century Chinese influence upon Japan require comment. First, although Japan was seemingly engulfed by Chinese civilization at this time, a closer look will show that the Japanese were very much in control of what and how they borrowed from abroad. The political leaders appeared full of confidence in their ability to carry out internal reforms modeled after what they had learned, but not slavishly imitated, from China. By this time, in fact, the Japanese were much more on their own with respect to China than in the previous age, since large groups of immigrants were no longer arriving from the continent. And while priests and artisans were welcomed from China, they were not so readily accorded status in the Japanese aristocracy. Second, it seems obvious that most histories have magnified the impact of China upon Japan because they have concentrated upon what transpired at the center of court activity and have neglected the rest of the country. Surely many areas were hardly touched by the influx of continental culture. Third, it is important to note that the Chinese civilization of the T'ang period was in many ways a rather special variant of the Chinese model. For instance, at no other time did Buddhism occupy so important a place in Chinese culture. Buddhism in fact colored the entire process of Japan's relations with China at this time (and later), for the Buddhist priesthood brought to Japan much more of the products of Chinese civilization than did even the official embassies of the period. Furthermore, after official relations lapsed, there were times when the only knowledge Japan received of China came through the reports of traveling priests. Thus the China which was exported to Japan was much more heavily colored by Buddhism than the ideal to which the Chinese subscribed. And this was to remain true for much of Japan's relations with China. For some reason, the strictly Chinese upper class, the Confucian officials, showed no inclination to travel abroad and certainly no compulsion to proselytize the Japanese. Only in the rarest instances did such men find their way to Japan and then only as refugees from political persecution. Thus, with the termination after 838 of Japan's official efforts to keep in touch with China, the strictly Confucian chapter of Japan's early phase of borrowing from China came to an end.

By the time the Fujiwara family had gained the upper hand at the court in Kyoto, a feeling of isolationism toward the continent had begun to set in. Japanese court society, while retaining many of the outward features of Chinese civilization, became increasingly un-Chinese in its values and manner of organization. With the rise of the provincial aristocracy and the spread of feudal institutions, Japan acquired a style of culture and a social and political structure which had no counterpart in China. Thus, from the ninth century, Japan and China drifted increasingly far apart. Yet during these years the Buddhist orders kept in touch with China, and it is to some extent the stimulus of what Japanese priests saw there that encouraged them to begin the propagation of the new Amida and Zen sects.

Japan's isolation from the continent was shattered by the Mongol invasions of 1274 and 1281. The dramatic repulse of these assaults by the warriors of the Kamakura shogunate proved a turning point in Japan's foreign relations. Heretofore the Japanese had depended almost entirely upon Chinese and Korean ships and crews to sail the East China Sea, but as part of the defense against the Mongols they had begun to build their own ships. With the disappearance of the Mongol threat, Japan revealed itself as an independent sea power. Japanese ships, largely freebooters known as *wakō*, began to rove the coasts of Korea and China.

From the time of the Mongol invasions, Japan's involvement in the affairs of the continent steadily increased. In 1342 the temple of Tenryūji began the practice of sending trading ships to China. Eventually, under the patronage of the Ashikaga shogunate, official trade relations were formalized between Japan and China, the Japanese accepting the role of tributary vassal to the Ming emperor. By this time, moreover, the nature of Japan's relations with China had changed. First of all, so-called "official relations" were conducted by the priests of certain Zen temples of Kyoto. Second, trade was now the all-important objective. Nor was such trade markedly one-sided, as it had once been. True enough, Japanese imports were mostly products of China's continued cultural superiority over Japan: copper coins, works of art, scholarly publications, medicines, and exotic stuffs. But the Japanese paid for such imports not only with raw copper, but also with their own manufactures, such as screens, fans, and peerless steel blades. Trade was becoming important for economic reasons. Japanese ports, such as Sakai, flourished on the China trade, as did many of the provincial lords. There were cultural by-products of this trade, but these were largely apparent in the field of art. Japan remained feudal and Buddhist.

The sixteenth century was Japan's greatest period of overseas trade expansion prior to modern times. By now the Japanese were masters of the sea, and Japanese freebooters ranged the China Seas as far as Annam. *Daimyō* vied for the opportunity to trade with the Portuguese or themselves fitted out vessels to send to the South Seas. But China was only indirectly involved in this activity. The Central Kingdom had by now declared the Japanese enemies of the empire. After Hideyoshi's invasion of Korea, animosity between the two countries reached the breaking point. Japanese were excluded from Chinese ports, and only indirect trade with China was possible. The Tokugawa rulers, after several attempts to make Edo the center of a controlled foreign trade, finally turned to a policy of isolation between 1636 and 1639. A thin trickle of trade eventually did build up through the monopoly port of Nagasaki, and a Chinese community of merchants was allotted a special residential quarter in the city, but Japanese relations with the Chinese were highly regulated and provided little cultural contact.

How surprising then that the Tokugawa period should witness a remarkable florescence of Chinese learning in Japan. Unlike the seventh-century chapter in Japan's emulation of China, the impetus behind the seventeenth-century flowering of neo-Confucianism was almost wholly a product of Japanese domestic needs and sprang not from any contemporaneous contact with China but rather from seeds already planted many centuries earlier. In the Japan newly unified under the Tokugawa house, shogun and *daimyō* both found in Confucianism the values for social and political order which they admired. Thus, while Buddhism went into a decline, Confucianism became the favored source of official morality and the basis of education. Within a short time Confucian scholars were employed by the shogunate and the *daimyō*. Confucian colleges sprang up in Edo and in many of the castle cities. And all this activity went on without the direct influence of China. Japan had discovered anew the value of the great Confucian tradition which had remained part of the East Asian cultural environment since the fifth century. Samurai applied themselves to the study of Chinese classics, history, law, and literature, and Japanese scholars of Confucian persuasion dominated the educational system and the intellectual world.

Yet left to their own devices the Japanese eventually outgrew their enthusiasm for Confucian scholarship. By the beginning of the nineteenth century Japan had almost totally lost touch with China. Trade at Nagasaki had nearly ceased. Chinese silks, which the Japanese had once sought so eagerly, were no longer in demand. The Japanese produced their own. In the intellectual field, new schools of thought challenged the supremacy of Confucianism. A newfound interest in Japan's own past called for the study of Japanese history and Shinto religious beliefs. Students of Western science had begun to attack the neo-Confucian cosmology. By the 1830s the Japanese had thoroughly absorbed Confucian ethics but had begun to grow restive under their subservience to Chinese culture. Once Japan's leaders acknowledged the superiority of Western culture, particularly science, the Japanese quickly abandoned their admiration for things Chinese. Within a few decades they could even pose as the superiors of the Chinese in adjusting themselves to the modern world. The Japanese invasion of China in the 1930s was frequently justified as an effort to "help" that country become a viable modern state.

Japan's relationship to China has not been that of constant empty-handed borrowing. On the one hand China itself went through cycles of cultural brilliance and decline, and on the other hand Japan swung between extremes of eager emulation and outright hostility toward China. It is this interaction of differential impact and receptivity played out through a constant process of technological growth in Japan which has made for the complex pattern of Chinese influence upon the country. And while we may consider Chinese influence one of the major sources of change in Japanese history, we must bear in mind that the "Chinese impact" was itself affected by the evolution of Japan's own cultural institutions.

JAPAN'S DEVELOPMENT
AS A MODERN STATE

Beginning in the 1840s, Japan plunged into the most turbulent era of its history. Within a brief century nearly every aspect of life, the government, economy, social organization, system of values, and manner of living, was radically transformed, not only for a narrow elite, but for the vast majority of the Japanese people. Again, as during the seventh century, deep-running internal changes were accompanied by the rapid influx of an alien culture. And again the historian is confronted with the question of how the two processes of change, one operating from within and the other from without, were related. Until recently the usual, or at least the popular, interpretation was simply that Japan had been overwhelmed by a wave of Western influence. Japan was merely one of many backward societies which had been awakened by the West and led into the modern world. The path to "modernity" was seen as leading over the terrain of two revolutions: the first, the revolution of westernization, transformed Japan into a world power in less than eighty years; the second, a revolution of democratization, was the gift of the American Occupation following World War II.

This simple image of a Japan inexorably shaped by foreign pressures has been challenged at many points by recent scholarship. The idea of westernization, as Prof. Richard K. Beardsley has pointed out in Chapter 2, requires particular rethinking, for it is obvious to us today that we cannot assume that all that happened to Japan after the 1840s was the result of Western influence alone. In the first place, Western civilization was itself involved in a process of change which was by no means confined to the countries of Western Europe. Second, Tokugawa society was developing under its own initiative along lines which foreshadowed to some extent the trend of the reforms which were adopted after 1868. Finally, many of the innovations which Japan adopted from the West in the early decades of contact themselves became self-generating of further change. In other words, the initial reforms, once they took hold in Japan, were themselves capable of preparing the ground for new stages of change, independent of direct Western influence.

Scholars have lately given thought to the nature of the social and intellectual foundations upon which modern society has come to rest, seeking to comprehend them in terms of some general "theory of modernization" or of more limited concepts of "political modernization" or "economic development." The work of the Conference on Modern Japan, for instance, has been directed to both a descriptive statement of changing conditions in Japan since the middle of the nineteenth century and the effort to discover recognizable patterns within these conditions. If the modernization of Japan is not simply a case of westernization, then what are the essential elements of the process which has transformed the country into a modern society? There is, of course, no simple answer, and perhaps the process must continually be defined at various levels of generality or from varying points of view. Some, for instance, have suggested that modernization has come in the wake of the increased application of rationality to human affairs, the result of man's effort to exert a conscious control over his environment and his own human conditions. Others have chosen to place their explanation upon another and more specific range of human activities: mechanization and industrialization in the economy, bureaucratization in government, egalitarianism in social relationships, and secularization in intellectual matters. Or it is possible to single out even more specific indexes of the factors which seem to be on the increase in modernizing societies: (1) urbanization and an urban-centered outlook of the total society; (2) heavy use of inanimate energy and of various complex economic functions; (3) social mobility and a relatively free participation of members of the society in economic and political life; (4) literacy and the spread of secular and scientific attitudes toward knowledge; (5) facilities of mass communication; (6) large-scale social institutions, such as government, business, and industry, organized bureaucratically; and (7) large areas of group interaction, culminating in nations or international organizations.[3]

Modernization is a process which, although it may have received its initial impetus in Western Europe, has now become a universal phenomenon. But historically it was in the West that societies first underwent the many interrelated changes which produced the modern nation-state, and it is certainly unthinkable that Japan should have undertaken the momentous reforms of the 1860s and 1870s had there not been a "Western impact" upon the Tokugawa state. Japan in comparison to England was a "late modernizer," a country which followed in the wake of the prior example of the West. It was not alone

[3] See John Whitney Hall, "Changing Conceptions of the Modernization of Japan," in Marius B. Jansen (ed.), *Changing Japanese Attitudes toward Modernization*, Princeton, N.J., 1965, pp. 7–41.

in this respect, and it is informative to study how its pattern of modernization compares with that of other similar societies. The examples of Turkey and China are particularly apt.

We can assume that no countries, not even the pioneer modernizers, were able to undergo the many changes of the last 100 or 200 years without encountering challenges that from time to time plunged them into periods of great political and social instability. For Japan, Turkey, and China these challenges were the more traumatic because they were so often brought on by the influence of foreign powers possessing superior technological and economic resources. The late modernizing societies of the East were each forced to undergo a series of crises of remarkably similar nature, and it was largely the differential abilities of each to meet these crises that accounted for their relative success or failure in negotiating the transition to modern nationhood.

The people of each of these countries had first to meet what we might call a crisis of identity; that is, they were required somehow to preserve their own will to survive and to remake themselves into viable nation-states. But the will to resist cultural annihilation was not sufficient in itself; each emerging state was obliged to protect its identity and thereby to face its crisis of security in a hostile world. The twin crises of identity and security were not easily met. Generally it was only after a vigorous leadership had emerged in command of a sufficiently widespread following to mobilize human and material resources that the new nation was able to compete in the modern world. Thus the creation of a new national identity and its protection came usually as the result of political revolution on a considerable scale. But once launched, the new state faced two further problems: first, the need for technological change and economic development; and, second, the necessity to evolve a national political process which could continue to rally the new citizenry behind the state and its goals. The abilities of Japan, Turkey, and China to meet these crises differed widely. And these differences were clearly the outcome of many factors, among them differing location, size, timing, and, particularly, the nature of the traditional society from which the new was obliged to emerge.

Today the contrasts between China and Japan are dramatic both in terms of the degree of modernization and in terms of the political system to which the two states subscribe. The causes of these differences are particularly interesting to speculate upon. The Chinese scholar Hu Shih has suggested that it was the Japanese political structure (i.e., the autocratic nature of Japanese government and the ability of the leaders to command the loyalty of the mass of the Japanese people) that accounted for the country's early rise as a world power. The sociologist

Marion Levy has pointed to differences in family systems which made for greater flexibility of social change in Japan. Edwin O. Reischauer has stressed the legacy of feudalism, which gave to the Japanese a political authority and class structure similar to that of Europe and hence was more responsive to Western influence. W. W. Rostow has suggested that economic conditions were closer to the point of takeoff in Tokugawa Japan than in Ch'ing China. And Robert A. Scalapino has stressed the factor of timing, for Japan came of age in a world in which the ideals of republicanism and constitutional monarchy were ascendant while China found the Soviet model closest to hand.

For whatever reason, the country's reaction to the impact of the West was dramatically rapid and positive. Japan was able to undergo the several crises of modernization with minimum disruption and delay. Between 1853 and 1877 it overcame the twin crises of identity and internal security. Between 1868 and 1890 the basis was laid for social, economic, and educational reforms which were to meet the crisis of economic development and national reorientation. By 1890 Japan could launch a program of heavy industrialization and at the same time assert its independence in international affairs. Between 1894 and 1905 it joined the imperialist powers on its own terms.

Given all the suggestions which have been offered to account for Japan's success in making the transition to modernity, there are two particular observations which require further statement. First of all, it seems evident that the level of attainment in political organization, social institutions, and economic development which Japan had reached in 1853 was a good deal higher than we once had thought. Second, much of the credit for Japan's smooth transition results from the rapidity with which she gained a sense of national identity during the traumatic early stages of the breakup of traditional society. Thus her exposure to Western influence prefaced reform, not revolution, as in so many other societies. A sufficient continuity in authority was maintained so that Japan's new leaders were able to direct a controlled change. It is in this respect that the symbol of the Emperor as the focus of national loyalty played such an important role. It was not by accident that the political event which ushered in the new Japan, the Meiji Restoration, was initiated as a traditionalist movement.

Japan from 1840 to the Present

As with premodern history, the periodization of the last 125 years of Japanese history is not so much a problem of making divisions as that of assigning "meaning" to agreed-upon periods. For the modern historian the commonly accepted periods are measured almost exclusively from political events. Between these dividing lines the historian has sought to identify some unifying factor, usually in terms of his estimate of the general political climate or of some significant feature of national activity. The Western historian has tended to assign meaning to the periods of modern Japanese history as if they constituted phases of adaptation to Western institutions and values. The nationalistically oriented Japanese historian has looked at the same history as a succession of steps in Japan's rise as an imperial power. The Marxist historian has seen the last 125 years almost exclusively in terms of the struggle between absolute government and the desire of the people for a larger voice in national affairs. The following survey of modern Japanese history attempts to avoid some of these cultural and political biases by relying upon the more neutral concept of political modernization.

The 1840s: Mounting Domestic Crisis

During the 1840s (the so-called "Tempō era") many groups in Japan were seized by a sense of domestic crisis. The Tokugawa shogunate had run into serious financial difficulties, while the shogun's major cities had become scenes of troublesome mass unrest. A large number of the *daimyō* also faced serious fiscal difficulties. Throughout Japan, voices of alarm were being raised. At Edo, Mizuno Tadakuni attempted ill-fated fiscal reforms, while the *daimyō* of Satsuma, Chōshū, Mito, and several other domains instituted drastic reforms to remedy their economies. Nariaki, Lord of Mito, urged the shogunate to undertake a program of military defense to build up the morale of the country.

The 1850s and 1860s: Precipitation of Political Reforms by the Foreign Crisis

Japan's leaders had long been apprehensive of the presence of Western ships in Japanese waters. The arrival of Commodore Matthew C. Perry in 1853 confirmed the existence of a foreign menace and linked the problem of domestic reform with that of national preservation. In the flurry of activity which followed Perry's appearance, leadership within the shogunate, the several domains, and the Kyoto Court worked feverishly toward creating a political order to meet the foreign crisis. In the interval from 1853 to 1868 three lines of policy competed for mastery of the country. The Tokugawa partisans sought revitalization of the shogunate; others suggested the elevation of the Emperor to a new position as head of a coalition of *daimyō*, in which the shogun would be obliged to share his powers; and still others called for the abolition of the shogunate and the unification of the country under the Emperor. The middle years of this short period were dominated by the effort of the shogunate and conservative *daimyō* leaders to preserve the existing balance of political power through some sort of coalition arrangement. Yet within the *bakufu* and the *daimyō* domains new leaders were emerging who were increasingly convinced that only a new national unity under the symbol of the Emperor could save Japan. The Restoration of 1868 was a victory for this extreme policy. In the few short years between 1868 and 1871 a new national leadership effectively abolished the system of territorial decentralization under the *daimyō* and established a central government under the Emperor. Japan emerged as a new nation, having succeeded in meeting its crisis of identity and momentarily at least its crisis of defense against the West.

From 1871 to 1881: Stabilization of the New State

During the seventies the Japanese resolved their internal differences over the ultimate form which the new state and society should take. Looking abroad, the Japanese saw that Great Britain, France, and Germany offered different and somewhat contradictory models to emulate. Within Japan a contest between statism (*kokken-shugi*) and popularism (*minken-shugi*) divided the politically literate stratum of society. While the leaders in government constantly worked to tighten their hold over the country, men like Itagaki Taisuki led local political movements and others like Saigō Takamori resorted to rebellion in the name of securing a broader base of participation in politics. In the face of such opposition, the leading faction in government used countermeasures both of control and of compromise. The creation of the Home Ministry in 1873, the training of a national conscript army, and the reorganization of local administration provided the instruments of control. At the same time, the government compromised with the opposition, and in 1881 it promised to adopt by 1890 a constitution which contained in it some provision for a national assembly. Japan's crisis of internal organization was essentially over.

From 1881 to 1890: Laying the Foundation of National Growth

This decade was characterized by growing stabilization of the country, assimilation of many technological and institutional changes, and increasing self-confidence and self-consciousness within the Japanese leadership. Early efforts at indiscriminate borrowing from the West were countered by a growing sense of nationalism. The promulgation of the Meiji Constitution of 1889 and the Imperial Rescript on Education of 1890 (we should add the Rescript to Soldiers and Sailors of 1882) combined to give lasting shape to a new state in which a modern technology of government adopted from the West was placed squarely upon a foundation of traditional nation-centered institutions and values.

From 1890 to 1919: Imperial Japan

Japan came of age as a modern state during these three decades, led by the imposing figure of the Emperor Meiji and the handful of "oligarchs" who had guided Japan through the crisis of national identity. The Japanese people had by now tasted the fruits of military victory over the Chinese and the Russians. War served as a stimulus to nationalism, unifying the country behind bold slogans and through the mass experience of suffering and sacrifice as the war dead were counted. An industrial economy was searching for overseas markets and colonial sources of raw materials. Expanding cities became the home of new classes of commercial and industrial workers, while schools and colleges, newspapers and journals were creating a new intelligentsia and extending the base of a national "public opinion."

The 1920s: Party Government and Social Unrest

The period of the 1920s has received more than its share of critical attention from both Western and Japanese scholars, for in many respects it contains the crucial problem of interpretation regarding the nature of the new Japanese state. By 1919, World War I was over and an era of democracy and good feeling was reportedly at hand. Should not Japan have emerged as a full-fledged democratic nation? And was it not a sign of some fatal weakness in Japanese society that party government should have "failed" and that Japan should have taken the road to militarism?

Perhaps it was Edwin O. Reischauer who most convincingly explained the decade of the 1920s as an era when Japan for the first time felt the impact of the fundamental reforms which had been adopted fifty years before. Thus this decade was less an era characterized by the failure of democracy and liberalism than a period of major adjustment to new problems brought about by an expanding population, the achievement of almost full literacy, increased industrialization, and the acceptance of new responsibilities as a world power. It was a time when new pressure groups revealed themselves in the Japanese political environment and the struggle between them was intensified. The political parties of the time were hardly the agents of democracy, but they did serve the very real purpose of providing channels of communication and compromise among the leading pressure groups. When world depression and mounting international tensions brought an end to the postwar era of goodwill, Japan was not alone among the nations of the world to take the turn toward military expansion.

From 1931 to 1945: Militarism and Totalitarianism

In 1931 Japanese forces occupied Manchuria, and Japan was set upon a path of conquest on the mainland of Asia accompanied by militarism and totalitarian regimentation at home. Although the term *fascism* has been applied to the Japanese government, the form which totalitarianism took in Japan differed greatly from that in Germany and Italy. Most obvious was the lack of a dictator, for Japan, even in the 1940s, retained its traditional political structure. The Emperor continued to serve as the ritual head of state, maintaining the balance among the many elite factions. When, in 1941, a single national party was created, it was justified as an organization dedicated to serving the Emperor (the Imperial Rule Assistance Association). Despite several attempts by dissident military groups to gain possession of the Emperor and stage their own revolution, it was the elite factions that maintained control of the source of legitimacy, building around the imperial symbol a style of national regimentation defined by some as the *consensus state*.

The Japanese today look back in horror at the suffering and degradation of the human spirit which militarism, fascism, and war forced upon the nation. It is only now that they are beginning to realize that the dark 1940s were, nonetheless, a time of significant social and economic change, when industrialization and the mass integration of the Japanese into the modern state structure were further extended. Japan came out of the 1940s morally and economically broken but significantly more "modern" by objective criteria.

The Postwar Years

The combination of military defeat, Allied Occupation, and the urgent desire of the Japanese for reform and reconstruction turned the postwar era into another period of headlong change. The upheaval which followed Japan's first modern defeat was probably as significant as that which followed the Meiji Restoration, and there are those who claim that only after 1945 could Japan be said to have become truly modern.

Be that as it may, changes in government, economy, and social conditions after 1945 were certainly of such scope and variety that they clearly marked the beginning of a new era. The new Constitution is merely the most obvious product of this era, but the remarkable physical and economic recovery gives evidence that the country may well have passed safely into the ranks of the stable modern communities.

There are of course many voices of pessimism refuting the possibility that Japan has gained a permanent stability. Many problems are still unsolved. Japan has had to face, in common with other late developers, a continued quest for its own identity and security within a fast-changing world in which the goals and opportunities have been determined in the main by the Western nations. In government, economic production, social legislation, and national ideals, Japan continues to face difficult decisions of whether to follow ready-made alien models or to seek some new amalgam between foreign influence and its own tradition. This dilemma continues in the post-World War II era, when the influence of a victorious Occupation must somehow be assimilated. In the years from 1868 to 1945 Japan reclaimed its sense of national confidence by a periodic return to its traditional sources of value. The destiny of a country which is Oriental in tradition and yet has traveled so far along the path of modernization can only be conjectured.

CHRONOLOGY OF JAPANESE HISTORY[4]

Date	Event
660 B.C.	Mythical date of the accession of Jimmu, first Emperor
ca. A.D. 300	Probable time of the establishment of Yamato hegemony
ca. 300–645	YAMATO PERIOD
405	Probable date of the introduction of writing from Korea
552 or 538	Introduction of Buddhism from Korea
587	Destruction of the Mononobe family by Soga-no-Umako
592–628	Reign of Empress Suiko
593–622	Regency of Prince Shōtoku (Shōtoku Taishi)
604	Seventeen-article "Constitution" of Prince Shōtoku (traditional date)
607	Founding of the Hōryūji; first embassy to China
645	Taika *coup d'état* and destruction of the main Soga family by Prince Naka-no-Ōe and Nakatomi-no-Kamatari
646	Promulgation of Taika Reform
663	Japanese defeat in Korea; ascendancy of Silla with T'ang support

[4] Among other sources this list is indebted to the chronology contained in Edwin O. Reischauer, *Japan Past and Present*, 2d ed., New York, 1953.

Date		*Event*
661–671	—	Reign of Tenchi, former Prince Naka-no-Ōe
669	—	Granting of surname Fujiwara to Kamatari
672	—	Jinshin War; accession of Emperor Temmu
702	—	Taihō Law Code promulgated
710	—	Completion of Heijō (Nara)
710–784	—	NARA PERIOD
712	—	Compilation of *Kojiki* (traditional date)
718	—	Yōrō revision of Taihō Code
720	—	Compilation of the *Nihon shoki*
724–749	—	Reign of Shōmu (d. 756)
741	—	*Kokubunji* (official provincial monasteries) established
743	—	Provision made for the private ownership of reclaimed land
752	—	Dedication of the Great Buddha (Daibutsu) of Tōdaiji in Nara
ca. 759	—	Compilation of *Man'yōshū*
770	—	Death of Empress Shōtoku and downfall of the priest Dōkyō
781–806	—	Reign of Kammu; revival of Taihō institutions
794	—	Completion of Heian (Kyoto)
794–1185	—	HEIAN PERIOD
801	—	Pacification of the Ezo (Ainu) in the north by Sakanoue-no-Tamuramaro
805	—	Introduction of the Tendai sect by Saichō (Dengyō Daishi) with headquarters at Enryakuji on Mount Hiei
806	—	Introduction of Shingon sect by Kūkai (Kōbō Daishi) with headquarters at Mount Kōya
810	—	Establishment of Kurōdo-dokoro (Imperial Chancellery)
838	—	Twelfth and last embassy to the T'ang (accompanied by the monk Ennin, who returns in 847)
866	—	Fujiwara-no-Yoshifusa, first regent (*sesshō*) not of the Imperial Family
866–1160	—	FUJIWARA PERIOD
887	—	Fujiwara-no-Mototsune, first Chancellor (*kampaku*)
905	—	*Kokinshū* edited by Ki-no-Tsurayuki and others
927	—	*Engishiki,* supplementary codes, compiled
939–940	—	Revolt of Taira-no-Masakado in the Kanto
941	—	Execution of Fujiwara-no-Sumitomo, pirate-rebel in the Inland Sea
995–1027	—	Supremacy of Fujiwara-no-Michinaga
ca. 1002	—	Writing of *Makura no sōshi* (Pillow book) by Sei Shōnagon

Date		Event
ca. 1002–1019	—	Writing of *Genji monogatari* (*The Tale of Genji*) by Murasaki Shikibu
1039	—	Kyoto invaded by Enryakuji monks
1053	—	Byōdōin built
1069	—	Establishment of Kirokujo (Records Office) to check the growth of the *shōen*.
1086–1129	—	Establishment by Shirakawa of *insei* (rule by the retired Emperor)
1156	—	Hōgen conflict: destruction of most leading Minamoto
1159–1160	—	Heiji conflict: military supremacy gained by Taira-no-Kiyomori (d. 1181) and his son Shigemori (d. 1179)
1160–1185	—	TAIRA (OR ROKUHARA) PERIOD
1167	—	Kiyomori named Prime Minister
1175	—	Founding of the Jōdo (Pure Land) sect by Hōnen Shōnin (1133–1212)
1180–1185	—	War between the Minamoto and the Taira (Gempei Wars)
1185	—	Defeat of the Taira and death of the child Emperor Antoku in the naval Battle of Dannoura
1185–1333	—	KAMAKURA PERIOD
1185	—	Establishment of *shugo* (military-governor) and *jitō* (military-land-steward) system by Minamoto-no-Yoritomo
1191	—	Introduction of the Rinzai branch of the Zen sect from China by Eisai
1192	—	Title of Shogun granted to Yoritomo
1199	—	Death of Yoritomo and assumption of control by his wife, Hōjō-no-Masako, and her father, Tokimasa
1205	—	Hōjō-no-Tokimasa appointed *shikken* (shogunal regent)
1206	—	*Shinkokinshū* compiled
1221	—	Shōkyū disturbance: suppression of uprising in Kyoto against Kamakura inspired by the retired Emperor Go-Toba; Kamakura able to appoint shogunal governors at Rokuhara in Kyoto (Rokuhara Tandai)
1224	—	Founding of the Shin (True Pure Land) sect by Shinran (1173–1262)
1232	—	*Jōei shikimoku* (Kamakura Law Code) issued by Hōjō
1253	—	Founding of the Nichiren sect by Nichiren (1220–1282)
1268–1284	—	Hōjō-no-Tokimune as *shikken*
1274	—	First Mongol invasion
1281	—	Second Mongol invasion
1331	—	Revolt of Emperor Go-Daigo; *Tsurezuregusa* written

Date   *Event*

1333   —   Desertion to Go-Daigo of Kamakura general, Ashikaga
            Takauji; destruction of the Hōjō at Kamakura by Nitta
            Yoshisada
1334   —   Kemmu Restoration under Go-Daigo
1335   —   Turning against Go-Daigo by Takauji
1336   —   Enthronement of rival Emperor by Takauji; death of
            Go-Daigo's supporter, Kusunoki Masashige; flight of Go-
            Daigo to Yoshino
1342   —   Practice of sending ships to China begun by Tenryūji

1336–1392 —   NAMBOKU PERIOD (PERIOD OF THE NORTHERN
              AND SOUTHERN COURTS)

1338–1573 —   ASHIKAGA (OR MUROMACHI) PERIOD
1338   —   Takauji, Shogun
1368–1394 —   Yoshimitsu (1358–1408), third Shogun
1386   —   Gozan Zen monasteries given official status (*kanji*)
1392   —   Reunion of the northern and southern courts
1397   —   Construction of the Kinkakuji (Golden Pavilion) by
            Yoshimitsu
1401   —   Tributary relationship with Ming China accepted
1444   —   Death of Zeami, perfecter of the nō
1449–1473 —   Shogunate of Yoshimasa (d. 1490), sometimes called the
              Higashiyama period
1467–1477 —   Ōnin War
1483   —   Construction of the Ginkakuji (Silver Pavilion) by Yo-
            shimasa
1488   —   Provinces of Kaga and Echizen controlled by members
            of the Shin sect (Ikkō-ikki)
1506   —   Death of the painter Sesshū
1542 or 1543 —   Arrival of the Portuguese at Tanegashima; introduction
                 of Western firearms
1549   —   Arrival of St. Francis Xavier (1506–1552) in Kyushu and
            start of the Christian missionary movement by the Jesuits
1560   —   Defeat of Imagawa Yoshimoto by Oda Nobunaga (1534–
            1582)
1568–1600 —   AZUCHI-MOMOYAMA (OR SHOKUHŌ) PERIOD
1568   —   Occupation of Kyoto by Oda Nobunaga
1571   —   Nagasaki established as port of foreign trade; military
            might of the Enryakuji destroyed by Nobunaga
1573   —   Shogun Yoshiaki deposed by Nobunaga; end of the Ashi-
            kaga shogunate

Date		Event
1576	—	New castle at Azuchi on Lake Biwa occupied by Nobunaga
1582	—	Nobunaga assassinated by Akechi Mitsuhide, who in turn is destroyed by Hashiba Hideyoshi (1537–1598)
1583	—	Osaka Castle built by Hideyoshi
1585	—	Hideyoshi named Chancellor; Shikoku pacified
1586	—	Hideyoshi appointed Prime Minister and granted the surname Toyotomi
1587	—	Submission of the Shimazu family of Satsuma to Hideyoshi; expulsion of the Christian missionaries ordered
1588	—	Confiscation of the arms of the peasantry (sword hunt)
1590	—	Destruction of the Hōjō family of Odawara; Hideyoshi supreme in Japan; Tokugawa Ieyasu (1542–1616) installed in Edo Castle as master of the Kanto; social classes frozen by three-clause edict; death of the painter Kanō Eitoku
1592	—	Hideyoshi's invasion of Korea with Katō Kiyomasa and Konishi Yukinaga as field commanders; start of missionary activity by the Spanish Franciscans
1595	—	Nationwide cadastral survey (*kenchi*) ordered and new land tax laws instituted by Hideyoshi
1597	—	Resumption of the Korean campaign; first executions of European missionaries and Japanese converts
1598	—	Death of Hideyoshi and withdrawal of troops from Korea
1600	—	Victory of Ieyasu at the Battle of Sekigahara
1600–1868	—	TOKUGAWA (OR EDO) PERIOD
1603	—	Title of Shogun acquired by Ieyasu
1608	—	Hayashi Razan, Confucian adviser to Ieyasu
1614	—	First siege of Osaka Castle by Ieyasu; persecution of Christianity resumed.
1615	—	Second siege and capture of Osaka Castle; destruction of the Toyotomi family; promulgation of the *Buke-sho-hatto* and *Kinchū narabini kuge-shū sho-hatto* (codes for the samurai and the Imperial Court)
1622–1623	—	Period of the greatest Christian persecutions
1623	—	Factory at Hirado abandoned by the British
1623–1651	—	Institutional foundations of the Tokugawa shogunate completed by Iemitsu, third Shogun
1633	—	Systematization of the *wakadoshiyori* (house-councilor) system
1634	—	Systematization of the *rōjū* (senior-councilor) system
1635	—	Systematization of the *sankin-kōtai* (alternate-attendance) system for *tozama daimyō*

Date		Event
1636	—	Ban on Japanese travel abroad
1637–1638	—	Shimabara uprising
1638	—	Expulsion of the Portuguese from Japan
1639	—	*Sakokurei* (seclusion order) promulgated; establishment of the *Shūmon aratame-yaku* (Inquisition Office)
1641	—	Dutch factory moved to Deshima at Nagasaki
1651–1680	—	Ietsuna, fourth Shogun
1651	—	Yui Shōsetsu plot against the shogunate; anti-*rōnin* measures
1680–1709	—	Tsunayoshi, fifth Shogun
1688–1704	—	GENROKU PERIOD
1693	—	Death of the novelist Ihara Saikaku (b. 1642)
1694	—	Death of the haiku poet Matsuo Bashō (b. 1644)
1701–1703	—	Chūshingura incident (Forty-seven Rōnin)
1704	—	Death of Ichikawa Danjūrō, first Kabuki actor of this name
1709–1712	—	Ienobu, sixth Shogun
1713–1716	—	Ietsugu, seventh Shogun
1716–1745	—	Kyōhō Reforms initiated by Yoshimune (1648–1751), eighth Shogun
1720	—	Relaxation of the ban on the importation of Western books; *kabunakama* (merchant guilds) recognized officially at about this time
1724	—	Death of Chikamatsu Monzaemon (b. 1653), playwright for the Jōruri and Kabuki theaters
1725	—	Death of Arai Hakuseki (b. 1657), scholar and adviser to the shogunate
1728	—	Death of Ogyū Sorai (b. 1666), Confucian scholar
1729	—	*Shingaku* expounded by Ishida Baigan
1745–1760	—	Ieshige (d. 1761), ninth Shogun
1760–1786	—	Ieharu, tenth Shogun
1769	—	Start of the supremacy of Tanuma Okitsugu (1719–1788) as *rōjū*
1783	—	*Rangaku kaitei* (Introduction to Dutch studies) written by Ōtsuki Gentaku (1757–1827)
1787–1837	—	Ienari, eleventh Shogun; reaction against Tanuma
1787–1793	—	Supremacy of Matsudaira Sadanobu (1759–1829) as *rōjū*, author of the Kansei Reforms
1798	—	*Kojiki-den* (Commentary on the *Kojiki*), completed by Motoori Norinaga
1804–1829	—	BUNKA-BUNSEI PERIOD
1804	—	Arrival of Nikolai Rezanov at Nagasaki

Date		Event
1814	—	Kurozumi sect founded by Kurozumi Munetada (1780–1850)
1825	—	Death of the print artist Utagawa Toyokuni
1826	—	Compilation of the *Nihon gaishi* (History of Japan) by Rai San'yō (1780–1832)
1837	—	Rice riots in Osaka led by the Confucian scholar Ōshio Heihachirō; Edo Bay and Nagasaki entered by the American ship *Morrison*
1837–1853	—	Ieyoshi, twelfth Shogun
1838	—	Founding of the Tenrikyō sect by Nakayama Miki (1798–1887)
1841–1843	—	Tempō Reforms undertaken by Mizuno Tadakuni, chief of the *rōjū; kabunakama* (merchant guilds) abolished
1843	—	Death of the Shinto scholar Hirata Atsutane (b. 1776)
1853	—	Arrival of Commodore Matthew C. Perry at Uraga; *daimyō* and court circulated for opinions by the chief *rōjū*, Abe Masahiro
1853–1858	—	Iesada, thirteenth Shogun
1854	—	Treaty of Kanagawa with the United States; mounting opposition to the shogunate's foreign policy; shogunal succession dispute
1858–1860	—	Strong action against the opposition taken by Ii Naosuke as *tairō;* succession question settled
1858–1866	—	Iemochi, fourteenth Shogun
1858	—	Commercial treaty with the United States; death of the wood-block artist Andō Hiroshige; founding of the future Keiō University by Fukuzawa Yukichi
1859	—	Start of the foreign trading community at Yokohama, Nagasaki, and Hakodate; execution of Yoshida Shōin, the antiforeign Chōshū scholar; Mito Nariaki placed under house arrest (Ansei purge)
1860	—	Assassination of Ii Naosuke by Mito samurai
1861	—	*Kōbu-gattai* (union of court and *daimyō*) policy attempted; ban on the building or purchase of large vessels lifted
1862	—	*Sankin-kōtai* relaxed; residence in Kyoto taken up by the *daimyō*
1863	—	British bombardment of Kagoshima
1864	—	Chōshū batteries at Shimonoseki destroyed by British, French, Dutch, and American ships; first shogunal expedition against Chōshū
1865	—	Imperial ratification of treaties with foreign powers
1866–1867	—	Yoshinobu (Keiki, d. 1913), son of Mito Nariaki, fifteenth and last Shogun

Date	*Event*
1867 —	Enthronement of Mutsuhito (Meiji); return of authority by Keiki to the throne

1868–1912 — MEIJI PERIOD

1868 —	January 1, opening of Kobe and Osaka to foreign trade; January 3, resumption of rule by the Emperor; Emperor's Charter Oath; establishment of Tokyo (Edo) as the new capital
1869 —	Return of domains to the Emperor by Satsuma, Chōshū, Tosa, and Hizen; *daimyō* reappointed governors of their former domains (now called *han*)
1870 —	Permission for commoners to take surnames
1871 —	Start of the postal service, conversion of the *han* into prefectures *(ken)*; establishment of the Department (later Ministry) of Education; Treaty of Tientsin with China; departure of the Iwakura mission for the United States and Europe
1872 —	Inauguration of railway service between Yokohama and Tokyo; compulsory elementary education
1873 —	Adoption of the Gregorian calendar; new land tax system; ban on Christianity lifted; establishment of the Home Ministry (Naimushō) under Ōkubo Toshimichi (1830–1878)
1874 —	Revolt of Etō Shimpei in Saga; Japanese expeditionary force in Formosa
1875 —	Settlement of the northern boundary with Russia (Japan exchanges Kurils for Sakhalin)
1876 —	Treaty with Korea; compulsory commutation of samurai pensions
1877 —	February–September, Satsuma rebellion and death of Saigō Takamori (b. 1827); death of Kido Kōin (Takayoshi; b. 1833)
1878 —	Assassination of Ōkubo
1881 —	Decree promising the convening of a national assembly in 1890; founding of the Jiyūtō (Liberal Party) under Itagaki Taisuke (1836–1919) and the Kaishintō (Reform Party) under Ōkuma Shigenobu (1838–1921); retrenchment policy begun by Matsukata Masayoshi as Minister of Finance
1882 —	Itō Hirobumi (1841–1909) in Europe to study constitutional governments; Bank of Japan established
1883 —	Death of Iwakura Tomomi (b. 1825)
1884 —	New peerage adopted

Date		Event
1885	—	Beginning of the Cabinet (Naikaku) system; Itō, first Premier
1888	—	Creation of the Privy Council (Sūmitsuin); new local administration law promulgated
1889	—	Promulgation of the Constitution; Gen. Yamagata Aritomo (1838–1922), Premier
1890	—	First general election for the Diet; promulgation of the Imperial Rescript on Education; telephone service between Tokyo and Yokohama
1894	—	Aoki-Kimberly Treaty to abolish British extraterritoriality in 1899; beginning of the Sino-Japanese War
1895	—	Treaty of Shimonoseki; Formosa acquired by Japan; Japan deprived of Liaotung by tripartite intervention
1896	—	Japan and Russia rivals in Korea
1897	—	Adoption of the gold standard
1899	—	Revision of treaties; extraterritoriality ended
1901	—	Death of Fukuzawa Yukichi (b. 1834), founder of Keiō University
1902	—	Signing of the Anglo-Japanese alliance
1904	—	Beginning of the Russo-Japanese War
1905	—	Treaty of Portsmouth; Japanese acquisition of south Sakhalin and the lease of Liaotung
1908	—	"Gentlemen's agreement" on emigration to the United States
1910	—	Agreement with Russia on spheres of influence in Manchuria; annexation of Korea
1912	—	Death of the Meiji Emperor
1912–1926	—	TAISHŌ PERIOD
1914	—	Ōkuma as Premier; Japanese declaration of war on Germany in World War I; capture of Tsingtao
1915	—	Twenty-one Demands pressed on China
1916	—	Death of the novelist Natsume Sōseki (b. 1867)
1917	—	Lansing-Ishii exchange of notes between the United States and Japan
1918	—	Beginning of "party government"; Hara Kei (Takashi) of the Seiyukai as Premier (assassinated in 1921)
1921–1922	—	Washington Conference; Japanese withdrawal from Siberia
1923	—	September 1, great Tokyo earthquake
1924	—	Abrogation of the gentlemen's agreement by the United States; Katō Takaaki as Premier
1925	—	Reduction of the army by four divisions; passage of the

Date	*Event*
	Universal Manhood Suffrage Bill and the Peace Preservation Law by the Diet
1926 —	Death of the Taishō Emperor and accession of Hirohito (Prince Regent since 1921)

1926–   SHŌWA PERIOD

1927 — Serious bank crisis

1928 — First general election under universal manhood suffrage; mass arrest of Communists

1930 — Signing of the London Naval Treaty; Premier Hamaguchi Yūkō wounded by an assassin (d. Aug. 26, 1931)

1931 — Outbreak of the "Manchurian incident"

1932 — Creation of Manchukuo; assassination of Premier Inukai Ki (Tsuyoshi) by young army and navy officers ("5–15 incident"); end of party government; Shakai Taishūtō (Social Mass Party) formed

1933 — Lytton Report on Manchuria; League of Nations quit by Japan

1935 — Resignation of Minobe Tatsukichi from the House of Peers

1936 — Assassination of Finance Minister Takahashi Korekiyo, etc. ("2–26 incident"), by rebellious soldiers of the 1st Division

1937 — Prince Konoe Fumimaro (1891–1945) as Premier; July, outbreak of war with China; bombardment of the United States gunboat *Panay* on the Yangtze River

1938 — Enactment of the National Mobilization Law; Gen. Araki Sadao (b. 1877), Minister of Education

1939 — Outbreak of war in Europe

1940 — Announcement by Premier Konoe of *shintaisei* (new national order); dissolution of the political parties; tripartite alliance with Germany and Italy; inauguration of the Imperial Rule Assistance Association; death of Prince Saionji Kimmochi (b. 1849), "last of the *genrō*"

1941 — Gen. Tōjō Hideki as Premier; December 7, attack on Pearl Harbor and start of war with the United States

1942 — Creation of the Greater East Asian Ministry; Japanese capture of the Philippines, Singapore, and New Guinea; Battles of the Coral Sea and Midway; Guadalcanal recaptured by the United States

1943 — Establishment of the Munitions Ministry

1944 — Fall of Saipan; Tōjō replaced as Premier by Koiso Kuniaki; Allied bombing of Japan

1945 — Landing of United States forces in the Philippines; surrender of the Germans; Potsdam Declaration; dropping of atomic bombs; entrance of the U.S.S.R. into the war against Japan; surrender of Japan

1946 — Gen. Douglas MacArthur appointed SCAP; disavowal of "divinity" by the Emperor; new Constitution promulgated; first postwar elections with women voters; Yoshida Shigeru as Premier; Occupation reforms, including purge of the "war criminals," dissolution of the *zaibatsu,* and a land reform law

1947 — Katayama Tetsu of the Social Democrats as Premier; Labor Ministry created

1948 — Second Cabinet formed by Yoshida; execution of Tōjō and six other war criminals

1949 — United States encouragement of Japanese industrial recovery and greater administrative autonomy; Joseph Dodge's budgetary report

1950 — Creation of the National Police Reserve by the Japanese; outbreak of the Korean conflict

1951 — General MacArthur relieved of commands; depurging of more than 80,000 persons; peace conference in San Francisco

1952 — Peace treaty in effect: end of the Allied Occupation; United States–Japan Administrative Agreement

1953 — United States–Japan Mutual Security Agreement; resignation of Yoshida as Premier

1954 — Hatoyama Ichirō as Premier

1956 — Ishibashi Tanzan as Premier; diplomatic relations with the U.S.S.R. restored; Japan admitted to the United Nations

1957 — Kishi Nobusuke as Premier

1960 — Widespread demonstrations against the approval of new United States–Japan Mutual Security Treaty; resignation of Kishi after the adoption of the treaty and his replacement as Premier by Ikeda Hayato; Asanuma Inejirō, head of the Socialist Party, assassinated

1964 — United States Ambassador Edwin O. Reischauer wounded by a mental patient in Tokyo; resignation of Premier Ikeda because of illness and his replacement by Satō Eisaku

JOSEPH K. YAMAGIWA

Language as an Expression
of Japanese Culture*

INTRODUCTION

The relationship between language and culture is intimate and revealing. Certainly one of the most distinctive aspects of Japanese culture is
its language. As branches of scholarship, philology and, more recently,
linguistics have concerned themselves with the analysis of languages and
comparisons between them. But, as in so many fields, it is only recently
(in this instance, as the interests of anthropologists and linguists have
coincided) that an effort has been made to study the interrelations of
language and other aspects of culture. The recentness of this line of
inquiry is underlined by the proceedings of a conference on the subject
reported in *Language in Culture*, edited by Harry Hoijer.[1] The conference was called largely because Benjamin Lee Whorf had raised some
fundamental questions about the relationship between language and
culture. In his article "The Relation of Habitual Thought and Behavior in Language," Whorf had written: [2]

> Which was first: the language patterns or the cultural norms? In main
> they have grown up together, constantly influencing each other. But in this
> partnership the nature of the language is the factor that limits free plasticity
> and rigidifies channels of development in the more autocratic way. This is
> so because a language is a system, not just an assemblage of norms. Large
> systematic outlines can change to something really new only very slowly,
> while many other cultural innovations are made with comparative quickness.
> Language thus represents the mass mind. . . .

* Acknowledgement is due Mrs. Karen Brazell for substantial assistance on certain
portions of this chapter. Suggestions by Professors Roy A. Miller and Samuel E.
Martin of Yale University were also of help in its preparation, as was the editorial
advice of Professor John Whitney Hall.

[1] Harry Hoijer (ed.), *Language in Culture: Conference on the Interrelations of
Language and Other Aspects of Culture*, American Anthropologist Memoir 79,
Chicago, 1954.

[2] Reprinted in Benjamin Lee Whorf, *Language, Thought, and Reality*, Cambridge,
Mass., 1956, p. 156.

The importance of language had already been stressed by Edward Sapir in his well-known work entitled *Language*. The following quotation from his article "The Status of Linguistics as a Science" expresses his views most aptly: [3]

Language is a guide to "social reality." Though language is not ordinarily thought of as of essential interest to the students of social science, it powerfully conditions all our thinking about social problems and processes. Human beings do not live in the objective world alone, nor alone in the world of social activity as ordinarily understood, but are very much at the mercy of the particular language which has become the medium of expression for their society. It is quite an illusion to imagine that one adjusts to reality essentially without the use of language and that language is merely an incidental means of solving specific problems of communication or reflection. The fact of the matter is that the "real world" is to a large extent unconsciously built up on the language habits of the group. . . . We see and hear and otherwise experience very largely as we do because the language habits of our community predispose certain choices of interpretation.

But the debate over whether language legislates thought norms or whether culture creates language in its image is perhaps equally dependent upon when and where we cut in upon the continuum of interrelationship between a whole culture and one of its parts, namely, language. Kenneth L. Pike suggests that language and culture are, respectively, the verbal and nonverbal elements in a unified complex of human behavior. Language and culture are not discontinuous: [4]

All psychological process, all internal structured responses to sensations, all of thinking and feeling, must also be considered as parts of human

3 Edward Sapir, "The Status of Linguistics as a Science," *Language*, vol. 5, pp. 209–210, 1929.
4 Kenneth L. Pike, *Language in Relation to a Unified Theory of the Structure of Human Behavior*, Glendale, Calif., 1954, vol. 3, p. 105.

187

behavior which will become structurally intelligible only when a theory, a set of terms, and an analytical procedure are provided which deal simultaneously and without sharp discontinuities with all human overt and covert activity. Language is but one structured phase of that activity.

The more organic conception of language as a part of culture is the one which most commends itself to those who would pursue the "cultural" approach to the study of Japan.

It is quite possible, then, to conceive of the Japanese language as reflecting verbally (and perhaps completely) all the nonverbal elements in Japanese culture; for every expression of Japanese culture, we may look for a corresponding feature in the language. Nor is language, regarded as a system of signs and symbols, isolated from other systems that also carry meaning. Verbal expressions, such as the formal greetings exchanged by friends, are often accompanied by gestures (a series of bows in Japan). Moreover, the gesture conveys part of the meaning not expressed verbally. The lowness of the bows, for instance, differs in accordance with the degree of deference intended. Sometimes a gesture may entirely replace an utterance. The extended hand, palm down and raised and lowered from the wrist, signifies a command or a request to approach the person making the gesture, just as in the United States a wave of the arm in a circular motion toward oneself says "Come!" or "Come on!" Thus linguistic expressions need not occur alone; they may be accompanied by kinesthetic signals possessing the same significance, or they may be replaced by gesture and symbol.

There is as yet no agreed-upon structural framework for a discussion of the relationship between language and culture. In this chapter we shall merely take up some obvious points of intersection in Japan between language and society, language and personality, language and history, language and the writing system, and language and ways of thinking. These relationships cannot be treated in all their complexity, but it is possible to indicate something of the "entanglements" in which the Japanese language participates with other elements of the whole culture.

The relationship between language and society in Japan is perhaps best illustrated in the use of honorific and humble forms of language that reflect the existence of a hierarchical system of social classes. An anthropologist such as Ruth Benedict made a great deal of the linguistic evidence of status stratification in Japanese society, and today the student of social change watches for signs of the breakdown of "feudal" relationships in the informality of speech and action that now seems to prevail in so many Japanese households. But if a new spirit of camaraderie seems to fill the air when Japanese fathers and sons and mothers and daughters talk to each other, the niceties of speech and gesture are still retained in more formal situations, as when a student talks to his teacher, a clerk to the president of his company, or a novice priest to his abbot. Japan, after all, is only 100 years removed from its traditional society and its many social compartments, as even the present language reveals. To some extent, then, language perpetuates social norms which contemporary society may wish to discard.

On the other hand, each individual as he finds his place in his culture shapes his own speech patterns. Each individual has his own personality, and each speaker his own "ideolect." This ideolect is shaped by a large number of factors. From his parents, nurse, brothers, sisters, and immediate relatives living in the area that surrounds his home, the Japanese child hears his first human sounds. As he grows up, his one-word exclamations and sentences become more and more complicated. Special habits of phonation, common to an area, may develop. The grammar becomes complex. False analogical formations are usually corrected, but if the child strives to improve his social status, he discovers the need of adapting his speech habits to those of the higher class to which he aspires. With education comes an increased vocabulary. At school and from the radio and television he begins to note and to pick up the features of speech standard in Japan. These tend to replace the forms of his dialect, at least in speech with persons from outside his dialect area and with those from areas (like Tokyo) where the standard language prevails. With experience in speech comes a richer acquaintance with the idioms, the phrasings and proverbs, of Japan. Loan words from foreign languages too become a part of his lexicon. If he goes on to the university, he may be able to read a newspaper with ease, and a newspaper may use in the course of a month some 14,000 different words expressed in one or more characters.[5] If he becomes a professional man, he gains control of a wide range of specialized technical terms appropriate to his field. If, on the other hand, he becomes a manual laborer, he may find himself using in greater proportion an arsenal of slang, even argot and cant, as he goes about his day's business. Whatever his occupation, he fashions his speech in accordance with the statuses of those he converses with. But since the range of his experiences cannot be the same as those of any other person, even of his own home village

5 This figure follows the report of the Kokuritsu Kokugo Kenkyūjo (National Language Research Institute) on the vocabulary found in all the issues of the Tokyo *Asahi* for June, 1949, as reported in *Goi chōsa: gendai shimbun yōgo no ichirei* (A survey of vocabulary: an example of word usage in a modern newspaper), Tokyo, 1952.

189

and of his own age and social group, and since in any case he is individualized by the special set of genes with which he was born and which shape his personality, small differences in speech separate him from his fellows. In effect he develops an ideolect, and this reveals not only the culture but the subculture in which he lives.

Age, class, area of birth, education, and occupation must all play their parts in shaping an individual's speech. The exact role played by each of these formative factors varies with each individual. Still, in speaking a particular language the individual finds himself conforming to one of the accepted social practices of the community—village, city, prefecture, and country—in which he lives. He conforms, in other words, to the usages of his language. But every major language such as Japanese has its variant forms. Uneducated speakers of Japanese living in two areas possessing widely different dialects may still have the utmost difficulty in understanding each other, for their respective dialects may have wide areas of mutual unintelligibility. How, then, are dialects related to the standard language and what does a person's use of dialect reveal about him as a member of society? Much of this is a matter of time and circumstance. In the past the speaker of a particular dialect may have been thought to be particularly virile by those whose speech was basically standard; today one who cannot speak the standard dialect may be thought to be eccentric or uneducated.

The history of language and language usage reveals a great deal about the development of a given culture. The degree of affinity discoverable between Japanese and the other languages of East Asia, for instance, is one of the major lines of evidence used to solve the question of the origin of the Japanese people and their culture. Contacts between Japan and China are revealed in the absorption of Chinese words and phrases. The history of this absorption tells us a great deal about what the Chinese impact upon Japan must have been at various points in history. Buddhist influence on Japan is revealed in the spread of special Buddhist phrases and Sanskrit words in Sinitic form. With the coming of the Portuguese and Spanish in the sixteenth century and the Dutch and English in the seventeenth century, a wide variety of European terms entered the Japanese language, though their range was exotic rather than practical. Then, after Commodore Perry's arrival in the second half of the nineteenth century, all sorts of Western vernacular words along with scientific terms in Greek and Latin were incorporated for very practical purposes. The Japanese people have probably been more receptive to foreign influence than have other groups in East Asia, and their language as used at any time in history clearly expresses this receptivity.

But language reveals cultural history in more ways than through changes in content and vocabulary. Changes in social structure, in mores, and in the organization of the learned professions are clearly revealed in language usage. Gaps between aristocratic and vulgar usage or between the language of literature and scholarship and the spoken tongue are important indexes to the social stratification of an age or to the possible monopoly of learning by an aristocracy or a priesthood. Vocabularies change also, not only through the influx of foreign words, but also through the agency of new groups and classes as they come to occupy new roles in the culture. Additions to the Japanese language made by the priesthood of the Kamakura period and the samurai of the Kanto region or by the merchant classes of the Tokugawa period are part and parcel of major social and intellectual turning points in Japanese culture.

If language reflects cultural history, it also has a hand in making it. The role of language in social or intellectual change is never completely passive, for a language can influence the capacity of a society to change under a variety of circumstances. In contemporary times the relation of language to social and technological modernization has been particularly important. The condition of the language in societies on the verge of modernization can differ greatly, depending on whether there is linguistic uniformity within national boundaries, whether the spoken and written systems are unified, and whether the language can be used for the education of all levels of society. In all these respects Japan was fortunate, though in one major respect, that is, in the nature of the writing system, it has probably been at a disadvantage.

Societies using an alphabet probably enjoy a major linguistic advantage over those that have adopted a system of charactery. A closer relationship exists between the smallest meaningful units of speech, the phonemes, and the letters of the alphabet than between phonemes and characters, whether the latter be hieroglyphic, Chinese, or syllabic. In the Turkish and Japanese cases, the trend has been to drop the more cumbersome system of writing in favor of a simpler one. In Turkey, the Latin alphabet has replaced Arabic writing since 1928. In Japan those urging romanization have never prevailed, but the system of characters is constantly being simplified, and romanization, now given a place in the curricula of the second and third grades in elementary school, is receiving wider acceptance. (In mainland China, too, experiments in alphabetization have been tried from time to time but have given way to the "character-reduction" approach. The total number of characters learned in the schools has been reduced from a prerevolution 7,000 to about 3,000.)

The persistence of outmoded patterns in the written script is a problem in all modernizing societies. It is probably true that rationalization of the writing system would effect major economies in the educational process of almost any society. Advocates of simplified spelling in English deplore the time spent in the schools in teaching and learning the mechanics of spelling, punctuation, hyphenation, capitalization, paragraphing, and the use of quotation marks, question marks, exclamation points, dashes, parentheses, and the like. The English composition course traditionally imposed upon college freshmen in the United States is a monument to the inability of the American school system to teach the fundamentals of writing English even after twelve years of schooling. In Japan the problem is even more complex because of the heavy legacy of a system of charactery, borrowed from China, coupled with the use of a kana syllabary which must be learned in two styles. It is usually estimated that some three years of a student's life are taken up in the study of the writing system itself. The language and the writing system have created many problems in Japanese education and society, but vested interests of various kinds have obstructed the adoption of an alphabet.

Of course, although the Japanese writing system today may seem cumbersome and ill adapted to the needs of mass communication and education in a modern society, we should remember that among Asian nations Japan has had one of the most flexible systems of writing. By comparison with the Chinese, the Japanese of the nineteenth century possessed a written language already much closer to the spoken form than either classical Japanese or classical Chinese. Moreover, the availability of katakana made the incorporation of foreign words comparatively easy. The present simplified writing system represents a compromise between tradition and modern necessity which retains a continuity with Japan's literary heritage at the same time that it is distinctly modern.

Is it possible, however, that Japan has retained too much of the dead weight of tradition in its writing system? Has language constituted a constraint upon the flexibility of Japanese thought or upon the understanding of concepts basic to science or to the development of individualism? The answer is by no means certain. The Japanese language and Japanese ways of thought have both changed through time and have both reacted to foreign influence, adopting particular forms and ideas and being reshaped in the process. To say with Whorf that the structure of the Japanese language "limits free plasticity and rigidifies channels of development" of thought or with Sapir that our view of the world is predisposed by the language we use would seem extreme. Both the language and the ways of thought are systems which interact and yet are also independent of each other. Neither is necessarily dominant in its relationship with the other. On the other hand, the anthropologist and the linguist can tell a great deal about the Japanese culture and social structure simply by an analysis of linguistic patterns; and if this is so, language must exert some sort of influence upon its users.

THE JAPANESE LANGUAGE: ITS LINGUISTIC ANALYSIS

Before pursuing the ways in which the Japanese language may serve either to mold or to reflect the character of Japanese culture, it is essential to learn something of the work of the linguist and the tools with which he describes or analyzes languages, including Japanese. Linguistics as a science of language study is of comparatively recent origin. Like other disciplines, it borders on a variety of other fields. At one extreme, it draws on physiology and psychology to analyze the biological aspects of speech production, while at the other it joins with anthropology and sociology in seeking to relate language to other cultural phenomena. Linguistics proper, which lies between these two extremes, is the study of language in terms of phonology, grammar, and lexicon, including meaning or semantics. There are, of course, several different avenues of linguistics: *Descriptive (synchronic) linguistics* describes languages as they are spoken at a particular point in time. It is concerned with the elements of language and ways of describing them scientifically. *Historical (diachronic) linguistics* deals with the chronological changes within languages. *Comparative linguistics* is synchronic when it deals with contemporaneous languages or dialects; it is diachronic when it compares languages at different chronological periods. It looks for language universals and typologies and for possible relationships between languages. *Applied linguistics* is the application of linguistic techniques and findings to such matters as language training, translation, the standardization of language, and the development and reform of writing systems.

Modern Japanese: A Descriptive Approach

Linguists handle their descriptive characterizations of language under two main categories: phonology and grammar. Phonology, in turn, has two branches: *phonetics,* which analyzes the way in which speech sounds are produced, transmitted, and heard; and *phonemics,* which studies how these sounds are used in language. Both branches are concerned with the discovery of objective criteria for dealing with the sounds and sound combinations from which languages are made.

How are we to describe the quality of sounds in standard Japanese, for instance? English books dealing with Japan frequently have a note on pronunciation which goes something like this: the consonants are pronounced as in English (with medial *g* always nasalized), the vowels as in Italian. While such a note gives the reader a fairly good idea of Japanese pronunciation, it is by no means a scientific description. Linguists have utilized their knowledge of the way sounds are produced (phonetics) to develop a descriptive system which does not rest on general comparisons. They are thus able to describe the sounds of any given language, be it Japanese, English, or Italian, without reference to any other language. Consonants are described according to the place and manner of their articulation. For example, the Japanese sound represented by *t* is a dental stop: *dental* refers to the place of articulation (the tongue is pushed forward against the teeth), and *stop* to the manner of articulation (the streams of air are completely stopped for an instant). The linguist distinguishes between the Japanese *t* and *d,* which are both dental stops, by the use of a third factor, called *voicing.* In a voiced sound, the larynx vibrates (as in the sound *d*), but in a voiceless sound (*t*) it does not.

The advice to the layman about Japanese pronunciation leads us to believe that the Japanese sounds represented by *t* and *d* are identical with the English sounds *t* and *d.* This is not true, although the linguistically unsophisticated person would be hard put to explain or perhaps even to hear the difference. The English *t* and *d* are alveolar rather than dental stops; that is, the point of articulation is the alveolar ridge (the ridge just behind the teeth) rather than the teeth. The same criteria —the point and manner of articulation and the distinction between voiced and voiceless sounds—can be applied to describe all the Japanese consonants.

When vowels are formed, the air moves through the oral passage without much obstruction, and the movement of the tongue is the major method of determining the sound. Vowels are described by two criteria: (1) the height of the tongue (according to three positions, high, middle, or low) and (2) the position of the highest part of the tongue in relation to the mouth (front or back). The application of these criteria to the five Japanese vowels shows that they may be given the following classification:

	Front	Back
High	*i*	*u*
Middle	*e*	*o*
Low		*a*

With the addition of a few other criteria (for instance, aspiration of consonants and the shape of the lips in vowels), linguists can describe any of the infinite number of sounds the human vocal apparatus can produce from an Arabic consonant to a Danish vowel. Yet, a particular language uses only a minute portion of the myriad sounds that are possible, and no two languages have exactly the same inventory of sounds. Japanese, for example, does not use either of the voiceless and voiced sounds represented by *th* in English (as in "cloth" and "clothe" or "thin" and "then"), nor does it employ the English vowels found in "bat," "but," and "bought."

Using the descriptions provided by phonetics, phonemics goes on to classify the sounds into *phonemes*. A phoneme is the smallest unit of speech that distinguishes one form from another. For example, the forms *tan* (shortness) and *dan* (step) are distinguished only by the initial consonants *t* and *d*; hence each of these sounds is a phoneme. Pairs of words which are distinguished by a single phoneme are called minimal pairs. The isolation of minimal pairs is the simplest and usually the most accurate method of establishing phonemes. All the Japanese phonemes can be identified in this manner, as in the following list:

pan̄	bread	*han̄*	half	*kō*	thus
ban̄	evening	*man̄*	10,000	*kyō*	today
tan̄	shortness	*nan̄*	difficulty		
dan̄	step	*wan̄*	bowl	*kan̄*	feeling
kan̄	feeling	*ran̄*	war	*kin̄*	gold
gan̄	wild goose			*kun̄*	mister
san̄	three	*shin̄to*	adherent	*ken̄*	prefecture
zan̄	remainder	*shitto*	jealousy	*kon̄*	this

koʔo * *shikaru*	scold a child
koō shikaru	scold thus

One other phonemic distinction that plays an important role in Japanese is pitch. Japanese does not have the stress accents found in English, nor does it have tones like Chinese, but there is a definite variation in pitch in any utterance. Usually incorrect pitch does not yield incorrect meaning; it simply sounds strange. There are, however, several pairs of words in standard Japanese in which pitch is phonemic. For instance, *káu* means "to raise animals," while *kaú* means "to buy."

Any language uses only a few of the possible sounds and combines these into meaningful units or phonemes. According to the method used above (which is not the only one), Japanese has twenty-two phonemes: five vowel phonemes, sixteen consonant phonemes, and one pitch phoneme. The phonological structure of a language also limits the patterns of sequences of phonemes. For example, at the beginning of an utterance the sound *t* in English can be used in the following consonant

* ʔ is a glottal stop.

clusters: *tr* (troop), *st* (stop), and *str* (street). The Japanese *t* can only be followed by a vowel. In fact, there are no consonant clusters in Japanese, and all consonants are regularly followed by vowels. (The "syllabic" consonant *n* is the only exception; it comes basically from the adoption of Chinese words containing a terminal *n*.) Because consonants do not occur at the end of syllables, all syllables are open; that is, they end in vowels. A vowel alone can make up a syllable, but as this regularly occurs only at the beginning of words, two vowels seldom come together. Thus, the sequence pattern of phonemes in a Japanese word is CVCV or VCV; the number of syllables can vary, but the pattern CV is consistent. As we shall see in the section "The Development of Japanese: A Historical Approach," these generalizations apply only to native Japanese before it was influenced by Chinese. Because of these differences in phonemic patterning, when Japanese borrows a word from English, the word must be modified to fit the Japanese pattern. This modification includes the breakdown of consonant clusters: the word "strike" (in baseball) becomes *sutoraiku*.

The area of linguistics known as grammar also has two branches: *morphology,* which deals with the structure of words; and *syntax,* which analyzes the way in which words are used in phrases and sentences. One task of morphology is to divide words into classes (parts of speech) according to their forms. Japanese words can be divided into two major groups: inflected and uninflected words. Verbs, adjectives, and specifiers (copulas) are the major classes in the former group, and nouns make up most of the latter. Japanese words are highly inflected; that is, a great number of suffixes (inflections) can be added to the verb stems. In addition, many of these inflections can themselves be inflected. This is in sharp contrast with modern English verbs, which have only four possible inflections; these, moreover, cannot be combined. The Japanese verb stem *tabe* (eat) can be inflected in the following ways:

tabe·ro	imperative	*tabe·saseru*	causative
tabe·ru	present and attributive	*tabe·rareru*	passive
tabe·reba	provisional	*tabe·masu*	polite
tabe·ta	past	*tabe·tai*	desiderative
tabe·te	gerund	*tabe·zu*	negative
tabe·tara	conditional	*tabe·yō*	tentative
tabe·tari	alternative		

These inflections may be combined to give such forms as *tabe·mashita* (ate) and *tabe·sase·rare·mashi·ta* (was made to eat). Japanese adjectives have many of the same inflections that verbs have. *Akai* (red) can be inflected: *akakereba* (provisional), *akakatta* (past), *akakute* (gerund), *akakattara* (conditional), etc. (English adjectives have a completely different pattern from English verbs: red, redder, reddest.)

Japanese nouns have no inflections. English nouns are inflected for the plural and the possessive (heart, hearts, heart's), but in Japanese there is usually no distinction between singular and plural: *kokoro* can mean "heart" or "hearts." Possession is most often indicated by the particle *no* (*kokoro no*, "heart's"), and number by the context or by grouping words.

Many languages have various methods by which one part of speech can be changed into another. In English, for example, some adjectives can be made into nouns by the addition of -ness (goodness, sweetness, etc.), and some nouns by the addition of -ish become adjectives (boyish, childish, etc.). The same process occurs in Japanese: some adjectives plus -sa form nouns (*atsusa*, "heat"), some nouns plus *suru* form verbs (*benkyō-suru*, "to study"), and some nouns and verbs form adverbs by reduplication (*toki-doki*, "occasionally"). Another way to form words is to create compounds. Japanese nouns, verbs, and adjectives can be combined in various ways to form compound words much as in English: *yama · kawa* (mountain stream) or *chika · michi* (shortcut).

A string of arbitrarily chosen words does not necessarily make sense; a meaningful sentence must have some means of signaling the relationships that exist between the words. This system of signals makes up the syntax of a language. In Japanese there are three types of syntactic signal: word order, particles, and inflections. We have seen how Japanese adjectives and verbs are inflected, but we need to examine word order and particles before we can understand how these three signal systems function in a sentence.

English speakers are well acquainted with word order; the subjects and objects of English sentences are usually distinguished by their position: "Jim hit Charles" differs from "Charles hit Jim" only in its word order. Japanese word order, however, is quite different from that used in English. In Japanese modifying phrases precede the words they modify (*shimbun o yonde iru hito*, literally, "newspaper reading man"—"the man reading the newspaper"), and the verb comes at the end of the sentence or clause (*Tanabe-san ga shimbun o yomimashita*, literally, "Tanabe-Mr. newspaper read"). A sentence may also end with an adjective with or without the specifier *desu*, "to be" (*Shimbun ga omoshiroi* [*desu*], "The newspaper is interesting"), or with a predicate noun and a specifier (*Sono hito ga Tanabe-san desu*, "That person is Mr. Tanabe"). Thus, among simple sentence patterns, three major types are: (1) subject, object, verb; (2) subject, adjective (specifier); and (3) subject, predicate noun, specifier.

The third type of syntactic signals consists of particles, uninflected forms which follow the word or phrase they refer to. In the examples in the preceding paragraph, *ga* and *o* signal the subject and object, respectively. For example, in the phrase *watakushi—mita hito,* the absence of the particle signaling the function of *watakushi* (I) makes it impossible to know whether the phrase means "the man I saw" or "the man who saw me." Some of the other Japanese particles are roughly equivalent to English prepositions, except, of course, that they are postpositions: *no* has the same possessive function as "of," *kara* means "from," and *ni* is often the equivalent of "to."

The Development of Japanese: A Historical Approach

A scientifically devised method of describing language makes it possible to chart changes within a language or to pinpoint comparisons between different languages. Historical linguistics starts with the problems of origin and typology, which in the case of Japanese are particularly elusive.

It is doubtful in fact that the origin of the Japanese language will ever be fully understood. But much is known in a general fashion about the way individual languages arise, develop, and either fade away or divide into new languages, and such insights can be usefully applied to the study of Japanese. The first concern of historical linguistics with Japanese is to "place" it within one of the large language families (groups of related languages which have descended from a single "parent"). Unfortunately, too little is yet known about the languages of East Asia to permit a conclusive mapping of language groups and their relationships. Nothing has yet been proved with any certainty about the relationship of Japanese to any other language. This is not to say that a number of hypotheses have not been made about the lineage of Japanese.

Today, Ryukyuan is regarded as a Japanese dialect. Although many other affinities have been suggested, most linguists regard the relationship between Japanese and Korean as being the closest among the affiliations with adjacent Asian languages. The evidence for this view, although meager, is nonetheless based on structural rather than on simple lexical correspondence and thereby is more convincing to comparative linguists. The existence of consonant and vowel correspondences between the two languages, identical root types, and a number of parallels both in morphology and in morphophonemics, that is, in the phonological changes that occur when morphemes (consonants, vowels, and combinations of consonants and vowels to which meanings may be attached) are placed in conjunction with each other, all seem to substantiate this relationship. Common to both Korean and Japanese also are a number of interrogative adverbs, particles following the nouns that they govern, similar forms in verbs and specifiers, and the phenomenon of reduplicating verb bases. The details have not been worked out, but various similarities with such languages and language groups as Gilyak, Ainu, Mongolic, Tungusic, and Turkic, that is, with the languages of the Altaic or Uralic-Altaic family, are hopefully being pursued. These languages all appear to have certain common characteristics: initial consonants are simple, verbs have numerous suffixes, verbal suffixes may be combined, postpositions are used, modifiers precede the word modified, and verbs come at the end of the sentence or clause.

In the past, scholars impressed by lexical similarities have tried to relate Japanese to the Malayo-Polynesian, "Austro-Asiatic," and "Tibeto-Burmese" families, but these supposed relationships have been discarded except for the persistent problem of similarities with Malayo-Polynesian (in the use of five distinct vowel phonemes, the pattern of open syllables, and a number of cognate words). A few scholars (particularly ethnographers) in their interpretation of linguistic evidence suggest that Japanese may have taken shape as various tribal or racial groups entered the islands at remote periods in the past. Such an approach would leave the question of southern influence at least open.

Since World War II much discussion regarding linguistic origins has accompanied the advances made in archaeology and ethnology. Of special interest is the work of Prof. Hattori Shirō of Tokyo University, who has applied the technique of glottochronology developed recently in the United States and has presented the evidence for the point in time when the Ryukyuan, Korean, Manchurian, and Ainu languages were separated from the Japanese language. Between Ainu and Japanese, he believes, the separation took place some 7,000 to 10,000 years ago. Between Japanese and Ryukyuan the separation came about 1,800 years ago.

NATIVE JAPANESE. Whatever the exact origin and lineage of Japanese, we do know that the language acquired an identity of its own prior to its heavy influence by the Chinese language. It is essential to be able to reconstruct as precisely as possible what "native Japanese" was like before its encounter with Chinese sometime after the end of the fourth century. The pattern of native Japanese has, of course, been highly resistant to modification and in the main shaped the way in which Chinese words were modified when they were adopted, but, contrarily, Chinese adaptations influenced the phonemic system and, to a lesser extent, the grammar of Japanese. In the modern language, native Japanese and Sino-Japanese forms are completely integrated, although it is usually possible to distinguish the native words from the Chinese loans and so to know what Japanese would have been like had it not been touched by Chinese.

Japanese has not always sounded as it does today. But as the writing system does not indicate pronunciation as alphabets can do and as there are no closely related languages with which to compare Japanese, it is difficult to ascertain exactly how the language did sound in the early historical period. We can, however, trace some changes in the phonemic pattern. We stated above that Japanese consists of open syllables with vowels always separated by consonants. This is still generally true, but the historical trend has been away from the CVCV pattern. The past tenses of many modern verbs have two consonants or two vowels together: *matta* (waited), *katta* (bought), *totta* (took), *shinda* (died), etc. In the Nara period these past forms all had alternating consonant-vowel patterns, but in the Heian period an elision occurred, so that vowels were dropped before the *t* of the past-tense stem. *Toritaru* (took), for example, became *tottaru*.

A morphological change in native Japanese has also resulted from the number of verbal suffixes. For example, in the Nara-Heian period there were six different suffixes to indicate past tense or completion: *nu, tsu, ri, tari, ki,* and *keri* (each of these forms was conjugated). These suffixes were common enough so that five of the six forms occurred in the first two poems of the *Kokinshū* (the imperial anthology of 905). There were presumably subtle differences of meaning between these suffixes to guide their usage, but many of these distinctions are lost to us now. Historically we can see these suffixes disappear one by one until in Tokugawa times only writers who were consciously using "classical Japanese" (usually poets) resorted to them. The modern past-tense suffix *ta* derives from *tari,* reducing the Heian choices to one.

SINO-JAPANESE. Japanese contact with China wrought great changes in the Japanese language. The introduction of the Chinese writing system was at best a mixed blessing. Because it took the Japanese so long to adapt this writing system successfully to their own language and because Chinese was held in such high esteem, educated men of the Nara and Heian periods neglected their own language in favor of Chinese as the language of government and poetry. At the same time that the Japanese adopted the administrative techniques, religious ideas, and many other aspects of Chinese civilization, they added the Chinese words which accompanied these borrowings to their vocabulary. (The Japanese dictionary *Genkai,* first published in 1884, listed more than 13,000 words as Chinese against nearly 22,000 words of Japanese origin.) Since Chinese words sounded very different from Japanese ones, it was not simply a matter of using them in a Japanese sentence; they had to be modified to fit Japanese phonemic patterns. Chinese words had a wider range of initial consonants and consonant clusters than Japanese words, including many medial vowels and diphthongs; Chinese words often ended in a consonant; and each word had a definite tone which was phonemically significant. In order to fit them into the Japanese CVCV phonemic pattern, Chinese pronunciation had to be greatly distorted: initial consonant clusters were simplified to a single consonant; when a *y* or an *i* occurred between a consonant and another vowel, Japanese divided the sound into two syllables; diphthongs were reduced to the nearest Japanese vowel; and final consonants (except *n*) were changed into vowels (*ng* to *u*) or made into new syllables by the addition of *i* or *u* (thus, *t'ang* was converted to *tau* in Nara Japanese and to *tō* in modern, *tiek* became *teki,* and so forth). The simple sound *kō* had to suffice for a range of more than eighty sounds in Chinese as divergent as *chiao, hsiao, quang,* and *k'ou.*

Japanese incorporated Chinese words into its vocabulary at different times and in different contexts (for example, Confucian or Buddhist). Hence the same word (expressed by the same character) was often imported with different pronunciations in Japanese, and most of the characters developed several pronunciations corresponding to the time and place of their introduction. The so-called *"go-on"* (Wu pronunciation) was introduced prior to the sixth century from central China. Later, the north Chinese pronunciation, known as *kan-on,* became the more prevalent source of borrowing. In literary Japanese certain preferences grew up over the use of *go-on* or *kan-on* (Buddhist terms tended to be read in *go-on*), but in modern Japanese these preferences have tended to break down.

Naturally the incorporation of Chinese words has had the effect of producing a proliferation of homonyms in modern Japanese: most pocket dictionaries list twelve different meanings for the compound word *kikan,* and more complete dictionaries list up to forty. (Each of these words is written with a different character; so there is no confusion in written Japanese.)

Chinese words are generally readily distinguishable from Japanese ones even after modification according to Japanese syllabic practice. These differences are evident because Chinese actually imposed certain innovations in the phonemic system of Japanese, bringing into Japanese the initial *r* (*ron*); the initial voiced consonants *g, d, z,* and *b* (*gaku, dai, zai, ban*); the final *n* (*zon*); long vowels (*shō*); and palatal *y* between consonants and vowels (*kyō, myō*). Thus, although the pronunciation of Chinese words was radically modified when they were adapted into Japanese, the process of modification substantially affected the phonemic system in Japanese as well.

The influx of the Chinese language into Japan also had its influence upon the development of Japanese grammar. In contrast to Japanese, which is a highly inflected language, Chinese does not use inflections, grammatical function being determined mainly by position and context and by function-indicating parts of speech. Since Chinese loan words came into Japanese uninflected, the Japanese had to devise ways of indicating syntactical function for these new words. To convert a Chinese word into an inflected verb, the verbal form *suru* (to do) was added (*ronzuru*, "to debate"). Similarly, "adjectival verbs" were formed by adding *naru* (the attributive form of a specifier meaning "to be"), which was later shortened to *na*. Japanese also borrowed devices for indicating parts of speech directly from Chinese. An example in common use in modern Japanese is the adjectival suffix *teki* (*gutai-teki*, "concrete").

Chinese thus influenced the development of Japanese: it expanded the phonemic system; contributed to the growth of new grammatical patterns; and gave Japanese a whole new vocabulary, especially in the areas of philosophy, religion, and government. With the passage of time, Japanese began to adopt words from other languages: *pan* (bread) and *tabako* from sixteenth-century Spanish and Portuguese, *bīru* from the Dutch word *bier*, *arubaito* from the German *Arbeit* (the Japanese meaning is "part-time job"), *areguro* (allegro) and many other musical terms from Italian, *guramu* from the French *gramme*, and *gurafu* (graph) and *sutoraiku* (strike) from English were all incorporated and transcribed with katakana. It would be extremely awkward, however, to adapt the many technical words of modern civilization into Japanese on the basis of such a cumbersome transcription, and it is here that contact with Chinese provided the Japanese with an alternative method of coining words. In the same way that the English or French can draw on classical Latin and Greek to form new words, Japanese can draw on Chinese to make new words. Psychology becomes *shinrigaku* (mind-reason-study), and linguistics is *gengogaku* (word-speech-study). There is no limit to the possibilities of such a system; new words are continually being invented, and old ones often fall into disuse, so that a complete, up-to-date dictionary of Sino-Japanese words is impossible to compile. One interesting aspect of this coinage of new words is that in many instances the Japanese preceded the Chinese in devising compounds for modern purposes. Thus in the last century Chinese has actually borrowed the Japanese Sinified compounds for such things as airplane, electricity, atomic bomb, and a host of other modern objects.

THE WRITING SYSTEM. Edwin O. Reischauer has written: "Perhaps the greatest single misfortune in the history of Japan was that, because of her geographic position, Chinese characters and not one of the Western alphabets became the basis of her writing system."[6] Most

6 Edwin O. Reischauer, *The United States and Japan*, rev. ed., New York, 1962, p. 154.

students trying to learn to read Japanese would agree, for despite the many simplifications which have taken place in recent years, the writing system remains complex and highly idiomatic. The cumbersome nature of the Japanese writing system stems from the nonalphabetic nature of Chinese writing and the fact that Chinese and Japanese are totally unrelated languages having vast phonological and grammatical differences. The Japanese attempt to write their own language by using Chinese characters presented major difficulties. It began about the fourth or fifth century, but it was not until the ninth century that the basis for the syllabic system used today finally emerged.

Essentially, what the Japanese did was to use the Chinese characters in three different ways: (1) as Chinese characters in their original meanings and Japanized sounds, (2) as symbols to stand for Japanese words and pronounced in Japanese, and (3) simply for their sounds as a means of writing Japanese. At first, of course, there was considerable confusion between the different uses to which characters were put. The phonetic use of characters (in standard abbreviated form) eventually separated out into the two varieties of kana. But the two symbolic usages for characters, whether pronounced according to Chinese (*on*) or Japanese (*kun*), were easily confused. In most cases one could tell only through experience or context how a given character was being used.

Thus, one of the most difficult features of written Japanese for a non-Japanese to accept is the multiplicity of pronunciations which a single character may have; considerable experience is required before a student learns when a character should be pronounced one way and when another. Where possible, the Japanese sentence attempts to provide pronunciation hints for the reader. Thus, when the character stands for a verb or an adjective, the addition of kana inflections becomes the key. For example, the character 下 (basically "down" or "under") is used with the appropriate kana in the writing of seven different Japanese verbs. These are distinguished by the use of hiragana as follows (the parts of the words indicated by hiragana are enclosed in parentheses):

Written form	Pronunciation	Meaning
下す	*kuda(su)*	give, confer
下さる	*kuda(saru)*	give, confer
下る	*kuda(ru)*	go down
下りる	*o(riru)*	go down
下ろす	*o(rosu)*	lower
下がる	*sa(garu)*	hang down, dangle
下げる	*sa(geru)*	hang

In addition, the character may be read as *shita* (below), *shimo* (bottom), *ka* (beneath), and *ge* (lower). Only experience can reveal whether the compound 下手 should be read *heta* (clumsy), *shimote* (lower part), *shitade* (act humbly), or *gete* (vulgar).

Since the Meiji Restoration and especially since World War II, the Japanese government, through the Ministry of Education, has entered the field to reform the Japanese writing system. The number of characters is now reduced to 1,850 so-called "*tōyō* kanji" (common-use characters), and newspapers and other publications are expected to limit their pages to this number. Of these, 881 have been labeled essential characters and are taught in the first six grades of the public schools. The government has also authorized the use of abbreviated forms (*ryakuji*) of many characters for simplicity of writing (140 out of 1,850), but there is still the problem of multiple readings of characters (the more common ones tend to have the greater numbers of variant readings), and few authors or academic writers are content to stay within the *tōyō*-kanji limits. And of course, in order to read any literature written before the twentieth century, one must know the older forms of the simplified characters and many more besides. In spite of attempted reforms, it has been estimated that Japanese schoolchildren spend two years more of their education in learning the mechanics of reading and writing than do children in the United States or Europe.

LANGUAGE AND SOCIETY

In our summation of the kinds of statement which linguists make about spoken and written Japanese, we have had to pass over the aspects of the language which appear to reveal in some fashion the peculiarities of Japanese social or intellectual life. What can the language we have just described tell us about Japanese culture? Is it possible, in fact, to state with any certainty that idiosyncrasies of the language are expressions of particular features of the culture? Certain features of Japanese (extreme sensitivity to levels of usage and a reluctance to make direct personal references) are so clearly a reflection of the nuances of social behavior that we should not have to question the linguistic evidence. But in other areas, for instance, the question of whether the structure of the language (particularly its syntax) and the nature of the writing system have a direct effect upon the working of the Japanese mind, we find ourselves in a very tenuous area of inquiry.

Honorific and Humble Speech

Let us start from what seems most demonstrable and work toward the more hypothetical. The study of levels of usage (honorific, polite, ordinary, and humble forms) and dialects (either regional or class) is related directly to certain differentiations within Japanese society. Undeniably spoken Japanese has traditionally contained a great wealth of expressions which denote relative social position. It is probably true that until modern times no "egalitarian" form of Japanese speech existed. Every expression made by one person to another automatically set the speaker in a relationship to the second as being superior, inferior, or equal and of being of one sex or another. Of course, English also has its levels of usage: the affirmative "OK," "yes," and "yes, sir," indicate at least three gradations, and there are many alternative ways of expressing any idea so as to convey different levels of politeness or familiarity. But Japanese not only has a greater number of gradations; it also has many more fixed devices for signaling these levels, and a speaker of Japanese must constantly choose among several possible levels.

Users of the Japanese language must therefore develop a special adeptness in selecting alternative styles of speech according to the requirements of the social situation. The variables in any given situation are the relative hierarchical positions occupied by the speaker, by the person or persons spoken to, and by the person or persons spoken of. Each speaker controls a battery of polite and plain (or informal) expressions, honorific or humble (self-deprecatory) forms, and a variety of dialectal variations. For most situations the usual polite forms are the ones to use; that is, *Ikimasu ka?* (Are you going?) is more common among educated persons of equal status than its more abrupt equivalent, *Iku ka?* On the other hand, the failure to use honorific or familiar forms when these are called for amounts to poor form. Honorific forms go beyond mere politeness to make explicit the actual or implied superiority of the person being addressed. Humble forms serve to deprecate the speaker and thus place the person spoken to on a higher footing. The use of honorific forms with reference to oneself is clearly a mistake, as is any mixture of honorific forms with forms that are deprecatory of the second and third persons. The failure to use familiar language toward a person who is obviously an inferior is equally poor form (that is, professor to student, husband to wife).

Let us see how all this works in practice. Suppose that a young Japanese said to his good friend, "I'll go." He would use *iku*, the plain form of the verb "to go": *"Ore ga iku."* If he were speaking to his father, he would probably use the polite suffix, *-masu,* and say, *"Boku ga ikimasu."* (Men commonly use three pronouns for the first person: *ore, boku,* and *watakushi,* in ascending order of politeness). If the boy were to speak to his friend about a respected teacher, he would properly use a separate honorific verb meaning "to go": *"Sensei ga irassharu"* (The teacher is going). Speaking to the teacher's wife about the teacher, he would use the honorific *irassharu* to show respect to the teacher and the polite suffix *-masu* to show respect to the person he was addressing: "*Sensei ga irasshaimasu.*" But if he were speaking directly to the teacher, both the honorific and the polite forms would be used toward the teacher: "*Irasshaimasu ka?*" (Are you going?) Women often use honorific verbs in the plain form when talking with their friends, thus showing respect as well as intimacy: "*Irassharu no?*" (Are you going?) When the subject of a statement wishes to show respect to a second person, he may do so by using a verb with humble meaning with the polite suffix *-masu*: "*Watakushi ga mairimasu*" (I shall go). This is a far cry from the sentence at the beginning of this paragraph: "*Ore ga iku.*"

This illustration shows that differences of politeness can be conveyed by the use of special nouns, verbs, and adjectives. Nouns may be made honorific by prefixing them with *o-* or *go-* (*otomodachi*, "your friend," "his friend," and even "my friend" when the friend enjoys an elevated status; *gorōjin*, an "aged man" or "woman"), by suffixing *-sama* (*dochirasama*, "who"), and by prefixing *go-* and suffixing *-sama* (*goinkyosama*, an "old man" or "woman," such as another person's grandfather or grandmother, who has retired from active life). The use of kinship terms is particularly subject to status niceties. Polite or honorific forms are used when one is referring to members of someone else's family. These are generally formed by the appropriate prefix-suffix combination (*o-* . . . *-san*), but in a number of instances entirely different words are used: my husband (*otto, shujin*), your husband (*goshujin*), my wife (*tsuma, kanai*), your wife (*oku-san*), my father (*chichi, oyaji*), your father (*otō-san*), my mother (*haha*), your mother (*okā-san*). A child will address his parents as *otō-san* and *okā-san*.

Certain nouns are honorific in and of themselves (*ōse*, "statements," "orders"; *donata*, "who"), and certain nouns suggest that the person referred to occupies a position inferior to that of the speaker (*omae*, "you"). Certain verbs also carry connotations that are honorific of the second or third person and are, therefore, not used with the first person: *agaru* (to eat, drink), *irassharu* (to come, go, be), *meshi-agaru* (to eat, drink), *nasaru* (to do), *ossharu* (to say), and *kudasaru* (to give). The verbs *nasaru* and *asobasu* are equivalents of the more common verb *suru* (to do) and may take the place of *suru* after nouns borrowed from the Chinese language: *Benkyō-nasatte imasu* (He is studying).

The passive and passive causative forms of verbs are frequently used to indicate honorific meaning: *Sensei no iwareru tōri desu* (It is just as teacher says). And of course there are a host of other ways of indicating levels of politeness, for instance, by circumlocution, indirection, and the like.

Certain verbs are humble in themselves and are used when the subject acknowledges the superior position of a second or third person: *itadaku* and *chōdai-suru* (to receive), *haiken-suru* (to look at), *mairu* (to come, go), *mōshi-ageru* (to tell, say), *sashi-ageru* (to give), *oyobi shimasu* and *omaneki itashimasu* (I invite), *gochisō ni narimasu* (I accept the food set before me), and *goran ni iremasu* (I show something to someone superior to me).

Finally, it is worth pointing out that certain forms containing the prefix *o-* have through usage become identified as units without an honorific connotation: *o-cha* (tea), *o-yu* (hot water), *gohan* (rice, meal), *o-kane* (money). Sometimes etymologically honorific forms have become petrified in greetings: *Ohayō* and *Ohayō gozaimasu* (Good morning!), *O-medetō* and *O-medetō gozaimasu* (Congratulations!).

Many Japanese claim that fewer distinctions of politeness are discernible in present-day speech and that a leveling process has occurred in the years since World War II. Certainly the bantering speech employed in many Japanese homes reveals a degree of friendly intimacy not associated with a rigid hierarchical structure. Practices tabooed in the past now are sanctioned in speech as well as in action. The niceties of the language of social intercourse in Japan are of concern to anthropologically and sociologically inclined scholars, who see in such ingrained patterns of speech indications of the distinctions which have characterized Japanese society. There is, however, an important syntactical function served by the system of denoting "respect" and "deference," namely, that it helps to serve the need for personal-pronoun indicators, which are used only sparingly in Japanese sentences. In fact, in direct speech a Japanese rarely uses the pronouns of direct address: *anata* (you) is still very much a formal term; *kare* (he, she) sounds stiff. The usual procedure is to speak in such a way that the reference is clearly implied (often by the use of appropriate verbal forms indicating level), or to repeat the name or title of the person being addressed. In modern Japanese, in fact, it is sometimes not clear how much respect or deference is intended by the use of honorific and humble terms. Some of the so-called "honorific" speech patterns are often used, it seems, only to denote syntactical differences or, in phrases like *Ohayō gozaimasu*, in petrified greetings.

The following extract from a letter of a student to a teacher, adapted from O'Neill and Yanada, *An Introduction to Written Japanese*,[7] demonstrates how plain, polite, and honorific forms are used together and how these serve to indicate personal references. As this is a letter of request to a superior, the language is very respectful. In the letter plain

[7] P. G. O'Neill and S. Yanada, *An Introduction to Written Japanese*, London, 1959, pp. 182–183; 213.

forms are given in regular type, polite forms are in boxes, honorifics are underlined, and humble forms are underlined twice. The same marking is used in the English translation.

> *Kore ni tsuite wa sensei ni* <u>onegai</u> <u>suru</u> *no ga ichiban ii to* <u>zonji</u>, *sō henji* <u><u>itasu</u></u> *tsumori* <u><u>de</u></u> <u><u>ori</u></u> [masu] *ga, sono mae ni sensei no goshōchi o* <u>itadakitai</u> *to* <u>zonji</u>, *kono tegami o kaki* [mashita]. *O-isogashii tokoro o shitsurei* [de gozaimasu] *ga, gohenji kudasaru yō* <u>onegai moshiage</u> [masu].

With respect to this matter, <u>I</u> <u>feel</u> that the best thing would be <u>to</u> <u>consult</u> <u>you</u>, Professor, and <u>I</u> <u>intend</u> <u>to</u> <u>reply</u> to that effect; but <u>I</u> <u>should</u> <u>like</u> <u>to</u> <u>have</u> <u>your</u> <u>understanding</u> before doing so, and [am] therefore [writing] to you now. [<u><u>I must apologize</u></u>] for troubling you when <u>you</u> <u>are</u> so <u>busy</u>, but <u><u>I</u></u> <u><u>should</u></u> <u><u>be</u></u> <u><u>grateful</u></u> for <u>your</u> <u>kind</u> <u>reply</u>.

Note that the English translation uses eleven pronouns, while there are none in the Japanese, although the noun *sensei* (Professor) appears twice. Yet this lack of pronouns causes no semantic confusion, since the antecedents are indicated by the use of honorifics and humble forms.

Informal Speech

Deprecatory and informal speech occupies the other extreme of the scale from the polite and honorific. Informal speech has the usual areas of usage among peers and young people and is basic in certain situations in which slang and even coarse language are permitted. It is also accepted as the language with which a patronizing superior addresses an inferior. Again we should remind ourselves that there are numerous ways in which the speaker of English can achieve the same ends: tone of voice, the use of abbreviated forms, and, in some cases, the resort to slang and vulgar expressions. Japanese lacks the refined nuances of the English vocabulary of profanity, but it is extremely sophisticated in its ability to provide vulgarities, deprecatory terms, and gruff expressions. We are here concerned primarily with the means of showing familiarity in conversation (student bull-session talks) or condescension.

First, there are a number of specific words which carry informal or deprecatory connotations: *ore* (I), *omae* or *temae* (you), *oi!* (hey!), *baka!* (you fool!). Beyond this the language of informality tends to be abrupt in syntax and to include substandard modes of pronunciation; it tends also to absorb certain dialectal habits considered impolite or low-class. In many "imprecise" utterances vowels or even whole morphemes are devocalized, that is, slurred, and in some cases lost: *asoko* (there) becomes *asko*, *watakushi* (I) becomes *watashi* or *washi*, *tokoro* (place) becomes *toko,* and *no* (thing, fact, one) becomes *n.* The particle *no,* possessive in meaning, may also be reduced to *n: boku n toko* (my place). Similarly, *-n* may be substituted for the *-nu* ending denoting a negative: *konai* (not coming) becomes *kon.*

Frequently found in informal speech are the contractions like *ja* and *jā* for *de wa* (in that case) or *sore ja* for *sore de wa* (also meaning in that case). *Da* replaces *desu: jikan desu* (it's time) becomes *jikan da.* To cover the entire range of abrupt or inelegant language would be impossible, since this language very quickly merges into slang and dialect.

Dialects

Radio announcers and schoolteachers in Japan are expected to speak standard Japanese (*hyōjun-go*), a model of "correct" speech which is closer to the Tokyo dialect than to any other. But everyday language varies considerably with the region where it is spoken. Such regional variations, or dialects, are becoming less and less pronounced as the radio, television, and compulsory education create a common language among all the Japanese. Yet it was only a generation or two ago that farmers from two different parts of the country frequently could not communicate with each other, and it is still possible for someone born and brought up in a single locality to talk to his friends in a dialect scarcely comprehensible to one who knows only standard Japanese.

We have already noted that Ryukyuan broke off as a separate dialect at least 1,800 years ago (with the result that there is a much greater difference between the Ryukyuan and mainland dialects than among the mainland dialects themselves), but how the main dialects came into being can only be surmised. A great deal of work has been done on the dialect geography of modern Japanese, however, and there is general agreement concerning its major divisions. As might be expected, these divisions follow fairly closely the cultural-geographic regions described in Chapter 1. There are three general dialect areas, Kyushu, Western, and Eastern, and several subdialects within each of them. Divisions are made on the basis of studies in phonology (including accent), grammar, and vocabulary. While the dialects have many lexical and grammatical distinctions, we shall have to limit our characterizations of them chiefly to pronunciation differences.

The Tōhoku dialect, spoken in northern Honshu (as at Sendai) is one of the so-called "*zūzū*" dialects, so named because the syllable *jū* is pronounced *zū*. In this dialect the vowels *i* and *u* are merged indistinguishably in the syllables *shi* and *su, chi* and *tsu,* and the consonants

JAPAN
Major Dialect Regions in Japan

EASTERN

WESTERN

HOKKAIDO

TŌHOKU

HOKURIKU

KANTŌ

IZUMO

CHŪGOKU

TŌKAI-TŌSAN

KINKI

HICHIKŪ

SHIKOKU

HŌNICHI

KYUSHU

SATSUGŪ

RYUKYU

N

miles
0   50   100   150

t and *k* are voiced in the middle of words. Thus when *d* or *g* occurs in the middle of a standard word, the Tōhoku dialect avoids confusion by adding a nasal, so that the standard Japanese *gojissen* (50 sen) becomes *gonzussen*. In the northern part of the Tōhoku dialect area the accent is similar to that in standard Japanese, but in the southern part the accent is not phonemic. In other words, *hana* (nose) and *hana* (flower) are pronounced with the same pitch pattern.

The Kinki dialect of western Japan includes the subdialects of Osaka and Kyoto. The phonology is like that of standard Japanese, but the accent is in many cases the reverse. The conjugation of some verbs is also distinctive in some areas of Kinki, especially in Kyoto. In Tokyo the verb to borrow is *kariru*; in Kyoto it is *karu*. These forms belong to different conjugations; the plain past tense of *kariru* is *karita*, and the past tense of *karu* is *katta*. In Tokyo the plain past tense of *kau* (to buy) is *katta*, whereas in Kyoto it becomes *kōta*. Tokyo *desu* is *dosu* in Kyoto and *dasu* in Osaka, while *gozaimasu* is *osu* and *omasu*, respectively. The Kinki dialect is also noted for the use of *-n* instead of *-nai* as a negative suffix: *iranai* (don't need) becomes *iran*.

One of the most interesting dialects from the Kyushu area is Hichiku, spoken on the west coast of the island, including the major cities of Nagasaki, Kumamoto, and Fukuoka. The Hichiku dialect has preserved some of the phonetic distinctions of ancient Japanese which have since disappeared in standard Japanese: *she* and *je*, *e* and *ye*, *zi* and *di*, *zu* and *dzu*, *uwa* and *gwa* all exist in various regions of the Hichiku dialect. A good deal can still be done to increase our knowledge of Japanese historical linguistics through the study of dialectal remnants.

In some ways more persistent than the regional dialects are the class or group dialects associated with a number of professions and hereditary families. Such dialects (usually a matter of special vocabularies) are often consciously perpetuated because their users are proud of the social distinction which their use infers.

To begin with, the language of the court defined an almost separate world with strong continuities going back to Heian times. The Emperor until Taishō times referred to himself with the pronomial form *chin*, borrowed from the Chinese language, an equivalent to the imperial "we" of the languages of Europe. When the character for this word was written or printed, it was the custom to leave a space after it, thus symbolizing the social distance separating the Emperor from his subject. Even today, in the more informal atmosphere created by the "disavowal of divinity" by the Emperor, a special honorific language is used in referring to him. The word *onshi* refers to an imperial gift, and the special character written to express the *-shi* is also reserved to express the verb *tamau* (to grant) when this verb is used with the Emperor as the grammatical subject.

The language of court society is filled with numerous archaisms and is particularly rich in honorific terms of address. Words for family members have numerous variations which indicate the rank of the family: *omō-san* (father) would be used by the upper nobility; *odei-san* (father), by the lower nobility.

Kabuki actors retain certain speech idiosyncrasies besides a considerable inventory of technical terminology. Geisha speech is characterized by a kind of bantering "cuteness" and by certain euphemistic phrases. Thus a geisha attending a party will use the term *murasaki* (the purple) for *shōyu* sauce and *nami no hana* (flowers of the waves) as a poetic equivalent for *o-shio* (salt).

The reduction of dialectal differences and the emergence of a standard speech gained a good start during the Tokugawa period, when Edo became the political center of the country and the *daimyō* and their large retinues traveled back and forth to it from the provinces. With the selection of Edo as the new capital of Japan it became inevitable that the Tokyo dialect should serve as the standard. The modern system of compulsory elementary education was first promulgated in 1872, but it was not until 1886 that uniform rules establishing the primary school system were proclaimed and not until 1905 that standard textbooks for the Japanese language were distributed throughout the country. At this time also, through uniform normal school training and the use of teaching manuals of various kinds, an effort was made to standardize grammar and establish a style of writing based on the spoken language. Regulations concerning the forms of kanji and kana and rules for spellings in kana were issued. The radio, movies, television, and other media of mass communication have in recent times helped the teachers to create in each community a citizenry that can speak a common language with those coming from other areas. This trend may mean that a person will end up retaining a dialect as well as learning this common language in which speakers of different dialects adjust their speech forms to each other, but this is a frequent occurrence in other countries as well. The common language (*kyōtsū-go*) is not exactly the same as the standard language (*hyōjun-go*) taken as the model in the schools, but it possesses in essence the features of the language of the middle and higher classes in Tokyo on which the standard language is based. Honorific terms, dialect forms, and special slang vocabularies remain as holdovers from the past, but in almost all respects Japanese has been moving toward standardization and uniformity over the past 100 years.

Nevertheless, language is a constantly changing institution, and if the spoken and written forms are merged, new influences tend to pull them apart again. And if old regional and class dialectal differentiations are disappearing, new ones are developing. In actuality the language of Japanese urban dwellers (particularly residents of Tokyo) or of the new business or intellectual elites is a far cry from what is taught in the schools. The speech of such persons is liberally sprinkled with foreign phrases and expressions, often made popular through imported movies or phonograph records. In upper-class families which have frequently traveled abroad or whose children are expected to be educated abroad, the father is called *papa* and the mother *mama*, and babies are taught to say *baibai* (bye-bye).

LANGUAGE AND WAYS OF THINKING

No matter how much Japanese has been standardized or modernized, it still is identifiably Japanese. It remains a language which retains much more of its traditional qualities than it has abandoned. And so we may ask whether the language, this most intimate possession of the Japanese people, is more than just a vehicle of communication. Is it possible that Japanese has an identity of its own and hence a capacity to put its imprint on the minds of each generation of Japanese? Does the Japanese language, in other words, have some part in creating and perpetuating the Japanese style of culture? We should hardly wish to deny such a role to language, yet convincing proof is hard to come by. In a field of conjecture as uncharted as this it might be best to leave the entire subject alone until sufficient empirical work has been done, but too many hypotheses have been set adrift, and too many clichés have become part of the folklore of cultural comparison to permit this. We shall take, therefore, the work of one noted philosopher and follow his inquiries into this complex question of relationships.

Professor Nakamura Hajime of Tokyo University in his work entitled *Tōyōjin no shii hōhō*, published in two volumes in Japanese in 1948–1949 and in English translation in 1960 and 1964, discusses what he calls the ways of thinking of the peoples of India and East Asia. For him religion plays a primary role in determining values and thought patterns. For Japan religion would include Buddhism, Confucianism, shamanism, and Shinto thought. The Japanese people, according to Nakamura, have a tendency to think primarily in terms of the particular social nexus in which they find themselves; they also show certain irrationalistic tendencies in their thinking and a general inclination toward the acceptance of actuality. Emphasis on the social nexus to which one belongs brings with it, says Nakamura, an overstressing of human relations; an acknowledgment of the rights of the group over those of its participating members; a close observance of family morals; an emphasis on rank and social position; a tendency toward ultranationalism; an absolute devotion to specific individuals, illustrated in particular by Emperor worship; sectarianism and factionalism; a willingness to defend through the use of force the ingroup to which one belongs; acute moral self-reflection; and, contrariwise, a lack of awareness of religious values. The irrationalistic tendencies of the Japanese, says Nakamura, are revealed in their neglect of logical rules, inability to think with logical coherence, intuitive and emotional approach to problems, inability to form complicated ideas, fondness for simple symbolic expressions, and lack of knowledge of the objective order. Dealing with the Japanese tendency to accept actuality, Nakamura discusses the habit of stressing the "intuitive sensible concrete" [8] rather than the universal and the attitude which emphasizes the fluid, incipient character of events.

Illustrating these points, Nakamura refers to various facets of the Japanese language. "Language," he says, "is basic to the life of a people; so basic that when a special language system comes into being, we may say that a people has come into being." On the relationship between linguistic forms and ways of thinking, he follows "what seems to be the general assumption that, to a certain extent, between the two there is a relationship of correspondence or parallel development—that language is a representation in sound of the concept which is produced as a result of the operation of thinking within our consciousness." Moreover, "if there is such an intimate relationship between the operations of language and thinking, it is worthwhile and indeed necessary to use forms of linguistic expression as a key in studying forms and ways of thinking." [9]

Many of Nakamura's observations on the relationship of linguistic forms to ways of thought in Japan are probably very much to the point. The tendency to emphasize the social nexus is undeniable, and this in many instances seems to bring with it a great emphasis on the structure of human relations within the context of any discourse. The answer to a negative question, such as "Aren't you going to school?" usually is "Yes, I'm not," because the asker of the question has implied that the person who is being addressed is not going to school. The answer is made in accordance with the supposed expectation of the questioner instead of with the fact involved. The elaboration of honorific and humble forms likewise points to a high degree of sensitivity to the social medium in which speech is being used.

But how far can we carry the interpretation of linguistic evidence? Is it true that a "respect for labor in vocational life resulted in the high

[8] Nakamura Hajime, *The Ways of Thinking of Eastern Peoples*, rev. ed., Honolulu, 1964, p. 350.
[9] *Ibid.*, pp. 5–6.

esteem of things produced as the fruits of labor?" [10] And is this to account for the fact that boiled rice is called *gohan* (with the honorific)? In his discussion of the attempt on the part of the Japanese to apprehend the absolute in the phenomenal world, Nakamura points to the use of the honorific prefix in everyday words like *o-cha* (tea) and *o-mizu* (water). This comes, according to him, from the tendency in Buddhism to admit the spirituality of grass, trees, and even nonliving things. Unfortunately for Nakamura's argument, the special use of the prefixes to which he is here referring is restricted even in Buddhist contexts to a few examples. There still remains the question of how forms like *gohan*, *o-cha*, and *o-mizu* became petrified in usage, and it would seem difficult to ascribe them entirely to Buddhism. What can we, in fact, deduce about the religiosity of the American who leaves his friends each day with the parting remark "Good-bye!" which comes from "God be with ye!"

While recognizing the existence of a most complex system of levels of usage in Japanese, we still must be able to tell with more than subjective insight what the significance is of the social interplay which Nakamura calls the "ritual in conversation." Can we go so far, as Nakamura does, as to say that since the first- and second-person subject is frequently omitted, the Japanese lack a "full awareness of the individual or of an independent performer of actions as an objective being"? Or can we agree with him that the "Japanese have no way to state, or to attribute actions to, a specific performer of action"?[11] We have seen that the absence of a stated subject does not mean that communication cannot take place; the forms of the verbs and other honorific elements offer sufficient evidence of who the subject is.

According to Nakamura, the irrationalistic tendencies of the Japanese are confirmed in their language by the use of the postpositional particle. "This part of speech," he says, "has the characteristic not only of expressing cognitive, logical relations, but also of expressing to some degree various delicate shades of emotion . . . emphasizing some specific meanings, evoking attention to some aspects of things, distinguishing delicate variations of emotions, and [leaving] rich overtones of meaning just because of this ambiguity." But to anyone who has read William Shakespeare or T. S. Eliot, Nakamura's statement that "the Japanese language is peculiarly sensitive in its grasp of emotion"[12] is hard to accept, and it is still a question as to whether it is the language that is the determining factor or the use to which Japanese speakers put it.

10 *Ibid.*, p. 509.
11 *Ibid.*, p. 535.
12 *Ibid.*, pp. 531–532.

What are we to do with the often-repeated claim that the Japanese language is notably deficient in words denoting intellectual and inferential processes of thought? This may have been the case in earlier times, but with the borrowing of Chinese, Buddhist, and Western terms virtually every philosophical system has been assimilated into Japanese culture and expounded in the Japanese language, and a Nishida Kitarō has been able to devise an original though eclectic philosophy of his own. The lack of relative pronouns, says Nakamura,[13] prevents "closely knit thinking in Japanese," but the Japanese language merely uses another device, attributive modification, to take their place, without damage to the communication of thought.

Again, the observation made by Nakamura that the Japanese language has a structure unfit for the expression of logical conceptions asks the language to perform under conditions for which it was traditionally unprepared. Here again, borrowing from Chinese and Western languages has in modern times remedied whatever deficiencies might once have existed, and if logicians could not have expressed themselves in ancient Japanese, the same probably could be said of Old English.

But Nakamura goes on to claim the Japanese have difficulty in forming complicated ideas for the reason that the Japanese language "is, generally speaking, very poor in imaginative words based on abstract and universal ideas."[14] Moreover, it is also "not adequate to exact objective statement," but rather is colored by an "illogical" quality. The problem here, obviously, is the question of whose Japanese we are to talk about. Too often Nakamura's complaints and those of others who have gone before him are lodged against an older form of the language which could not possibly contain the lexicon of modern science and philosophy. And too often they fail to recognize that different means may be taken in different languages to express the same or similar things. The Japanese language today is certainly adequate for the requirements which are put to it. And if the Japanese of the 1590s or the 1890s was less adequate, it would seem that it was more the fault of the culture (the users) than of the language itself.

None of the foregoing can possibly deny the proposition with which we started this discussion, namely, that language is an important and revealing aspect of culture. But what is at issue is the exact function of language as an ingredient of culture and the way in which it is interrelated with the thought process. It is mainly when writers like Nakamura place the blame upon language for certain "inadequacies" of the Japanese mind that we feel uneasy. Turn these statements around,

13 *Ibid.*, p. 534.
14 *Ibid.*, p. 557.

so as merely to claim that linguistic expressions or syntactical forms are the result of the cultural requirements and conventions of a given period in history, and the proposition seems less questionable.

It is perfectly true that the Japanese language until modern times has not been used to carry the burden of logical syllogisms or closely reasoned briefs on legal cases, but is this the fault of the language or the influence of the culture? It is quite true that the Japanese people until modern times were not called upon to express themselves in the kind of rigorous reasoning which was begun in the West by the Greeks. But to say that the Japanese mind had not been put through complex and sophisticated processes of reasoning by Buddhist and Confucian thinkers would be to ignore a large area of Japanese intellectual history. There is also a fascinating though dangerous game that can be played with vocabulary. Why is it that the Japanese have a dozen different words for rain during varying seasons, whereas English differentiates, by use of adjectives, only in the quality of precipitation? What is the significance of the use by the Japanese of the expression *sumanai* (literally, "I can never repay") for the idea of "I am sorry" in English? And what meanings can we squeeze from the study of a host of other words which are special to the Japanese aesthetic vocabulary (*sabi*, for instance) or expressions which seem to reveal an entirely different conception of man and nature (for example, *hara ga tatsu,* "to get angry"; literally, "the stomach rises")?

Admittedly also, Japanese lacked many areas of vocabulary as the country faced the prospect of building a new nation-state. The concept of "nation" was not even available and had to be freshly coined: *kokka.* Beyond that, whole categories of new conceptions had to be clothed in newly created words: the people, citizens, freedom, rights, political party, individualism, and a host of others. And while the Japanese intellectual or political leader was impatiently running the Japanese through vocabulary drills of new and unfamiliar words, a large residue of old words standing for old attitudes and ways of thought remained in use.

Loan words add suppleness to a language, which may thus become a medium for the development of fresh and complicated concepts and ideas. These ideas may in turn create a need for new vocabulary and even for new grammatical structures. Language and thought may thus bring about changes in each other's development, but in the process it would be difficult to assert that either takes precedence over the other. Unquestionably, by comparison with other, more scientifically controlled studies in language, the whole problem of meaning—the accretion of new meanings when new words are added to a language and the effect on a language when concepts new to a culture are acquired—is hardly touched by scientific analysis. Newly accepted terms and concepts may be incompletely understood when newly adopted into a language. Even well-established terms may not be understood by more than a fraction of the community. We therefore terminate this portion of our discussion with what has by now become a cliché, that language and thought, as well as language and the other aspects of culture, bear a close relationship to each other. The relationship between language and thought, however, requires further, most careful analysis.

LANGUAGE AND MODERNIZATION

Whether or not the Japanese spoken and written language has any inherent weaknesses, it has undeniably been an adequate tool of communication for the Japanese people as they have overcome the many problems of modernization which they have faced since 1868. The difficulties in language reform met by other Asian countries remind us of the importance of language as a vehicle for social and political change and as a necessary foundation for national development. The many ways in which the Japanese adjusted and simplified their linguistic arsenal as they came into the modern world resulted in a remarkably supple language, capable of expressing virtually everything required in modern life and phrased in grammatical forms that repeat or closely resemble those of speech. A hundred years ago this was certainly not the case.

For the Westerner residing in Japan in the 1860s it was probably not at all apparent that the Japanese would be capable of modernizing their language. For several decades, in fact, higher learning in Japan was based on English or German texts and even on English or German instructors. The Japanese medical student, to take an example, was required to write his dissertation in German, so that until well into the twentieth century the entire medical profession tended to express its technical ideas in German or at least in Germanized Japanese. This is no longer necessary. The Japanese can now write medical textbooks in Japanese, having absorbed the medical vocabulary originally derived from the West, either in kana transcriptions or in character translations. Behind this achievement lie many decades of learning and institutional growth, involving the expansion of the Japanese medical profession, including the creation of medical schools dedicated to the training of Japanese students (and using the Japanese language) and the proliferation of hospitals on the practical side and of research institutes on the theoretical—all the foundation work, in other words, to make modern medicine an integral part of the Japanese technological world.

Of the many changes required of a traditional language system before it can serve its purpose in a modern state, one of the first involves the unification of the spoken and written styles. Although this came about with relative ease in Japan, we should not assume that the achievement was painless or effortless. In fact, if we follow the so-called *"gem-bun-itchi"* (unification of spoken and written systems) movement in Japan, we shall see that nearly half a century was required. Japan was fortunate in having an early start and an intellectual leadership which recognized the importance of a common language for vigorous national growth.

The language unification movement in Japan is sometimes dated from 1866, when Maejima Hisoka, the man who later became known for his reform of the Japanese postal system, proposed to the Shogun that Chinese characters should be abolished and written materials follow speech. When, half a century later, Shiga Naoya published the first part of his famous novel *An'ya kōro* (Road through the dark night), what might be called a pure colloquialized style, still literary in the sense that the discursiveness of everyday speech was avoided, was at last realized in fiction. The path between Maejima and Shiga was neither straight nor direct.

In the first years after Maejima's proposals, while there was fairly common agreement that language reform was necessary, there was little agreement on what should be done. Some felt that a colloquialized style should be expressed in romanization. Katō Hiroyuki, who later became president of Tokyo Imperial University, and Nishi Amane, a student of literature who had studied at Leiden University, advocated a rather high colloquial style. They wrote using the form *de gozaru* to express the verb "to be." Shimizu Usaburō used the form *de aru* in his translation of a work on chemistry, while Ueki Emori employed the polite form *-masu* in a work on human rights. Only certain newspapers, along with some women's and girls' magazines, tried a truly colloquialized style.

The years 1883–1889 were marked by massive influence from the West upon Japan. Pressing for agreement between speech and writing, Mozume Takami published his *Gem-bun-itchi* in 1886. The Kana-no-Kai (Kana Society) was formed to further the use of the kana in writing Japanese, and the Rōmajikai (Romanization Society) campaigned for the use of the alphabet. But it is among the novelists that we see how much progress was being made. Following the example set by the raconteurs of the day, Futabatei Shimei and Yamada Bimyō became the first writers of fiction to attempt a spoken-language style. Considering how closely all former writers, in narration and description, had followed the forms of the classical literary language, Futabatei's *Ukigumo* (The drifting clouds) was a milestone in the history of the effort to make writing sound like speech. But in the nationalistic half-decade between 1890 to 1894, culminating in the Sino-Japanese War, writers like Ozaki Kōyō and Kōda Rohan went back to the seventeenth century and took the novelist Ibara (Ihara) Saikaku for their model, thus combining elegant and popularized elements in their writing; Mori Ōgai attempted a combination of Japanese, Chinese, and westernized elements; and others tried a style based on the literal translation of European writing. Under these circumstances the movement to colloquialize writing made virtually no headway.

The next half-decade, from 1895 to 1899, found Ueda Kazutoshi, who had returned from a tour of study in Europe and was newly installed as professor of philology at Tokyo Imperial University, arguing strenuously for a colloquialized style using the standard language taught in the schools. The use of *de aru* gained ascendancy when Ozaki Kōyō's new novels, *Aobudō* (Green grapes) and *Tajō takon* (Endless feelings, endless regrets), won wide popular favor. And so, when during the first decade of the twentieth century European naturalism strongly influenced Japanese fiction, the absorption of a colloquialized style in fiction gained many converts. The spoken-language style was popularized by such leading literary men as Natsume Sōseki and Terada Torahiko. Moreover, the textbooks issued by the Ministry of Education in 1903–1904 employed the forms of the standard language in a colloquialized style, and compositions by schoolchildren, it was decreed, should follow the spoken language.

By the years 1910–1922 virtually every writer in Japan had turned to the colloquialized style. In addition to Natsume and Mori, numerous authors whose names are now well known—Nagai Kafū, Tanizaki Jun'-ichirō, Mushanokōji Saneatsu, Akutagawa Ryūnosuke, Kikuchi Kan—experimented with the new style. Mushanokōji in particular was successful in using the forms of everyday speech, Arishima Takeo adopted Western phrasing, and with the appearance of Shiga's *An'ya kōro* a truly concise colloquial style materialized for fiction. When, in 1922, the Tokyo *Asahi* and *Nichinichi* began to publish their editorials in the style of the spoken language, the new style had gained a major victory.

Yet the history of the adoption of colloquial language by the writers of fiction in Japan tells only a small portion of the story of the development of Japanese as a modern language. As in the medical profession, every aspect of Japanese life was obliged to pass through phases of some sort of tutelage when intellectual horizons and the accompanying terminology were expanded almost entirely in a foreign medium. Only gradually did the new vocabulary become domesticated, and the new structural forms necessary for the conveyance of new ideas take shape. To gain final acceptance and assimilation of these innovations required a complex and widespread interaction between the absorption of new ideas into the culture and the mass communication of new language forms and content. To achieve this goal required more than just the evolution of a colloquial style among novelists and journalists. The complex interplay of reforms in compulsory education, the effect of new textbooks, and the influence of military conscription and military training, of the spread of newspapers and popular journals, of the radio and cinema, and of travel abroad and visits from foreigners which lie behind the condition of the Japanese language today is beyond quantification. The Japanese language has been a major vehicle of modernization, but without the feverish activity of the Japanese people, dedicated to absorbing and domesticating the technological and ideological features of modern society, there would have been little incentive for language reform. The fact that language was an equal partner in modernization with many other aspects of Japanese culture is perhaps the outstanding characteristic of language in Japan during the past century.

JOSEPH K. YAMAGIWA

Literature and
Japanese Culture*

APPROACHES TO THE STUDY
OF JAPANESE LITERATURE

Japan's literature, no less than the literature of any other nation, is one of its most expressive products, for it reveals the sentiments and thoughts of its people and their attitudes toward their intellectual or aesthetic values. Japan today is one of the most literarily inclined countries in the world. The number of books published annually is second only to that in the Soviet Union, and the country far exceeds the United States in the number of new titles and in the total number of copies of books sold each year. Japan ranks high in the readership of its newspapers and journals and in almost any other index of national interest in the written word. The author, too, whether the strictly literary variety or the scholar-critic, occupies a prominent position in the eyes of the public. It is not at all unusual for one or more of the individuals with the highest annual incomes to be men of letters and not, as in the United States, actors or entertainers. Visitors to Japan may be amazed by the number of bookstores to be found even in small towns and, above all, by the large number of patrons who purchase books or stand for hours and browse without purchasing. Clearly the written word is highly prized, and reading an extremely popular pastime.

The study of the literature of a given people need not by any means be limited to the work of the literary specialist or critic. There is much in the total written or published output of a society which does not interest the specialist in literature. Such a person tends to leave to others the works of history or the essays on philosophical or religious subjects, and he is not likely to concern himself with the writings of the political economist, the polemicist, or the journalist. The field of literary study, in other words, has its particular interests and its accepted boundaries. And anyone whose primary concern with Japanese litera-

---

*The author wishes to acknowledge the assistance of Mr. Noah S. Brannen and Dr. Yoshio Iwamoto in the early stages of the preparation of this chapter. Critical suggestions by Prof. Donald Keene were also of great help.

ture is to gain some special insight into Japanese culture must be prepared to look beyond these traditional disciplinary boundaries. While of late members of the literary profession have followed many unusual lines of inquiry, for instance, into value preferences and reading habits, it is more common for them to confine their field of interest to subjects defined by the term *literature* itself.

But what is literature? The answer is not simply given. In fact, countless generations of writers in the West from Aristotle and Horace to such more recent poets and critics as Alexander Pope, William Wordsworth, Percy Shelley, T. S. Eliot, and I. A. Richards have debated the content of literature and the precise qualities which make a piece of writing literature rather than something else. A composite view of their thought does not assure us of a satisfactory definition, but it can surely help to identify the main qualities which have been looked for in literature by our best-known critics.

One of the most fundamental and distinguishing features of literature upon which these critics agree is that it employs a special kind and quality of language. While scientific language is, ideally speaking, *denotative*, aiming at an exact concordance and correspondence between the word and what it refers to, literary language is highly *connotative*. In literature, language itself is used creatively and imaginatively. Charged with nuances, associations, and memories of past usage, literary language conveys a richer load of feeling and emotion than does the language of science. It is not merely referential but has an expressive side, conveying the tone, attitude, and special sensitivities of the writer. Moreover, all kinds of rhetorical devices, such as meter, alliteration, patterns of sound, and inner contrasts and oppositions, as well as consistencies and harmonies of a subtle variety not found in straightforward expository writing, are used in the writing of literature. Language, then, employed with an emphasis on expressive form, especially evident in poetry but no less present in prose, is a major ingredient of literature. Literature, in other words, is an art which demands appreciation for these qualities as well as for the expository content of its writing.

Another distinguishing trait of literature, one which is closely related to the qualities of language referred to above, is its imaginative character, or what some critics have called its *fictionality* or *inventiveness*. The statements in novels, poems, or dramas are not literally true. They are not logical propositions and must be accepted by the reader in the spirit which Wordsworth called a "willing suspension of disbelief." However much literature may be drawn from real life, the time and place of a novel are not those of real life. Close scrutiny will reveal that even the most realistic novel, the very "slice of life" of the naturalist, is constructed according to certain artistic conventions which do violence to reality. Thus, a system of aesthetic values is implied, and a work of literature must demonstrate these values to merit acceptance.

A third feature of literature, particularly the kind which has been appreciated generation after generation, is its universality of theme which can appeal both emotionally and intellectually to readers separated by wide social, cultural, or historical distances. Literature is basically humanistic, and it extracts from the particular circumstance the qualities of the human condition which transcend the moment and touch the imaginations of successive generations. William Shakespeare and Johann Wolfgang von Goethe continue to attract their readers because they deal with basic problems, those of good and evil, truth and falsehood, which are as pertinent today as they were in the past. Universality of theme is an elusive literary quality, since few authors have expressed themselves consistently in masterful terms. Yet this quality is surely one which the critic is apt to look for in making his judgment of the "excellence" of a work of literature.

Literature, finally, is charged with emotion. This is perhaps most true of poetry, but emotion is not absent in fiction and drama. The very expressiveness of literary language implies emotionality. The power of literature is the capacity to speak through emotional rapport with the author as much as through the intellect. It is for this reason that literature provides a penetrating revelation of the feelings as well as the thoughts of a given writer and permits the most direct communication between writer and audience.

From the above it can be seen that literature must tend to confine itself to certain genres. Poetry of course is the most venerable receptacle of literary expression, but drama and prose, in the form of novels and essays, are equally respected media. The Japanese literary output is similar in its major genres to that of Western literature. Thus the genres themselves are easily compared. But this is less true of such matters as language, style, and content where great differences exist and comparisons become extremely difficult.

THE CULTURAL RELEVANCE OF JAPANESE LITERATURE

As we have noted, Japanese literature is not often studied primarily for what it reveals of Japan's culture and history. As an object of disciplinary specialization, it is studied in its own right for its intrinsic values. The main objective of studies of this kind is the description and analysis of literary works themselves. If literary scholars are concerned with the relationship of culture to the literary product, it is not so much for what literature reveals about the culture as the reverse. As to the relationship between culture and literature, these scholars are quite sharply divided between those who believe that a literary work should be studied on its own terms without reference to the cultural background of the author and those who believe that it is more satisfactory to move from the cultural environment to an analysis of the work of literature.

The first group of literary analysts, upholders of the *intrinsic* approach, believe that the study of literature should, first and foremost, concentrate on the work of art itself. Among the most articulate upholders of this belief have been the New Critics of the United States. Proponents of this approach agree that it is the form of a work that should be the proper focus of their study; they are united in ruling out of their consideration the data of historical period, social context, or biographical information concerning the author. On the contrary, their attention is focused on the analysis of diction, "key words," rhythm, meter, and other elements of style which emerge from the literary work itself. Such concern for the form and aesthetic content of individual works of literature has been helpful in directing attention to the historical literature of Japan as individual works of art and not merely as "the products of an age." The New Critics have urged the student to ask what it was that the author originally hoped to achieve and what it was that the original audience received from its reading. In other words, they have sought to focus attention upon the work of art in terms of its intrinsic value system, and this approach is of the utmost importance when a work of literature is a product of a foreign culture.

The other, and quite legitimate, approach to literature has been carried forward by the proponents of what we might call the *extrinsic* method of analysis. Such an approach seeks to study and interpret literature in the light of its social context and its antecedents, thus providing a causal explanation which professes to account for a piece of literature in terms of its historical and environmental origins. Scholars using this approach have varied from those who put primary stress upon the historical milieu or the social environment of the author to those who look for the main determining factors of literary creation in the biographical details of an author's life or in his psychology, the climate of ideas, secular or theological, of his age, or some quintessential spirit of his time. Such scholars have looked outside the work of art itself to find explanations as to how it came into being, why it was written, and what it means.

Both approaches are obviously useful to the student of Japanese culture if explanations of "meaning" of Japanese literature are taken as being indicative of certain qualities and conditions within the culture itself. The intrinsic approach permits us to inquire into what it was that the Japanese at any given time looked for in their literary creations and what the range of their sensibilities might have been. The extrinsic approach gives us certain clues to the relationship between cultural conditions and artistic achievement.

It is of course the latter approach which provides the most persistent and popular method of studying literature as the revelation of a culture, its values, and its goals. Assuming that "literature is an expression of society," and certainly one cannot totally deny that both the writer and his work are creations of a society in some specific period of history, some scholars have attempted to demonstrate how various pieces of literature or literary genres reflect certain characteristics of their times. Historians are especially prone to regard literature as a means of gaining direct access to the ideas and insights of a particular historical age. Thus, we find them claiming that the poems in the *Man'yōshū* (collected ca. 759) mirror the naïveté and the early exuberance of a developing aristocracy. The literature of the classical age which produced the famous *Genji monogatari* (after 1002) is believed to be closely linked to the real conditions of elegance and sophistication of life at the Imperial Court of Kyoto. Literary historians read into the products of the feudal age, particularly such works as the *Heike monogatari* or the nō drama, a spirit of pessimism occasioned by the civil conflicts and the waning influence of the court. They see in these works both a glorification of the life of the warrior and a religious sentiment expressing the impermanence of life. Literature of the Tokugawa period (1600–1868), particularly the works of Ibara (Ihara) Saikaku and Chikamatsu Monzaemon, is said to express the pleasure-seeking values of the newly prosperous merchant class, which for all its wealth was excluded from political influence. And finally the literature of the Meiji period (1868–1912), marked by a great diversity of types and sentiments, is explained as the product of a society in transition, struggling to resolve the conflict between traditional values and the challenge of Western ideas. Each such evaluation may well be overdrawn, but a given piece of literature is by its very nature to some extent a social document. In the study of Japanese culture, because of the inaccessibility of so much of the more technical material in the fields of philosophy or religious exegesis, literary works have tended to play a more important role for the non-Japanese intellectual or cultural historian. The editors of *Sources of Japanese Tradition* [1] have provided a glimpse of the variety of writings which lie in abundance for use by the intellectual historian once he can master the Japanese language. The religious essay, the historical tract, and the philosophical exposition are yet to be extensively used by Westerners as a means of inquiry into the Japanese historical mind.

To return to the problem of the relationship of a literature to its culture, literature not only can serve as a mirror of social values, mores, and ideas; it is also itself a source of influence upon society. Literary works are not necessarily the passive recipients of the stamp of a given age: they themselves help to form the intellectual or cultural climate. Individual literary works may be highly influential in molding group behavior or in influencing personal motivation. Evidence of this influence is abundant, especially in periods of mass readership. During the Tokugawa period, government censorship of certain types of literature, particularly the love-suicide plays, was motivated by the influence which these plays had upon popular morals. In modern times Marxist or Communist writers have produced novels and plays whose social and political messages have received wide acceptance.

The interrelationships between literature and culture are obviously manifold, and the task of the scholar who would assess literature both in its own terms and as a revelation of the society which produced it is most complex. This is particularly so when we as outsiders to Japanese culture attempt to assess the meaning of Japanese literature or to extract from it its social significance. In another sense, however, the outsider can bring to a study of Japanese literature certain qualities of judgment and evaluation which may prove useful. The comparative approach to a national literature is necessary if one is to rise above the level of parochialism in his critical judgments. Such an approach can broaden the reader's perspective and improve his understanding and

[1] Tsunoda Ryūsaku, William Theodore de Bary, and Donald Keene, *Sources of Japanese Tradition*, New York, 1958.

appreciation of the way literature manifests itself in a variety of cultures. Questions which have traditionally been asked by the students of one national literature can provide fresh lines of inquiry into another. The identification of marked differences between two literary traditions can set in motion a whole line of inquiry into the reasons why a culture has stressed one style of expression rather than another.

Perhaps the ultimate aim of a comparative approach to literature would be to devise a uniform set of criteria for classifying and judging all literatures. Yet, universal standards are extremely difficult to establish and to apply, and it is certainly too early to expect a full repertory of agreed-upon standards by which the critic can bridge the cultural differences between Europe and Japan. In practice, the Japanese critic still relies heavily upon his own systems of evaluation to judge his past literature, and conversely the Western critic is prone to view Japanese literature through eyes colored by moral and aesthetic expectations deriving from his own historical tradition. Thus it has taken nearly half a century to move from the highly tendentious approach of William George Aston, whose *History of Japanese Literature* was so critical of many of the more creative Japanese literary forms and whose appreciation of Japanese poetry or the classical nō drama proved so weak, to the present generation of men like Donald Keene, Edward G. Seidensticker, Howard S. Hibbett, and Robert H. Brower, who are able to interpret with great subtlety and sympathy the peculiarly Japanese elements in Japanese literature both past and present.

This new insight by Westerners into Japanese literature developed slowly and only after the appearance of an adequate number of competent translations from Japanese into the languages of the West. At the turn of the century, Aston, though he wrote a history of Japanese literature, nonetheless believed that what he wrote about was inconsequential as great literature. With Arthur Waley's translations of the nō drama (1921) and the *Genji monogatari* (1935), classical Japanese literature found its first real audience in Western countries.

Contributing to the recent interest in Japanese literature and the willingness to evaluate it as a major contribution to world literature has been what we might call a *changing aesthetic* both in world literature and in Japanese literature. At present the literary worlds of Japan and the West have coalesced in many ways and have been fused at a number of points. There has been a sharing between France and Japan of considerable importance. French impressionism found a parallel in the Japanese *haibun,* which was a wedding of the poetic qualities of the haiku and prose. Earl R. Miner has shown in *The Japanese Tradition in British and American Literature* the stimulus that Amy Lowell received from the haiku in *Pictures of the Floating World* and *What's o'Clock*. Ezra Pound was another poet affected by Japanese poetry. William Butler Yeats, one of the great dramatists of modern times, found inspiration in the nō drama, particularly its structural and technical aspects. And more recently, Western dramatists and movie producers such as Joshua Logan and Paul Green have responded enthusiastically to Japanese techniques and forms in their theatrical and cinematic presentations.

But perhaps the reverse current, the influence of Western literature on Japanese writers, is more readily apparent. The history of Japanese literature after 1868 is in many respects the story of Japanese response to Western influence on the form and content of literary expression. As translators rendered into Japanese the historical fiction and drama of Lord Lytton, Sir Walter Scott, and Shakespeare, the science fiction of Jules Verne, and the political novels of Benjamin Disraeli, Japanese writers quickly followed suit in their own manner. Tsubouchi Shōyō called for an intensification of realism, as opposed to the moralistic, comic, or decadent fiction that had been popular in Tokugawa Japan. Russian naturalism was introduced in the works of Futabatei Shimei. European romanticism caught the imagination of Japanese poets. Émile Zola, Gustave Flaubert, and Guy de Maupassant stimulated a Japanese brand of naturalism, all in the early decades following the Meiji Restoration.

Japanese literature today reflects all the reactions to realism found in the West: the psychological approach of Edith Wharton and Thornton Wilder; the Freudian interpretation typified by D. H. Lawrence; the neoromantic movement exemplified by Romain Rolland, Hermann Hesse, and Joseph Conrad; impressionism as exemplified by Marcel Proust; symbolism in its many forms, all have had their impact in Japan. As communication between West and East improved, each literary movement in Europe quickly had its counterpart in Japan. Yet at the same time we should recognize that both literatures were moving toward each other in spirit, and the passage back and forth across the oceans increasingly was weaving Japanese and Western literature into a single fabric.

Today, therefore, it has become more and more difficult to distinguish a distinctive Japanese literature from that of the West—if we ignore the difference in language. In the field of the novel, for instance, though a few modern writers (Tanizaki Jun'ichirō, Nagai Kafū, Mishima Yukio) have consciously dipped into their native literary heritage, many authors and critics feel that there is little or no connection between themselves and pre-Meiji literature. There are many reasons for this, including the desire to be "up to date," but the chief reason for the present alienation of the Japanese from their literary tradition lies in the nature of modern society. Japan's industrial modernization has been accompanied by a drastic change in ideas and mores, and aesthetic values in literature have consequently been affected by conditions similar to those which have conditioned Western literature. When a modern Japanese reads, say, Leo Tolstoy, he reads an author who has become in effect a part of his own tradition. In fact, it is probably easier for him to understand the problems of a young man growing up in contemporary Germany than those of a boy in eighteenth-century Edo. The younger generation in particular considers the literature of the world to be its own. The cliché that for many Japanese today the *Genji monogatari* is more easily understood in Arthur Waley's English translation than in the original is probably an exaggeration, but it nonetheless makes an important point. Speaking at the University of Michigan on "The Literary Climate in Japan Today," Mishima borrowed Goethe's phrase and, applying it to Japan, noted, "It is highly Asiatic for one to yearn for the West," and expanded this remark as follows:

> The mode of living in Japan today is a hopeless confusion of the East and West. One eats his bowl of rice on the tatami, wears his tie and coat, jams into the subway, and goes to his Le Corbusier supermodern office building. We all bear such confusion and even ignore it. If so, why shouldn't the novelist also express the same confusion in his works?

Modern Japanese literature may well have become thoroughly identified with the trends of world literature, so that its appreciation requires no great stretch of the imagination by readers alien to Japanese culture. Yet it retains its identity if only because it is written in its own language, a language which is peculiar to the Japanese people and hence confines the work of the Japanese writer to those familiar with his language. While the drama and the cinema sometimes rise above the necessity of using words, language is the sole medium by which literature per se can exist and be communicated to its audience. The peculiarities of the Japanese language, then, have exerted a constant influence upon Japanese literary expression, encouraging or accentuating certain types of expression and inhibiting others, and a knowledge of the language is an essential prelude to an accurate assessment of Japanese literature.

The outstanding historical fact about the Japanese language is that it has had to maintain itself in a world environment dominated by quite different languages. Both in ancient and in modern times, Japanese has been a minor language in a world dominated first by Chinese and then by English. Furthermore, in each situation the differences between Japanese and the dominant language were so great as to make fusion and assimilation extremely difficult.

Another historical fact of great importance is that the Japanese did not devise a system of writing prior to their adoption of the Chinese characters. Thus, early Japanese literature was oral and had to be handed down by word of mouth. The exact date of the introduction of Chinese writing is not known, though it may have been the beginning of the fifth century. The earliest extant Japanese literary work (written in Japanese sounds which were simulated by Chinese characters) is a chronicle known as the *Kojiki* (Record of ancient matters). It is said to have been set down from the oral tradition in the year 712. Though largely a collection of prosaic legends and myths, this work does show an embryonic urge of the Japanese to poetic expression. With the influx of Chinese culture and literature in the Nara period, however, the male members of the aristocracy in particular had begun to write in Chinese and even to write Chinese verse. Their poems, naturally, were stilted and showed the difficulty which the Japanese experienced in bridging the cultural distance with China. A collection called the *Kaifūsō*, compiled in 751, is the earliest monument to the Japanese effort to write Chinese poetry.

Since written Chinese was not a phonetic system, the Japanese were obliged to use Chinese characters as phonetic signs to record their own language. This technique, found in the *Kojiki*, was somewhat improved in the texts of the *Man'yōshū*. But the *Man'yō* style was altogether too unwieldy for easy use. Since the characters were employed in their original form, both as phonetic signs and for their full meaning, one was never sure of how to read a given line of poetry. A simpler means of writing was needed before a Japanese literature could develop. This requisite was met by the evolution of the kana, or syllabic script. Two varieties of kana were developed; one, the more angular variety, was known as *katakana*, and the other, more cursive, as *hiragana*. Each set contained forty-eight symbols derived by extreme abbreviation from an appropriate-sounding character. Although the Chinese language continued to be used, mainly by men in the transaction of governmental and official business, the writing of religious or philosophical treatises, and the creation of the stiffish Chinese poems, the hiragana in particular became the medium for a free-flowing native literature, consisting principally of fiction and diaries, composed most successfully by the women of the Heian Court.

The writings of the Heian period were in most respects a direct reflection of court speech, but in the Kamakura period, the language of literature went through a considerable revolution under Chinese influence. Since literature was written increasingly by priests and men trained in the Chinese tradition, the Chinese language began to infiltrate written Japanese, chiefly in the form of loan words. Eventually a literary style called *wakan konkōbun* (mixed Japanese-Chinese style) was developed; it was to persist as the major literary form until modern times. As this new style became more generally accepted, increasing numbers of Chinese words were borrowed, especially in the areas of philosophical and religious vocabulary.

The influence of this heavy borrowing from the Chinese language is difficult to assess. Aside from adding to the complication of the writing system, it affected the character of Japanese literature itself, causing the development of various literary forms distinguished by wide differences in style. Sinified Japanese was never suited to all literary genres or modes of expression, tending to be employed for expository purposes, so that a relatively pure Japanese style was retained, particularly for use in poetry and drama. So subtle and pervasive has been the influence of Chinese on the Japanese language, however, that certain syntactical elements considered to be a part of Japanese literary style in the pre-Meiji period represent direct borrowings from Chinese grammar.

After 1868, of course, the influence of European literary and educational concepts called for a prompt reintegration of the written and spoken languages. In literature the *gem-bun-itchi* movement called for the use of the vernacular as a literary language and received the support of most writers by the turn of the twentieth century. The greater agreement reached by the spoken and written languages in its turn helped to produce a new national literature. With the introduction of a colloquial style the novel came into its own again, and revolutionary changes resulted in poetry and drama. At the same time, however, Japanese found itself immersed in a world of European languages. The effects on literary style and content have already been mentioned. On the language itself the chief effects have been apparent in the number of loan words adopted (in their grotesque kana renderings), the many movements to abolish or simplify the kanji, and, more recently, the modification of Japanese syntax.

The course of development of the Japanese language has obviously had its effect upon Japanese literature. If language is an "ineffable constant element" in the literature, as Brower and Miner have suggested,[2] it is also a living and changing thing. Changes in literary style

2 Robert H. Brower and Earl R. Miner, "Formative Elements in the Japanese Poetic Tradition," *Journal of Asian Studies*, vol. 16, no. 4, p. 504, 1957.

accompany changes in language. Certain characteristics of the Japanese language must, in part at least, account for certain features of Japanese literature. For language is both brush and pigment to the writer, and the "quality of language" determines what best the writer can do with it. The five-seven-five-seven syllabic cadence of traditional Japanese poetry, for example, is intimately related to the syllabic structure of the language, in which words that are "native" (as opposed to those of Chinese origin) characteristically assume the consonant-vowel-consonant-vowel pattern and do not end in abrupt consonants. Thus, syllabic count becomes a most important structural feature of Japanese prosody, whereas in English poetry, in which stress is the decisive factor, it plays a less significant role. This CVCV pattern also lends qualities of assonance and sonorousness to Japanese poetry which are more pronounced than in English verse.

Japanese poetry has never developed rhyme. With the exception of loan words (especially from Chinese) ending in "syllabic" *n*, every Japanese word ends in one of the five vowels. Obviously, rhyme would become an unbearably monotonous device. On the other hand, the highly assonant nature of the syllables, coupled with modulations of pitch, produces a harmonic cadence of great gentleness that can best be compared to the liturgical chant of the synagogue or the cathedral. Since what is heard are differences in pitch rather than differences in stress or loudness, the syllables rise and fall as notes might in music.

An element of the syntax which obviously influences the character of Japanese poetry is the great number and frequency of use of particles: bound forms, usually of one or two syllables, which indicate relationships or emphasis. Particles of exclamation, so abundant in Japanese poetry and especially in the haiku, are the chagrin of the translator, who can usually come up with nothing more than a series of monotonous "ohs" and "ahs" and a few exclamation points.

The inflections of verbs, adjectives, and specifiers constitute another distinctive element of the Japanese language. Inflections remain in the modern language, but to the Western interpreter those of classical Japanese are joined with numerous inflected suffixes that express extremely subtle distinctions of mood. Thus, the translator finds that the forms *sumeri, sumitari, suminu, sumiki,* and *sumikeri,* all based on the verb *sumu* (to live), may each be rendered in the past or in the past perfect. Moreover, suffix can succeed suffix, as in *sumitarikeru* or *sumeri-shi.* With such a system of inflections, it is easily possible to compose an entire five- or seven-syllable line with a form based on a single verb.

Alliteration as a poetic technique was never widely exploited by the

Japanese poet. The reason is probably found in the highly assonant quality of the language, which would seem to make any conscious effort to reduplicate sound both superfluous and monotonous. It is only the rare poem that seems to make use of alliteration, although the device is found fairly often in the poetic parts of the drama.

Brower and Miner have pointed to Japanese substantives as a unique source of poetic imagery. At least in classical Japanese poetry, nouns representing such abstract qualities as "truth" and "beauty" did not exist. On the other hand, Japanese nouns came to have a "greater potential of nuance and connotation" than ours of the West; they are "incipiently literary images." [3] This is seen particularly in the semi-metaphoric use of place names, a device which is rarely employed in Western literature. Place names acquire poetic associations—imagistic suggestions and euphemistic qualities—which make them poetry to the Japanese. The problem of connotation is particularly complex, for each language tradition develops its own aura of connotation and association around particular words, phrases, and images. In Japan as in the West, words may evoke memories of both native and foreign (usually Chinese) usage.

Finally, Japanese language and literature contain usages and forms which reflect the peculiar features of Japanese society and mores. Particularly noticeable are the differences denoting social position, polite and abrupt forms, honorific and humble words, distinctions between men's and women's speech, and words denoting family relationships; all reveal a great subtlety of status distinctions which are less easily found in European languages.

CHARACTERISTICS OF JAPANESE LITERARY EXPRESSION

The determinants of the social and historical context and the peculiarities of language and usage have all had their effect upon Japanese literature, but is it possible to go farther in the search for distinctive features of Japanese literature? Are there, in other words, any broad and generalizable "characteristics" of Japanese literature? Are there perhaps some "constants" which run through Japanese literary history and are still identifiable in the highly westernized literature of the present day? These are difficult questions to ask of the literary critic, though he has not been reluctant to answer them if the tentative nature of his observations is assumed.

[3] *Ibid.*, p. 505.

The scene of the firefly hunt in Tanizaki's *Sasameyuki* may be used as a starting point:

This viewing of fireflies, certainly, was not like flower-viewing, something that satisfied the visual sense. Rather it was, she thought, something that forced one to meditate and at the same time was somewhat childish, taking the participants into the world of the fairy tale, a world which, perhaps, should be converted into music instead of into pictures. The feelings one experienced ought to be put into the music of the koto or piano. . . .

Here in a contemporary novel we can see preserved the elements of a literary tradition which predates the Meiji period. It is in fact reminiscent of similar scenes in the *Genji monogatari,* in which the author's intent is essentially aesthetic and little more. Note also the diffident attitude the author displays to time and its duration; the scene has almost no setting in time and no duration. The plot is not advanced by it nor retarded. There is no purpose, no meaning—nothing beyond the aesthetic enjoyment of the moment. Let us read further:

Sachiko had had no idea how far they would go before they would begin to make their journey back, for Kōsuke had said nothing of returning home, but when she inquired whether they shouldn't be turning back since the wind was becoming fresher, he replied that they were already on the road home; only, they were taking a different way from the one they had followed on the way out. Even so, since it was taking such a long time to return home, Sachiko realized that they had unconsciously gone a long way in their excursion. When, suddenly, she was told that they had finally reached home, she found herself at the back gate of the Sugano house. Each had in his hand a container with a number of fireflies, and Sachiko and Yukiko were keeping some of theirs in the sleeves of their garments.[4]

Here a third characteristic of Japanese literature appears in the particular use of imagery. Imagery is, of course, the property of all literary traditions, but in Japanese literature it seems to be based more firmly on a feeling of identity with nature than in the West, where nature is more often regarded as fearsome and antagonistic. The basis for the Japanese identification with nature may perhaps be found in the animistic impulses of Shinto or in the philosophy of Taoism imported from China. The special rapport which the Japanese poet feels with nature was intensified by the Buddhist concept of the oneness of all existence. Japanese imagery usually does not include the concrete personifications of Western literature, such as Shakespeare's "morn, in russet mantle

4 Book 3, Chapter 4; translation by the author.

clad," or Samuel Daniel's "Care-charmer Sleep, son of the sable Night."

Much of the Japanese literary tradition is concerned with the perpetuation of an imagistic vocabulary. To help the poet and reader to enter swiftly into an aesthetic appreciation of nature, there has been developed a particular use of symbols. Many of these can be described as nature symbols; both the *uguisu* (bush warbler) and the *ume* (plum blossom) herald the beginning of spring. As the tradition developed, the nature symbols became more subjective, coming to stand for certain human emotions and longings, mostly of love: the *hototogisu* (cuckoo) became the symbol of sadness or unrequited love, the *kari* (wild goose) represented sadness or longing, and pairs of *oshidori* (mandarin ducks) symbolized conjugal affection.

The influence of Buddhism brought another use of symbolism. Standing for the evanescence of life were *tsuyu* (dew), *awa* (foam on the water), and *sakura* (cherry blossoms). All of these, lovely as they are, last but a moment in time, and then they are no more. A particularly touching expression of this type of symbolism is illustrated in the following haiku:

Asagao ni	In the morning glory
Kyō wa miyuran	Shall I perhaps see
Waga yo kana.	My life today.

But even in such a use of symbolism there is no indication that the poet was looking for metaphorical or allegorical meaning. Symbols in Japanese poetry are an aesthetic rather than a philosophic medium. They serve to give poetic intensity and verbal economy to poetry. To quote Brower and Miner:

> Japanese poems often exist as descriptive lyrics of single expressions and are quite satisfactory artistic wholes, without the necessity for the private meaning conveyed, say, as a message of love. Western allegory is usually monolithic —without the meaning of the metaphor, there is little significance to the poem; Japanese allegory, on the other hand, is often Janus-headed, with one preoccupied face turned toward the images of the natural scene and with the other giving a knowing wink to some dear girl or fellow priest.[5]

Perhaps the most obvious "constant" in Japanese poetry is the alternation of lines containing five and seven syllables. Through examination of the poems preserved in the *Kojiki, Man'yōshū,* and *Kokinshū,* we are able to determine something of the way in which this poetic alternation became established. It appears that the earliest Japanese poetry

[5] Brower and Miner, *op. cit.,* p. 513.

contained a varying number of syllables per line. After a long period of development, the poetry finally began to show a preference for the alternation of five syllables and seven. The use of a terminal seven-syllable line came even later. In the *Man'yōshū*, some of the *chōka*, or "long poems," run to as many as 150 lines. The use of *hanka* (envois) as a kind of refrain at the end of the *chōka* probably helped to establish the form later called the tanka, for the *hanka* were identical in form with the tanka, a "short poem" of thirty-one syllables, with five lines containing five, seven, five, seven, and seven syllables, respectively.

To many critics it is the seventeen-syllable haiku, with the lines running five, seven, and five syllables, which best sums up the distinctive character of Japanese literature. "The *haiku* element," as Yasuda calls it in *The Japanese Haiku*,[6] is something uniquely Japanese. Included in this concept are the obvious insistence on form, the aesthetic identification with nature, and the particular use of imagery which characterize Japanese poetry. This element can be seen too in prose, notably in such writings as the *Oku no hosomichi* by Matsuo Bachō, the novels of Ihara Saikaku and Natsume Sōseki, and the modern novels of Kawabata Yasunari. It represents the quality of subjective identification with nature—a peculiar balance between loss of personal identity and subjective interpretation. It stands for a lyric (as opposed to a symphonic) development of the theme, but one in which small graphic details are curiously joined with an imaginative suggestiveness, as in a *suiboku*, or black-and-white painting. It insists upon brevity of statement, whether in a seventeen-syllable poem or in a short novel.

PROBLEMS OF TRANSLATION INTO ENGLISH

Most of the nuances of Japanese literature which we have just identified must be perceived in the original to be fully appreciated. Since the Western reader's encounter with Japanese literature will occur through the medium of translation, his view will, at best, be an oblique one. The Japanese language is particularly difficult to translate into English without considerable loss. Fortunately, translations from the Japanese have improved greatly over the efforts of fifty or more years ago. For example, the translations of the tanka made by Arthur Waley and Sakanishi Shio are far superior to those of F. V. Dickins, who, in attempting to convey all the overtones of the originals, translated each tanka into an eight-line stanza containing four rhyming iambic-pentameter couplets!

6 Kenneth (Shōson) Yasuda, *The Japanese Haiku*, Tokyo and Rutland, Vt., 1957, pp. 54–60.

The lucid renderings of modern prose and drama by Keene, Hibbett, Seidensticker, and Ivan I. Morris account in large measure for the popularity of such authors as Tanizaki and Mishima in the West today.

The difficulty of translating Japanese into English, however, is almost superhuman. Two languages could hardly differ more widely even on the purely mechanical plane. To take a simple illustration, the Japanese sentence *Ano kado / ni / tatte iru / hito / ni / kikimashō*, if rendered word for word, would run "That corner / on / is standing / the / person / of / let us ask." In a smooth English translation, it would be "Let's ask the person standing on that corner." In other words, the order is almost completely reversed in the process of translation.

Little wonder, then, that word-for-word correspondence between the two languages is seldom possible. With languages so different in syntax and vocabulary it often happens that Japanese words must be omitted from a sentence if the translation is to sound like English. For example, one would never think of translating *Okāsan no tokoro e kite* as "Come to Mother's place," even though the word *tokoro*, meaning "place," is in the original. The sentence simply means "Come to Mother!" and whether it is affectionately or sharply spoken depends on the tone of voice. Conversely, an accurate translation of Japanese at times requires the inclusion of several English words for which there are no corresponding words in the original; that is to say, paraphrasing is required. If meaning is difficult to capture accurately in translation, the problem of the portrayal of style is even more difficult, for here the translator must constantly choose between faithfulness to the language of the original and deference to the language of the translation. And beyond this, how is one to achieve in the translation of a Japanese poem the lyricism and euphonic effects of the original? Like a black-and-white reproduction of a painting in color, a translation into English from Japanese can achieve a semblance of success only when the original has a limited color range.

What are some of the chief difficulties faced by translators of Japanese literature? There is of course the matter of vocabulary. Japanese abounds in honorific terms and forms for which there are no English equivalents. What about the Japanese reticence in the use of personal pronouns, which constantly requires the translator to substitute names and articles? Japanese has an extremely rich vocabulary on some subjects (such as the variety of teas, for which the single prosaic word "tea" must suffice) and a limited choice of words on others (such as Western clothing, which usually comes out *yōfuku* in Japanese). Thus the "literal" or the "explanatory" translation becomes heavy and unnatural, and the smooth translation is often inaccurate. When the English vocabulary is deficient, adjectives and descriptive phrases invariably are required in the English renderings to bring out the full meanings.

The problem of "word overtones" occasions yet another difficulty. Words with particular connotations for the Japanese reader may express nothing or something quite different to the reader of the English version. The cuckoo (*hototogisu*), for instance, is a favorite subject of Japanese poetry, but unfortunate connotations of the word in English have caused the translator considerable difficulty. Such flower names as *sakura* (cherry blossom), a symbol of the warrior's spirit, *ume* (plum blossom), the first sign of spring and the symbol of burgeoning love, and *asagao* (morning glory), the emblem of things transient, do not have the same evocative powers and meanings for Japanese and English readers, let alone the range of erotic or vulgar word plays.

A special problem which arises in translating classical Japanese poetry into English is the rather high frequency of certain rhetorical devices. One of these is the *makura-kotoba,* or "pillow word," a term used to describe words which have evolved in the poetic tradition in a qualifying relationship to other words. Thus, *chihayaburu,* meaning "thousand-swift-brandishing," became a fixed epithet for the Shinto gods; the word *kusa-makura* (grass pillow) came to modify *tabi* (travel); and so on. These pillow words were used partly for their rhythmical value, but they carried important overtones of meaning. They were employed with great frequency in the early poetry: about 130 can be identified in literature prior to the eighth century; 500 are found in the *Man'yōshū*; and 300 in the second great classical anthology, the *Kokinshū*, compiled in the first years of the tenth century.

How is one to render a satisfactory translation of such a poem as the following from the *Man'yōshū*, in which the pillow words are enclosed in parentheses?

(*Umasake*) *Miwa no yama*	Mount Miwa (reminding one of fine sweet wine)—
(*Aoniyoshi*) *Nara no yama no*	Between the mountains of the Nara mountains
Yama no ma ni . . .	(Reminding one of green and red oak leaves) . . .

Here we have two place names, Miwa and Nara, each preceded by the traditional pillow word which is always associated with them. The pillow words in this poem are not entirely descriptive, but neither can it be said that they are entirely meaningless. In the case of Miwa, the pillow word *umasake* is related to the literal significance of another word, *miwa*, which means "royal sacrificial rice wine." And, because the place name Miwa by accident was homophonous with the sacrificial wine *miwa*, *umasake* became its special pillow word. Obviously the literal sense is not important. The association of the pillow word *aoniyoshi* with Nara is explained differently. A kind of oak tree peculiar to Nara became so closely identified with the city that it was given the name *nara*. The leaves of this tree are said to be a distinctive combination of red and green. *Aoni* means "green-red." The next two syllables of the pillow word, *yoshi*, are to be taken as particles of emphasis (they are also included, no doubt, for rhythmic purposes). Thus, *aoniyoshi* was fixed as the special pillow word for Nara. Of course such a complicated explanation could never be included in the translation of a poem. The elaborately interpretive translation may squeeze every drop of meaning from the original, but the result is certainly not "literature." Such efforts have been of use chiefly for the advanced student of the literature or the language.

Another poetic device is the *jo*, or "introduction," a phrase from one or two to several lines long that serves to modify the immediately following word. The *jo*, however, bears no really intimate relation to the meaning of a poem as a whole. Rather, its meaning is limited to the word that is modified. To cite an example:

Ashibiki no	Long
oshidori no o no	As the tail of the mandarin ducks
nagaki . . .	Which drag their feet . . .

Here the first two lines, translated "as the tail of the mandarin ducks which drag their feet," merely modify the following word *nagaki* (long) and serve no other purpose than to "introduce" this word. It is to be noted that *ashibiki no* (which drag their feet) is a pillow word applicable more frequently to mountains.

Still another poetic device is the *kake-kotoba*, or "pivot word," a sort of pun in which a single sequence of syllables is made to pivot from one meaning to another in the course of a sentence. A crude example in English might be:

In the snow
Neither the footprint of the doe
Nor the *bear*-est trace
Of passers to and fro . . .

It is obvious from this example how ludicrous any attempt to incorporate *kake-kotoba* in a translated poem would become. The rendering of a pivot word usually requires a double translation, as in the following example: [7]

Shirazarishi	More than in the days of yore
Inishie yori mo	When I knew you not
Aoyagi no	Oh, green willow threads
	more than ever
Itodo zo kesa wa	This morning are my thoughts
Omoi midaruru.	Entangled.

In this poem the syllables *ito* in *itodo* mean "threads," but they participate at the same time in the word *itodo*, meaning "more than ever." We are thus obliged to render them twice. Also, *aoyagi no*, meaning "which is [reminiscent of] green willows," is used as a pillow word for *ito*, and the term *midaruru* (to be entangled) turns out to be an *engo*, or "associated word," called to mind and used because the word *ito* (threads) has been used.

Although the subject matter of a poem must necessarily delimit the range of vocabulary which is employed within it, the Japanese poet, like his counterpart in other literatures, has sought to exploit the full range of associations and connotations emanating from the words used early in a poem. Perhaps there is nothing especially Japanese about the deft use of associated words to give added meaning to all the words used in a poem, but the concern with such words suggests that Japanese poets, at least in classical times, were particularly sensitive to diction. The poem that we have quoted above contains three of the devices found frequently in Japanese poetry.

Beyond these technical and mechanical difficulties of translation what is one to do with the subtleties of rhythm, word color, and shades of difference expressed in the original through the choice of different particles? Some translators have attempted to simulate the rhythms of Japanese poetry with varying degrees of success. Yasuda in *The Japanese Haiku* and *A Pepper-pod* not only preserves the five-seven-five syllabic structure of the haiku but even considers it to be the most fundamental of poetic rhythms, equally applicable to the English language. Compare his translation of a haiku of Bashō with an original English "haiku" of his own creation called "Crimson Dragonfly." [8]

[7] Edwin O. Reischauer and Joseph K. Yamagiwa (trs.), *Tsutsumi chūnagon monogatari*, p. 172.
[8] Kenneth (Shōson) Yasuda, *A Pepper-pod*, New York, 1957, pp. 110 and 111.

Shizukasa ya	How silent and still!
Iwa ni shimiiru	Into the heart of rocks sinks
Semi no koe.	The cicada's shrill.

Crimson dragonfly,
As it lights, sways together
With the leaf of rye.

The tribulations of the translator of Japanese literature into English could be expounded at much greater length, but the magnitude of the problem is apparent. Literature can speak directly from author to reader. In translation, however, the author must depend upon his interpreter and is at the mercy of the inadequate fit between two languages. It is for this reason perhaps that it is in the longer prose pieces, the stories, novels, and plays, where the overall effect can accumulate, that the rendition of substance and sentiment has best been achieved and the Japanese writer has most successfully communicated with the Western reader.

PERIODS OF JAPANESE LITERARY DEVELOPMENT: GENRES AND REPRESENTATIVE WORKS

Since Haga Yaichi published his history of Japanese literature (*Kokubungakushi jikkō*) in 1900, most literary historians have adopted his system of dividing Japanese literary history into five periods. These follow rather closely the periodization found in Chapter 3, "The Historical Dimension," except for the duration of the earliest stage of literary development. Haga's periods, which we adopt in this section, are as follows:

1. The archaic period, to A.D. 794
2. The classical age, from 794 to 1186
3. The medieval age, from 1186 to 1600
4. The early modern age, from 1600 to 1868
5. The modern age, from 1868 to the present

The Archaic Period: To A.D. 794

The origins of Japanese literature are obscured by the failure of the early Japanese to devise a system of writing. For many centuries the poetical, historical, and religious expressions of the Japanese people were perpetuated as an oral tradition and hence were subject to the anonymity of the reciter. The introduction of Chinese writing, though it ultimately provided a means of writing Japanese, proved to be difficult to assimilate and for many years represented a literary and intellectual tradition which competed with Japanese. The Chinese characters were not suited to the recording of the Japanese language. Hence it tended, like medieval Latin, to retain its identity, serving as a carrier of Chinese thought and Buddhist doctrine. The literate Japanese was for centuries chiefly Chinese-educated. But gradually, by the phonetic use of Chinese characters, compilations which represented the final deposits of the oral tradition were written down.

Composed in Japanese were the *Semmyō* (Imperial proclamations) and *Norito* (Shinto prayers of thanksgiving and imprecation), both of which reveal the close relationship between ritualism and statecraft practiced by the early Yamato chieftains. Historical or local records liberally filled with myth and legend are found in the *Fūdoki*; these were collected by provincial officials and presented to the central government in the first half of the eighth century. At about the same time appeared the *Kojiki* (Record of ancient matters), which is the earliest collection of Japanese myths, legends, historical stories, and genealogies centered in the Imperial House. Covering the period from the supposed creation of the world through the year 627, it offers highly valuable materials to students of the ancient Japanese language, history, and folklore. It also contains some of the earliest Japanese poetic efforts. The *Nihon shoki* (Chronicle of Japan), compiled in 720, covers Japanese history from its beginning to 697. Written in Chinese, it is less revealing of the native literary style, though the content is in most respects entirely Japanese.

The outstanding literary product of the archaic period is the *Man'-yōshū*, an anthology of poetry of strictly Japanese authorship and inspiration. Covering some 350 years of poetic writing and a wide variety of subject matter treated by at least 450 different authors, it contains a total of 4,516 poems. Somewhat comparable to the *Book of Odes* in the Chinese tradition, it attempts to draw on the poetry of "the common people" as well as that of the nobility. The collection represents a high point in ancient Japanese lyricism. By contrast to the later, more restrained poetry of the classical period, the *Man'yōshū* ranges widely in style and subject matter, including feast songs; poems on travel, nature, love, and the evanescence of life; poems expressing patriotism and pride in noble lineage; narrative poems; and, occasionally, derisive poems. The verses display a direct and frank approach to the experiences of life and tell of the joy, love, grief, and indignation felt by a relatively unrestrained people. The forms employed include many examples of the thirty-one-syllable tanka; some 262 long *chōka*; and a few *sedōka*, or "head-turning poems," consisting of two parts, each with the five-seven-seven syllabic pattern and usually representing some sort of exchange, often a question and an answer, between two poets.

The outstanding poet of the *Man'yōshū* is Kakinomoto-no-Hitomaro (end of the seventh to the early eighth century), a kind of poet laureate who excelled in both the *chōka* and the tanka. His work included love poems, hymns of praise, and travel poems, but it was for his elegies written upon the death of members of the Imperial Family that he became most famous. His poems display a deeply emotional fusion of nature and man; the grandeur and magnitude of the ocean are blended with the naïve yet passionate feeling of lovers in such a poem as the following:

> Like the swaying sea tangle,
> Unresisting would she lie beside me—
> My wife whom I love with a love
> Deep as the *miru*-growing ocean.

> (Nippon Gakujutsu Shinkōkai, tr.)

In contrast to the *Man'yōshū* is the *Kaifūsō* (Remembrance of things past, 751), a collection of Chinese poems composed in lines of five or seven Chinese characters each. Imitative of Chinese verse, these poems are stiff and formal and are often concerned with subjects alien to Japanese experience. The *Kaifūsō* may demonstrate a high state of literacy among the Japanese nobility of the time, but it is also indicative of the hold of the Chinese tradition over the Japanese with scholarly aspirations. Chinese verse maintained its popularity with the courtiers of the following Heian period and had its writers throughout Japanese history.

Notable because they became an ingredient of later Japanese drama are the rites of the Shinto shrines. The *kagura*, the oldest form of shrine dance, was traditionally considered to have been handed down from the antics performed before the cave in which the Sun Goddess is said to have hidden herself. Another form of ritual dance, the *gigaku*, was imported from the continent in about the seventh century A.D., as part of Buddhist ceremonial. Characterized by the use of enormous masks, the dance was accompanied by a three-piece orchestra of flute, hand drum, and cymbals. The *bugaku* (dance music) was also imported from the continent in the seventh century, as a ritual court dance. Two forms —the *samai* and the *umai*—came to Japan, the former supposedly from India through China, the latter from Korea. Virile and bold, these dances require long, vigorous steps accompanied by stately changes in posture. They survive in the *gagaku* performances at the Imperial Palace today.

The Classical Age: From 794 to 1186

Two noteworthy events presaged the flowering of Japanese literature during its classical age: first, the transfer of the court to the new capital of Heian; and second, the development of a simple method for the writing of the Japanese language in the perfection of the kana syllabary. There was a gradual assimilation of Chinese words into the native vocabulary but no heavy borrowing as in later periods. The cultivation of elegance, refinement, and grace which so obsessed the court nobility was reflected in the literature. The dominant genres of the native literature were *monogatari* (tales), *nikki* (diaries), and poetry, and though there were both men and women writers of note, the men tended to be restricted to their governmental pursuits and to the composition of stilted, formal poetry in Chinese. Thus, it was the women who were free to experiment with the more versatile kana script.

The fullest development of the romantic *monogatari* form is found in the *Genji monogatari* (*The Tale of Genji*, ca. 1002–ca. 1019). This great work is distinguished not only as the masterpiece of classical Japanese fiction, but as perhaps the earliest "novel" of world literature. The author, Murasaki Shikibu, was lady-in-waiting at the court of an Empress. The novel itself, which is of great complexity and magnitude, deals mainly with the amorous attachments of Prince Genji, the son of an Emperor by a consort of inferior rank. It has been made available to readers of English in the superb translation of Waley. Although some may find the recounting of Genji's many love affairs monotonous, the novel is consciously written to provide a subtle variety within its unifying structure. Each of the ladies with whom Genji becomes involved possesses a distinct personality which sets the mood of the chapters in which she appears.

Other tales treating romantic subject matter appeared both before and after the *Genji*. The *Sagoromo monogatari* (ca. 1055), written by an unknown author and modeled on the *Genji*, deals with the love affairs of a commander of the guards. Compared with the *Genji monogatari,* it has a pedestrian quality. The *Ochikubo monogatari* (Tale of a sunken room), written about 980, describes court life with considerable realism in the telling of a Cinderella story.

Legendary tales were also a favorite theme of Japanese classical writers. The *Taketori monogatari* (Tale of a bamboo cutter), a simply written fantasy, is one of the earliest of the *monogatari*. Written in the ninth century, it is the story of a divine maiden, found in a bamboo stem, who brought renown to a bamboo cutter but resisted the attentions of the young nobles of the country to return to the moon. The *Utsubo monogatari* (Tale of a hollow tree), written about 970 by an unknown author, deals with the adventures of a man who journeys to Persia and returns to Kyoto with a magical koto (zither). His grandson, found living in a hollow tree, wins fame and position as a musician of extraordinary skill.

Another variety of *monogatari* could hardly be classed as novels; they consisted of short lyrical tales which served as vehicles for the presentation of poetry. Exemplifying this style are the *Ise monogatari* (Tales of Ise, ca. 880) and the *Yamato monogatari* (Tales of Yamato, ca. 970). The former describes a series of amorous incidents mainly in the life of the hero and poet Arihara-no-Narihira, each featuring one or more tanka; the incidents are loosely joined to the story of a trip Narihira makes from the Heian capital to the grand shrines at Ise. The latter is a disjointed collection of stories set in a variety of locales and written in a loose style.

The *nikki* and the *zuihitsu* (miscellany) flourished as more casual literary forms during this period. The development of these two genres is due mainly to the fact that the peace and luxury of the Heian period afforded court writers sufficient leisure to reflect upon their personal experiences and the daily events of the narrow circle in which they were participants. Of the diaries and miscellanies, those written by women who served at the Heian Court have proved the most interesting to later audiences, but it should be remembered that the male courtiers also wrote diaries of a more serious nature, often of great historical value. Belonging to the genre of *nikki* are the *Tosa nikki* (Tosa diary, 935), by the poet Ki-no-Tsurayuki; the *Sarashina nikki* (Sarashina diary, 1059–1060), by the daughter of Sugawara-no-Takasue, who traveled from Sarashina in Shinano Province to Heian and became a lady-in-waiting at the Imperial Court; the *Kagerō nikki* (Gossamer diary, 990), by the wife of Fujiwara-no-Kaneie; the *Murasaki Shikibu nikki* (978–1015), by the author of the *Genji monogatari*; and the diary of Izumi Shikibu, a poetess at the Heian Court. The miscellany is best represented by the *Makura no sōshi* (Pillow book, about 1002), in which the author, Sei Shōnagon, comments with wit and humor on the life of the aristocracy. This work ranks with the *Genji monogatari* as one of the two great masterpieces of the classic age of Japanese literature. Together with the *Genji*, it serves as a lively source of information on courtly life during the Fujiwara period. But it is the style and good nature with which Sei Shōnagon describes a "tiresome lover" who gets up in the morning, searching for his belongings in a clumsy way, or the difficulty the court ladies had in composing poems after an outing to hear the cuckoo, that distinguish her as a writer.

Toward the end of the eleventh century male writers (priests or courtiers) began to write historical accounts in the *monogatari* style. The *Eiga monogatari* (Tale of glory, ca. 1092) and the series of *kagami* or "mirrors"—the *Ōkagami* (Great mirror, ca. 1200), *Imakagami* (Present mirror, ca. 1170), *Masukagami* (Clear mirror, ca. 1332), and *Mizukagami* (Water mirror, ca. 1171)—are all mainly historical tales. In these narratives the description of events is often accompanied by the writers' criticism of events and characters.

The poetry of the classical period is known chiefly through the *Kokinshū*, an imperial anthology of 1,111 poems compiled in 905. These poems are generally more refined but also more limited in their emotional impact than those in the *Man'yōshū*. The subjects are as varied, but there is a formality reflected in the highly studied style. The greater use of puns (*kake-kotoba*) and associated words (*engo*) adds to the artificiality. While the moon in the *Man'yōshū* is a cheerful sight (as in the poems of Akahito), to the writers of the *Kokinshū* it is often a symbol of sorrow. Buddhist influence is felt in the pessimistic attitude toward life, yet there is still little real religious sentiment. The tanka by this time has become a polished poetic form, and the *chōka* is less frequently resorted to. Thus the range of emotional expression has been narrowed, and the expression itself has become more polished. The preface to the *Kokinshū*, written by the chief compiler, Ki-no-Tsurayuki, author of the *Tosa nikki,* mentions by name six great poets of the period whose works are found in the anthology. Of these, Arihara-no-Narihira (825–880), hero of the *Ise monogatari,* Ono-no-Komachi (ninth century), and the priest Henjō (816–890) are the most important. Narihira shows exceptional technical skill in his poems of love and nature, treating these subjects in an impersonal, lyric mood which has characterized much of Japanese literature down to this day:

Tsuki ya aranu	Is there no moon?
Haru ya mukashi no	Can it be this spring is not the same
Haru naranu	As that remembered spring?
Waga mi hitotsu wa	And this alone, my mortal body,
Moto no mi ni shite.	Remains as ever without change? [9]

The Medieval Age: From 1186 to 1600

With the ascendancy of the provincial military aristocracy (the *bushi* or samurai) a new dimension was added to Japanese life. Both Nara and

[9] Brower and Miner, *op. cit.,* p. 525.

Heian declined as cultural centers, while the Buddhist monasteries and provincial headquarters of military families provided refuge and patronage for the arts and letters. Buddhism also reached a deeper level of the Japanese consciousness through the faith expressed in Amidism, the asceticism of Zen, and the militant attitudes of the Nichiren sect. Literature of the early medieval age reflects both the passing of court society and the new values of the military man. Many authors express a nostalgia for the elegance of the past and a pessimism concerning the present. At the same time, the war tales of the day fed the interest of the *bushi* in the exploits of their ancestors.

In the early medieval age, most literature was written by people who had renounced the world and sought the solace of a life of retirement from social and political upheavals. If the literature of the preceding period was essentially the work of women, that of this period was by and large the work of priests. Their writings are infused with an otherworldly mood, concerned as they are with the transience of earthly things. The language also was changing, for the priests were thoroughly familiar with Chinese. Thus the old dichotomy between the native language and Chinese became less pronounced, as Chinese words were increasingly assimilated into the Japanese language.

The *gunki monogatari* (war tales) which became popular in the Kamakura period reflect not only the interests of the *bushi*, but also the sentiments of the priesthood, which wove its didactic lessons into epic tales of battle and intrigue. The most remarkable work in this genre is the *Heike monogatari* (Tales of the Heike, early thirteenth century), which covers the years from 1132 to 1213, dwelling especially on the collapse of the Taira house as it faced the Minamoto during the years 1177–1185. Used for recitation by players of the biwa (a four-stringed lutelike instrument), the *Heike monogatari* has come down to us in many variant texts. The work is episodic, with the thread of the great civil war and the refrain of lament over the decline of the Taira elite knitting the fabric together. The *Heike monogatari* has provided a storehouse of plots for subsequent Japanese literature, from the nō drama of the fourteenth century to Akutagawa Ryūnosuke and Yoshikawa Eiji in the twentieth century. The stories of Kesa and Moritō, the exile of Mongaku, the death of Atsumori, and the drowning of the child Emperor Antoku are among the riches of this Japanese classic. Other war tales include the *Hōgen monogatari,* dealing with the wars of the Hōgen period (1156); the *Heiji monogatari,* telling of the wars of the Heiji period (1159–1160), in which the Taira defeated the Minamoto; and the *Gempei seisuiki* (Record of the rise and fall of the Minamoto and Taira, ca. 1247). The latter, a variant of the *Heike monogatari*, also narrates the struggle between the Taira and Minamoto houses but with less literary interest. The last of the true war tales, ironically named *Taiheiki* (Record of the great peace, 1370), is an embellished political history and account of battles fought between 1318 and 1367. It tells of the rise and fall of the Emperor Go-Daigo and the rise of the Ashikaga house.

The influence of Buddhism, with its emphasis on renunciation and didacticism, is reflected in the *Uji shūi monogatari* (Gleanings at Uji, late twelfth century), a collection of some 194 tales, including Buddhist moral tales, humorous anecdotes, and traditional fairy stories. The *Jikkinshō* (Selection of ten teachings, 1252) contains stories illustrating ten moral principles drawn from Buddhism. The literary activity of the Buddhist priests also extended to writing such miscellanies as the *Hōjōki* (Ten-foot-square hut, 1212) and the *Tsurezuregusa* (Idle jottings, 1331). In the *Hōjōki*, written by a retired priest, Kamo-no-Chōmei, the tone is pessimistic; the author describes natural calamities which beset the capital at Heian, his absorption in nature, life in his ten-foot-square hut, and his meditations on the transience of all things. The *Tsurezuregusa*, written by Yoshida-no-Kenkō, a celebrated poet and court official who became a Buddhist monk and went into retirement, is a collection in 243 sections which range in length from a few lines to three or four pages. It covers a variety of subjects, from architecture to a gentleman's tastes. Tinged with melancholy, it is filled with worldly wisdom.

The *otogizōshi* (fourteenth to seventeenth centuries) are short and often fantastic adventure stories, sometimes of the nature of fairy tales. When read aloud they appear to have been rendered in a chant. An example is *Sannin hōshi* (Three priests, sixteenth century), in which three priests decide to explain what made them abandon the world. It turns out that the stories which two of the priests have to tell bear a close relation to each other, for it is the lady loved by one of them (who had once been a samurai) who is slain by the second (who had been a robber). But the first priest bears no ill will toward the second, since in his view it was karma that drew them together and made them both priests. A diary entitled *Izayoi nikki* (Diary of the waning moon, 1280) by Abutsu-ni, a court lady turned nun, describes with feminine warmth and delicacy the journey that took her to Kamakura to contest the seizure by her stepson of a manor, left to her by her husband, which she believed should pass to her own son.

In the realm of poetry, this period offers several collections of tanka which follow the style perfected during the preceding age. Yet there is a change of mood, for the pessimistic tone of Buddhism has thoroughly permeated the verses. The outstanding collection of poetry of the thirteenth century is the *Shinkokinshū* (New collection of poems ancient and modern). If the influence of Buddhism is hardly noticeable in the *Man'yōshū* and manifested in a conscious but superficial fashion in the *Kokinshū*, it is deeply and widely apparent in the *Shinkokinshū*. The mystical and philosophical teachings of the revived Tendai sect are particularly evident, for Tendai continued to be popular in court circles. The influence of Chinese poetry, especially of the T'ang poet Po Chü-i, is also visible. Among the outstanding contributors to the *Shinkokinshū* were two courtiers, Fujiwara-no-Shunzei (Toshinari), who lived from 1114 to 1204, and his son Fujiwara-no-Teika (Sadaie), who lived from 1162 to 1241; the latter was mainly responsible for the compilation of the anthology. Shunzei's style reflects the melancholy and loneliness of the Buddhist believer of his day. These qualities produced a peculiar state of mind that is described by the Japanese term *yūgen*, the "mystic profundity" that comes from contemplation of the secrets of the universe.

Another great poet of the period was the priest Saigyō, whose 1,571 poems in tanka form are collected in the *Sankashū* (ca. 1190). Saigyō was a courtier who renounced the world, left his wife and possessions, and spent his life traveling about Japan viewing beauty spots and composing poetry about them. His pattern of life set the example for later poets, particularly Bashō. As a poet who wrote of man in nature, Saigyō contrasts with Teika and Shunzei, whose chief preoccupation was to reflect a vast scene in a small incident. Saigyō experienced and expressed the feeling of man for deserted or unspoiled nature. Having taken the tonsure, his eye saw with a religious allusion, as in this poem:

Kokoro naki	Even for someone
Mi ni mo aware wa	Free of passions, such sadness
Shirarekeri	Can be known—
Shigi tatsu sawa no	Evening in autumn
Aki no yūgure.	Where a snipe rises out of the marsh.

Although the tanka continued to be the chief poetic form of the thirteenth and fourteenth centuries, another form, known as the *renga*, or "linked verse," was gaining popularity. Originating as a kind of pastime in which two or more poets contributed alternating units of five-seven-five and seven-seven syllables, it eventually became an elaborate form with intricate rules governing the sequence of subjects to which successive contributors were expected to refer. The 100-verse *renga* composed at Minase in 1488 by the priest-poet Sōgi and two of his disciples is considered to be the greatest creation in this style of expression.

The latter half of the medieval age (the Muromachi period) was noted not only for the development of the *renga* style of poetry but also for the perfection of a unique form of drama, the nō. Emerging as a unified art form during the late fourteenth century, it was characterized by the use of masks and by formal, symbolic dance forms. The main characters of the nō represented human spirits or demonic or nature spirits returned to earth to reenact some dramatic scene (usually one which brought about their own or someone else's death). Played upon a simple stage modified from the Shinto dance stage, nō utilized elaborate brocaded costumes, stylized stage properties, a chanting chorus, and a musical accompaniment of flute and hand drums. Two men in particular, Kannami Kiyotsugu (1333–1384) and his son Zeami Motokiyo (1363–1444), patronized by the Ashikaga shoguns, perfected the art of nō both in theory and in technique. Their plays are still produced in the traditional manner and have come to represent the aristocratic tradition in the theater. The sentiments in these plays are invariably noble, awesome, or tragic, and the style of presentation is religious in tone, inspiring the feeling of *yūgen*. At about the same time, the *kyōgen* were developed as comic interludes to relieve the seriousness of the programs of nō performances. While nō plays are written in the stately literary language of the classical period, the *kyōgen* used the vernacular of the day. Acting relied heavily on comic mime to create a light and humorous quality known as *okashi*.

The Early Modern Age: From 1600 to 1868

The cessation of civil warfare after 1600 ushered in an era of more than two centuries of peace during which the arts and letters flourished in great abundance and variety. The samurai class, now secure in their castle towns, turned in large numbers to literature and especially to scholarship. But the most significant development was the appearance of a new creative class, the urban common people, whose popular literature catered to a growing portion of the Japanese. During the Edo period literature secured a mass audience through the medium of printed books and the popular theater.

Perhaps the most distinctive feature of the Edo literary scene was the clear-cut separation between two levels of activity, the aristocratic and the popular. The *daimyō* and their samurai adherents patronized or participated in a cultural life which continued the aristocratic traditions of the Ashikaga period. Their drama was that of nō-*kyōgen*, their poetry the tanka and Chinese-style verse, their prose the writings of the Japanese or Chinese classical ages. The most distinctive activities of the samurai were the study and elaboration of Confucian texts and the writing of national and local histories. Belles lettres as such was less esteemed, for it was "uplifting" accomplishments to which the samurai aspired. And so, during the eighteenth and nineteenth centuries, although the samurai laid the foundation of modern historical scholarship and philosophy and kept alive the traditions of nō and classical poetry, it is literature and drama in the popular genres which have attracted the attention of later admirers. Though often less than edifying, qualities of freshness and human interest gave them a universal appeal.

One literary form, the short poetic verse known as the haiku, managed to bridge the gap between the noble and lesser classes. A form which had evolved from the *renga*, it was acceptable as a vehicle for serious poetry at the same time that it proved simple enough for mastery by the masses. Variously called *hokku* (beginning verse) and *haikai* (light verse), the haiku grew to prominence as the main vehicle of Japanese poetic expression in the sixteenth and seventeenth centuries. Since it consisted of only seventeen syllables, word economy and suggestion were its main essentials, and though it first was used to express comical and witty sentiments, it came to be employed for the composition of profound imagistic poetry by its greatest practitioners.

The man who perfected the haiku as a serious poetic form was Matsuo Bashō (1644–1694), a poet who followed the Saigyō tradition by renouncing the world and adopting a simple life which freed him for frequent travel in search of poetic experience. He is best known for his *Oku no hosomichi* (The narrow road to Oku), which is a narrative, studded with haiku, of his trip to Matsushima and other places. The trademark of Bashō and his successors was the simple pictoral image which carried overtones of deep philosophic suggestion:

Kareeda ni	On a leafless bough
Karasu no tomarikeri.	A crow is perched—
Aki no kure.	The autumn dusk.

Bashō's approach to his subject is, in the manner of the Zen monk, not intellectual but intuitive, requiring the physical and mental attitude of relaxation, meditation, and concentration. The feeling or mood found in his poems is often described by the Japanese as one of *sabi*, the particular quality which derives from aging or weathering. The mantle of Bashō was handed down to Taniguchi (Yosano) Buson (1715–1784) and Kobayashi Issa (1763–1827), but the haiku form was confined to no particular group or period. From this point it became the most common form of Japanese poetry, lasting even into modern times. It was, in fact, to influence such modern Western poets as Pound, Yeats, and the imagist poets of the 1920s.

While haiku were written by serious poets, the general public came to prefer the comic—and, to some degree, erotic—qualities embodied in two forms known as *kyōka* and *senryū*. These forms employed the same lines of five-seven-five-seven-seven and five-seven-five syllables, respectively, as the tanka and the haiku, but their lack of seriousness makes them easily distinguishable from the latter types. While poems in this style were mostly frivolous in intent, they sometimes carried messages of social or political protest beneath their surface form.

The Edo period saw the rise of a popular drama in its two forms, the *bunraku* and the Kabuki. The origins of the *bunraku*, or puppet drama, can be traced in part to the Jōruri, a kind of storytelling to the accompaniment of the three-stringed samisen and acted out by the use of puppets. The beginnings of Kabuki are found in the half-religious, half-erotic dances begun in Kyoto by a woman named O-Kuni. As the form developed, it expanded its dramatic content. *Onna* Kabuki (women's Kabuki) was performed by women who were also available as prostitutes, and *wakashū* Kabuki was performed by boys who served as catamites to their patrons. The Kabuki as we know it today began with the *yarō* Kabuki (men's Kabuki), which developed as a reaction to the immorality connected with the *onna* and *wakashū* Kabuki. By 1652 women were banned from the stage, and a tradition of male actors for feminine roles developed. Kabuki reached its first heights in the Genroku period (1688–1703). The Osaka Kabuki was dominated by the master playwright Chikamatsu Monzaemon (1653–1724), who excelled in both the *sewa-mono*, or "domestic pieces," and the *jidaimono*, or "period pieces." The Edo Kabuki is epitomized in the work of the actor-playwright Ichikawa Danjūrō I (1660–1704). The Ichikawa family made famous the robust, virile type of Kabuki associated with Edo which was called *ara-goto* (rough stuff), as against the *shosa-goto* (dancing and posturing style) performed at Osaka. In 1878, Danjūro IX and the playwright Kawatake Mokuami rebelled against the artificiality of language and costume in the traditional Kabuki and performed the first of a series of *katsureki-geki*, or "plays of living history," which were more realistic, but the spirit of these plays was too studied to endure for long.

Paralleling the development of Kabuki was the puppet theater (later known as *bunraku*), which stayed closer to the Jōruri tradition. *Bunraku* took its name from the Bunrakuza, the famous nineteenth-century

Osaka theater where these plays were so successfully performed. The puppet theater was fashioned into a serious and extremely popular dramatic tradition through the fortuitous collaboration of Takemoto Gidayū, a Jōruri chanter, Tatsumatsu Hachirobei, a puppeteer, and Chikamatsu Monzaemon, the playwright. Many of Chikamatsu's best plays were written for the *bunraku,* and the fact that the puppets, though capable of extremely realistic action, could speak only through the voice of the Jōruri reciter who sat at the right of the stage, had a considerable influence upon the form of Chikamatsu's writing. In particular, it made his style more lyrical and less realistic.

Another conspicuous development in the popular literature of the period was prose fiction. The *sōshi* (story book), the evolution of which spans the interval from the fourteenth to the seventeenth centuries, was the immediate forerunner of the modern novel. The distinction between the *sōshi* and the *monogatari* is mainly historical: the *monogatari* was a product of the classical age and was written for an aristocratic audience. The *sōshi* was written primarily for the people at large. It formed a popular literature written chiefly for entertainment but not without some concern for style and attention to the realities of daily life. A good deal of moralizing was apt to enter these stories as well. *Sōshi* of the Edo period were of many types and levels of literary worth. They are usually categorized into groups according to their content, authorship, or publishing house.

Of the prose writers of this period the best known by far is Ibara (Ihara) Saikaku (1642–1693), who pioneered in developing the *ukiyozōshi* (stories of the floating world). In them he describes in a vivid, racy style the lives and loves of men and women of the merchant class. His *Kōshoku gonin onna* (*Five Women Who Loved Love*) and a number of other stories have been ably translated into English and show Saikaku handling with considerable literary elegance subjects drawn from contemporary society, which previously had been considered unworthy of literature. His style relies heavily on the techniques of pivot words, puns, and allusions utilized by the masters of *renga* poetry. Among the writers of *kokkeibon* (humorous stories), the most famous was Jippensha Ikku (1765–1831), whose *Dōchū hizakurige* (translated into English under the title *Shank's Mare*) tells of the escapades of two roustabouts, Yajirobei and Kitahachi, as they travel down the Tōkaidō from Edo to Kyoto. In this work one finds a remarkable realism of description enhanced by the use of dialect in dialogue. *Seken musume katagi* (*A Wayward Wife*) is probably the best work of Ejima Kiseki (1667–1736), who wrote in the style of Saikaku but with somewhat more realism and feeling. His works, translated by Hibbett, are excellent revelations of the mood of life in the merchant quarters of Osaka and Kyoto. We have mentioned just a small fraction of the prose output of the Edo period, which ranged from pornography to moralistic picture books and from tales of the gay quarters to highly didactic stories in the Chinese style such as those by Takizawa (Kyokutei) Bakin (1767–1848).

The Modern Age: From 1868 to the Present

Japan's struggle to modernize itself under Western influence is reflected in every phase of its literary activity after 1868. Of the many revolutionary changes affecting Japanese culture during the Meiji period, the one which had the deepest influence upon literature was probably the breakdown in the hierarchy of the social classes. The samurai class, which had stood at the top of society, gradually lost its special position and distinctive way of life, while the merchant class, theoretically lowest in the Tokugawa scale, began to climb the social ladder. There could now be a national literature for all classes. Magazines and newspapers became new organs for the dissemination of literature. New horizons opened in thought. Bridges were built between Japan and world literature, and a new drama and a new poetry developed. But it was in the field of the novel and the short story that the most remarkable development occurred.

During the 1890s the Japanese writer rapidly abandoned traditional forms and substituted Western ones. The haiku and the tanka and the theater of the nō, *bunraku,* and Kabuki were felt to be inadequate to express the complexities of the new life, and it was fiction rather than poetry and drama to which the Japanese turned in their first efforts to modernize their literature. Scores of translations and inferior imitations were the result. Nevertheless, this was "a liberating wave of imitation," for after having suffered the imitative period, Japanese writers were able to rediscover the values of their native literary tradition, and modern Japanese literature emerged as a combination of native and Western elements.

The modern period of the Japanese novel may be said to begin in 1885 with the publication of *Shōsetsu shinzui* (The essence of the novel), by Tsubouchi Shōyō (1859–1935). This professor at Waseda University and translator of Shakespeare and Scott saw the salvation of the Japanese novel, which had become bogged down in moralism or pornography, in the adoption of the more realistic Western view of literature.

Ukigumo (The drifting clouds, 1887–1889), by Futabatei Shimei (1864–1909), is considered the first successful attempt by a Japanese to write in Western fashion a novel dealing with an individual's search for identity. The novel reflects the strong influence of such Russian naturalists as Fyodor Dostoyevsky, Ivan Turgenev, and Ivan Goncharov, but it is unmistakably Japanese in the situation it portrays. *Futon* (The quilts, 1907), by Tayama Katai (1871–1930), and *Hakai* (The breaking of the commandment, 1906), by Shimazaki Tōson (1872–1943), are two other important pieces of fiction written in the style of the early naturalist movement in Japan. The latter also carries the first overtones of the social protest which was to infuse so many works at a later date.

Experimentation with Western techniques and ideas began with highly imitative writings, but eventually it resulted in a fresh approach to the Japanese aesthetic tradition and in the creation of an entirely new "native" literature. A balance between Western influence and the rediscovered native tradition was the aim of most of the gifted novelists of the late Meiji period. Natsume Sōseki (1867–1916), a professor of English literature at Tokyo Imperial University, achieved considerable success in combining the style and philosophy of George Meredith with the traditional aesthetic ideas of *yūgen, sabi,* and *okashi.* He left such intriguing novels as *Botchan* (Sonny, 1906), *Wagahai wa neko de aru* (I am a cat, 1905), *Sanshirō* (1908), *Kokoro* (The heart, 1914), *Michikusa* (Grass at the side of the road, 1915), and *Meian* (Light and darkness, 1916). Writers such as Mori Ōgai (1862–1922) and Nagai Kafū (1879–1959) returned to traditional Japanese literature for thematic inspiration, even though Mori had studied in Germany and Nagai in France and evidence of Western influence is discernible in their novels. Mori was the author of such short stories as *Maihime* (The dancing girl, 1890); *Gan* (*The Wild Geese,* 1911); *Abe ichizoku* (The Abe clan, 1913); and *Sanshō Dayū* (1915), named for its hero, a wealthy landowner living in Tango Province, north of present-day Kyoto, as well as of several important critical essays and translations. Kafū is represented by his lyric, sensual stories and by his translations of French symbolist poetry found in *Sangoshū* (Coral collection, 1913). Akutagawa Ryūnosuke (1892–1927), who so meticulously shaped the short story into a delicate work of art, was strongly influenced by Edgar Allan Poe and Gerhart Hauptmann, but he also drew upon such medieval Japanese collections of stories as the *Uji shūi monogatari* to find the delicate balance of ancient and modern so characteristic of his works. Akutagawa left numerous superb short stories, such as *Rashōmon*, named for a gate in Kyoto (1915); *Hana* (The nose, 1916); and *Shinkirō* (A mirage, 1927).

Contemporary writers who strive to express traditional Japanese values include Tanizaki Jun'ichirō (1886–   ) and Kawabata Yasunari (1899–   ), whose works reveal an atavistic tendency to return to tradition and rely more and more on the aesthetic principles of "old" Japan.

Kawabata's *Yukiguni* (*Snow Country*) is an almost plotless, impressionistic tale of the love adventure of a geisha and a businessman from Tokyo who have several encounters in the idyllic seclusion of Japan's mountains. Kawabata combines aural, musical effects with visual impressions to form a rich descriptive fabric.

Tanizaki, who today enjoys the reputation of being Japan's greatest novelist, began writing in the satanist vein. *Shisei* (Tattooing, 1910) is the story of a tattoo artist who searches for the perfect human back on which to compose his masterpiece. In tattooing on a beautiful girl's back the likeness of a spider, he manages to infuse the diabolic spirit of the insect into the girl. His translation of *The Tale of Genji* into modern Japanese exemplifies his withdrawal into a Japanese environment, from which he wrote of the deep and destructive obsessions of his characters, usually for Western agents of degeneration. His novels translated as *Some Prefer Nettles* (1955), *The Makioka Sisters* (1957), and *The Key* (1960) have received high praise outside Japan. *The Makioka Sisters,* the title in English by which *Sasameyuki* (The delicate snow) is known, is in particular notable for the heroine's many meetings with candidates for her hand in marriage, recalling Prince Genji's affairs with a legion of lady loves.

Of all the qualities of modern Japanese fiction, a particular sensitivity to psychological problems and to the minute details of daily life seems most clearly to exhibit the "Japanese touch." This is true of the novels of Tanizaki and Kawabata. Certain forms have best embodied these characteristics, for instance, the *shi-shōsetsu,** or "private fiction," which consisted of extremely personal accounts of the author's experiences. Dealing with incidents and ideas which are sometimes bookish and overly literary, they are always charged with a kind of hypersensitiveness. Shiga Naoya, in his short story *Kinosaki nite* (At Kinosaki), depicts a highly introspective young man, himself recovering from injuries in an accident, who displays an almost morbid preoccupation with death. Everything he sees—a bee on a roof, a rat with a skewer thrust through its neck, a lizard struck by a stone—is dead, about to die, or seen at the moment of death. The *shi-shōsetsu* need not always be written in the first person, but it is in almost every case autobiographical to some degree. In Japan it has been condemned by some critics, who demand that this introspective and subjective "I" fiction be replaced by some form of *honkaku-shōsetsu* or "real novel," filled with real, full-bodied characters.

The *shinkyō-shōsetsu,* or "mental-life fiction," is closely related to the "I" fiction. Itō Sei, translator of *Ulysses,* borrowed from James Joyce

* Also commonly pronounced *watakushi-shōsetsu.*

the idea of the stream of consciousness to give this form a new basis. But Natsume Sōseki had already shown himself a master of the art of writing psychological novels. In his *Kokoro* the plot hardly moves at all. Even in the interchange of conversation between the protagonist, who is a teacher, and the young man who narrates the story there is little communication. Step by step, through the eyes of the first-person narrator, the reader is brought deeper and deeper into the thought and mind of the teacher. It is this probing into the inner recesses of the human mind that marks this type of fiction.

Finally, in certain novels dealing with experiences in World War II, the Japanese have produced some works, graphically describing the impact of death, flight, and fear, which will perhaps challenge the best war literature of any country. In 1948 Ōoka Shōhei produced *Furyoki* (Record of a prisoner of war), the story of a stranded Japanese soldier in the Philippines, wounded, sick, and looking for water, examining his own mind. The soldier reflects, "As long as one's own life hangs on the action of the enemy, to kill or to be killed—one has the right to kill." But within his conscience he finds the unconditional demand "not to kill." Ōoka followed his early success with *Nobi* (Fires on the plain), published in 1952. The vivid description of what happens to the minds and bodies of sick and starving men makes this work rank among the more moving books coming out of the war. Although the sensitivities are Japanese, the characterization in Ōoka's works reveals the influence of Stendhal.

We shall not detail the works of the proletarian school, or of the existentialists, or of the modern "rebels without a cause," whose activities parallel, and to some extent are motivated by, Western examples.

When compared with these epoch-making developments in fiction, poetry and drama have not prospered in modern Japan. Perhaps while modern Japanese fiction had a great deal more to learn from the West than to teach it, Japanese poetry and drama had already attained their perfection and uniqueness and hence were in a position to influence rather than to be influenced by the West. Somehow conditions in Japan seemed less congenial for the development of these forms. The social changes of the latter half of the nineteenth century, occasioned principally by industrial expansion and political and educational reforms, enabled greater and greater numbers of persons to gain sufficient leisure and education to enjoy popular fictional literature. The novelists flourished. The poets, on the other hand, tended to isolate themselves from the general public. Fiction thus gained enthusiastic readers among the newly risen middle class, while poetry either remained the monopoly of a few aristocrats, priests, hermits, and sinologues or degenerated into a low-level pastime in the continued composition of *senryū* and *kyōka*.

What seemed to be a conflict between the old and the modern in the Western world was, in Japan, also a conflict between indigenous and foreign elements. Poetry, because of the highly specialized forms it had taken, proved to have little flexibility. Some Japanese poets attempted to express the complex sensitivities of modern man within the confines of the tanka and haiku forms, but such poetry could hardly be true to the traditional poetic principles of *sabi* or *yūgen* and yet be modern. On the other hand, imitation of the newly introduced Western models remained superficial and, by and large, betrayed a lack of originality and spontaneity. Preoccupation with form, as evidenced in the poet's attempt to write in the colloquial language and to free himself from syllabic restrictions, resulted in a neglect of content. The "new poetry" was often a mere arrangement of images, without depth of thought or emotion based on moral, religious, or philosophical concepts. Since knowledge of Western literature came chiefly through translations, both poets and readers overlooked the Western poet's concern with such linguistic matters as rhyme and alliteration, which, to be sure, are untranslatable. It was inevitable that Western poetry, rich in its own allusions and connotations and expressed in a strange metrical system, should not be understood and hence could hardly be imitated.

As in the case of poetry, so in drama, the restrictions imposed upon the playwright by tradition served to stunt rather than to help the growth of a modern dramatic art. Masks, flute, drum, monologue, chanting, slow gestures, the symbolic use of fans and sleeves, etc., all contributed to make the traditional stage forms of the nō and the Kabuki more symbolic than representational. Nor were the old media suitable for the adaptation of westernized plays. Trained in viewing Kabuki, the spectators for their part were interested primarily in the performance of the actors rather than in the protagonists' characters or in the plot construction. The old playwrights had tended to sacrifice the intensity of a dramatic conflict to the finesse of postures and actions. Though based on contemporary events, the *shimpa,* or "new school" drama of the 1890s tended to emphasize melodramatic elements and thus failed too to present the complexities of character and plot. The use of Western costumes and scenery and the staging of the Occidental mode of life in translated plays were felt to be unnatural and failed to appeal to the spectators once their curiosity had been satisfied. What the general public preferred were the period pieces, the *jidaimono* and the *sewa-mono,* to works on contemporary subjects. Otherwise, it was drawn to inexpensive movies and to variety shows. Not until the Japanese developed their own cinema did the drama manage to bridge the separation between tradition and modern interests.

Why had fiction met this task so much more quickly and successfully?

Unlike poetry and drama, fictional literature did not have to contend with the weight of tradition. A prose style which incorporated informal conversation had already developed in the lighter literature of Tokugawa Japan. Once the heavier classical style of the narrative and descriptive passages had been reformed, few restrictions remained. The serial publication of stories and novels in popular and inexpensive magazines enabled the prose writer to acquire a large reading public and consequently to lead, relatively speaking, an economically secure and stable life once he had established himself. The readers of fiction, for their part, did not have to cope with such stringent rules as they did in reading poetry or drama. The flexibility of prose further enabled the writer to express freely the turbulent social upheavals of the modern period and to delve into his personal experience, thus resulting in the rather rampant popularity of the *shi-shōsetsu* genre among prose writers. In addition, prose was more easily exploited for propaganda purposes, political or religious, than poetry or drama. Of great importance also, Western fiction was less artificial in translation than Western poems or plays. Thus the process of assimilation to Western models was easier and faster in fiction than in poetry and drama. Literature provides one of the most interesting examples of cultural change in Japan under Western influence and modern inducements. It is especially revealing of the differential effects of foreign influence and of the differences in aesthetic adaptability found in the several literary genres.

JOHN WHITNEY HALL

The Visual Arts and Japanese Culture*

PROBLEMS OF APPROACH AND EVALUATION

Japanese art has received the serious attention of students of Japanese culture both because it ranks high in world art according to connoisseurs and because, apart from its aesthetic qualities, it makes clear and tangible statements about Japanese culture and values at various times in the past. Art has the capacity to speak both for "art's sake" and for the culture which produced it. Art, and by this we should wish to include architecture as well as painting and sculpture, constitutes a rich repository of visual manifestations of cultural values, often more tangibly and seemingly more directly comprehended than works of literature or philosophy. Certainly more easily appreciated than creations in the fields of government or law, art can furnish a means of entrance into the emotional and intellectual life of past and present Japanese. It provides visible evidence of influences from the past or from outside the culture. But the student of Japanese art, whether he is interested in it as pure art or as a revelation of nonaesthetic values, is involved in many difficult problems of evaluation, interpretation, and comparison.

The vocabulary of art appreciation is by no means standardized, nor is there agreement on how to determine the aesthetic and cultural content of works of art. In every instance in which a Westerner approaches an object of Japanese culture he faces a problem of comparative judgment. How does one go about viewing and judging a Buddhist statue, a ceramic bowl, or a wood-block print? Is a single, universal scale of evaluation of art objects applicable to both Japan and Europe? Is the vocabulary of art history and art criticism appropriate to Europe transferable to Japanese subject matter? How useful, on the other hand, is the technical vocabulary of art appreciation developed by the Japanese themselves? Such are some of the continuing questions which confront the art historian.

Much of the interpretive literature in the field of Japanese art is

* The historical portion of this chapter has relied heavily on syllabus material prepared by the late James Plumer.

impressionistic, subjective, or based upon stereotyped rationalizations devised by Japanese interpreters of their own art or by Western admirers of an unfamiliar but exotic tradition. The common tendency of both is to read idealized concepts or exaggerated claims into Japanese materials. The Japanese are eager to demonstrate certain "unique characteristics" of their artistic temperament, while Western observers are apt to look for qualities which they consider "Oriental." The products of the Japanese artist or builder, of course, stand on their own merits and remain mute evidence of the individuals and culture which produced them. The problem is one of assessing the intent and realization of the artist and the relation of his work to the society which nurtured him. Only then can it speak for the culture as such.

To look at Japanese art in this way is not an easy task for the Western observer, whose views cannot by any means coincide with those of the makers or first viewers in Japan. His unfamiliarity with Japanese life and history limits him. Many objects from Japan that he looks upon as art—pure, simple, and useless—may be partly or primarily objects of use or of religious instruction or be linked to music and dance traditions quite unfamiliar to him. Beyond this, the ability to appreciate the art of an unfamiliar culture is partly a matter of self-awareness. One must become conscious of one's own biases, of the questions one habitually brings to a work of art (for instance, what person or scene does this represent?), and thus learn to ask new questions when the customary ones are inappropriate. For the artist cannot hope to produce a work that is a satisfying answer to all possible questions, nor does he want to. He chooses to call attention to certain aesthetic features by stressing them, meanwhile suppressing or ignoring others (as, for instance, perspective may be sacrificed to pattern); perhaps he stops with this statement, or perhaps he seeks to evoke a reaction to make an intellectual point (as by creating an earthly, fleshlike Bodhisattva to suggest that salvation is close at hand for all mankind).

Japanese artists naturally addressed themselves to problems and questions (whether aesthetic or ratiocinative) that were current in their time and used current canons to guide their choices of what they wished to communicate. We, removed in time, distance, and culture, cannot blindly apply our own traditions of appreciation to interpret the message in a Japanese work of art and so arrive at exactly what the artist intended. But we can go far by viewing the work attentively and testing various "questions" (rather than asking only our stereotyped habitual ones). A unique advantage of aesthetic materials is that the vocabulary of the message is usually (unless altered by time) as clearly evident to us now as it was to the maker, if only our eyes are alert. The maker may have incorporated any of a number of elements in his vocabulary (and ignored others, consciously or unconsciously). He manipulated subject matter, materials, colors, sizes, or textures, organizing or interrelating these to suggest harmony, contrast, or tension. It is the viewer's task to try to understand the message the artist sought to convey.

Like all fields of cultural analysis, that of art appreciation and art history has its formal boundaries and traditional methods of handling its subject matter. The works of art or architecture which are recognized as worthy of consideration and appear in illustrated histories or surveys of Japanese art have become fairly standardized over the years. This condition is a product of two selective processes. One is the accident of history, which has preserved some and destroyed many other works of art. The other is the result of the impact of two sets of human values, first those of the Japanese people, who, generation after generation, have seen fit to preserve or restore on a selective basis products which they have felt most worthy; and, second, those of the professional critics and art historians, who have chosen to call attention to certain pieces. Thus the art of the past is retained in the present in a selective and somewhat idealized fashion. To some extent, then, one must recognize a discrepancy between the interests of the professional art critic and the cultural anthropologist or historian, whose special motivation for viewing art is to gain certain insights into Japanese culture and society. A work of art need not be intrinsically of the highest quality to serve as an index to social conditions or philosophical or religious ideas. Similarly, a work of the highest intrinsic worth may be too individualistic to be indicative of more than an artist's private creativity. To this extent, then, even the content of the word "art" may differ among scholars. To some only the "fine arts" are worthy of consideration; others include "folk arts" in their purview. The cultural historian or anthropologist is apt to go much farther in including objects that are not particularly aesthetically refined in his area of concern.

Called "Japan's greatest and completely original creation in general world architecture," the shrines of Ise demonstrate the elements of simplicity and "naturalness" which have characterized the Japanese tradition in architecture.

a

b

(a) The great tomb of Emperor Nintoku erected during the late fifth century is a prime example of the "keyhole" style burial mound. Its outer measurements are 900 by 1,400 feet, and the central mound is nearly 100 feet high. (b) Yasukuni Jinja (the Shrine of the War Dead) in Tokyo with its torii of riveted bronze symbolizes the perpetuation of Shinto beliefs as an element in Japan's modern nationalism. (c) A portable shrine containing the spirit of their protective deity is raised aloft by the youth of a farming village before the entrance to the regional head shrine as part of a harvest festival.

c

a   *b*

(*a*) The city of Nara housed the greatest achievements of Buddhist art under the influence of *T'ang* China. The figure of Gakkō, part of the triad of statues at Yakushiji, is one of the most sophisticated products of the Tempyō period workers in bronze. (*b*) A fine example of one of the fierce protective deities of the Buddhist pantheon, the Shūkongō-shin at Hokkedō is one of the few large statues sculptured in clay. It is brilliantly colored.

Considered one of the most beautiful Buddhist statues preserved in Japan, the Miroku Bosatsu of Chūgūji, Nara, is now thought to date from the Asuka period (i.e., before A.D. 645). It is carved in wood and typifies the formal quality of early Buddhist iconography in Japan.

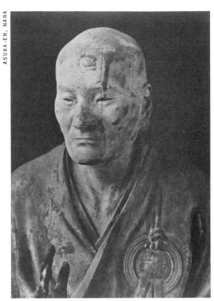

a

b

(*a*) The strength and realism of Kamakura religious sculpture is well exemplified in this wooden statue of Muchaku by Unkei, contained in the Hokuen-dō of Kofukuji in Nara. (*b*) While Buddhist art had declined by the Tokugawa period, wood carvers excelled in more secular and decorative themes, as this detail from a wall panel in the Tōshōgū at Nikkō shows.

(*c*) Hōryūji monastery founded in 607 is considered the most perfect group of Buddhist buildings in Japan. This is also a supreme example of seventh-century Chinese architectural style. Remarkably preserved through the ages (though rebuilt and repaired), it exemplifies the ability of the Japanese to preserve their most respected historical moments.

ASUKA-EN, NARA

c

K. B. S. PHOTO

a

K. B. S. PHOTO

b

G. OGINO

c

(*a*) Ginkakuji (the Silver Pavilion) set on the slopes of Higashiyama in Kyoto and surrounded by a garden of trees, rocks, and water, was the retreat from which the eighth Ashikaga Shogun Yoshimasa (retired 1472-1490) patronized the arts of nō, painting, and tea ceremony. (*b*)Famous for its use of only sand and stones, the garden at Ryōanji exemplifies Ashikaga period aesthetics under Zen influence. (*c*) Zen priests meditating at Shōkokuji, Kyoto, carry on the monastic tradition which played such an important part in the art and scholarship of the Ashikaga period.

The keeps of Himeji *(a)* and Matsumoto *(b)*
castles exemplify the castle architecture
of the sixteenth century. Under the
protection of these towers were built the
palaces of the territorial *daimyō*,
elaborately decorated with gold screens.

a

b

a

b

c

Common architectural and aesthetic features, with roots in the "Shinto style" of Ise, join the famed detached palace at Katsura (a), built near Kyoto during the early seventeenth century, farm houses in central Japan (b), and contemporary domestic architecture (c), a style which took shape during the Tokugawa period.

The polite accomplishments of calligraphy (d), flower arrangement (e), and tea ceremony (f), once the monopoly of the upper class, are now part of the repertory of the well trained Japanese lady. The latter two were developed into sophisticated art forms in the Zen monasteries of the Ashikaga period.

d

e

f

青山疊々水重々
萬里來同槲几中
不用區々飛杖錫
卧遊奇勝飽無窮

淋漓元氣出自毫素峯密競秀
渟滾滂沱石頑而後木老而陰
谷有紫芝澗饒堂林仁智之資
樂此必無衡茅真唐東海隅
油具微疵玩品潰菴敢題夢解
據定黄絲

a

(a) The best known Ashikaga master of ink painting in the Sung style, Sesshū (1420-1506) excelled in landscapes done in bold brush strokes. The poems written at the top of the scroll contribute both sentiment and calligraphic interest.

The wood-block print was brought to a high level of technical and artistic achievement during the Tokugawa period. Early prints relied on strong lines and fairly simple colors, as illustrated in Kaigetsudō's *Courtesan (b)*. Suzuki Harunobu (1725-1770) made important advances in wood-block technique and use of color *(c)*. Wood-block printing is one of the few traditional art forms to retain its vitality into modern times *(d)*.

NIHON KE ZAI SHIMBUNSHA

b

BENRIDO

c

d

Nō, the aristocratic dramatic form developed during the fifteenth century, is here illustrated from a scene in Dōjōji. The actor wears the mask of a female demon.

These scenes from the Bunraku (a) and Kabuki (b) theatres illustrate two forms of the popular drama of Tokugawa times. The black form behind the male puppet is one of three manipulators.

a

b

Tokugawa exemplars of the decorative Yamatoe style of Japanese painting were
Tawaraya Sōtatsu (early seventeenth century) and Ogata Kōrin (1658-1716).
Sōtatsu's painting illustrated here *(a)* includes a fine example of Japanese
calligraphy using mostly *kana*. Kōrin's *Iris* is painted on a six-paneled
gold screen *(b)*.

a

b

Finally it should be recognized that the art historian, like the literary critic, may vary in his approach to works of art, depending upon whether his prime interest is intrinsic or extrinsic. Is an object to be "explained" chiefly in terms of itself as an isolated work of creativity, or is it to be seen in terms of its artistic or cultural milieu? The first approach is more apt to rely on observations regarding form, technique, and intrinsic aesthetic qualities; the second, to inquire into the "meaning" intended by the artist or the function of the object within the culture that produced it. The second approach would seem to be related more directly to the aims of the general student of Japanese culture; and, to be sure, the majority of the treatments of Japanese art to date have been studies in the extensive tradition. But the fundamental importance of the intrinsic study of Japanese art cannot be overlooked, for it is largely through such study that the vocabulary of comparative aesthetic judgment is refined and the grounds for appreciation of Japanese art in relation to the art of other traditions are laid. The section which follows summarizes the content of the standard "art-history" approach to premodern Japanese art. It takes as its main areas of concern painting, sculpture, and architecture.

PREMODERN ART: THE MAJOR GENRES AND CHANGING CULTURAL CONTEXTS

Art historians have devised a fairly standard system of nomenclature for the various "art periods" in Japan. These follow the lead of the divisions used by the political historians except that a few additional periods are added to take care of certain changes in art style, such as Hakuhō (early Nara), Tempyō (late Nara), Jōgan (early Heian), Kitayama (early Ashikaga), and Higashiyama (mid-Ashikaga). As in the case of the eras used by cultural historians these periods serve as useful, but generally somewhat arbitrary, conventions of periodization. It must be remembered that the exact dates of such periods are not significant for the art field. Terms such as *Kamakura, Yoshino, Ashikaga*, and *Edo* are based solely on political criteria. And while it is undeniable that shifts of government or ruling groups did affect artistic endeavor, especially in times when art reflected very closely the nature of the ruling class, this has not always been the case.

These comments are not meant to imply that the standard art periods adopted by the Japanese are totally without meaning, but rather that it is dangerous to read too much into them. The tidemarks of developmental rise and fall of various individual genres, for instance, are not by any means contained within these across-the-board divisions, nor can

the precise dates be taken to indicate sharp changes in artistic performance. Art periods can most appropriately be thought of as blocks
of time surrounding peaks of high artistic achievement. Within such
blocks, then, it is possible to speak of certain dominant styles which to
some degree reflect climates of thought and religious inspiration. Insofar
as these artistic modes have been associated with changes in political
or social structure or have shown evidence of foreign cultural influence,
it is possible to search for significant relationships between changing art
styles or content and the changing cultural environment, but it must
be remembered that the conventions of standard art periods are used
in a selective fashion. Any survey of Japanese art and architecture is
therefore apt to be told in terms of highlights and high points.

Pre-Buddhistic Period

Archaeologists have revealed in considerable detail the physical remains
of two early cultures distinguished by their contrasting ceramic traditions: Jōmon and Yayoi. The culture of the Jōmon people, because of
their remoteness in time, is not easily reconstructed. Yet enough remains
of the dwellings, artifacts of common use, bodily ornaments, and religious symbols to reveal a primitive, sub-Neolithic society based upon
hunting and fishing as a way of life. Jōmon pottery vessels are distinguished by their crude technology but extraordinary variety and elab-
orateness of design. Figurines and a few phallic symbols reflect something of personal simplicity of religious beliefs. Scholars have been
tempted, though with doubtful justification, to read into Jōmon life the
customs and beliefs of the present-day Ainu and to see in this prehistoric period a "superstitiously dark" orientation to the world, both seen
and unseen.

Yayoi culture with its wheel-made pottery, rice-based economy, and
clear indications of intercourse with continental Chinese civilization,
contrasts sharply with Jōmon. Excavations of Yayoi communities, such
as that at Toro, reveal a life distinctly less primitive in its social and
economic organization, and the presence of bronze mirrors, bells, and
weapons is indicative of the stimulus which the Yayoi people were
receiving from the continent. With the maturation of the iron-based
culture distinguished by Sue ware and great burial dolmens, the line of
cultural development begun by the Yayoi people reached its highest
level. It is to this Tomb (or Yamato) period culture that the attention
of the art historian is drawn.

Yamato culture was distinguished politically and socially by the
emergence of powerful ruling families able to recruit the labor of large

bodies of workers. The tombs of earth or stone, in their great size and difficulty of construction, are illustrative both of social differentiation and political influence. Artifacts and works of art were now the products of distinct social units that carried on traditional occupations at the behest of ruling families. Many of these groups (such as weavers, arms makers, and jewelers) were of continental origin. Two products of the Yamato period seem particularly significant in their revelation of qualities which appear to be antecedent to certain later Japanese art styles. These are the architecture of public buildings (especially Shinto shrines) and the pottery figurines known as *haniwa*.

Although the present shrines at Ise, dedicated to the ancestor of the Imperial Family, are no doubt modified from the originals which they claim to reproduce, they nonetheless stand for a mode of architecture which is distinctly Japanese (in contrast to that of China). Bruno Taut, the German architect, has made the remark that "The shrines of Ise are Japan's greatest and completely original creation in general world architecture." [1] Certainly, the emphasis upon the use of wood in its natural, unpainted state, the simple, straight lines of walls and roofs (especially the simplicity of the torii entrances and wooden fences), and the effort to harmonize buildings with the natural forest environment reveal aesthetic principles cherished by Japanese in their household architecture as distinct from their public architecture which tended to show Chinese influence.

Haniwa figures are less easily judged for their contemporary significance and aesthetic value. Created for religious purposes to place in or about the tombs of the Yamato rulers, they reveal a hasty and even crude workmanship. Yet the art historian directs our attention to the deft simplicity of workmanship in the *haniwa* as an indication of a directness and purity of conception which he purports to find typical of the Japanese artist and artisan of later generations, and his views have gained considerable support as wall paintings of this period with similar aesthetic qualities have come to light in recent years. All these products of the Tomb age combine with the recorded myths of early Japan to reveal a picture of an unsophisticated, though certainly not primitive, culture whose members adopted a direct and relatively untroubled attitude toward nature and the unseen world. Later Japanese artists, writers, and philosophers have frequently sought to return to this period as a source of Japan's most private aesthetic tastes and religious attitudes. In the idealized picture of the age created by Japanese scholars of the late eighteenth and nineteenth centuries (especially Motoori Norinaga) the Yamato age was looked upon as an ideal natural order,

[1] Bruno Taut, *Houses and People of Japan*, rev. ed., Tokyo, 1958, p. 139.

when the Japanese lived simply and attained a state of natural goodness and morality. So also, contemporary artists in search of a native "primitive art" have looked to the products of this age for inspiration.

Asuka (or Suiko) Period.

The introduction of Buddhism to Japan (traditionally dated 552) provides a convenient date from which to record the beginnings of a new complex of art genres and styles of continental origin, but Buddhism was in fact only part of the vast wave of continental influence which engulfed Japan at this time. Nor is the date 552 significant in and of itself. Japan's response to Chinese civilization had a long history, revealed first in the articles of daily use, such as mirrors, dress ornaments, and agricultural implements. Korea had also long served as an intermediary in the transmission of Chinese cultures to Japan. But the influence of Buddhism and the establishment, after the turn into the seventh century, of direct contact with China greatly accelerated the adoption of the continental style in religious artifacts and public architecture.

Chinese architecture of the time contrasted with that commonly found in Japan in its greater use of stone and its employment of heavy, upright pillars for the support of broad tiled roofs. Buddhism as an organized religion brought with it an elaborate temple architecture (largely that of the Chinese court style) and a complex iconography. These elements gradually spread among the ruling class in Japan, beginning in the Yamato area. Much of the early temple and palace architecture and the Buddhist statuary was undoubtedly produced by Korean or Chinese artisans until the new techniques were mastered. The works of the Asuka period must be thought of as emerging from a culture still largely unaffected by continental influence. The few great temples or palaces erected during this age undoubtedly stood out dramatically from their surroundings and were of strictly continental inspiration.

Fortunately there has been preserved near the present city of Nara a monastery founded in 607 by the imperial prince Shōtoku. Known as the Hōryūji, the extant buildings of this monastery consist of the main gate, cloisters, a five-story pagoda, and a Kondō, or main hall. Even if all were burnt and rebuilt 100 years later, as is now thought possible, they form the oldest group of wooden buildings in continuous use anywhere in the world. In the Kondō there have been preserved many art objects of the time, particularly images set up for worship and still so used. Notable among these is the central group, a bronze trinity formed of a seated Sakyamuni (the historical Buddha), flanked by a pair of standing Bodhisattvas (merciful interceders or saviors). This was cast by a craftsman of part-Korean ancestry known as Tori Busshi, in the stiff manner witnessed about a century earlier in the stone cave sculptures at Yunkang in China. One should note that an imported philosophical symbolism rather than native aestheticism governs the placement of this statuary, a symmetrical trinity centered in a foursquare frame consisting of a heavenly king guarding each cardinal direction and sheltered under heavenly canopies.

Asuka religious sculpture appears to the viewer today to impart a naïve and pious sentiment. But the stiffness of the statues should not be assumed to reflect technical immaturity. This quality is undoubtedly bent to the purpose of presenting the liturgical subjects as aloof, ethereal beings (as well as reflecting the style which had developed in the Chinese cave sculptures). Facial expressions, even of fierce deities, are illumined with a kind of inner joy. Stylistically they show, as in Chinese Wei dynasty schools, the "archaic smile," parallel cloth folds, and serrated drapery ends.

Suiko period painting is seen only in fragments, such as the scenes of gods, men, animals, and landscape details, found on the miniature lacquered Tamamushi (Jade-Beetle) Shrine. These objects reveal a type of brush painting which is rather formal and stiffly stylized, though again the media may have a great deal to do with this quality.

Noteworthy features in temple architecture, all traceable to Wei China, include a high stone platform with steps (upon which main buildings were built), sturdy wooden pillars, and tiled roofs with wide eaves and simple bracketed supports. The pagoda, a unique feature of the Buddhist temple, combining the architectural traditions of the Han tower and the Indian stupa, fulfills the dual purpose of free-standing steeple and reliquary.

Hakuhō (or Early Nara) Period

No sharp line divides the Hakuhō period from the preceding one. The date 645 is politically significant in that it marks the beginning of the Taika Reform. After that date the central government consciously facilitated the introduction of Chinese technology and arts into Japan. Nonetheless, it was not until the beginning of the eighth century that T'ang influence on Japanese culture was to produce its high flowering. During the last half of the seventh century, the Japanese were engaged chiefly in the process of absorption, experimentation, and preparation for what was to follow. Examples of sculpture and architecture in the Buddhist tradition of this half-century show a greater smoothness and lightness of design within proportions which are basically those of the Asuka period. One of the most famous statues in all Japan has long been dated from this period. It is the Chūgūji polished-wood Kannon seated in the Miroku (Maitreya) posture of princely ease, one foot on a lotus support, the other horizontal, the right fingertips touching his smiling face. The double topknot on his head was once shielded by a crown long missing. (Most recently this statue has been updated to the Asuka period, so that the best example of this period may be the Yakushiji trinity, whose place, once secure in the Nara period, now seems better fixed as Hakuhō.)

The painting of this era may be judged from a later copy of "Prince Shōtoku with Two Sons" in the Hōryūji, from traces of figure drawings on the Tachibana Shrine, and from the remains of the Hōryūji Kondō murals that have scarcely survived the wear of centuries and a disastrous fire in 1949. These paintings are remarkable for their portrayal of a strong influence (in painting technique and in the gestures of the figures) from India as well as the expected Chinese manner (revealed particularly in the draperies and designs). In them also one sees early efforts at landscape depiction.

The three-storied pagoda of the Yakushiji, with its alternating roof pattern, dates from this period. It is one of the most delicately styled buildings of its kind in Japan and demonstrates the growing architectural skill of the Japanese. Thus in wood carving, bronze casting, painting, and architecture the Japanese were becoming less and less a distant provincial outpost of continental art. The groundwork was being laid for the remarkable burst of artistic virtuosity which was soon to come.

Tempyō (or Late Nara) Period

The period from the completion of the first permanent imperial capital in Japan in 710 to the dedication of the Great Buddha of the Tōdaiji in 752 stands out as one of the great eras of artistic achievement in Japanese history. The burst of creative activity in the fields of public architecture and Buddhist art was part of a broad complex of cultural changes which began in 645 and had as its ultimate aim the creation of a centralized imperial-aristocratic state. Administrative reform brought into existence a machinery of government which centered on the Emperor and operated through an elaborate bureaucracy, housed in the capital and extended to the provinces. Land control and tax collection were standardized, so that the imperial government was supplied with heretofore undreamed-of financial and labor resources. Temples and shrines were patronized and provided with state support and new economic resources. Communications within Japan and to Korea and China were vastly improved. For the moment Japan became an important member of the cultural world of East Asia, which had its political center in the Chinese capital of Changan and its spiritual center in India.

Before surveying the major artistic achievements of this period it is necessary to remind ourselves again of certain problems in evaluating the relationship of the art of this period to the culture as a whole. The art historian's picture of the Nara age is inevitably selective. The arts and artifacts which remain to elicit his admiration are almost exclusively those of the elite, that is, a relatively narrow court aristocracy located in and about Nara. It is a picture which says almost nothing about conditions in the provinces outside the capital. It says little about the nonaristocracy or even the lower aristocracy. We have yet to gain an adequate idea of what percentage of the total national effort the Nara achievement represented. In view of the "reassertion" of Japanese tastes and customs which had become visible before this period was over, we may surmise that outside the capital or a few major provincial administrative centers the "continental fashion" fell off rapidly. Nara, in its grandeur, was an oasis of cosmopolitan art in an otherwise traditional and rather folkish Japanese plain.

Another problem confronts the attempt to visualize, on the basis of remaining artifacts, how Nara looked in its heyday. Today the visitor to old Nara who views the monasteries or studies in museums the remnants of eighth-century Japan may well be led astray by what he sees. Seemingly so much remains of Nara's past, and in such an excellent state of preservation, that he is apt to assume that what he sees is indeed the way Nara looked 1,200 years ago. Let the observer remember, then, that Nara in its day (like Tokyo today) was the cosmopolitan center of the country. It was a city bright with color and bustling with activity. The message of peace and religious contemplation which comes to those who today visit the Tōshōdaiji or the Yakushiji is to a large extent the work of centuries of weathering. The "religious piety" manifest in the darkened features of a Buddhist icon is heightened by the work of centuries of incense smoke. The quiet unworldly attitude of the attendant priests in temple courtyards reflects the passage of time which has bypassed the Nara sects in favor of newer and more evangelical varieties of Buddhism. The early Nara was a city created not for religious or artistic purposes, but as an administrative and court center. Its style was based on the great Chinese capital of Changan. Its plan was bold and symmetrical, as were the state laws and ordinances adopted at the time. Public buildings were highly colored, with pillars of red and roofs of colored tile. Public officials bustled to and fro in uniforms, each color designating a rank. The Buddhist priesthood was as deeply involved in public activities as in private meditation, for priests were prominent in state affairs. Temples also were colorful. Their exterior beams were tinted red, while inside the statues gleamed with gold or bright primary colors.

Finally let us remember that despite the many buildings and statues still dating from this period found in the vicinity of present-day Nara, these represent but a bare fragment of the total output of the age. Only an example of two of the public buildings (in the Tōshōdaiji group) or palace architecture (the Hokkedō of the Tōdaiji) are to be found. Rice fields have now reoccupied the great rectangle, two by three miles, laid out with symmetrically patterned streets to form the official city. Time has softened the image of the former capital city of Nara.

Among the Buddhist statues reflecting the style of the Nara age the most characteristic is the great black-bronze trinity of the Yakushiji: a nine-foot seated Buddha with an eleven-foot pair, Nikkō and Gakkō (deities of Sun and Moon), on either side. (The problem of dating this group has already been aluded to, so that we may in fact be speaking of a late Hakuhō creation.) The gently swaying stance and curving drapery of the flanking figures provide a remarkable contrast to the imposing immobility of the central figure. T'ang technique and taste are revealed in the skillful mastery of the bronze medium, realistic or illusionistic handling of the human form and dress, and a remarkable fluidity of line.

The grand scale and dignity of eighth-century architecture are best seen at the Tōshōdaiji, the monastery built in 759 under direction of the Chinese priest Chien-chên. The T'ang style of building is typified by this assemblage: roofs are proportionately lower, eaves wider, and interiors higher than in previous styles as a result of newly evolved bracketing techniques. The Kondō, with huge wooden frontal colonnades rising from a stone platform, contains three enormous lacquer sculptures, rising more than twenty feet to the tips of their halos (the work of Chinese and Japanese sculptors). Of these the central seated Roshana Buddha with 1,000 tiny Buddhas in his halo may well provide, in a smaller scale to be sure, the best approximation of what the Great Buddha of the Tōdaiji must have been. The mood is that of calm and imposing dignity befitting the spirit of Vairocana, unifier of the universe.

The chief focus of artistic and religious activity of the eighth century was, of course, the Tōdaiji with its fifty-three-foot cast bronze Roshana. The temple, patronized by the Imperial Family, held a supreme position in the Buddhist hierarchy, being the chief among a network of state-sponsored provincial temples (*kokubunji*). The statue of Roshana (or Vairocana), completed after seven years, was dedicated in A.D. 752 by Emperor Shōmu in a magnificent ceremony attended by visitors from as far away as India. Damaged in successive fires, it is now replaced by the cumbrous Daibutsu (Great Buddha) of today. Only a few petals of the original lotus-seat dais remain. Little remains as well of the original Tōdaiji buildings save the eighth-century Sangatsudō of the Hokkedō (Lotus Sutra Hall). This building holds most of the surviving Tempyō period sculpture of the Tōdaiji. The entire assemblage, containing a wide variety of products of the lacquerer, clay modeler, painter, and metal caster, all brought together under the direction of priest and architect, exemplifies the harmonious integration of the arts so characteristic of the Nara age. It illustrates also the vitality of Buddhist imagination as it took on many new forms represented by the multiplicity of iconographic renditions.

One of the most remarkable survivals of the Tempyō period, and certainly the most useful to the cultural historian, is the Shōsōin. A storehouse of the Tōdaiji, established to contain the personal effects of Emperor Shōmu, it is a literal treasure trove of art objects which are at the same time objects of use from the Imperial Palace. Here in good condition, to list a few, are musical instruments, saddles, stirrups and bridles, swords, rugs, brocades, glass ewers, lead-glazed ceramics, ivory rulers, rhinoceros-horn cups, a lacquered game table with push-button counter-storage drawers, jade flutes which will still play, willow baskets that will hold water, furniture, writing utensils, and many other domestic articles used at the court and by the priesthood. No other collection shows so clearly the multiplicity of cultural influences (Chinese, Indian, Persian) which played upon the Japanese aristocracy of this age. No other shows so vividly the luxurious life of the Imperial Family and the varied capacities of the public artisans of the time. The Shōsōin building itself is an important archetype of the early Japanese storage house, a type of "log cabin" using logs hewn in triangular cross section and laid to permit a "breathing" action, held above the damp earth by nine-foot posts almost three feet thick.

Jōgan (or Early Heian) Period

For reasons of state a new capital, Heian, was set up forty miles from Nara on the site of the present Kyoto in A.D. 794. This move did not drastically change the nature of government, the composition of society, or the way of life of the Japanese, high or low. Heian itself was built in a style not so different from that of Nara, though larger. The city plan and style of architecture for public buildings were essentially Chinese. Nonetheless, it is possible to detect certain changes of mood and interest in the religious art and architecture of the ninth century.

In Buddhist art, the spread of new esoteric sects, Tendai and Shingon, fostered a complicated and difficult iconography, using elaborate symbolism and diagrammatic representations. Typical of the changes introduced by the new sects were icons, often many-armed and many-headed, representing Sino-Hindu concepts of deities that only the specifically instructed could grasp. Such are the six-armed seated Nyoirin Kannon of the Kanshinji near Osaka and the three-faced, four-armed Brahmā at the Tōji in Kyoto. More traditional subjects, following the style established in Nara, were treated in a freer and more earthy fashion. The compelling beauty of the eleven-faced Kannon at Nara's Hokkeji nunnery, is achieved out of a single block of imported fragrant sandalwood. Its flowing drapery tempers the heavy frame and accentuates the lengthy arm reaching downward toward every worshiper who seeks salvation. One senses increasing mysticism in the representation, a greater mastery over wood and of the chisel, and a more symbolic use of line in these works of the early Heian period.

The few surviving paintings of the Jōgan period are masterpieces of powerful esoteric iconography. Some are benign ones like the Amida on a lotus at the Hokkeji and the Brahmā on a smiling six-tusked pink elephant at the Saidaiji; others are terrifying like the Yellow Fudō, tusked and glaring, standing with ready rope and sword at Miidera. The better-known Red Fudō at Mount Kōya, seated on the rocks with a halo of red-tongued flames and a dragon wrapped around his weapon, is equally awesome. The esoteric sects also brought into vogue a type of painting known as the *mandara* (mandala), a stylized pictorial representation of complex ideas of the relationship of the Buddha nature to the visible universe and other cosmological concepts.

Probably the domestic architecture of the aristocracy of the period was undergoing the refinement which became apparent in the public buildings of later centuries. Early Heian official buildings continued, with greater freedom and adaptation to Japanese needs, the Chinese style inspired from the T'ang dynasty. Examples such as the Kasuga Shrine of Nara or the modern reconstruction at the Heian Jingū in Kyoto, show the continental use of red-painted woodwork, as well as extensively bracketed eaves supporting lightly curved tile roofs. The Japanese carpenter was beginning to assimilate the heavy T'ang style to the convenience of Japanese court life.

In the temple architecture of this period certain new styles of building with symbolic significance for the esoteric sects were introduced (notably a new form of single-storied pagoda called *tahōtō*). But the most conspicuous change was in the location of monasteries. Enryakuji (the Tendai headquarters on Mount Hiei) and Kongōbuji (the Shingon headquarters on Mount Kōya) were both set in mountainous surroundings of great natural beauty. Buildings were no longer arranged symmetrically, but to fit the mountain terrain. Now cinnabar-painted temples were set against the background of tall evergreens. The existing buildings of Enryakuji and Kongōbuji are, of course, of a much later date, so that Murōji near Kyoto offers us the best approximation of what the early monasteries may have been like.

Fujiwara (or Late Heian) Period

With the assertion of Fujiwara mastery over the Heian Court, the nature of Japanese government, as well as the tastes and interests of the courtiers, changed markedly. By the beginning of the tenth century the Japanese court had already abandoned the practice of dispatching official embassies to China or the sending of students abroad for study. The Sinicized bureaucracy adopted two centuries earlier was relegated to ceremonial status, while a few organs of effective government revealed an actual power structure which rested on the domination of a handful of aristocratic families: the Imperial, Fujiwara, Minamoto, Heike, Ki, Sugawara, and a few others. These great families and the temples and shrines patronized by them now drew their income from extensive provincial estates (*shōen*) over which they acquired the rights of proprietorship and taxation.

Court society no longer looked so slavishly to China for inspiration, though Chinese learning was still highly prized; and the elements of court life, dwellings, secular painting, and literature, gave evidence of a "reassertion" of non-Chinese tastes. Whether this reassertion was consciously arrived at or merely reflected a willingness to accept in high society tastes and ways of life which had characterized the mass of the lower aristocracy who could not achieve the Chinese ideal, we do not know. Probably a fusion of values was taking place; the result was both an "assimilation" of Chinese influence and a reassertion of certain Japanese styles.

But the changes were most notable in the more domestic arts. Works in Buddhist architecture, iconography, and painting showed no marked break with previous eras. One of the most characteristic buildings of the age and certainly one of the most beautiful of all Japanese temples in the Chinese style is the Byōdōin, built under Fujiwara patronage at

Uji, near Kyoto. Much time and skill and great revenue from the provinces were lavished on its central Hōōdō (Phoenix Hall) and the Buddhist objects it contains. The Byōdōin permits one to recapture the spirit of Fujiwara opulence at its height. The building, a great hall with open pavilions to left and right, simulates a bird with outstretched wings just landed on the shore of the lotus pool in front. On the ridgepole of the hall are two large and handsome bronze birds, the *hō* and *ō* that when symbolically united become the magic phoenix. Within is the gilt wood seated image of Amida, attributed to the sculptor Jōchō, with dais, nimbus, halo, and canopy of intricate flowering and flamboyant design. Pillars are lacquered and inlaid with mother-of-pearl. High on the walls, separately hung, are low-relief carvings of more than fifty Bodhisattvas, many with musical instruments, all once brilliantly colored. Below these on wooden panels are paintings of deities descending to earth from Amida's Heaven.

Despite the continued strong Chinese influence in the Byōdōin, there are certain features of the assemblage which demonstrate a change in aesthetic mood and religious setting. The placement of the Hōōdō on the edge of an irregularly shaped pond and the delicacy of the architecture are responsive to new religious beliefs, particularly the new worship of Amida, the Buddha of the Western Paradise. The spread of the concept of Amidism in court circles of the tenth century reflected a lessening of the remoteness of Buddhist beliefs and a greater reliance on the comforting doctrines of salvation and belief in the existence of a paradise. Typical of the religious paintings of this age were the scenes of Buddha and his host hovering above the earth waiting to receive the soul of the dying believer. Frequently courtiers lay in their deathbeds holding a fine thread the other end of which was attached to the hand of the painted Buddha. The Byōdōin, dedicated to Amida Buddha, floated as if in a paradise beyond the lotus pond set in front of it.

More indicative of the innovations in architectural design hinted at in the Byōdōin was the style of aristocratic palace architecture known as *shinden-zukuri*. The *shinden* style, while retaining a basically Chinese method of construction, softened the overall effect by its tendency to omit the cinnabar coloring on exterior woodwork, its use of bark- or reed-thatched roofs, and a studied asymmetry in the distribution of rooms and causeways about a garden and pond. Portions of the present Imperial Palace of Kyoto (a nineteenth-century construction) carry out this style, which shows a quiet restraint in interior decor and a more natural integration of the building with the surrounding landscape. A similar modification of Chinese symmetry and similar sensitivity to the natural setting are revealed in the famous shrine of Itsukushima, built on piles extending out into the water of Miyajima.

Considered most characteristically Japanese among the paintings of the period was the long horizontal narrative scroll (*emakimono*), which became popular along with the revival of native literature. Among great surviving examples of these brush drawings and paintings are the "Ban dainagon" scroll, a story of palace fire and intrigue; the "Shigisan engi," a story of a miraculous flying warehouse; the "Genji monogatari," a love story; and the "Animal Caricatures," actually warnings in a humorous vein of the pitfalls that beset the priesthood. This last, attributed to Toba Sōjō, abbot of the Kōzanji near Kyoto, exhibits some of the finest ink brush drawings produced in Japan. In style, the *emakimono* reveal some of the characteristics of the narrative court literature which flourished at the time: a secular concern with court life, a greater reliance on inspiration derived from native subjects, a stylized quality of representation, a brilliant use of color, and a formalized perspective which looks down from a slight angle above the horizontal. And it is these features which distinguish the "native style" of painting (Yamato-e) as it developed in contradistinction to the modes of painting introduced from China.

Kamakura Period

In many ways the political changes which culminated in the establishment of the Kamakura shogunate marked the greatest social and cultural turning point since the Taika Reform. With the founding of the Kamakura military government a new class (the warrior provincial aristocracy, or samurai) came into prominence. For the first time two distinct social classes with differing tastes and interests (the courtiers of the capital and the provincial military aristocracy) patronized the arts. Consequently new patterns of life, new provincial cultural influences, new tastes and values, and even new religious sects gained currency. The dominant style of life in Japan after the twelfth century has been called *feudal*. It certainly reflected the rise of the samurai class and the increasingly important function of the Buddhist monasteries as the refuge of arts and letters, but it was not a time of complete "provincialism." Kamakura became a major cultural center; there was renewed contact between Japan and China, which was then in a period of artistic ascendancy under the Sung dynasty. Thus, many currents affected the variety and content of Japanese art, making it difficult to characterize the age in simplistic terms.

By the twelfth century, also, another feature of Japanese art production had begun to have an effect. This was the influence of schools or guilds of craftsmen consisting of groups of artisans working together under the direction of a master artist. Such groups, which dated from the late Heian period, were by Kamakura times quite strongly in evidence, and artists themselves appeared to become more self-conscious of their role in society. The chief artist was by Kamakura times more apt to be identified by name with his products, and stylistic differences between synonymous schools provide the material for art criticism.

In the realm of Buddhist art several great accomplishments stand out to set the spirit of the age. One was the national effort expended in rebuilding the Tōdaiji in Nara (the temple had been burned during the wars preceding the establishment of the Kamakura shogunate); the other was the casting of the great Amida Buddha at Kamakura. These and related sculptural works reveal two significant changes in mood: (1) a conscious renaissance of the Tempyō style and (2) an accompanying veering from idealism to realism. In Nara and Kyoto, Unkei (1148–1223), master sculptor, architect, and temple restorer, held sway with his six sons, directing dozens of carpenters, wood-carvers, and laborers. His work is representative of the new injection of earthly vigor and realism into the traditional forms of Buddhist iconography. His greatest project, six 30-foot images ordered by Yoritomo for the restored Tōdaiji, were later lost by fire. But a giant guardian pair, Niō, still stand in the great South Gate. Scarcely less famous is the pair of demon lantern bearers—stunted, muscular, and ferocious—carved by Unkei's son Kōben for the Kōfukuji.

Unkei's best-preserved project, done with his sons, is the Hokuendō of the Kōfukuji. The building is a refined emulation of the eight-sided Yumedono. Inside is a seated eight-foot Buddha Miroku flanked by a pair of six-foot standing figures, two philosophers (Seishi and Muchaku). Single images attributed to Unkei alone are a seated Jizō (guardian deity) in Kyoto; a three-foot Dainichi (Maha Vairocana), on which he labored for a year while in his twenties; and at least one of the 1,000 Senju Kannon, all nearly life-sized, at the Sanjūsan-gendō in Kyoto. In the same hall is the bony, half-naked holy man Basu. Elsewhere in Kyoto, the lifelike priest Kūya who brought the name of Buddha to the people in the streets, long attributed to Unkei, is now identified as the work of Kōshō. Unkei's work is typical of the age in its advanced use of the craft guild system and the highly developed mastery of the technique of joinery and assembly that made possible the mass production of sacred images of great size.

Two sculptures remaining at Kamakura are illustrative of the spirit of the Kamakura age: (1) The great bronze Buddha Daibutsu rises forty-nine feet above the worshiper, imposing and serene under the sky since tidal waves long ago destroyed its temple. This statue, by unknown casters, though erected in emulation of the Nara Great Buddha, portrays well the mood of Amidism which nourished the religious awakening of the times. (2) A squat portrait of the warrior-aristocrat Uesugi Shigefusa in tall hat and formal dress illustrates the new interest in political and religious leaders which was to result in a genre of portraits in sculpture.

Even more than sculpture, the Buddhist paintings of the period emphasize new sectarian interest. "Amida's Welcome," as in the famous Kyoto three-screen version, shows Buddha rising as it were directly beyond the hills of Japan, so real is the blue-green landscape. Heaven and Hell in the side screens seem almost incidental. The narrative scrolls, even when dealing with the sacred and miraculous like the "Travels of Ippen Shōnin" or the "Tale of Saigyō," devote much space and brushwork to the hills and trees and valleys of this world, although landscape is never painted for itself. Adventure is depicted as in the "Kibi" scroll (perhaps a Heian work, now at Boston), and war in the "Heiji" scroll (also at Boston) or the "Burning of the Sanjō Palace." Here and in other paintings the action of bulls and horses is superbly portrayed. In the combination of broad areas of high color with a dashing brush stroke, as in the "Tale of Michizane" at Kyoto's Kitano Shrine, the Yamato-e style of Japanese painting is brought to a high point. Three examples of portraiture will indicate its scope: Yoritomo, the first Shogun, with a fine face topping the massive blackness of his robe; the child who became Kōbō Daishi floating on a lotus in a dream; and the priest Myōe contemplating birds and squirrels from the branch of a crooked tree. The last named, though touched with light color, shows the beginnings of the monochrome ink style which developed to a high point in later centuries.

In temple architecture the Kamakura period witnessed a variety of styles, some reviving eighth-century Nara features, some showing the effects of new classical Chinese influence, and some incorporating new features imported by Zen priests from south China. In all there was revealed a deeper understanding of wood and grain and of bracketing, vertical and cantilever supports, and ingenious joining techniques. Of the rebuilt Tōdaiji, only a few structures still remain. The South Gate and the Great Buddha Hall demonstrate the heavy and somewhat ornate, but certainly imposing, style characterized by the elaborate exterior bracketing which permitted the freeing of the interior from the heavy crossbeams. In the "classical revival" style was the rebuilt Kōfukuji. The great five-storied pagoda particularly shows the combination of traditional structures and new size. Typical of the new Zen-inspired style was the Shariden of the Engakuji at Kamakura, probably the sole building of the period still left in the city. Built to house a tooth of the Buddha, its dark, rather somber style is accentuated by the use of natural materials.

Ashikaga (or Muromachi) Period

While the Japanese of today look to the Heian period as the classical age of the arts and letters, the aristocratic culture of that period has passed so far into history that it has proved a remote and unapproachable ideal. From the contemporary point of view, of much greater significance are the arts and tastes of the Ashikaga age, many of which are perpetuated today as the chief "traditional" modes of Japanese aesthetic expression. In painting (sumi-e), in drama (the nō), in the domestic arts (ceramics, landscape gardening, the tea ceremony, flower arrangement), and in domestic architecture (the tearoom), many of the basic forms and aesthetic canons respected in Japan today, had their origins in this age. The particular circumstances which gave rise to the flourishing of new art forms in an age of political unrest reflect the final absorption of the culture of the court nobility into the samurai sector of society. The establishment of the Ashikaga shogunate in Kyoto and the ascendancy of the provincial military houses over the proprietorships of the aristocracy completed the rise of the samurai as the dominant class throughout Japan. While the warrior aristocracy emulated the life of the court nobility, it also patronized new art forms and asserted its own particular tastes. Into this milieu were injected powerful influences which were derived from the spiritual and cultural leadership of the Zen monasteries and the new direct contacts with China.

The entire mood and spirit of the arts of the Ashikaga period contrast markedly with those of the aristocratically dominated Nara and Heian ages. By the fourteenth century the characteristic atmosphere was one of mysticism and restraint. Lavish displays of luxurious living were not lacking, but no longer did a small aristocracy have the capacity to draw upon the resources of the entire nation. There were no efforts to build a large and completely new capital city. There was less color, less visible display of social distinction. The Zen monasteries provided a meditative atmosphere. The Ashikaga shoguns, when not engaged in warfare, were apt to take pleasure in the cloister as an escape from the harsh realities of the world.

The two great patrons of art among the shoguns were Yoshimitsu

(r. 1368–1394) and Yoshimasa (r. 1449–1473). The former, who brought to a high point the prestige of the shogunate, possessed sufficient power to play the autocrat. Around him he created a life of splendid ostentation. His monument was the gilded Kinkakuji, a villa on the edge of a pond set in a spacious deer park. Here he collected works of art from across the world and wore his brocaded robes received from the Emperor of China. Yet for all the display and search for novelty which excited Yoshimitsu, he and his followers were men of disciplined taste. The Kinkakuji for all its splendor was designed to take its place in a natural setting.

Yoshimasa, who lived through the declining years of the shogunate, drew about him, as if in compensation for the hopelessness of the political situation, an even more sophisticated coterie of priests and artists. His monument, the Silver Pavilion (Ginkakuji), expresses that mystical quality which the connoisseurs of the time looked for in all the arts, from the drama to ceramics. The effort to find an "inner meaning" in nature and in the artistic creations of man demonstrated to a high degree the fusion of the aristocratic tastes of the classical period with the deep introspective quality of Zen Buddhism.

By Ashikaga times the art of Buddhist sculpture had passed from its place of foremost importance. The Kamakura tendency toward realism may in part be responsible for this decline. But a more probable reason is that Zen Buddhism, with its emphasis on contemplation, simply made the icon less necessary for purposes of ritual. The talents of the woodcarver were turned to other tasks: portrait statues, ornamental panels, and nō masks.

Architecture of the Ashikaga period is characterized by the use of natural wood and the subordination of building to the surrounding natural setting. Typical of the time are the fragile beauty of the Kinkakuji and Ginkakuji and the quiet courtyards of the great Zen monasteries on the outskirts of Kyoto. The two shogunal pavilions were essentially viewing towers from which to contemplate the surrounding gardens of water, rocks, and pines. Both were planned and laid out at great expense to recapture the world of natural effects and to suggest to meditative minds the relationship of man to nature. This demand for harmony between man-made building and natural setting is even today one of the cardinal principles of Japanese architecture. Resting on canons which stressed simplicity arrived at through careful selection and design, it was achieved by a fusion of native architectural styles exemplified in the Shinto shrine, certain Chinese technological features, and the aesthetic principles which emanated from the Zen monasteries.

The temple architecture of Zen monasteries is illustrated in the partially preserved or restored buildings of the official "five temples" (*gozan*) at Kyoto (actually there were six), consisting of the Nanzenji, Tenryūji, Shōkokuji, Kenninji, Tōfukuji, and Manjūji. Set among the wooded outskirts of the city, these large monastic establishments contained several subtemples and many central buildings. The dominant architectual style, characterized by unpainted pillars and woodwork and large expanses of white plaster walls, showed a strong influence from south China. The mood of austerity was accentuated by the demeanor of the black-robed priests.

Painting was undoubtedly the greatest art of the Ashikaga period. Although largely derivative of Chinese landscape style, the new manner of ink painting appeared to fit the mood of the time and inspired Japanese artists (many of them Zen priests) to a remarkable mastery of Chinese techniques and even to fresh creative imagination. In the new monochrome style known as "water and ink" (*suiboku*) vivid colors were replaced by black on white. Painting now depended upon skilled brushwork—bold strokes, flat washes, and dark splashing, varying from jet black to complete transparency—and on the use of line and balance. The painter who brought this technique to its first height was Shūbun, a priest of Shōkokuji, who was named official painter of the Ashikaga shogunate during the mid-fifteenth century. More famous, however, was the priest Sesshū, who traveled in China to acquire a mastery of the *suiboku* techniques. Sesshū painted Japanese landscapes with considerable realism and is credited with putting a native stamp on his work. His longest scroll, less than a foot high but some fifty feet long, now in the Mōri Collection, unrolls to show a pilgrim path over land and sea from early spring to deep winter. Quite different is his "Ferryman," in which a few impressionistic "ink-splash" strokes hint of mountain range, river expanse, and mist and space. A painting by Sesson, one of Sesshū's successors, shows a ship in a storm approaching a rocky shore. Ryōzen is known for a white heron by the water done by inking in the currents around it; Josetsu, for a "Fool Catching a Catfish with a Gourd"; and Geiami, for a fool "Laughing at the Moon." Kaō depicted a "Sage on a Tiger"; Shūkō, a sage on a donkey seated backward. Such themes were drawn from the religious vocabulary of the Zen monasteries, and in the stroke quality itself was intended a statement of the direct approach to religious perception.

But not all painting of the Ashikaga period was religious in inspiration and purely Chinese in style. The Yamato-e tradition of decorative work, particularly the pictorial scroll, continued to be popular and was perpetuated at the now declining Imperial Court. During the middle of the fifteenth century the most important painter in this style was Tosa

Mitsunobu. A fusion of the Tosa tradition with Chinese-style *suiboku* painting resulted in the formation of the Kanō school of pseudo-Chinese decorative artists begun by Motonobu (1476–1559). Thus there was started the strictly decorative and secular school of professional painters who dominated the Japanese scene from Motonobu's time until the end of the nineteenth century.

Another of the great art forms of the Ashikaga period was the landscape garden. Laid out in conjunction with the temple and pavilion architecture commissioned by the Zen priesthood and military aristocracy, these gardens sought in various degrees of realism or abstraction to depict nature in miniature. By far the most famous single garden is the abstraction of sand, moss, and rock at the Ryōanji, something of a tour de force which reproduces the feeling of a *suiboku* painting. More characteristic are the large "walking" gardens of the Kinkakuji and Ginkakuji, built around irregular pools. The moss garden of the Saihōji contains one of the most nearly perfect examples of waterfall and stream created without water (*kare-sansui*) out of rock and sand and, of course, moss.

At the center of much of the aesthetic connoisseurship of the time was the social pastime which was built up around the drinking of tea. The tea ceremony (*cha-no-yu*) was developed into a ritualized form of social entertainment which laid heavy emphasis on art appreciation. As such it became a vehicle for the dissemination of art tastes in a variety of fields, such as ceramics and lacquer ware. Developed to a high point of sophistication by the Shogun Yoshimasa, it was taken up by the military aristocracy whether in the capital or the provinces. The use of ceramic bowls now became common in Japan, first through the import of Sung celadon and "Temmoku" ware, but later using the fine products developed in many local kilns. In these years Seto stood out in quality and ability to approach Chinese craftsmanship. This kiln has given its name to the common word for pottery in Japan (*setomono*).

Another art form which stimulated numerous subsidiary arts was the nō drama. Although the drama itself belongs to the domain of literature, music, and dance, the visual effects of the drama were carried by gorgeous brocaded costumes and by imaginatively carved masks. The work of the skilled weaver in silk and hemp and the dyer and worker in gold and silver thread is well illustrated in the former. The nō masks constitute one of the most exquisitely developed genres in all Japanese art history. Masks ranging in representation from demons or demonic humans to the ingenuous beauty of young womanhood, masks which tell the range of human emotions from humor to tragic suffering, were carved with utmost economy of line and balance between realism and dramatic stylization by artisans attached to the houses of military lords.

The popularity of *cha-no-yu* and nō drama during the Ashikaga period is indicative of yet another dimension to the culture of the time. By the sixteenth century one can note a marked increase in the volume and distribution of works of art throughout Japan. The development of overseas trade which joined Japan with Korea, China, and Southeast Asia, the growth of internal trade and production, and the rise of numerous provincial centers of political power all helped to extend the demand for works of beauty or for more elegant living. No longer did the capital constitute the one center of craftsmanship. Groups of artisans were patronized in numerous provincial centers where they worked for local military lords or produced for distribution through a flourishing guild system. The "aristocratic life" was to some extent becoming more common.

Momoyama Period

With the disappearance of the centralizing power of the Ashikaga shogunate during the sixteenth century, Japan became divided politically into the numerous territories of military lords (*daimyō*) who competed among themselves for regional or national supremacy. The last half of the sixteenth century saw the appearance of large numbers of castle towns (*jōkamachi*), which served as administrative headquarters and garrison posts for these regional hegemonies. Castle towns, dominated by the rugged castle walls and moats and the great many-storied keeps of the *daimyō*, housed the regional military aristocracy and protected the attached service class of artisans and merchants. No longer did Nara or Kyoto, as national capitals, dominate the cultural scene. Although with the winning of national hegemony by Nobunaga and Hideyoshi, their castles at Azuchi and Momoyama became for a time the chief centers of political authority and the focal points of art patronage, these centers differed only in degree from the scattered regional strongpoints of the provincial *daimyō*.

The *daimyō* made up a new group of provincial military aristocracy whose lives had been spent, for the most part, in the battlefield. While their newly won prestige and wealth gave them the capacity to build lavish palaces or patronize artists on a grand scale, their tastes were not so sophisticated or finely developed as those of the courtiers of Kyoto or the military aristocracy of the Ashikaga period. Characteristic of the Momoyama period in architecture are the great castles, such as Osaka (a recent reconstruction) and Himeji (one of the finest remaining examples of the time). Palaces (which adjoined the castles) are characterized by eccentrically curved roofs, elaborately carved panels, bright colors, lacquered pillars, and lavish gold screens. It is the latter, the Momoyama screens (*byōbu*), which are considered the most typical examples of the taste of the period.

The dominant school of painters was the Kanō school, which under Eitoku (1543–1590) and Sanraku (1559–1635) brought to a height the decorative style known as *shōhekiga* (decorative wall painting). Much use of gold leaf for background and bold colors combined to give a flamboyant overall effect, but, as in the equally colorful carvings of the time, the individual parts of these works of art (the brush stroke or the carved line) reveal a direct and abbreviated stylization characteristic of Japanese workmanship. Examples of the work of this era have for the most part been destroyed by warfare, but parts of Hideyoshi's castles or temple structures built under his patronage remain in "Hideyoshi's gate" at Tenryūji, the Jūrakudai at Nishihonganji, and the Chishakuin monastery, all in Kyoto.

Above all, the Momoyama period was a time of rapidly changing tastes and pursuit of novelty. With the arrival of Portuguese traders and Jesuit priests, a fad for "things Western" spread throughout *daimyō* society. Hideyoshi's two ambitious military expeditions into Korea resulted in the influx of new artistic concepts from the continent and the introduction of numerous artisan communities, especially potters from Korea.

Tokugawa (or Edo) Period

The establishment of the Tokugawa shogunate in 1603, the elimination of Hideyoshi's remaining influence in 1615, and the closing of the country to foreign contact in 1639 marked successively the passage of Japan into a state of peaceful and isolated existence which was to continue for more than two centuries. A time of relative prosperity as well, the Tokugawa era witnessed a widespread florescence of the arts and letters. The art of this period is so complex in its social base and so many-sided that it can no longer be described in terms of a single dominant, or even a cluster of dominant, genres. Particularly with the rise of the mercantile urban classes (the *chōnin*) there came into being two quite different cultural patterns, that of the samurai and that of the commoners, each deserving the attention of the art historian.

The cultural and artistic life of the still dominant samurai class tended to perpetuate, without great modifications, the major aristocratic genres of the Ashikaga and Momoyama periods. Much of the Tokugawa product was derivative and lacked the spark of originality. In architecture the ornate mausoleums of Nikko and Ueno, the lavish castle-palace interiors of the Nijō in Kyoto, and the massive reconstructions of the Komponchūdō on Mount Hiei and the Daibutsu hall of Tōdaiji bring to a climax the heavily decorative styles and techniques of the Momoyama period. For the regional lords the efforts of lacquerers, potters, weavers, metalworkers, and other artisans were poured out in great quantity.

Typical of the artistic life of the Tokugawa military aristocracy was a formalization and codification of earlier traditions. The tea ceremony and nō drama, perpetuated as the prerogative of the ruling class, became increasingly stereotyped. So also were many of the canons of taste which accompanied the tea ceremony. The Kanō school of painting continued to dominate the realm of professional decorative painters, perpetuating with little imagination the technique and themes of the founders of the school. Sculptors made no noteworthy innovations.

Yet within the sector of aristocratic art a number of significant achievements and innovations are recorded during the Tokugawa period. In architecture the detached palaces of Katsura and Shūgakuin stand today as perhaps the noblest expressions of Japanese domestic architecture, combining excellence of architectural line, use of natural materials, integration with a garden setting, and an overall restraint which is typical of the best of Japanese tradition. Katsura, in particular, designed by Kobori Enshū, has attracted worldwide attention and inspired many a modern architect.

In painting three new lines of development deserve attention. At one extreme the great stylizers and simplifiers such as Sōtatsu and Kōrin developed the ultimate in decorative beauty of screens and other furnishings out of the Yamato-e tradition. At the other extreme men like Maruyama Ōkyo instilled new vitality into the Chinese monochrome tradition. Maruyama's style reflected the increasing rationalism of the age and achieved realism through techniques of perspective and modeling learned from the West. Finally, fresh currents from China together with the spread of Confucian philosophy among the Tokugawa samurai led to the popularity of the "literati style" (bunjinga or nanga). Indulged in by amateurs more often than professionals, this style which cultivated a deliberate sense of "sketchiness" was especially suited to the expression of philosophical ideas. Yosa (Taniguchi) Buson (1716–1783) and Ike-no-Taiga (1723–1776) combined realism and idealism to express poetic moods of man's relationship to nature. Others in this tradition, Gyokudō (1745–1820), Mokubei (1767–1833), and Watanabe

Kazan (1793–1841), were all men of varied talents with highly formalized Confucian approaches to their painting.

In sharp contrast to the arts of the upper class were the creations of the *chōnin* stratum of Tokugawa society. Denied by its lowly status the noble sentiments and philosophies which were the property of the political and cultural leaders of the time, the *chōnin* concentrated on the world of entertainment. *Chōnin* arts emerged from an environment dominated by the popular drama, the courtesan, and the vulgar novel. The chief art form proper to *chōnin* culture consisted of the so-called *"ukiyo-e"* (paintings of the floating world), wood-block prints produced mostly to illustrate novels, advertise night spots and dramatic productions, or commemorate places of beauty along the travel routes frequented by the many tourists of this more affluent age. The new *ukiyo-e* school was deeply folkish in its inspiration, though it may have been influenced in its wood-block technique by a knowledge of Chinese prints acquired at Nagasaki. Printing techniques were rapidly devised to meet the popular demand, and the whole medium brought painter, engraver, and printer together into a guildlike relationship characteristic of Japanese artisanship. Considered a "vulgar art" in their day, the *ukiyo-e* have in modern times received much attention, especially from Western critics.

During the Tokugawa period the *ukiyo-e* tradition passed through a cycle of development from crude beginnings to sophisticated flowering and to ultimate decadence. Early artists relied on the strength of their lines as well as on colors. Gradually, as an increasing number of blocks were used, each for a separate color, there was a consequent weakening of the strong black line. The integrity of the school was all but lost by the end of the period with the introduction of aniline dyes from the West. Individual Tokugawa artists, though versatile, have often become associated with specific subject matter. Sharaku's actors are superb theatrical characterizations; Harunobu's lovers rival Hindu miniatures in delicacy of technique and sentiment; Kiyonaga's courtesans, their garments boldly calligraphic, are at once alluring and sedate; Utamaro produces the "picture girl"; and, finally, Hokusai and Hiroshige, with increasing use of Western perspective, though avoiding shadows, capture the colorful everyday scene.

Two important consequences of the Tokugawa age of peace and relative prosperity evident in all social strata were the standardization of the canons for domestic architecture and the lavish development of the minor arts. The ordinary Japanese dwelling developed in this period is now recognized as a prime architectural creation of Japanese culture. Key features are the use of plain wood and materials in modular sizes;

resilient straw floor matting (tatami); thick sliding panels (fusuma) to shut off hallways; light papered partitions (shoji) to shut off or open up room space; sliding weather partitions (*amado*) removable so as to unite house and garden; separate bath (*furo*) and sanitation (*benjo*) facilities; the alcove (tokonoma) for the display of special art objects; the storage units for bedding and clothes (*oshiire*); the low, wide-eaved roof which protects against summer sun but permits the entrance of winter sunlight; and the attached garden designed of trees, rocks, occasionally flowering shrubs, and a trickle of water.

Encouraged both by the military aristocracy and the wealthy merchants, a host of Japanese artisans produced goods of high artistic integrity and technical competence in wood, lacquer, metal, porcelain, and textiles. Ingenious little nests of boxes called *inrō,* netsuke (miniature ivory, bone, and wood figures of men, mice, and other creatures) for use as toggles, and sword guards of iron with gold or silver inlay of this period are now avidly collected. These last are of infinite variety but of minor significance as compared with the splendid hand-forged steel sword blades of earlier periods, the pride of the samurai. Many of these blades rank with great examples of painting, sculpture, and architecture as national treasures in the eyes of the Japanese. Great ceramic traditions thrived at provincial kilns. Multicolored Tokugawa porcelains of Kakiemon and Nabeshima, developed to cut in on the Chinese trade with Europe, rivaled the earlier Ming wares of China; and the stoneware of Karatsu and Seto equaled the best folk pottery of the continent. These minor art forms were to develop into the folk traditions which have managed to weather the impact of Western art and industrial production and remain today a major heritage of Japan's artistic past.

JAPANESE ART GENRES: AN ANALYSIS OF THEIR CONTENT AND SPECIAL CHARACTERISTICS

Having briefly surveyed the standard premodern art periods as distinguished by the art historians of Japan, we may now turn to a number of questions of a more analytical nature concerning the content of major Japanese art genres and the qualities of aesthetic appreciation stimulated by them. As noted at the outset of this chapter, the Western observer is inevitably presented with certain difficulties in appreciating Japanese art because of the many differences in medium, content, and convention which it contains. Although much of Japanese art appears to speak directly to all observers, there are many problems of art vocabulary which require translation into terms understandable to the Western observer.

The Westerner viewing Japanese art finds many unfamiliar media and materials (in architecture, the tile roof or the tatami floor; in sculpture, the dry-lacquer technique) and many unexpected art forms (calligraphy or landscape gardens). Many features of Western art which we come to expect as part of the artist's standard range of vocabulary are missing in Japan, while others disregarded in the West are particularly stressed. A few examples may help to illustrate this point. Westerners are rarely trained to exploit or appreciate texture as a primary visual ingredient of art; it remains a tactile and secondary element, whereas in Japan texture is frequently stressed, for instance, in pottery, architectural decor, and textiles. Westerners, since the Renaissance at least, have come to expect originality or uniqueness of their artists in the choice of subject and treatment. They must learn to look for the quality of virtuosity so frequent in Japanese art whereby different artists limitlessly repeat identical subjects (such as bamboo leaves) just so that each effort has its subtle differences of rendition. The comparative art critic may find numerous generalizations of this type regarding the differing qualities of artistic tradition in Japan. Familiarity with the particular genres which make up Japanese art, the background of the artists, the purposes for which they produced, and the variety of themes and media available to them will make possible a more effective and truer appreciation of the worth of Japanese art.

In particular, a familiarity with the several genres in terms of the qualities intended by the Japanese artist and the conventional modes of the technique and critical vocabulary which shape Japanese art is necessary if the Western observer is to see below the surface which so often misleads him. The art of calligraphy, when first viewed, may seem to require incredible virtuosity to the outsider; he may think it incomprehensible that anyone could or should bother to master the complicated structure of the Chinese ideograph. Yet for those trained from childhood in the mastery of brush and character, there is no mystery. Novelty alone, the unusual bodily and facial shapes of Buddhist icons, for instance, may impress the non-Japanese observer with a sense of the grotesque unless he is reminded that such forms conformed to strict canons which every artisan had mastered in his time.

In the previous survey of art periods a good deal has been said about the three main categories of architecture, sculpture, and painting. For this reason there will be no need to dwell on particular works of art in these fields but rather to seek an understanding of the particular features of these traditions which reveal their aesthetic meaning. To this analysis it will be helpful to add a discussion of certain other art forms, notably calligraphy and ceramics, which are so close to the heart of the Japanese aesthetic sensibility.

Architecture

Japanese architecture, both public and domestic, contrasts in almost all its essential features with Western architectural tradition. In Japan the dominant materials are wood, paper, plaster, and the thatch or tile roof. Stone or brick buildings were not constructed prior to modern times. Thus Japan makes nothing of the arch and dome, the glass window, or the vaulted interior. Great crowds are not sheltered inside the largest temple buildings but rather are gathered before them in such a way that the façade of the building is accentuated. The skill of the Japanese builder traditionally turns to such features as the use of wood columns, careful joinery, and open spaces flexibly joined. Basically, as we have seen, Japanese architecture is compounded of two different (though in some ways similar) traditions: the native Japanese and the Chinese. The line of continuity from the early Shinto shrines includes interiors of palaces of the Heian period, Momoyama and Ashikaga period teahouses, and the style of domestic architecture standardized during the Tokugawa period; it has as its key ingredients the use of natural wood, straw, and paper and the harmony of building with the natural environment. The Chinese style, much grander, using tile roofs and painted pillars, brought to Japan a technology based on "representation" (to use Taut's word).[2] In the Chinese tradition it is the roof and the symmetrically designed building supported by massive pillars which are the prime architectural ingredients. As we have seen, architecture intended to be publicly imposing, whether it be the Buddhist temple, the government office or palace, the castle, or the storehouse, has tended to take the continental style, while the native style has been preferred more often in domestic dwellings or the residential interiors of palaces and other public structures.

For buildings in either the continental or the native styles the chief architectural feature which attracts the observer from a distance is the roof. The roof in its size or shape often indicates the purpose for which the building is used. A city like Kyoto, before the intrusion of modern ferroconcrete structures, looked from above like a vast sea of gray-black tile punctuated here and there by the massive roofs of a temple or palace and occasionally a pagoda. The slightly convex, thin-lined roof of the teahouse or detached palace (such as Katsura) which typifies the Japanese domestic style immediately reveals the change of mood

[2] *Ibid.*, p. 146.

between it and the heavier continental style with its concave lines and upswept ends.

On approaching Japanese buildings more closely the architectural elements which stand out are the wood joinery and the use of materials. In wooden buildings, in which plaster merely fills in the spaces between pillars and beams, the wooden skeleton provides both the visible feeling of stability and the sense of ornamentation. The visible construction, in its simplified Japanese style or the more elaborate Chinese, reveals the functions of the different wooden elements and (as in the elaborate bracketing which supports the Chinese tile roof) exemplifies the ingenuity of the designer. Much of the external beauty insinuated even into Chinese styles of structures in Japan comes from the contrast in color and texture between wooden structural pieces (darkened or painted vermilion) and white plaster. A further contrasting feature of domestic architecture is the external wooden rain panel (*amado*), as in the Katsura design.

Upon still closer observation, the chief elements which make up the aesthetic vocabulary of Japanese architecture are the skill of the carpenter in the use of natural materials and the contrast of the materials themselves. Exemplified in the teahouse is the subdued statement of mood through color, the underscoring of design through diversity in the texture of materials such as tatami, plaster walls, structural pillars, ceiling woodwork, the refined woods of the tokonoma, and the paper of the shoji. Such elements, requiring the sophisticated utilization of natural woods, constitute one of the chief aesthetic contributions of the Japanese style of architecture. The Japanese carpenter is particularly proud of his ability to plane off a surface to accentuate the grain or to polish wood to bring out its color.

One useful method of gaining an appreciation of the qualities of Japanese architecture which are looked for by the Japanese themselves is to study the more obvious efforts to be "arty." Certain examples of Japanese architecture which the Western observer first notes as quaint and Oriental are of an essentially sentimental and exaggerated taste from the Japanese point of view. Such features as a very heavy and ornate roof, complex and nonfunctional bracketing, an overuse of contrasting materials, and gnarled-tree woodwork in the tokonoma all point up the features which the Japanese most prize in their architecture by overdoing the effect. The careful observer comes to be able to distinguish the good from the bad: the refined beauty of the Hōryūji or the Shin-yakushiji in contrast to the overornateness of Nikko, the restraint of Katsura in contrast to the garish "naturalism" of a room in a Japanese country inn.

A final feature of Japanese architecture, though unrelated to its strictly aesthetic quality, which might be mentioned is its remarkable capacity to preserve itself despite the destructibility of the materials. Japan today shows some of the oldest wooden buildings in the world. Buildings such as the Hōryūji have withstood weather and earthquake for more than 1,200 years. Associated with the capacity to preserve public buildings is the custom of frequent repair. Buildings such as the Ise Shrine or the Kyoto Imperial Palace are in effect "preserved" by rebuilding according to the original specifications. The Japanese government has in recent years carried out a program of restoration of architectural monuments by careful dismantling and reconstruction after decayed parts have been replaced. The durability of Japanese architecture (in contrast to that of China) may also reflect the long continuity of homogeneous political leadership and cultural values which the Japanese have historically maintained. It reminds us that the turbulence of Japanese military history was provided until recently only by civil war, with less extensive destruction to certain institutions and property than in wars of invasion.

Sculpture

As we have been able to note, the art of sculpture in Japan has been confined largely to two rather distinct genres, Buddhist icons and decorative objects, the latter being designed either for the embellishment of architectural forms or for minor domestic uses. Despite the frequent mixture of these genres, it seems proper to differentiate them because of the clearly different intent of the sculptor in each genre. Buddhist iconography has tended to be highly ideographic and symbolic. It is produced within the limits of a strict iconographic canon and permits freedom only in its embellishment or its overall sentiment. Although sculpture took on remarkably forceful naturalism during the Kamakura period, Japanese sculptors in most periods seemingly were more strongly attracted to symbolism and convention. Secular carving (renditions of flowers and animals in decorative panels, for instance) has also tended toward stylization and conformity to rather narrow conventions of style. In studying the course of development of the sculptor's art in Japan we have noted a conspicuous rise and fall in the genre of Buddhist sculpture. Buddhist iconography in Japan lost its vitality by the late Kamakura period. Secular sculpture in wood and ivory was perhaps most advanced in the Momoyama age. The major product of the fusion of these two approaches to sculpture may well be the nō mask, which combined the deep symbolism of the Buddhist icon with the simplicity and stylization of the Japanese secular carver of wood.

In assessing the quality of Japanese sculpture and judging its worth the Western observer must again orient himself in terms of unfamiliar media and subject matter. Few Japanese sculptors ever worked in stone except for crude roadside images. Bronze was used in the early Buddhist icons, and iron, gold, or silver metalwork became highly developed in the Momoyama and Tokugawa periods. A specialized technique of modeling with lacquered fabric was used in the middle stages of Buddhist art. But it was chiefly wood which the Japanese sculptor used with success, freeing himself from the limiting dimensions of a single tree bole by remarkable skill in joinery. Wood was used sometimes in its natural state but was most frequently painted with black or red lacquer and then often covered with gold leaf.

The iconographic symbolism of Buddhist sculpture is naturally quite technical. Fundamentally the observer must realize that although the human form is borrowed by the sculptor, his basic intent is to create a visual manifestation of an abstract idea: compassion, nobility, fierce bravery, suffering. The statues of the Asuka or Tempyō ages cannot be judged from a naturalistic point of view. They do not portray specific fleshly beings but symbolize unearthly, ethereal, abstract beauty in every detail of shape, line, and texture.

The work of the secular sculptor is less symbolic and depends more on the skill of execution and on the boldness of stylization. To take the wood panels which adorn the walls of the Tōshōgū at Nikko as an example, they show extreme virtuosity in the technique of carving, together with stylization that draws on the great ornamental painting of the period. Flowery virtuosity rather than intense feeling is noteworthy in the treatment of waves, iris, bamboo, and birds. Note also that most subjects are flowers, birds, and animals. The secular tradition (except for a few portrait statues) entirely lacks interest in the human form whether clothed or nude. Like the Yamato-e painter, the secular carver in Japan has placed his emphasis on color and simplified line, giving a two-dimensional decorative effect.

Painting

Painting in Japan as much as any of the major genres of art shows a diversity between continental and domestic tradition. From the continent have come styles of Buddhist religious painting and the landscape and portrait style of the Sung and Yüan dynasties. These contrasted with the more decorative and secular Yamato-e tradition in choosing religious subjects in their philosophic concepts. Both styles are similar technologically, however, in the materials utilized and in many of the basic techniques of the artist. While the Japanese artist has painted on wood and plaster, he has made most frequent use of silk and hard-sized absorbent paper. Brushes are pointed, except for a few wide varieties for the application of washes. The color medium has been watercolor (soluble or in glue suspension). Japanese have not used oil or tempera prior to modern times.

The area or field available to Japanese painters often differs considerably from what the Westerner expects within his own traditions. Customary proportions are set by the room panel (fusuma), the folding screen (*byōbu*), the hanging scroll (kakemono), the long, horizontally rolled scroll (makimono), and various miniature forms (fans and *shikishi* squares). Few of these closely duplicate the proportions of the Western framed painting hung at eye level or parallel its use as a wall filler. Paintings on panels, screens, and fans are most often decorative in intent and conceived in relation to their architectural or utilitarian purposes. The horizontal scroll (emaki) generally contained pictures to illustrate passages of literary text. Paintings done for their own sake, to be hung and viewed independently, are found chiefly on the kakemono.

Japanese paintings, however, appear to suffer not at all from being so often bound to utilitarian objects. On the contrary, artists challenged and transcended these apparent limitations with immense aesthetic impact. Two recurrent devices may be mentioned, because they contribute so strongly to the flavor of Japanese art. In the first instance, an artist "breaks the frame," running his lines of composition outward to suggest a complete work somewhat larger than the area actually available. This device offers a remarkable amount of freedom and calls the viewer's attention to overall structure as against subject matter. Perhaps it had a rather practical origin. The artist's visible border, in effect, does not circumscribe his composition. As one unrolls a horizontal scroll in his hands, he never views the work entire and whole; so the artist, unless content to break the whole into successive panels, must provide strong organization at every point without benefit of side frames, while simultaneously luring the eye past the section actually visible.

In the second instance, the artist exploits what is termed *dynamic negative space* in modern Western art. He leaves large sections of his apparent field untouched. The subject of central interest, in some cases, catches the eye not merely because it dominates lesser subject matter within the frame but because it stands alone in space; yet all this space is required, and none can be cropped away without impairing the fit of the subject to its new frame. Alternatively, the areas of virgin space are arranged to make the observer interpret them, perhaps as fog, water, or certain parts of the body in a portrait. Literally blank areas, thus, carry meaning essential to the perception of the whole. In ink drawings, especially, such calculated restraint on the part of the artist forces the observer to be an appreciative yet unconscious participant in the creative process.

The watercolor technique of pointed brush on paper has also had an effect upon the quality of representation achieved by the Japanese artist. Paintings tend to emphasize line or are built up by the careful use of ceaselessly practiced, conventionally limited brush strokes. In fact, the Japanese artist is generally trained to master conventional representation of natural objects (leaves, birds, grasses) before he ventures to sketch or paint from life. Painting from life is almost nowhere to be found. Even works seemingly depicting specific locations or real birds or flowers are seldom sketched directly from nature (Sesshū may be an exception in his paintings of Ama-no-hashidate or the Tōfukuji). Artists made sketches, to be sure, but they generally painted from their "remembrances in tranquillity." Painting tends therefore to be of conventionalized and idealized subjects, with the emphasis of the artist directed toward virtuosity of brushwork or balance of line and color.

In all types of Japanese painting (except the extremely stylized decorative art and *ukiyo-e*) brushwork is one of the major elements of appreciation. In the rendition of a pine needle, a bamboo stem, or the branch of a tree, the artist will use a single stroke of the brush to provide both form and modeling. Much of the interest of such a technique to the viewer is the feeling which he derives of the "movement of the brush." The dynamism of most Japanese paintings comes as much from the texture of the brushwork—hasty splashes, bold lines, delicate threads—as from the overall tension of design. Brush virtuosity and economy of effort, in which one brush stroke serves more than one purpose, are highly prized. Since watercolor technique does not permit the artist to paint over a stroke once he has committed himself, control of the brush becomes essential.

Because of the tendency toward imaginary or idealized renditions of their subjects, Japanese artists have generally emphasized design and color balance rather than naturalistic reproduction; figures of animals or humans are frequently thrown into distorted shapes (especially in Buddhist painting) to accomplish the desired balance. A strong tendency in Japan, even while under the shadow of China, has been for delight in pattern and design to surge up through and replace the intellectualities that dominate Chinese styles. The combination of brush conventions and subject stylization has produced, as in the work of Kōetsu, Kōrin, or Sōtatsu, some of the most distinctly original works of Japanese painting.

As in the case of sculpture, the many accepted subjects of painting have been determined largely under influence from China. Buddhist painting depicts deities, esoteric charts of Buddhist concepts (*mandara*), or pictures of heavens and hells. Secular painting may depict portraits of important individuals, natural landscapes, flowers and grasses, certain animals (tigers or horses), birds, fish, and human beings in social or military activity. Conspicuously absent in the aristocratic tradition is the human face or body as an object of aesthetic interest. Paintings of female beauties or pornographic scenes became increasingly common in the Tokugawa period, as the erotic interest in the human form developed, but it was not until Japanese artists had studied in the West that the nude became a subject acceptable in genteel circles.

Calligraphy

Accentuating many of the special features which the Japanese looks for in painting is the genre of calligraphy, in itself considered an art no less prized than painting. Because of the nature of the Chinese language (its use of complex ideographs of varied forms) writing, from at least the time of the adoption of the brush, has been looked upon as something to be appreciated aesthetically. In China calligraphy was probably ranked above painting in the esteem of connoisseurs, for in that society it was the art par excellence of the scholar. Much of this attitude toward calligraphy has influenced the Japanese. Until recent times young men applying for positions in business were required to write out their applications by brush so as to "reveal their character." Public figures were accustomed to reward their admirers with specimens of their brush writing. Accomplishment in calligraphy has been the mark of the gentleman and scholar. Artisans or professional artists, who have produced most of the other arts, have rarely been admired for their calligraphy, for it has taken a combination of leisure and erudition to produce the great calligraphers.

In Japan the art of calligraphy has developed along two particular lines: the writing of Chinese characters and the writing of Japanese script, or kana. The former has had its absolute level of attainment in China, and few Japanese masters have been credited with the ability to match in virtuosity or inventiveness the best Chinese calligraphers. Writing in kana is a much more restricted undertaking. It produces calligraphy of a delicate, grasslike quality which has no counterpart in China.

An understanding of the art of calligraphy can contribute greatly to the acquisition of a feeling for Japanese painting, especially in the Chinese tradition. The media, lampblack ink, absorbent paper or silk, and the pointed brush, are also the favorite media for painting. Many of the qualities derived from brush, ink, and paper and exploited by the calligrapher have been carried over into painting. The absorbent paper requires a sure hand, which in turn necessitates long hours of practice. (The drawing of a long stroke with the utmost confidence is no less a matter of technique than the execution of a difficult run on the piano.) The analogy of the calligrapher to the musician is not too farfetched. Like the performing musician, the calligrapher finds his subject matter set. The ideograph is there to be mastered; the only freedom permitted the calligrapher is that of "interpretation" and individual accentuation. But such interpretation (or deviation from the norm) can be successful only after the achievement of complete mastery of accepted technique. Calligraphy as taught through the centuries in China and Japan has been a matter of memory and discipline: the "wearing out of brushes."

What is looked for in a piece of ideographic writing? In general, calligraphy constitutes an abstract art depending not upon the content of what is written but on an aesthetic vocabulary based on black ink in varying texture and density on white paper, on the quality of the stroke, and on the overall balance of composition. Appreciation of calligraphy requires sensitivity to a number of qualities, among which the following are perhaps basic: (1) *Internal balance*: each character is written within the confines of an imaginary frame. The distribution of asymmetric strokes within the frame creates an equilibrium of internal tensions. The asymmetry of the strokes assures the creation of a dynamic balance. (2) *Rhythm of brushwork*: because the brush passes over the paper, stopping momentarily at node points and moving rapidly from node to node, it is possible to "feel" the rhythm of the movement of the brush. The "quality of the brush stroke," whether it moves rapidly or deliberately, is a matter of aesthetic interest. (3) *Variation*: in the mind of the writer and the viewer, behind each written character is an ideal type. The calligrapher varies his product according to the message he wishes to convey and his personal idiosyncrasies, setting up a tension between the ideal and his own interpretation. Finally, of course, there is the matter of overall balance of dark and light, the appropriateness of ink quality to paper, and the placement of signature and seals which makes up the entire composition. The total impact of a piece of calligraphy can, as a consequence, be very powerful, developing to a high point the many abstract qualities prized in painting as well: balanced tensions, contrast against open spaces, rhythm and quality of line, variations on a familiar theme, texture, and the like. Above all, the viewer will ad·mire the evidence of discipline and control over brush, ink, and paper which can result only from a lifetime of dedication to technique.

Ceramics

Of the minor arts ceramics is perhaps the most prized and richly developed by the Japanese. Most examples descend from the large Chinese family of ceramic techniques and styles, and few ever reached the heights of perfection attained by the best wares of China; yet Japanese ceramic products have attracted worldwide attention for quality as well as for their neat adaptation to daily use. The West's warm reception of Japanese pottery and porcelain in recent years, however, is still but a slender link across a broad gulf that separated the ceramic traditions of the West and Japan, both at the kiln sites and in their places of use. Food habits, conventions of entertainment, and traditions of interior decor have all put their distinctive stamps upon the potter's craft in our different cultures. Perhaps one of the outstanding differences between attitudes toward ceramics is found in the degree to which individual pieces are considered worthy of close appreciation as works of art. We should remember that Japan has lacked the tradition of the large banquet table spread with silver, glass, and dishes of uniform design. It has its own variety of preferred types: the hand-held rice bowl, the handleless cup, the small dishes for serving individual portions of fish or vegetables. It lacks the need for glasses, goblets, and plates that accompany the meat and wine cuisine of the West. The use of chopsticks has also affected the style of table dishes used by the Japanese, though not necessarily in the same way as in China.

Three social institutions in particular have placed their mark upon the ceramic tradition in Japan: the tea ceremony, flower arrangement, and the formal meal. The particular practice of ceremonial tea drinking which originated in the Ashikaga period and was fully developed during the Momoyama era made the appreciation of ceramic or lacquer vessels one of the chief aesthetic ingredients of its ritualized experience. The conscious restraint of architectural effects in the tearoom, particularly the quiet neutral tones of plaster walls and tatami, created an appropriate setting for studied appreciation of individual pieces of pottery. In the tea ceremony a conscious attempt is made to utilize a variety of ceramic types which contrast but also blend with respect to color, size, texture, and degree of firmness. A porcelain water jar of blue Ming ware will be combined with bowls of dark earthenware, the whole being highlighted perhaps by a touch of red in the cake dish.

During the ritual each bowl is admired individually by the guests. The tea ceremony has also accentuated certain ceramic shapes, notably the large teabowl for serving powdered tea.

The *cha-no-yu* tradition in Japan has been an important repository of certain highly prized aesthetic values. The teahouse has nourished appreciation of such qualities as *sabi, wabi,* and *shibusa,* all indicating a quiet, somber, reflective approach to art. The most-admired pieces of tea ware thus are apt to be earthenware pieces of an unpretentious nature. Bowls are cherished for a particular drip of the glaze, a "flame mark" caused in firing, or a subtle quality which suggests repose.

Balancing the tendency toward the somber in *cha-no-yu* is the less formal tradition of steeped-tea (*sencha*) drinking. Here the emphasis is more on elegance and polish. Ceramic vessels are of porcelain and frequently highly colored. But the attention to texture, color, contrast, and variety of kiln types is as detailed as that in the more formal ceremony.

The attention given to the arrangement and appreciation of cut flowers and shrubs in Japan has also had an effect upon the ceramic tradition. *Ikebana,* as the art came to be known, developed along many lines according to the various requirements for which floral displays were needed: formal arrangements for religious offerings or important social occasions, casual arrangements for the everyday decoration of the tokonoma, carefully studied "informal" arrangements for the tea-room. The vase or bowl and the plants, all integral elements of an arrangement, are treated as a composition under rigorous canons. A vessel of neutral color but interesting shape tends to be preferred. The vase is not simply a container for a cluster of colored flowers, but rather an object of appreciation along with the flowers or branches it contains.

The formal Japanese meal consists of individually served portions of a variety of fish, fowl, and vegetables, each course arranged to please the eye as well as the palate. The dishes required are, for the most part, small plates, sauce cups, sake cups, rice bowls, chopstick rests, and the like. In the Japanese meal much of the visual effect is produced by harmony or tension in color and texture, considering both the dish and its contents. In the course of a meal the host will use containers of earthenware, porcelain, or lacquer in a wide variety of hues, weights, and sizes; and each will stand scrutiny as a work of artistic quality. A well-known restaurateur will be as proud of his stock of dishes as of his cuisine. The formal banquet can provide the fullest range of Japanese ceramic art, combining the well-known "folk" wares of Oribe, Imbe, Iga, or Karatsu with the fine porcelain of Imari, Kutani, and Kyoto.

The Chinese and Japanese in Japanese Art

We have noted that for almost every major genre of Japanese art the initial stimulus and much of the subsequent inspiration have come from China. Japan has "invented" relatively few major art forms. Has Japan, then, been primarily an imitator of continental modes and style? There can be no doubt that Japanese artists and connoisseurs have looked throughout the centuries to China as the fountainhead of the arts and letters. Japan today is a rich storehouse of Chinese art, preserving many varieties now lost on the continent. For a Japanese artist or calligrapher, to be mistaken for a Chinese has been considered the highest praise to which he could aspire. Japanese artists have traditionally despaired of attaining perfection in art forms mothered by China. Their valued works, in fact, consistently differ from those of China in style, subject matter, technique, and artistic intent. One may well ask whether the Japanese simply failed to comprehend Chinese models and achieve equal peaks, for there is much in Japanese art which is at its best only good, but not great, imitation of China. From such a view, one might conclude further that certain Japanese preferences, such as introspective aesthetic values (*wabi* or *sabi*), were cultivated in exasperation over their failure to produce works of the same grandeur as those of China.

Yet the fact remains that, in any array of Japanese works, those closest to the Chinese model are often not the best in the lot, by either majority opinion or the judgment of specialists. The most splendid or most ingratiating works have unmistakably Japanese qualities. Some of these qualities have already been pointed out in "Shinto" architecture, Yamato-e paintings, subtly carved nō masks, and kana calligraphy. In all of these there recur qualities of stylization, decorativeness, restraint, and a propensity to favor design and shapes and color balance over more intellectually contrived meanings. As to the decoration of architecture and objects, however, the Chinese passion for the bright and garish (as well, perhaps, as the bold and the noble) is transmuted in Japanese hands, being refined and quieted and keyed into the material of the object. In sculpture the Chūgūji Kannon, in painting the "flowers in baskets" of Ogata Kenzan, in architecture Katsura, in pottery the graceful but folkish Imbe ware, these illustrate the particular values most admired by the Japanese artist. But there is an even more profound quality which appears to lie closest to the beauty of the "Japanese approach" to art. It is the sensitivity which the Japanese artist has shown to his materials and to his natural environment. The capacity of the carpenter to remain true to his materials and the humility with which dwellings are placed in the natural setting are perhaps adequate examples.

It is rather interesting that this complex of values has never really been articulated by the Japanese art theorists. Whereas modern Japanese art critics making comparisons with the West have written of Japanese simplicity, harmony, or appreciation of the "natural quality" in materials, such terms are not in the vocabulary of the premodern Japanese. It is hard to doubt that such values were deeply and unconsciously felt, for they flow from the unreasoned and unrationalized work of the artisan or carpenter as much as from the self-conscious artist; yet they were taken for granted.

On the other hand, there is a dimension of Japanese aesthetics which has been consciously articulated and provided with a carefully devised vocabulary. This is the syndrome of tastes which have been cultivated in the tea ceremony and are related to the more multidimensional values of connoisseurship illustrated by the qualities found in the teahouse and tea vessels: *sabi*, the quality of depth which comes from aging; *wabi*, the feeling of melancholy and humbleness which comes from a realization of one's insignificance in the scheme of nature; and *shibusa*, that particular austerity of taste which combines the subdued colors and multiple textures of the tearoom into a harmonious but dynamic assemblage.

What is the source of these "uniquely Japanese" qualities? Art critics claim to see the roots of the Japanese artistic temperament in the *haniwa* and Shinto shrines of protohistoric days. Reference to such concepts as "national character" or "folk tradition" only restates the problem without explaining it. For in whatever way the Japanese artist or artisan has differed from his Chinese counterpart, we must look for a reason in the differing material, social, and intellectual styles of living which separate the two countries. While the Japanese artist has borrowed many Chinese forms, he has been motivated differently, either because he has failed to appreciate the deeper philosophical ingredients of the Chinese original and has substituted his own greater appreciation of visual effects or because he has been inspired by the different conventions and necessities of his society. In either case, the best of his work has its own individuality and its own integrity.

MODERN CURRENTS: JAPANESE TRADITION AND WESTERN INFLUENCE

Since the middle of the nineteenth century Japanese culture has come under the influence of yet another powerful cultural tradition. During the last century Japan has found itself oriented increasingly away from the Asian continent toward the West. In most ways this new encounter has placed greater strains and stresses upon the native artistic fabric than the previous contact with China. No more apt example of the clash of Japanese and Western tastes and values can be found than in the realm of art.

Japan today is one of the few Oriental societies which have reacted positively to Western culture and have absorbed, to the point of having assimilated, a number of Western aesthetic traditions. A study of the slow, painful process by which the Japanese have acquired new techniques such as oil painting, new visual approaches such as perspective, and new subject matter such as the nude and the art of social protest reveal dramatically the many fundamental cultural differences which have separated East and West in the area of aesthetic expression.

The Western critic of modern Japanese art (that which is modeled upon the West) sees in it much that is derivative of the West, both in technique and in inspiration. A frequent comment is that technique and style may be mastered, but content and ability to convey fresh meaning are lacking. In a similar view those who are familiar with the best of the "old art" of Japan find the "heart going out" of the traditional genre. Changes in the political behavior, social structure, and international status of the country inevitably affected the artistic output of the Japanese people.

Perhaps we should note at the outset that the recent encounter between East and West in Japan has not by any means been completely one-sided. In Japan there have been strong advocates of "native values." There have been movements to strengthen and clarify the features of Japanese art most congenial to the native temperament. Okakura Kakuzō, in *The Book of Tea,* has extolled the virtue of "simplicity," the "love of nature," and "repose." Hasegawa Nyozekan has pointed to the "cultural democracy" of the Japanese. The modern Japanese state gave rise to an artistic chauvinism which kept pace with its expanding political frontiers. In recent years there has been a marked impact of Japanese tastes in architecture, gardens, and ceramics on the United States, calling forth such expressions of interest as the series of articles on Japanese aesthetics in *House Beautiful* (August and September, 1960). Before this the Japanese print had influenced painters of the postimpressionist school in Europe.

But if some Japanese artists and critics have asserted the superiority of the Japanese tradition, the majority of Japanese producers have been overwhelmed by the recent social revolution and the cultural impact of the West. Their reaction has to some extent seemed inevitable. In the new Japanese state and society of the twentieth century, the artist or artisan has found himself in a vastly new environment. With the passing of the traditional society based on aristocratic leadership, the old patterns of patronage and support for craftsmanship have been altered. The artist, as in the West, has become increasingly a man apart, admired for his individuality. The machine has made possible the cheaper production of artifacts once produced by handicraft. The artisan has had to adjust himself to a competitive domestic and world market, while new tastes in clothing, food, and shelter have drastically altered the demand for art commodities. The introduction of new values and standards of art appreciation, together with the new mass participation of the Japanese in the setting of tastes and demands for goods, has brought about a confusion of values which has been particularly disruptive to the Japanese artist.

Whether Japan has been obliged to suffer a greater trauma than the countries of the West as they preceded Japan on the path of modernization is a moot question and depends largely upon whether one concludes that there have been fundamental differences between the traditional societies of East and West or whether one is inclined to accept all "traditional societies" as basically similar. The modern dilemma facing Japan in the arts has been the question of what to do with the old in the face of the new, how much of the old arts can hold true today, and what can be adapted and what must be discarded. (In other words, it is a question of what of the old art was part of the old social and economic fabric that is being discarded.) The Western observer, witnessing the clumsy attempts of the Japanese to work in Western genres, is apt to express the desire that the Japanese "stay within the boundaries of the traditions they know best." Many a tourist regrets (along with Lafcadio Hearn's earlier lament) the "passing of old Japan." But can a country such as Japan aspire to world power with one part of its culture while retaining its traditional values and patterns of workmanship with another part?

What resolution has Japan made of these varied demands? The most important lines of adjustment have taken the following distinct forms: artificial preservation, fusion of new and old art forms, revitalization of old forms in the new environment, and attempted assimilation of foreign techniques. By artificial preservation we mean the nationally and privately supported programs of art collection and preservation in museums, national monuments, and endowed institutions. For instance, much of the best of Japan's old arts (and also a certain number of producing artists!) have been designated "national treasures" or "important cultural objects" by the government. Subsidies are made available for the maintenance and repair of works of art and for the livelihood of artists. In this way the best of the past is preserved in the Japanese memory, while skills such as puppetry, the nō drama, certain pottery styles, etc., which would otherwise die out, are perpetuated. The Japanese public need not remain ignorant of its artistic heritage.

In a few areas, Japanese artists are succeeding in fusing tradition with modern influence. This has come about either by adapting old arts to new themes and purposes (for example, the lively development of the "modern" wood-block print) or modifying Western techniques to Japanese circumstances (some of the best of modern Japanese architecture fits into this category). The process of fusion has not been easy for the Japanese. The traditional potter lacks an understanding of the requirements of modern society and of ways to produce for them. If he modifies his product, he generally copies in meaningless fashion what his dealer requests of him. The young artist attuned to cosmopolitan urban life may lack the technique to achieve his intent. Fusion must be the work of individual genius, such as that of Kiyoshi Saitō, the print artist, or of generations of experimentation, as in the examples of some of the more recent ceramic products.

A still different line of adaptation has been the injection of new vitality into traditional crafts. The recent movement to revive the folk arts, particularly ceramics, supported in practice and theory by the Englishman Bernard Leach and the Japanese potter Hamada Shōji, has resulted from a combination of two fundamental developments. First, there has been a reeducation of the Japanese public to the worth and utility of works of excellent craftsmanship produced by artisans working in folkish (and, therefore, traditionally unesteemed) conventions. Second, there has been education of the artisan communities to the need to retain integrity in the face of their adaptation to new patterns of production. The revitalization of the kilns of Bizen, Mashiko, and Karatsu or the weavers of Tamba has had its counterpart in the appearance of well-patronized "folk-art" stores in the major cities.

How successful have the Japanese been in the mastery of Western art forms? Certainly the Japanese artist today has come a long way from the first feeble attempts to portray perspective or to paint the female nude. But a visit to a modern art exhibition is still apt to be disappointing to the Western connoisseur. To the comparative student of culture, however, such an exhibition can be of great interest in pointing up the differential pattern of comparative success and failure in the Japanese attempts to master Western art. In general, the most successful artists have been long expatriates, such as Isamu Noguchi and Yasuo Kuniyoshi, or practitioners in the more abstract fields of expression. Japanese success has been pronounced in fields of architecture and industrial design. (Note the works of Tange Kenzō or the products of the camera and electronics industries.) Painting in oil and sculpture (especially of the human form) have probably been least successfully mastered, indicating their association with religious or artistic conventions in the West which have yet to be assimilated into Japanese life.

Bit by bit Japan has become part of the international world of modern art. Her artists are represented in world art exhibitions, not merely as curiosities, but because of the respect they merit from a world audience. The Japanese film industry in particular has won wide recognition with *Rashōmon, Ugetsu monogatari,* and other products. At home in Japan "Western-style" objects of art and artifacts of daily use have found their way into the houses of Japanese of many classes. The import from abroad is no longer a necessity if the Japanese chooses to live in Western style. But still in most areas of Japanese life two cultures—traditional and Western—remain apart, and complete assimilation has rarely been achieved. To this extent the Japanese artist must live a split personality or commit himself to one mode of creation or another.

In conclusion let us return to the question of what the nature and condition of the arts in Japan can reveal about the Japanese and their culture today. Professional interpreters of Japanese culture have claimed for the Japanese a "unique sensitivity" to nature and beauty. Many Western travelers to Japan are heard to echo this view, and in the world at large the image of the country as a land of natural beauty with people living in charming impracticality persists. Yet Japan has mastered the most practical features of modern civilization; her engineers and scientists rank high in the world at large. A modern city, such as Tokyo, seems dedicated less to beauty than to economic competition. The cluttered, ungainly quarters of Japanese cities centering on railroad stations or factory installations are proof that for the Japanese as for others "modern necessity" often comes before considerations of aesthetic satisfaction.

Where then does the persistent view of Japan's unique orientation to beauty originate? There is little doubt that the average Japanese lives closer to a traditional culture in which beauty has been emphasized than does the average American. The perpetuation of numerous handicraft skills means that his shops are more apt to include products made by hand with great integrity. There remain as well numerous social conventions which accentuate the aesthetic attitude: seasons for flower viewing or moon viewing, the custom of decorating the tokonoma, the arts of the tea ceremony and flower arrangement. While the majority of Japanese react to these stimuli in a conventional manner, giving forth stereotyped expressions of appreciation, they are undoubtedly induced to comment upon purely aesthetic experiences more frequently than the average American. The crowd of Japanese country tourists at a temple in Kyoto is more apt to be lectured to by the guide on the aesthetic principles manifest in the garden than would the visitor at Mount Vernon be told about the visual qualities sought by George Washington in the arrangement of the elements of his estate. The visitor to Japan is more apt to find visual beauty emphasized along with other aesthetic factors (room decor in a restaurant) or to encounter more numerous evidences of overt respect for the arts (the art departments of department stores). The educational process also appears to emphasize art training to a remarkable degree. By contrast with the United States, where only a mild attention is paid to the cultivation of amateur arts (such as piano, watercolor, and ballet) as a means of developing the well-rounded child, in Japan the availability and the technical competence of instructors in *sumi* painting, calligraphy, tea ceremony, flower arrangement, dance, and music (koto or piano) are extremely high. The perpetuation of these aesthetically oriented social pastimes and the continual demand for them as means of cultural training strongly color the aesthetic reactions of the mature Japanese. The businessman who finds leisure in his successful years is as likely to indulge in ink painting as in golf. Or he may well take up both.

If then we admit a particularly strong emotional, aesthetic quality to Japanese modern culture, as Japan becomes more and more generally a typical member of the community of modern industrial societies, what particular qualities can remain to Japan? What stamp may the country place upon the increasingly uniform products of modern painting or architecture? The answer, though only conjectural, is certainly indicated by the contribution which Japan made historically to East Asian continental art and in the particular lines along which her artists and artisans have been most successful in recent times: dexterity in decorative techniques, sensitivity to color, sensitivity to nature and to materials, a capacity to suggest through restraint. These may well continue to be the forte of the Japanese artist.

RICHARD K. BEARDSLEY

Religion and Philosophy *

INTRODUCTION

To study traditional Oriental philosophies one must be prepared to study religions, for the Far East, especially Japan, never produced a strong branch of rationalist and secular philosophy such as flourished in the Occidental world from Greco-Roman times on. Yet religions in the Far East have a rather unjustified reputation for being mysterious and obscure, to the point of driving away many who have no special penchant for the abstruse and esoteric.

Far Eastern religions include, it is true, doctrines and concepts of a highly involuted character, some mystical and some not; these doctrines have much importance in Japanese religious history. But at the opposite pole quite solemn and significant religions flourish almost completely unsupported by philosophical speculation. The Japanese have been able to combine both sorts on an equal basis in their religious life. When a Western observer who has been reared in the quite different context of Christianity examines Japanese religions, several considerations at first puzzle him as incongruities: that most Japanese can follow more than one religion at once; that they value equally religions that are of such different degrees of philosophical elaboration; and, especially, that they do not particularly look on any of these religions as a main source of ethics.

The Western observer's problem is not so much to immerse himself in subtle or abstruse thinking as it is to look at religion the way a Japanese views it, to ask: In what ways are the Japanese religious? Or to ask the question which runs through this survey: What is the role of religion (as defined by the Japanese themselves) in Japanese culture? This approach will put him on common footing, at least, with most Far Easterners should he wish then to proceed farther toward the outer fringes of Far Eastern philosophy.

Yet this method of inquiry seems to entail some difficulty for Westerners, who tend more often to ask what religions the Japanese

* John Whitney Hall is the author of the section "Confucianism" in this chapter. Grateful acknowledgment is made to Morioka Kiyomi for suggestions contributing to other sections.

believe in or how religious the Japanese are rather than ask how the Japanese express religion. Such questions, innocuous or rewarding in the West, where ideas about religion have been shaped for two millennia by Christianity, simply do not evoke answers that fit the forms, the content, or the functions of much of religious life in Japan. These questions take for granted, for example, that doctrine and the specifically liturgical acts of prayer and devotion are the ineluctable core of any religion. They are not. Religions in Japan in fact often neglect both doctrine and liturgy and yet serve very adequately and richly as religions.

How is one to recognize and identify religion without dogma or liturgy, to proclaim it religious? The matter is not difficult if we reflect that any religion has not one but three aspects and should be viewed from all of them: its ideology, its organization, and its participants. The *ideology* may be shaped into a doctrine, but not necessarily so. It consists of assumptions, attitudes and valuations which ordinarily are recognizable as religious because they concern supernatural beings, forces, or principles; to use another expression, ideology is the mythic ingredient of religion if we understand the term *myth* to mean unquestioned, even if unprovable, basic convictions that guide and inform one's life. *Organization* exists to maintain the ideology and to actualize and express the aims implied in its myths. In Christianity and some other religions, the organization is the church, either as an abstract, hierarchical structure containing positions and roles for its professional devotees or as the bodily collectivity of all members. Not all religions have a church, but all have a form of organization. Finally, a religion is defined in terms of the views or beliefs and behavior of its *participants,* whether they are actually performing rituals or merely going through acts that are guided and informed by religious conviction or organization.

These three aspects of religion, ideology, organization, and participants, bear a mutual relation to each other, as if they were corners of a triangle. Because the church exists to interpret ideology to the participants, a linear arrangement is often assumed, as follows: doctrine → church → members. But one finds also that the attitudes or wants of the participants tend to mold the ideology and, in turn, that their perception of ideology directly guides their behavior. So the three aspects do not comprise successive strata but instead are mutually interrelated points, as in a triangle.

Besides being considered in the three aspects just named, religion in action at the *local level* where it touches people's everyday lives may need to be taken into account separately from religion at the *national level*, where overall organization is most visible and doctrine may be most explicit. At either level, however, we should be aware of all three aspects, perceiving (1) the way persons participate in (2) groups organized to reaffirm or achieve (3) aims implied by the assumptions that constitute the charter, the myth, or the doctrine of their organization.

MULTIRELIGIOUS JAPANESE CULTURE

The view just recommended requires the examination of each Japanese religion as a part of total culture and society rather than as an independent phenomenon. We must think of religion as being shaped by a culture, granting also that religious ideas may help to shape a culture. Probably no one will object to this condition, though customary thinking and phraseology that speaks of "adopting" religion or of "replacing" religion 1 with a "borrowed" religion 2 tempts one to consider religions as interchangeable parts that can be inserted in or removed from otherwise intact cultures. In actuality religion is one of the qualities of society, coloring it and taking on its color reciprocally; the two are separable only for certain analytic purposes. This fact, once clarified, makes the subject of religions in Japan more readily penetrable.

Many choices of religious expression have been available to the Japanese: Shinto, Buddhism, Confucianism, Christianity, and a group of sects called here *New Religions* in accord with their common Japanese appellation. Only Shinto and the New Religions are unique to Japan; the others have wider communities, and their origin, as well as their center of gravity, is outside the country. Because of the prominence of religions of foreign origin and certain admixtures of doctrine or practice at the national level, the Japanese attitude toward religion is often described as eclectic and syncretic. Whether such a description is correct depends on one's viewpoint. Organizationally and ideologically, religions that have coexisted for centuries in Japan still remain separate and distinct systems. Buddhism and Shinto are readily distinguishable from each other; what is remarkable about this fact is the absence rather than the prevalence of doctrinal or organizational syncretism. As to eclecticism, whatever cults have been imported from abroad certainly have been reworked to suit the Japanese cultural context rather than remaining foreign bodies attached to Japanese life.

Hence, eclecticism and syncretism are not conspicuous in two aspects of religion, the ideological and the organizational. When we consider individual participation, a combination, if not a merger, of religions meets our eye. Almost all Japanese engage to some extent in Shinto practices but also participate in Buddhist ritual, and they very well may simultaneously follow the practices or evince the assumptions of a third religion. This leads to oddities, such as appear in the table below, which totals places of worship and membership of the various religions in the country. The table, compiled in 1961 but necessarily using census methods developed in countries where each person adheres to only one religion at a time, should not be taken as a record of separate organization and membership in the case of these religions in Japan. The apparent total religious membership in 1961, for example, considerably surpasses the total population of the country in that year, which fell short of 90 million.

STATISTICAL SUMMARY OF RELIGIOUS BODIES AND MEMBERS IN JAPAN, 1961

Religion	Sects	Shrines	Temples	Churches	Members
Shinto	142	80,699	2	24,652	78,632,009
Buddhism	169	4	75,640	4,720	61,741,546
Christianity	38	...	...	3,865	669,074
Other	30	6	4	1,187	4,553,596
Total	379	80,709	75,646	34,524	145,596,225

SOURCE: Ministry of Education, *Religions in Japan*, Tokyo, 1963, pp. 122–123. Shrines are ordinarily Shinto, temples Buddhist, and churches Christian. The exceptions shown here reflect genuine confusion as to how religious groups should list themselves in categories provided by the Ministry of Education. From one year's enumeration to the next, figures fluctuate remarkably.

A good many persons, obviously, were counted twice in the table, not through error but because (Christians excepted) participants in one religion followed another at the same time. Various inaccuracies, incidentally, creep into a tabulation such as this; for example, some persons respond to the census inquiry by naming just one religion, whereas others name all the religious bodies with which they have some connection. Hence, no table can give an exact comparison of membership, although this table shows as well as any the rough proportions of the size of each. Moreover, it tells at least by implication that though Japan may possess no higher total of religious bodies than some heterogeneous Western nations, her people participate in ways basically different from the one-only pattern of Westerners.

Just how these religions share membership is best illustrated by a living example rather than by additional tables. Let us take a hypothetical contemporary rural community, an administrative village, or mura, as a single instance. The mura consists of a number of hamlets, which may be designated A, B, C, D, and E. Two sorts of religious structures exist: Shinto shrines (miya) and Buddhist temples (tera). They differ in appearance and location. A torii, or gateway with a double crossbeam, marks the entrance to the shrine alone; from the torii a road or path leads to a succession of small buildings set on a common axis with it. As a minimum, a small building (honden) serves as the focal point of ritual, though a roofed platform (haiden) may be set in front of it for offerings and dances; other structures may be distributed in the precincts on or near the torii-honden axis. These structures usually are built in Japanese style and sit in a secluded dell or on top of a hill. Chinese architecture, in contrast, marks the usual temple: a cluster of buildings, each under a curved roof laid with heavy tiles, is set within a compound that often includes a cemetery. One hall houses an altar for prayer, another is the home of the priest and acolytes, and others may exist within the compound. The temples may sit within a hamlet or somewhat removed but on similar terrain. They and the shrines are distributed among the hamlets of our hypothetical mura as follows:

Hamlet	A	B	C	D	E
Shrine	a	b	c_1, c_2	d	e
Temple	x	y			z

As the above summary indicates, each hamlet has its own, named shrine; hamlet C, it happens, possesses two, each much like the other except for distinctive names. These shrines are part and parcel of their respective communities. Only the households that live in hamlet A serve shrine a at its festivals, and similarly with hamlets B, C, D, and E. Yet the dates for festivals, which are seasonal affairs, generally coincide for all shrines, so that all the households of the mura have a nearly identical shrine festival calendar. Some of the festivals are relatively unimportant and quiet, but important dates are prepared for long in advance and celebrated joyously, with the young men of the hamlet taking the lead, intoxicated and noisy, up to the final prayers that terminate the festival. The prayers give thanks for welfare, good crops, and good health and ask that protection continue. Every household is represented by one member at the prayers. There are no anthropomorphic images or icons fundamental to the shrine; a statue is in the heart of certain shrines, whereas others may show only a bronze object or even a stone, but the statue (or the stone) is merely a "receptacle" or "lodging" for the active spirit of the shrine. Prayers are addressed to a formless spirit or spiritual force, which may be worshiped uniquely at this one shrine but is just as apt to be worshiped widely at shrines throughout the region or the nation; similarity of name implies no organizational affiliation, however, for the shrine belongs to the hamlet rather than to any outside, higher religious organization.

The three Buddhist temples of the hypothetical mura, on the contrary, represent their nationwide sects in the local community, being branches or subbranches of a *honzan* ("main mountain," a term preserving a conventional image of each temple as a mountain or its cavern within which the Buddha's doctrines are preached). This means that the association with any particular hamlet is fortuitous. Each temple's parish reaches out to include anyone who wishes to belong to it, though naturally most parishioners live nearby; but the parishes intersect or overlap each other, particularly when the temples are of different sects. A single hamlet might be host to two temples, as to two shrines; but the temples would be of different sects, rather than one being a branch of the other, and hamlet members would be in the parish of one or the other but not of both. In short, temples belong not to hamlets but to their sects. Buddhist sects present mutually exclusive versions of doctrine and so have mutually exclusive bodies of communicants; though this implies personal and individual choice of doctrine, the actual practice is for a household to belong to a parish and be counted as a unit. Households that shift from the parish of one temple to another do so for neighborly convenience or other social reasons that have little or nothing to do with doctrinal matters. In every case, parishioners rely on the priest of the temple mainly to perform services for the dead in their respective ascending family line (male), either at the funeral or at specified intervals thereafter; so temple affiliation is a mark of respect for the preference of one's ancestors as much as a matter of one's own convictions. The priest ordinarily sees his parishioner at the latter's home to "chant a sutra" by way of services; there is no parishwide assembling of a congregation corresponding to the Sabbath service of

Christian and similar churches, though the priest not only goes through the temple's own ritual schedule in the temple but may provide a service there for any family that wishes it or may advertise sermons for all comers.

From this summary, it should be clear that shrine and temple are both "needed" for a full religious life, inasmuch as they perform non-conflicting and nonoverlapping functions. Shinto ritual proceeds from confidence in the existence of protective forces of supernatural quality, which extend their beneficence over things and affairs of this world, meaning especially the local Japanese world. This protection spreads outward from a sacred point to an area of lesser or greater expanse, depending on the importance of the enshrined power, and it includes everyone and everything belonging to the community or communities under this blanket of protection. In a sense, every Japanese is under the aegis of several shrines: his local village shrine, various district shrines, and, at the summit, large national shrines. Whereas the shrine offers security in the present world, the temple has as its primary province the problems of existence after death, and its communicants support it either out of personal concern for their fate upon dying or, more laudably, out of loyalty and veneration for their ancestors. In the temple, they consolidate family ties, not community ties; and, in fact, the presence of the priest is more essential than the presence of a temple, for the simple apparatus necessary to ritual—a book of sutras as scripture, some candles, bells, and incense—is easily and regularly maintained at home for ritual that uses a special cabinet (*butsudan*) or, on major occasions, the decorative niche (tokonoma) of the main room as an altar.

Nothing prevents any villager from adhering as a communicant to some other religious body or doctrine in addition to his community shrine and family temple. Within the hypothetical mura described here, there may be congregations of several of the New Religions. Since members join these cults out of personal volition, communicants come from households scattered throughout the mura, forming a congregation for regular or irregular services held, perhaps, in someone's home. Confucianism, described in the section below as a philosophy, has no cult centers for ordinary Japanese, nor is it thought of as a religion offering a spiritual interpretation; yet it is part of village life insomuch as virtually all elders, at least, know and respect Confucianism as a philosophy that has deeply influenced their conduct. Only Christianity has some difficuty in establishing communicants without conflict in this village, because its converts ordinarily must abjure any part in the Buddhist prayers for their father's ancestors and, unless some household member joins the community festival and prayers at the shrine, they invite alienation from the community. Christians stand apart because their religion monopolizes not only their faith but their group affiliation.

SHINTO

Ideology

The concepts of Shinto have been part of Japanese culture since prehistoric times. They form a pattern which has not spread outside Japan. Particular features of this pattern are common enough in the religion and folklore of the world at large, however, to assist interpretation and comprehension: notably, a concept of ritual pollution and its purification (from disease, injury, or death; from sexual intercourse or the blood of wounds, menstruation, or childbirth; or from antisocial acts, such as murder or adultery, that lead to such pollution) as a necessary prelude to communication with supernal powers; and the concept of supernal powers, resident in places or objects as much as in persons or divinities. In Shinto the pollution from things is *imi*, from improper acts, *tsumi*; its cleansing is *harai*; one uses prayers (*norito*) or the ritual of celebration (*iwai*) to express gratitude or give pleasure to the protective power (*kami*). Often enough, visitors to a shrine use set prayers of gratitude or hope, but one may express one's personal, immediate feelings as well. Though the basic elements are not unique to Shinto, not only have they been worked into a unique system, but they appear also to have developed through several phases.

The meaning of *kami* is elusive but important. An objective explanation was attempted by Motoori Norinaga, one of the leading scholars of the Shinto revival movement of the late eighteenth century: [1]

I do not yet understand the meaning of the term *kami*. Speaking in general, however, it may be said that *kami* signifies, in the first place, the deities of heaven and earth that appear in the ancient records and also the spirits of the shrines where they are worshipped. It is hardly necessary to say that it includes human beings. It also includes such objects as birds, beasts, trees, plants, seas, mountains, and so forth. In ancient usage, whatsoever was outside the ordinary, possessed superior power, or was awe-inspiring was called *kami*. Eminence here does not refer merely to the superiority of nobility, goodness, or meritorious deeds. Evil and mysterious things, if they are extraordinary and dreadful, are called *kami*. It is needless to say that among human beings who are called *kami* the successive generations of sacred em-

[1] Quoted in Ministry of Education, *Religions in Japan*, Tokyo, 1963.

perors are all included. The fact that emperors are also called 'distant *kami*' is because, from the standpoint of the common people, they are far-separated, majestic, and worthy of reverence. In a lesser degree, we find, in the present as in ancient times, human beings who are *kami*. Although they may not be accepted throughout the whole country, yet in each province, each village, and each family there are human beings who are *kami*, each one according to his own proper position. The *kami* of the divine age were for the most part human beings of that time, and because the people of that time were all *kami*, it is called the Age of the Gods (*kami*).

Motoori's conclusions came from his study of early records, such as the *Kojiki* (A.D. 712) and the *Nihongi*, or *Nihon shoki* (completed in 720), which not only were intended to be histories rather than analyses of religion, but also embody in a fairly conscious manner Chinese concepts and styles of reference to mythological matters, which confuse the issue. By our standards these records offer a very faulty historical perspective. Research that has accumulated since Motoori's time now makes it seem likely that the concept of *kami* gradually widened and altered as the nature of society changed over a span of centuries and that we can get a clearer understanding of the nature of *kami* by considering its probable phases of development, all of which are presented in flat perspective in Motoori's catalog of concepts quoted above. It is not easy to trace ancient beliefs with certainty, but the following scheme, even if partly conjectural, is in accord with current scholarly opinion. To deal with all existing varieties of *kami* would take much space without adding much clarification; it will suffice to examine only one major category, the *ujigami* or *kami* of a shrine which is the ceremonial center of each village or group of villages (and larger communities) and which is the source of supernatural protection for the entire religious community. We reserve a more detailed description of the shrines until later; here we are concerned with the presiding *kami*.

In an early period (probably in the agricultural villages of the Yayoi culture) it seems likely that such *kami* were localized, nonpersonified powers that protected the entire community in the way just described. Such a pattern of communal guardianship has been known throughout the historic epoch; so there is no reason to doubt that it began earlier. Motoori says, "in ancient usage, whatsoever was out of the ordinary . . . was called *kami*," and the *ujigami* of many villages through the present time has been no more specific in shape or character than this. Such an *ujigami* has no form or personality but is merely a force residing in an out-of-the-ordinary spot: a mountain peak or a point of land, a special grove or pile of rocks, and the like. This invisible force might, however, occasionally or regularly be embodied in an object or be reached by addressing it through this object. A wordplay or pun makes this linkage between spirit and object possible: the object, whatever its nature, was and still is called *mitama* (sacred jewel), and any spirit force may be called *tama*. A sacred jewel, however, might not even exist for some spirits; its proper location, where it exists, is in the shrine; and because the spirit may move to it, the shrine may be located where convenient for communal ritual, not necessarily in the spirit's natural point of residence.

It probably was later that human beings could become *kami*, as Motoori notes. Perhaps in the protohistoric or semihistoric periods, when "chiefs" or similar distinguished persons and their lineages rose as an elite responsible for defending and taking the initiative in managing the community, they guarded the community's sacred objects and so became not only the trustees but the chief representatives or priests of the community. From this, it is only a short step to being identified with the object and its spirit, becoming the spiritual as well as the military, temporal guardian of the community. Illustrative passages in some of the *Fūdoki* (local records of the eighth century A.D.) tell that a tribe or clan, when submitting to the Emperor, handed over to him the jewel it possessed, or that he took away the jewel upon conquering the group. In this phase of development, we see how the community's *kami* could become identified with a prominent lineage (*uji*) or its legendary progenitor, hence become an *uji-kami* (*ujigami*), and even acquire a personal name.

We do not know whether the *ujigami* previously had a different designation. At any rate, the development cited here is consistent with another aspect of belief, namely, the veneration of ancestral spirits, which seems indubitably an old, persistent trait of Japanese culture. It is hard to be sure whether the guardian-aristocrats came to expect all their villagers to pay respect to their personal ancestors or whether these ancestors simply became identified with the community as its principal forebears. Ancestors even in more recent times, when, under Buddhist influence, they became known as *hotoke* (Bodhisattvas), have been conceived as merged in a general body, not as individually identifiable spirits. Aboriginal concepts, it is believed, varied somewhat but did include the concept of a collectivity of ancestors; in the protohistoric or semihistoric periods, then, this concept converged with that of the *kami*, fusing into a concept of a guardian spirit with a human personality or, to reverse the terminology, a concept of deified human beings, referred to by Motoori. In modern times, various *ujigami* shrines are identified with legendary founding families or ancient chieftains, representing the developed *kami* concept just described.

The same period or a slightly later one saw the development of myths narrating the activities of high celestial deities. These were the myths drawn on by compilers of the *Kojiki* and *Nihongi*, in which each deity has clearly unique traits and quirks of temperament, besides being genealogically linked together as human beings are. The myths show internal inconsistencies, repeating incidents as seen from different and conflicting viewpoints; different myths also attribute different natures and functions to a single deity. It is especially interesting, since we know that the myths were compiled, organized, and altered to legitimize the preeminence of the Imperial House over others by Chinese historico-mythological methods, that Amaterasu, the direct divine ancestress of the Yamato line, is presented as the highest deity only part of the time. Part of the time she is one of a pair. In a myth group regarded as "the Izumo group," Kammusubi is the paramount ancestral deity (presumably of the Izumo line). From the entire body of historical myths it is fairly clear that this deity in his military aspect (as Takagi) and his ritual aspect (as Omoikane) was on a par with Amaterasu, all of which may be translated into earthly reality by the assumption that the Yamato and Izumo groups, at the time of writing, were allied together. Only later, apparently, did Yamato gain the suzerainty recorded in other parts of these mythical histories. Moreover, these myths show the capacity of *kami* to appear under varied manifestations, the same deity being differently named for different functions.

When Buddhist theology first made its appearance in Japan, it was viewed as a further elaboration of normal (i.e., Shinto) mythology and ritual. Later, in 584–585, the two rites were set against each other, being supported respectively by opposing houses; the Mononobe family, champions of the Nakatomi line that held Shinto priestly authority, was ranged against the Soga family, which championed both the new Buddhist religion and centralization of the state. Still later, in 1318, in a conscious syncretism, the founders of Dual (*ryōbu*) Shinto interpreted the celestial *kami* as avatars or manifestations of the Buddha. This syncretistic faith was unable to displace Buddhism and Shinto as separate belief systems. The two religions worked out a generally effective pattern of coexistence, even though in certain respects they entered periodically into competition or, conversely, in many localities the Shinto shrine and the Buddhist temple were merged. Both religions were instruments of the state; so each incurred hostility as well as support for reasons ostensibly religious but, in truth, more political than metaphysical. Political manipulations, however, occurred mainly at higher levels and affected popular adherence only slightly. Shinto remained community-centered, with local shrines to local spirits or with larger regional shrines (or their local branches, created by literally dividing the *mitama*, or central sacred objects, of the original) to heroic and celestial ancestors. The Tokugawa house sought to use the latter concept by building the country's most splendid shrine at Nikko and employing it for veneration of the family line. Then, with the emergence of a concept of nationhood in the late eighteenth century, such nationalist scholars as Motoori Norinaga, Kamo Mabuchi, and Ban Nobutomo reexamined traditional myths and developed comprehensive interpretations that supported the reinstatement of the Emperor as the rightful prime ruler of all Japanese. The new Meiji government, taking over from its predecessors the Jingi Kan (Office of Shrine Affairs), compiled a nationwide list of shrines that merited public support, ranked them, appointed guardians on salary as public officials, and issued regulations for services, all under the Kyōbushō (Department of Religious Affairs), later the Bureau of Shrines and Temples, under the powerful Home Ministry (1877). Thus was created a State Shinto, drawing upon traditional concepts, attitudes, and practices to form a nationalistic organization as part of the state. Its contrast with preexisting forms of Shinto is better seen by comparing organization than by comparing ideology.

Organization

The most typical shrine is the local or regional shrine. It is community-centered; that is, all residents within its area are covered under its protection. No one is considered as withdrawing from membership unless by leaving the community he automatically ceases to be a participant. Though a guardian may officiate at services, he never becomes the core of the organization, any more than do the *miko,* or female attendants (virgins, under a strict interpretation of tradition), who give dance performances or assist at other parts of ritual. Authority is vested, if at all, in the *miyaza,* or community shrine council, that sits, if possible, in the shrine grounds for its meetings. In some communities, the right to such a seat was traditionally the best symbol of old-timer status; this council was not infrequently the only regular forum for civic affairs. Most of the actual labor and expense for upkeep and ceremonies are normally borne by the Youth Association, another community organization. As the ultimate testimony to the linkage of shrine organization to the community, we find that migrants to Hokkaido have tended to found a shrine (a branch of a shrine in one of their localities of origin) as an expression of the coming of age of the community. A few all-Japanese communities of migrants to Hawaii have shrines, similarly founded; but almost no migrants elsewhere, to California, Brazil, or the Philippines, carry on shrine worship, for Japanese migrants do not settle there in wholly Japanese communities.

Individual Belief and Actions

Apart from ensuring that his household is represented in shrine festivities and other occasions relating to the *kami,* a person is not required to worship actively in order to be assured of protection under the *kami.* Each person must be presented to the community shrine, however: babies at birth after a suitable period of decontamination for the mother, children upon changing to a new age-grade (now generalized as the Shichigosan ceremony for children in their seventh, fifth, or third years), and brides at marriage. Moreover, one is free to seek protection from any special or regional shrine. As examples, innkeepers and others in the entertainment world (*mizu-shōbai*) tend to pay special visits to red-painted shrines of Inari, a one-time patron of rice farming whose protection has now spread instead to these more urban pursuits; and villages form *kō,* or social groups that collect dues to pay the travel expenses of their members in rotation to famed national shrines, such as those at Ise or Izumo. Almost any traditionally oriented person, happening to visit a shrine, brings home from it a *fuda,* or bamboo slip to ensure the welfare of the house and its inhabitants. Apart from worship at shrine structures, country households participate also in regular seasonal ceremonies to *kami* with special functions, such as the mountain *kami* who moves to the fields as the earth *kami* in spring, fructifies the seed, and then returns to the mountain in fall.

BUDDHISM

Ideology

The original doctrine of the compassionate Buddha, like that of Jesus or Mohammed, was addressed to Everyman, that is, to mankind at large. This sense of universal mission to all men has never disappeared, though the doctrine has undergone many changes, surviving mainly through Southeast Asia, Tibet, Mongolia, and Japan and, more sporadically, in China. The ideology of Japanese Buddhism consequently must be studied without neglecting the larger perspective of universal Buddhism. Historically, views that gained wide sway in Japan are apt to be the interpretations of Chinese sages, not original Indian doctrines. Nonetheless, Japanese culture placed its unmistakable imprint on

Buddhism, reshaping its ideology as well as its organization by a distinctive turning of logic and emphasis.

Primitive Buddhism taught that "enlightenment," a mystic experience, was the only escape from the suffering of earthly existence. Without enlightenment, one must undergo endless reincarnation and suffer earthly evils. One must strive to achieve release from existence by becoming a Buddha (an enlightened one); the only route is the Eightfold Path: right aims, right views, right speech, right conduct, right living, right effort, right mindfulness, and right concentration. One's progress along this path is determined by one's karma, or "chain of causation," forged in earlier incarnations by one's steps in the right direction or away from it.

Before this doctrine reached Japan, it already had two interpretations that were the basis of a major schism. The Hinayana school held that each seeker must make his way along the path by personal, unaided effort; from this school came the Theravada sects of Southeast Asia. The Mahayana school held that the difficult process of groping toward release is eased by Bodhisattvas (enlightenment beings). In the simplest terms, the Bodhisattvas are those who have, in effect, done all that is needed to become Buddhas but have voluntarily stopped short of their final goal to show compassion to others and help them. This Mahayana doctrine of compassion and vicarious enlightenment had a strong influence in the northern Buddhist countries: China, Korea, and Japan.

Buddhism experienced several phases of development in Japan that may be viewed equally well as a reorientation of doctrines or as phases of a wider popularization. At least three main phases must be distinguished. During the first, lasting from the presumed date of first introduction in A.D. 552 or 538 to medieval times, the appeal was primarily to the intellectual and social elite: either the teaching was scholastic, devoted to cataloging a vast hierarchy of transcendent saints and deities converted from paganism and to working out their distinctive functions; or else it leaned toward esoteric ritual. It must be granted that Buddhism was initially welcomed for its character as a disciplined, organized church that could enlist elite converts to support the newly emerged central state which was its sponsor. The profundities of its philosophy passed over the head of the usual convert at first, though aristocrats gradually increased their sophistication. Approaching the medieval period, a social revolution brought feudalism out of the ruins of the aristocratic regime. The new rulers, dominant by force of arms, were interested in Buddhism but cared little for subtleties of doctrine and supported, instead, a new set of sects which came into being in the twelfth and thirteenth centuries: the Amidist sects that stripped ritual operations to the bare essential of declaring faith in Amida Buddha, the ardently nationalist sect of Nichiren that simplified doctrine to absolute reliance on one sutra, and the Zen sect that cut scholastic learning away from the search for enlightenment and relied instead on personal discipline for insight. It was not until civil wars were terminated in the late sixteenth century, however, that these sects broadened their membership far beyond the samurai class. This final step of popularization among commoners was not accompanied by notable doctrinal developments among Buddhist scholars but rather by a reorientation of sect affiliation among the various classes. Before tracing all these changes in greater detail, we must look at the characteristic modes of organization achieved by Buddhism in Japan.

Organization

The priest, as a trained specialist, is the central figure in Buddhist worship; the temple is at the same time a home for a priest or a group of priests and acolytes and a hall for ritual that can be performed as well with or without a congregation. A characteristic Japanese flavor pervades the organization of temples within their sects. Temples of any one sect in the countryside stand ranged in a genealogy of descent that links them all to the sect's main or original temple just as branch houses are linked to a main house. Throughout the Tokugawa period, a temple was apt to be identified with a noble family; in the Shin sects, especially, in which celibacy was not expected, the head priest's son succeeded to his position and identified his place in the sect by his household's genealogical or fictional (*oyabun-kobun*) kinship to the head temple. The *ie* (house-structure) norm of corporate family organization was more explicit in Shin sects than in others but tended to prevail in all sects until after World War II, when each temple was listed as a legal entity independent of any other temple and empowered to choose its sect affiliation at will. (See Chapter 2.) As to the relation of the priest to his parishioners (*danka*), he simply services the household in religious matters as a specialist paid each time he performs; his real concern is with the dead rather than the living, and certain features of a funeral, such as the conferring of a new name on the deceased, make it not too fanciful a suggestion that the priest is the godparent for the ancestors. By traditional custom, a person is supposed to find among his neighbors a sponsor or godparent who supplies a new personal name as he enters a new age group. Having acquired several sponsors throughout his life, when he dies his funeral is a final age-grade ceremony in which the priest and he, now deceased, are the principals.

The sects now popular in Japan are heavily founder-centered; stress has been placed on having faith in the procedures or doctrines outlined by the founder rather than on independently searching for truth. The group cohesion normal to Japanese life supports such an attitude of veneration for, dependence on, and obedience to the founder, first, and then to each succeeding head speaking with absolute authority in his name. Commentators have noted that even Zen sects, which revived an aspect of original Buddhism by basing their search for enlightenment on *jiriki* (one's own efforts) rather than *tariki* (help from another, such as a Bodhisattva), have exhibited a strong inclination toward *tariki* in Japan by rigidly pursuing the regimen expounded by one or another master in the past.

Finally, it bears reemphasizing that Buddhist organization throughout Japanese history made it a formidable counterbalance to the state, creating the classic church-state tension. In its early days (741) a branch temple (*kokubunji*) was built by imperial decree at each provincial capital (*kokufu*) to further the spiritual welfare of the state and its officers and to reinforce official authority (a function paralleling that of the traditional shrines). As temples gained affluence and power in Nara, however, the court was moved to Kyoto; but monasteries that were clustered on nearby Mount Hiei, possessing their own lands and ultimately their own men-at-arms, interfered again and again in temporal affairs. Not until the Tokugawa house unified Japan under its absolutism and alternately fed and starved the temples to make them serve as one of its instruments of control over the populace was the conflict resolved.

Individual Belief and Actions

Few adherents remain in any of the six sects that made Nara a splendid temple-adorned capital town in the early days of Buddhism: Sanron (625?), Jōjitsu (625), Hossō (654), Kusha (658), Kegon (736), and Ritsu (754). Three have died out, leaving Jōjitsu, Kegon, and Ritsu. These sects, of relatively scholarly appeal, were overshadowed during the Heian period by the founding of the Tendai sect (805) by Saichō on Mount Hiei northeast of Kyoto and the Shingon Sect (806) by Kōbō Daishi on Mount Kōya some forty miles southwest of Nara. The Tendai sect undertook to bring the Shinto *kami* within the Buddhist pantheon by declaring that, like all other gods within Buddhism, the *kami* had been converted from paganism and were now guardians of the Buddha; but the Shingon doctrine argued that the *kami* were not converts but were actual manifestations of Buddhas and Bodhisattvas though either interpretation made it possible for Buddhist priests to manage shrine activities and even to build temples and shrines on the same ground, the respective functions of Buddhism and Shinto were not basically confused. The direction of funerals became the prerogative of Buddhist priests, whereas weddings and other nonpolluting celebrations remained in the province of the shrines. In these sects that have remained popular since the Heian period, however, Buddhism was already oriented to the veneration of ancestors, unlike its orientation in China.

The intricacies of doctrine and elaboration of ritual that characterize the foregoing two sects did not prevent their acquiring great temporal power, but to a greater extent from pious donations of land by the nobility than from popular support, and even these touched few persons in the villages below samurai rank. The medieval sects remain the largest in membership today. Two Amidist sects, Jōdo (founded by Hōnen Shōnin in 1175) and Shin (Jōdo Shin, founded by Shinran in 1224), take second and third rank in membership today, with more than 7,500,000 and more than 9,000,000 adherents, respectively. Amida Buddhism gives full scope to the elaborate iconolatry that emerged within the Tendai sect, with thirteen Bodhisattvas, or deities, of whom five are especially singled out for veneration: Dainichi (Maha Vairocana), the cosmic Buddha, around whom are gathered, at cardinal points of the compass, Miroku (Maitreya), the Buddha of the future; Shaka (Sakyamuni) or Gautama, the historical Buddha; Ashiku (Akshobhya), the source of life; and Amida (Amitabha), the dispenser of infinite compassion. But Amida Buddhism gains its greatest appeal from its offer of salvation on relatively easy terms. Simply by uttering the phrase *"Namu Amida Butsu"* (Hail, Amida Buddha) with full faith and conviction, one may gain release to the Western Paradise or Pure Land (Jōdo). This theme of divine compassion and mercy rather than rigid self-discipline in the Eightfold Path gave Amida Buddhism a new and appealing spiritual quality.

Nichiren, founder of the Nichiren or Hokke sect (1253), sought his key to truth in the Lotus Sutra that asserts the unity and inseparability of the universal Buddha (Dainichi), the eternal Buddha (Amida), and the historical Buddha (Shaka). His followers invoke this sutra, chanting *"Namu myōhō renge-kyō"* as their central ritual. But also, in keeping with Nichiren's denunciation of other teachings as perversions of truth, they tend to be the most actively proselyting sect in Japan today, and it is from the Nichiren sect that various near-fanatic movements have sprung, most recently the Sōkagakkai with its policies of forceful recruitment and political action. With adherents totaling more than 9,000,000, the Nichiren group of sects has slightly the largest membership of any in Japan.

Zen sects (introduced from China in the period 1191–1227) lived through a period of monkish quiescence before they rose to prominence partly by supplying sage advisers to perplexed officialdom. They emphasize meditation (the Sanscrit meaning of Zen) as a disciplined but purely introspective approach to the goal of sudden enlightenment (satori). Disciples of Zen deny that insight into truth and the real nature of things can be expressed verbally or communicated through intellectual concepts. Consequently, Zen makes room for mystical intuition (stressed by Eisai, 1141–1215) and thoughtful but nondoctrinal living (stressed by Dōgen, 1200–1253). Some argue that Zen is really a revolt against Buddhism, smacking of Chinese Taoism; but adherents claim that Zen has stripped away the accretion of Mahayana trappings to return to original Buddhist teachings. In any event, the sect encourages contemplation on the part of a communicant; its doctrine that all of nature expresses the fundamental truths has made it hospitable not only to a cloistered life but to a life of action as well, not only to fencing and archery but to calligraphy, poetry, and painting. Simplicity, austerity, and self-discipline are valued, not to demonstrate humility or self-abnegation but for their contributions to intellectual directness. All these qualities gave Zen a rather special appeal to warriors aiming at fortitude and discipline and to intellectuals. Zen sects continue to be favored among intellectual and leisured groups today, though the membership as a whole covers all divisions of society, as does the membership of any other sect.

Universal Buddhist affiliation dates from the Tokugawa period, when, combining the drive to extirpate Christianity with the opportunity to utilize the systems of temples throughout the country to perform desired governmental functions, the Shogun Iemitsu decreed that every household must register with some temple. Temples thus kept the near-equivalent of a total census of population and had a decided advantage in retaining adherents. Buddhism was consequently strengthened in numbers, but it was in no danger of escaping from government control. In fact, looking back at the feudal and civil-war periods when fortified monasteries kept troops of men-at-arms, collected feudal rent from their estates, and imposed their might on affairs of state, the contrary was true. The Tokugawa regime carefully stripped away autonomous secular power from the church. Buddhism as a social entity became an organ of the state; attention was diverted from religious functions, and secularization was accompanied by corruption of the clergy. The religion was not devitalized, as the Meiji government learned when, in the zeal of promoting Shinto it confiscated temple lands and attempted to incorporate all temples that had some association with shrines into the State

Shinto system. Public resistance made a more permissive policy necessary. Nevertheless, Buddhist sects have had difficulties in maintaining
temples in the face of relative indifference on the part of parishioners,
and few notable developments have occurred in the past century.

Through the centuries, the meaning of Buddhism to its devotees has
changed considerably. One infers from the tone of pronouncements
uttered by Prince Shōtoku (Shōtoku Taishi) and other early converts
among the aristocracy that the doctrine of the Eightfold Path opened a
glorious vista, adducing arguments based on self-interest (i.e., one's own
escape from painful carnality) in support of public and private morality,
humility, and altruism, all of which virtues were useful to the limping
progress of the newly formed state. In the medieval period and especially during the civil wars, when rapine, famine, and disease were
seldom forgotten for generations, one or another Buddhist outlook
gathered strength, offering rare intellectual comfort and solace to persons of some sensitivity. One could rest assured of very little in this
world's secular life, but, as the medieval nō plays poignantly show, one
could hold faith in Buddhism's spiritual doctrine of retribution or the
accumulation of merit (karma). Still later, as the peasantry was gathered
universally within the fold of the Buddhist temples during the Tokugawa period, Buddhism tended less to be keynoted by the air of melancholy and despair characterizing it in medieval times. Instead, the
priests and rituals and temples were worked into the pattern of everyday needs. The temple was a social center for elderly people of the
village; to some extent, also, it organized recreational activity among
the young and among married women. The priest held roles of father
confessor, marriage counselor, amateur psychiatrist, and confidant vis-à-
vis his parishioners, depending somewhat on his own capacities. And,
above all, the ceaseless round of ceremonies honoring family ancestors
validated and stabilized faith in the corporate household, a fundamental
institution of traditional Japan.

After the mid-nineteenth century, these functions continued, but the
temple's stature weakened gradually as other facilities for sociability,
recreation, education, etc., appeared and as the social matrix altered.
All Buddhist sects suffered under regimentation between the 1880s and
the 1940s; but though this regimentation was ended by the Occupation,
they were struck an even more severe blow by the agricultural land
reform law. Each temple was treated as a legal person and permitted to
own and cultivate no more land than any other self-sustaining farmer;
under this definition, few temples escaped losing property, and almost
all were reduced to a state of penury, for the American pattern whereby
each congregation contributes voluntarily to the support of its own

church was very little developed. Since the Occupation began, temples have attempted various adjustments to the new circumstances, never with very sympathetic support from officialdom; many have tried to rise to the challenge of the "Social Gospel" represented by Christian sects, conducting kindergartens, nurseries, infirmaries, and other public service activities, and some sects (especially the Shin sect) are actively evangelizing both in Japan and overseas. But signs of vitality are not to be sought entirely in innovations and nontraditional activities. The Zen sect retains vitality without making obvious concessions to modernization, whether because of its freedom from doctrinal positions or, more likely, because its introspective methods, which bear interesting parallels to the aims and techniques of psychoanalysis in the West, serve modern wants in Japan. Thus, though Buddhism as a whole is enduring lean days, there are lively exceptions.

The organization called the Sōkagakkai deserves special comment, having thrust itself into prominence within a decade after World War II both as a religious and a political movement. Technically, it is not an independent religion but a lay movement within the Nichiren group of Buddhist sects, founded in 1941, suppressed after 1943, and revived in 1956. Using vigorous proselyting campaigns, it raised its estimated strength to almost 3,000,000 members by 1962. In its religious aspects, it enlists the laity to win converts for its Nichiren-shō sect; it has expected its members to abstain from all other religious participation, an unusual stand for a Japanese faith to take and one which is being relaxed even within the Sōkagakkai. The movement teaches unquestioning faith in the power of one sutra (canonical verse) emphasized by the medieval monk Nichiren; in return, it promises that the believer's life will be filled with "beauty, good, and benefit." Benefit is concretely interpreted to mean health, success in business, and Buddhahood in this life. Several features attracted public attention and alarm beginning in about 1956. One was the Sōkagakkai's militant techniques of conversion: its lay members went out, often in groups, to proselyte either by suasion (*shōju*) or by intimidation (*shakubuku*), the latter being a "hard sell" of such vigor and persistence that new converts were sometimes literally frightened into joining and the recruiters ran afoul of the police for property destruction or trespass into homes. These methods have been somewhat softened recently, but the movement is now large and prosperous enough to attract converts through another noteworthy feature: its tightly disciplined and showy organization. Members are assigned by age and sex to quasi-military divisions and squads with differentiated functions, such as proselyting or the organizing of social events, welfare activities, and instruction of members. A third notable feature has been the movement's entry into politics as a sort of interest group, with the declared intention to establish its faith (the Nichiren-shō sect) as the national religion. This activity stems from the assumption that government must inevitably be imperfect until conjoined with religion. The movement's authoritarian discipline permitted it to concentrate the votes of members upon one candidate in a selected district; Japan's electoral system makes such concentration successful in the national House of Councilors as well as in the assemblies of the larger cities. In the 1962 national elections, nine candidates for the House of Councilors ran as "independents" sponsored by the Sōkagakkai; all nine won seats, increasing the number of Sōkagakkai seats to thirteen and making this movement a "third force" in politics. The voting records of these councilors are relatively conservative, but as electoral candidates they seem to catch floating votes from people who identify their own interests neither with labor nor with big business. All these unusual features of the Sōkagakkai have roused many Japanese to apprehensive concern, not because of the movement's present status so much as because of its growth momentum; but there are now signs that it is slowing down.

CONFUCIANISM

Confucianism has acquired a poor reputation in certain quarters in Japan and especially among Western students of contemporary Japanese history. The Confucian ethic is credited with having abetted much of the conservative, status-conscious, and nationalistic sentiment of the prewar era. It is blamed for much of the "undemocratic" residue of behavior in postwar Japan. In education especially, the question of whether instruction in "morals" should or should not be reintroduced into the curriculum hinges upon whether one desires or objects to a reemphasis of Confucian-based social values. Yet there were times in Japan's past when Confucianism was a liberalizing force (in contrast to Buddhism), and it is claimed by some pro-Confucian scholars that Confucius himself was a progressive thinker for his age. The social role of Confucian thought in Japan has not always stemmed from the "inner necessity" of Confucianism itself, nor has all the conduct which is ascribed to Confucian influence necessarily been motivated by Confucian principles. Social and political behavior derived from deeply ingrained cultural traditions in Japan have at times only been rationalized by an overlay of Confucian vocabulary. The Confucian principles of social ethics are so broad and universal that they have tended to envelop many values which have been common to status-oriented agrarian societies in general and especially in East Asia. Any study of Confucianism in Japan should attempt to clarify the difference between the real and apparent influence of Confucian thought upon Japanese culture.

Ideology

We may begin our inquiry regarding Confucianism by asking whether it should be thought of as a religion. Confucianism in recent times has lacked most of the essential attributes of religion. It has no special priesthood, no places of worship, no clearly defined creed. In the past, in China and during certain periods in Japan, Confucianism acquired some of these religious attributes. Members of the high bureaucracy or instructors in the Confucian classics acted as a sort of priesthood, and there were state rituals and "temples to Heaven" or shrines dedicated to Confucius and the sages. At the private level the ritual veneration of family ancestors could also constitute a religious dimension of Confucianism.

In Japan all these visibly religious aspects of Confucianism have been played down. Yet to a Japanese of a century ago or even perhaps to a man of the old generation today, the teachings of Confucius were accepted as one of the three religious systems (the others being Shinto and Buddhism) which governed his life. Confucianism, especially in its later neo-Confucian guise, did in fact fulfill intellectual and emotional needs as a satisfying religious belief, and in old Japan it was possible for a man who had dedicated his life to the study of the classics to consider his study all-sufficient and even to choose Confucian (as against Buddhist) burial for himself. It has been more common, however, for Japanese to incorporate Confucianism into a triangle of beliefs, one dealing with the homeland and the family (Shinto), one with death and the afterlife (Buddhism), and the third with social conduct in the present (Confucianism).

The body of beliefs which make up the ideology of Confucianism is extremely large and varied. It is contained in a group of writings (a set of classics and commentaries upon them) which has grown through the ages, although half a dozen men stand out as the foremost contributors to doctrine. Confucius (551–479 B.C.) was the originator and the one who drew together and interpreted the first set of basic texts (many were anthologies of earlier philosophic or literary works). Mencius (373–288 B.C.) by compiling the *Analects* provided the prime source of knowledge about Confucius himself. Tung Chung-shu (ca. 200–120 B.C.) was the foremost Confucian organizer and institutionalizer. Chu Hsi (A.D. 1130–1200) and Wang Yang-ming (1472–1528) marked the beginning and end of the great period of synthesis when Confucianism absorbed certain religious concepts from Buddhism to become a more comprehensive system of belief. Later Confucian teachings were almost exclusively of this synthetic or neo-Confucian variety, and it was this stream of doctrine which made its deepest inroads on Japan of the immediately premodern period.

Confucius' relationship to the doctrine which bears his name is similar to that of Jesus to Christianity. The works and thoughts of Confucius have been added to, distorted, carved in stone, and dogmatized in a manner utterly out of harmony with the intent of the original teacher. Eventually a body of thirteen classics was adopted as the basic scriptures. Most of these works are obscure in the extreme, some of them antedating the time of Confucius. They have consequently been encrusted by layers and layers of commentary. Under the impact of the neo-Confucian movement, four books, the *Analects*, the *Mencius*, the *Great Learning*, and the *Doctrine of the Mean*, with the new commentaries upon them (notably by Chu Hsi), were adopted as the scriptural core.

The doctrine which emerges from the classics and the commentaries provides, first of all, a cosmological answer to the nature of existence and man's position in the universe. In the simplest fashion this cosmology can be described as follows (Chu Hsi's metaphysics is considerably more complex): existence is the result of a heavenly creator (T'ien) which gives rise to the laws or principles (tao or li) governing all existence; cosmic phenomena are produced by the interaction of universal forces (yin-yang or their more sophisticated counterparts); man's destiny is to fulfill his inner motivation and to follow the "path" ordained by Heaven for human society.

Being more than a cosmology, however, Confucianism provided a philosophy of human action and a moral code for society. It was the Confucian belief that a "good society" could be achieved on earth. Since man is inherently good and hence perfectible, society needs only guidance and exemplary leadership. The individual requires proper training and practice in upholding the values of a good society. Basic to such a society are the virtues of benevolent or considerate action (*jen*, or *jin* in Japanese), loyalty (*chung*, or *chū*), filial piety (*hsiao*, or *kō*), and other forms of morality which serve to uphold the five basic social relationships (between ruler and subject, father and son, husband and wife, elder brother and younger brother, and friend and friend). To its ethic Confucianism gives the sanction of its cosmology, for the social virtues it extols are believed to emanate from the will of Heaven.

The Confucian scriptures provided a code of conduct both for the individual and for the guidance of "rulers." Confucianism looked forward to a well-ordered society in which a benevolent sovereign inspired his officers and subjects to proper conduct at all levels. Proper government should be "good government" to which all persons could give their full loyalty. Eventually, as might be expected, Confucian theory became interwoven with Chinese governmental practice, so that theory tended to be applied in a strictly traditional manner. It is from this that the traditionalism and authoritarianism of Confucianism were derived. Thus, although not inherent in the works of Confucius himself, Confucianism tended more and more to provide the rationale for an authoritarian, bureaucratic, and status-conscious political and social order. In the Far East, Confucianism has generally been associated with conservative orders in both ancient and modern times.

Organization

Confucianism in Japan has existed more as an ideology than as an organized state or family cult. One reason for this may be that Shinto has traditionally functioned at the two levels at which Confucianism took on religious overtones in China. In Japan, both the cult of the sovereign and that of the family have been handled under Shinto ritual. The exceptions to this statement may be found in the Nara and Tokugawa periods. During the first, Japan adopted the Chinese form of bureaucratic government and with it some of the ritualism of the Chinese Emperor. During the second, Confucian advisers to the government (*jusha*) sought to introduce Confucian ritual into the shogunal administration. Neither succeeded in replacing the more common forms of Shinto ceremony that supported sovereignty.

The Confucian impact on Japan came about through ideas which had their most visible or organized application in two institutions: (1) legal codes or political maxims and (2) the curriculum of education. Since the early seventh century, when Shōtoku Taishi set down an administrative code based on Confucian concepts of loyalty to the sovereign, successive generations of Japanese rulers have sought to regulate the conduct of officials and subjects through Confucian precepts. The Nara law codes, the Tokugawa social codes, and the didactic elements of such modern political documents as the Meiji Constitution, the Imperial Rescript on Education, and the Rescript to Soldiers and Sailors have all drawn heavily upon Confucian ethical vocabulary. Education in premodern Japan, except what was provided for the Buddhist monastic novice, was almost entirely based on Confucian texts. This became a matter of great importance during the Tokugawa period, when the base of education among samurai and upper-class peasants and merchants expanded enormously, leading to a deep penetration of Confucian values.

During the Tokugawa period, the reliance by the shogunate and the *daimyō* on the principles of Confucianism as the basis of their statecraft led to the patronage of a large body of Confucian instructors and educational institutions. This apparatus was swept away after the Restoration of 1868. Although the Tokugawa Confucian College (the Shōheikō) became one of the foundation stones of the modern Tokyo University, the temple to Confucius at Yujima today is a forgotten relic of the once-powerful position of sponsored Confucianism in Japan. In the modernizing world of postrestoration Japan, the Confucian scholar per se had little status. Yet the social values of loyalty, filial piety, and respect for authority remained high in the value system of the new "imperial Japan."

Individual Belief and Actions

The importance of Confucianism in both early and recent times has been that it has furnished guidance for a dimension of individual behavior not satisfied by either Shinto or Buddhism. Confucianism provides an idealized set of values for social conduct neglected by Shinto (which assumes a customary corporate society based on communal or family harmony) and by Buddhism (which is more deeply concerned with individual redemption). Hence it is largely from Confucianism that ideas of socially proper conduct were formulated.

It is undeniable that Confucian thought has leaned toward conservatism. Its primary concern has been with the "regulation" of society and individual behavior. The concept of loyalty (*chū*) and respect for parents (*kō*) which stood as the foundation of Tokugawa moral instruction, of *dō* (one's proper way) or *mibun* (one's proper station) were based upon a view of society which was fundamentally static and authoritarian. Such principles, of course, are not necessarily confined to Confucian doctrine. Japanese society has commonly subscribed to them, so that we can hardly credit all authoritarian behavior as Confucian-inspired.

Yet despite the normal tendency of the Japanese to subscribe to the basic values of Confucianism, there has never been a complete acceptance of all Confucian doctrine in Japan. In feudal Japan and even in the Tokugawa period, the training of the samurai set before him ideals of military discipline and disregard of human life which contrasted with the civilian orientation of Confucianism. In recent times modern science and liberal political philosophy have clashed with Confucian social doctrine. The homiletic stories of loyal or filial conduct used to educate Japanese youth in the morals (*Shūshin*) classes served well in the authoritarian environment of prewar days but are in bad repute today.

The question facing contemporary Japan is what to put in the place of the Confucian values upon which prewar Japan relied so strongly. Democracy as a social system has entered the postwar era largely as a liberalizing and antitraditional influence. It has placed, as yet, little emphasis on the "responsibilities" of freedom as complementary to the privileges of an open society. Modern Japanese youth impatient for all the freedom of expression and action which they believe to be their newly gained right look only with scorn upon the values of social order and moderation which they associate with the "feudal" past. The older generation, frightened by defeat in war and the reforms of the Allied Occupation, seem to find themselves powerless to evoke a responsible order.

What is certain today is that Confucianism as a cosmology and system of values has almost entirely succumbed to the course of modern change. Confucian cosmology lost its grip on the Japanese mind with the spread of science and the rationalistic philosophies of the West. Confucian social values have been irreparably weakened by the failure of a state and society once supported by such values to save Japan from a crushing defeat in war. Meanwhile, the modern Japanese must attempt to find some new synthesis of moral values to meet the needs of a new and more democratic society.

CHRISTIANITY

Japan's first experience with Christianity, in her so-called "Christian century" (1549–1640) ended just past the threshold of the absolutist regime of the Tokugawa shoguns. The Tokugawa regime, besides extirpating the Christian doctrine by every means at its command, placed so deep an imprint of its own on Japanese society that almost nothing carried over from the earlier period to the present except a tradition of martyrdom and a few communities of underground cultists, or hidden Christians, near Nagasaki. Christianity itself evolved in the interval of two centuries, making it necessary to distinguish between the Roman Catholic creed implanted by sixteenth-century missionaries and the primarily Protestant evangelism of the nineteenth and twentieth centuries. Thus, the two Christian periods present relatively sharp contrasts.

Their comparison, however, raises a point of more than casual interest. St. Francis Xavier, a Basque friar, arrived in Japan from Malacca, then a Portuguese colony, in 1549 and was soon followed by other

Catholic missionaries. Their efforts at conversion were made mainly in western Japan, but they won a following there estimated as high as 600,-000 before extirpation became the firm policy. Assuming this estimate of converts to be near the true mark, one may well ponder the reasons why Christianity gained a sixteenth-century foothold proportionately firmer than it holds in the twentieth century, when its total of members of all sects has risen to 669,074 (1961). Christianity now claims 0.66 per cent of all Japanese; at that time closer to 4 per cent had accepted Christianity.

Various reasons existed for tolerating or embracing the Christian creed. Before the Tokugawa regime ended the long period of civil wars, several lords and military leaders had accepted conversion themselves, while others, including the redoubtable Oda Nobunaga, encouraged it in other Japanese as a counter to the political and military power of Buddhist sects. The excitement of a foreign culture, represented by the traders and gun-bearing soldiers as well as by missionaries, was something of a lure. Yet the crux of conversion in Catholic as well as later Protestant teachings was the individual appeal for salvation, an act of conscience which, as we shall see, tends to alienate the convert from his most central social and emotional ties and which must have been a wrench then as now. Moreover, repression began as early as 1597, with the crucifixion of twenty-six Christian missionaries and converts at Nagasaki; though it was sporadic for some time, the very pertinacity of Christians in their beliefs and practices called forth greater severity until ultimately, in 1640, every household was compelled to register as a parishioner of a Buddhist temple. Homes were searched for Christian emblems, suspects were forced to trample on icons, patrilineal relatives of converts were killed or punished, and marriage was interdicted into lineages of known Christians. The rebellion at Shimabara Peninsula near Nagasaki, recurrent through 1637 and 1638, was partly an agrarian uprising but became mainly a Christian rebellion; the government suppressed it with bloody ferocity, massacring 37,000 Christians. Considering the variety of reasons for unrest in the area, such severities do not measure the appeal of the Christian creed alone, yet its sixteenth- and seventeenth-century success did strengthen incentives to renew missionary work when opportunity next appeared in the nineteenth century.

Since a group of four American missionaries arrived in 1859 to revive Christian teachings, Christianity has regained its earlier numerical position but scarcely more. A general and sufficient explanation is hardly possible, yet observers have called attention to a variety of factors. It is still difficult to reconcile Christian doctrine and practices with traditional Japanese culture. Of course, increasing numbers of

Japanese feel no powerful commitment to this culture, regarding many of its features as old-fashioned or feudal. Yet, it is claimed, what commitment they have may be to a secular, nonreligious life rather than to Christianity. Another notable factor has been one or another form of opposition to the free exercise of religion. The United States-Japan Treaty of 1858 authorized freedom of religion for foreigners residing in Japan, but until 1873 the old signboards prohibiting the propagation of *Kirishitan* teaching made it clear that Christianity was not for Japanese. State support of Shinto, expressed in a catalog of cult ceremonies compulsory for all Japanese, posed problems of conscience for both pastors and parishioners for some decades. Finally, in 1941, the government forced all Protestant Christian denominations to combine under one administration or cease activity, and the years of World War II were inhospitable years for Christians in Japan.

From yet another viewpoint, a reconciliation between Christianity and Japanese culture was impeded by foreign sponsorship, financing, and management of evangelism. Most Christian denominations in Japan are branches of their mother churches abroad even today, and policies have been set by the mother churches that provided funds. Doctrinal differences between sects at home may mean little to prospective Japanese converts, yet missionaries who must report to boards in America naturally have difficulty in softening doctrinal distinctions in Japan. In 1956, 3,571 foreign missionaries represented 38 sects of Christianity; so much diversity was still no match for that of the 142 Shinto and 169 Buddhist sects, but on the other hand neither Shinto nor Buddhism was being taught by priests in a ratio of one foreigner for every two native-born Japanese, as was Christianity. From this viewpoint, the rise of a Japanese movement called Mukyōkai (Nonchurchism), initiated by Uchimura Kanzō on the premise that the essential roots of Christian belief are in the individual conscience and require no church, is a phenomenon of considerable interest. In the second decade of the postwar period, also, Japanese churchmen have reached posts of authority in considerable numbers.

Ideology

The balance of foreign control over Christian sects in the country makes unnecessary or redundant any outline of the basic doctrinal premises of this religion in Japan. A feature that sets both Protestantism and Catholicism (though not the Russian Orthodox Church) far apart from alternative religions in Japan is their advocacy of what has been called the *Social Gospel*: dedication to education (from kindergarten through the university level), medicine, and other avenues of social uplift as a corollary to the search for spiritual grace. In simple terms, Christianity is activist where traditional Buddhism and Shinto take a position of passivity or retreat; the Christian position accords with the expectation that man can mold and improve the external world rather than with the premise that he must accommodate himself to immutable external realities. This basic stand has drawn into Christianity businessmen, intellectuals, and others whose presence among the leadership groups of changing Japan has made Christianity influential far beyond the degree suggested by its low number of adherents.

Organization

Most sects of Christianity in Japan today are Protestant and so, in principle, are congregation-centered. This emphasis differs significantly from the community-centered quality of Shinto and the temple-centered quality of Buddhism. That is, ultimate authority over both doctrine and procedure is vested in the congregation. When the congregation dissolves, the church vanishes; although the minister is in the role of leadership, he retains this role at the pleasure of the congregation or its representatives. This principle tends to be distorted and honored more in the breach than in the observance insofar as the pastor is in missionary status, holding a pulpit by the authority of a congregation abroad rather than the congregation he preaches to. Even so, a sense of congregational solidarity provides a certain bond for Christians which, because of its voluntary nature, is difficult to match in most traditional Shinto or Buddhist organizations.

Individual Belief and Activity

The few studies of Christianity in Japanese life suggest strongly that its exclusiveness is Christianity's chief disadvantage in drawing converts. Stated in other words, persons who are strongly attracted by everything that Christianity represents nonetheless hesitate to be converted because of repercussions on their lives outside the church. Should a convert refuse to join his family at the household *butsudan* (the cupboard in which ancestral memorial tablets are kept) to participate in ceremonies on the death anniversary of an ancestor or to join in offering prayers for his welfare and goodwill? The ancestor was Buddhist, not Christian; yet the convert often is impelled to symbolize his new orientation by dismantling the household *butsudan*, in effect denying loyalty to past generations. Again, what happens to his status as an active community member if his household sends no representative to shrine ceremonies? Personal conversion affects his household, his neighborhood, and his community to a great extent. Within many local communities, it has been difficult for an individual person to accept Christianity without upsetting the lives of those around him, and villagers tend, not without reason, to classify a whole household rather than given members as being Christian or non-Christian. It is not infrequently decided that conscience permits one to join shrine and temple ceremonies as a civic or quasi-political act while professing Christianity in private, but a mass, conventional solution that would neutralize the problem has not appeared. Such problems are decidedly less serious under urban conditions. A situation in which one is independent of one's neighbors and kindred in day-to-day living and in which one's home may have no *butsudan* reduces or eliminates many issues that beset conversion to Christianity and lets the issues of conscience stand out as important. The consequence is that Christian evangelism has advanced almost exclusively in cities, making slow progress in small towns and among the villages of Japan.

NEW RELIGIONS

One wonders, at first, how the Japanese are able to group many religious sects into a single category called New Religions. The group is extraordinarily heterogeneous and troublesome to summarize as to place, circumstances, or origin, tenets, ceremonies, organization, and so on. Upon examination, however, a family resemblance is found. In this group, as contrasted with either Shinto or Buddhism, which are their progenitors, common characteristics appear in ideology, organization, and membership. Their doctrinal position tends to be activist, inasmuch as it recognizes ill health, poverty, and unhappiness as curable evils rather than as simple facts of existence and offers here-and-now help against them. In organization, their central element is the congregation of believers; though the congregations do not necessarily serve as the centers of power and authority and though in the minds of their followers the cults are as much founder-centered (rather than doctrine-centered) as are Buddhist sects, the sects act through their congregations and exist only as long as the latter exist. It happens that women have frequently been important either as founders or as builders of the sects in their early phases. Members become such by conversion and conviction and support a sect as an act of individual volition rather than automatically belonging on account of membership in a particular community or household; not faced with the dilemma of Christians, however, New Religion converts may continue to practice other religions. They seek security, comfort, and assistance either in general spiritual terms or, sometimes, in very practical terms. Christianity, not

Buddhism, Shinto, or Confucian doctrine, is the nearest to being equivalent to these features of orientation, organization, and participation. Yet very few New Religions have any recognizable historical relationship with Christianity. The question that follows is why, since they are Japanese in origin, such functional parallels with Christianity should characterize them.

Certain of these sects are superficially well known through their own propaganda and the public press, whereas others have gone almost unnoticed. Only quite recently has analytic attention been paid to the New Religions, and explanations of their similarities or differences still leave questions unanswered. A couple—Kurozumi (1814) and Tenri (Tenrikyō, 1838)—came into existence fairly early; a larger group sprang up when freedom of religion was restored after World War II; but the major group either rose in a brief two-decade period, 1870–1890, or descended from sects that emerged then, by splitting off, by recombining doctrinal elements from various sources, or, in a few cases, by making outright innovations that cannot be traced directly to any traditional religion.

If a blanket explanation is attempted, it surely must be made in more than religious terms. Quite tentatively, the New Religions of Japan may be compared to movements of both a religious and a non-religious nature observed in Europe and among indigenous peoples of Africa, Oceania, and the Americas at a time when tension-ridden sociocultural change has awakened them to expectations of better lives but not yet taught them political approaches to achieving them. These religious movements, we are tempted to say, are prepolitical reactions to change, some aimed at hastening the desirable future, others at cherishing and returning to the comfort and security of tradition. Among primitive peoples, this reaction has been known as revitalism or revivalism, because it has so often looked back to a more desirable past; in Europe, some movements have clutched at vanishing tradition, but others have envisioned a future utopia or millennium often destined by some miracle to be brought to pass overnight. This reaction is primitive only in lacking sophistication about the nature of society and its processes; it may well be a symptom of healthily rising expectations, though in Japan and elsewhere it appears to be most common among people of limited education who have the greatest obstacles of an economic or other nature to achieving their dreams. It is not surprising that the movements to which they flock offer the millennium through faith rather than rational understanding or economic effort. Nor is it surprising that the earlier Japanese movements arose in the more prosperous areas of western Japan but not among the more prosperous economic groups there. This suggestion, however, is a thin speculation attempting to explain how and why New Religions differ categorically from the older religions of Japan. It is now time to examine their characteristics in greater detail.

The table below gives only a partial list of movements that may be placed in this category. The Sōkagakkai organization, often included among the New Religions, has already been treated as a special movement within Nichiren Buddhism. Some existing movements that are now small in size or very new may rise to great prominence in a relatively few years, but not necessarily at the expense of others, for although a few movements tend to foster exclusive adherence by their members, most carry on the Japanese tradition of welcoming a new convert no matter how many other religious affiliations he has. The logic of the latter position is that any religious activity may supplement or reinforce another, as Shinto and Buddhism have done for millions of persons. The exclusivist viewpoint does not have fertile ground in Japan.

NEW RELIGIONS OF JAPAN

Sects with Shinto roots	Genealogy	Category*	Membership†
Izumo Taisha	ancient nucleus	PH	2,300
Kurozumi	1814	F	860
Tenri	1838	F	2,350
Konkō	1860	F	630
Taisei	1870	PH	140
Misogi	1872, as Tofukamikō	F	80
Fusō	1873, as Fuji-ichizan Kyōkai	M	650
Mitake	1873	M	710
Shinri	1880	PH	570
Shinshū	1881	F	580
Shūsei-ha	1876	PH	40
Jikkō	from Fujiko (1564) via Fujidō	M	470
Ōmoto	1892	F	
Seichō-no-ie	from Ōmoto: syncretist	F	1,500
P.L. (Perfect Liberty)	from Mitake and Fusō via Tokumitsu: syncretist	A	600
Sekai Kyūsei	from Ōmoto: syncretist	F	400
Tenshōkō-taijingū (Dancing Religion)	1946	F,A	110

* F = goals through religious experience or faith; A = goals through ascetic practice or induced rapport; PH = goals through philosophical meditation; M = goals through mountain worship.

† In thousands.

SOURCE: Adapted from Ministry of Education, *Religions in Japan*, Tokyo, 1963.

Ideology

The larger number of New Religions are clearly kindred to Shinto in their theology; they may reinterpret the position or function of deities or even add a nontraditional supreme deity or supreme principle, but these innovations do not cast doubt on the source from which they have been drawn. A good proportion assert that their truth is to be learned through a mystic experience—sometimes a hallucination or trance—and seek to achieve this experience for every follower; others are content that the founder mystically acquired the doctrine, during a spell of illness, a trance, or the like. Some ask only faith; others urge ascetic or magical practices. The so-called "mountain cults" (Mitake, Fusō) use pilgrimage to the sacred mountain as their touchstone for achieving rapport with the sacred spirit. As Ronald Dore [2] observed of Buddhist sects, that followers distinguish them not by differences of doctrine but by differences of their respective founders, so with the New Religions. They can be distinguished ideologically, but this is not the paramount basis for joining one and not others.

Organization

Women loom prominently in many of the New Religions, as they never did in more traditional religions. A woman appears as the founder, proselyter, or manager in nearly 50 per cent of these cults. Few of the founders themselves had much education; a handful had risen to wealth, then lost it; but most were in near-poverty throughout life, unless enriched through their sects. The founder, if a visionary person, tended in various cases to be eclipsed by the competent manager who took the reins of the organization in his own hands.

The terms set for membership are quite varied. It is true that all comers are generally welcomed, but new entrants or even established members may be expected to undergo denial and self-sacrifice. Volunteer labor in behalf of the leader of the Tenri sect is an example, and, in keeping with the sect's utopianism, it offers members most elements of a new society: separate communities and various facilities even up to the provision of a university. Regular services of ritual, singing, prayer, or testimonial characterize some but not all New Religions; the congregation usually assembles in one member's home unless its size requires a larger hall.

[2] Ronald P. Dore, *City Life in Japan*, Berkeley, Calif., 1958, p. 347.

Participation

The variability of activities almost defies generalization. Whereas some sects expect regular attendance at meetings and may urge their members to participate actively, as with ritualized singing and dancing or rhythmic body swaying or with testimonials, others do not even expect members to attend lectures regularly. No studies are available to permit a general summary of the class status, prevailing occupations, or other characteristics of the participating congregations. The motivation to join depends greatly on the tenets of the sect; many members of Tenri and others seek healing and welfare through faith in divine reason or in guardian spirits, while members of the Mitake sect are interested in divination and purification. The Sōkagakkai, though a Buddhist sect, has a clear resemblance to New Religions that stem from Shinto, not least in that it frankly promises an increase of material wealth to its followers. In some sects, no more concrete result than gratification and expansion of the spirit is anticipated.

MATERIALISM AND NIHILISM

To this point, we have examined only the religious philosophies that are well represented in Japan. Moreover, though we have sketched in their idea systems to comprehend what these religions mean to the Japanese people at large, this outline has been extremely spare and curtailed. In what follows, dealing with the modern period, secular philosophies are necessarily central, and we must take account of their effect among the educated or intellectual elite even when such effects are harder to trace among the masses. Two watersheds for intellectual currents are notable: the Meiji Restoration and World War II. In the Meiji period, Japanese were first given access to systematic philosophies of the West, and, at the same time, a secular educational system was set up. To educated Japanese whose lives were being transformed by new ways from Europe, the philosophies that had developed in association with that culture were of lively interest. As for other Japanese, even if they had never so much as heard of a single European philosopher by name, they too were brought into contact at least with the philosophy of naturalism implicit, say, in the physical sciences, thanks to the universal and compulsory principle of elementary schooling. Thus, conditions of the Meiji period promoted the wide dissemination of quite novel viewpoints and values.

Then, defeat in World War II sucked the life out of certain traditional or neotraditional values. Viewpoints that thereupon sprang to life were not innovations, for they had been present for a half-century or more in Japan; they replaced the doctrines that had been damaged or shattered in the train of military defeat. A great many Japanese, however, acquired a new skepticism. They found no sure footing in various areas of life, especially those affecting individuation. So the war, rather than simply leading to the triumph of nontraditional philosophies, was notable for raising many unanswered and unanswerable questions about the nature of man, society, and the universe which no prefabricated philosophy has been able to satisfy to everyone's satisfaction.

During the first period defined here, what selection of European philosophies was favored? In universities, though the available range was rather wide, there was a marked preference for German intellectual concepts. College students had among their student songs one very popular lyric entitled "Dekansho," an acronym from the initial syllables of the names Descartes, Kant, and Schopenhauer. Perhaps one may reasonably point to a feature held in common by all these philosophies and by the official or Japanese state viewpoint: they embody a dualistic conception of mind as an entity apart from matter (unlike the materialists' monistic assertion that "minding," like breathing, is no more than a function of matter in living creatures). This concept was fully compatible with crucial nationalist doctrines, for example, with the assertion that *Yamato-damashii* (Yamato spirit) was what made the Japanese a common and unique people or with the insistence that a deathless entity called *kokutai* (national polity) constituted the heart of the nation. Though these and other elements of national doctrine were not consciously or systematically derived from dualistic European philosophies, they were in conformity with them, and most educated persons, whether college-trained or self-taught, before World War II felt some obligation to be conversant with these lines of Western European thought.

Other lines of European thought were by no means excluded among the same intellectual circles, though the political climate seldom favored their being stressed in university training. Dominant among these philosophies was materialism. Marxism, in the long run, was to exert the greatest impact, although British economic and rationalist works were also translated and widely read. Such world-shaking events as World War I and the Russian Revolution, coinciding with the domestic, economic, and social tensions that marked the so-called "liberal decade" of the 1920s, helped to stimulate the circulation of translations from Karl Marx, Friedrich Engels, Vladimir Lenin, and other liberal or radical thinkers. The heritage of their ideas persists today even in certain common phrases for social or economic phenomena that were first translated from their works: e.g., if one wishes to refer to the middle class, a most common phrase is *chūsan-kaikyū,* which connotes "bourgeoisie" rather than "middle class"; especially since World War II, *hōken-teki* (feudal) is the more common synonym of *kyūryū* (old-fashioned). Thus, materialism as well as German idealism can be said to have gained fairly wide currency after the Meiji Restoration, without yet coming into acute conflict with older, traditional religious philosophies. This conflict was postponed rather than eradicated or avoided altogether, however. When it came into the open after World War II, the materialistic members of the Western philosophies tended to be in a decidedly advantageous position.

To assess the destructive impact of the unconditional surrender ending World War II, we must recall that the Japanese prewar government, preparing with every resource for all-out warfare, had mobilized religion and ethics along with property and manpower. "Thought-control" legislation was intensified. The government argued that, though Japan was admittedly short of material resources, her Yamato spirit (Shinto), the boundless protection of divine forces (Shinto), and the absolutely dedicated fealty of her people (Confucianism) would enable her to overcome all opposition. Concepts derived from non-Japanese traditions were enlisted: e.g., the missions to drive the imperialists from their Asian colonies (Marxism) and to unite all Asians as brothers of a single race (racism). Not only did this philosophical edifice topple with defeat in 1945, but the Occupation subsequently banned state support or guidance of Shinto, excised Confucian ethics from the school curriculum, identified the state with its citizens rather than with a god-protected entity (*kokutai*), and struck mortally at the concept of the house (*ie*) as an entity by supporting guarantees of individual liberty. Yet, although the Occupation intended, by these steps, to trample basic wartime assumptions underfoot, it found these assumptions already laid prostrate by defeat itself.

Among other peoples, historically, one may find occasions when a national ethic has survived military disaster without crumbling; a few can be called to mind that may even have waxed stronger under adversity. Whether total warfare and unconditional surrender in modern times rule out comparison with any historical precedents may be debated. So, also, one may debate the inferences drawn from such comparisons. If the Japanese cooperated closely with the Occupation to uproot wartime teachings instead of clinging to them more tightly after they had failed the test of fire, does this prove that the Japanese are essentially practical and pragmatic about their convictions? Or does it prove that these particular convictions were part of an artificial system thrust by fanatics on the nation as a whole through techniques of propaganda rather than being self-generated expressions of deep belief? Argument of this sort may be profound or profoundly futile. What is incontestably true is that defeat left a large realm of uncertainty among postwar Japanese, not merely proving that certain nationalistic premises were unreliable, but leaving people widely skeptical about the trustworthiness of any premises at all.

Materialism, of course, offered a ready interpretation for the military debacle, and many persons now contemplated it more seriously than before. Yet this viewpoint was not the only one to present itself as a substitute for what the war had taken away. Various local religious cults and the spectrum of the New Religions drew much interest and increased participation, particularly during the lean postwar years when they promised healing against disease and welfare and comfort rising out of poverty. A Christian campaign of evangelism in 1949 drew tremendous throngs, though it gained relatively few long-term converts. Perhaps most notable of all, however, is what may be called in philosophical terms *nihilism*, a refusal to accept wholeheartedly any system of interpretation of the universe. Extreme expressions of this attitude are relatively rare, though one may suspect their influence in the rising curve of juvenile delinquency among better-educated groups or in individual and group advocacy of carnality and other immediate-sensory pleasures. Most persons who are disturbed by the lack of final answers nonetheless retain direction and day-to-day stability in both an emotional and an intellectual sense from their families, friends, and jobs and from their sense of being all one people with a remarkable history of accomplishment. It is true that from seven to nine out of the ten persons polled in various opinion surveys deny that they possess any religious convictions. Nonetheless, most Japanese assert quite positive and definite values, whether personal or social.

Two illustrations may convey an intimation of the pragmatic and immediate quality of the positive orientation referred to here. First, when the Emperor publicly renounced the doctrine of his personal divinity, it was with the approval and urging of the Occupation, and the Occupation also ensured that political power should not be focused on him or his surrogates; otherwise, the Occupation treated the imperial institution with great respect and care as a symbol. But attacks have become more frequent and virulent against the imperial institution, emanating from the Japanese themselves, even while conservative elements have taken steps to shield or even reinstate the institution as something more than a symbol. At issue, in large part, is the latest religiopolitical role of leadership of the Emperor; opponents deplore not merely the political threat it poses but, even more strongly, the nonrationalistic assumptions that support it. Theirs is an outspokenly antireligious viewpoint in many cases.

Second, a nonreligious orientation clearly animates one of the most positive and optimistic keynotes of present-day Japan. Running through the traditional philosophies is the assumption of fixity and changelessness in the environment, to which men must adjust themselves. Buddhism most explicitly treats the world and its evils as immutable facts which can be dealt with in only two ways: by transcending the state of carnal existence or, in Zen, by cultivating such detachment that existence is no longer a problem. In either case, it is man that must accommodate himself or be modified, not the world about him. In contemporary Japan, this detached or melancholic outlook is rarely evident, having been replaced by the brisk confidence that man can and must remold his environment to suit his wants. Among the most commonly heard phrases is the one that refers to creating "a brighter life" in the future. Whether indigenous or borrowed, recent or old, this activist viewpoint is very much at home in Japan today.

Religious philosophies have yet the chance to reassert themselves with new interpretations appropriate to modern life. The New Religions, though clearly not yet answering the wants of the large majority, do present updated doctrines of a mystic or supernatural character. A nonreligious orientation, however, characterizes the main segment of the Japanese at the moment, according to their own assertions. Viewpoints range along a spectrum from indecision or neutrality to active agnosticism. A certain number of those who disavow religious beliefs are skeptical of or antagonistic to any system of values; for convenience, we have called these persons *nihilists*, and we must recognize the considerable force of this outlook at the present time. But matched against it and probably much more prevalent is the persistent and active mood described above which, if it were more explicitly articulated, might be termed *humanism*, the conviction of man's central value to himself, expressed in inchoate form by vast numbers of those who are unconscious of adherence to any explicit, traditional philosophy in Japan and equally unaware of the historical precedent of humanism abroad.

RICHARD K. BEARDSLEY

Personality Psychology*

INTRODUCTION

The study of personality and its determinants is still in a formative stage. It is judged so not only because its basic concepts have yet to be defined satisfactorily (a state of affairs not unusual in scientific fields), but also because theoretical work began only recently. Clinicians whose purpose is to relieve the distress of mental patients have developed extensive and detailed information about personality disorders without necessarily agreeing on the underlying theory of personality itself. As one approach to clarifying theories of personality, some researchers have taken to studying persons living in contrasting cultures and ethnic groups. Here they overlap the interests and methods of anthropologists, who also have become interested in how varied cultures can affect the outlook of persons reared in them. This joint field of study, personality in culture, had barely begun before World War II. Hence it was something of a pioneering step to apply its concepts and techniques to the wartime analysis of Japan under the sponsorship of the United States government. Interest in Japan has continued to be keen among students of personality in postwar years, though actual research has been limited mostly to work done by the few persons qualified both in the Japanese language and in personality psychology. Thus, we are dealing with a field that is young in Japan and elsewhere and underpopulated with researchers.

Though systematic research in this field is recent, behind it lie literally thousands of more or less perceptive characterizations of personality or group character made by commentators on their own or alien cultures as far back as the days of Herodotus in the fifth century B.C. Certainly an immemorial curiosity as to what one's own people or one's neighbors are like represents, in part at least, an interest in group personality. But systematic studies of group personality, however limited and defective, rise a step above casual, intuitional characterizations, however perceptive, in subjecting themselves to the disciplined methods of measurement and verification and in accepting standards other than

* Acknowledgment is gratefully made to George A. DeVos for manuscripts and discussions, and also to Edward Bordin, Wagatsuma Hiroshi, and Sofue Takao for comments and ideas that influenced the presentation of this chapter.

subjective preference to determine the scope and accuracy of an assertion or to arbitrate between conflicting and contradictory assertions. Personality psychology is committed to empirical, inductive methods of analyzing a national or an ethnic group; for this reason it can make only limited use of the accumulated reservoir of observations.

It need not be assumed that all observations on personality in Japan are automatically invalidated unless they are based on controlled psychological testing. We shall, in fact, draw on certain "commonsense" observations in this survey. But personality theory does teach us to be cautious, to reject some assertions based on untenable assumptions, and to be aware that obvious surface impressions may assume quite altered significance as we dig below the surface with psychological methods. An example dealt with below is the division of power between the sexes in Japan, often cited as an example of male supremacy on the basis of misleading surface impressions. To understand how and where caution and discrimination should be applied, we must survey some of the assumptions and methods used to sharpen insight into psychological phenomena; in the course of this survey, we shall be able to show why psychologists, accustomed to using individual persons rather than groups as their basic unit of study, are immediately involved in the study of culture, a group phenomenon, as soon as they attempt to compare individuals from contrasting ethnic groups.

Clinical evidence overwhelmingly supports the concept of personality as something that grows out of an interaction of several elements rather than being complete and fixed at birth. An inborn or inherited propensity is one element, but only one among others, and it is a potential rather than a fixed and definite quantity or quality. At least as important are (1) the changing state of maturation and (2) the external environment. A few comments on each will show how these factors interlock with each other, preventing the would-be analyst from isolating and assessing the inherent potential personality by itself.

First, we must recognize that potential character traits can be expressed only at some stage of maturation of the individual who is presumed to possess them. Second, we must take account of the external environment to understand maturation, for the following reason: in speaking of a person as mature we mean that he has developed well-organized and satisfying responses to persons and things about him; so it follows that the term *maturation* refers to the interactions of a person with his external environment. Maturation is a process of advancement through which each person fits himself to his surroundings as well as working on the surroundings to shape them to his wants. To understand this advancing interaction, psychologists have developed such important concepts as gratification, cognition, and perception.

Research on personality in culture deals with these concepts as they are affected in different and contrasting environments. Since most such research has used psychoanalytic or Freudian versions of these and other concepts, this theoretical point of view is given here. According to this viewpoint, individual behavior is motivated by one or two basic drives: a drive to secure emotional warmth, love, and attention (mediated sexually in one or another fashion); and a drive for expression (mediated through aggression or achievement). Seeking to gratify these drives, each person comes to manifest *widely integrated dispositions for perceiving or otherwise responding to himself and his environment.* This is to say, he is developing and expressing his personality. The phrase shown here in italics may, in fact, serve as a definition of personality. A differently worded definition, also useful for our purposes, is "those ways of behavior or techniques of solving problems which have a high probability of use by one individual."[1]

In studying such individual dispositions or "ways of behavior [and] solving problems," the concept of gratification helps to divide the maturation process into stages; the concepts of cognition and perception help to explain how these dispositions are fitted to the external environment. We shall now examine these concepts.

An infant, beyond doubt, perceives and seeks gratification through modes different from those of an adult. So personality cannot be conceived apart from its degree of maturation except as a vague predisposition. Clinical observations among Europeans led Sigmund Freud and his followers to the concept of definite stages of psychosexual maturation common to every person between infancy and adulthood. The stages are continually being reexamined both by research within our own culture and by crosscultural research. To speak again in Freudian terms, researchers are asking whether the search for gratification always

[1] Anthony F. C. Wallace, *Culture and Personality*, New York, 1961, p. 7.

focuses earliest around *oral* functions, later around *anal* (and digestive) functions, and, ultimately, around *sexual* functions; that is, whether these anal, oral, and sexual stages of maturation, with their respective substages and variants, appear among all mankind irrespective of heritage and environment. Whatever their stand on this question, researchers generally agree, at any rate, that psychological maturation is most fruitfully viewed as proceeding by definite stages, just as biological maturation advances by stages.

If, as stated above, the integration of dispositions for particular responses to environment constitutes personality, then the character of one's environment is clearly vastly important to the structuring of personality. Clinical study suggests strongly that modes of perception, response, and satisfaction adopted at an early age (roughly within the first six years of life) set the permanent ground plan of a person's personality structure. Some hold that, once this ground plan or base has been formed, even quite radical subsequent changes of environment cannot affect it but can only alter the superstructure; others regard this view as overly restrictive and dogmatic and would grant that considerable change can occur in basic personality structure if environmental pressure strongly impinges at one of the critical turning points of maturation, such as adolescence, when the individual experiences far-reaching reorientation. What both sides fully agree on is that the nature of the environment is just as critical to the shaping of personality as is the basic nature or the stage of maturation of the person concerned.

This reasoning makes it clear that the sociocultural milieu, a dominant part of everyone's external environment, is extremely pertinent to personality research. Different cultures have different effects on their members, whether taken as individuals or as collectivities. Researchers whose interest is in collectivities, however, are not unanimous in their view of the relation of personality qualities to the surrounding institutional environment. A point of difference pertinent to what is to be discussed below hinges on whether people of a single society can be assumed to have a definable national character. One view assumes that persons who interact smoothly must be able to do so because they share an inner stock of common orientations, perceptions, and goals as well as customs, institutions, and language. In other words, underneath the traits that distinguish one person from another there must be a shared *personality profile*, which may be defined as national (or group) character. Some researchers take exception to this assumption. To them, the possibility of a common profile is a problem to be demonstrated, not an axiom to be taken for granted. Their picture of a society is of individual persons, each of whom gradually constructs an extremely individual cognitive map of his cultural environment to guide him in seeking to gratify his drives. His personal map, they point out, need not be identical with those of his neighbors even in skeletal form; in fact, it is most apt to differ in fundamental ways from those of the persons with whom he has the closest interaction. Persons with distinct and individual cognitions of their milieu interact smoothly because their maps share certain points of intersection, not because matching features are entered on the maps of male and female, parent and child, superior and subordinate, and so on; to play their interacting but reciprocal (not identical) roles these varied persons need different maps. The scolded child cannot have the same image of himself and the situation that is held by his scolding mother; she scolds because her outlook differs from his outlook, even though it intersects his at points critical to their relationship.

We need not pursue the differences between viewpoints in detail. Adherents of the "group-character" hypothesis concede that the unity of profile expectable in a small homogeneous society will not necessarily be found in large diversified societies in which relations such as those between parent and child vary with region, socioeducational level, and other factors. Researchers actually at work in Japan, rather than concentrate on this major but difficult question, are paying greater attention to discovering whether constant features of the sociocultural environment give rise to constant or regular psychodynamic mechanisms impinging on most or all Japanese; they are working, as it were, on segments of the major problem. Hence they examine socialization to see how the intergenerational transfer of psychological orientations takes place; they want to know how culture institutionalizes modes of coping with diverse personalities and how individuals internalize and integrate modes of coping with their diverse culture; they try to associate personality disorders with social conditions, examining each disorder for identifiable patterns; and so on. This study of mechanisms accumulates much enlightening information but does not require any beforehand assumption as to the existence or the nature of a single "Japanese national character."

Before dismissing the relation of the individual to his environment, we must note that individuals are not simply products of their cultural systems alone; as organisms they are members of other systems as well. To illustrate the analytic problem with a fanciful example, one may imagine a whole population that exhibits extreme stomach concern because it is constantly hungry or shows strong startle reactions because it is daily beset by earthquakes. Everyone in the society might share these features of behavior, even though they were not directly produced by the culture. In fact, unless the population had devised ways to cope with stomach concern or startle reactions, making them part of their potential for solving problems rather than mere organic responses to stimuli, there would be little point in dealing with these phenomena as personality traits. Let us take a less fanciful, actual example: patterns of drunkenness among Japanese men. Some men are little affected even by hard drinking, but it is more usual for a man to feel and act inebriated on only two or three thimblefuls of sake: first his face flushes brightly, then his speech and actions get out of control, usually in a good-natured, jolly direction. It would be difficult to gainsay the cultural-psychological suggestion by Ruth Benedict that Japanese men become inebriated precipitately as a custom-sanctioned escape from strict social constraints that build more acute psychic tension than in other societies. But if we want to account for curious phenomena such as vascular flushing of the face, or even ask about the mechanism of inebriation, we might become aware of contributing organic factors—e.g., a low level of riboflavin or another nutritional element in the typical diet, or physiological peculiarities of the liver—which in fact might require much more cautious psychological interpretation. Such investigation has not been made, it seems, but this phenomenon of drunkenness reminds us that the investigator of sources of personality traits should be ready to look at noncultural and nonpsychological systems. For the researcher in personality and culture, the individual remains important as the locus where the cultural system intersects with noncultural systems (psychological, physiological, geographical, and others). Cognitive and emotional factors, germane to the psychological system, are so constantly active in this intersection that they receive a special amount of attention.

A final few words of introduction should be given to methods of getting information and to their advantages and limitations. Psychological fieldwork bearing on culture and personality consists basically in recording how people behave or solve problems and how they feel about this behavior; the researcher not only must exercise ingenuity, especially to ascertain feelings, but he must try to make the behavior or the situation not too complex or to hold some factor constant. Perhaps he secures a detailed life history in which the constant factor is the person, while the variables are the person's experiences. Perhaps he observes children, either controlling the conditions under which they interact or concentrating on certain frequent and universal situations. An example of the latter is the study of toilet training, which once was so strongly emphasized to the near-exclusion of other factors as the major determinant of personality by enthusiastic researchers that other scholars drew back in some skepticism from this new field of "bathroom anthropology."

Or the researcher may devise a standard test or interview. Much Japanese research is based on tests of this kind. Especial use has been made of projective tests, which may consist of any stimulus (pictures, inkblots, incomplete sentences) that elicits spontaneous, emotion-colored reactions from the person serving as subject. They are called *projective* because the subject projects himself into the picture or statement on the test. Responses to verbal interviews are open to a degree of error anywhere but nowhere more than in Japan, where restraint in speaking one's mind is very common; also, it must be remembered that both the questions presented to the subjects and the interpretation of their answers may be unwittingly twisted or miss vital points, simply because they are verbal and are aimed at predetermined targets. Some researchers favor projective tests which raise the fewest verbal obstacles to a clear understanding of unverbalized and uncon-scious attitudes and sentiments. The Rorschach Test (a standard set of cards showing irregular and suggestive inkblots to elicit imaginative descriptions from the subject) is frequently used to ascertain how a person goes about perceiving and interpreting puzzling features of his world; it is a reliable test in the hands of experts, yet it was devised to test personality disorders, with the result that all responses are inter-preted with a vocabulary couched in terms of aberrations. Another much-used test, the Murray Thematic Apperception Test (T.A.T.) elicits interpersonal attitudes with a standard set of pictures showing one, two, or several persons together in simple settings. It is very useful for examining such universal relations as the mother-son or woman-man relation, but few responses deal with relations far outside the family circle.

Sociological and anthropological techniques of observation and inter-view are never quite so free as projective tests from the possibility of an observer's bias or failure to ask the right questions. They do give information, however, on the relation of individuals to social institu-tions—community, state, religious bodies, etc.—that are as yet quite untouched by projective tests. In the effort to combine the virtues of each approach, certain "group-dynamics" techniques developed in the United States are now being used in Japan by various researchers centered on a group at Kyushu University. Their studies have but begun, and much greater attention is needed in this area, for most current tests and methods were developed in the United States, where individual relationships hold stage center, whereas Japanese social and personal relations clearly make room for supraindividual organizations as significant entities at every point on the spectrum.

For all that current techniques fall short of total coverage or ideal performance, their information yields valuable insights. A special virtue is their capacity to provide checks for hypotheses and conclusions arising from unrelated research techniques. Some of the debate that swirled around Ruth Benedict's much-admired pioneer study, *The Chrysanthemum and the Sword* (1946), might have been stilled had there been more specifically psychological information at the time. Miss Benedict made an anthropological analysis of the family, state, and other institutions, characterizing them as "authoritarian" and "hierarchical" and viewing them as, on the whole, burdensome to the individual through their rigidity and intensity. Then she used available materials—interviews and content analyses of novels, films, etc.—to identify in Japanese attitudes a receptivity to authority and hierarchy, whether in connection with familiar institutions or in the face of new organization problems. She put the two analyses together as representing the predominant cultural-psychological pattern of Japan. Though her methods were admired in Japan, she drew attack for emphasizing out-of-date institutional forms, for too sweepingly characterizing a diversified society, and (with vehemence) for overlooking subjective attachments to family, community, state, etc., that are quite independent of authoritarian constraints. Especially on the last-named point, both she and her critics were handicapped by a lack of information on Japanese society as perceived subjectively by its members. The techniques discussed here are intended to supply just such information, and their early application in Japan owes much to the stimulus given by Miss Benedict's controversial contribution.

Whether or not a pan-Japanese personality profile may be possible in theory, data are certainly insufficient for one at present, and the following two sections are of considerably more modest scope. The first section examines some of the impressionistic allegations about Japanese personality, noting in passing the guidelines set by personality or culture theory for judging the acceptability of commonsense observations on the Japanese people as a whole or as members of certain subgroups. A nonpsychological but systematic research source providing useful information is introduced in this section: the extensive periodic questionnaire surveys carried out by newspapers, government offices, and others. A major example, the surveys of the Mathematical Statistics Research Institute of the Ministry of Education, is cited. The second section draws more directly on research into personality done by American and Japanese scholars and groups. Besides William Caudill and George A. DeVos among Americans, Japanese-centered research is being done by groups such as the Human Relations Research Group (centered at Nagoya University) and the Association for Group Dynamics (centered at Kyushu University) and by persons such as Doi Takeo, Hoshino Akira, and Sofue Takao. This section is focused on the psychological implications of typical social situations and reviews certain patterns of orientation and response that personality research has brought to light among Japanese.

SELF-PERCEPTION AND SOCIAL GROUPS

Self-perception is a lifelong, continuing process of rediscovering "what is me?" Each person, to answer this question, draws on many sources and forms a composite answer to guide him in various distinct roles. The social groups he belongs to contribute significantly to his composite self-image; he forms ideas of what he is or should become by analogy with what his fellow members are and even shapes himself to fit the model he perceives in them or in the nature of the group itself. Of considerable importance in this connection is a person's ethnic or national group. For the Japanese, with their long history as a distinct people in an exclusive island home, ethnic identity is exceptionally clear and unambiguous. Different individuals are apt to draw somewhat different conclusions as to what "being Japanese" means, for each weaves his diverse personal and subgroup experiences into his percep- tions of the ethnic group; even so, we may look here, if anywhere, for sources of mutually shared predispositions and attitudes. Many ob- servers seeking universal Japanese character traits have, indeed, begun and ended their search at this level.

As is made evident by the very diversity of opinions and interpreta- tions that have accumulated over the years, it is not easy to define or analyze the group image even of a people as clearly differentiated as the Japanese. One reason is that passing fads or currents of thought color the observers' viewpoints, altering their objectives, their sources of data, and their lines of reasoning. Analyses made even recently some- times are guided by outworn assumptions that conflict with the findings of psychology or other social sciences. Impressionistic interpretations thus must be used selectively and with caution. An example or two will serve to illustrate this warning.

One group of interpretations tries to link temperament with political phenomena. Errors are obvious in the more extreme examples which appear at moments of international tension, when outsiders "prove" the Japanese to be amoral and treacherous while their own apologists "demonstrate" their unique pride and devotion. But milder instances, such as the conclusion drawn from Japan's long record of militarism that the Japanese temperament is unusually tolerant of strife and violence or is most comfortable under extreme regimentation, may be just as weak in basic assumptions or reasoning. The conclusion cited itself may be credible, but it cannot be supported by ascribing the behavior of Japan as a nation to the personal temperament of the Japanese as an ethnic group. This assumption, that nations mirror their people's character, did not so obviously fly in the face of facts a century or so ago as compared with this century, when totalitarian regimes have risen to force reluctant peoples into their mold.

The charge to be leveled against such politicotemperamental interpretations may apply equally to analyses in fields that seem quite distant, such as that of aesthetics. In this field, for instance, an observer notes a strong sense of imagery, of emotional and sensory nuances, as a pervasive feature of Japanese literature. In poetry and prose, he argues, logic runs second to feeling by contrast with, say, Euro-American literary standards of objective coherence of narrative and description. He then explains that such attention to emotion is linked to, and presumably derived from, the rich capacity of the Japanese people for sensing and expressing feeling.

The argument is perhaps too bluntly summarized here, but our purpose is not to take issue with the validity of the observer's comparisons, the selection of his evidence, and his choice of descriptive labels; rather, it is to charge both interpretations cited here with being guilty of basic methodological error. These interpretations encourage thinking that runs quite counter to the findings of psychology and other social sciences in tracing literary imagery, militarism, or any other sociocultural phenomena to alleged roots in temperament. Where does such temperament originate? Psychological studies indicate, as we have seen, that specific temperamental qualities emerge under the influence of external conditions. They are not inborn but are shaped and molded into existence especially by pressures from the sociocultural surroundings. Creative persons by definition are outside the run of the mill, whether in literature, politics, or some other field, yet the qualities of temperament they exert upon their society were developed in response to the same processes that contributed to the shape of less distinguished personalities. When their accomplishments over a considerable period of time fall into a distinctive, consistent pattern, it seems reasonable to seek sociocultural determinants of their capacity to make similar contributions. This most important analytic step, omitted from or reversed by analyses that treat militarism, poetic imagery, etc., as the result of temperament, is precisely what interests psychological researchers. Not content with a conclusion that a given cast of character is just "the nature of the race," they must examine the question of whether the alleged specific qualities do in fact appear frequently and, in addition, what conditions brought these qualities into existence. The temperamental characteristics discussed below are analyzed in this fashion.

Certain temperamental features that seem at first glance irreconcilably disparate can be reasonably well accounted for when we ask how they may have come into existence. Not a few observers have described the Japanese, for instance, as prone to self-deprecation and immensely insecure about themselves and their society. Extreme humility about themselves is deduced from their eagerness to emulate things from abroad— from their "instinct for copying." But other observers have been equally struck by almost the exact opposite: an arrogant assertion of Japanese superiority over others—the spirit of defiant pride that underlay both daring strategies and brutal tactics in military operations through World War II. The apparent sharp contrast between these attitudes is among the features that have made Japan seem outstandingly paradoxical.

Yet a resolution suggests itself if we take account of Japan's special historical and geographical position. Few areas of comparable population anywhere in the world have had such culturally homogeneous people who were so long isolated from other peoples. As far back as history goes, these islands were the home of an essentially single people who spoke one language and had a common body of customs, institutional traditions, and values. In isolation, the Japanese missed what most peoples have experienced, a constant rubbing of elbows with outsiders, a constant pressure to see themselves with outside viewpoints, to resist or submit to the intrusion of other peoples and cultures without losing their identity. When they did have such contact or mingling, it was an intense and overwhelming experience, for the outsiders were either the Chinese in their most resplendent periods, the T'ang, Sung, and Ming dynasties, or the technologically advanced Europeans of the nineteenth and twentieth centuries. Putting ourselves in the position of Japanese with this background, our own self-perceptions might well have considerable ambivalence or oscillation. After long periods when an ethnic self-image might lie latent without critical examination, it could not stand firm and impregnable against the competing images of outsiders. Japanese might well oscillate between seeing themselves as the heirs of age-long civilization and viewing themselves as ignorant simpletons. Ambivalence and hypersensitivity feed on each other, and it has been extreme and contradictory expressions of these sentiments that have caught attention: deep humility and self-denigration at one point, exceptional arrogance at another. Where such attitudes have marked Japanese conduct, it is not as inborn qualities of character, but as the crystallization of the insecurities affecting the entire people caught in these particular historical-geographical circumstances.

As each decade and century adds its share to the accumulated fund of ethnic experiences, the meaning of history changes, and likewise such features of personality. Japan of the mid-twentieth century is not the isolated nation she was formerly. Her people are participants, to varying degrees, in culture that is not exclusive to Japan but international. The Japanese who live among structures of steel, concrete, and glass, work at chemistry, electronics, or international trade, and relax with jazz, tennis, or night baseball need derive no sense of being "un-Japanese." Objectively, moreover, even cultural differences need not connote inferiority in an era when Japanese arts and crafts of traditional style find international buyers as eager for them as for cameras and radios made in Japan. All these developments are working changes in Japanese self-perceptions. Through their mass communications media and often in person, Japanese can and do examine the curiosities of foreign lands, sometimes still with hypersensitive tinges of envy or of superciliousness but increasingly with interest devoid of self-consciousness. A good many Japanese young enough to know only the recent years approach the world as members of a people who have won their share of international prizes for fine films, scientific achievements, and beautiful girls. Admittedly, few can yet identify themselves without reservation in such confident terms. Sentiments of insecurity that are by no means residual or superficial lie behind the great emotional weight and heroic effort invested in making the Olympic Games of 1964 in Tokyo an unqualified success. Few Japanese, even in areas remote from Tokyo, were untouched then by the tense air of anxiety and pride, not merely in being hospitable to capacity crowds, but in passing inspection as an equal to any previous host nation. In general, however, the level of emotional uneasiness is lower than in any earlier generation as the Japanese approach the point of regarding themselves as merely one among many peoples, unconcerned about being greatly better or greatly worse than their international neighbors. The epochs of Japanese history still charge the Japanese self-image with meaning but are decreasingly apt to touch off hypersensitive responses of arrogance or self-deprecation.

Aspects of Japanese social structure help to resolve another set of contradictory temperamental features. Are the Japanese docile, self-abnegating, restrained? Or are they volatile, mercurial, explosive? Observers have remarked on both sorts of characteristics, which suggest rather different temperaments—or different circumstances. We suggest that the issue is one of different circumstances impinging on Japanese as group members, calling for different performances of the members' roles. Social life throughout Japan is noted for the solidarity of group associations. To be Japanese is to be involved in close, complex, and enduring relationships with one's family, one's neighbors, and other specific associates. Even persons who, in recent terminology, are "dry," meaning that they have shed emotional attachments to past traditions cherished by the "wets," nevertheless accept close-knit group ties to family, office clique, schoolmates, or business and professional associates. Such groups are not merely sets of friends who have chosen each other for compatibility but are derived from kinship, birthplace, school or business, etc., and maintain superior-inferior relations based on age and other factors.

Tradition has stabilized such groups by expecting each member to subordinate his personal wants to the requirements of the group. What would be an act of extreme personal self-sacrifice in another society can be passed over in Japan as a dutiful but not unexpected act of group loyalty. In a hierarchical group the person on top may well develop the habit of command, while others have the habit of docile obedience; in other groups several or all members share in decisions and management, but self-restraint still prevails. So much is true of relations within the group. In external relations, however, tradition has not only condoned but applauded explosions of ferocity to gain group aims or ward off threats. In extremity, group loyalty may underlie violence even to the point of self-destruction. Murder and assassination have served the ends of factions. On a grander scale, in the Pacific theater of war during World War II, troops threw away their lives for the Emperor in last-ditch, suicidal "banzai" charges, while "kamikaze" pilots were trained in the art of crashing their bomb-laden planes on enemy ships. Captured troops were conspicuously rare until the last weeks of that war, and, at intervals up to twenty years after hostilities ended, reports have been confirmed of Japanese soldiers who evaded capture and lived in the jungle thereafter like hunted animals. These are special cases, to be sure, yet their extreme nature and frequency make it difficult to disregard them. One seeks in vain for an explanation more satisfactory than that of self-destructive loyalty to one's group. Hence, we may conclude that both violence and docility should be credited to exceptionally intense group affiliation in Japan.

The motivation to accept such close affiliation and give it a central position among one's values can be viewed on several levels. Unconscious psychodynamic factors seem to come into play, as is suggested by the data on guilt and masochism discussed in the following section. Conscious motivations also are at work and may be discussed here. In terms of practical economics, one may pay out loyalty in order to survive with group support in a society where public aid is yet only marginal against illness, old age, or destitution. Again, as Ruth Benedict emphasized, group responsibility for each member gives him sponsored entry into social intercourse; a person's standing among new acquaintances is uncertain until his introduction shows which group vouches for him. Miss Benedict viewed group affiliation, nevertheless, as a burdensome and only occasionally gratifying necessity. Her insistence on the pain of group affiliation, perhaps reflecting the American attitude of condescending pity for the "organization man," brought retorts from Japanese commentators stressing that loyal members also derive personal satisfaction from the affectionate fellowship of other members and the esteem of the world at large. Economic and social sponsorship are positive objective motivations, and emotional gratification is a reinforcing subjective motivation for preserving one's group relationships. Not all Japanese accept these benefits as outweighing the constraints on personal freedom implied by group membership, but the restive ones seem to be in the minority, as is suggested by responses to several queries in the five-year survey of public opinion conducted by the Mathematical Statistics Research Institute of the Ministry of Education. One question asked respondents to state which of two bosses they would prefer to work under: (1) an unreasonably difficult taskmaster during office hours who, however, would help employees with their problems outside the office; or (2) a supervisor who, though fair and reasonable during working hours, would not take trouble over employees' outside problems. Respondents at the rate of 85 per cent in 1953, dropping to 77 per cent in 1958, preferred the boss who was willing to extend personal attachments outside the office.[2] Their reasons for this preference were not probed and can only be a matter of speculation, yet this majority answer from a cross-sectional sample shows how many Japanese lean toward attachments of diffuse functions with specific persons or groups.

The question may be raised whether Japanese think of group loyalty as being worthwhile because one needs social connections if one hopes for personal gain. Another query in the survey just cited suggests that social climbing is not a significant incentive. The query asked respondents to indicate how they believe most people succeed. Less than 10 per cent attributed success to good social connections, whereas about 40 per cent thought hard work was the answer and 30 per cent thought that getting good breaks was most important. These responses, in other words, support the view that group affiliation is valued not for social climbing but for social security. There is other evidence to show that the strong drive for achievement, discussed below, operates within a group context, that one exerts himself to achieve for the benefit of the group rather than using the group for his own advancement.

[2] Nishihara Kazuyoshi, *Nihonjin no iken* (Japanese opinions), Tokyo, 1963.

It is tempting to speculate that this phrasing of success and failure may offer a clue to special Japanese patterns of suicide, a phenomenon of psychological concern. It is, of course, difficult to learn the reasons for successful suicide attempts, only those who failed to kill themselves being available for interview, but interpretation is not reduced to sheer guesswork. Suicide is evidence of great personal tension or derangement; but it is more than that, as Durkheim showed in an extensive study of suicide in various European nations.[3] Sociocultural groups differ considerably from each other in so personal a matter as when and why one takes one's own life and how one goes about it. The most distinctive feature of Japanese suicide is not its high rate, despite common opinion to the contrary (Scandinavian rates exceed those of Japan, for instance), but its pattern of a high rate in youth. In most countries, suicide rates rise gradually in middle and old age groups. This pattern occurs also in Japan, but, in addition, the Japanese incidence shows a sharp peak and subsequent decline between the late teens and the early thirties; the rate at the age of twenty-five is as high as the rate among persons in their sixties (50 per 100,000). Both sexes are affected, though the female rate is somewhat lower, as at all ages in Japan and elsewhere. Suicide thus stands as the leading cause of death for the otherwise healthy age group between, say fifteen and thirty.[4] The fact seems to be that in Japan more than elsewhere many young people perceive themselves as caught by intolerable problems permitting no release other than through self-destruction. Can we define these problems?

In this age range a good many objectively definable problems come to a head. The high school and university systems set absolute limits to the number of applicants who can pass rigorous entrance examinations, condemning considerable numbers of applicants to failure. Also, boys enter employment, beginning jobs with little prospect of ever being able to make a second choice. Marriage is another nearly irrevocable step, taken usually after only a brief acquaintance with one's eventual spouse. Even if we have identified correctly the key problems—education, jobs, and marriage—and might demonstrate that they are more critical in Japan than elsewhere, however, our question is not fully answered, for it is the subjective view of such problems that makes suicide the only perceived solution, and we are forced to speculate at this point.

[3] Emile Durkheim, *Suicide: A Study in Sociology*, John A. Spaulding and George Simpson (trs.), Glencoe, Ill., 1951.
[4] Satō Kōji and Sonohara Tarō, "A Proposal for an International Study of Suicide," *Psychologia*, vol. 1, pp. 71–73, Kyoto University, 1957.

The closeness of group affiliation, we suggest, may have a significant bearing on youthful suicide, for it may drastically curtail alternative solutions to personal problems. Provided that a person can get along without family or other group attachments, he may run away from otherwise intolerable situations; provided that he can rely on his internal standards to judge his capacity and accomplishments rather than needing reassurance from others, he can bear up under difficulties without even running away. But evidence suggests that neither provision holds true for many Japanese. Living alone without group support is subjectively as well as objectively difficult for persons deeply conditioned to putting group needs ahead of their own wants, and the same conditioning makes persons emotionally dependent on external reinforcement of their self-images. Hence, one cannot ease the guilt of failure to meet group expectations by running away, for one carries one's guilt along and at the same time removes the supports for one's superego. In a personally intolerable situation, such as is created by unpleasant marriage prospects, one is torn between self-love and love of family; if damage to the family is unthinkable, aggression has to be turned not outward toward others but inward upon oneself. This reasoning needs to be supported by evidence of appropriate psychodynamic processes; we shall discuss the process of introjection, such as might lead to suicide, in the following section.

In recent years more than ever in the past, self-perception has come to pose a sharp enigma: What am I by myself? Heretofore, group membership roles answered most questions of identity, but wartime defeat discredited the classical corporate family and most other traditional norms of group identification, and wide-ranging postwar reforms had the common intention of liberating the individual person. Such liberation posed unfamiliar problems to persons whose identity had been clarified by their relation to the group (as an arm is defined by its belonging to the body). To be sure, the conundrum of individuation existed earlier; the changes after World War II, however, gave it a keener cutting edge. In everyday life each person encounters situations that remind him to be aware of his position and functions apart from any permanent, lifelong group.

It is generally agreed that young persons of the postwar generation have been wrestling with problems of individuation to a greater degree than their elders, but it is not easy to measure differences in the level of concern. First, young persons in their teens and twenties tend to be much more self-centered than older persons while they learn to handle problems rising out of their biological and social maturation; concern over individuation in Japan cannot easily be separated from the more universal phenomenon of concern over maturation. Second, although both popular and intellectual literature vociferously reiterate the problems of youth in this regard, such articulate opinion may or may not accurately reflect average attitudes. One method devised to minimize the gap between average opinion and the opinions articulated through literature is the method of "content analysis" applied to the popular press. An example pertinent to the problem of individuation may be cited as an illustration. This study [5] analyzed the content of letters written to life-counseling columns of Japanese newspapers and, for comparison, letters written to comparable columns of American newspapers. One finding was indeed that mature persons were most apt to ask advice about interpersonal relations within the family without making themselves the central figure of their letters. Letters from young persons, however, concentrated on their own individual problems, and a high percentage, especially from girls, asked advice about their physical features (their short stature, stubby nose, too large breasts, etc.) as if they had just begun to take inventory of themselves. It need surprise no one that teen-age girls worry about their appearance, yet the content of American letters was significantly different. Letters from young persons there, though also self-centered, complained less about their own defects than about the attitude of other persons toward them. In other words, both groups of youngsters hoped by some means to win greater comfort and affection, but the Americans expected others to make the adjustment, whereas the Japanese youngsters were ready to mold themselves to achieve their desires. Japanese parents and grandparents, we may believe, had also accommodated themselves to their surroundings rather than the other way around in their youth, but not with such individuated goals of seeking personal love and attention. The new generation applies old habits to new interests and goals.

ACHIEVEMENT AND INTERPERSONAL RELATIONS

To this point we have paid greater attention to the organization of society around the individual than to the structure of the individual personality. In this section, we shall examine evidence which shows mechanisms that may contribute to the shaping of personality along one pattern rather than others, and we shall survey the influence on each other of personalities so shaped.

Ruth Benedict was the first to suggest that the pressure brought to bear on the ordinary Japanese throughout his life shifts in a pattern

[5] Katō Hidetoshi (ed. and tr.), *Japanese Popular Culture*, Tokyo and Rutland, Vt., 1959.

significantly different from that of an ordinary American. The American situation, she suggested, puts rather strong pressure on the very young during their initial socialization under the anxious sponsorship of self-conscious parents; a second period of heavy pressure begins after full maturity and increases with old age as persons face retirement and the breaking up of their families. The intervening period offers relatively ample scope for self-expression and self-gratification, from one's school years onward through autonomous adulthood. Thus, she conjectured, American life moves through an arc curving up from the strictness of infancy and early childhood to the freedom of adulthood and then moves downward toward the constraints of old age. Americans, consequently, are eager to grow up but shun the idea of getting old. In her view, Japanese life reverses this arc into a U shape, putting persons under pressure after infancy and childhood and then relaxing the pressure toward old age. The Japanese baby and young child enjoy gratification within relatively loose constraints. Then, as the youngster (boy or girl, equally) advances through school, he comes under stricter surveillance and constraints that intensify and persist through marriage and the years of household responsibility. Old age, finally, brings relaxation from these pressures yet does not interrupt the warmth of family attachments; so this period offers gratifications comparable only to those of infancy. Since expectations and emotional attitudes follow the arc established by the social system, she said, people leave infancy regretfully and look forward happily to grandparenthood.

Miss Benedict's cleanly phrased hypothesis sets an organizing background to hypotheses of a less sweeping character, though as we proceed it is useful to look back and ask how closely reality follows the U arc she proposed on the basis of limited information, especially after nearly two decades of sweeping sociocultural restructuring in Japan. We may begin by asking what attitudes especially define high-pressure adulthood among Japanese. Are there perceptions that cut across all the varied roles of this complex society and, in harmony with the U arc Miss Benedict suggested, set adulthood apart as a segment of life?

One quite arresting result from a number of studies has already been mentioned briefly. This is a very positive attitude toward achievement and hard work. Pervasively valued as an adult trait, this attitude is also encouraged in principle if not practice at almost any age above sheer infancy. The expectation that adults should be eagerly industrious neatly fits Miss Benedict's stipulated peak of responsibility in these years, but let us see evidence for this value as applied to youth. We may take responses to one Thematic Apperception Test (T.A.T.) card that pictures a boy sitting, face supported by his hands, and gazing at a violin on the table in front of him. A high percentage of Americans, when presented with this card, imagine that the boy really wants to go out to play but is nonetheless about to practice on the violin because his mother (or someone else) strongly wants him to do so. Such a response is infrequent among Japanese, whose usual reaction is better represented by the following, the answer of a boy of sixteen:

> I like music and I used to go to a teacher to receive violin lessons. One day he told me that I'd better give up the violin because I was not doing well. However, I vowed to myself that I would become a good player. I practiced day and night as hard as possible and finally my teacher had to admit that I was playing well.

Such a story, more usual from persons over thirty-five years of age even in Japan, is an atypical response for any age group of ordinary Americans. (Americans respond to other cards with high achievement expectations; they are achievement-oriented, as are the Japanese, but are motivated in a somewhat different fashion.) Other Japanese responses to this card show that the person anticipates aid and encouragement especially from his mother or another family member.

Inspiration from one's father, incidentally, has an emotional shading of respect quite unlike the influence suggested from one's mother. Hers is a warm, loving image; the paternal image is cooler and more aloof. Various T.A.T. responses indicate that a father can exert as effective an influence dead as alive; this conclusion might be reached apart from projective tests, for widowed mothers often call on their sons to gaze on a photograph or other symbol of the deceased father or inspire them by bringing a giant enlargement to a school athletic meet. The test data, however, assure us that such acts are not empty symbols. An example of the T.A.T. responses, given in this case by a man, aged twenty-three, to a close-up view of an elderly man behind a young man, is:

> He is thinking of his dead father. This is the image of his father. This . . . he is recalling his father and making up his mind to strive toward success. I don't know what his profession is. Anyway, he has ambition now.

The strong, positive motivation toward achievement is again confirmed by an extensive study of first- and second-generation Japanese in the United States,[6] which showed, by use of a comparison with middle-class Americans, close compatibility of values and attitudes

[6] William Caudill and George A. DeVos, "Achievement, Culture, and Personality: The Case of Japanese-Americans," *American Anthropologist*, vol. 58, pp. 1102–1126, 1956.

between the two groups. The study further indicated, as we have noted, that this drive is fostered in somewhat different ways among the two ethnic groups. Commenting on the basis of the Japanese motivation to achieve success, Norbeck and DeVos [7] point out that socialization in a family intended to endure for generations inculcates devotion to long-range goals and that this same socialization makes Japanese sensitively dependent on outside opinions and expectations to buttress their self-evaluation. Ambition is rooted in this disposition to look far ahead and this need for outside reinforcement of the superego.

Such a conclusion, based on studies both in Japan and among Japanese abroad, is of considerable interest for the light it throws on the national achievements of the Japanese over the past century and longer. We have already taken note of the sensitiveness of the Japanese people to foreign opinion, calling on certain historical facts for an explanation. This account of psychodynamic factors that make the Japanese not merely sensitive but ambitious fills in the picture more clearly. The family socialization fostering the drive toward achievement constitutes a pattern that must have had a similar influence on personality a number of generations back, well before the Meiji Restoration permitted the Japanese to turn their energies to modernization. Ambition is by no means a quality developed *de novo* out of the new sociocultural milieu in which modern Japanese live. Instead, it appears to be one of the personality elements which Japan was able to utilize very well to accomplish her remarkable transformation.

The failure to achieve success may confer upon Japanese not only a sense of inadequacy but feelings of guilt. Before examining the link between guilt and achievement, we should note that early personality-in-culture studies included the Japanese among a group of cultures that were said to rely for social control entirely on shame (one's reaction to his image as measured in the eyes of others) and to lack any sanctions operating through a sense of guilt (self-judgment through internalized standards). Hence, to discover that guilt is also a means of social control (in addition to shame, which exists beyond any doubt) is a matter of more than passing theoretical interest, for it throws doubt on the validity of sweeping distinctions between shame cultures and guilt cultures, especially if guilt plays an important role. In accumulated Japanese psychological materials, feelings of remorse do, in fact, appear frequently and play a significant role. Hitherto, however, they have been difficult to identify because they are not linked to a

[7] Edward Norbeck and George A. DeVos, "Japan," in Francis L. K. Hsu (ed.), *Psychological Anthropology: Approaches to Culture and Personality*, Homewood, Ill., 1961, p. 35.

universalist ethic using transcendent symbols comparable to Judeo-Christian concepts of sin and grace; Westerners accustomed to looking for such symbols and failing to find them in Japan have been unable to see that Japanese do suffer guilt or even to see that an ethical system exists. As we shall see, guilt and shame are not so clearly separable in Japan as in societies carrying the Judeo-Christian heritage, but one readily perceives guilt defined in psychological terms, as is well explained in the following: [8]

> The Japanese seem to suffer from guilt which is not associated with any complex of supernatural sanctions, but is instead derived from the system of loyalties which cements the structure of their traditional society. Guilt in Japanese is hidden from Western observation because we do not understand Japanese familial relationships, and because conscious emphasis on external sanctions helps to disguise the underlying feelings of guilt which, severely repressed, are not obvious to the Japanese themselves. The keystone toward understanding Japanese guilt is held to be the nature of interpersonal relationships within the Japanese family, particularly the relations of the children with the mother. The Japanese mother, without conscious intent, has perfected techniques of inducing guilt in her children by such means as quiet suffering. She takes the burden of responsibility for their behavior and, as also with bad conduct on the part of her husband, will often manifest self-reproach if her children conduct themselves badly or in any way fail to meet social expectations. When a person does wrong he thereby hurts his mother, and he also hurts other familial members; as a result, he suffers unhappiness and feelings of guilt.

A selection from T.A.T. responses may give an effective illustration of the roots of guilt. The following response was called to the mind of a farm woman, aged twenty-two, by a picture showing a man standing, arm thrown across his face, near a bed in which a female figure lies supine:

> He got married for love with this woman in spite of opposition from his parents. While they were first married they lived happily. But recently he has been reflecting on his marriage and the manner in which he had broken through his parents' opposition . . . and the present wife . . . he attempts to brush away the blame within his breast. One night on the way home he buys some insect poison, gives it to his wife to drink and she dies. What he has done weighs on his mind. He gives himself up to the police. He trustfully tells his story to them. He reflects on how wicked he has been in the past. He completes his prison term and faces the future with serious intent.

The chief actor in this story suffers not from condemnation by others

[8] *Ibid.*, p. 27.

but from his own conscience—he feels guilty. His "wickedness," however, has a social rather than a religioethical foundation: his defiance of his family was his first wrong step, of such gravity that (in this fantasy, at least) it is balanced by murder. Marriage by itself is not evil, but it becomes so by transgressing the family ethic and brings a reaction of remorse rather than shame.

In the apt phrase chosen by Norbeck and DeVos, "quiet suffering" carries a silent admonition from one person to another. The narrator's phrasing in T.A.T. stories showing how guilt is induced makes it clear that the errant son or husband of the story repents and reforms because he got the message, as in this simple excerpt: "His father dies, which inspires the [hitherto stupid or lazy] son to work hard. He becomes successful." In short, guilt is the vehicle that carries the message to the intended receiver. Admonition, however, is only one of the uses of illness for communication, which is discussed more broadly below.

With this recognition of the existence of guilt in Japan we may return to the way in which it is linked with achievement. A person may overcome his sense of guilt by achieving success, it seems—the corollary of falling prey to guilt by failing to achieve. A good many T.A.T. responses tell, at least briefly, of a miscreant who, driven by remorse, reforms, works hard, and wins success. Punishment may be mentioned or omitted. Such a story, for instance, may present a lazy boy who feels remorse after stealing from a neighbor and then, without referring either to punishment or to the return of the stolen money, tell how he won praise for hard work at school thereafter. By implication, it is immaterial how closely the culprit's achievement is related to his wrongdoing. We are led to conclude that guilt emerges not from the act itself, as evil, but from the social position of the wrongdoer. His lazy, rebellious, or criminal behavior is wrong when it injures the group he represents, especially his family. This injury is what makes it wrong. Hence, he may balance the wrong by working to reflect credit on his family.

By such logic it becomes only secondarily important that a person be punished or forced to make amends and almost irrelevant that a given crime receive a given penalty. The miscreant's repentance and return to good behavior are the more vital matters. It will help to see how this theory, extracted from spur-of-the-moment stories, is executed in fact, as can be done by examining Japanese proceedings in criminal and civil law. A few studies comparing judicial practices in Japan with those elsewhere, especially in the United States, are most helpful. These studies indicate that Japanese prosecutors and judges tend to view legal penalties as discipline rather than as retribution for wrongs and so treat offenders in ways different from normal practice elsewhere. It is the Japanese prosecutor who is the more apt to dismiss a case without trial when he thinks the offender is truly repentant. A Japanese judge is apt to use the minimal sentence within his discretion or to suspend sentence if he believes the offender intends to reform, and he will moderate his sentence considerably when the intent behind a crime is innocent or extenuating. In other cases, the defendant with good intentions or penitence may be sentenced much more lightly than another person guilty of the same act. In short, the judge tries to treat the offender rather than to remedy the offense. There are intellectual and philosophical grounds for this view, of course; law in Japan and elsewhere is split between two rather incompatible functions on which thoughtful men take different positions. Some conceive of the law as society's instrument of retaliation against harmful acts; penal codes tend to be built, for the most part, around this conception. Others conceive of the law as society's instrument for rehabilitating offenders; parole systems and other devices rest on such a concept. On the whole, Japanese members of the legal profession lean toward the second view, wishing to strengthen the therapeutic and preventive potentialities of the legal system. They advocate better facilities for investigating the background of the persons they must sentence; they urge that judges be given greater discretion in suspending sentences and greater power over the supervision of probation. Their position is backed by legal and sociological research, but at the same time it testifies to an orientation basically parallel to the views expressed in Japanese T.A.T. stories about wrongdoers and their reform.

We have examined at some length the sense of guilt and related matters, showing that guilt is an important instrument of social control and discipline within the family and other areas of Japanese society. Guilt is a spur to the drive to achieve success, induced if needed when other socialization processes fail to keep this drive strong. It does not need to be constantly active, for the person vulnerable to it tends to drive himself rather than waiting to be driven to meet expectations. Parents build these features into their children's personality structure by unconscious means, believing all the while that "you cannot train a child under four" and lovingly excusing the child's mistakes. Conscious training is not associated with their praise and love for a child who learns to walk and talk early or their silent suffering of the child who rejects these feats. Therefore, childhood on the surface is as Ruth Benedict judged it, relaxed, open, and free from pressure; but under the surface the child learns that achievement brings love and so acquires the drive that is put to a strenuous test later, when external pressures begin to bend the course of his life into the U arc she pictured. Interpersonal relations within the family are crucial to instill this drive and will engage our attention through the remaining pages of this section.

We may return to the ways of communicating attitudes that underlie personal relations. First, let us recognize that persons talking together communicate at several levels. While the words themselves are carrying part of the message, other parts are conveyed by the choice of one word over another, the tone of voice, the rate of utterance, glances, gestures, and any number of possible motions and positions of the body. When an emotion is the most important part of the message, its most effective communication may well be wordless. People come to depend on wordless communication, then, for certain sorts of messages or for a whole category of communication. The Japanese show a disposition to teach or guide children by handling and manipulating them rather than by shouting instructions at them from a distance; teachers of the traditional arts demonstrate a technique, then leave the apprentice to acquire it by reiterated practice, for they consider verbal directions a nuisance rather than a help. People accustomed to learning through demonstration and manipulation are apt to be quite sensitive to wordless messages that convey emotion. It is interesting to note how often Japanese memory works in terms of physical sensations. With surprising frequency, Japanese who are asked to call to mind a single outstandingly pleasant memory from childhood remember especially the comfort, security, and emotional warmth of being carried in a sling or hood on a parent's or grandparent's back, as is the Japanese custom when out on the streets with a small child. Wordless messages, moreover, offer no interpretive problem to the receiver if sent in culturally standardized settings by a person sharing similar psychodynamic processes.

A T.A.T. excerpt cited above implied that a father's death served to reprimand his son and induce reform. More often it is a mother who, hurt by the obstinacy or selfishness of a son or daughter, falls ill or dies. The errant child, frequently grown and away from home, perceives and responds to this message of admonition or warning. As William Caudill quotes the comment of one professional Japanese nurse, however, sickness offers the chance to explain many things that seem embarrassing or inopportune when put into words, and illness may have a much milder message, such as the desire for love, which can be answered by giving loving attention. Varying messages can be conveyed by the person who falls ill, with confidence that the intended receiver will perceive the urgency and orientation of the communication. Researchers in psychology studying the process identify the mechanism as being what is technically known as introjection: attributing to oneself or incorporating within oneself the image one has of another person or object. This mechanism permits the incorporator to deal as he would like with the unattainable or shunned object by acting upon himself. Introjection is familiar to both parent and child; therefore, if a parent, upset by his child's failure to meet his standards or comply with his wishes, introjects the image and falls ill, the child comprehends that the suffering is occasioned by his own misconduct and accepts the guilt he has previously failed to feel.[9]

Results of T.A.T. tests suggest that self-doubt and feelings of guilt may be symbolized in fantasies of illness; among all the responses offered by men and women of one farm village, men referred to the illness or death of a loved person in almost one story out of ten and generally ended on an optimistic note, whereas about one out of every five responses from women spoke of these subjects or about grief and concern over sickness and death and ended on a brooding note. A sufficient explanation of the contrast between men's and women's stories may be sought in their respective social situations. Most of the men tested were living in their natal village, whereas their wives had moved there only upon marriage; especially for the young wives, who contributed a good share of such stories, their household status was in some degree probationary. The insecurity suggested in their frequent stories of grief or illness may reflect the insecurity of their actual lives.

Despite such strong hints of insecurity about themselves, coupled with formal inferiority of social status, women actually play an important integrative and directive role in their households. This social role is combined with a psychological disposition to assume responsibility for the behavior of household members. Time and again, when commenting on a family problem situation presented in a projective test, female respondents throw blame on a woman pictured in the test situation, even going to the length of misinterpreting or restructuring the problem to do so. Women's self-blame is expressed in ways that make clear their sense of ultimate responsibility for men's behavior, e.g., the self-reproach or illness over an errant son which we have noted above.

Such stories, however, grade into examples with a masochistic orientation. That is, in stories dealing with illness, the purpose shifts from admonishing a loved person for willful or errant conduct to attempting

9 George A. DeVos and Wagatsuma Hiroshi, "Psychocultural Significance of Concern over Death and Illness among Rural Japanese," *International Journal of Social Psychiatry*, vol. 5, pp. 5–19, 1959.

to draw a loved person's love to oneself by suffering. A particularly clear example is seen in the following story by a farm girl, aged seventeen, responding to a previously mentioned T.A.T. picture showing a woman recumbent and a man standing near her:

[Gazes at the picture a long time.] Although this couple was married and lived happily, the wife was not healthy. She went to bed with a cold. Her husband took care of her and did not go to work at his office. One day he thought she was somewhat better and went to work. When he came home that night he found his wife dead. From her diary lying there he learned that she had grieved over her husband [being absent from work] and had committed suicide by taking poison. (He is now crying with grief.) Having lost his wife, he continued to work very hard and . . . he led a lonely life by himself without ever forgetting his dead wife.

Slight twists to this otherwise familiar plot give this story its masochistic flavor: suicide in exaggerated self-reproach for an emergency already past; the wife dying to draw her husband's love, with no other apparent purpose. Such a masochistic flavor appears not infrequently in stories from women—a phenomenon that arouses little surprise when one considers the prevalence of this pattern in popular fiction aimed at women in Japan. Among the favorite themes of movies, television drama, and magazine fiction is that of the quiet suffering of a girl, young wife, or elderly mother whose self-sacrifice makes her a lovable person and wins copious tears from the responsive female audience. The T.A.T. story cited here, though artlessly exaggerated, follows an accepted, well-worn formula.

Insofar as Japanese have been drilled similarly to repress certain basic drives and freely express others, they share a basis for emotional intercourse which, being difficult to put into words, may mislead outsiders who have been drilled to a different pattern. Caudill suggests on the basis of picture tests similar to the T.A.T.[10] that Japanese in general have a higher tolerance than Americans toward expression of sensual gratification. Sensuality is more ego-syntonic, or consciously acceptable to the ego and so not needing repression. To use a nontechnical illustration, an American man is apt to be made uncomfortable and embarrassed by the massage and other sensuous stimulation that accompany an ordinary haircut in Japan; he has been drilled to repress gratification under such circumstances. An American mother may unconsciously repress the sensory satisfaction which a Japanese

10 William Caudill, "Patterns of Emotion in Modern Japan," in Robert J. Smith and Richard K. Beardsley (eds.), *Japanese Culture: Its Development and Characteristics*, Chicago, 1962, pp. 115–131.

mother can consciously accept in nursing her baby. On the other hand, Caudill suggests also that Americans in general tolerate a higher level of direct aggression than do Japanese. Black-and-white distinctions are not intended by these interpretations, of course; with respect to aggression, one may find that Japanese move away from a dispute at an earlier point than Americans yet compete with similar pleasure in contact sports, and only further study can inform us to what extent enthusiasm for rough-and-tumble is associated with or separate from reticence in other forms of aggression. Nevertheless, Caudill's findings on psychophysical impulses and reactions offer a clue to social institutions that are persistently puzzling to persons trying to comprehend Japan.

This sort of approach may offer an insight, for example, into the role of geisha in traditional and modern Japan. These professional female entertainers endlessly fascinate foreign visitors to Japan, perhaps largely because they seem enigmatic. Formally, the geisha are organized in troupes or companies under a mistress and are hired to entertain a dinner party of men with dances, music, games, and banter; but they also exert talent in contriving a warm, intimate atmosphere animated with flirtatious talk, seductive postures, and fleeting caresses before they leave the premises and the party comes to a halt. A good many observers, supposing the party should have an aftermath after what seems almost equivalent to sexual foreplay, are puzzled that the male guests seem to go home contented. But it is possible to view the so-called "geisha party" in any one of several ways on psychophysical grounds. Foreigners usually assume that the center of interest is heterosexual interaction between the girls and the guests and that the presence of geisha is desired to offer sexual stimulation, if not sexual completion. If Japanese can accept as being within ordinary limits sensory stimulation that seems to Euro-Americans to belong on the intense plane of sexual arousal, as Caudill suggests, however, then the Japanese guests may accept the geisha as they accept the cuisine, for the pleasure of the moment and no more. We need not stop conjecture even here but can suggest that the male guests often are less concerned with the girls themselves than with using them to impress other men at the party with their own powers of sexual attraction—a "little-boy" mode of behavior classed by developmental psychologists as typical of the phallic phase of maturation. The reasons for this view will be made clear below. Japanese are not all of one kind; there surely are some who enjoy dinner parties mainly because of the girls, some because of the men, and some because of the physical comforts. On present evidence, the last two groups probably include a majority of Japanese men or, at any rate, a higher proportion than would a gathering of Americans or Europeans.

Here we must take note of wider, nonphysical aspects of seeking gratification. The noted Japanese psychiatrist Doi Takeo [11] has called attention to attitudes and emotions described by the noun *amae* or the verb *amaeru*, which have connotations perhaps not matched by any English equivalents. Depending on context, the verb denotes "to be cuddlesome, coquettish, lovable; to act like a spoiled child; to take advantage [of someone]." As Doi points out, all these meanings are apt to be gathered together in a single personality type or a single syndrome of behavior. Whether the attitude invites love (by being cuddlesome), selfishly demands attention (by acting spoiled), or feeds on another person (by taking advantage), he believes its central meaning refers to dependency needs. Moreover, he notes, the words *amae* and *amaeru* appear quite frequently in diagnoses of patients in Japan. This dependency, he suggests, originates in the nursing period; and oral dependency is the type most often recorded by Japanese psychiatrists, both because they are sensitive to it and because it fits their Japanese patients. Thus he underlines the clinical meaning of the behavior people describe with the word *amaeru*.

Despondent personality configurations have caught the eye of other researchers in Japan. Studying ordinary families and communities rather than patients at clinics, as Doi has done, several have identified dependency as most characteristic among men, which at first seems to be in conflict with the Japanese use of the term *amae* more often in reference to women. Caudill, DeVos, and others conjecture that personal relationships within the family foster dependency in the first instance, while outside relationships also can be structured to preserve dependency well beyond the age at which American males begin to resist and repress the urge. Any child is inevitably dependent on his mother in infancy; she may unconsciously preserve psychological dominance over a male child merely by punctiliously following tradition, treating him with tender concern that befits her social subservience to him, as explained below; his dependency then is transferable, also unconsciously, to others in adulthood. The last is possible because institutionalized male roles in Japanese society tolerate self-centered, juvenile dependency as one way of performing the role. No man need apologize for expecting help and self-abnegation from women at large; for treating people brusquely and willfully, when at work, but turning

---

11 *"Amae*: A Key Concept for Understanding Japanese Personality Structure," in
ibid., pp. 132–139.

around to exercise exquisite Japanese courtesy toward his superiors or anyone else in a position to offer nurture; and so on. Some men, in ways that harmonize with dependent predispositions, give strong hints of arrested psychic development: those, for instance, who ignore women except as comforting maternal figures or as sources of sensual gratification (compare the role of geisha above); those who quickly lose physical self-control upon tasting alcohol; or those who give way to tantrumlike outbursts. All such behavior is far from being universal among men; it also remains to be proved that most or all of these characteristics accompany a single personality type. What can now be said is that such performance occurs with noteworthy frequency.

Women's inclination to dependency is more difficult to assess without specific psychological evidence because their social roles are institutionalized with little tolerance of dependency. Within the family, most girls are expected to care for their own needs early and to discipline themselves against intruding on the prerogatives of others. In adulthood and outside the family, they must be largely self-reliant, in addition to learning how to exert indirect pressures and win others over by emotional warmth, if they are to have their way. The very fact that women are given so little scope for institutionalized dependency perhaps accounts for their reliance on *amae,* in the sense of cozening and wheedling or being lovable enough to be granted favors which they cannot demand on equal terms with boys. Hence, the Japanese themselves associate *amae* with women.

According to empirical evidence at hand, the mother-child relation seems the most intense personal relationship within the Japanese family. It was difficult to perceive this relation as long as investigators sought the key to personality in formalized customs, such as toilet training or cradling, but it comes clearer as attention is paid to less formalized contacts and modes of gratification. How long does a child sleep with its parents, if it is not separated from the beginning? How is the baby fed? Who carries the infant, and how? Who bathes the child or accompanies it in the bath? Answers to such questions teach us much about the way in which personal bonds are formed. The mother's position is strategic for controlling these early facets of socialization, and the Japanese mother forges strong bonds with her children by using her position effectively. In the traditional household, especially, her position is weak with respect to everyone except her children, for only her own progeny postdate her arrival as an outsider in the midst of the emotionally unified group already making up the household. But her children are her own care; their birth frees her from various household duties to devote herself to their needs, and they may well be the only persons in the house who unreservedly need her; so she has both opportunity and incentive to bind her children to her in outright dependency. The mother-child relation in a traditional house, however, separates into two: a relation with the expected heir, who often is the eldest son; and a relation with noninheriting daughters and sons. The heir will probably be in lifelong close contact with her; the others will probably leave the community and will certainly leave the house. She is apt, thus, to give her most unreserved love and service to the prospective heir and, by doing everything possible for him, to diminish his capacity to shift for himself. By being just a bit less scrupulous in sitting up at night to wait for other children to come home, by not unfailingly hanging up their clothes for them, arranging their schedules, and seeing that they have coins, handkerchief, matches, an umbrella, or whatever else they may need as they leave the house, she may give the other children a better chance to escape total dependency.

Projective test data suggest the way in which the mother's concern for her daughter differs from her concern for her son (the tests fail to probe differences in the quality of her concern for different sons). Women's stories touching on the mother-daughter relation show concern over physical care and the health of the daughter; stories of sickness possibly signal some sense of guilt over the mother's partiality toward her sons. But stories about the mother-son relation focus on achievement on the one hand and rebellion on the other. Why does the mother nourish her son through infancy, make herself responsible for his successful training or education, and worry over his marriage and job to such an extent that she assumes the ultimate blame for his failure? We have looked into the psychological function of self-blame, and we have seen the social reason for her special attention to a first son, but we also can perceive her motivation to help her children succeed, through the concept of aggression. Normally, the mother's chief gratification in life must be vicarious, for she herself must be submissive and satisfy others, not aggressive and self-gratifying. This constraint on her self-expression is usually interpreted, and correctly so, as a disadvantage of being a woman in Japan; but her sociological weakness carries the seed of psychological strength which gives her power over those who depend on her, even to the extent of quelling rebellion by her own suffering. To achieve vicariously through her children is a task that takes its physical toll but gives an outlet for otherwise bottled-up aggression and, if she has successfully forged the bonds of loving control, must also occasionally give her the exhilaration of victory.

We have already noted that men, in return for their mothers' hovering care, see their mothers in a very warm light. From their fathers they draw inspiration, and they offer in return a deep sense of honor; but the relation is more symbolic and distant and less charged with warmth. So accustomed are men to getting maximum satisfaction from a maternal source that many seem to seek in marriage, also, a maternal relation. The husband is markedly dependent on his wife, she reciprocates with the same watchful care she will eventually give to her child, and all the world around them reinforces this relationship with praise. Sex need not be the focus of such a relationship. Sociologically speaking, a strong sexual relationship is potentially harmful to the vertical unity of a stem family and is discouraged; psychologically speaking, tests give little evidence of a strong sexual bond between husband and wife. (Yet it is hazardous to conclude merely from sparse or absent testimony that the bond is unimportant.) Data on farm men show little or no evidence of active sexual possessiveness toward their wives; it does not enter their heads that a wife might be unfaithful (nor need it, in fact, for the country wife faces almost insuperable practical difficulties in arranging enough privacy and time to carry on an affair). Responding to the same tests, wives contemplating the thought of extramarital relations by their husbands exhibit anger but give no sign that they are disposed to take action. The most that can be said from all this is that sex is not a focal area of husband-wife relations. Nor is this conclusion really contradicted by a consciously expressed advocacy of letting people marry for love, for although they approve of romantic love marriages for other persons, their T.A.T. responses show that in their own cases such a marriage exposes them strongly to a sense of guilt toward the family.

CONCLUSION

We have surveyed aspects of Japanese character first by drawing on ordinary information and second by utilizing special psychological testing techniques. It must be evident, however, that in this field one cannot abstract the individual persons who feel, believe, and act from the culture that envelops them; consequently, one cannot fully separate the two approaches. On the one hand, an analysis of ordinary observations of Japanese in their normal cultural setting is quite apt to go astray unless it is made against a background of psychological theory and harmonized with basic concepts of personality; on the other, the psychological testing devices must incorporate elements of the cultural setting to be fruitfully interpreted.

Most of the interpretations presented here must be considered tentative. As far as possible, this survey has used analyses based on tested evidence rather than on subjective opinion. The field of personality in culture has both theory and investigative methods to employ in gathering and evaluating evidence in order to reduce subjectivity. But since it is extremely new and dependent on the effort of a few persons suitably prepared for research in Japan, the evidence remains rather slender even on the subjects most thoroughly studied to date. Enough progress has been made to permit informed conjecture, but too little to provide many solid conclusions. Interpretations reach their highest probability in areas of special interest to psychology, e.g., interpersonal relations, but even here they remain working hypotheses on which further study is desirable.

An attractive feature of this line of research is its capacity to illuminate questions of fundamental interest to other fields of study of Japan. The personality processes that give the Japanese a drive to achieve in pursuit of long-range goals, not solely for personal gain but for the advancement of collective group welfare, is one such question. It assists the economists who are concerned with the emergence of industrial or commercial entrepreneurs, the political scientists who are interested in leader-follower relations, and the sociologists who deal with group integration, to name a few examples. In time, no doubt, further inquiries will be pointed toward problems pertinent to these and other fields.

A second area of exciting promise offered by psychologically oriented research in Japan lies in its capacity to enrich the discipline of psychology. At the same time that this work is contributing insight into Japanese culture, it is broadening the scope of crosscultural testing of psychological concepts and methods. Several specific lines of research not discussed in this survey exemplify this dual contribution. For instance, psychiatrically trained workers are undertaking a psychosomatic analysis of Zen religious training, which should make Zen more readily comprehensible and simultaneously contribute to the psychology of learning and cognition. Research into child training in Japan, as we have suggested, provides a check on the concepts of developmental psychology. Japan's high rate of sociocultural change over the last three generations makes it an ideal testing ground for research into the durability of the basic determinants of personality. Sociopsychology will be enriched by findings from the study of Japanese juvenile delinquency, which is a phenomenon of worldwide growth in modern and modernizing nations. Methods of treating mental illness in Japan, where

381

the cultural heritage provides a background of assumptions and approaches shared by the Japanese clinician and his patient but quite unlike the Euro-American background, give the opportunity for new insights in the field of psychiatry. In short, while psychological research is needed to understand Japan, Japanese research offers an extraordinarily rich proving ground for further development of the various fields of psychology.

JOHN WHITNEY HALL

Education and Modern National Development[*]

INTRODUCTION

The field of education, like that of law or medicine, refers more correctly to an area of professional activity (teaching and its attendant functions) or to an aspect of culture (the learning process and its institutional embodiment) than to a disciplined branch of academic inquiry. Only certain types of professional educators (usually the comparative educationalists) are interested in education for what it reveals about a people and their culture. Joining them are scholars from a variety of other disciplines, sociologists, historians, psychologists, or philosophers, who use educational data to gain insight into group or individual attitudes, into the ideological aspects of national development, or into the formative backgrounds of political or intellectual leaders. Education, seen either as system or as content, is one of the most revealing features of a culture. The history of education, particularly in a rapidly changing society such as Japan, provides a constant measure of the values which the culture has believed worth preservation or the changes which it has adopted in the face of new conditions.

Every nation which has passed over the threshold of modernization has had to achieve a breakthrough in the fields of education, language, and mass communication. The truth of this statement has long been recognized as applying to the countries of Europe, for which the adoption of national vernaculars and the spread of literacy beyond the aristocracy were intimately associated with the whole process of cultural renaissance and nation building. With respect to Japan, the importance of the development of a uniform written language based on the vernacular and the creation of a centralized educational system has been fully recognized only in the last few years, particularly as the emerging nations of Asia and Africa have begun to reveal profound difficulties in overcoming similar problems. What was once accepted as an ancillary

[*] This chapter in indebted to syllabus materials prepared by Ronald S. Anderson. It also had the advantage of a prepublication reading of Herbert Passin's *Education and Society in Japan,* New York, 1965.

aspect of Japan's modern revolution—an indication of her thoroughness in emulating the West—is better seen today as one of the most basic aspects in having provided the intellectual foundations of a modern society.

For Japan in particular, the creation of a national education system served a vital function in giving the country the capacity to modernize and to gain popular acceptance of the basic aims of the new state. A study of the educational system (both formal and informal) affords an insight into the manner in which the Japanese responded to Western influence. Education played a tremendously important role first in disseminating knowledge about the West and the new sciences and second in circulating the technical skills and political and social attitudes required of a modern citizenry. Although scholars have tended to emphasize the role of government in forcing the pace and dominating the spirit of modern Japanese educational development, the willingness of a people to take their education seriously and often to make personal sacrifices for it is not something which can be explained solely by the actions of a government bent on improving its human resources.

We need not doubt that the Japanese leaders and even the people at large entered the latter half of the nineteenth century with a great zeal for learning and a willingness to strive for the acquisition of new ideas through education. A dramatic emphasis on education, in fact, preceded the Restoration of 1868. Statistics on numbers of schools, numbers of students, and incidence of literacy all show a sudden increase during the 1850s and 1860s. The famous clauses in the Charter Oath of 1868 which stated "Base customs of former days shall be abandoned" and "Knowledge shall be sought throughout the world" expressed both a recognition of the inadequacy of things the way they stood and a desire to follow the Western model in seeing them remedied. The desire was fulfilled. Today Japan possesses one of the most advanced state and private educational systems in the world. The attendance rate in public primary schools is more than 99 per cent, the literacy rate is more than 98 per cent, and 7 out of every 1,000 Japanese attend a university. Education in Japan is, and has been for many decades, a serious busi-ness, in fact, one of the most competitive areas of Japanese life. This is in part a legacy from the attitudes toward learning popularized by the Confucian mentors of the seventeenth and eighteenth centuries, but it also is a product of the everyday world in which the Japanese have had to compete for social status and economic opportunity. In modern Japan education has great relevance. Not only is it important to the country's national aspirations to excel as a world power, but also to the individual who seeks his own advancement. For Japanese society has shown itself both intensely competitive and ready to reward special training or talent—not without limit or exceptions, yet to a startling degree for a society considered "traditional" only a century ago.

The prime concern of public education especially in modernizing states is literacy. Japan started the quest for a literate, self-conscious citizenry with considerable assistance from the Tokugawa period, for it is estimated that more than 40 per cent of Japan's males (including nearly all those in the higher orders) were literate at the time of the restoration. By the end of the first decade of the twentieth century Japan had passed beyond the 95 per cent mark in literacy. Thus it was less the question of literacy than of that of educational policy and cur-riculum content that was in the balance.

School systems, whether state-controlled or privately supported, are the embodiment of certain normative aims and public or individual expectations. Educational philosophy puts its mark upon the style of education and hence upon the popular mind: upon the citizen's atti-tudes toward his government and its leaders, toward the outside world, and toward the world of knowledge in general. These attitudes can differ drastically, depending upon whether schooling is offered pri-marily to afford individual self-fulfillment or to inculcate nationalism and dedication to state aims. As the predominant policies governing public education in Japan have swung between these differing poles, one sees a sympathetic reaction in the attitudes and convictions by which the Japanese of a given period have lived. Conversely, the policies affecting the educational system at any given time have tended to be strongly related to the predominant political philosophy of the moment or to the international environment encompassing Japan.

The consequences of education, of course, are not limited to the public political arena. Formal systems of schooling and public attitudes toward education exert a powerful influence upon the whole frame of mind and habit of thinking of a people. Both among those with minimal education and among the intellectual elite, the style of education and its basic philosophical premises (whether they be liberal, statist, or Marxist) put their stamp upon the style of reasoning, the questions asked and the answers accepted, and the intellectual behavior of the society. The cast of the academic mind, in other words, has much to do with the basic "thinking process" as it is transmitted to the nation's youth. But perhaps of even greater importance is the attitude with which a people have approached the subject of learning, especially when it involves the willingness to accept change. This also is a matter of the quality of mind. Few national elites in recent history have been subjected to and taken seriously so varied an assortment of philosophies, ideologies, and schools of inquiry as have the Japanese. Yet few Asian peoples have been so successful in maintaining a sense of national identity while entering the world community of nations as learner rather than as instructor. How the Japanese have managed to do this is certainly one of the most significant questions the student of Japanese education can ask. And it is probably in the data of education that the answer is most readily available.

One of the outstanding features of the "Japanese mind" throughout history has been its persistent inquisitiveness and flexibility in the face of new and demonstrably superior intellectual systems. In the course of their intellectual development the Japanese have taken up with Confucianism and Buddhism and later with Christian, Hegelian, liberal, Marxist, and modern scientific systems of thought with great enthusiasm. Placed under similar circumstances, other societies have resisted or even rejected intellectual intrusions uncongenial to their traditional values. While the Indians or the Chinese, for instance, have experienced various traumas of withdrawal from their particular religious orthodoxies, the Japanese somehow have managed to accept (or at least acknowledge) quite readily the entire range of thought currents emanating from the West. In doing this, they have remained persistently eclectic, despite cycles of feverish imitation or resurgent xenophobia, so that the result has often been a distinctly Japanese adaptation (misadaptation, some would say) of Western ideas or methods, an adaptation in which the Japanese have somehow been able to preserve a modicum of their individuality. It would seem that the Japanese, from the time of their first contact with the West, have been both more receptive and better able to salvage elements of their tradition than today's Chinese, for example, and have avoided the extreme dilemmas of an all or nothing choice between old and new, native and foreign.

The method by which the Japanese have retained a sense of their identity in the midst of a world of changing habits and conflicting intellectual demands and attractions is clearly reflected in the field of education. It had its less happy aspect, as we know, in the period of ultranationalistic resurgence which reached such a pitch during World War II. But we shall have to look most carefully and, if possible, dispassionately at the problem of nationalism in education, for while we may condemn the extremes to which the Japanese carried their delusions of national self-importance during the 1930s and 1940s, it would be hard to deny the importance to a late modernizing country of the sense of national identity in the face of the forces grinding toward uniformity and conformity in the modern world. Today in a Japan which has disavowed so much of its past, in fact, has given up that vital link of self-identification with its belief in its own political uniqueness (the *kokutai* idea), we see accentuated the symptoms of insecurity, uncertainty, and search for self-identity which were latent in the earlier years of the country's rise as a modern state. It is not by accident that the focal point of the postwar ideological struggle for personal and national security should be found in the educational system and among the youth of school age. Nor is it an accident either that the Japanese intellectuals who show the most profound bewilderment and uncertainty today are members of the generation which grew up with the bitter experiences of war, defeat, and disillusionment so strongly engraved upon their minds.

The Japanese today are five generations removed from the men who opened the country to the West and placed it on its present course of national development. Japan's educational system has its full quota of public elementary and secondary schools and public and private colleges and universities. In addition, it has built up a rich endowment of cultural and intellectual facilities: libraries, museums, concert halls, theaters, and the like. The volume and range of coverage of scholarly journals and publications are perhaps unmatched by those of any other country. Certainly the organs of mass communication, from newspapers and television to comic strips, are among the most fully developed in the world. Moreover, the educational system itself was thoroughly overhauled at the end of World War II by the American-dominated Occupation. Superficially the American observer would find little to differentiate "Japanese education" from his own. Yet more fundamentally, a study of education in Japan will reveal that Japanese school life, national attitudes toward education and the learning process, and the school and university systems themselves differ widely from what we are familiar with in the United States (though less perhaps than from the systems of some European countries). And these differences are significant, for they reveal a dimension of Japan's cultural personality which we need to be able to grasp.

JAPAN'S EDUCATIONAL HERITAGE: CONFUCIANISM, *BUSHIDŌ*, AND APPRENTICESHIP

Education in Tokugawa Japan is only now receiving the attention it deserves from Western scholars. In the works of Ronald P. Dore and Herbert Passin we now have the bases for understanding what Japan's educational heritage was in terms of its availability to the several social classes, its content and consequent effect upon the culture, and its influence in preparing the various segments of the population for the reforms of the early Meiji period. The common tendency until now has been to dismiss Tokugawa education as "feudal" and "Confucian" and, except for the *terakoya* (the small parish schools), which admittedly provided the basis of the Meiji elementary school system, to assume that Japan literally had to start from scratch after 1868 to build its modern educational system. The truth is that Tokugawa education did much more than lay the foundation for primary schooling; above all, it instilled a favorable attitude toward education throughout a wide segment of the population. Nor should Confucianism, that supposed philosophy of social and political conservatism, be so lightly discounted, for whatever its political limitations, it provided a sound base upon which a modern educational system could rest. Confucianism firmly believed in the importance of education, and it was under Confucian tutelage that the Japanese after the sixteenth century erected a system of schooling with extensive textual and pedagogical support. Confucianism taught attention to the affairs of government and social order. As in the case of the scholasticism of Europe, its knowledge of the psychological and physical worlds may have been faulty, but its categories of thought were useful and at least orderly.

To say that education in Tokugawa Japan was Confucian is only to acknowledge the fact that the Japanese had based themselves on the only fully developed system of knowledge common to East Asia, namely, that of China. Given the country's historic dependence upon China, this was to be expected. And while certain types of schooling were available in Buddhist monasteries and like institutions, almost inevitably the Confucian literature that came into Japan from the fifth century onward made up the bulk of the textual material which formed the basis of instruction. Traditional Japanese "book learning" was fundamentally Confucian. So also were the basic attitudes toward edu-cation, especially regarding the importance of moral instruction and the cultivation of proper attitudes toward the state and the family. During the Tokugawa period this reliance on Confucian or Chinese practices reached its height, but it also began its decline, as Japanese thinkers began to take up the study of their own "classical heritage" of works written in Japanese or to experiment with the fragments of Western science which managed to seep through the wall of seclusion. But it is also true that even the decidedly un-Chinese tendencies in Tokugawa thought seldom broke out of the enveloping framework of Confucian rationalism.

Whether entirely Confucian-inspired or not, there was a great expan-sion in education and in the pursuit of learning during the Tokugawa period. The achievement of peace and comparative prosperity under the Tokugawa shoguns gave the Japanese the leisure and the means to stress the arts and letters. There were changes in the structure of society as well, particularly as greater and greater numbers of persons turned to urban living, which stimulated the desire for education. For some education was a means of self-cultivation, but for most it had become the practical requisite for better performance of the role of soldier, bureaucrat, merchant, or village headman. By the end of the seventeenth century Japan was beginning to achieve literacy on a wide scale. This meant that the ability to read and write, indeed, the capacity to enjoy literature or to be amused by short stories, had passed out of the hands of a small minority composed of priests or aristocrats. For one thing the samurai class (by definition expected to be literate) constituted a sizable 5 to 7 per cent of the population. Added to this were a growing class of urban commercial families and a wealthy stratum of villagers who not only found the ability to read and write necessary for their business or administrative duties but also had the leisure to indulge in the reading of the classics or the composition of poetry. Historians have in fact talked about an intellectual renaissance during the seven-teenth century, and while the analogy with Europe may be somewhat farfetched, it is true that some of the most creative products of the Tokugawa period were in the field of letters and philosophy. Not many of these products have continued to attract the attention of present-day scholars. (It is the popular literature which we now admire.) But we should remember that Tokugawa scholars produced literally hundreds of national and local histories and thousands of treatises on political economics and social morality. While these works are no longer informa-tive to us today, they reveal a remarkable degree of intellectual sophis-tication, given the limitations within which they were written.

Learning in Tokugawa Japan was first of all a requirement for the samurai class. Education was both a badge of social distinction and a practical necessity for a class which had turned from military to bureaucratic pursuits. It was thought sufficiently important, in fact, so that by the eighteenth century enough government-supported schools and colleges had been established to assure at least a minimum education for the entire class. Chief among the schools patronized by the Tokugawa shoguns was the one begun in the Hayashi residence in 1630 and dedicated to the teaching of Confucian ethics and philosophy. In 1690 it was enlarged and renamed the Shōheikō. It served as the main Tokugawa college and, with its excellent library, became the seat of official scholarship and of the orthodox Chu Hsi branch of neo-Confucian doctrine (*shushi-gaku*) favored by the shogunate. The Hayashi family continued throughout the Tokugawa period to serve as hereditary rectors of the college. The Shōheikō became the model for a large number of schools established by the several *daimyō*—perhaps three hundred of them by the end of the Tokugawa period—for children of the samurai in each domain. Members of the samurai class, at least by the beginning of the nineteenth century, had a course of study available which began with the local domain school, then continued for some at the Shōheikō or other private academies for more advanced training, and might even include special study in Edo or Nagasaki.

Education for the samurai, though it may have had its literary overtones, was essentially the schooling of a ruling class. As such it was expected to instill both technical competence in reading and writing and a knowledge of principles of the social and political order and a strength of character and personal discipline becoming a military officer. The basic code of the samurai stated in its very first clause that the gentleman must cultivate both letters (*bun*) and military training (*bu*). And whatever the authorities may have meant by the term *bun,* in actual practice the content of education was left to Confucian-trained teachers who were as much concerned with the ethical message of the text they expounded as with the linguistic skills it instilled in the students.

Confucianism provided the philosophical rationale for both public and personal morality. The leading educational theorist at the outset of the Tokugawa era, Hayashi Razan (1583–1657), drew from the Confucian classics the ethical principles for statecraft and a loyal officialdom, justifying the shogun's authority and the special status of the samurai. To a later Confucianist such as Kaibara Ekken (1630–1714), the aim of education was to promote filial piety and benevolence, the supreme Confucian virtues of personal conduct. For him the end of personal cultivation was to bring the individual into harmony with the social order by practicing the five classic virtues of benevolence, justice, courtesy, learning, and integrity of character. Women were to cultivate chastity and submissiveness. Despite the abstractness and overly didactic quality of so much of the Confucian borrowing from China, in the early years of the Tokugawa period at least, the message was remarkably revelant to the political needs of Japan. The texts and theories with which samurai education was nourished helped immeasurably in easing the transformation of the samurai from the rough military man he was at the outset of the period to the officer and "gentleman" he had become within two or three generations.

But the exhortations of shogun and *daimyō* would have had little influence in raising the standard of literacy among the samurai or in encouraging erudite studies in general had not the age also required men of scholarly training. The increasingly bureaucratic nature of government, the premium placed upon the ability to read and write, in fact, the competition for preferment on the basis of some sort of administrative competence created a constant demand for education. The requirements of the age also put their stamp upon the kind of "military training" which the samurai received. For with the elimination of all possibility of further civil war, the samurai put his muskets upon the wall and turned his sword and bow into less warlike instruments. His zeal for military preparedness was converted into a passion for social and moral discipline. Swordsmanship and archery were gentled into pastimes calculated to deepen the concentration of the mind, while military training itself stressed the achievement of qualities of decisiveness and vigorous leadership. *Bushidō* (the code of the samurai) became a way of life as much for civil administrators as for the officer in the field.

Education for the common people, though not formally provided for by the authorities, was not by any means neglected. The Tokugawa government encouraged, though it did not subsidize, common schools (*terakoya*). These were rudimentary affairs, conducted in local temples or the homes of priests or laymen, and provided elementary schooling, watered down from the samurai version, for a few of the common people. The parish schools relied on the simplest of Confucian texts and emphasized certain practical subjects, such as calligraphy, oral reading, arithmetic on the *soroban* (abacus), and etiquette. The teachers were priests, both Buddhist and Shinto, unattached samurai, Confucian scholars, or educated merchants or villagers. In all there may have been some fifteen thousand *terakoya* in existence at the time of the Meiji Restoration. It is these schools which literally formed the basis of Japan's modern elementary school system.

At an educational level above the *terakoya* there came into being a variety of semiofficial schools known as *gōgaku,* or country schools. More numerous than the domain academies and colleges, these schools provided a more advanced level of instruction in both Confucian studies and practical subjects. They were usually open to both samurai and commoners, but their main purpose in most localities was to improve the quality of the men who headed the organs of local government, the village headmen or the town ward heads.

Most diverse in size and subject matter were the large number of private boarding schools, called *juku* or *shijuku.* Most of these were quite small, depending upon a single master who surrounded himself with a few disciples and gave instruction in his particular scholarly specialty or in some particular accomplishment. Such private schools met a variety of educational needs and operated at a variety of levels. They became particularly popular toward the end of the Tokugawa period, as samurai and commoner alike sought special skills or gained the leisure to indulge in further education. An estimated fifteen hundred *juku* were in existence in Japan in 1870. And many of the outstanding leaders of the Restoration received their inspiration for political action at the feet of such *juku* teachers as Yoshida Shōin (1830–1859), the fiery Chōsū activist, or Fujita Tōko (1806–1855), the Mito loyalist.

It is sometimes asked why, if Tokugawa education was essentially Confucian, it should have produced such different results from what it did in China. The answer, in part, is that Japanese education was not simply Confucian. Perhaps what most differentiated the educational and intellectual climate of Tokugawa Japan from that of China at the same time was that, though Confucian principles were admired by the Japanese, they were never considered the only basis of pedagogy or the only source of educational philosophy. The Tokugawa commitment to Confucianism was strong, but it was never absolute, and it was actually on the decline after the beginning of the nineteenth century. As a doctrine providing religious certainty and comfort, Buddhism was by no means dead, and Shinto was in the course of a strong resurgence. To those inclined to secular learning, studies of Japanese literature or Western sciences competed more and more strongly with the Confucian classics. Perhaps the eclecticism of the early nineteenth-century Japanese intellectual stemmed from the fact that all intellectual systems (except Shinto) were to some extent alien. Finding his psychological security increasingly in the rediscovery of "Japanese" values (pride in country and Emperor or dedication to military discipline), he could take a more relaxed view of Confucianism and its practical consequences. Securely dedicated to particularistic national values which had their source in the incarnate symbols of the Emperor or the warrior's code, he was relatively free to accept or discard the metaphysical systems upon which his "schooling" rested. Toward the end of the Tokugawa period, the parallel spread of Western learning (Dutch language and science) and "imperial learning" (chiefly Japanese history and literature) gave witness to a growing intellectual ferment.

Aside from its strong Confucian element, there were other aspects of education that affected the quality and style of learning which the Tokugawa Japanese received. It has been said that education in Japan was conducted in a *feudal* atmosphere. The term is not particularly appropriate, but it does serve to identify certain features of the pedagogical system which contrast strongly with the principle of universal education to which the Japanese eventually turned. Tokugawa education was first of all class-based. There was a frank adherence to the view that education was more necessary to the highborn than to the low, and classroom procedures were organized to give privileges to samurai over commoner and high samurai over low. That this attitude toward education was not at all unique to the Japanese needs no elaboration. (We need only to compare Japan with England of the same time.) And that such class restrictions in education were breaking down in nineteenth-century Japan, particularly in the *shijuku* and in the non-Confucian branches of study, is also important to bear in mind.

There is another side to this complex of attitudes toward education which remained more strongly characteristic of the Japanese instructional system even after 1868, namely, the assumption that knowledge was something acquired by apprenticeship from a master. Thus, even in the larger schools, the transmission of knowledge was accomplished through a system of personal or highly intimate associations between student and teacher. The student was often bound over to the teacher by his parents, or at least he was obliged to acknowledge his absolute authority over his mind and body. Of course, the apprentice system, in the strict sense of the term, was most commonly used as the means of imparting a trade or manual skill. But the same basic approach to learning, whereby the master disclosed increments of his special knowledge in carefully controlled lessons which the student then took on faith and learned by rote and in which the student once graduated became the lifetime disciple of the master, pervaded all branches of education. It is this approach to learning which tended to drive all skills, whether artistic or intellectual, into restricted channels transmitted generation after generation within certain families or "schools." It made for rigidity and imitativeness. And although this practice is no longer common in the academic world in Japan, certain arts, such as the nō drama, the tea ceremony, flower arrangement, and most of the traditional crafts, are still transmitted in this fashion. It is still true that one of the persistent comments about differences between the American and Japanese attitudes toward learning is that there is a heavier reliance in Japan on rote learning and on the acquisition of a professor's "system." Emphasis on originality was not part of Japan's educational heritage.

Still another feature of the educational process which was accentuated both by the master-disciple system and by the heavily religious orientation of learning in Tokugawa Japan was the assumption that education should "train character" as well as impart useful information. Training in certain arts was considered useful as a way of developing self-discipline or inculcating proper social attitudes. We have already noted that the substance of learning ((Buddhist or Confucian) was largely ethical; one of its foremost aims was to make the student virtuous by teaching him the wisdom of the past and so to shape his character as to meet the needs of his society. Calligraphy, the basis of literacy, was taught for its character-forming (mental-disciplinary) effect as well as for its practical value. Teachers were supposed to be models of virtue; they were honored as much for their character as for their erudition. Such attitudes of reverence toward teachers, unthinking devotion and willingness to take directions, were to have both their admirable and less desirable results. For if Japan in the early years of its modernization was fortunate that its people were filled with a zeal to follow leaders of a remarkably enlightened quality, the zeal to follow led to disaster during the 1930s, when those leaders had been replaced by men of more xenophobic aims.

In final assessment, then, we see that Tokugawa education showed a great diversity and complexity of institutional and ideological facets. The volume of education was remarkably large, as indicated both by the number of persons estimated to be in school (perhaps 1,300,000 in the late 1860s) and the quantities of publications consumed by the Tokugawa reader. While most schooling was highly moralistic and didactic, it was also practical, and furthermore there had already come into existence by the end of the period several levels of instruction which recognized varying social and occupational needs. Moreover, there was diversity in subject matter which made it possible to choose unorthodox fields of study without great stigma. And, finally, things were changing. This above all seems to characterize the late Tokugawa scene, for in all aspects of education, in school attendance, in the number of schools, in variety of courses, in heterodox subjects being pursued, it was in the years beginning with the 1840s that the greatest changes appear to have taken place. As Japan came increasingly into contact with the West, the counteractions (both defensive and acquisitive) were rapid and decisive. The vigor with which the Japanese samurai drew his sword upon the foreigner as well as the inquisitiveness with which he sought to penetrate the secrets of Western power were remarkable testimony to his intellectual alertness.

THE MEIJI RESTORATION AND EDUCATIONAL POLICY

Education was very much in the forefront of the thinking of the leaders of the Meiji Restoration, who once they came to power worked quickly toward the formation of an educational policy consistent with the aims of the new government. Some of the earliest decisions made by the restoration government were concerned with state ideology, education, and popular instruction. But the educational aims of the new government and the nature of the policy which should guide the training of the new subjects of the Emperor were by no means agreed upon. The Japanese of 1868 faced critical decisions regarding education and the role of the state in the setting of public attitudes. What was to be the philosophical basis of a formal educational system? Should it be Western in content and conception, or should it attempt to retain traditional elements? What should be done about the religious content in education? What of the competing claims between Confucian- and Shinto-based morals? Or should Japan adopt an entirely new ethical system from the West? Was some sort of compromise possible in which the Japanese could become modern and yet retain their traditional social values? What, indeed, was the relationship between Western morality (and more specifically Christianity) and Western success in modernization? In the early years after the restoration there was no clear consensus of how to deal with these questions, except that all leaders were agreed that education should further national development and patriotic unity around the symbol of the Emperor. The years between 1868 and 1890 saw a struggle over matters of ideology and educational theory while the practical steps of creating a new school system and eliminating the remnants of illiteracy were steadily carried forward.

The struggle over a national educational policy closely paralleled the broader search for a new political ideology. The issues were comparable, and the resolution to both came in the same style of compromise between new Western concepts and traditional state- and family-centered values. The struggle for control of educational ideology was far more complex than a simple competition between liberal and statist views or between "Western" and "Japanese." Despite the relative placidity of the world of the 1870s and 1880s, which got along without the bitter antagonisms engendered by the spread of Socialist ideas, there were still the alternatives between British and German systems or between Shinto and Confucian principles. In fact the first assault on educational policy after 1868 came from a strong group of "Shinto scholars" who wished to eliminate Confucian influence from education altogether. During the years 1868–1869 they urged the idea of a "restoration" of Japanese imperial values. Their influence was countered by the advocates of Western scientific training coupled with a liberal state philosophy, and for the time being the partisans of westernization won the day. Confucian scholars were everywhere pushed into the background. Yet the possibility of a coalition of ideas which would combine a strong Shinto-based support of the Emperor with Confucian principles of personal and public morals, particularly the values of patriotism and filial respect, was always latent in the Japanese quest for national recognition. The final resolution of these interests was achieved during the 1880s, particularly with the promulgation of the "modern" though strongly Emperor-centered Constitution in 1889 and the Imperial Rescript on Education in 1890. The rescript fused elements of Shinto statism, Confucian ethics, and a modern attitude toward learning into a comprehensive statement on the purpose of education and the responsibilities of the citizen in the new state. It stressed the idea of education for service to the state and loyalty to the newly conceived fatherland.

How this compromise came into being is best told along with the story of the creation of Japan's modern school system. Immediately after the restoration, the new government closed all Tokugawa schools to permit the planning of a completely new school system. It was quickly realized, however, that the new had better utilize the foundation of the old. In 1869 a university (*daigaku*) was established by amalgamating the Shōheikō and other Tokugawa colleges into a single institution dedicated to the teaching of "Imperial, Confucian, and Western studies." In July, 1871, a Department of Education was created and vested with authority over all educational and cultural matters. The new Department boldly promulgated in September, 1872, an Educational Ordinance (*gakusei*) containing a national plan for the establishment of universal education.

The new system was modeled after the elaborate and systematic educational structure perfected by the French. The country was to be divided into eight university districts, each provided with 32 middle schools, and each middle school district was to be provided with 210 elementary schools. This made a planned total of 53,760 elementary schools (one to every 600 persons). The number is twice as large as the number of such schools which were in use in Japan in 1960. The ordinance also established four years of compulsory education for both males and females between the ages of six and ten. Schools were to be administered by prefectural and local officials. They were to receive subsidies from the national treasury, however, and to be subject to an elaborate system of central inspection.

Statistics compiled in 1873 show that in that year more than 13,000 primary schools were in operation and that 46 per cent of Japan's male children and 17 per cent of the girls were in school—far short of the goals of the ordinance but nevertheless a remarkable start. Though the centralized administrative system adopted in the ordinance was French-inspired, the curriculum at the elementary level came to be modeled after the American "common school" system. The reason for this goes back to the Iwakura mission of 1872, when the First Senior Secretary of the new Department of Education, Tanaka Fujimaro, and five of his assistants traveled through the United States. At that time they were introduced to the works of Horace Mann and Henry Barnard and were sufficiently impressed by the American elementary school system to decide upon its adoption in Japan.

While the Iwakura mission was en route to Washington, the Japanese chargé d'affaires, Mori Arinori, impressed by the success of American public education and anticipating that this subject would be of major interest to the mission, addressed identical letters to a number of prominent Americans, requesting their advice for Japan. He received twelve detailed answers from college presidents, professors, state superintendents of schools, a clergyman, and a member of Congress. (These have appeared in a book under the title *Education in Japan,* published in New York in 1873.) The Japanese were confirmed in their belief that education was one of the most sensitive areas of national policy. They were astonished, however, to have their enthusiasm for complete renovation of the Japanese system dampened. One of the replies, from a professor of mathematics at Rutgers College, Dr. David Murray, stressed the importance of adapting the educational system to the national culture. These words from a farsighted cultural relativist surprised the Japanese, who wanted quick results and were willing to adopt foreign practices on a more wholesale basis. In 1873 Tanaka was appointed Vice Minister of Education, and he promptly employed Dr. Murray as the first national Superintendent of Schools and Colleges. Murray and Tanaka subsequently worked out the content of the first national educational program in Japan.

In the flush of reformist zeal which seized Japan during the 1870s, Tanaka was actually inclined to be more extreme than his American colleague. It is interesting to see Murray, the firm believer in cultural relativism, resisting Japanese attempts at indiscriminate borrowing. For instance, he opposed Mori Arinori's plan to adopt English as Japan's language of education, and he urged that textbooks be written as soon as possible in Japanese to replace the foreign ones which had of necessity been put in service. Murray's emphasis on the training of Japanese teachers also had as its goal what he called *naturalization of education.* Instruction in classroom teaching was given in the new normal school which had been established in Tokyo in 1872. There an attempt was made to draw upon the philosophy and practice of Johann Heinrich Pestalozzi, the Swiss educator, whose influence was then most pervasive in the United States. The Pestalozzian system insisted that instruction be in conformity with the natural development of the child and that learning could best be achieved through sense experience with actual objects, models, and specimens rather than mere memorization of abstractions. But above all the philosophy of education had moved away from the goal of service to the state and had put its emphasis squarely upon the individual and the fulfillment of his potential. One could not move much farther from the fundamental aims of education under the Confucian system.

The Educational Ordinance of 1872 had obviously been overly ambitious. Despite the efforts of Murray and Tanaka, the early stages in establishing a universal school system came slowly and not without opposition. The physical problem of building and staffing new elementary schools in itself was a severe drain on village finances, and this together with the discontent caused by the new military conscription system caused farmers to riot in a number of locations. They preferred the private parish schools, which seemed to offer more practical training and a more familiar standard of values. In 1878 Murray found that even in Tokyo almost 70 per cent of the primary pupils were attending private schools.

Tanaka's solution was to emulate the United States still further. With the help of Murray, he drafted a new Educational Ordinance in 1879 which made a popularly elected school board in each town and village responsible for the establishment and maintenance of schools. The result was disastrous to Tanaka's intentions. The people interpreted the new law to mean that the government was losing its interest in education and passing the burden of supporting schools to them; they closed some of the new elementary schools and consolidated others to save money. Fewer children went to school, and the education of girls was particularly neglected.

The decentralization reform failed, and with it the liberal policy encouraged by Tanaka and his American advisers fell into disfavor. Already Tanaka had come under heavy attack from more conservative members of the government, particularly over the issue of morals instruction. The Emperor Meiji himself had encouraged his Confucian lecturer, Motoda Eifu, to prepare a rescript on educational policy (issued in 1879) which recommended a return to Confucian values. Murray had returned to the United States in 1878, and Tanaka resigned in 1880. Yet in many ways a revolution had already taken place in Japanese education. Throughout the country now, children sat at desks and used blackboards and wall maps. They studied translations of American and European texts, such as Robinson's *Arithmetic* and McNally's *Geographies*, instead of memorizing the *Thousand-character Classic* and the *Analects* of Confucius. The Japanese language was being modified and standardized so as to form the basis of universal elementary education and the means of communicating modern scientific ideas.

The year 1880 then marked a major shift in Japanese elementary education policy. In that year the Ministry of Education by ordinance made "morals" (*shūshin*) a required course. Military drill was also introduced into the curriculum, under retired army officers, to strengthen the moral and intellectual training of the students. In December, 1880, schools were forbidden to use books containing "material dangerous to national peace or injurious to public morals," according to standards set by the government. The Ministry of Education began to compile a full series of standard texts in all subjects, with consequent control over their content. Confucianism, momentarily abandoned in favor of Western individualistic ideas, was seen to have relevance still in the modern world.

In 1885, Mori Arinori was appointed Minister of Education. One of his first acts was to write, in 1886, a series of new educational ordinances which provided a uniform system of elementary and higher education under the centralized control of the Ministry of Education. These were to be the basis for Japan's national educational system from this time to 1945. The new system was frankly statist in its orientation. As Mori stated in one of his speeches, "In the administration of all schools it must be kept in mind, what is done is not for the sake of the pupils but for the sake of the country." Even the regulations covering Tokyo University, now designated *Imperial*, stated that the functions of a university were to teach the arts and sciences essential to the state. There is good reason to believe that the Educational Ordinance of 1886 was written in consultation with Itō Hirobumi, who was at that time drafting a Prussian-type Constitution, and that it was designed to harmonize with the doctrine of the supremacy of the state which Itō planned to embody in the Meiji Constitution. At any rate, the educational system, like the Constitution, drew heavily on German philosophy for its rationale.

As so often happened in Japan, shifts in internal policy often reflected changes in the world environment. At about the time that American influence was waning in the late 1880s, a new philosophy of education was gaining popularity in Germany, that of the idealist philosopher Johann Friedrich Herbart. His ideas fitted the new trend in Japan far better than those of Pestalozzi, for he advocated moral instruction as the main object of education. In Herbart, then, the Japanese had found a modern educational philosopher whose ideas permitted a return along the Confucian path. Soon Japanese educators were going to German rather than American universities to study the new educational philosophy, while German philosophers were called upon to replace the Americans in Tokyo Imperial University.

After 1886 the elementary school system was avowedly dedicated to the training of the moral and patriotic individual. The period of compulsory schooling (relaxed to three years) was again set at four years; one middle school and one normal school were established in each prefecture, and a corps of inspectors were appointed to superintend the national schools. Mori's ordinances of 1886 paid particular attention to teacher training. Students at the normal schools were given state scholarships and were committed to teach for a fixed period after graduation. Students were required to live in dormitories under military-type discipline. (A retired army officer was made director of Tokyo Normal School.) Military calisthenics were introduced as a means of building physical fitness. From about this time, too, the school uniform came into general use, identifying the student for his special role of dedication to learning.

Mori, as the guiding force behind these changes, has been considerably misunderstood. To say that he was a nationalist was only to say that he was Japanese. He was more. He like Itō, the framer of the Constitution, wanted to make Japan modern and also great. The desire to excel made him reject the individualists who would dissipate the energies of the state. His desire to make Japan modern caused him to oppose the Confucianists who would return Japanese policy to an even more rigid authoritarianism. It is only as we realize the nature of the opposition Mori faced from the "right," from men like Motoda Eifu, that we can judge to what an extent the system of 1886 represented a compromise in the direction of modern (though certainly collectivist) education.

By the late 1880s, then, state educational policy and the national school system had been stabilized so that the system provided utmost efficiency in the inculcation of the latest scientific knowledge but was strongly infused with nationalistic spirit. After Mori's death (he was assassinated in 1889 by a radical nationalist) it was only a slight moving of the pendulum to the principles expressed in the Imperial Rescript on Education, which along with the Constitution became one of the fundamental documents of modern Japan. In the same year the practice of sending portraits of the Emperor to schools to be used as objects of reverence was begun, and the ingredients of patriotic indoctrination were fully in place.

THE EDUCATION SYSTEM OF IMPERIAL JAPAN

Although minor changes were made in the system presided over by the Ministry of Education, the 1886 ordinances had laid the basic framework of the first modern educational system in Asia. Thereafter the most notable changes were of degree, not kind: expansion of facilities and increased volume of instruction. In 1908, six years of elementary education became compulsory for all children. Beyond basic elementary schooling, several alternative educational programs came into being, the choice depending on such factors as sex, means, ability, and objective. Eventually, this settled into a pattern of five alternative programs, often called *tracks* or *ladders*, which came to characterize the state educational system of imperial Japan.

Academic Track

The academic track was highest in public esteem. Limited to a select group of able students on the premise that the quality of education, especially at the higher level, could only be maintained if it was restricted to the best minds, it led eventually to one of the state or private universities. But while the philosophy of selection was elitist, this was not an elitism based on birth. Though students could gain some advantage from family background, particularly if it involved wealth, entrance into each level of the academic course was openly competitive and so offered an avenue of free mobility for the most talented. The course consisted of a six-five-three-three ladder, leading from the regular six-year elementary school (*shō-gakkō*) to the preferred five-year middle school (*chū-gakkō*), next to the highly selective three-year higher school (*kōtō-gakkō*), and then to the few professional three-year universities (*daigaku*). (It should be noted here that the distinction between junior college, college, and university with which we are familiar did not emerge in Japan. Japanese higher schools thus covered our last year of high school and the first two years of college. They might best be thought of as junior colleges. The universities extended their training one year longer than our four-year colleges.) Entrance examinations at each level after the first were strenuous and provided a rigorous screening. Only some 10 per cent of the male graduates of elementary schools were able to enter the exclusive academic track by passing the examination for the government middle schools, at least one of which was found in each prefecture. Middle school was terminal for about 72 per cent of these students. A more successful group, about 19 per cent, went on to the higher schools, and the rest were diverted to normal schools or technical schools.

The government higher schools, of which there were thirty-two, cultivated a strong school spirit and sense of exclusiveness, since only about one out of seven candidates sitting for the higher school examination had been able to gain admission. Dedicated to preparation for the universities, the higher schools provided preprofessional training and some general education at roughly the junior college level.

If they survived the university entrance examination and had the means, higher school graduates pointed toward one of the nine imperial universities (including one each in Korea and Taiwan), one of the twelve lesser-esteemed single-faculty government universities, or one of the twenty-five private universities. Though the ambitious might try for Tokyo Imperial University as the most prestigious and most apt to provide direct access to government jobs, so difficult was the entrance examination that only the ablest were able to win a place. Those who failed to enter often studied on their own and tried again, or else they went to one of the other universities. The total enrollment of the universities was limited in 1938 to just under 73,000 and almost entirely to men. The ranking imperial universities produced research and scholarship of a high order, equivalent to the best in Western universities. In them were found libraries, laboratories, and research facilities of good quality and a faculty a large portion of whom had gained experience abroad.

Girls' Track

The traditional attitude toward women in Japan combined with European educational philosophy to curtail educational opportunities for girls. From the third year of elementary school the curriculum differed for girls. Women were almost completely barred from the higher rungs of the academic ladder, though a handful (210 in 1937) were admitted to some of the imperial universities. Girls desiring more than an elementary education went on to their own separate four- or five-year secondary schools called *kōtō-jogakkō*. These were attended by only about 8 per cent of the graduates of elementary schools, mostly daughters of families with some means. The schools paralleled the boys' middle schools in grade level, but because the education of girls was considered less important than that of boys, the academic standards were lower. Greater emphasis was placed on social and homemaking accomplishments. Girls had fewer hours of the basic subjects: national language, science, mathematics, history, and geography. Specialized training was given in the finishing school type of subject: sewing, music, dancing, flower arrangement, and the tea ceremony, the traditional household arts prerequisite to becoming a good wife. But girls with serious academic desires were not always satisfied. The government provided no universities for women, though it did establish two girls' higher normal schools for the advanced training of women teachers. For the rest, girls seeking higher education went to the sixty private girls' colleges, often missionary-founded, where they obtained a liberal arts training stressing language and literature, with some offering courses in homemaking. These were generally three-year institutions, roughly equivalent to the boys' higher schools, or to American junior colleges. This was the highest level normally open to women.

Normal Schools

A separate track was devoted to the specialized requirements of teacher training. The government placed great reliance on teachers as agents of the state and took particular pains with their education. It paid their expenses and exacted a period of service in return, ten years for male normal school graduates and five years for women, according to the regulations established by Mori in 1886. Later this period was reduced to 4½ years. From 1886 on, normal school students were given military training and special indoctrination in loyalty and patriotism and were kept in dormitories under strict supervision. Women attended separate normal schools.

Technical Schools

To provide for the vocational training of those unable to aspire to the professions and government services, the Japanese national system created a technical school track. At the secondary level, it consisted of five-year vocational schools (*jitsugyō-gakkō*) for the training of middle-grade technicians. The schools prepared for careers in agriculture, commerce, industry, fisheries, the colonies, and the like. They accommodated approximately 10 per cent of the elementary school graduates.

At the higher level, technical institutes (*semmon-gakkō*) provided three to five years of college-level instruction which prepared skilled technicians for business, industry, and government. They were frequently of better academic quality than the regular higher schools, but they were not accorded the rank of higher education. They were, in fact, more like junior colleges in the United States, being equivalent in grade level to the last year of high school and the first two years of college, and provided terminal education. The majority of the 300 prewar technical institutes were colleges of industry and of commerce. Others, counting as many as a dozen each, were colleges of agriculture, fisheries, medicine (second grade), and pharmacy. There were also at this level a few colleges of music, art, textiles, foreign languages, theology, and physical education. Though of lower prestige than the universities, these institutes provided higher technical and semiprofessional education each year to three or four times as many students as the universities trained.

Youth Schools

The last and least pretentious track was that of the *seinen-gakkō*, or youth schools. Created in 1935 to improve the training of large numbers of workers or potential soldiers, they provided a two- to seven-year part-time or full-time continuation of education for laboring youth who had finished the elementary school but did not have the opportunity to go farther. In 1941 this group, together with those attending higher primary schools, constituted three-fourths of the nation's young people. The government appropriated a considerable budget to provide them with a simple, practical form of vocational training, hoping thereby to increase the nation's agricultural and industrial productivity. Teachers were especially instructed in youth normal schools, where they learned the techniques of vocational training and morals instruction. Military training for boys comprised one-third of the school week, and home economics and sewing were stressed for girls.

During World War II the youth schools were devoted almost exclusively to national propaganda and military training. They were inspected by subordinate army officers. Some were practically converted into military factories. About fifteen thousand were scattered in makeshift quarters over the country, mostly in rural sections. Beginning in

April, 1939, the government made attendance compulsory for all boys up to the age of nineteen who were not attending middle schools. At the same time, elementary schools were renamed *kokumin-gakkō* (citizens' schools) and were given a curriculum dedicated largely to the war effort.

The Ministry of Education

The agency within the government which had responsibility for the state education system and authority over all accredited institutions of learning was the Ministry of Education (Mombushō). Established as a Department in 1871, it was renamed a Ministry in 1885 and reorganized in 1915 and again in 1934. It exercised indirect control over elementary and middle schools (through the education departments of prefectural or local governments) and direct control over all higher schools and universities, whether public or private. Its responsibility extended to educational policy, academic calendars, programs of study, textbooks, entrance qualifications, teachers' qualifications, salaries, budgets, allocations of special grants, and almost every conceivable function. The Minister of Education was a political appointee, the appointment like that of other Cabinet members being made by the Emperor. He was aided by a Vice Minister, who as a career bureaucrat managed to provide continuity in the direction of the Ministry and in the educational system. In the prefectures, governors acted as the local deputies of the Minister.

The permanent bureaus of the Ministry in 1937 were the following: General Education, Thought Supervision, Textbooks, Religions, and Educational Research. In addition, there were a wide variety of sections dealing with such subjects as budgets, school architecture, physical education, and personnel. The Ministry maintained its own school and university inspectors, who took precedence over inspectors maintained by the prefectural or local levels.

Private Schools and Colleges

To leave the impression that education in prewar Japan was entirely supported and controlled by the government is, of course, misleading. Even in 1959 private schools accounted for less than 0.3 per cent of all the students enrolled in the elementary grades. But beyond the elementary level conditions were different. In 1940 the proportion of students at the academic higher school level who attended private schools was 11 per cent, and at the university level more than 60 per cent were in private institutions. Private vocational or technical high schools, as might be expected, served the largest portion of Japan's youth; some 70 per cent of those in school at that level were enrolled in such schools.

As Professor Dore has pointed out,[1] these figures reveal one of the most significant features of Japanese education, prewar as well as postwar. For despite the elitist philosophy adopted by the Japanese, the elementary school system was standardized for the entire society. The cultural differences which distinguish the graduates of public schools in England or private schools in New England were not found in Japan. For all Japanese youth, whether they eventually entered one of the exclusive imperial universities or a less prestigious private university, the early school years had been identical, based on the same texts and principles.

Private institutions thus contributed to Japanese education largely at the secondary and university levels. And since a large portion of the private secondary schools were dedicated to the preparation of students for entrance into the desired government universities, it was chiefly the private universities which provided something of an alternative academic environment to the great state institutions. These universities had varied histories and backgrounds. Several were founded by Christian leaders or by mission groups, while others were founded to stress particular subjects: foreign languages, philosophy, law, the arts, or particular religious doctrines.

Of the private universities, Keiō and Waseda gained the best reputations. The first, founded by Fukuzawa Yukichi, had its start before the restoration and for many years was dominated by Fukuzawa's philosophy of individualism and liberal political beliefs. From the start Keiō stressed the training of young men for careers other than in government and politics, although as it turned out a large number of the early followers of Itagaki Taisuke and his Liberal Party had their training at Keiō. Waseda, founded in 1882 by Ōkuma Shigenobu, was established as a training ground for men who might enter opposition politics on the side of Ōkuma's Reform Party. Both of these universities eventually became large multifaculty institutions training chiefly for business, journalism, government, and medicine. The desire to compete for entrance into desirable jobs led even these "opposition" universities along conservative courses.

Even with the existence of private institutions which could supplement the government system of higher education, many young Japanese found

1 Ronald P. Dore, "Education: Japan," in Robert E. Ward and Dankwart A. Rustow (eds.), *The Political Modernization of Japan and Turkey*, Princeton, N.J., 1964, pp. 199–201.

the opportunities in Japan too limited or too intellectually restricted. Study abroad was a frequent solution for those who had the means. In prewar Japan many wealthy or titled families made a regular practice of sending sons to Oxford or Yale. Women with scholarly ambitions frequently traveled for study to Europe or the United States. Medical doctors and scientists often took up postdoctoral studies in Germany, while artists and musicians attempted to reach the source of their inspiration in France or Italy.

PREWAR EDUCATION:
SOME PROBLEMS OF EVALUATION

By the 1930s it had become common for Western, and particularly American, observers to look with disfavor upon the Japanese educational process. Once it appeared that Japan was moving along the path of militant nationalism which had proved attractive to Germany and Italy, foreign critics noted with alarm the increase in nationalistic indoctrination which was finding its way into Japanese schools and texts. American Occupation personnel charged with setting government policy after 1945 looked upon the educational system as one of the chief strongholds of ultranationalism and militarism, and it made education one of the prime targets of reform. To them the primary ills of the old system were its centralization, elitism, and nationalism. Education, in other words, had collaborated fully with the forces which had driven Japan to war and nationalistic hysteria.

There is little that can or should be said in defense of the role education played in Japan from 1930 to 1945. By the time of Pearl Harbor the entire school system had been converted into a gigantic factory for the production of soldiers or of well-indoctrinated workers on the home front. Even within the universities the voices that might have questioned the myths of Japanese uniqueness and world mission which formed the bases of the "New National Structure" movement were silenced. Education had become little more than an organ of state policy. To say that this condition of degradation, this surrender to the blind forces of national avarice, was a sign of weakness is certainly permissible. To say that it was inherent, indeed inevitable, in the education policies adopted in 1886 is another matter.

In holding up the American educational ideal to the Japanese, as is so often done, it is well to remember that the United States developed its system of education as a result of certain unique social and economic conditions. Japan in creating a modern national system followed a pattern which was more common in other "advanced countries" of the

West than that of the United States. Nor does it seem likely that Japan could have avoided its course of centralization and state control, given the financial and administrative problems faced by the young nation prior to the twentieth century. The "failure of democracy" was not confined to Japan alone and was a product of complex world conditions which did not leave the United States totally untouched.

Looked at without the specter of the war years in mind, the Japanese educational machinery was remarkably efficient in doing what had been asked of it. A literacy rate that was the highest in Asia and comparable to those of the most advanced Western countries, a citizenry intelligent in its behavior and educated to high standards of lawful conduct and personal hygiene, farmers willing to profit from the results of scientific experimentation, businessmen able to adjust their policies to world market conditions, an intelligentsia inquisitive and avid for information through newspapers, journals, books, and travel, an intellectual elite which by the 1920s was contributing to world literature and scientific advancement, these were some of the remarkable achievements of the Japanese educational system.

It should be remembered also that the state system of education was not the only means of acquiring an education in modern Japan. Private schools and nongovernmental universities provided alternative opportunities stressing different goals and values. Large numbers of Japanese went abroad for study and were exposed to different philosophies and ideologies. Japan in fact was subject to strong currents of dissident ideologies, including socialism and communism. In the school system the philosophy of John Dewey had its impact in the 1930s.

But it is also perfectly evident that prewar education had overall idiosyncrasies and special characteristics which, whether for good or bad, became accentuated during the tense war years after 1930. First and most obvious was the influence exerted upon the process of education and style of mind by the Japanese language itself. Despite the remarkable success which the Japanese had in modernizing their language, the retention of the ideographs (kanji) perpetuated a host of educational problems. Many observers have concluded that the complexity of the Japanese language has been a formidable barrier to easy elementary education and has restricted the rapid and exact communication of ideas either within the culture or from outside it. The habits of rote learning required in mastering the characters, it is also claimed, have been carried over into other fields of learning and have tended to encourage uncritical acceptance of officially approved ideas and dogmas. Not all of these claims have been substantiated scientifically, but there can be no doubt that the written language is one of the most thoroughly

Japanese aspects of the culture, favoring the easy perpetuation of traditional values and visibly branding as foreign whatever new ideas arrive from abroad. Language reform, by which is generally meant simplification of or elimination of characters from the script, continues today to be a significant educational issue.

Another notable feature of prewar education in Japan was its admittedly elitist orientation and hierarchical structure. This was true both of the organization of the educational system and of the attitude toward learning. The inordinate prestige of the imperial universities (especially that of Tokyo), the rigid curricula of the universities, and the German-style authoritarian method of instruction made for rigidities in the thought process of both student and teacher. In university faculties the tendency toward the formation of cliques was fostered by the strong status differences between institutions and the habit by which a system of thought was handed down from a master professor to his disciple students. Such leader-oriented doctrinalism was not confined to the schools but was carried over into the professions (law, medicine), business, and government. Similarly, the prestige of Western scholarship produced an inordinate emphasis on ready-made packages: German historicism, Hegelian philosophy, economic determinism, and the like. Couple this factionalism with the fiercely competitive desire of the Japanese to gain the "best" education, accentuate it by an exacting entrance examination system, and we have the ingredients of a rigidly hierarchical attitude toward the whole process of learning.

The notably practical orientation of prewar education was undoubtedly a product of Japan's position as a nation and of her internal economic and institutional conditions. The country had little opportunity to consider education as a means of developing the "well-rounded man." While Japan as a nation was obsessed with the objective of "catching up" with the West, education for the individual inevitably stressed practical knowledge and techniques. The liberal arts approach to higher education was in a sense a luxury which could not be afforded, indeed, cannot even today. University students understandably pointed to law (for government service), medicine, science, economics (for business), and technical professions. University faculties were weak in the speculative and social sciences. Political science, anthropology, and sociology, though taught, were slow to develop as experimental disciplines.

Unfortunately we know too little about the relationship between the manner in which the mind is trained to absorb information and the results of education in terms of individual or group behavior. Unquestionably the Japanese educational system and the mind it produced were prone to systems and doctrines and less at home with free or open methods of inquiry. The tendency to "take on faith" or to commit oneself totally to a system had its wellsprings in the Confucian tradition and was further nourished by the Germanic borrowings after the 1880s. But the tendency of the Japanese to give himself wholeheartedly to some doctrine or ideology may have had deeper causes. As we have noted, the Japanese were historically dependent upon systems of thought emanating from outside their culture. Is it not possible that such a dependence could have led to a more complete embrace, beyond the purely technical details of a given system, once a commitment had been made? Is not the Japanese thinker more dependent upon the system to which he gives himself not only to provide a practical means of solving specific problems, but also to create the framework for his entire intellectual identity? For what is he to cling to if not to an all embracing and intellectually satisfying system? The alternative in modern times (except for those of religious conviction) has been a reliance on some version of Japanism, with nationalistic or aesthetic overtones. The comfortable assurance which is granted the Western scholar of being part of the mainstream of world history at the same time that he can freely choose his methods of inquiry was denied the Japanese, or so he has felt.

At any rate, the Japanese academic world of the 1930s was greatly torn by the conflict of ideologies. We are more apt to remember the extremes of the right, but we should also recall the dramatic activity on the left which so shocked the Japanese Establishment. Marxism, socialism, and communism found open and vigorous acceptance in the universities during the 1920s. Perhaps because of the weakness of opposition parties in Japan and the lack of development of an independent group of journalistic critics of the regime, it was in the universities that the most active expression of opposition developed. By the time the Establishment took seriously the spread of communism into the universities, the penetration had gone remarkably deep. One can hardly recapture the sense of fear, frustration, and resentment which swept the campuses in Japan during the dragnet operations in 1925, 1928, and 1929, when students and professors were picked up in such large numbers, some to be tortured by the special "thought police," most to be released but thoroughly frightened. By 1935, with the dishonoring of Professor Minobe Tatsukichi, state organs of intellectual control had brought the country into a condition of visible conformity around the ideals of Japanism.

Few countries in the world outside the totalitarian states managed to mold the minds of their people as thoroughly as did the Japanese after 1940. The main educational instrument in this program of nationalistic indoctrination was the course of study in morals, which occupied an increasingly important part of the Japanese curriculum. Morals instruction and courses in Japanese history tended increasingly after 1930 to create distorted and myth-centered images of the nature of the Japanese state. Two concepts in particular formed the keystones of the new nationalism. First, through the idea of *kokutai* the Japanese were given to believe that they possessed a special form of national organization presided over by a sovereign who was unique among rulers. Second, the relationship of subject to sovereign was considered that of child to parent, the entire Japanese state being conceived of as a vast family living together in complete harmony under the father superior. By the late 1930s, especially with the publication of *Kokutai no hongi* (*Cardinal Principles of the National Entity of Japan*), the argument that Japan had a mission to combine the unique historical quality of the Japanese state structure (a divine Emperor and supremely loyal subjects) with the best of Western culture (science but not political or individual morality) into a revolutionary new amalgam and to spread its influence throughout the world was seriously being taught in the schools. At the same time, university professors were lecturing on the beauties of the imperial institutions or were bending their disciplines to support the claim that the Japanese were racially and culturally superior. In view of the rapidity with which these men abandoned such ideas after the war and in the light of the difficulties the state had in stamping out "dangerous thoughts" during the 1930s, we should perhaps credit the Japanese with at least some resistance to intellectual regimentation. But we cannot forget easily the conditions that permitted the final military and intellectual debacle of the 1940s: the surge of ultranationalism which drove out all reason, the arrogance of the public official or of the state-dedicated scholar, the brutality of the soldier, the encroachment on freedom of inquiry by the thought police, the intellectual regimentation, and the mental and physical exhaustion brought on by the war. These are the nightmares which haunted the postwar reformers and still trouble the Japanese intellectual today.

THE OCCUPATION REFORMS

To the degree that Japan had built its wartime morale upon myths of imperial invincibility, the collapse of Japanese arms brought total disillusionment to the Japanese people and discredited the system of education which had misled them. Because of the close link between education and the "secular religion" of the state, defeat in war brought both systems down at the same time. Few areas of Japanese culture were dealt so severe a blow; in few areas did defeat leave such a vacuum. Conversely, Occupation authorities fastened upon educational change as one of their prime areas of reform and rehabilitation. Few saw the irony in the plan to use education forcibly to democratize a people that had just been educated to a pitch of ultranationalism.

On the surface the two educational systems which confronted each other in 1945 could not have seemed more dissimilar: the American representing the idealization of egalitarian, secular, and liberal arts education; the Japanese the epitome of elitist education turned to nationalistic ends. Yet with an almost disconcerting eagerness the Japanese embraced the Occupation-sponsored reforms which revamped their school system and substituted a radically different policy of education. Whether it was true, as many of the Japanese who greeted the Occupation officials claimed, that the wartime intelligentsia had been silenced but not completely won over to ultranational aims is perhaps beside the point. The Japanese seemed eager for a change. The result was something of a surge of mutual admiration: the Japanese hopefully adopting the touchstone of democracy, the American educational advisers flushed with a sense of mission and warmed by the realization that their views were being respected. Such was the prelude to the remarkable overhaul of the Japanese educational machine which occurred after 1945.

The Potsdam Declaration of July 26, 1945, had provided the basis for Allied postwar policy in Japan. It said in part: "There must be eliminated for all time the authority and influence of those who have deceived and misled the people of Japan into embarking on world conquest." This was to be accompanied by a removal of "all obstacles to the revival and strengthening of democratic tendencies among the Japanese people. Freedom of speech, religion, and of thought as well as respect for the fundamental human rights shall be established."

The Occupation was administered by means of a machinery of limited military government working through the existing Japanese civil government. Military Occupation government thus took the form of a series of special staff sections attached to a General Headquarters and located in Tokyo. The Civil Information and Education Section, organized on September 22, 1945, was given responsibility for guiding the reorientation and reeducation of the Japanese people. It dealt with the Japanese central government authorities (the Ministry of Education), issuing policy directives for execution by the Japanese.

The first educational directive of the Supreme Commander for the Allied Powers (SCAP), entitled "Administration of the Education System of Japan," was issued on October 22, 1945. It merely spelled out two general policies as the major educational aims of the Occupation:

(1) prohibition of the dissemination of militaristic and ultranationalistic ideology and discontinuance of military education and drill; and (2) encouragement of the inculcation of democratic educational concepts and practices aimed at developing an educated, peaceful, and responsible citizenry.

A second SCAP directive, "Investigation, Screening, and Certification of Teachers and Education Officials," dated October 30, 1945, required the Japanese to set up machinery for screening the nation's half a million teachers. It contained three major provisions: (1) the immediate removal of all teachers "known to be militaristic, ultra-nationalistic, or antagonistic to the objectives and policies of the Occupation . . ."; (2) the disbarring for the time being from the field of educational activity all ex-soldiers; and (3) the establishment of suitable administrative machinery for "the investigation, screening, and certification of all present and prospective teachers and educational officials." Ultimately about one-fourth of the existing teaching staff resigned or was purged.

A third SCAP directive affecting education, issued on December 15, 1945, was entitled "Abolition of Governmental Sponsorship, Support, Perpetuation, Control, and Dissemination of State Shinto." It prohibited "the dissemination of Shinto doctrines in any form and by any means in any educational institution supported wholly or in part by public funds. . . ." It also required that all textbooks and teachers' manuals be censored and Shinto doctrines deleted and that teachers henceforth be barred from taking students to Shinto shrines for worship or observing Shinto rites. It forbade the circulation of two texts, *Kokutai no hongi* and *Shimmin no michi* (The way of the people). The directive did not interfere with the private worship of sect Shinto. On December 31, a fourth directive, entitled "Suspension of Courses in Morals, Japanese History, and Geography," was sent to the Japanese government. The three courses were promptly dropped, and the texts in these courses were withdrawn. Those in geography and history were rewritten by 1947. The morals course, the principal vehicle for nationalistic indoctrination, was not restored to the curriculum until after the Occupation had ended.

These Occupation directives were essentially surgical in intent. The legal basis for a new policy of education was ultimately placed in the new Constitution, promulgated in November, 1946. Article 20 said: "The State shall refrain from religious education"; Article 23, "Academic freedom is guaranteed"; and Article 26, "All people shall have the right to receive equal education correspondent to their ability, as provided by law. All people shall be obligated to have all boys and girls under their protection receive ordinary education as provided by law. Such

compulsory education shall be free." These guarantees of the Constitution were subsequently implemented by a series of educational laws,
the most important of which was the Fundamental Law of Education
of 1947, a definitive statement of educational policy. It replaced the
Imperial Rescript on Education (which the Diet now expressly repudiated) and differed from it in crucial respects. Sovereignty was now
stated to rest with the people, and the objective of education to be
found in the "full development of personality" and "independent spirit"
of the people. The School Education Law of March, 1947, which accompanied the fundamental law, provided in detail for the carrying
out of the aims of the new education. The control of schools was
decentralized by the School Board Law passed in 1948, which created
elected and local school boards with power to modify curricula and
textbooks. The stage was set for the full-scale modification of the whole
field of education in Japan.

The story of the Occupation reforms is not told, however, merely in
terms of SCAP directives and constitutional guarantees. In no other
area of SCAP policy did the nature of American intent and Japanese
receptivity raise so many fundamental questions. On the American side
idealism, sometimes of a starry-eyed variety, was carried into the field
by SCAP officials. Educational advisers suggested to the Japanese policies
which were in some instances still only experimentally accepted in the
United States. More than this, one may well ask whether policies which
had emerged from the experience of professional educators in American
culture could invariably be the most effective ones to introduce into a
tradition so different as that of Japan and whether, if introduced, they
could take root without modification. The years since the Occupation
have disclosed many problems which stem as much from cultural differences as from any unwillingness of the Japanese to understand the
basic philosophy behind the attempted reforms.

THE NEW EDUCATION SYSTEM IN OPERATION

The ideal of equal educational opportunity was vigorously pushed by
the Occupation reformers. This ideal called for the reorganization of
the entire educational establishment from a multitrack system into a
single-track educational ladder, up which all the youth of the nation
might climb. A standard six-three-three-four system was instituted in
which the first two levels, six years of elementary schooling and three
years of lower secondary schooling, were made compulsory. This raised
the number of compulsory years from six to nine. The nine years were

open to all children and were to be free. No entrance examinations were to be required. Coeducation was adopted as a basic principle of equality, and the number of women receiving higher education was expected to increase steadily.

Naturally, the extension of the compulsory period by three years, accomplished over a three-year period (seven years compulsory in 1947, eight in 1948, and nine in 1949) was a great strain on the economy of a country that was still suffering from war and defeat. It required provision for some 1,030,000 new pupils in lower secondary schools. Because of this influx and the purge of instructors, there was an immediate shortage of teachers. New candidates had to be recruited and were given a six-month training course to fill the gap. By 1950, all children of lower secondary age were in school.

Under the new system, a single comprehensive type of upper secondary school was created to replace the several specialized types (agriculture, commerce, academic, etc.) of prewar days. The latter were allowed to continue but were required to offer a minimum national curriculum of general education subjects. Especially in rural areas, the Ministry of Education recommended the creation of a comprehensive upper secondary school to meet the needs of all the youth in the community, whether they were heading for an academic or a vocational career. Schools could nominally become "comprehensive" by offering the academic plus one other course, most commonly either agriculture, technical, or homemaking.

The ideal of providing terminal vocational education in an upper secondary school side by side with the general or academic college preparatory course did not work out as well as expected. The pressure for entrance into the prestige universities continued to be so great that the majority of students preferred the academic course whether they were qualified or not. It soon developed that only 30 per cent of those taking the academic course were able to go on to a university, while the remaining 70 per cent had to go directly into jobs, still poorly prepared. The devalued vocational courses were thus denied support, and staff and equipment suffered. There has consequently been a tendency to return to specialized one-course schools and also to revive the sharp prewar distinction between types of schools, the academic being favored socially and financially and the vocational taking a lesser, depreciated role.

The prewar university in Japan was an advanced and sophisticated institution with a proud tradition of German-type scholarship. It placed primary emphasis on research and specialization and left all general education or liberal arts training to the higher schools. The

U.S. Education Mission, to promote greater equality of opportunity in higher education and to improve the offerings of the universities, recommended the creation of a greater number of national universities, general education as a required part of every student's program for a broader humanistic training, freedom of universities from governmental control, and academic freedom for university teachers.

In the reorganization of higher education, 249 institutions of varied types—universities, colleges, technical schools, normal schools, etc.— were consolidated and reclassified to produce a unified system of 68 national four-year universities (somewhat similar to state universities in the United States) at the apex of the six-three-three-four system. Each prefecture was required to have at least one university offering general education and teacher education besides the usual disciplines. In addition, provision was made for prefectures and municipalities to have their own "local universities" and private groups to have their "private universities."

By 1963, there were 591 higher educational institutions of all kinds, or fewer by 67 than in prewar days but greater by 91 than the number in 1957. The 591 included 270 *daigaku* (colleges or universities), public and private. Among these were 72 national universities, 34 local universities, and 164 private universities. Of the 72 national universities, only 29 of the older ones, including former imperial universities, had graduate schools. In addition, 16 of the local universities and 58 of the private universities had graduate schools. Among the 321 junior colleges were 28 national, 41 local, and 252 private institutions.

The quality of these institutions was naturally quite varied. Those based upon former imperial universities and the prewar single-faculty government institutions, together with the oldest private universities, have been able to maintain excellent standards and develop strong faculties. Those comprised of former normal and technical institutions, in small and more remote prefectures, suffer from inadequate plant, equipment, staff, and national support. There is a serious question whether some prefectures can support the overhead plant cost of education at the university level over a long period.

One of the major problems of higher education has been the inadequate correlation between the new preparatory education and the highly specialized graduate study, which is still largely conducted in the old style. To many, the whole university reorganization appears to have lowered the standards of higher education, and some of the newer national institutions carrying the name of university have clearly not fulfilled expectations. On the other hand, the opportunity to receive college training has been extended to rural youth near their homes and within their means. Vested interests and local pride have begun to come to the support of these smaller institutions. Some of the newer ones have begun to provide trained personnel for local commerce and industry. Others are specializing in such areas as fisheries and engineering, which will enable them and their graduates to make a distinctive national contribution.

As the local universities have become more successful, they have contributed to some extent to the breakup of the prewar academic hierarchy. The prestige of universities formerly far outclassed by Tokyo University has risen somewhat, and teachers from national universities have been willing to join the staffs of local universities. But the attempted decentralization of universities and the de-emphasis of Tokyo University's preferential position have been only partially successful. Students from all over Japan still try to enter Tokyo, and a diploma from there is still the best passport to certain sorts of governmental service or positions in finance and business. The entrance examination continues to be a major hurdle to all prestige universities.

In the effort to emphasize liberal arts training, the Occupation reforms required that all college students take thirty-six units of general education evenly divided among humanities, social sciences, and natural sciences. In effect, this was accomplished by fusing the former higher school with the university to provide the general education curriculum. This fusion has led to numerous problems. There was discrimination against the former higher school staff as not being of university caliber, and there was continuing opposition to the requirement of general education as taking up precious time that should be devoted to specialization. Since the requirements cannot easily be abandoned, certain professional faculties, especially engineering, in some institutions, have begun to require an additional year of college. In the case of the junior college, opposition to general education has succeeded in reducing the requirement from twenty units to twelve, leaving twenty-four for specialized education and twenty-four for electives.

One major result of the new educational system (undoubtedly aided by the postwar economic prosperity) has been a national increase in the level of education. It is estimated that the 591 institutions of higher education had a combined enrollment of more than 600,000 in 1963. The number of students applying at all levels has grown year by year, so that the demand for education still greatly exceeds the capacity of the schools. There continues to be crowding at the compulsory level, with double sessions and a class size often well over the legal limit of fifty students. At the college level, even in some of the new national universities in rural districts, there are still greater numbers of applicants than of openings. At the preferred schools, such as the select few secondary schools and the former imperial universities and prestige private universities, the number of applicants is from five to twenty times the number than can be accepted. The result has been that stiffer and stiffer entrance examinations have been devised for selection. Students have gone back to the practice of taking examinations several times, cramming in between, in the hope of success. In the first-rank universities, more than 70 per cent of the freshmen are repeaters (so-called *"rōnin"*), having crammed outside school for one, two, or more years before they finally passed the examination. This condition is accentuated by the different levels of instruction which mark the new higher schools and the largely unchanged universities.

In the area of faculty training and educational policy formation, the new system has required numerous changes. Reeducation of the teaching force was essential if the vast body of teachers trained in the old normal schools was to be able to handle the new curricula and new interpretations of social and individual values. First through the higher normal schools, then through local normal schools, teachers of elementary and secondary schools were instructed in the new educational philosophy and in the new methods, curricula, and texts. At the university level the major change was accomplished through weeding out a portion of the prewar faculty. Throughout the Occupation period educational advisers from the United States spent much time discussing educational objectives with Japanese educators at all levels. Many Japanese leaders also visited the United States.

The new atmosphere of freedom in education produced some unexpected results. The unionization of teachers and professors, actively sponsored by the Occupation as a means of improving the teachers' welfare, proceeded very rapidly. By 1947 the Japanese Teachers Union (*Nikkyōso*), 500,000 strong, was the largest single union in Japan. Membership had grown to more than 600,000 by 1960. Affiliated with the overall General Council of Trade Unions (Sōhyō), it began to demand a voice in setting educational policy and even put up representatives in national and local elections for the Diet or for prefectural or municipal office. Furthermore, many of the new young recruits to the ranks of secondary and higher education, having silently fed on antigovernment and Marxist thinking during and at the conclusion of the war, were vigorously anti-Establishment in their thinking. Leadership in the teachers union was thus manipulated by politically active individuals who were allied with the Socialist Party and who adopted a "teacher's code" which was openly Marxist in content. On occasion teachers of Communist sympathies took over local unions or schools.

From the academic point of view, while the craze for "democracy" gave rise to a confused groping toward freedom in all academic matters, the dominant ideology which replaced the prewar nationalism was at the outset Marxism. Textbooks once written under Ministry direction were now freely selected by local boards. The new history and social study texts more often than not were now written to illustrate how the Japanese had been exploited by monopoly capitalism and oppressed by the "Emperor system." American influence on Japanese educational policy had relatively little success in communicating the meaning of democratic education and free inquiry to those who did not already comprehend it. For among men who have instinctively looked for holistic intellectual systems, democracy provided only an attitude and a set of rules for behavior in an open society. It lacked a body of revealed knowledge which could explain how man had reached his present state and what precisely needed to be done to improve it.

As an organ of educational policy and control, the Ministry of Education, which once had controlled curricula, texts, and teacher training and had ensured conformity through national inspectors, was greatly modified in the new system. By the passage of three laws, the Board of Education Law of 1948 and the Ministry of Education Establishment Law and the Private Schools Law of 1949, the Ministry's functions were decentralized. School control was transferred to locally elected school boards; and the Ministry was transformed into a professional advisory body, charged with giving guidance, providing expert consultation services, and establishing certain objective standards.

The role of the new school boards at the prefectural level was to operate prefectural schools (upper secondary schools) and assist local boards. Prefectural boards certified all teachers and administrators in the prefectures, approved all textbooks, gave advice and guidance to local boards, and procured foodstuffs for the lunch program at local schools. Otherwise, as in the United States, local boards were sovereign over public compulsory education, establishing and maintaining schools, appointing and dismissing teachers, determining curricula, choosing textbooks, buying instructional materials, and providing in-service training for teachers. Both types of boards, prefectural and local, selected their respective superintendents, decided educational policy, and drew up the education budgets for their schools. Most of these powers had hitherto been the prerogative of the Ministry of Education and its prefectural agents.

The new school board system had difficulty from the start. Local areas had little understanding of what was required of such boards. Teachers were eligible for election to the boards, and since most teachers were members of the Japanese Teachers Union, those who gained seats were often accused of representing not the interest of the public, but that of the union. The concern of many parents that leftist indoctrination had taken over in the schools lent support to the conservative government's drive to place the selection and control of local boards in the hands of local political leaders, mayors, and governors and ultimately to return it to the Ministry of Education. A bill making boards appointive and reducing their size and responsibilities was brought before the Diet and, despite violent Socialist opposition, was passed in June, 1956. Simultaneously the government managed to pass legislation which would prevent teachers from joining political parties and engaging in political activity. In short, there has been a partial return to greater central control over education and the teachers.

The relationship between the Ministry and the teachers remains greatly changed from prewar days, however. Teachers are free to think, plan, and experiment. Supervision by school inspectors with power to fire or demote was replaced by professional "assistance" from a teachers' consultant, who no longer assessed a teacher's work, though he might give advice and suggestions for improvement. Here again, the freedom given appeared to be too wide, especially when teachers took advantage of it to protect themselves from interference in their political activities. It is ironical that in the years following the Occupation, as attempts were made in the Diet to pass legislation which would place greater powers of "supervision" in the hands of school authorities, it was the Japanese Teachers Union which most vehemently sought to uphold the "freedoms" provided by the Occupation directives. Vigorously opposed to what it called attempts to reinstate "authoritarian methods" in school administration, the union was quick to come to the defense of its members against any violation or alleged violation of their rights. One of the latest rounds in the battle between the Ministry and the unionists on the teaching staff was the inauguration in 1958 of a nationwide program of teacher efficiency rating. The program was aimed at placing much greater power in the hands of the principal as the chief rater. The union staged such vigorous protests and teacher strikes against the system that after three years of turmoil in the schools, while a truce was agreed upon, the rating program was able to exercise little effect.

EDUCATION AND ITS PROBLEMS TODAY

Education in Japan today has regained its autonomy of development, and few Japanese give much thought to the fact that the present system was derived from reforms imposed upon the country by an alien authority after defeat in war. To the American observer the remarkable thing is that so much of the Occupation program appears to have taken hold, and not simply because a superior power willed it. There appears to have been sufficient desire for certain reform features, particularly the expansion of educational opportunity and the elimination of propaganda, so that the postwar directives were accepted for the better. Other features were naturally criticized, at first surreptitiously and later openly. The objectives and ideals expounded by American educationalists must now compete freely in Japanese academic and governmental circles. And the Japanese have discovered that American educational policies have themselves moved far away from the naïve assumptions of the postwar era.

In Japan today, education remains one of the most vigorously discussed areas of national policy, for every Japanese knows that education is essential to the country's ability to compete in the world and yet that it was through education that the discredited nationalistic values were inculcated and that the war effort was rationalized. Frequently, therefore, the clash of opinion between conservatives and their opponents in politics has focused on the issue of education. At the base of these differences remain the fundamental issues of the balance between freedom and responsibility in a democratic system. Conservatives pointing to the moral confusion of Japanese youth and the irresponsible political behavior of students and teachers have urged a return to at least some of the stabilizing elements in the old system: some degree of ethical instruction, increased instruction about Japan as a nation, greater centralization of control, and greater selectivity and adaptation to the practical needs of the country. Their opponents have frequently insisted upon a freedom which approaches irresponsibility. That the conservatives will predominate is indicated by the fact that over the loud protests of Socialists, the teachers union, the majority of the press, and many intellectuals (and of course students), a modified social ethics course was made compulsory in 1958.

What has most concerned the conservative leadership in Japan has been the seeming lack of direction except toward radicalism among faculty and students. There has been, therefore, some conservative interest in a revival of a stabilizing code comparable to the Imperial Rescript on Education. Nonetheless, the only attempt to adopt one in recent years was unsuccessful. In 1951, Minister of Education Amano Teiyū drafted an "Outline of Ethical Practice for the Japanese People," popularly called the "Amano Rescript." This code gave a perfunctory nod to the Fundamental Law of Education in mentioning the dignity of human personality but the heart of the document was its assertion that "the State is the parent body of the individual. Without the State there would be no individuals." Dr. Amano went on to describe the position of the Emperor as a "moral focus." Confucian hierarchical relations were advocated as "the basic pattern for just relations in a just society." The public outcry against the Amano statement forced its author to abandon his plan of setting it up as a universal code of morals at the time the Occupation came to an end. Succeeding ministers of education, Okano Kiyohide and Ōdachi Shigeo, have made public pleas for a return to the morality of the imperial rescript. And in January, 1956, Minister Kiyose Ichirō openly attacked for the first time the philosophy of education underlying the Fundamental Law of Education. He called for its amendment, because, he argued, it lacked national consciousness and disregarded the idea of filial piety. Behind these open statements in favor of greater centralization and discipline in education has been the gradual tightening up of the system through indirection (budget controls, in particular).

It would seem inevitable that the Ministry of Education should exert "greater responsibility" over the nation's schools. Certain trends along this line have already been mentioned: the required morals course, the appointed school boards, the compartmentalization of social studies, and the imposition of a stricter control on textbook writing and publications. To these must be added such other recent evidences of recentralized Ministry control of all educational processes as (1) the publication in 1958 of new courses of study for the elementary and lower secondary schools in the *Official Gazette* (*Kampō*), thus giving them official sanction and requiring universal application instead of the "suggested" nature of the earlier courses of study; (2) the nationwide requirement that principals rate all their teachers, on a vague (and necessarily subjective) scale; and (3) the Ministry's move in 1958 to make a financial contribution toward the salaries of school administrators in order to increase their "obligation" to the Ministry. But at each step of this process the Ministry has been strongly resisted by such pressure groups as the Japanese Teachers Union and the National Student Federation (Zengakuren). In addition, most of the newspapers of the country, liberal and conservative alike, intellectuals in general, and professional educators in the universities in particular have opposed recentralization. There is in fact a strong vested interest in the new system which has made any sweeping reversion to prewar conditions improbable.

Japan still has a difficult problem ahead in resolving the ultimate aims of its educational system. In contrast to the Imperial Rescript on Education, which provided a set of absolute values for all, the Fundamental Law of Education seems to many to be vague and legalistic.

Among those who were educated in prewar days there is a tendency to depreciate modern schooling as being inferior to their own, too lax, too free, and deficient in morality. But their sons and daughters, who received their education in postwar days, do not necessarily share this sentiment. For more than a decade they have been exposed in the classrooms and textbooks to new ideals, such as respect for the individual, equal opportunities, and civil liberties, or more likely to ideas of the class struggle and the need to work for a freer society. A 1958 psychological study of a sample of elementary teachers, using a specially constructed Japanese teacher attitude scale and a Japanese F scale (test for authoritarianism), showed that contemporary elementary teachers tended to verbalize attitudes sympathetic to a more open approach to education. Though such attitudes might not necessarily carry over into classroom behavior, especially under the mounting "reverse-course" pressures, it is clear that, at least at the elementary level, Japanese teachers have accepted nonauthoritarian objectives.

For the student, the classroom in postwar Japan would seem to have become a more friendly and congenial place. The character content of written Japanese has been considerably reduced, and the student has been encouraged to think for himself and to participate in free discussion. To some extent he has learned to respect more than one opinion or to defend his own against others. He has been denied the certainty that his was the best and most successful nation and that his way of life was without peer, but he may have gained the excitement of discovering his country as a part of world history.

Nevertheless, the college and university student more frequently finds himself in a strangely bewildering world. Confronted by the example of the emerging nations of Asia in which students have often carried the burden of revolutionary leadership, having inherited the spirit of the postwar reaction against authority of all kinds, he nonetheless finds himself in a society and an economy which despite notable inequalities are reasonably stable and prosperous. This situation helps to account for the pattern of student organization and behavior which has given rise to the "student movement" of postwar Japan. Freed from compulsory military service and untouched by the many government-sponsored patriotic organizations of prewar years, the students have organized themselves freely for self-government and even political purposes. Characteristic of the activities of the Zengakuren has been a highly politically motivated leadership with a rather large but lethargic general membership. Organized in September, 1948, after a nationwide strike in which 200,000 students purportedly participated, the Zengakuren has been a constant participant in the political conflicts on the national stage. The segments of Japanese youth most sensitive to the political issues of the day find themselves frequently on the attack against authority, either of the government or of their own universities. The great surge of demonstrations of May and June, 1960, if we subtract the hard core of professional agitators who took the lead, reflected the desire of Japanese youth to stay in the forefront of the struggle to prevent a return to authoritarianism.

The great dilemma in post-Occupation Japan has arisen over the degree of political extremism which appears to be necessary or justified to preserve national and intellectual independence. Postwar Japan finds herself in the grip of cold war tensions which have exerted strong pressures on the minds of the Japanese people. These tensions have tended to distort the issues in the field of education, identifying the neutralist or the pro-Communist with the institutions of decentralization and non-interference by government in education and making of the advocate of greater control the blackest of protofascists. It has become difficult to differentiate between politically motivated anti-Ministry agitation and that engaged in for idealistic reasons. Thus the core of "democratic" values which had been set down in postwar Japan has been, in many instances, whittled away by both the left and the right. Meanwhile, the "liberal alternative" to these extremes seems never to have been very clearly understood. The professional advocate of *demokurashi* is almost as stereotyped in his behavior and thought as his more extreme opponents.

Ironically, it has been in the area of higher education, the universities especially, that the impact of liberal principles has appeared to be least secure. In some ways the most neglected of the educational institutions by the postwar reforms, the universities have suffered a loss of prestige and of financial support. The university professor today still must engage in a variety of side activities to make a respectable living. His environment, both physical and intellectual, has changed little from the dingy, ill-serviced quarters he inhabited prior to the war. If anyone has felt the class conflicts at first hand, the professor feels he has. Moreover, with few opportunities to secure free research funds (foundations are almost nonexistent), the university professor finds the academic world still narrow and Ministry-dominated.

These conditions in part explain the strong political coloration of academic faculty thinking and activity, for there is still much to win and a great deal to lose. Such a faculty must feel acutely the discrepancy between the surge of postwar prosperity and their own less enviable position. It is easy to become cynical and embittered and to pass these sentiments on to students. Hence the quickness with which the intellectual points to marks of government insincerity or submission to "American imperialism" and the slowness to find fault with the behavior of Communist powers.

The academic mind appears still to be caught in a serious conflict. It is perhaps most aware of the uncertainty of world conditions. In the immediate postwar years the world was not so deeply divided. One could be sure, it seemed, that democracy in its American guise had defeated Japan and Germany, and that given a chance it could resurrect Japan as well. Today there is no such surety, and the emotion-charged image of a modernizing Red China has further confused the issue. To many, in fact, there seems to be greater demonstrable certainty in the principles of Marxism than in the less highly systematized principles of open inquiry that stand against intellectual authoritarianism. The willingness, even desire, to submit to intellectual systematization, the persistent belief that intellectual inquiry should be linked to social action, these are some of the continuing characteristics of the academic leadership which confront the growing national pressure for "normalcy" under greater governmental control. Perhaps the resolution of this conflict will not come until greater numbers of the postwar generation of youth, educated under new values, begin to assert their leadership in the field of ideas.

RICHARD K. BEARDSLEY

Japan's Political System *

Of the several aspects of Japanese culture, none is so immediately related to problems of national stability, security, and well-being as the
political system. In the corporate makeup of a nation, political affairs
comprise much of the essential bone structure and the related nervous
and muscular systems. Government with its attendant functions is basic
to the existence of a nation, for it provides the "mechanisms for the
identification and posing of [national] problems and the making and
administering of decisions in the realm of public affairs." [1] It holds the
key to a nation's ability to meet the great crises which confront it from
time to time or to adjust itself to the more routine pressures of changing internal and external conditions.

The political system can be studied in many ways; and, in fact, most
of the social sciences are able to contribute in one way or another to
an understanding of the problems of institutional evolution, group
structure, decision making, and personal behavior which touch on the
realm of political affairs. The discipline which makes the study of political systems its special competence, however, is political science. And
just as the subject of politics yields to the methodology or special interests of a variety of disciplines, so also among political scientists does
one find a variety of approaches to the common subject matter of political affairs. One is always in danger of oversimplification or of misplaced
emphasis in any attempt to make a simple differentiation between types
of scholarly methodology, but it is useful to think of the work of the
political scientist as being divided along two sets of intersecting coordinates. Along one line we find at one end the historically minded
writers whose work is mainly description of past political events and of
the process of institutional evolution or of policy change in government.
At the other end are the scholars of political structure whose concern
is with the interrelated parts of the political system and their functional

* Lectures and writings of Robert E. Ward, in particular, have influenced the viewpoints in this chapter. The author gratefully acknowledges debt to Nobutaka Ike for
preparing a syllabus manuscript in this field.

1 Robert E. Ward and Roy C. Macridis (eds.) , Modern Political Systems: Asia, New
York, 1963, p. 8.

differentiation rather than with the way in which a system arrived at any particular form. Along the other line we have at one end the scholars (the vast majority, in fact) who are concerned with a single political system, as against those at the other end who indulge in comparative analogies between two or more systems.

Japan has received the attention of all types of political scientists both in the West and among the Japanese. It is probably true, however, that comparative assumptions have bulked large in any treatment of Japanese political affairs simply because of the historical circumstance which has made Japan a "developing" state in modern times and has placed its political development constantly in the shadow of Western norms. We might stop to think, for a moment, how different the writings on Japanese government would be were Japan the leading power of the modern world and the Japanese "Emperor system" the accepted ideal of political organization (as, in fact, the ultranationalists of the 1940s had hoped).

As one might expect, the literature on Japanese government and politics is particularly rich in historical and descriptive studies. Of these, the works of scholars in the Japanese faculties of law tended to be legalistic and narrowly confined to the study of formal administrative institutions. Interpretive studies of the political process have come more often from the pens of Western political scientists or historians with particular social interests. Prior to World War II and immediately thereafter these conditions produced two very marked currents of interpretation. Western scholars who had busily charted the course of political evolution of the new constitutional monarchy were much concerned over the strong authoritarian tendencies in Japanese government, the continuation of elitist and extralegal channels of influence, the "failure" of party government, and the upsurge of militarism. Japanese scholars were simultaneously writing about the absolutist nature of the Meiji state, the failure of the social revolution, the rise of fascism, and like undesirable features of the modern state. Obviously one group of scholars was holding up the model of liberal-democratic government, while the other was basing its criteria for judgment on the Marxist theory of stages of social development.

The work of political scientists in more recent years, particularly in the West, has by and large tried to avoid the use of particular political regimes or ideologies as models for comparative or analytical purposes. It has attempted instead to develop new and politically neutral conceptions of political organization and change. As in the field of economics, political scientists have divided their attention between the problems of development and those of structural and functional analysis. Japan has been studied from both of these points of view, since Japanese politics are still very much in the process of "modernization," yet at the same time the political process is sufficiently stable and complex to require the most sophisticated tools of cross-sectional analysis.

The developmental approach starts with two generalized political models representing "traditional" and "modern" systems and then seeks to understand the process of change which leads from the first to the second. The process may simply be talked of as "political modernization," or it may be discussed under such general conceptions as "transitional politics" or "nation building" or in terms of more limited problems of leadership, bureaucratization, "political socialization," and the like. Since the study of Japan's political modernization had received a considerable start prior to the end of World War II, at a time when the main models for comparison were drawn from existing European systems or from Marxist theory, the most recent impetus to developmental theory has tended to come from studies of the emerging nations of the postwar era.

The fact that Japan has lost her "underdeveloped" status among the nations of the world and that her early development took place in an environment which was neither colonial nor fraught with ideological conflicts between democracy and socialism has given her case a number of unique features. Developmental theory, especially of the recent nation-building variety, has consequently been of less than direct relevance. Conversely, the "Japanese lesson" in modernization seems almost as remote to the other nations of Asia as do the prior examples of the nations of Europe. Japan's experience in political modernization appears to be of a different order and style from that of the emerging nations today.

Of course this is true only in a relative sense, for in fact the Japanese of a century ago faced formidable problems of political and social organization very much on the order of those now confronting the new states of Asia and Africa. A recent study by members of the Committee on Comparative Politics of the Social Science Research Council of the process of political modernization in Japan and Turkey concludes that, though different in timing, circumstance, and political ingredients, the two cases showed significant similarities in the nature of the problems each faced and in the pattern by which these problems were solved.[2]

Students of political modernization have been less deeply concerned than economists, for instance, with the preconditions which appear to stimulate the conscious drive toward national self-assertion. The circumstances of "takeoff" have generally been too diverse for generalization and have been left to the explanations of the historian. The *process* of modernization is more amenable to generalization, however, and it has elicited a number of theories of wide applicability. The example of the colonial countries has given rise to the conception of "dual societies," in which the colonial rulers in control of a modern superstructure depend upon the continuation of the traditional society to maintain a political order. By analogy it has been possible to conceive of the modern political apparatus in Japan as having had an almost autonomous existence to which native practices had to be assimilated. Another pattern of modernization is seen in the example of China, which in its confrontation with the West struggled to protect its inner value system from contamination while admitting the necessity of emulating Western economic and political technology. Writers have discussed the tensions which marked the early phases of Japan's political modernization in terms of the dichotomy between Western science and Eastern values. But the Japanese never seemed to resist very hard or for very long the stimulus of Western examples. Thus, scholars these days are more apt to look upon the coexistence of a traditional political behavior and modern techniques as constituting a dynamic "reinforcing dualism" that furthers both stability and flexibility during the traumatic phase of transition politics.

Ward and Rustow have distilled from the comparative study of Japan and Turkey a remarkably useful typology for "late-developing" nations undergoing political modernization. Given certain conditions which permit political development, i.e., a social and institutional base of sufficient strength to maintain national order over the transition period and yet of sufficient flexibility to respond to the needs of modernization, they have described the problems which such nations must overcome before attaining a stable modern polity in the following terms: [3]

[2] Robert E. Ward and Dankwart A. Rustow (eds.), *The Political Modernization of Japan and Turkey*, Princeton, N.J., 1964.
[3] *Ibid.*, pp. 465-466.

The crisis of identity.
The crisis of security.
Problems of leadership and followership.
The crisis of economic development.
Problems of popular relationship to the political process.
  The crisis of integration.
  The crisis of penetration.
  The crisis of participation.
The crisis of output and distribution.

Reference to Chapter 3 will help to explain how Japan managed to meet each of these crises with remarkable directness, so that by 1890 the country was already on the way to solving its problem of economic development. If, then, we conceive of the World War II years as being characterized by an inadequate handling of the problems of economic distribution and popular relationship to government, we can look upon the postwar years, particularly after 1952, as bringing about the solution to these final problems of development. Following this approach, we shall expect the political condition of Japan today to reflect a prime concern with problems of output and distribution. The crises of identity and security and the struggle for the achievement of a viable nation structure and an adequate political machine have long since been faced. It is for these reasons that many political scientists today are inclined to leave to historians the first fifty years or so of Japan's modern political history and to immerse themselves in the complex problems of contemporary political organization. We need only remind ourselves that Japan is already on its second modern Constitution and hence its second modern political revolution. The political scientist finds more than enough scope for his inquiries within the context of the second of these revolutions. Japan has in fact come a long way from the initial confrontation with the crises of identity and security which are still troubling most of the emerging nations of the world today.

It is for this reason that we turn in this chapter to the structural analysis of contemporary Japanese politics rather than to the developmental story. The problems of "transition politics" are touched on in a number of parts of this book, under history, education, economics, and, to some extent, law and anthropology. We do not intend to play down the story of Japan's political modernization but wish, in the interests of methodological variety, to introduce an approach which has recently gained in popularity.

Structural analysis, to which so many political scientists are presently attracted, places the feet of the observer squarely in the present and attempts to assess the political system in terms of the universal need to achieve "more effective, more adaptive, more complex and more rationalized organizations." [4] Moreover, it conceives of the political system in the broadest terms and not simply those of government and state policy. Any society or the groups that compose it must reconcile differences of opinion, give attention to collective problems, and arrange to act on them, not only at moments of crisis, but in the routine operation of everyday affairs. All this activity is essentially political and, in sufficiently large and complex societies, requires a coordinated structure of mechanisms to ensure some coherence and unity of action. It is the task of the political scientist to isolate these mechanisms and discover how they originate, how they are related to the society as a whole, and how they function. Some of the structures or institutions by which societies handle public affairs appear as formal organs of government. Others are outside the government (e.g., political pressure groups) and range from formal organizations to vaguely defined bodies of people. Formerly, political science gave most of its attention to the organs of government and the exercise of power through them, but interest has now expanded, under the broader conception of politics, to the many informal and unofficial factors that affect each society's apparatus of decision in public affairs. To use an analogy, it is as if, to understand the output of a political or governmental machine (its performance as an apparatus for social decision), one were to study the materials and plan used to build it as well as the materials fed into it for processing.

To say that the structural-functional view is primarily contemporary in its focus does not mean that it restricts its data to current affairs. In fact, it incorporates into its particular way of looking at politics much of the content of the developmental approach. It must take up, to begin with, the historical heritage and ecological setting of a society, its socioeconomic organization, and its doctrines and value systems, but it does so with the intention of discovering the political import of these matters, which comprise the foundation or working environment of politics today. This approach involves also the study of parties, interest groups, and the structure of leadership in political affairs. It of course requires the examination of the organs of government proper and of the nature, quality, and effectiveness of the decisions that are taken by the collectivity. But it tries to bring to bear on these subjects special insights into the process whereby people in the contemporary world have effectively organized their political affairs.

What constitutes the "area of public affairs," who participates in decisions in this area, and how the resolution of interests is achieved

[4] Lucian W. Pye, *Politics, Personality, and Nation Building*, New Haven, Conn., 1962, p. 38.

are matters on which different societies rarely coincide. They may be considered to be determined in general by certain fundamental or historical factors in any individual society, together with the changes which are forced upon that society in the course of its history. Each political system, consequently, is unique, but there is nonetheless a chance of determining general principles that apply to the area of public affairs, problems that are common to all, and qualities that pertain to various categories of political science. Conversely, the use of such generalities to explain the operation of any given political system is the mark of the contemporary effort at political analysis.

Above all, the structural-functional approach eschews the question of whether a system is democratic or authoritarian, socialistic or imperialistic, but seeks its criteria of comparative judgment in the assessment of efficiency in functional terms. An efficient political system has an element of stability balanced against an element of change. To endure and operate efficiently it should respond to pressures from without and within, so as to meet new problems or changing conditions which may, in fact, even alter its structure and functions. Moreover, an effective modern political institution must set a context of acceptance and stability for such a response in order not to invite revolutionary groups to disrupt the system by violence. Twice in the past century, in Japan's case, radical pressure imposed on the political system has overtaxed the organs of government and forced their dismantling and rebuilding, once by groups within the society and once by an outside conquering power. Whether the apparatus for political decision in present-day Japan offers a sufficiently flexible response to existing pressures for change and sufficient stability to avoid another disruption is one of the chief problems calling for our examination in this chapter.

THE SETTING: FOUNDATIONS OF THE POLITICAL SYSTEM

Historical Setting

The political system of Japan, like any other, reflects its historical past and, increasingly in the modern era, the atmosphere created by events around the world. It must be seen in its historical context or setting. The present Japanese government is young, being based on the Constitution promulgated in 1946, after World War II, at the direction of an American-dominated Occupation. Because of its youth, it is regarded as still not fully tested, and its traditions as still being under formation. Yet the present system is not completely new, for it has built into its foundations many stones remaining from the edifice which housed the

Constitution promulgated in 1889 in the name of the absolute monarch, the Meiji Emperor who had been restored to authority in 1867. And this is not all. The Emperor who now is the symbolic head of state, Hirohito, is literally the descendant of the world's most ancient dynasty, which originated in hazy protohistoric times, probably within the first or second century A.D. Thus, the apparatus of state is a blend of the very youthful with the very old, showing in its operation a mingling of conservative forms and values with relatively chaotic and extreme behavior more characteristic of young regimes.

Historically, of course, it was the Tokugawa regime which provided the immediately premodern institutional background from which Japan's modern government emerged. The Tokugawa regime, as Chapters 3 and 11 remind us, had prepared a heritage of considerable proportions for its successor regimes. It drew all parts of Japan together under a single rule and held them together for 2½ centuries. Although the Tokugawa shoguns by no means headed a modern state but instead were "first among equals" in a land divided into many independent domains, their regime in time created a central bureaucracy of trained administrators to staff a wide variety of offices performing specific functions. In addition, each domain built up bodies of bureaucrats whose skills were to prove vital to the new imperial government after 1868. Thus the Tokugawa rulers, both central and local, had worked out methods for recruiting men of ability and for training successors to office, all without seriously compromising the basically contrary principle of birthright, which was the key to high position in a feudal system. The machinery of administration was carefully structured and effectively applied. Judicial precedent, as will be noted in Chapter 11, had begun to accumulate a body of law and practice, even though its application favored the elite. Such developments, within a government vastly unlike its successor, nonetheless gave substance to the administrative apparatus of the Meiji government that may have meant the difference between failure and success in coping with the critical problems of the new regime's first decades.

After forcing the overthrow of Tokugawa rule, the men who seized power intended little more at first than to nurture domestic welfare by restoring the Emperor's ancient supremacy while adding adequate protection against the new threat of foreign encroachment. To accomplish this double task of domestic reform and national defense, however, they found themselves driven to revolutionize the nation on many fronts. From key positions in the government, the "oligarchs," as they eventually came to be known, reached out actively into commerce, industry, education, religion, and even family structure, creating ministries,

435

bureaus, and other organs of state to deal with each of these sectors. They extended government into new areas, not simply to quench a thirst for power, but, step by forced step, as a means toward the goal of strengthening Japan's capacity for self-defense, freeing her of obnoxious treaties that gave extraterritorial rights to intruding nations, and dignifying her standing as a world power. Nevertheless, their actions did greatly enlarge the scope of public affairs and create new organs of government. By the time they finished, the product of their labor was a modern constitutional state which was able to preserve its main outlines even through the drastic reformation which was imposed upon it by the occupying powers after World War II.

The fact of continuity in no way constitutes a denial of far-reaching postwar change in the political system and its product. Among historical factors relevant to this change, some are of a quite general nature, but others are peculiar to Japan. As to the former, the postwar government was formed in a world environment quite different from that of the nineteenth century. Tokugawa Japan, committed to government by and for the elite 7 to 10 per cent of its population and mobilizing the rest only to provide rice rent and services, could not survive in an age of exploration and colonial empire building, whereas the Meiji nation-state, first gaining strength and firmness by authoritarian tactics that mobilized its entire population and then launching itself on colonial adventurism, echoed the prevalent nineteenth-century pattern of imperial statehood. By the mid-twentieth century, however, imperialism everywhere was retreating under calumny and attack and the world was applauding other state concepts, including the democratic, welfare-oriented state. Defeat and occupation by the Americans thus ensured that attempts at change would be toward a democratic pattern.

The present political system is often assumed to be primarily the result of Occupation policy. Yet the comparative stability which this system has manifested of late would hardly have resulted had not local and historical factors in Japan at the conclusion of the war proved receptive to radical change. Japan at the end of 1945 was in ruins, figuratively and literally, and in deep need of rebuilding. She had paid a high price to wage World War II. Some 46 per cent of her cities were blasted or burned, 20 per cent of her homes had vanished, and her industry was cut by 25 per cent or more. The wartime death toll was 1,800,000 persons. The overseas empire was a total loss. Japan had fallen to the status of a second- or third-class power, with as many enemies within her former Greater East Asian Co-Prosperity Sphere as outside it. Her people were wounded, confused, and deeply distrustful of the system that had brought them to catastrophe. They were ready to welcome the plans for "democratization" brought in by the Occupation forces.

Consequently a virtually free hand to experiment with directed social change was given to the Occupation, nominally comprising all the Allied Powers but in fact a creature of the United States. The first mandate of the Occupation was demilitarization. Taught a lesson by the failure of demilitarization without other supporting changes in Germany after World War I, the Occupation coupled demilitarization with decentralization and democratization.

Article 9 of the revised Constitution unconditionally renounced war as an instrument of national policy; this singularly explicit declaration of demilitarization has occupied the center of many a political storm since 1947, when the Constitution went into effect, without yet having been amended. Perhaps this provision, had it stood alone against subsequent events or pressures to resume prewar habits, would not still survive intact, but its purpose gained support from other measures. Article 9 often has been upheld or denounced as a symbol in the dissension between right and left, the real targets of attack being other parts of the network of changes brought about in Japanese society and government.

The Occupation implemented demilitarization as such by dismantling plants for military production and by conducting war crimes trials to purge militarists from positions of public authority. At the same time, it tried to awaken or strengthen the interest of groups that would constitute antimilitary clienteles by giving them a vested interest in new or revised institutions. For instance, it made a point of strengthening women's rights, of giving rural tenant farmers ownership of their land, and of guaranteeing labor the right to organize unions.

From the beginning, the Occupation had intended to revise the Japanese Constitution that dated from 1889, and when a completely new Constitution was drafted, the Occupation's foremost concern was to protect its provisions. This document was extraordinary and must be viewed against the particular historical background of the time. It was first drawn up in English, not in Japanese; hence its very wording embodies connotations that, although clear in the context of Anglo-American history, are at best cloudy in a Japanese milieu. It is a document that, beyond establishing the organs of government and their functions, purports to guarantee a long list of citizens' rights, legitimizes specific groups of interests, and provides for mass participation in public life. Its preamble, which begins "We the Japanese people," establishes political values which are not yet fully assimilated by the Japanese. The Constitution therefore deals with hopes for the future rather than just a pattern for the present, to an extent perhaps without parallel in such documents. Whether these provisions were efficient or realizable on the Japanese scene was a matter of secondary concern to the Occupation. It is of interest to us today to discover whether they were realistic from a functional point of view.

Yet this was not the end of Occupation influence upon Japanese political policy. In 1948, while Japan was still occupied and these initial reforms were yet being completed, the world situation brought about a marked shift in Occupation policy. The cold war was on, and a portentous reversal of the power balance was taking place in Asia. China, a strong partner of the United States and its Allies during World War II, was shortly to fall under a Communist regime, whereas Japan, the former enemy, suddenly emerged as a political bastion of the Western powers in the Far East. To realize this potential, the United States could no longer continue its 1946–1948 policy of stern discipline laced with punitive measures. The Occupation shifted its aims as the Asian continent was lost. (This trend was accentuated after the outbreak of the Korean conflict in 1950.) It muted the keynotes of its 1946–1948 policy—demilitarization, decentralization, democratization—and pulled out the stops on a new set: rehabilitation, relaxation of reform, and even rearmament. The Occupation now had to promote Japan's rapid recovery of economic strength and political stability to the point of concluding a final peace treaty. That meant slackening or removing its checkreins on any political and social forces in Japan that could be counted on to oppose Soviet plans for aggrandizement in the Far East, save for extremists who would undo all the gains of the preceding three years. Accordingly, the Occupation eased its manner, adopting an advisory and supervisory role from 1948 until its termination in 1952.

Summing up modern Japan's varying historical settings in terms of their influence on the political system, we find a clear theme of interplay between liberalizing and conservative influences. The former prevailed for relatively brief intervals, though long enough to change the course of development on several occasions, yet over the long haul liberalism has been a lesser force, just strong enough to check the conservative drift toward authoritarian rule. Between 1868 and 1881 pressure for liberalization forced the decision to create a constitutional monarchy; in the 1920s again, administrative scandal and economic crises led to a greater popular voice in government, symbolized by such changes as the adoption of universal manhood suffrage in 1925; finally, the brief but potent first three years of Occupation, from 1945 to 1948, were a period of liberal preeminence. But the pendulum swing toward conservatism filled the longer periods in between: from about

1882 to 1918, in the hypernationalist 1930–1945 period, and again in more muted tones since 1948. First the Meiji oligarchs, proud of their sense of mastery over the state they themselves had created, then the hypernationalists, drawing their heroes from the Japanese past, and, latterly, the well-connected leaders of the conservative Liberal Demo cratic Party have held leading roles longest in the political arena.

Geographic and Demographic Foundations

Placement on islands at the Pacific edge of Asia rather than among alien peoples in midcontinent has had an undeniable bearing on the shaping of the Japanese political system. Almost 100 miles of sea gap have freed Japan for most of her history from anxiety about aggressive neighbors and protected her from becoming multiracial, multilingual, or multicultural through population drift. Premodern Japanese rulers were blessed by geographic location with a high degree of external security. Had their frontiers been more vulnerable, perhaps the lengthy internal dissensions, such as marked Japan's political history through a long period up to the Tokugawa unification, would have been cut short; and "dual government," permitting a regent or a military house to hold administrative power apart from the legitimate Emperor, would have been impractical. Japan might then have had a series of dynasties, as did most continental peoples.

Speculations such as these are untestable and need not be discussed at length here; it is sufficient if, by merely looking at them in passing, we recognize that location has undoubtedly influenced political culture. Moreover, the influence of geography has differed sharply from one period to another. For example, in premodern agrarian periods before the population explosion Japan seemed a fertile enough land, its many mountains serving as convenient protective barriers for local territorial lords, whereas in modern Japan the mountains have become barriers to communication and have proved lamentably deficient in mineral resources; the relative lack of industrial raw materials has been one factor that has made Japan heavily dependent on foreign resources and foreign trade, with a consequent effect on her international political posture.

Demographic factors clearly have an impact on political and governmental decisions. Before World War II, for instance, the government adopted strong though contradictory population policies, favoring a high birthrate but claiming then to be driven by overpopulation to contest with other states for territorial acquisitions overseas. The fact that both policies were more or less spurious (other influences controlled the high

439

birthrate and kept emigration rates low, as far as can be seen) does not diminish the fact that demography was of political concern. Again, in the postwar period, the government's anxious promotion of economic growth to take care of the postwar population bulge may have been somewhat misplaced, for economic expansion has been such that labor shortages loom in a greater number of sectors of the economy than are threatened by labor surpluses. In any case, the demographic situation, whether correctly estimated in relation to the government or not, has prominently affected government action. Moreover, Japan's high population, approaching 100 million in the foreseeable future, must inevitably be weighed in the thinking about governmental support of social security, health or unemployment insurance, transportation improvement, and a host of other matters. For his part, finally, the elective official cannot be unaware or unconcerned about other demographic matters, such as migration into or out of his constituency or the shifting ratio of rural to urban voters within his district.

Social Foundations

The characteristics of Japanese culture and society set a great many of the fundamental problems with which the political system must deal. There is space here to discuss only certain features of special political import as examples. To start with, the homogeneity of the Japanese ethnic and cultural tradition (see Chapter 2) is reflected in a sense of community interests uniting people comfortingly behind their leaders in facing the outside world. Japan has not known historically, nor does it experience today, great conflicts of interest arising from differing ethnic or cultural backgrounds. On the other hand, with respect to domestic policies, only recently has geographic and social mobility become intense enough to erode long-standing regional sentiments and reduce the gulf between upper and lower social classes; and it is still sometimes to the politician's interest to play on regional and class sentiments and keep them alive in the face of forces that tend to diminish them.

But if the Japanese "voting public" is comparatively homogeneous, it is also affected by the usual repertory of differing pressures and interests. There is a 97.8 per cent rate of literacy and wide saturation of newspapers, magazines, and radio-television broadcasting, in addition to one of the world's fullest systems of schools and universities, as a result of which most Japanese are exposed to a great deal of information about the world and about public affairs in Japan. The public, whether intensely interested or not in political information, has wide general access to such information. One consequence is that the government can use the facilities, if it so chooses, to inform the electorate of its policies. Another, arising especially from the many American television programs regularly run in Japan, is that Japanese of all localities and all ages see with their own eyes enough of the "affluent society" to bring quite concrete and specific expectations into the voting booth.

The prevalent condition of life for the average Japanese has also changed considerably in recent years. Urbanization, steadily increasing for more than a century, is now passing the 70 per cent mark. Only about one-quarter of the total labor force is primarily employed in agriculture, forestry, and fishing, while in the cities themselves a shift is occurring from manufacturing to service occupations. These shifts accompany growing freedom of social mobility for persons with talent and energy and obviously or subtly affect public attitudes on a multitude of matters. The average Japanese is being cut away increasingly from traditional or habitual expectations about his life and hence is apt to be less automatic in his political beliefs or behavior.

A remarkable overall rise of national income, totaling approximately 237 per cent (after allowance for inflation) between 1948 and 1962, has brought much improvement of living standards in the countryside as well as in the cities, and this too has its political significance. If, as is now supposed, Japan has evolved a "consumer economy," the government, claiming credit for its policies aimed at economic development, can expect to benefit by the new public confidence generated by this good living. For its part, the government has inaugurated several important public assistance and social insurance programs, as well as medical treatment and health insurance. These programs are evidence of an upswing in policies concerning the public weal, though their deficiencies still bring them under critical fire. What is at least as significant is that certain extensive sectors of the population still have little share in these gains: small and medium businessmen, workers classed as "temporary employees," the teaching profession, and farmers are among the less fortunate. Until now, major political parties have not concentrated their efforts on getting support from these groups or ministering to their discontent, no doubt because such groups have not yet become vociferous. Thus, there remain danger spots and incentives to political extremism in the midst of a general atmosphere of apparent well-being.

As one might expect in a country which has undergone so many drastic changes in recent years, differences in political outlook between generations are marked, though they become less pronounced as one moves upward from the middle range of education and income. Well more than half of Japan's university students, by most estimates, support political parties and programs of the left, and Marxist extremism characterizes the two large student and teacher organizations, the National Student Federation (Zengakuren) and the Japanese Teachers Union (Nikkyōso). Because students of less militant opinions rarely have their political views reflected in the press, their proportion is hard to estimate, yet almost any youth group of high school age or above, when polled, shows markedly stronger "progressive" opinions than do older persons. In the past it has been common that with maturation and job or family responsibilities, youthful dissenters have tended to conform to the way of thinking of their elders, but many elders today fear that the sobering effect of such responsibilities will not be enough to cancel out the allegedly demoralizing influences of the reformed postwar educational system. It is still too early to be sure, but as yet voting patterns have shown no marked shift to the left as new cohorts reach voting age.

The problem of making correlations between social background and political behavior is now complicated by the mobility of Japanese society. Class structure is difficult to characterize succinctly, for it is undergoing rapid mutation; so its bearing on the political system is complex and not a little puzzling. Until the war almost unquestioned prestige was conferred on the descendants of premodern and early modern elite groups; although such prestige still exists in traditional sectors of the country, even there it must compete with the prestige carried by others by virtue of professional or technical skill or wealth. Whereas the former may hold conservative political sympathies, the latter are apt to have a progressive leaning. This trend is even more marked among the newly rising "middle class" of salaried workers, who, especially in larger companies, may vote Socialist in greater numbers than the wage workers of their companies and certainly are less conservative than upper executives.

Ideological Foundations

The views of the Japanese on the world, their society, and themselves as participants in political affairs are far from fitting one mold, yet it is possible to identify certain prevalent attitudes toward such important matters as legitimacy in government, the concept of national identity, and the accepted patterns of participating in the political process. The last 100 years have brought many cycles of profound change in these attitudes.

As to legitimacy, any government that hopes to achieve stability without the constant exercise of force must claim rightful existence on some basis that is acceptable to the whole society. When the Tokugawa regime toppled in 1868, for instance, in large part through its failure to handle economic and military problems, those who took over did in fact develop more effective policies for these problems, yet their most effective rallying cry was not the promise to manage the economy better but the assertion of their intention to restore the Emperor as the rightful leader of Japan. The phrase *sonnō jōi* (revere the emperor, expel the foreigner) was an appeal to traditional legitimacy. Obviously, legitimation of rule in the person of the Emperor was of prime importance to the new Japanese state, and it was so treated in the Meiji Constitution and again half a century later, when the Allies, to make sure that formal surrender and submission to the Occupation would not be repudiated and resisted by the people, determined to maintain the Emperor as the recognized symbol of state. Nonetheless, by 1946 it appeared feasible to invoke a different principle: the "social contract" (as Jean Jacques Rousseau named it), whereby government is conceived to exist by virtue of a tacit agreement with each individual governed. While the Emperor remained as a tangible rallying point for his people, he was declared in the new Constitution to "derive his position from the will of the people with whom resides sovereign power" (Article 1). Insofar as this principle enjoys a measure of acceptance in Japan today, it demonstrates that governmental legitimacy is an issue subject to change along with the changing values of the society. Yet legitimacy through popular sovereignty is not a concept that is readily understood by the majority of the Japanese or fully believed in by those in power.

The unity of the Japanese people under the Emperor in the nineteenth and twentieth centuries was reinforced by strong feelings of nationalism. In Europe, nationalists sometimes were commoners in revolt against irresponsible aristocratic regimes (as in France or Germany) or sometimes were subject peoples in rebellion against alien masters (as within the Hapsburg or Ottoman empires); in either case, their assertion of the right of a homogeneous people to unified self-government could be realized only by shattering an earlier regime. But the Japanese already had their autonomy, and their nationalists sought not to upset the regime but to support it against the outer world, first to repel would-be foreign aggressors and later to venture out into the competition for empire. What made their resemblance to nationalists elsewhere strong was their sense of striving upward from a position of inferiority to attain their rightful international standing. For this they were prepared to accede to the government's demand for loyalty, disciplined industry, and the sacrifice of individual wants. In postwar years, the nationalist spirit flickers only weakly and in isolated individuals or small groups; it is yet early to forecast its extinction, however, until the arrival of a test, such as a crisis thrust on Japan from the outside. that might revive it. The strong feeling of national identity and the desire to excel has continued to characterize the Japanese people, but the experiences of the war have caused them to react violently against the "flag-waving" style of national pride.

No simple generalization as to how the typical Japanese views his relation to government will fairly fit the present situation. The present condition guarantees a wide range of civil rights, some more nearly ideal than realizable, and provides for universal adult suffrage and the secret ballot, but in practice much flux and ambivalence remain since the drastic reworking of the political system during the Occupation period. Traditionally, governmental prerogatives were permitted to override the rights of groups and individuals. Several features of the republican political system or of the democratic philosophy of government had absolutely no basis in Japanese political tradition. Parliamentary representation, the use of the ballot, and the organization of parties were all alien to the Japanese until after 1868, though they are now accepted as part of the habitual system of political expression. There are now more numerous signs of pluralist views, which deny exclusive or supererogatory authority to the government on important questions, but neither the citizen nor the official easily finds a position for government other than at the peak of hierarchical authority. Government, for instance, does concern itself with public welfare, but its bureaucrats administer welfare measures more nearly as paternalistic guides or directors than as servants of the people. Thus there is still little disposition to call policy makers or administrators to account as stewards of a program; as professionals, they are conceded to be the best judges of their programs, and the citizen's function in exercising his franchise is to select the professional who seems well connected and best attuned to his wants and then leave to this expert the function of choosing among programs and ways of implementing them.

If the use of the ballot as a means of popular participation in government is still not fully assimilated into Japanese political practice, neither are open debate over issues and the resolution of conflicts over policy by majority decision. In government, decisions are arrived at among professionals, whether bureaucrats or politicians, more often by consensus (the traditional Japanese method) than by adversary debate aimed at winning majority support. These consensus decisions are a collective product that tends to obscure the responsibility of particular persons for particular policies and thus to inhibit the open expression of individual leadership. Since small confidence is reposed in the principle of majority decision after open debate, minorities face the choice of

444

settling for fringe compromises, meekly capitulating in consensus, or protesting against the "tyranny of the majority." In critical disagreements, this protest may still break out into violence. In the abstract, the public deplores violence, yet in particular cases the culprit who is unswervingly sincere or who repents his rash action finds a measure of forgiveness even among the opposition.

In sum, few citizens feel an impassioned responsibility for politics; their tendency is to leave matters to the professionals, at least between elections. Having voted for the man rather than for his program, most electors not wedded to an ideology make few demands for farsighted policy or strong leadership; hence, few candidates work hard to present an image of statesmanship or develop a stand on many issues but, instead, deal pragmatically with issues apt to gain their reelection on the basis of personal connections and compromise. It is probably in the attitude toward government and political leaders and in the practice of political decision making that some of the greatest contrasts between politics in Japan and in the United States are to be found. And these contrasts provide political scientists with constant substance for discussion as to their meaning and whether or not the remnants of traditional political behavior in Japan should be deplored or accepted as inevitable or desirable.

POLITICAL INPUT:
HOW PERSONS AND PROBLEMS
ENTER THE POLITICAL PROCESS

The Election Process

SUFFRAGE. Japan's political system since 1889, being that of a constitutional monarchy with an elected Diet, has made the electoral system one of the prime methods by which the individual citizen has been given a public voice in government. Despite anti-Establishment criticism that the government has been slow in meeting the desires of the people for an expanded and politically significant vote, it is also true that there has been a steady expansion of the electorate since the first election in 1890. At that time the lower house was elected by male citizens twenty-five years of age or over who had paid ¥15 in land tax (for one year) or in income tax (for three years) and who had resided in the electoral district for at least one year. Only about 450,000 persons, or 1 to 2 per cent of the population, comprising mainly large landowners and some businessmen, met these qualifications. Restrictions, especially in tax qualifications, were gradually relaxed under pressure from urban districts and business interests, and the domination of the landowning interest in the Diet was overcome by amendments to the Election Law in 1900 and 1919. In 1925, universal manhood suffrage gave all males twenty-five years of age and older (excepting soldiers, indigents, and some others) the right to vote; any male thirty years of age or older was eligible for office. More than 13 million persons (about 20 per cent of the population) were entitled to vote in the election of 1928. The next large increase in the electorate occurred in 1945, when women first won the right to vote and the age limit dropped to twenty years. Qualified voters now comprise more than 50 per cent of the population.

Expansion of the electorate, along with other changes, has given elections growing importance in the political system. Besides making politicians in general more sensitive to public opinion, it has opened the way for proletarian political parties avowedly dedicated to the cause of depressed classes. Moreover, whereas elected representatives, comprising the lower house prior to 1946, did not control major decisions, these representatives, now comprising the entire Diet, are designated in the constitution as "the sole law-making organ of the state" (Article 41). Initiative and referendum rights in local and national government in theory give additional scope to the power of the voting public. In practice, nonetheless, the Diet is overshadowed by the bureaucracy in initiating and framing legislation; and, as noted above, representatives are rarely responsible to their constituents for definite positions on specific matters. In rural constituencies, especially, office seekers come to terms less often with individual voters than with local bosses or persons of influence, who control blocs of votes in return for parceling out patronage to faithful persons or neighborhoods.

THE ELECTORAL SYSTEM. The strength of the individual voter is greatly affected by the way districts and constituencies are set up. Let us examine for illustrative purposes national elections for the House of Representatives. Election districts in Japan have varied in size from time to time, being small and numerous under the 1899 law (257 districts) and again in 1919 (454 districts) and large in 1900 (97 districts) and 1945 (53 districts). The present districting, of medium size with 118 districts, provides for the election of 467 members of the House of Representatives. Each district sends 3 to 5 representatives (except that the Amami Islands send only 1), yet each constituent has but a single vote to cast. To be elected, a candidate must be among the top 3 to 5 in the number of votes polled, depending on the size of the district. This system, a multimember-constituency system, tends to favor the majority party, while a proportional-representation (multivote) system would give greater advantage to minor parties.

Different features of this system cause dissatisfaction on different sides, so that efforts to change it since its adoption in 1947 and confirmation in 1950 have all failed. For instance, the conservative Liberal Democrats would prefer smaller districts, while Socialists would gain more from larger ones. However viewed, the system gives rise to unusual problems. Should too many candidates be entered by the campaign manager of one party in a race in his district, the spread of votes may weaken the position of all, whereas if too few candidates are entered, they may pull enough excess votes to have elected still another candidate. In the first case, a weaker party's candidate may squeeze into a winning position because the opposition manager's optimism split the stronger party's strength too finely; in the second, his caution will give a seat away to a weaker party's candidate by default. This dilemma cannot rise in a single-member–constituency system like ours; the multi-member system also discourages running a very strong candidate teamed with weaker ones from the same party, for this would mean that the popular man would hurt the others by drawing off more votes than he actually needed for election. This compromise system operates inherently to the disadvantage of strong candidates and strong, disciplined parties, since it requires competition among members of the same party.

Reapportionment of representatives has not taken place since 1947, although the country has experienced large-scale population shifts, particularly into urban areas. Cities had not yet recovered their wartime evacuees in 1947, and they have since received a large influx of migrants into their industries and businesses, sometimes doubling in the 1950–1960 decade while rural election districts showed almost no change. Since no reallocation of seats in the lower house has been made to reflect these changes, there are such gross inequalities of the sort familiar in American state legislatures that metropolitan areas are seriously underrepresented. One vote in a rural election district near Kobe, for instance, is worth about three votes in Kobe's election district itself. Failure to reapportion has not been an oversight, of course. The conservatives, now holding a comfortable majority in the House of Representatives, have their main strength in rural districts, where any change would jeopardize their advantage, and so have no intention of permitting such a change in the Election Law.

The upper house, or House of Councilors, of the Diet consists of 250 members who are elected, but on a basis different from the representatives. In the nation at large 100 members are elected; the remaining 150 are elected from the forty-six prefectures, each of which returns 2 to 8 members.

Local government consists of two levels, prefectures and municipalities (cities, towns, and villages). The governors and assemblies of prefectures and the mayors and assemblies of municipalities all stand for public election. Prior to the postwar period, a large proportion of local government offices, as well as membership in the upper house of the Diet, was appointive and out of reach of the voting public. Thus the postwar reforms extended by a considerable degree the operation of the electoral process in an effort to make government more "responsible."

VOTER PARTICIPATION. Voting is made easy by the automatic registration of qualified voters. Even so, the Japanese record of participation in elections is very high. In 1961, 56,600,000 persons (more than 60 per cent of the population) were entitled to vote. Six national elections between 1949 and 1960 drew 73.5 to 76.9 per cent of all qualified voters. These rates compare more than favorably with recent American national elections, in which 60 to 64 per cent of all registered voters got to the polls. Rural voters in Japan, with rates of 80 or 81 per cent, outdo urban voters, whose rates drop to 66 to 74 per cent. It is interesting to note that, whereas normally in the United States national elections draw the greatest numbers of voters, it is normal in Japan for local elections to draw even greater numbers than general elections, rising from 85 to 95 per cent in both city and rural localities. While this high rate can be taken as evidence that Japanese, in line with a long tradition, still generally consider their personal interests to be most significantly tied to their local communities, it is also true that personal obligations to candidates are apt to stir voters to participate. Country people vote at the highest rates, partly from a sense of duty to help their community make a good showing in public; the high rate is no proof of their greater personal interest in formal politics. Conversely, city voters have tended to turn their interests from local to national elections as the realization that the latter can exert a significant impact on local welfare has gradually grown.

Political Parties

Political parties in Japan have existed since as early as 1874, and the present conservative party (Liberal Democratic, or Jiyū Minshutō) has an ancestry dating from the early 1880s, if one allows for periods of suppression of parties (1884–1889, 1940–1945), while its principal rival, the Socialist Party (Shakaitō), can be traced similarly at least from 1925. Thus, party organization was not innovated during the Occupation. But since World War II parties have had much stronger status and functions than before, when they fought against odds to justify their existence as anomalies in an authoritarian government, competing against each other in the House of Representatives, where they could exert little more than negative effect on the affairs of state. In the postwar climate, by contrast, in which an important amount of governmental action issues from the new House of Representatives, parties play a significant and positive role.

It is a bit unfair or misleading, however, to view Japanese political parties with some of the presuppositions derived, say, from American party behavior. First, there is an entirely different relative balance; Japan's party system is neither a two-party system nor a multiparty system in the usual sense, for through its various advantages the conservative Liberal Democratic Party enjoys persistent and strong preeminence over all others. In national elections since 1947 this party has consistently won 60 per cent or more of the total vote for seats in the House of Representatives and controlled slightly less than two-thirds of the seats in the House of Councilors. Conservative strength is even greater at the levels of the prefectures and municipalities. In both local and national elections, a good many candidates run as independents but must be classed with the conservatives, so that actual conservative strength includes virtually the entire percentage of votes or seats not won by opposition parties, most of which are of progressive or left-wing affiliation. These progressive parties have shared about 25 to 39 per cent of the votes (19 to 35 per cent of the seats) in the House of Representatives, never more than 25 per cent of the votes (22 per cent of the seats) in the prefectural assemblies, and only 13 per cent of the votes (5 per cent of the seats) in the municipalities. It is true that progressive strength has gradually been curving upward at each of these levels, yet these several parties are far from offering a serious challenge to the majority position of the conservatives, particularly since their attempts to form coalitions have been unsuccessful and they are split as far apart from each other as they are from the conservatives. As the Japanese say in wry jest about their postwar party situation, it is a "1½-party system."

A second presupposition about parties in the United States that fits Japan even more poorly is that parties are organizations of the voting public. No Japanese party is a mass-membership party. The Liberal Democratic Party, claiming a registered membership of about 1,500,000 in 1959, is believed by most observers to have much fewer members, perhaps 300,000. This membership is very active only during campaigns; at other times, the branches that are claimed to exist in 54 per cent of the local municipalities are mostly dormant. The Socialist Party's membership reportedly totals about fifty thousand, organized in less than one-third of the cities, towns, villages, and districts. Membership in the Communist Party may rise to about ninety thousand (it maintains both registered and nonregistered members; so its membership is especially difficult to estimate). These totals indeed form a small proportion of the electorate. In fact, it would be no great exaggeration to say that professional politicians and administrators comprise most of the membership of Japan's political parties; the parties are consequently more in the nature of parliamentary parties operating mainly in Tokyo. The usual voter, like a bettor at a horse race, may take a more or less keen interest in the fortunes of contenders running under the "colors" of a party but hardly considers himself a fellow member.

A third misleading presupposition based on American experience is that a political party is a cohesive organization. Formal organization does exist in Japan but rather as a façade; the reality for most parties lies in clusters of political factions—evanescent and shifting, as personal affiliations are made or broken—that confederate for convenience and visibility under a party banner. The bonds between clusters are loose and fragile; so the major parties have a complicated history of splitting and recombining under various names that makes it difficult (and not entirely realistic) to trace back any party as if it were a coherent and durable organized entity. Within both of the main parties, the Liberal Democrats and the Socialists, there is much disagreement on major features of policy and program. The Liberal Democrats tend toward pragmatic, professional politics rather than toward either a clear stand on basic issues or a clear ideology; the Socialists are strongly ideological and share a great deal of theory but split on many questions of translating theory into practice.

To perceive reasons for this instability, it is helpful to study the history of parties. The earliest organizations that might be given such a name were a few discussion groups of intellectuals in the formative period of the new Meiji government; if they can be called parties, it is because their members wanted them to serve the people in exercising some voice in government. In 1881, Itagaki Taisuke organized the Liberal Party (Jiyūtō), espousing popular sovereignty, and Ōkuma Shigenobu formed the Reform Party (Kaishintō), advocating government by a constitutional monarchy. Though each had a political platform, these parties were primarily the personal followings of the two leaders and were formed mainly with the pragmatic intention of gaining entrance into government. Such political parties were used as a wedge to break the Satsuma-Chōshū monopoly of high office in government and were joined mainly by opposition groups. Both for this reason and because of the implicit role of parties as instruments for giving the populace a voice in government, they were viewed with distaste and suspicion by the autocratic oligarchs of the government. The two original parties nonetheless developed a technique of obstruction, through negative action on budgets and no-confidence votes, that by 1896 made the government tempt them to come to terms by offering positions to their leaders. Meanwhile, at local levels, parties exercised some influence by moving members into bureaucracies. Thus, before 1900 the pattern was set of parties as harassing forces primarily loyal to a particular leader whose rank rivaled that of the oligarchs but who was usually at odds with the governing cliques (even though the leader might participate in a coalition government).

Party leaders comprised only one of several leadership groups: (1) civilian oligarchs of the government, (2) professionalized military leaders, (3) occupants of the higher ranks of the bureaucracy, (4) leaders of big business (*zaibatsu*), (5) the hereditary peerage, and (6) political party leaders. The Constitution of 1889 clearly limited their role in the House of Representatives. The other groups in government (except for the *zaibatsu*, who were more indifferent to politics) were unitedly opposed to any significant extension of party power. Nonetheless, the party leaders, speaking for "the people" in a national and international climate of rising political expectations, exploited their limited role to such good effect that they won increasing power. From 1924 to 1932, the power of political parties was high enough to call forth the belief that parliamentary government was winning over authoritarian rule. Yet, as Professor Ward observes: [5]

> . . . it would be a serious error to regard this as a triumph of "liberalism". The programs and performance of the parties that achieved a brief victory in the late twenties were not very liberal by either American or Japanese standards. Ideologically, these parties were quite conservative. They were much more interested in achieving and exploiting power than in implementing democratic policies, either domestically or in foreign relations. They produced few outstanding leaders and, by neglecting or outraging major sections of Japanese public opinion, they contributed to the authoritarian resurgence of the thirties.

Under the "authoritarian resurgence" that led from the assassination of Prime Minister Inukai Ki (Tsuyoshi) on May 15, 1932, through increasingly regimented years to crushing military defeat in 1945, Japan became totalitarian in its political structure but had no parallel to the Nazi or Fascist parties of Germany or Italy. Party power was increasingly repressed, and the parties themselves were forcibly dissolved in the active war period between 1940 and 1945. The Imperial Rule Assist-

[5] Ward and Macridis, *op. cit.*, p. 29.

ance Association (Taisei Yokusankai), which was organized by Premier Konoe Fumimaro to replace the parties, was not a party in even the broadest sense. Rather, it served as a mechanism for regimenting political figures of all types under government control. Thus the evolution of the parties was cut short at the still relatively youthful stage reviewed above, and it is hardly surprising that their postwar character, even in a situation of greatly expanded power, bears the stamp of this heritage rather than conformance to the structure and function of parties in one or another of the nations of Europe or America.

LIBERAL DEMOCRATIC PARTY (JIYŪ MINSHUTŌ). This party, of a conservative orientation, was amalgamated in 1955 from the Liberal and the Democratic parties. As noted before, it is more or less a parliamentary party with rather modest and mainly professional membership even though it is well experienced in sweeping the winning places at the polls. Centered in Tokyo, it has as its officers leading professional politicians; the office of president usually is held by the Prime Minister. A party congress meeting in Tokyo selects officers and wields ultimate authority, though a Diet delegation, or caucus of members holding seats in both houses, is influential. The party, especially through its Political Research Committee, sets its policies and uses the delegations in the Diet to implement them in legislation, enforcing almost automatic voting conformance on matters agreed on in party circles, under threat of expulsion to rebels.

Its finances are more a matter of speculation than of knowledge, but there is no doubt that large sums are consumed, especially in election campaigns. Reports filed as required by law reveal that contributions in 1958 totaled more than ¥2.37 billion ($6.6 million); a higher rate was reported for the first half of 1959, an election year. Some 60 per cent was received in contributions from business firms at ¥10 million or more each. Outside observers differ in speculating about the amount of support received in addition, either in covert fund raising by the party or in support of individual campaigners or factions; this sum is perhaps as much again as the declared receipts. The conservative party is popularly regarded as wealthy through its close connections with big business. There certainly is justification for both parts of this view: financial means appear to surpass those of other parties (one estimate is that Liberal Democratic expenditures on the 1960 general election campaign amounted to ¥10 million per candidate), and both the party and its members get business support, especially from the *zaibatsu*. The further assumption, however, that big business is concerted and homogeneous in its political interests is surely oversimplified.

Being a loose coalition of factions held precariously together for campaign and legislative strategy, the Liberal Democratic Party itself is less homogeneous than is implied by the foregoing summary of organization. At least eight major factions composed of sixteen to fifty-five persons each were identifiable in 1962, each willing and anxious to have its leader supplant Ikeda Hayato as Prime Minister and party president. The delicate balance of power among these factions, reflected in compromise appointments to office and compromise policies, makes each faction leader an important person. Since four or five must agree in order to carry any important decision, dissidence among factions cannot be ignored. Consequently, most important matters are decided on the basis of complicated compromises, which by fully satisfying no one leave the party in a constant state of precarious adherence to its policies.

Analysis of the social and professional backgrounds of 298 Liberal Democrats holding seats in the lower house of the Diet in 1958–1959 provides additional insight into the character of party leadership.[6] These men were professionals, elected to the same office for an average of 4.6 terms. Their average age was fifty-seven years; 81 per cent were college graduates, of whom half were from national or public universities or colleges, especially Tokyo University. More than half of the total (52 per cent) had business backgrounds, usually of an executive nature, while only 19 per cent claimed backgrounds in agriculture—an interestingly negative correlation with the party's sources of voting support, in which the rural share is high. Previous careers as bureaucrats were recorded for 26 per cent. Many were experienced officeholders at lower levels: in prefectural assemblies (18 per cent) or at the city, town, and village level (26 per cent).

These findings throw some explicit light on characteristics often alleged in more general and sweeping terms. Liberal Democratic Party leaders do, indeed, have strong personal associations with business. The allegation that excessive weight in party councils is carried by ex-bureaucrats of an age to have been made authoritarian and reactionary through prewar experience can be supported in some measure from these figures, but interpretation should also take into account the fact that a law-enforced retirement age in the postwar bureaucracy stimulates a drift of retired bureaucrats into elective politics without discernible selection as to political persuasion or temperament.

By American standards, the program of the Liberal Democratic Party as of the early 1960s was not notably conservative but had a clearly pragmatic character, suitably vague at many points. Its compromise

6 Data on Liberal Democrats and Socialists are based primarily on Robert A. Scalapino and Masumi Junnosuke, *Parties and Politics in Contemporary Japan*, Berkeley, Calif., 1962, pp. 161–177.

character and its missions reflected internal as well as external strategies of expediency. The program stressed, with pride, the party's role in maintaining prosperity and called for an annual economic growth rate of 9 per cent (tied to a policy of doubled national income between 1960 and 1970 enunciated by Prime Minister Ikeda); it paid heed to public welfare and called for a scheme of road construction. Most open to attack from the Socialist side was the party's full support of the United States–Japan Mutual Security Treaty, of close association with the United States, of a pro-Western international policy, and of the establishment of political neutrality in the public schools and universities.

JAPANESE SOCIALIST PARTY (NIHON SHAKAITŌ). Only since 1945 have parties of the left been significantly strong in Japan, but in this period they have formed the major opposition to conservative coalitions and even briefly (1947–1948) put their leader, Katayama Tetsu, into the Prime Minister's Office at the head of a weak coalition Cabinet. Centered in Tokyo like the conservative party, the Socialist Party is a coalition since 1955 of formerly separate right-wing and left-wing factions. The chairman of the Central Executive Committee (in place of a president) is head of the party. An annual congress charged with setting basic party policies dependably provides a more vitriolic show than the Liberal Democratic Party congress, for the strong doctrinal commitment of both wings of the party (or of all five main factions) repeatedly forces a debate on whether the party should stand for class interests instead of national interests, what relation it should develop with the workers' unions, and other long-range issues. Members who hold seats in the Diet are rigidly obliged to vote in conformance with party policy on matters on which policy has been established.

Less opulent than the Liberal Democratic Party, the Socialist Party reported contributions and campaign expenditures of barely more than one-tenth of the amount reported for the same period (1958–1960) by the conservatives. According to the report, following a major contribution (¥21.3 million) from the General Council of Trade Unions (Sōhyō), there were large contributions of ¥3 million to ¥5.3 million, but 47 per cent of all contributions were in much smaller amounts. Estimates of campaign expenditures in 1960 fell near ¥2.5 million per candidate. Although some businesses do contribute to both the Socialist and the Liberal Democratic parties, the Socialists hope to regularize individual membership fees, failing which their financial position must be considered precarious.

Owing to factional divisions, the Socialist Party has an uncertain orientation and leadership, though it has achieved the reputation of being the "most Socialist" of all such parties in the world, and doctrinal issues most often form the basis of the splits among its factions.

Social and professional backgrounds reported by 168 Socialists holding seats in the Diet furnish a composite picture quite in contrast at key points to that of the Liberal Democrats reviewed above. They, too, were professionals but with a lower average tenure of office (3.8 terms). Their average age was fifty-two; 62 per cent were college graduates, about half from national universities but fewer from Tokyo University than was the case with the Liberal Democrats. Only 18 per cent had business backgrounds, 10 per cent came from agriculture (e.g., as leaders of cooperative associations), and 50 per cent reported union backgrounds. Only 4 per cent had previous careers as bureaucrats. Roughly comparable to that of the Liberal Democrats was the amount of previous elective officeholding at lower levels (27 per cent in prefectural assemblies or in cities, towns, and villages). This professionalized body is clearly linked more closely with labor than with business, in contrast with the Liberal Democrats. Yet, as is clear from their reported college training, the Socialist leaders are by no means workers who have risen through shops, factories, and mines; rather, they are professional, educated spokesmen for masses whose life experiences are very different from their own.

Although domestic policies opposed to big business and solicitous of small businessmen and low-income groups are part of the Socialist platform, greater stress has been laid on the foreign planks of their platform, which oppose Japan's pro-United States and pro-Western stance and favor a "positive neutralism." The latter position calls for at least the abrogation of the United States–Japan Mutual Security Treaty, the withdrawal of United States Armed Forces, and measures of disarmament. The party wants closer relations with the Chinese People's Republic and the U.S.S.R. Placed in direct opposition to the Liberal Democratic government on all these foreign-policy issues, the Socialists have felt driven to mass demonstrations, riots, and violence that have attracted worldwide attention to their confrontation and brought not a little criticism for their tactics.

JAPANESE DEMOCRATIC SOCIALIST PARTY (NIHON MIN-SHU SHAKAITŌ). Briefer mention may be made of this party, a right-wing Socialist splinter from the main Socialist Party that was formed in 1960, although it has attracted the interest of American students of politics both because of its moderate stance and because of its promise of developing a pragmatic program focused more strongly on issues than on doctrine (as with the Socialists) or on tactics for garnering power (as with the Liberal Democrats). It is organized much like the Socialist Party. With experienced politicians at the core, its candidates were somewhat better financed than the Socialists in 1960 (an estimated ¥5 million was spent for the average candidate). The party leans on the moderate labor groups. Its leadership has fewer members with union and college backgrounds and a higher proportion of former elective officials from lower levels. The party program strikes a moderate note between those of the two larger parties, eschewing neutralism but seeking the modification of the United States–Japan Mutual Security Treaty in foreign policy and the implementation of socialism for the masses, not merely the working class, in domestic policy.

Beginning with 40 seats shared among its members just before the 1960 election, the Democratic Socialist Party had a serious setback, winning only 17 seats from that election. Its future looked insecure and was not brightened in the 1960 local elections, in which, from having a grip on 135 out of 2,657 seats in the forty-six prefectures, the party dropped to 86 out of 2,688 seats. It remains to be seen whether the party, having neither the vested electoral strength of the conservatives nor the aggressive and even flamboyant image of the Socialists, will thrive in the long run.

OTHER POLITICAL PARTIES. The Japanese Communist Party, readmitted to legal existence with other parties in 1945, has continued to run candidates in every general election since then. These candidates drew 3 to 4 per cent of the total vote and have been able to occupy up to 4 seats in the lower house. The party thus has no significant strength in elective assemblies, national or local, yet by infiltrating its members into influential positions in unions and other organizations it gains indirect but noteworthy power. Very tightly organized, it has a party congress, but final authority is wielded by its Central Committee. It maintains both registered and nonregistered memberships, thought to total about ninety thousand today, a drop from its postwar peak of 100,000. The party is financed by undisclosed means, generally assumed to include some Soviet and Chinese support; in 1960, it spent a roughly estimated ¥1 million per candidate. Its program, along the Socialist line but more extreme, is especially marked by anti-American features.

The situation of extreme political ferment immediately following the war, when 363 "parties" participated in the 1946 election, has calmed down greatly. The great bulk of these parties have gone out of existence. Apart from a considerable number of candidates who run as independents (many of them of a conservative character, as has been noted, but separated from the Liberal Democratic Party for tactical reasons), however, certain candidates at national or local levels are supported by nationalist or other more or less extreme groups.

Worth mention for its impact on the electoral scene, although not a political party in any strict sense, is the religious movement Sōkagakkai. It may be regarded as a lay movement for conversion to the Nichiren-shō sect of Buddhism, formed about 1941 and suppressed during the latter half of World War II, but rising with remarkable vigor to a claimed membership of almost 3 million by 1962. Its religious doctrine is hazy and puzzling as to details, but its adherents strive for faith in beauty, good, and benefit; the last-named virtue includes physical healing and business success. The sect clearly stands for the achievement of these values in this world, and it advocates and practices direct action for the social welfare of its members. A declared aim is to make Nichiren-shō the national religion of Japan. The sect's leadership expects and receives from its members well-disciplined performance of various functions, including proselyting, fund raising, and social welfare activities, together with prayer and other religious observances. The Sōkagakkai entered politics as the Kōmeikai in the 1955 local elections with surprising initial success, then got 3 out of 4 of its candidates into the House of Councilors in 1956; by 1962, it had 15 members seated in the House of Councilors. In the 1963 elections, its membership in the prefectural assemblies rose from 3 to 56 of the total of 2,688 in forty-six prefectures. What attracts wide attention is the disciplined response of the members, whose strategically directed votes have placed almost every person in office who has stood as a candidate. The Socialist Party leaders show concern not merely out of fear of being overtaken in numbers, but also because Sōkagakkai candidates, after being elected by "floating votes" from economically depressed and discontented "little people" whom the Socialists would like to woo, turn around and vote with the conservatives on most issues other than ones bearing on war (the United States–Japan Mutual Security Treaty), violence (amendment of the Police Law), and reparations.

SUMMARY OF POLITICAL PARTY FEATURES AND PROBLEMS. To a great extent, the major Japanese political parties take their color from the individuals and factions of professional politicians that form their heart. They cohere as parties because of tactical considerations and despite much internal dissension on issues or programs in order to compete in the Diet and campaign most effectively. Thus what unity exists among the Liberal Democratic factions is virtually forced on them by the existence of the Socialist Party, and vice versa. The Liberal Democrats are pragmatic, the Socialists doctrinal; yet the very insistence on theory makes it harder for the latter to reach agreement on specific political issues than for the practically oriented conservatives to do so. Under such circumstances it is difficult for a party to achieve a particularized cohesive program rising out of long-range issues. Leaders must give first attention to the uneasy coalition that supports them, a fact which produces blurred compromises; and second attention to opposing the major rival party, a fact which produces inflexible positions, far apart, with little recognition of common ground on which to pursue conduct of state.

Each major party, having professional politicians as its bones and flesh, is primarily and narrowly concerned with what goes on in legislative circles in Tokyo. Neither is an organization with mass membership; neither has grass roots or carries its full national personality clearly into prefectural and municipal or village elections. The voting public, therefore, is not enticed into developing a close sense of identification even with the party it may regularly support. Each party is aware of the hazards inherent in such a psychological distance but has found no means of reducing it effectively.

Despite the limitations implied in these paragraphs, postwar Japan leans heavily on its political parties to furnish leadership for the nation. When, at the end of World War II, the peerage and military elites were eliminated and the advisers to the Emperor were cut off from direct participation in the political process, leadership functions devolved on three main groups: political parties, the civil bureaucracy, and business. Whatever the conditions in the "triumvirate" that may inhibit men from rising to their highest capacity of courage, foresight, and dispassionate judgment, these three groups are nonetheless the primary sources upon which Japan now relies for statesmanship and guidance.

Political Interest Groups

The process of decision making in an increasingly complex modern society alters on the one hand as governmental interests and activities spread out over both old and new sectors of society (to regulate, promote, and integrate them), and on the other hand as the people who are directly or indirectly touched by its presence grow more aware of and interested in government. In nontotalitarian states, political parties and public elections of legislators who represent geographical segments of the society are mechanisms that feed the desires and interests of constituents into the decision-making process of the government. A gap remains, however, inasmuch as a single legislator from each geographical segment or voting district can represent only a fraction of the increasingly diverse and specific interests in his constituency. At least in theory, the voter may express his individual views on issues in various ways, but a group expression is often more continuous and more effective. Political interest groups, consequently, multiply to fill the gap and, in behalf of specific interests, to speak to administrators, legislators, and the public. Some form of interest representation exists in any society, but it is in the more modern societies that the political interest group becomes "systematically organized, relatively impersonal in style, continuous, public, and focuses on larger targets" rather than on "personalized, episodic, private, local, and diffuse" objectives.[7]

Japanese interest groups fall into both modern and premodern categories. As might be predicted from the large, diversified, and relatively impersonal quality of metropolitan centers, modern political interest groups are about as frequent and conspicuous there as in large modern cities anywhere. Modern interest groups have been appearing in rural Japan also, however, as the pace of modernization in agricultural and forestry areas continues. Conversely, though interest groups of the traditional sort are most frequent outside cities, they have not by any means disappeared from urban areas. Hence, while we suggest an urban-rural distinction here, it is only approximately true, although the nation as a whole can be said to exhibit a dualistic character with respect to political interest groups.

Some interest groups are local because their problems are within the competence of local or prefectural governments. In the countryside, for instance, there are a multitude of irrigation cooperatives, while the larger cities can be viewed as a network of groups organized around professions and trades, some subdivided by wards and shopping districts. Local battles to be resolved by the city council or the village assembly or by conferences among mayors may be fought at this level. The existence of parallel interests in other parts of the country, however, often leads to federation to reach objectives at the national level or may link local groups to national organizations that have some common interests. In this context can be seen some of the contrasts between traditional and modern patterns, which pose a dilemma of choice to politicians, attracted as they are to any unit or group that holds out the promise of a bloc of votes and the possibility of financial support. In the country, especially, the astute old-time politician would attempt to build a *jiban,* an area within his electoral district where he could depend on large blocs of votes for himself or for persons or measures designated by him. To control his *jiban* he needed an organization of lieutenants who were persons of influence locally, and through them he would distribute favors or money in return for voter loyalty, as well as using "pork-barrel" techniques of channeling advantages to his locality. A

[7] Ward and Macridis, *op. cit.,* p. 80.

jiban is naturally more difficult to maintain in a city, where voters move in and out at a greater rate and have more diverse interests; and the *jiban* system was hurt by the postwar adoption of multimember electoral districts for the House of Representatives. Problems first encountered in the cities are now facing politicians in districts that are predominantly rural but in which industrial or business development is occurring (notably those areas chosen for industrial decentralization). Local politicians cannot represent equally all the diverse interests, some local and some national, held by voters in such districts. *Jiban,* consequently, are weakening or even becoming obsolete in a great many rural localities.

On a national scale in the countryside prior to World War II, the Imperial Agricultural Association (Teikoku Nōkai) served for the distribution of subsidies to agriculture and for communication between the Ministry of Agriculture and farmers; it was politically conservative and was assumed to be dominated by landlords. Tenant unions emerging in the 1920s tried to force the reduction of land rents through court action, demonstrations, and violence; the Japanese Farmers Union, founded in 1922, inherits this tradition and is connected with various socialist causes and parties. Since the war, other associations and cooperative federations exist for marketing, purchasing, insurance, and forestry and act as interest groups. Federations of agricultural cooperatives, which were formed in large part to gain governmental consideration for their economic interests, are active lobbyists. So much local financing is received as subsidies and grants-in-aid from the central government that national associations of towns and villages or their assemblies (and even those of cities), though formed as part of the apparatus of government, make representation to the national government an important part of their activities. The average farmer, however, is seldom consciously touched by these new federations and formal associations, and the rarity, in rural communities, of systematically organized groups with explicitly defined political programs is in considerable contrast to their increased appearance in cities.

Business and labor organizations stand out above all others as the most systematic, large-scale, and clearly defined interest groups of Japan. The largest businesses are associated in the Japanese Federation of Employers' Organizations (Nikkeiren), while the economically hard-pressed smaller employers are joined in the Political League of Small and Medium Enterprises (Chūseiren). The Japan Management Association (Dōyūkai) and the Federation of Economic Organizations (Keidanren) also operate by raising money to help finance election campaigns, especially those of conservative candidates; by influencing public opinion through publishing or using the mass media; or by making contact with political leaders. The most influential among these groups, and perhaps foremost among all the pressure groups of Japan, is the Nikkeiren.

Labor is characteristically organized in a large number of enterprise unions (units limited to one company and including most or all of its permanent employees) instead of industrywide trade unions. Most unions are linked into nationwide federations, headed by officials whose outlook is strongly flavored by Marxist conceptions. The Japanese pattern of labor organization, added to traditions that give negotiations with management rather different functions than in the United States and coupled with the left-leaning character of their federations, leads labor to stress political action, as compared with collective bargaining, in the effort to gain its objectives. In any case, thousands of unionized employees of railroads, schools, and other enterprises have the government as their employer. Thus, Japan's labor federations are active and powerful pressure groups. The most political in its orientation is the largest federation, the General Council of Trade Unions (Sōhyō), representing 3,800,000 members, or about half of the unionized workers in Japan. Its major rival is the General Council of Japan Labor Organizations (Dōmei Kaigi, formerly Zenrō), representing 1,400,000 members. The latter is linked with the Democratic Socialist Party; it is politically more moderate and puts greater stress on economic action than Sōhyō, which is the prime backer and financer of the Socialist Party and has taken stands parallel with those of the left-wing Socialists. Besides these two federations, the Japanese Teachers Union (Nikkyōso) and the National Student Federation (Zengakuren) have maintained very active political programs; each has figured in certain incidents of violence and vociferous demonstrations for Socialist causes or against government policies.

The belief is widespread that lobbies representing various interest groups regularly resort to corrupt techniques of influence; some instances have been revealed in inquiries or trials. Perhaps more general still are two types of relationships with individual government officials. Of the first type are the "captive" politicians who have turned to a pressure group for access to a bloc of votes and campaign contributions and who are expected, while in office, to give attention to its interest. A study of labor interest groups in 1959 identified 49 of the 467 representatives and 48 of the 250 councilors in the Diet as being primarily representatives of particular unions. In less extreme instances, of course, the interest group is only one among numerous groups behind the candidate it supports. The second type of personal relationship occurs with bureaucrats. Labor unions and leftist interest groups have fewer opportunities of this sort than business, agricultural, and professional groups; e.g., an organized farm group may have close relations with high-level officials in the Ministry of Agriculture and Forestry. In some such cases, the Ministry may have sponsored the formation of the group in question in order to have a channel of administration and communication to its clientele throughout the country. While such a group is today less the creature of its sponsoring ministry than it may have been in the 1930–1940 decade and may assume other functions, its ties with a group of ministry officials in Tokyo will naturally remain close and direct. Then, when a bureaucrat retires from government service, usually on an inadequate pension, he may be enlisted into an important position in the group he used to regulate or service and negotiate in its behalf with his former ministry colleagues. Failing such a position, he may run for elective office with support from the interest group. Such practices are alleged to give rise to a good deal of personal influence in the bureaucracy.

As is evident, much of the action of interest groups has tended to follow personalized lines and be covert in nature. Since it is not easily studied, the extent of borderline or corrupt practice is difficult to ascertain. In various areas there has been some shift, on the part of pressure groups, toward increasing their emphasis on impersonal appeals to public opinion through published information and announcements, as against a direct approach to government personnel. In any event, although there still is a serious imbalance in the access enjoyed by different interest groups to government, their operation has helped to make government more responsive to the wants and concerns of the people at large, who are now a much more important element of the political process than before the war.

THE ORGANS OF GOVERNMENT

The government, providing the machinery by which decisions in the realm of public affairs are formally made and administered, becomes the focal point of inquiry into the political system in the sense that it is the fortress or the high ground which the interests or groups that vie for influence seek to occupy. Those who control some or all of the mechanisms of government hold sway over official functions to a lesser or greater extent and so exercise control over the means of political achievement. At the same time, one cannot merely by examining the blueprint or ground plan of government expect to understand its performance, for there is interaction as well between the government and the wider political system of such a nature that the most visible offices and institutions may be relatively weak or isolated from subsurface levels where the important power is wielded. Frequently the performance of government is responsive to pressures or traditional practices which remain in the informal sectors of the political system without having been given space in the official charter. Such a variance between formal plan and actual performance is definitely true of Japanese government and will require our attention along with our inquiry into the formal organs of government.

The Constitutions of Japan

Among the rules agreed on to keep political contention within tolerable limits in a society, those considered more fundamental than others tend to be separated into bodies of law that are difficult to alter. These bodies of most venerated principles are generally brought together in constitutions. In modern times, Japan has lived under two constitutions of vastly different complexions. The first, which is usually named for the Meiji era, was promulgated in 1889 and took effect in 1890. It remained the basic law until the end of World War II. The second, now known simply as the Constitution of Japan, was promulgated in November, 1946, under most exceptional conditions following Japan's defeat in that war. It is of some importance if we are to understand the issues that swirl around the present Constitution to perceive how it compares with the Meiji Constitution in terms of political ideology and the structure of government which it defines.

THE MEIJI CONSTITUTION. Japan's first Constitution reflected the conviction of the leaders who came to power in 1868 that effective domestic control and external security required a stable and modern system of government. Rejecting in form at least the traditional styles of government to which Japan had been accustomed, it nonetheless seemed to consolidate the position of the oligarchs, most of whom were drawn from the Satsuma and Chōshū domains, ensuring the perpetuation of their authority. Out of consideration for international public opinion and for opponents within the country, it made modest concessions to the principle of representative government. The government it created was thus strongly authoritarian, yet it was also significantly different from previous Japanese patterns and within the range of variation acceptable among European states at a time when international opinion tolerated nations that were not notably liberal provided that they were capable of resolute action.

The Meiji Constitution was conceived of as a gift from a benevolent Emperor to his people. It represented a theory of the state (*kokutai*)

463

whereby the Emperor embodied the state and was the source and repository of all state powers. It thus played up to and was reinforced by his spiritual authority, which was based on the elaborate myth of legitimation that claimed that rule over Japan was entrusted to the Emperor through his ancestors descended in unbroken continuity from Amaterasu Ōmikami, the Sun Goddess. In theory, thus, the Constitution established an extraordinarily centralized system of government, for all ministers and officials acted only as agents of the Emperor.

From the point of view of Japanese political tradition, the most novel feature of the Constitution was the establishment of a bicameral legislature. Membership in the House of Peers, the upper house, consisted of imperial princes, princes and marquises, collegially elected representatives of the lower orders of nobility, imperial appointees, members of the Imperial Academy, and representatives of the highest taxpayers. The House of Representatives, the lower house, was popularly elected from constituencies. The question of how much power the legislature should be given was one of the crucial issues upon which the oligarchs differed significantly from their political critics.

The Emperor had power to determine the organization of all branches of the administration. The most important agency was the Cabinet, created in 1885, which was headed by a Prime Minister appointed by the Emperor on the advice of the *genrō* (elder statesmen). Twelve ministers headed departments, of which the most important for centralizing the government were those of Home Affairs and Education. The former controlled the bureaucracy, local government, and the police force. The latter directed the entire educational system, which was increasingly used for political indoctrination. To the Cabinet was delegated the Emperor's nonmilitary authority. At first, each minister was individually responsible to the Emperor, but the impracticality of this arrangement led to collective responsibility. The Emperor's military authority, however, was separately delegated to the general staffs of the Army and Navy for command and operational functions. The ministers of War and the Navy were theoretically selected by the Prime Minister, but during two crucial periods, 1900–1913 and 1930–1945, the general staffs gained control of their appointment. This meant that the military services could exercise considerable influence in the composition of a Cabinet if they chose to do so.

The authoritarian and elitist bent of the Meiji Constitution was marked not only in the conditions placed on civil rights (see Chapter 11), but in the limitations on the power given to the houses of the Diet. Statutes, though passed by the Diet, were subject to an absolute imperial veto, or they could be nullified if the administration failed to provide implementing funds in the budget. The Emperor had the right to convoke, open, close, and prorogue the Diet and to dissolve its House of Representatives. He declared war, made peace, and concluded treaties. The judiciary exercised its power in his name. The very important power of the budget was not held at the initiative of the Diet, for the Diet had power only to approve. Nonetheless, by the shrewd exploitation of this slender right, the House of Representatives gradually won a greater share of political power, for by refusing to approve the budget (whereupon the government was limited to operating with the budget of the previous year) it could tangibly hamper the government's plans.

In practice, thus, government became something other than what was originally intended in the Meiji Constitution, though it retained its basically authoritarian, centralized character. The Constitution was supplemented by other legal documents affecting government organization: the Imperial Household Law, imperial ordinances, and statute laws. The first of these could not be supplanted or amended by the Diet, and the second merely required approval by the Diet; only the third originated in the Diet in theory, but in fact most statute laws were devised and proposed to the Diet by administrators responsible only to the Emperor. Insofar as the decision structure of government gradually altered, however, it changed less through legislation than through evolving procedures, such as the negative power over the budget exploited by the House of Representatives, or through the emergence of decision-making bodies that had no constitutional or legal authorization.

These extralegal bodies were either advisory to the Emperor or held executive authority delegated from him; in either case they were out of the reach of both the Diet and the Cabinet, and the imprecision of their limits of authority, in most cases, contributed to overlapping, obscurity, and rivalry in the operation of the government. The main advisory body was the informal group of elder statesmen (*genrō*) and its successor after 1926 (*jūshin*). The *genrō* were for the most part "retired" Meiji leaders who had been the real power behind the throne. Their opinions were asked on most important state decisions. No Premier was ever appointed except on their recommendation, and several *genrō* became premiers. Other advisory bodies were those holding imperial household offices, the Imperial Family Council, and the Privy Council. The Lord Keeper of the Privy Seal and the Imperial Household Minister together controlled access to the Emperor, since all appointments for imperial audiences had to be made through them. The military authority of the Emperor was delegated to the Supreme Command, comprising the chiefs of the General Staff and the Navy Staff, the field marshals and fleet admirals, the Minister of War, and the Minister of the Navy, without whose advice the Emperor was, in the end, unable to act. Moreover, even though the two military ministers acted as members of the Cabinet, their function as members of the Supreme Command responsible only to the Emperor came to mean that the military could act independently of the Cabinet or against it, whereas the Cabinet, bearing collective responsibility, could not function so long as the General Staff or the Navy Staff failed to name a person (an officer on active duty) as Minister of War or Minister of the Navy.

Judicial authority was constitutionally included in the sovereign power of the Emperor. Members of the judiciary accordingly viewed their function as protecting his sovereignty. Authority in local government was derived from the central government, for the Prime Minister appointed governors of the prefectures on the advice of the Home Ministry, and the elective representatives in prefectural assemblies had no power over the governors. In municipalities, although some measure of autonomy existed in that municipal assemblies were elective and in turn elected the mayor, career bureaucrats usually ran the local government under the wide authority of the Home Ministry. The Ministry could dissolve all representative boards at local levels, although their members were popularly elected.

In sum, the Meiji Constitution established a highly bureaucratic system of government with diversified arms that encouraged professional specialization. It ensured a high degree of centralization, yet it permitted obscure and complex delegation of authority, so that the Emperor, supreme in theory, was isolated and removed from authority in practice. Although the Constitution did make minimal concessions to popular participation in government, it did not effectively impede the resurgence of authoritarianism spearheaded by the military from 1932 on. It is noteworthy, moreover, that in the "moment of truth" of the young officers' revolt of February 26, 1936, after which the military elite achieved ascendancy, the nonmilitary governmental bodies made no appeal to the people to help prevent the slide into militarism.

THE CONSTITUTION OF JAPAN AFTER WORLD WAR II. The first draft of the new Constitution was published in Japan on March 6, 1946; it took effect on May 3, 1947, as an amendment to the Meiji Constitution. The story behind its drafting is quite extraordinary and enters into the continuing controversy over its retention and amendment, for it is with reason called an imposed document, and its roots lie in Anglo-American tradition, not in Japanese tradition. To achieve the American policy of democratization, American higher officials under Gen. Douglas MacArthur, Supreme Commander for the Allied Powers (SCAP), generally agreed that substantial changes in the

Meiji Constitution would be needed. But when a Japanese committee appointed by the Cabinet in November, 1945, failed to present a draft very much different from the existing Constitution, the Government Section of SCAP produced in English the first draft of the present Japanese Constitution. The Japanese translation was then submitted to the Japanese for revision and adoption. On March 5, 1946, the Cabinet acceded under pressure to accept the Japanese translation as its own. Minor changes preceded its submission to the Diet, which overwhelmingly adopted it, though only after extensive debate. It was then promulgated by the Emperor on November 3, 1946, to take effect six months later. Any other course for the Japanese was almost out of the question, for it seemed likely that rejection would precipitate even more radical changes, not excluding possible abolition of the imperial institution.

The Constitution, in a preamble and eleven chapters comprising 103 articles, provides for a system of government that blends in unique fashion elements familiar in American and British tradition. Although it preserves most of the prewar constitutional organs of government, its allocation of decision-making powers and procedures dramatically transforms their relationships. The preamble speaks in the name of the people, "in whom resides sovereign power." It strips the Emperor of all political authority; it creates both houses of the bicameral Diet through popular election and vests superior legislative and financial power in the lower house; it ensures that the Cabinet, in which executive authority is concentrated, is responsible to the elected representatives; and it creates an independent judiciary in the American pattern, vesting its Supreme Court with the power of judicial review of "the constitutionality of any law, order, regulation, or official act." With respect to local government, on which the Meiji Constitution was silent, it introduces the principle of local autonomy, granting rights and independence of government in sharp contrast with previous practice. It specifies in ambitious and idealistic detail a long list of the rights and duties of the people. In Article 9 of Chapter II, unique among the world's national constitutions, it renounces war as a sovereign right.

It is remarkable that this Constitution continues unchanged and that it has been a workable document, considering the decisive changes it has imposed on the reluctant leaders of the Japanese government. Taking also into account its origin and the fact that its very terminology, based on foreign concepts, is not immediately lucid in Japanese, it is not surprising that there has been constant pressure for revision. Revisionists, most numerous among the conservative leadership, advocate constitutional recognition of Japan's right to self-defense, redefinition of the status of the Emperor, reform of the House of Councilors, an increase in the authority of central government over local entities, an easier system of constitutional amendment, and other changes. Most proposed changes are fairly moderate, none openly advocating a wholesale return to the system which this Constitution replaced. A Constitutional Investigation Commission appointed in 1956 under the Secretariat of the Prime Minister's Office is believed to be about ready to submit recommendations. The issue continues to be controversial in Japanese politics, for the progressive groups have united in opposition to amendment, alleging that even one apparently innocuous change will open the path to repeated and drastic reactionary revision.

The Constitution provides only the skeleton of government organization and is supplemented by a number of basic laws, more readily amended than the Constitution, that prescribe the actual nature and operations of major organs of government. These include the Imperial House Law, the National Diet Law, the Law of the Courts, the Cabinet Law, the Finance Law, the Public Office Election Law, and the Local Autonomy Law. These more specific laws combine with the Constitution to give form to the present government of Japan.

The Emperor

The Emperor's official functions are clearly restricted to acts that have only ceremonial importance. His position is made subject to "the will of the people," and he acts only on the initiative of responsible government officials, in accordance with their decisions. He is regularly informed about matters of state, but his opinion about them is not officially requested. Succession to the throne must devolve on the eldest son down the direct line of descent; adoption with the Imperial Family is not permitted. The Imperial Family no longer possesses most of the extensive property it held through World War II but depends for its main support on an allowance voted annually by the Diet. Even so tenuous a position, much weaker than that of the British monarchy, is resented by many Japanese, especially among the younger generation; yet there has appeared no alternative symbol to provide a rallying point for the national loyalty of the Japanese citizenry. In this role, the continuance of the imperial institution has an importance that is valued by many reflective Japanese.

The National Diet

The Diet is constitutionally the most powerful organ of the state, with the sole power to make laws. The government, in consequence, is a parliament-centered apparatus. The Diet's two houses, the House of Representatives and the House of Councilors, are formed by popular election. The organization of the upper house, or House of Councilors, represents a compromise of views in the drafting of the Constitution, the Americans favoring a unicameral legislature, while the Japanese leadership wanted an appointive upper house or one representing professions and certain portions of the electorate. In the compromise, the House of Councilors comprises 250 members, of whom 150 are elected from the forty-six prefectures treated as electoral districts, 2 from the smallest in population and up to 8 from Tokyo and Hokkaido; the remaining 100 are chosen "at large," from all Japan treated as a single electoral district. Members' terms are six years long and are staggered so that half of the members are elected at three-year intervals. In practice, some men of national stature win election in the national constituency; but the system makes it possible for national-scale pressure groups to back selected candidates, and the upper house is consequently as partisan as the lower house.

The House of Representatives consists of 467 members elected as described above from 118 multimember districts for a four-year term. No postwar Diet has continued for its full term before being dissolved by the Cabinet; so terms in actuality depend on political relations and are of indeterminate length. A Speaker and a Vice Speaker are chosen from among the members, normally from the majority and the minority parties, respectively. Committee organization has become important in accomplishing the business of the House; as in American practice, members are assigned to the committees, which generally parallel the divisions of the Cabinet, and chairmanships are allotted according to relative party strengths in the House.

The upper house is distinctly subordinated to the lower house. A bill is normally passed by both houses to become law, but the lower house can override rejection by the upper house with a two-thirds majority of those present. The lower house originates the budget, and its decision prevails on a simple majority vote if a joint committee of both houses cannot reconcile differences. Similarly, a majority vote is sufficient to ensure selection of the Prime Minister or ratification of a treaty against opposition by the upper house. Serious disagreements between the two houses have been rare, a circumstance that leads revisionists to claim that the upper house as now constituted makes little or no distinctive contribution to the legislative process.

Though granted much new power, the Diet has not been quite the predominant driving force of government that it could be in theory. Two features of its operation illustrate this verdict. First, its "lawmakers" actually make few laws but debate, publicize, and sometimes amend legislation that is initiated elsewhere: in the bureaucracy, the Cabinet, or the policy research committees of the political parties. According to one survey that studied 1,890 bills enacted by postwar Diets, only 30 per cent were private bills (sponsored by members) and many of these had been previously drafted by bureaucrats or by party councils. A parallel situation, of course, is not unfamiliar in many Western legislatures. Second, in plenary sessions the Diet usually just passes on decisions made in committee, with rigid voting discipline enforced on the members of each party. Since the dominance enjoyed by the conservative party makes passage or rejection of a bill readily predictable once it has come to a vote, the "progressive" minority has had to develop skill in preventing a measure from coming to a final vote. The progressives, in fact, face a grave dilemma, for the unlikely prospect of their winning a majority in the foreseeable future makes them a perpetual minority. Either they will be eternally steamrollered by the disciplined vote of the conservatives if they follow normal parliamentary practice, or, alternatively, they may resort to obstructionist methods, going as far as systematically planned violence in the Diet or on the streets. The tumults which have arisen from the nonparliamentary tactics adopted in cases of last-ditch opposition are such that public confidence in the legislative process and party government has frequently been seriously shaken.

Apart from legislation, the Diet has a good many important functions. Through hearings and inquiries it is supposed to exert continuous supervision over the quality of governmental performance. It audits government accounts, and it is solely responsible for raising and spending public monies and so scrutinizes the annual budget bill with great care. Finally, since it chooses the Prime Minister from among its own members and has the sole right to bring about the resignation of the Cabinet or forcing a general election by a vote of no-confidence, the Diet has ultimate authority over the executive arm of the government.

The Cabinet

The primary executive body, the Cabinet, is responsible to the Diet. The number of its members is not fixed; in 1963 the Cabinet consisted of seventeen political leaders headed by the Prime Minister. Twelve presided over ministries: Foreign Affairs, Finance, Education, Justice, Welfare, Agriculture and Forestry, International Trade and Industry, Transportation, Labor, Construction, Postal Services, and Local Autonomy. The remaining five, ministers without portfolios (departments), headed various agencies of the administration.

The Prime Minister and a majority of his ministers must be members of the Diet; all must be civilians. Since in the Diet, which selects the Prime Minister by vote, the decision of the House of Representatives prevails in case of disagreement, the Prime Minister normally comes from this house, and so do most members of his Cabinet, whom he selects after he has been chosen. Intraparty tensions, not to mention other political considerations, make his choice a delicate and exacting one. Although no law constrains his selection, the Prime Minister is usually the head of his party, thanks to a coalition between factions; so he must distribute ministerial plums in such a way as to gain maximum support for his own position. A strong Prime Minister, such as Yoshida Shigeru, fairly frequently reshuffled Cabinet posts without disaster to himself; in general, a Cabinet is more ephemeral in tenure than a Prime Minister, lasting ten or eleven months to his twenty-five or so (the average between 1946 and 1960). All postwar Cabinets have been conservative but one, a weak Socialist-conservative coalition under Katayama Tetsu that lasted less than ten months in 1947–1948; hence, in a period of conservative dominance of the legislature, the House of Representatives' no-confidence vote has not normally caused the fall of a Cabinet. Rather, Cabinets have fallen either because of intraparty maneuvering or because of public unrest over policy or a scandal in government. Since Cabinet changes have meant only that one group of conservatives comes in to replace another, stability in major policies has been greater than might be expected from the frequent turnovers.

Cabinet posts are prized; so the pursuit of harmony within the party through spreading these rewards around would be one important function even if there were no others, but the Cabinet has notable formal responsibilities as well. A major task is preparing the annual budget. Others are the general conduct of government administration, domestic and foreign; preparing and submitting the vast majority of the bills considered by the Diet; and informing the Diet and the people of the state of the nation. Besides having a strong hand in formulating major policies, the Cabinet implements the law with its orders, convokes extraordinary sessions of the Diet, arranges for general elections, and appoints justices of the Supreme Court. It thus enjoys extensive executive powers.

The cabinet cannot, as in former days, run roughshod over other organs of government. Its members are collectively responsible to the Diet, all being jointly answerable for the various official decisions or policies; and they must attend sessions and answer questions about their administration when officially requested to do so. The Diet may refuse to support legislation and force the resignation of the Cabinet. It is true that the Diet, or at least the members of the majority party, in practice tends to accept Cabinet leadership and give firm support, both to have access to party favors and patronage from these high party officials and to avoid the high cost of campaigning for reelection in case a standoff impels the Cabinet to dissolve the Diet. But the docility of majority-party members as holders of Diet seats does not resolve their discords as members of factions within the party. The Cabinet continually faces pressure from dissident groups within its own party, and this if nothing else inhibits high-handed action.

A different set of checks on the Cabinet comes from the professional bureaucracy, headed by career civil servants who occupy posts as vice ministers in each major ministry. These vice ministers, meeting regularly, form the so-called "little Cabinet" and, being expert and well informed, make many decisions that are passed on to the Cabinet for routine approval. The Cabinet, with temporary ministers, would be very much more at the mercy of the bureaucrat leaders, were it not for the counterbalance provided by a professional and technical staff of more than 20,000 that is attached directly to the Prime Minister. This Prime Minister's Office reduces the Cabinet's dependence on the regular bureaucracy and permits a more balanced interaction.

The Bureaucracy

Japan's ministries, agencies, and local governmental entities, employing about three million persons, or one of every fourteen members of the working population in 1960, have been experiencing the postwar bureaucratic expansion that has affected other nations. In 1940 the same general categories of employees (excluding the military and certain others) were less than one-tenth as numerous. Yet it is only the scale and not the fact of bureaucracy that is new, for bureaucratic administration has been an important element of the political system since the Meiji Restoration and before. Of course, the vast majority of government employees fill posts which have little political power. The bureaucratic pyramid slopes in rapidly, leaving no more than about four thousand higher officials (first, second, and third grades of the administrative service), the products of rigorous training and selection through the civil service examination system.

A bureaucratic career is considered an honorable and desirable one for able young persons in Japan, both for its historical association with elite status and for the security and other advantages it offers today. It is respected in part because high performance is required of candidates hoping to rise to advanced rank in the more important ministries of the central government, such as those of Finance, International Trade and Industry, and Agriculture and Forestry or the recently established Ministry of Local Autonomy. A strong graduation from one of the ranking universities is generally desirable. The prewar monopoly held by a very few universities over access to higher government positions has diminished (among the prewar administrative elite, for instance, the Law Department of Tokyo Imperial University furnished 92 per cent, with another 4 per cent coming from the Law Department of Kyoto Imperial University), but Tokyo University graduates, who still occupy three-quarters of the higher posts, even now comprise a clique that results in preferential advantage to younger graduates from the same school. Besides needing a brilliant school record, aspirants to higher rank take the higher civil service examination even before graduation. Examinations now are less narrowly legal, technical, and based on detailed memory of the law than formerly, when the volume of the six law codes (the *Roppō*) was the aspirant's bible, and grading is not made solely by the law faculties of the monopolistic schools; but postwar attempts to broaden the examinations still have not transformed them into liberal arts intelligence tests.

The candidate who has passed the higher civil service examination, if appointed, is apt to enter government service as a sixth-grade employee. His career is likely to be exclusively within one ministry, for rivalry among ministries almost precludes transfers or other forms of cooperation. Just as the examinations require competence but inhibit originality, so good performance requires efficiency and obedience and is apt to repress initiative. Because of the rigorous selection process, however, the bureaucratic offices obtain quite able men. Moreover, considering Tokyo apart from other areas as the administrative and cultural heart of Japan that draws the indisputably prime candidates, the various regions are approximately equal in the quality of performance of employees in branch offices of the central government or in local bureaucracy. There are no conspicuous backwaters of inefficiency or incapacity.

Higher bureaucrats are very much a part of the political system. As in other modern nations, fewer and fewer of the problems presented for political decision are strictly nontechnical in all aspects; professional politicians need the help of experts in tax or banking or construction or agronomic or chemical fields; and when they turn, as they do, to

473

bureaucrats possessing such training, the bureaucrats do more than carry out policy: they help to make it. This purely professional involvement, however, is only the first of the bureaucrats' contacts with politics. It is understandable that groups that will be affected by bureaucrats' intervention in the decision process should attempt to influence those in key positions; and all the more so in Japan, where bureaucrats have willingly entered areas of indecision and uncertainty left open through weaknesses on the part of postwar legislatures. These organized pressure groups offer various forms of persuasion, from gifts and entertainment down to outright bribes, for which bureaucrats are as good targets as politicians. Finally, many bureaucrats become involved in politics, thanks to the system of early retirement and low pensions which leave them able and anxious for subsequent employment. Substantial numbers run as candidates for elective office; as noted earlier, 26 per cent of the Liberal Democrats in the lower house in 1959 had formerly been career bureaucrats, though only 4 per cent of the Socialists had a bureaucratic background. A count of Cabinet members holding office between 1954 and 1961 shows a bureaucratic background in the case of 35 per cent. A political second career is inviting, in part because the retired bureaucrat can obtain campaign support and costs from groups or individuals associated with his former ministry, and in part because his ability and his knowledge of government in Tokyo will be of advantage to him as a politician and so contribute to his appeal as a candidate. In short, an ex-bureaucrat should make an efficient legislator or elective administrator; a good many observers, however, express alarm at admitting bureaucrats into the precariously democratic legislative organs of government, for bureaucrats as a class are alleged to be elitist, authoritarian, and antidemocratic.

There is considerable objective evidence for this allegation. In Japan, the bureaucrat is the spiritual descendant of the samurai, whose obligation and loyalty radiated up toward his lord and out toward members of his own class but not down toward the common crowd. Samurai bureaucrats were not of the people, having been born to a higher status. The oligarchs who set up the framework of modern Japan, coming from this class themselves, established a departmentalized bureaucracy with no thought but that it should serve the state, its members being respected as servants of the Emperor. Even after civil service examinations were used to recruit candidates from the public schools, bureaucrats had little or no reason to feel an identity with the civilian populace; and ordinary people tended to accept the primacy of the state and their own role as lesser subjects of the Emperor under his stewards, the government officials. There was in Japan no precedent for the conception introduced by Americans into the new Constitution in 1946, declaring the bureaucracy to be "the servants of the whole community," and the relatively few persons on either side of the status gap who now try to substitute such a concept for ingrained habit patterns are still apt to find themselves out of step and frustrated.

Local Government

Prior to enactment of the new Constitution in 1946, all administration outside the capital was regarded as an extension of the central government. Prefectures and communities had no autonomous powers of decision or self-management. The present system stems from a determined move by American policy makers in the Allied Occupation to push political initiative down to a level close to the people, emphatically decentralizing it in order effectively to democratize it. Whether or not the policy makers fully appreciated some of the problems arising from the difference in scale as well as in tradition between Japan and the United States, many problems do prevent decentralized local government from operating as planned, although the system set up in Chapter VIII of the Constitution and the Local Autonomy Law of 1947 is still the legal basis. It is a highly decentralized system, in terms of Japanese tradition, but still technically a unified system as contrasted, say, with the federal system of the United States.

In each of Japan's forty-six prefectures the voters elect a governor and, separately, a single-house assembly. Each city, town, or village within the prefecture elects its own mayor and single-house assembly. Below the central government there are only these two tiers except in Tokyo, a unit of special problems and special provisions in every field, including government. None of the territory of Japan is unincorporated; all belongs to one or another of the local units. In both the prefectures and the smaller units, the governor or mayor is empowered to dissolve the assembly, while the latter in turn has the right of a no-confidence vote. These units are granted extensive powers of self-government, including, of course, taxation and control over their budgets. The national government is forbidden to interfere in the area of these powers. These rights are utilized with considerable energy by prefectures and cities but less so by towns and villages, and all local levels deviate from the specified legal norm.

Local officials, for one thing, are more often occupied with the business of national ministries at their local level than with their own affairs. This is so, in part, because they depend on the national government for subsidies, grants-in-aid, or loans for anywhere from 20 to as much as 80 per cent of their essential revenues. This dependence is one obvious by-product of the fact that their tax base is not broad enough to support the cost of essential local administration and services. Many communities have been amalgamated into larger units to spread the cost of government, and proposals for regional groups of prefectures are under consideration, in part to ameliorate this serious impediment to genuine local autonomy. Quite apart from financial problems, however, officials are still habituated, on the one hand, to following informal consensus-group patterns of administration and, on the other, to looking to the national bureaucracy in Tokyo for detailed guidance. As an illustration, village assemblies typically do business by negative consensus, that is, by offering no-objection approval of measures submitted by the mayor (and usually drafted by the vice mayor, a career bureaucrat); and, at all levels, laws, ordinances, and charters tend to be carbon-copied from models handed down from Tokyo. A good many useful-sounding committees set up according to these models remain inactive while professional bureaucrat employees accomplish the work.

The Judicial System

Since Chapter 11 will be devoted to a specialized survey of law in Japan, very little comment is needed here. The present court system, by its clear separation from all organs of government administration, is the basis of a separation of powers which did not exist before the new Constitution was adopted. Formerly, the courts and judicial personnel were conceived as being more or less responsible, along with other administrative agencies, for carrying out government policies and decisions, whereas now the courts stand apart and equal to the legislative and executive branches and have the power of reviewing the actions and policies of both these branches. Voters each tenth year review the appointments of Supreme Court justices, who hold life terms. The fifteen justices of the Supreme Court, which has complete administrative control over all inferior courts, are appointed by the Cabinet, except that the Emperor appoints the Chief Justice nominated by the Cabinet. We should not be surprised to learn that the Supreme Court has not indicated a disposition to make vigorous use of the power of judicial review of legislation, for the concept of the autonomy of the judicial function of government is perhaps one of the most alien to the Japanese tradition. In their normal functioning as courts of justice, the courts operate very nearly as planned; but adjudication is not as commonly resorted to in Japan as in the West, indicating that there persists among most Japanese a strong inclination toward compromise, conciliation, and mediation by informal methods rather than adversary litigation in courts.

Governmental Performance and Its Evaluation

The function of a political system being to regulate and make decisions in public affairs, it should be possible to examine the "output" of the Japanese system to see how decisions are guiding the society and meeting its needs. Such an examination should be made in terms of the situation in which the society exists as well as of the historical determinants that have provided or denied it resources for meeting its needs. In the past, observers and critics of Japanese politics have too often simply applied British or American ideals to their evaluation of the political performance, as if Japan's system arose from identical backgrounds and faced similar circumstances, or as if the West supplied the universal ideal to which all people must aspire. Japan's situation and heritage are Asian. Only recently, as measured by the life expectancy of contemporary societies, has either been international enough to include political association with Western nations. During 100 years of contact with the West the political system of Japan has been hammered repeatedly into one shape and then another in response to situational pressures or internal demands. We must attempt to avoid judging its present performance as if these factors of situation and heritage did not matter.

The foregoing sections have described the Japanese political system from a structural-functional point of view without attempting a systematic assessment of the quality of the system and its performance as a mechanism for handling political affairs. Our description has not been completely neutral, for it is almost impossible to describe a political system, particularly one which has undergone such major changes, without characterizing its operations at any given point as being more or less authoritarian, more or less centralized, and so on. Evaluation of political performance is one of the major concerns of the political scientist, though he has yet to agree upon a common basis for expressing his judgment. Until recently, it would seem, evaluation was most often tied to some existing political system or ideal, so that an existing system was judged as being more or less democratic, socialistic, or totalitarian. Recent attempts to devise a "politically neutral" method of judgment follow through on the analogy between a political system and a processing machine, inquiring into the nature and quality of the "product" resulting from the input into the machinery we have just described.

Looking at the political system in this fashion, we shall wish to review some of the sharply negative judgments which have commonly been made about Japanese government in its several guises prior to the end of World War II. Government under the Meiji Constitution has been called authoritarian, with the implication that it fell far short of permitting the kind of open society with free access to political and economic opportunity which the Japanese people deserved. Yet considering the time (1890), the international mood (imperialism), and the internal condition of the country (popular lack of political experience), it is hard to imagine that the kind of government which the critics had in mind would have been possible or even have served the needs of the country, which then required strong leadership, a resolute foreign policy, and tutelage in political affairs. Likewise, to look upon the first three decades of the twentieth century as exemplifying a "failure of the party system" puts before the Japanese people an unrealistic (and perhaps even unsuitable) ideal. Moreover, such criticisms fail to recognize the very real advances made by the Japanese during these decades as they became politically conscious individuals with an increasing sense of both the possibilities and the limitations of political action provided under the Constitution. The decades of the 1930s and 1940s are the hardest to assess objectively, for the judgment that a more "democratic" political system would have prevented the drift toward totalitarianism and war is dangerously hypothetical. From hindsight we have discovered that the war years did as much as anything to break down social distinctions and to force the Japanese people into mass participation in national (and hence political) affairs and consequently prepared the ground for many of the postwar political developments. Above all, we cannot imagine the Occupation reforms having been imposed with any degree of success upon a Meiji Japan, for while there were a few vocal and active critics of the Establishment who would have applauded such reforms in the 1880s, the vast majority of the people and their leaders would only have been confused by the grant of unexpected freedoms.

This does not mean, of course, that Japan's political development followed an inevitable course and that each stage in its history must be accepted without comment. Japan had its alternatives of political style and emphasis at every turn in its recent course of development. That the Japanese put primary emphasis on national security and the protection of vested interests above that of benefit to the masses of the people was a conscious choice which bore its results in the kind of society (and the kind of tensions) which emerged in the 1930s. That this preoccupation with national security and the reluctance of privileged groups to relax their powers was overplayed certainly helped to push Japan into the disastrous years of militarism. But to assume too hastily that the cure for these extremes was simply a matter of injecting "greater democracy" into government is too easy a diagnosis.

Today, however, the model of democracy is relevant to Japanese politics. It becomes reasonable to inquire how the political system measures against democratic standards not because democracy is a predestined "need" for Japan, but because after six years of forceful "democratization" the Japanese themselves have come to expect of their political system a government by popular participation which would be accountable to the people, offer equality of public opportunity, and provide for a diversity of interests. There are now realistic goals which the Japanese hope to enjoy, though they disagree over means between the blueprint drawn by the Occupation and the idealized or pragmatic programs which characterize the various political parties. Let us then review the performance of the Japanese political system in terms of the Occupation-sponsored principles to which so many of the Japanese subscribed.

The Occupation aimed certain programs at the foundations of society to build support for democratic government. It struck at what were deemed gross inequalities by initiating, in agriculture, land reform; in business, the dissolution of the *zaibatsu* cliques; and in education, uniform access to all levels of schooling. It struck at regimentation of interests by liberalizing school curricula and decentralizing school administration, by modifying family organization, by guaranteeing various civil rights, and by prohibiting a state religion. Finally, it concentrated its efforts on the political system itself to make way for a popular and responsible government. Much of the social revision endures and has been accepted by the Japanese as desirable foundation stones of their present political system.

In the political realm we have seen that constitutional and legal opportunities for popular participation in government remain intact and provide as liberal a framework as those of any nation. In addition, informal avenues for participation, especially political interest groups, continue to multiply, a proof that at least a proportion of the citizenry is making use of opportunities to influence government. Yet, as we have seen, there remain marked inequalities of access to power by interest groups, some being much weaker or more poorly financed than others, some having the ear only of the minority party. Voting rates are extremely high, but much evidence shows that both traditional and new patterns generally regarded as incompatible with democracy make the right to vote fall short of its intended significance; boss rule, community pressures, and traditional loyalties very often submerge independent judgment. These inequalities and undesirable political practices are recognized today and are the butt of many of the popular attacks upon the existing system.

These criticisms, moreover, cannot altogether be ignored by the government. The elaborate legal and structural apparatus intended to make government responsible to the people is still largely intact. In consequence, the government and its members take much greater care to inform the people and cultivate public approval than before the war; a candidate for election, especially, cannot habitually disdain the electorate and still win high office. On the other hand, the candidate or bureaucrat often cultivates limited group interests to a greater degree than he does the figurative average voter, and, in addition, the bureaucrat is fairly well insulated from control by public opinion. By this token, governmental responsibility by no means fulfills the spirit of the legal safeguards or the expectations of the Japanese, and special private interests do have disproportionate influence, as much through the progressive as through the conservative factions in the legislature and as much through the bureaucracy as through the Diet. Though greater speculation than evidence is offered on the subject, many persons are convinced that their franchise means nothing against the monopoly over political power shared by big business, the bureaucrats, and the conservative politicians—and this is the tune played in the political commentary of the popular press, which rarely departs from its antigovernment stance.

Yet in many ways the Japanese have less to complain about than appears on the surface. Government welfare policies are remarkably fully developed. Taken on its own terms, Japanese government has long been concerned with promoting economic development, not forgoing welfare programs and direct intervention in the process. Amid the rubble of defeat in 1945, the government put high priority on rehabilitation and economic growth. The growth has been spectacular, at least as measured against the impoverishment, inflation, and insecurity of the situation immediately after the war. The progress is reflected in lengthened life expectancy, vast improvement in the average standard of living, and the emergence of a self-conscious middle class. The conservative party takes credit and proclaims further development to be its prime goal. But if such a claim is granted, the government also must be held in part to account for the uneven enjoyment of prosperity and the erratic and partial regulation of the economy. Sizable groups remain at a depressed and insecure level of living, such as the "temporary-employee" class and many small farmers; conversely, some groups, notably big business, have enjoyed special advantages at the expense of the general public, for whom living costs are very high. One should not deny that effective political leadership has contributed to fundamental gains, however, and it is also necessary to recognize that the postwar government has developed and implemented a new sense of economic responsibility to the people, first by facilitating wide sharing of economic gains and second by initiating social security, insurance, and health programs.

Education also has been a matter of government concern and has undergone remarkable development. Beginning with changes sponsored by the Occupation, including the liberalization of public school instruction and the expansion of colleges, development has gone forward to place Japan high among all nations in the proportion of her population attending college. The pressure on capacity is still high; colleges were able to enroll only one in four applicants in 1962; yet the number of students, 564,454 in 231 colleges in 1957, was far above the prewar enrollment of 81,999 students in 47 institutions in 1940. Along with its support of education, to be sure, the government has aroused criticism for its tendencies to control political expression or even to curb free speech on the campuses and to recentralize the entire educational system under the Ministry of Education. One of the issues of sharpest controversy is that of politics in education.

In international affairs, Japan has faced complex problems with variable success. The government has usually put a high priority on foreign trade; exports have expanded and altered their character to compete in more profitable markets, while the necessary imports also have been obtained. Usually, though not always, the exchange has brought a profit, and in 1964 the government acceded to long-standing pressure from abroad by ending restrictions on most forms of currency exchange. Problems of trade discrimination and new competition nonetheless continue to harass the foreign-trade field. In foreign policy, most of Japan's relations have been normalized from their wartime and postwar difficulties by the conclusion of peace treaties. A diplomatic agreement with the U.S.S.R. in 1956 was at least a partial solution of problems that blocked a peace treaty, and treaty relations now are lacking only with the Chinese People's Republic, North Korea, and North Vietnam. Japan holds a seat in the United Nations. Under a succession of Liberal Democratic governments, she has leaned toward close relations with the United States and the Western European bloc of nations. A cautious increase of armament for defense has been accomplished. Whether all these developments represent success is difficult to judge in view of the uncertainty of future international developments, and certain of the policies named, particularly rearmament and alliance with the United

States, have precipitated some of the most spectacular parliamentary crises of the postwar era between conservative and progressive parties.

The political system in Japan today may then be characterized as basically democratic, with strong features of welfare statism and bureaucratic control. The system has met with considerable success the problems of postwar reconstruction and of the need for the Japanese people to regain their confidence in themselves and their government. The main question which today confronts the political analyst consequently concerns the future. The present system is the result of drastic reforms imposed by occupying forces and a certain amount of later "readjustment." Can the present government retain its ability to satisfy the heightened expectations of the Japanese people in the realm of politics? And can the state retain its moderate international stance? Several problems becloud any evaluation of these questions, but the main one is whether the present system can handle the so-called "confrontation" (as it is called by the Socialists) or polarization of parliamentary factions within Japan. Conservative leaders deeply distrust the Marxism espoused by almost all progressive leaders; the progressives, denied access to power and its responsibilities that might moderate their stance, hold a rather rigid and narrowly doctrinal position on government and society and treat the conservatives as "class enemies." The wide and fixed gap between these two camps admits little opportunity for maneuvering or adjustment on practical issues. This rigidity is a continual threat to the stability of parliamentary procedure and, moreover, raises the issue of what happens to legislative processes altogether if, in the event of a serious national crisis such as a prolonged depression, enough votes switch to put the Socialists in a position to practice "tyranny of the majority." In the political scientist's terms, then, the Japanese political system must still seek to develop the machinery for bringing political factions together on a more realistic basis, and this in turn requires further easing of the social and economic differences which persist to polarize Japanese politics. Whether this is achieved through democratic processes or through the more drastic measures (such as nationalization) demanded by the Socialists depends both on the future balance of economic and social conditions in Japan and the international environment of the Japanese state. To a considerable degree the concept of democratization still serves as a measure of Japan's ability to meet her political needs, yet we have learned not to expect the Japanese style of democracy to duplicate the American or any other existing model.

B. JAMES GEORGE, JR.

Law in Modern Japan [*]

INTRODUCTION

Other chapters in this book have traced Japan's modern history and touched upon the many problems of transition from Tokugawa "traditionalism" to the "modernism" of the years following the Meiji Restoration. In the realm of political affairs in particular, a good deal of attention has been given to the dramatic changes in political system and ideology which have occurred over the past 100 years. Underlying this treatment of cultural change, of transformation in education, government, and economics, however, has been a major problem of interpretation: to what extent was Japan *justly* influenced by the West? Having made the distinction between "westernization" and "modernization," the question remains, what elements of Western civilization go beyond the parochial limits of Europe and the United States to become the ingredients of some universally inevitable "modern society"? In most areas the answer is by no means clear, for it is extremely difficult to detach the essential (or universal) principles of a particular approach to government or to problems of social organization from the cultural dress with which these principles have clothed themselves.

To be more specific, the Japanese during the late nineteenth century were strongly attracted to the principles of individual dignity and freedom which they saw exemplified by so many Western individuals and customs. Yet how were the Japanese to avail themselves of these qualities? Was it enough to change the laws or the political system? Or did the Japanese need to consider adoption of the Christian religion, which seemed to be at the heart of Western beliefs about the individual. In the realm of political affairs a similar dilemma faced both the participants in politics and those who observed from the side. Was there a particular course which Japan's political development should follow? Was there a political system which was both "modern" and "right" for Japan?

[*] Suggestions offered by Prof. Dan F. Henderson were of help in the preparation of this chapter. Footnotes to the text appear at the end of the chapter.

484

The answers to these questions have never been simple or clear-cut. Those who have given unambiguous and positive answers have generally done so through haste or bias. Yet the uncommitted who say "one system is as good as another" are of no help to us either. In politics the vocabulary which has been used to state the various alternatives faced by the Japanese is still couched pretty much in terms of existing systems: absolutism, feudalism, democracy, socialism, fascism, communism, and the like. The effort of some political scientists to cut through these systems into a realm of general theory which will permit the description of a given political organization in functional terms and project the desired goal of political activity along a scale of increasing modernization has just begun, and their findings have not been fully perfected or generally accepted.

Law offers something of an exception in the area of comparative institutions in being able to present a more structural field of analysis with more generally agreed-upon norms and universals. Law, of course, is a most sensitive and revealing aspect of society, affording a means of insight into the values, rules, and procedures by which the society lives and regulates itself. It thus provides one of the most useful case studies of the way in which Japan has met and digested the many influences which have beat upon her since the middle of the nineteenth century. But the legal field has a further advantage. In the concept of "the Rule of Law" there is a widely accepted universal standard which can be used as a measure in comparative and developmental treatments. Here is a subject for which the scholar's vocabulary is being created and standardized by the actual participants in legal affairs. Moreover, there has been a meeting of minds between representatives from diverse cultures and historical backgrounds on terms and definitions. For this reason, though law is a particularly specialized field, it is presented in this volume for what it reveals of the process of political change and modernization in Japan.

485

The format of this chapter differs somewhat from the others (mainly in the use of supporting footnotes). Since many of the subjects covered in it have not received the general attention of Western scholars, it was felt that a more direct form of documentation was desirable. Furthermore, the chapter introduces a greater volume of substantive material, again on the ground that this is not generally available to the introductory reader.

THE DEVELOPMENT OF THE RULE OF LAW AS THE AIM OF A LEGAL SYSTEM

The concept of the Rule of Law is one to which much attention is currently being devoted in legal circles throughout the world. The term appears in the Anglo-American tradition for the first time in the writings of A. V. Dicey, a nineteenth-century English constitutional lawyer. Dicey sought to distinguish the English legal tradition from the French tradition embodied in the *droit administratif,* which rested in part according to him on the idea that:

> . . . [T]he government, and every servant of the government, possesses, as representative of the nation, a whole body of special rights, privileges, or prerogatives as against private citizens, and that the extent of these rights, privileges, or prerogatives is to be determined on principles different from the considerations which fix the legal rights and duties of one citizen towards another. An individual in his dealings with the State does not, according to French ideas, stand on anything like the same footing as that on which he stands in dealings with his neighbour.[1]

In contrast, Dicey submitted that the unwritten English Constitution rested on the Rule of Law, which had three fundamental characteristics:

> It means, in the first place, the absolute supremacy or predominance of regular law as opposed to the influence of arbitrary power, and excludes the existence of arbitrariness, of prerogative, or even of wide discretionary authority on the part of the government. Englishmen are ruled by the law, and by the law alone; a man may with us be punished for a breach of law, but he can be punished for nothing else.
>
> It means, again, equality before the law, or the equal subjection of all classes to the ordinary law of the land administered by the ordinary Law Courts; the 'rule of law' in this sense excludes the idea of any exemption of officials or others from the duty of obedience to the law which governs other citizens or from the jurisdiction of the ordinary tribunals. . . . The notion which lies at the bottom of the 'administrative law' known to foreign

countries is that affairs or disputes in which the government or its servants are concerned are beyond the sphere of the civil courts and must be dealt with by special and more or less official bodies. This idea is utterly unknown to the law of England, and indeed is fundamentally inconsistent with our traditions and customs.

The 'rule of law,' lastly, may be used as a formula for expressing that with us the law of the constitution, the rules which in foreign countries naturally form part of a constitutional code, are not the source but the consequence of the rights of individuals, as defined and enforced by the Courts; that, in short, the principles of private law have with us been by the action of the Courts and Parliament so extended as to determine that position of the Crown and of its servants; thus the constitution is the result of the ordinary law of the land.[2]

In the aftermath of World War II members of the legal profession in a number of countries expressed their concern for the preservation of the concept of an orderly Rule of Law in a world so recently ravaged by unbridled authoritarianism by banding together in the International Commission of Jurists, dedicated to the support and advancement throughout the world of the Rule of Law. The Commission has defined the Rule of Law as:

> The principles, institutions, and procedures, not always identical, but broadly similar, which the experience and traditions of lawyers in different countries of the world, often having themselves varying political structures and economic background, have shown to be important to protect the individual from arbitrary government and to enable him to enjoy the dignity of man.[3]

In 1959 representatives of fifty-three countries gathered in Delhi to consider the question further and issued the so-called "Declaration of Delhi." Some of the specific conclusions in support of the declaration will be set forth later, but the preamble amplifies further the term *Rule of Law* as:

> . . . [A] dynamic concept for the expansion and fulfillment of which jurists are primarily responsible and which should be employed not only to safeguard and advance the civil and political rights of the individual in a free society, but also to establish social, economic, educational and cultural conditions under which his legitimate aspirations and dignity may be realized.[4]

Members of a committee of the American Bar Association further elaborated their ideas of what the Rule of Law means:

1. Freedom from private lawlessness provided by the legal system of a politically organized society;

2. A relatively high degree of objectivity in the formulation of legal norms and a like degree of evenhandedness in their application;

3. Legal ideas and juristic devices for the attainment of individual and group objectives within the bounds of ordered liberty;

4. Substantive and procedural limitations on governmental power in the interest of the individual for the enforcement of which there are appropriate legal institutions and machinery.[5]

Though most of these statements on the Rule of Law bespeak the Occidental legal tradition,[6] that tradition characterizes almost all the legal systems of the world today, and the evolution of most legal systems has meant a gradual elimination of official whim as the guiding criterion of justice and the steady expansion of a system of codified, impersonal laws impartially administered. The history of legal institutions in Japan is a case study in an evolving Rule of Law.

SOURCES OF JAPANESE LAW

Tracing the origins of any legal system is a difficult task, but to search out the beginnings of Japanese law is especially so because of the relatively late development of a written language and the consequent lack of early legal and administrative documents. It is fairly obvious, however, that the legal history of Japan prior to modern times may be broken down into three separate periods: a primitive era before roughly 700, the period of reception of Chinese law between 600 and 1200, and the feudal period between 1200 and 1868. After 1868 Japan entered the "world stream" of legal development, characterized by the introduction of various principles derived in the main from the West.

Whether or not there was "law" in the primitive period depends of course on the definition used. In his study of primitive law Hoebel states:

A social norm is legal if its neglect or infraction is regularly met, in threat or in fact, by the application of physical force by an individual or group possessing the socially recognized privilege of so acting.[7]

Such law performs four functions:

The first is to define relationships among the members of a society, to assert what activities are permitted and what are ruled out, so as to maintain at least minimal integration between the activities of individuals and groups within the society.

The second is derived from the necessity of taming naked force and directing force to the maintenance of order. It is the allocation of authority and the determination of who may exercise physical coercion as a socially recognized privilege-right, along with the selection of the most effective forms of physical sanction to achieve the social ends that law serves.

The third is the disposition of trouble cases as they arise.

The fourth is to redefine relations between individuals and groups as the conditions of life change. It is to maintain adaptability.[8]

Within such a framework Japan had a system of law during its primitive era. There were apparently rather firmly fixed rules of proper conduct within the family or local clan and community. Many of these rules were in essence canons of religious worship, and none was written down. Land was held by the household or the community, and birth determined status in the community. By the end of this first period, Japanese law appears to have made one of the significant shifts in emphasis away from primitive law, that of emphasis on procedure:

> Privilege-rights and responsibility for the maintenance of the legal norms are transferred from the individual and his kinship group to the agents of the body politic as a social entity.[9]

Then, with the introduction of Chinese political and philosophical institutions, Japan made the transition to mature law that Diamond finds significant in his *Primitive Law*:

> The law has ceased to live in the outer, everyday world, to be variable, changed easily by changing circumstances; it lives in a world of its own; it progresses chiefly by logical application of an observed underlying principle to new facts; it is stereotyped and difficult to change except by legislation, which is little resorted to. . . .[10]

As Japan fell under the religious, cultural, and political influence of China, major changes were wrought in her governmental and legal structure. The sophisticated Chinese system was embodied in the Taihō Code of 702 and the Yōrō Code of 718. It was characterized by centralized administration, imperial proprietorship of all rice land, compulsory military service, and taxation in kind. The administrative legal codes and the land laws were to provide a basis for subsequent administrative procedure for more than a millennium, but the political system itself eventually proved unworkable. Imperial centralization soon gave way to private hereditary ownership of land and to regional government maintained by private military power, the seedbed in which feudal systems of law flourish.

The first stages of feudalism, particularly during the Kamakura and Muromachi eras, saw individual small landholders committing their lands to a military leader in return for a promise on his part to protect them. Those who received the right to use such lands were required to perform military service under the military lord.[11] While the older precedents of "imperial law" provided a basic foundation upon which regional variations were placed, for practical purposes the laws which the individual now felt were increasingly those which the feudal lord under whom he dwelt promulgated and administered. When once again the country was unified under a strong central power after 1600, a centralized system of feudal law came into being, dominated by the codes and institutions of the Tokugawa shogunate.[12]

Henderson summarizes a number of characteristics of this legal system which in varying degrees have left their impress on the modern Japanese legal system.[13] The basic assumption was one of the inequality of individuals by virtue of a hierarchical class system. The military took precedence over civilians, and women occupied a legal position little better than that of chattels. The group was conceived to be the basic unit of society, and the individual's relationship to the group and to the leader of the group was one of duty, not one of right.[14] Since this was so, benefits were often conferred or decisions given as a favor and by the discretion of the chief of the unit and not according to any fixed and established rules. Conciliation of disputes was resorted to wherever possible. The rules set out to guide various bodies of people were most often couched in general terms as moral rules and precepts, and since these precepts were known and accepted by most persons, it was considered unnecessary to promulgate specific explanations of how the rules would be enforced. Administrative and bureaucratic regulations were numerous, however, and quite specific in designating what was expected or prohibited for the individual. Because departures from these moral or regulatory standards would be obvious, the emphasis of the criminal provisions was not on what was criminal but on how the offender should be disposed of; the Code of 100 Articles is concerned primarily with steps that can be taken to discover the truth from the offender's lips and with methods of executing him, not with what conduct is forbidden to him. Matters of property and family law were customary and for the most part local, and therefore they were not dealt with at all in the formal codes, whereas matters affecting succession to official or military posts, including restrictions on marriage, were carefully prescribed, being vital to overall allocations of power. Within these limits Wigmore is rather persuasive that "the highly organized judiciary system began to develop by judicial precedent a body of native law and practice which can only be compared with the English independent development after the 1400's." [15] But Tokugawa law carried down to the very end the conception of class hierarchy and differentiation. Thus, while the legal practices which took care of intraclass or group problems were able to serve the individual better on a basis of standard procedure and objectivity, questions which involved differences between classes provided almost no protection for those in the inferior status.

At the time of the restoration the Emperor Meiji and his advisers set out to modernize the country and to centralize governmental power. The legal machinery inherited from the shogunate was inadequate for either purpose. In 1870 the Meiji government created a Bureau for the Investigation of Institutions, and one of its first products was a translation of the French Civil Code. As young legal scholars returned to Japan from abroad, the universities began to teach English, French, and German law. Older men appointed to newly created judicial offices looked to whatever legal resources they could find, usually French codes in translation, while the younger judges advocated the application of whatever decisions, statutes, and jurisprudential writings they had studied abroad. During this period deep divisions appeared within the legal profession itself which had serious effects on the status of lawyers in later generations [16] and which at the time caused an uneven administration of justice. Citizens and subjects of most foreign nations enjoyed extraterritorial rights by treaty, and whenever the Japanese government pressed for new treaties abrogating such extraterritoriality, the Western governments replied that they could not comply until domestic Japanese law should become fixed enough so that their citizens could comprehend and respect it. The result finally was an agreement that new treaties would be entered into, but the new codes of Japanese law would have to be drafted and enacted before the treaties would become operative.

Because of this pressure, the Japanese government looked about for ready-made systems which it could adapt quickly and easily to Japanese conditions in order to present to the world at least the façade of a modern state founded in law. The Anglo-American common law was not an appropriate source for such a system, because large segments of its doctrine were to be found only in volumes of appellate case reports from a number of jurisdictions and because it appeared to rest in large part on a traditional division of functions between judge and jury whereby the judge determined matters of "law" and the jury matters of "fact," a distinction unknown in Japanese tradition. In contrast, French law had been codified from the time of Napoleon and was administered by a corps of professional judges who were in theory bound not by precedent but only by the language of the codes, a combination of attributes which appeared to fit well into Japanese patterns. Consequently, it was France to which the Japanese government turned for its inspiration in code making. The French government sent as an adviser Prof. Gustave Boissonade, who was instrumental in the preparation of a Penal Code [17] and a Code of Criminal Procedure,[18] adopted in 1880 and 1890, respectively.[19] A German, Hermann Roesler, also assisted in the preparation of the first Commercial Code.[20]

A draft Civil Code was also prepared under Boissonade's direction and was promulgated in 1890, to take effect in 1893. But because the code was so thoroughly French in its derivation, strong opposition developed among those who wished English jurisprudence to be taken account of in the drafting process, and in short order what had commenced as a squabble among conflicting schools of legal scholarship turned into an issue in which conservatives and liberals took political sides. Consequently, the effective date of the code was postponed to the end of 1896 and was further delayed while a new drafting committee, which included representatives of the "English" faction, considered other alternatives.[21] Their draft, which became the Civil Code of 1898, rested primarily on the German codes which had just been developed and which reflected the needs of a modern industrial and commercial society far better than the French codes, which were then more than seventy-five years old. At the conclusion of the initial codification period, formal Japanese law was structured according to the classification scheme of the civil law, not the common law, and traditional Japanese law was preserved primarily in only those parts of the Civil Code covering family law and succession.[22]

In the pre-World War II period only two innovations were made resting on the common law: the jury system in criminal cases and the trust. Neither proved successful. The Jury Law of 1923, in force from 1927, was required to be applied in serious cases and was optional in others, but the career judges felt that the system violated Article 24 of the Meiji Constitution, which prohibited the denial of the right of Japanese subjects to receive a trial from judges appointed according to law. Furthermore, very few Japanese citizens accused of a crime wanted to receive judgment from their neighbors. Moreover, the system was disadvantageous to the defendant. The costs of the jury were superimposed on other costs of the criminal proceeding, and the defendant's right of appeal was limited to questions of law, in contrast with his right to relitigate questions both of fact and of law at the appellate level following a nonjury trial in the court of first instance. Since the defendant had the right to waive a jury trial in all cases, the right was ever increasingly exercised, and the system fell into actual disuse. The law was suspended in 1943 and has not since been reactivated.[23]

The trust is a legal device by which, typically, the property of one person is held or managed by another person or corporation for the benefit of third persons or institutions. The Trust Law of 1922 was enacted primarily to clarify the legal status of trust companies, which had come into being in the early twentieth century. The statute was broad enough to cover purely private transactions, but it seems not to have been made use of except by corporate fiduciaries.

When Japan surrendered to the Western Allies in 1945, the Occupation authorities immediately suspended the administrative and legal measures on which the Japanese militarists had relied in implementing their wartime policies. The Potsdam Declaration had required the Japanese government to "remove all obstacles to the revival and strengthening of democratic tendencies. Freedom of speech, of religion, and of thought as well as respect for the fundamental human rights shall be established." To effectuate this statement of policy, the government was required to suspend all measures restricting political, civil, and religious liberties; to allow full discussion of the Emperor and the imperial system; to remove restrictions on the collection and dissemination of information; and to abolish all restrictions based on race, nationality, creed, or political views. The press and religious institutions were freed from governmental control. Traffic in women for prostitution was abolished as a practice in violation of human rights and of individual liberty and dignity. A new Constitution was promulgated, and substantial revisions were made in a number of codes and laws. Many of these changes and innovations will be touched on in the following pages; suffice it for now to say that they represented efforts to engraft ideas derived from the common-law system and from American constitutional experience on a system derived from civil law. The degree of success or failure must be judged in the context of each particular experiment, but it has been in the postwar period that the greatest advances have been made toward the achievement of the Rule of Law as urged in the Declaration of Delhi.

THE STRUCTURE OF THE LEGAL SYSTEM

The Courts

In the *Conclusions* of the Delhi Conference the judiciary is stated to be a key factor in the Rule of Law:

> An independent Judiciary is an indispensable requisite of a free society under the Rule of Law. Such independence implies freedom from interference by the Executive or Legislative with the exercise of the judicial func-

tion, but does not mean that the judge is entitled to act in an arbitrary manner. His duty is to interpret the law and the fundamental principles and assumptions that underlie it. It is implicit in the concept of independence set out in the present paragraph that provision should be made for the adequate remuneration of the Judiciary and that a judge's right to remuneration settled for his office should not during his term of office be altered to his disadvantage. . . .

[I]t is essential that the powers of the Legislature be fixed and determined by fundamental constitutional provisions or conventions which . . . organize judicial sanctions enforcing the principles set out in the [legislative] clause and protect the individual from encroachments on his rights. . . . The safeguards contained in the constitution should not be directly undermined by devices which leave only the semblance of judicial control.

To ensure that the extent, purpose and procedure appropriate to delegated legislation are observed, it is essential that it should be subject to ultimate review by a judicial body independent of the Executive.[24]

It is only in recent years that the Japanese judiciary has substantially attained these goals.

In the Tokugawa era there was no clear dividing line between law and administration. Individual disputes were settled within the bounds of and for the purpose of advancing official policies. Every effort would be made to settle the matter locally by conciliation, and only when private conciliation efforts failed would the problem be presented before a local magistrate. If the dispute presented a problem of serious proportions, it might thereafter be brought before central offices of the shogunate in Edo.[25] There disputes between persons from different territorial jurisdictions might be adjudicated, review made of death sentences imposed on vassals in daimiate courts for political offenses, and advisory opinions issued for the guidance of local officials. Official practice manuals were also prepared and sent to local magistrates. But the magistrates were merely instruments for attaining objectives set by the shogunate itself.

This blurring of the lines between law and administration continued under postrestoration law. Prior to the institution of the Meiji Constitution, judges were still appointed on the same basis as other administrative officers. The Meiji Constitution preserved the existing system; Article 57 provided: "The judicial power shall be exercised by courts of law according to law in the name of the Emperor. . . ." Within this provision the Diet organized a system of courts under the Ministry of Justice consisting of summary police courts (*ikeibatsu-saibansho*) at the lowest level;[26] district courts (*ku-saibansho*), with jurisdiction to try minor civil and criminal matters by informal proceedings; local courts (*chihō-saibansho*), which served as appeal courts from district courts and exercised general civil and criminal trial jurisdiction; courts of appeal (*kōsa-in*), which heard appeals on law and fact from local courts; and the Daishin-in (often translated as the Court of Cassation after its French counterpart), which heard appeals on points of law from inferior courts and had original jurisdiction in certain cases involving peers.[27]

Another weakening influence on the judicial power, in addition to its position as a suborgan of the Ministry of Justice, was the existence of a separate system of litigation in an administrative court. Article 61 of the Meiji Constitution provided:

> No suit at law, which relates to rights alleged to have been infringed by the illegal measures of administrative authorities, and which shall come within the competence of the Court of Administrative Litigation specially established by law, shall be taken cognizance of by a court of law.

By virtue of this provision, objections raised to administrative measures, bureaucratic interpretations of statutory law or promulgation, and the application of administrative regulations had to be channeled through administrative organs and reviewed by the Court of Administrative Litigation (Gyōsei-saibansho),[28] patterned after the French Conseil d'État. Since all members of the regular judiciary were employees and functionaries of the Ministry of Justice and since the Ministry in turn was merely one part of the total executive machinery, the result was that at least in theory the Court of Administrative Litigation was more powerful than and superior in authority to the law courts whenever a question of administrative abuse was raised. Certainly as a practical matter the disabling of regular courts to referee disputes between the subject and his government made it possible for the militarists, following their accession to political power, to accomplish changes in governmental structure and to institute administrative measures destructive of the liberties of individuals and opposition groups, free from scrutiny by courts of law; the limited and cumbersome review procedures provided for the Court of Administrative Litigation removed any effective check on such activities as far as that court was concerned.

The situation has been drastically changed under the present Constitution. The judiciary is formally recognized as a third independent branch of government. Article 76 provides that "the whole judicial power is vested in a Supreme Court and in such inferior courts as are established by law." "No extraordinary tribunal shall be established, nor shall any organ or agency of the Executive be given final judicial power," which is a direct and final blow at the prewar administrative court system. "All judges shall be independent in the exercise of their conscience and shall be bound only by this Constitution and the Laws." Article 78 limits the removal of judges to cases of public impeachment or judicial declaration of physical or mental incompetence; the executive arm is specifically denied any power to discipline judges. Article 81 confirms the role of the judiciary: "The Supreme Court is the court of last resort with power to determine the constitutionality of any law, order, regulation, or official act." The Supreme Court is given rule-making power by Article 77 and has exercised it by issuing various rules governing practice before it and inferior courts and by issuing rules of criminal and civil procedure.[29]

Except for changes in name and the abolition of police courts, the postwar judicial system bears substantial resemblance in both structure and jurisdiction to the earlier system. At the bottom of the ladder are summary courts (*kan'i-saibansho*), with petty civil and criminal jurisdiction. The courts of general trial jurisdiction are district courts (*chihō-saibansho*). The most significant addition is the system of family courts (*katei-saibansho*), with territorial jurisdiction corresponding to the district courts, competent to handle domestic relations problems, juvenile delinquency cases, and criminal trials against adults who have contributed to the delinquency of minors. In its approach of conciliation and protection it fits Japanese social traditions far better than the district courts with their more formal and public proceedings. Above the district and family courts are the high courts (*kōtō-saibansho*) and the Supreme Court (Saikō-saibansho), with appellate jurisdiction. Qualifications of judges and organization of the courts are provided for in the Court Organization Law (Saibanhō).[30]

The change in status of the Japanese judiciary has created problems within the judiciary itself concerning its role in law making and law evaluation. As suggested above, feudal Japanese law rested in the almost unfettered discretion of the judicial administrator; each case was considered unique, and no very effective system was devised to correlate the decisions reached by individual magistrates. When the civil-law system was adopted, there was no substantial change in judicial attitude toward judicial precedents, for under the civil law the legal norms are in theory all contained in the code provisions, and the judges merely apply the appropriate provision to the facts of the particular case. This was most congenial to Japanese administrators and judges. If a court deciding a particular case included in its formal judgment statements expressing its interpretation of the underlying code provision, this in no way bound or had to be taken cognizance of by the same or another court deciding another case; the court deciding the later case was free to draw a different conclusion about the proper interpretation and application of the statute from that arrived at in the first. The relative rank of the courts did not matter; a court of appeal could ignore interpretive statements in an earlier opinion of the Daishin-in with impunity, and both decisions would be cited as equal authority by scholarly commentators. Indeed, scholars themselves felt free to maintain that the "true" law under the code was quite contrary to what the courts had declared the code coverage to be, an attitude quite different from that of their academic counterparts in England or the United States, who may disagree with an interpretation adopted by the appellate judiciary but who still recognize it as the existing norm until either the judiciary reverses the prior decision or the legislature or constitutional convention acts to abrogate the judicially created standard.

The postwar Constitution, however, requires more of the judiciary, in that the Supreme Court at least, if not all the courts, is required to pass on the constitutionality of legislation. The role has proved an unaccustomed one and has been sparingly exercised. But if the Supreme Court passes on a constitutional question by formal decision, lower courts and judges are bound by the decision and cannot rule to the contrary. Though this paramountcy of the Supreme Court is technically required only in constitutional cases, one can observe an increasing tendency toward following Supreme Court precedent in other cases as well, and the Supreme Court appears to consider the fact of differing interpretations among the several high courts as reason to pass formally on the interpretation of rule and statute. Only time will tell, but an American lawyer receives the impression that judges, prosecutors, and lawyers use precedent in a way strikingly similar to that in the Anglo-American tradition and that in time the Japanese legal system may resemble far more closely that tradition than its original civil-law precursor. At present the academic community is the principal stronghold for the earlier ideas that decisions may be ignored at will and that the scholar's opinion may outweigh that of the Supreme Court as "law"; even here some of the younger writers, particularly those who have studied in the United States, are coming more and more to recognize that prior judicial decisions, even under a code, do determine the coverage of law.

Since the Constitution refers only to the Supreme Court's power to interpret the constitutionality of legislation, there has been disagreement over whether or not inferior courts also have the power to determine constitutional questions in default of a Supreme Court decision. The Supreme Court has ruled that they may do so, but it is not clear

whether this ruling is based on the Constitution itself or on the statutes
which create the lower courts and define their jurisdiction; if it is the
latter, the Diet could restrict the power to decide constitutional questions if it chose.

The Court has also found it necessary to preserve its powers against
encroachment from the legislative branch. The first occasion arose in
1948 as the aftermath of the Urawa Mitsuko case. Mrs. Urawa had been
deserted by her husband and was in extreme want; she decided to kill
her three young children and commit suicide. She gave poisoned fish
to the children, who died, and drank the gravy herself, but when the
poison failed to take effect she turned herself in to the police.[31] The
district court gave her a three-year suspended sentence, and the procurator waived appeal, which made the judgment final. The Judiciary Committee of the House of Councilors of the Diet began an investigation
of the case, contending that the decision was based on the "feudalistic"
thought that the grim necessities of life might be sufficient motive for
a "quadruple suicide." In May, 1949, the Supreme Court sent a formal
statement to the House of Councilors, urging that the Constitution did
not permit other governmental bodies to interfere with the exercise
of the judicial power vested exclusively by the Constitution in the
courts. The Judiciary Committee replied:

> The power of determining unconstitutionality of laws, vested in the
> Supreme Court, is only the negative function of exercising a veto on applica-
> tion of laws violative of the Constitution in individual concrete cases. Con-
> sequently, the forming of an opinion by the Supreme Court on a constitu-
> tional question other than judicial matters, in relation to the Diet and the
> Cabinet, which is not at all a concrete judicial case, is a usurpation.

The second was the Suita City "silent-tribute" case, in which during
the pendency of the proceedings the presiding judge failed to prevent
and control a demonstration in the courtroom by persons sympathetic
to the defendants, in which they enforced a period of silence in memory
of the war dead in the Korean conflict and applauded the termination
of hostilities. Japanese trials are conducted in the form of a number of
brief hearings at which testimony is heard, each hearing being followed
by an adjournment of several days or weeks. After the courtroom demonstration but while the trial court continued its serial trial proceedings and prior to adjudication of the case, the House Judiciary
Committee summoned the Procurator-General and the Chief of the
Administrative Section of the Supreme Court before it to testify about
the details of the incident but in consideration of the earlier Urawa
case did not summon the trial judges themselves. The Impeachment

498

Committee of the House of Representatives endeavored, however, to call before it the presiding judge of the trial court; he refused to attend. Thereupon the Chief of the Administrative Section of the Supreme Court suggested to the committee that to investigate the handling of the trial of a case which was still pending might constitute an improper influence on the ultimate decision of that case. In both of these cases the formal documents suggest a draw, but public and scholarly opinion in general has supported the position taken by the representatives of the judiciary, and the Diet has refrained from using its investigating and impeaching powers in recent years in connection with specific judicial decisions.

The Supreme Court has adopted limitations on the scope of its reviewing power similar to those developed by the United States Supreme Court. One is that there be a case or controversy. In 1952 the secretary-general of the Social Democratic Party brought an action contending that the laws providing for the establishment of defense forces for Japan in the guise of a National Police Reserve were unconstitutional. The Court rejected the case on the ground it need only decide concrete cases, not express opinions on abstract constitutional issues.[32] Implicit in the ruling is the idea that a taxpayer has no standing to challenge the constitutionality of expenditures of tax revenues. Another limitation is that political questions will not be decided by the Court. After Prime Minister Yoshida dissolved the House of Representatives in 1952, one of the candidates who lost his seat in the ensuing election brought suit contending that the dissolution was in violation of Article 7 of the Constitution because there was neither a no-confidence resolution nor a rejection of a resolution of confidence. The Court threw the case out on the same grounds as the National Police Reserve case.[33]

The Court has been most sparing in its exercise of the power to declare legislation unconstitutional, and not all of its decisions have been as strong in favor of individual rights as one would have expected decisions of the United States Supreme Court to be in similar circumstances.[34] Nevertheless, since this power of review and interpretation is new and unfamiliar in Japan, advances must come slowly, as indeed they have in India and West Germany, where constitutional review also is a recent innovation. On the whole the prognosis is favorable in Japan.

The Procuracy

During the feudal period there was no class of officials directly comparable to a modern prosecuting attorney or procurator; apparently any official was empowered to commence proceedings. When the first formal system of criminal procedure was adopted in the Meiji period, it was patterned directly on the French system, in which the state is represented by the *procureur* in all criminal prosecutions. Prior to 1945 procurators had substantial powers as employees of the Ministry of Justice to gather evidence and require cooperation from anyone to further their investigations. During the trial of cases they sat on the bench with the judges, who ranked no higher than they in authority and who were also subordinates in the Ministry of Justice. In practice considerable deference was paid to the opinion of the procurator in charge of the case. Though under the present Code of Criminal Procedure many of the investigating powers of the procurator have been curtailed, nevertheless his basic functions have not been essentially changed. The judge has now been moved into a superior position as part of an independent judiciary, however, and the status and powers of defense attorneys have been increased to such a marked degree under the present Constitution and code that procurator and defense counsel occupy approximately the same relative position in the trial of criminal cases. The result is a truly adversary proceeding.

At the head of the procuracy is the Procurator-General, a senior official in the Ministry of Justice. A number of administrative and training personnel serve directly under his supervision. The procurators themselves are assigned to offices corresponding to the territorial jurisdiction of the several high courts, district courts, and summary courts; each office processes the cases which will be tried in the court of corresponding territorial competence. Aspects of their duties will be considered in greater detail in the section "Criminal Procedure."

Attorneys

The *Conclusions* promulgated at Delhi naturally turned to the legal profession itself as one of the instrumentalities for promoting the Rule of Law. The views embodied in them which represent both the civil and the common law are:

> It is essential to the maintenance of the Rule of Law that there should be an organized legal profession free to manage its own affairs. But it is recognized that there may be general supervision by the Courts and that there may be regulations governing the admission to and pursuit of the legal profession.
>
> While there is some difference of emphasis between various countries as to the extent to which a lawyer may be under a duty to accept a case it is conceived that:
>
> (1) Wherever a man's life, liberty, property or reputation are at stake he

should be free to obtain legal advice and representation; if this principle is to become effective, it follows that lawyers must be prepared frequently to defend persons associated with unpopular causes and minority views with which they themselves may be entirely out of sympathy;

(2) once a lawyer has accepted a brief he should not relinquish it to the detriment of his client without good and sufficient cause;

(3) it is the duty of a lawyer which he should be able to discharge without fear of consequences to press upon the Court any argument of law or of fact which he may think proper for the presentation of the case by him.

Equal access to law for the rich and poor alike is essential to the maintenance of the Rule of Law. It is, therefore, essential to provide adequate legal advice and representation to all those, threatened as to their life, liberty, property or reputation who are not able to pay for it. . . .[35]

The attainment of such goals of course requires the existence of constitutional provisions and statutes which guarantee a legitimate scope of activity to lawyers, but it also requires a profession the members of which command a substantial degree of respect in the community because of their competence and their adherence to moral and ethical standards. It has been only in relatively recent times that the profession in Japan has begun to attain these qualifications.

There was no regularly established legal profession prior to the Meiji era. Private persons could not bring prosecutions, and their private disputes were disposed of by reconcilement and conciliation.[36] The *nanushi* (mayor or headman) of the village represented his villagers in disputes with outsiders over boundaries and irrigation rights, accompanied individual townspeople to court when they were engaged in litigation with residents of other villages, and acted as a kind of notary in connection with sale, leasing, and encumbrancing transactions to which his villagers were parties. In performing these functions he resembled an attorney, though he was also charged with official responsibility for prosecuting crimes and punishing minor offenders within the area of his administrative jurisdiction.

In Edo and Osaka there appeared a group of persons called *kujishi* [37] who advised townspeople and visitors how to carry out their negotiations with tax and administrative officials. They became notorious for their bribery of officials, the high fees which they charged, and their instigation of improper litigation and were in due course banned from Edo. But the ban was inapplicable to those who were also proprietors of inns. The Edo Tax Office was located in a part of Tokyo in which there were many temples and pleasure spots and consequently many inns to accommodate visitors. Though in ordinary practice the *nanushi* or the head of the litigant's house was expected to accompany the litigant before the competent official, when one visited a place other than his place of residence, the proprietor of the inn at which he stayed became in legal effect a temporary head of household and therefore accompanied the litigant. Thus the proprietors of the inns near the Edo Tax Office came more and more to advise and represent their transient patrons in tax and other administrative matters. These *kuji-yado*,[38] as they were called, were held in no more esteem than their predecessor *kujishi;* an 1854 text describes them as persons "who accompanied stupid people to court and wrote documents for them." [39]

After the restoration the roles of *daigennin* (advocate) and *daishōnin* (notary) came into being, apparently on the French pattern. An official examination was instituted in 1876, but it was difficult enough that few passed, and most of those who had practiced as *daigennin* continued their professional activities without using the title. The status even of licensed *daigennin* was low, and it was not until late in the nineteenth century that they were accorded the same courtesies by courtroom attendants and admitted to the courtroom under the same conditions as were the procurators. During this period various bar associations were formed. The conflicts between the English school and the French school were also evident here, however, and on several occasions the public procurator was forced to intervene and straighten out the situation. The first formal Lawyers Law was enacted in 1893, and at this time the word *bengoshi* came into currency. In ensuing years constant efforts were made to raise the standards for admission to the profession, but unlicensed *daigennin* remained in practice, and the continuous disputes between and among the public and private bar associations made it difficult to strengthen admission requirements. The modern Lawyers Law was enacted in 1933 and revised after World War II.[40] The chief postwar changes were those which took responsibility for regulating the profession from the Ministry of Justice and lodged it in the Japan Federation of Bar Associations (Nihon Bengoshi Rengōkai). Matters of discipline and disbarment are in the hands of the federation and not in those of the judiciary.[41]

The private practitioner continues to occupy a relatively minor social position when compared with his counterpart in Western countries. The stress on the right to counsel in the present Constitution and Code of Criminal Procedure, however, has meant a major increase in the standing and responsibility of the profession in criminal cases. Private attorneys serve as a responsible check on procurator misconduct. Nevertheless, their role still continues to be of lesser significance on the civil side than one would expect in a modern industrial nation of 97 million people. There were in 1962 only 6,800 attorneys in Japan organized into fifty-one bar associations. Most are concentrated in the larger cities, where they do mainly commercial and property work.[42] Practice is usually on an individual basis, with nothing resembling the large law firm in United States practice.

This minor role in civil-law matters is chiefly the result of the traditional disinclination of the Japanese to litigate even in instances of direct and substantial injury to person or property and their continued resort to reconcilement and conciliation.[43] While there is no reason why an attorney cannot be sought out as the third-party mediator, the traditional disfavor with which the lawyer is viewed, particularly in rural areas, makes it unlikely in fact that his services will be so utilized; the low figures for the lawyer population outside metropolitan areas tend to confirm this.[44] Furthermore, the regular attorney has to compete with various specialists in tax and patent matters and with the *shihō shoshi* (legal scrivener or notary on the European pattern) for business which in other countries would fall to the attorney.[45] Larger corporations tend also to maintain their own legal departments staffed with graduates of law faculties who are not formally qualified as lawyers, which further reduces the "preventive practice" on which lawyers outside Japan rely so heavily.[46] Until and unless these conditions change, this minor role in society will most likely continue to prevail. Obviously, it would seem, even mature and modern legal systems can differ considerably in the manner in which they handle the details of legal procedure.

Legal Education

There were no formal law schools until the 1880s, when the Ministry of Justice established its own school to teach French law. Soon thereafter law departments were established in the leading imperial universities and at private universities like Chūo, Waseda, and Keiō. Under the first Lawyers Law graduates of the imperial schools could be admitted to practice without special examination, but in time this special treatment ceased, and examinations came to be required of graduates of any law school before they could be admitted. Only a relatively small percentage of those enrolled as attorneys had taken formal law training at the universities, however, which meant that law faculties increasingly purveyed general education, combining law with political science and economics. No practical training of any kind was offered. Efforts were made to establish an apprentice system under the 1933 Lawyers Law, but it did not actually function effectively prior to the war. This was merely the other side of the lack of development of a separate and respected legal profession in Japan.

In 1949 the Lawyers Law and the new Court Organization Law provided for the creation of the Legal Research and Training Institute (Shihō Kenshūsho) under the supervision of the Administrative Section of the Supreme Court.[47] Each year approximately half of the persons receiving university diplomas in law sit for the examination; out of the 8,300 candidates in 1960, only 345 (4.16 per cent) passed. Successful candidates undergo a two-year training program consisting partly of academic instruction paralleling in many ways portions of the curriculum of the American law school and partly of apprenticeships in courts, in procurators' offices, and with private attorneys. At the end of the second year a second examination is administered, which most of the trainees pass, and the trainees then become full-fledged judges, procurators, or attorneys.

In contrast to the English and American tradition in which judges and prosecuting officials are selected or elected from among experienced members of the bar, Japanese judges and procurators usually become such at the outset of their careers and gain no other type of experience during their active professional lives. There are a number of reasons for this, including the European patterns of career judiciary and procuracy on which the Japanese system is based, the laws governing appointment to government service which as administered make an appointment from outside the particular branch of the profession difficult, a rather exclusive attitude on the part of each group toward outsiders, and severe financial drawbacks for the private attorney who accepts a belated appointment to government service.[48] While there is much talk of a unification of the legal profession to promote mobility in professional activity, such a unification is not likely to occur until basic changes have been made in the laws governing the profession and even more basic changes in the attitudes of the legal profession itself.

Those who contemplate a teaching career may, if their records are strong enough, be appointed as assistants to a full professor in a particular field. If they prove promising, they may receive appointments as assistant professors and in time will become full professors. Under the present Education Law, master's- and doctoral-degree programs are maintained at a number of law faculties, but their graduates are rarely called to teaching positions at outstanding schools and have no advantage in writing the national bar examination. Consequently, very little useful function has been served to date by these advanced-degree programs. It is unusual to find a law teacher who has had any experience in practice; this, coupled with the European training of many members of the teaching profession, means that in numerous cases law is taught as an abstract body of learning unrelated to the realities of practice before courts and administrative agencies.

CONTEMPORARY DEVELOPMENTS
IN JAPANESE LAW

Constitutional Law

Under the pre-Meiji emperors and shoguns there was of course no understanding of the function of or desire for a constitution in the modern sense.[49] With the influx of new ideas under the Emperor Meiji, however, there was substantial pressure to provide a constitution. Upon prolonged investigation Prince Itō Hirobumi recommended that a constitution be promulgated on the lines of the Prussian or Bavarian constitutions, which on the surface appeared to grant substantial rights and liberties to the citizenry but actually left the scope of such rights and liberties to administrative or legislative judgment. Since this suggestion suited nicely the desires of those in authority, the Meiji Constitution of 1889 was so drafted and promulgated. Its preamble indicates the tone of the document:

> Having by virtue of the glories of our ancestors ascended the throne of a lineal succession unbroken for ages eternal; desiring to promote the welfare of, and to give development to the moral and intellectual faculties of our beloved subjects, the very same that have been favored with the benevolent care and affectionate vigilance of our ancestors; and hoping to maintain the prosperity of the State in concert with our people and with their support, we hereby promulgate . . . a fundamental law of State, to exhibit the principles by which we are to be guided in our conduct, and to point out to what our descendants and our subjects and their descendants are forever to conform.

In form all organs of government, including the legislative, were responsible to the Emperor. Though individual subjects were guaranteed freedom of abode and change of abode (Article 22), freedom from entry and search of the dwelling (Article 25), privacy of written communications (Article 26), and freedom of speech and press (Article 29), all of these were limited by the phrases "within the limits of law" or "except in cases provided for by law." Freedom of religion (Article 28) was permitted to the people "within limits not prejudicial to peace and order and not antagonistic to their duties as subjects." Those who controlled the imperial machinery controlled the nation.

One of the chief reform measures under the Occupation was the adoption of a new Constitution. In legal form it was an amendment to the old Constitution made pursuant to the machinery for amendment contained in the preamble of that document; thus some writers have maintained that the form of state (*kokutai*) [50] has not been changed under the new Constitution. But the preamble to the new document indicates clearly that a fundamental change has been made:

> We, the Japanese people, acting through our duly elected representatives in the National Diet, determined that we shall secure for ourselves and our posterity the fruits of peaceful cooperation with all nations and the blessings of liberty throughout this land, and resolved that never again shall we be visited with the horrors of war through the action of government, do proclaim that sovereign power resides with the people and do firmly establish this Constitution. Government is a sacred trust of the people, the authority for which is derived from the people, the powers of which are exercised by the representatives of the people, and the benefits of which are enjoyed by the people. This is a universal principle of mankind upon which this Constitution is founded. We reject and revoke all constitutions, laws, ordinances and rescripts in conflict herewith. . . .

Under the present Constitution the Emperor is no longer "at the head of the Empire, combining in himself the rights of sovereignty" (Meiji, Article 4), but rather is "the symbol of the State and of the unity of the people, deriving his position from the will of the people with whom resides sovereign power" (Article 1). The Imperial House Law passed by the Diet controls the succession (Article 2), not a law created by the Emperor himself (Meiji, Article 75). The Emperor's powers are strictly controlled (Article 7), and even gifts to and from the imperial household require Diet approval (Article 8). Hereditary peerages are abolished [Article 14(2)–(3)]. A large number of rights and freedoms are granted (or reserved) to the people without scope for legislative or executive qualification (Chapter III). The Diet is the highest organ of state power and is the sole law making organ (Article 41). Executive power is in the Cabinet (Article 65), which is responsible to the Diet [Article 66(3)]. The judiciary, as indicated above, is now independent (Chapter VI). Amendments to the Constitution must be ratified by the people and must be immediately promulgated by the Emperor as part of the Constitution (Article 96).

The document was drafted in some haste, and a number of provisions taken from American experience had no near counterpart in earlier Japanese law. Other provisions were incorporated to cure what were felt to be abuses under the earlier system. Among the former group, interpretive questions have arisen which the courts have had or will have to resolve; several will be alluded to in the materials on family law, criminal law, and criminal procedure. Among the latter group, one of the major areas of dispute has been that over the meaning and coverage of Article 9, which renounces war as a "sovereign right of the nation and the threat or use of force as means of settling international disputes" and states that armed forces and "other war potential will never be maintained." Rapid change in world circumstances made this, practically speaking, a questionable restriction, and Self-Defense Forces were created with American support and blessing. Contemporaneous with the San Francisco Peace Treaty the two countries executed the Mutual Security Treaty under which American armed forces continued to be stationed in Japan. Violent political debates raged over the constitutionality of these measures under Article 9. At length at least some light was shed on the question by the Supreme Court, which in the process revealed a divergence of opinion among the members of the Court themselves as to its role in deciding such questions.

The case, now usually known as the "Sunakawa case," [51] arose when left-wing students and labor union members joined the residents of Sunakawa Village in protesting by force the projected extension of runways of Tachikawa Air Force Base, which would take some of the arable land of the village. A number of the group surged into posted areas of the air base and were arrested and forcibly removed. Seven of them were prosecuted under article 2 of the Law for Special Measures Implementing the Administrative Agreement between Japan and the United States Authorized by the Security Treaty, which made anyone entering United States Armed Forces' facilities when prohibited or refusing to leave when requested subject to not more than one year of penal servitude or a fine of not more than ¥2,000 or a minor fine. Were this law not in effect, defendants could only have been prosecuted under article 1(32) of the Minor Offenses Law for entering a prohibited place, which would have been punishable only by detention or a minor fine. The defendants contended that they were being subjected to heavier penalties only because their conduct affected United States forces, that only the Mutual Security Treaty gave such forces special protection, that the presence of United States forces amounted to the maintenance of war potential in violation of Article 9(2) of the Constitution, that the special law therefore rested on an unconstitutional agreement, and that its application would deprive them of liberty and impose a penalty other than through "procedure established by law" (*hōritsu no sadameru tetsuzuki ni yoranakereba . . . keibatsu o kaserarenai;* Article 31).

The Tokyo District Court accepted their general line of argument and found them not guilty. Under Article 1 of the Mutual Security Treaty the United States was to "maintain forces to contribute to the maintenance of international peace and security in the Far East and to the security of Japan against armed attack from without, including assistance given at the express request of the Japanese Government to put down large-scale internal riots and disturbances in Japan, caused through instigation or intervention by an outside power or powers." The spirit of the Constitution required that Japan put her trust in the maintenance of peace through international cooperation of peoples and by military force administered only by the United Nations; presence of United States troops under the treaty amounted to the maintenance of war potential in violation of Article 9. Even though Japan was obligated under international law by virtue of the treaty to permit American forces in Japan, their presence nevertheless violated Article 9, and the effort to apply the special law violated Article 31. The government immediately appealed to the Supreme Court.

The Court reversed the district court. All the justices signed the brief statement of reasons for the decision, which construed Article 9 as preventing only aggressive war and not self-defense, upheld the Mutual Security Treaty as an interim measure for the defense of Japan, construed the treaty and supplementing agreement as leaving control of American troops in American hands, and suggested that the question was a political one which was primarily for the Diet and which the Supreme Court should not review unless the treaty was "obviously unconstitutional and void."

A number of the justices, however, felt it necessary to submit supplementary opinions explaining their reasons for voting for the official decision. Chief Justice Tanaka thought that the district court erred when it tied the special law to Article 9, but that in any event Article 9 was meant as an expression of international law which rejected only wars of aggression and considered wars in self-defense legitimate. Justice Shima felt that the question of what might be done by way of self-defense was one to be resolved through ordinary governmental action and that the Court could not say under the circumstances that there had been an abuse of discretion under the Constitution in resolving the problem as it had been. Justices Fujita and Irie insisted the entire matter was a political one and invoked the "political-question" analogy in American practice, the *acte de gouvernement* of French law, and the "act of state" in English decisions. Justice Tarumi would not have upset the administrative decision and suggested also that Article 31 did not clearly cover questions of the propriety of substantive criminal legislation under the Constitution but rather might be limited to the question of whether existing criminal-procedure statutes and rules had been applied or correctly applied in the particular case; he felt, however, that the lower court's judgment was illogical under either alternative. The several opinions of Justices Kawamura, Ishizaka, Kotani, Okuno, and Takahashi agreed that the Mutual Security Treaty and the special law were constitutional but disagreed with any implications in the formal statement of reasons that the Supreme Court lacked the power to review treaties under the Constitution; they suggested that there was no more reason to defer to the Diet in the case of a treaty than in the case of legislation.

Thus, the statements made in the Sunakawa case and the refusal to decide the National Police Reserve case on the merits [52] suggest that the Supreme Court will not invoke Article 9 to strike down the maintenance of defensive forces and material. But the Court is obviously divided in its attitude toward its relation to the Diet in reviewing matters of treaties and international affairs and perhaps in disagreement as well over the extent to which it can review substantive legislation under Article 31.[53]

Family Law

For centuries the family (*kazoku*) was the key unit in Japanese society. A patriarchal system prevailed, and continuity of the family was considered necessary in order that succession to property might be secure and that proper rites might be performed for the sake of the ancestors. Women were given a position markedly inferior to that of men. The woman entered the husband's house on marriage and might be sent away for a number of reasons. Adoption was recognized as a proper way of ensuring the continuation of the household line. All acts of all members of the household were under the strict control of the head of the house. These characteristics survived the Meiji Restoration and were incorporated in the Civil Code of 1898. Though the family system was gradually altered as Japan became more and more urbanized and industrialized, the traditional system continued to be embodied in the legal system until after World War II.

The basic unit under the Meiji code was the house (*ie*). This term did not have reference to a building or to a group of people living together but rather to a legal institution which came into being when the family was legally recorded in the family register (*koseki*). After the family was registered, it made no difference where its members actually resided, but changes in the status of members had to be recorded in the register before they took legal effect.

The legal representative of the house was the head of the house (*koshu*); under him were his relatives in the house and their spouses (article 732). The head and the members of the house all bore the family name of the house (article 746). The head of the house was bound to support its members (article 747). Members could acquire property in their own names, but if there was doubt about ownership, the property was presumed to be that of the head of the house (article 748). Members could not fix their places of actual residence against the will of the head of the house and could be ordered upon reasonable notice to move their residence wherever the head directed. The head was not responsible for them during any period of noncompliance, and continued disobedience could bring expulsion (*riseki*; article 749). The head had to consent before a natural child (*shoshi*) could be adopted (article 735), before blood relatives in another house could be admitted or readmitted (article 737), before relatives of persons already admitted could be admitted (article 738), before members could be married or adopted (article 750), or before they could be divorced by agreement (article 809). Failure to obtain approval or contracting a disapproved relationship could bring expulsion, in which case the expelled individual had to establish his own house (article 742). Incompetent members of the house were placed under a form of guardianship known as the family council (*shinzokukai*), which also supervised the affairs of minors and in certain cases determined on whom the headship of the house should devolve (articles 944–953, 886, 888, 751, 982, 985). The head of the house could not resign unless either he was sixty years of age or over or incapacitated to act by reason of illness or otherwise and unless succession to the headship had been accepted by a competent heir (articles 752, 753).

The chief victim of this system was the new wife of a member of the house. The system of marriage matches (*miai-kekkon*) was preserved and love matches made difficult by the requirement that the head of the house approve the marriage and the registration of the marriage. Even if the marriage relationship were approved and consummated, approval of registration might be withheld until it was determined that the girl was a dutiful daughter-in-law and a good worker or capable of bearing healthy children, or until her own parents concluded that she was entering a good home, for the head of her house had also to approve the marriage. Until the registration was finally consented to and carried out, she was subject to being packed ignominiously back to her parents, perhaps with a child of the "nonexistent" marriage. Under such circumstances she would have a technical right to compensation,[54] but the aggrieved Japanese wife rarely sought legal advice in domestic relations cases, as her American counterpart would have done.

Even after the marriage was finally registered, the wife was at a legal disadvantage compared with the husband. She was bound to live with her husband (article 789). Contracts respecting property could be entered into before marriage, but they had to be separately registered before the marriage was registered to be effective (article 794). The husband managed the wife's property (article 801), though she had to consent to the contracting of loans, transfer of property, and furnishing of security (article 802). If it was uncertain to which spouse property belonged, it was presumed to be that of the husband (article 807).

Divorce could be effectuated by consent (article 808), though the consent of the head of the house was also necessary. Since once the marriage had been registered the wife was a member of the husband's house, however, this meant that she was bound by that consent which was given. Being instilled with a submissive attitude toward husband and elders, she ordinarily complied without objection. Or, if she did not agree, the provisions for judicial divorce were weighted heavily in favor of the husband. Adultery was legal ground for divorce only when committed by the wife [article 813(2)], and the provisions that authorized divorce if the spouse had been "subjected . . . to ill treatment or gross insult which renders cohabitation unbearable" [article 814(5)] or if the "lineal ascendants have been subjected to ill treatment or gross insult by his (her) spouse" [article 814(8)] were readily invokable against the daughter-in-law who refused to consent to the divorce. In either case legal custody of the children went to the father unless there was a specific agreement to the contrary (articles 812, 819), which meant in practice that the husband's wishes were controlling. The only time the man was at a legal disadvantage was when he married a woman who was the head of a house and entered her house (*nyūfu kon-in*), in which case the legal disabilities which usually attached to the wife attached under the several code articles to the *nyūfu*. If the heiress was provided for, however, by adopting a male on condition that he marry the girl (*mukoyōshi-engumi*), the usual marriage rules applied, though the adoption might be revoked if the marriage ended in divorce.

Children remained under parental control until they came of legal age (20 under article 3) *and* had an independent livelihood. They had to live where directed by the parent unless the head of the house (if not the parent) directed otherwise (article 800). A child could not enter the armed forces without parental permission (article 881) and could not engage in any business or occupation without such consent (article 883). The parent managed the property of the child and of the child's wife, if any (articles 884, 885), though a mother had to consult the family council first in order to take a number of actions respecting her children's property (article 886), and a father or mother had to ask the family council to appoint a special representative if there was a conflict of interest between the parent and the child (article 888). The duty of care was that which the parent exercised over his own property (article 889), but at the child's majority only an accounting for the surplus of income over the costs of rearing the child and managing his property was required (article 890). The parent had the power of discipline and could place an unruly child in a house of correction with the permission of a court (article 882).

Children included children born during wedlock (article 820), a natural child (shoshi) acknowledged by its father (article 828) through registration or mention in a will (article 829), and adopted children (yōshi; article 837). The child or the descendants of a deceased natural child could sue to force the mother or putative father to acknowledge him (article 835), and the shoshi was automatically legitimated if the natural parents later married each other (article 836).

There were certain limitations on adoption. No ascendant or person older than the adopter could be adopted (article 838). If there was already a male heir presumptive, no other male could be adopted except as a husband for a daughter (article 839). A guardian could not adopt his ward during wardship or until after the final accounting had been rendered (article 840). Consent had to be given by the adopter's spouse (article 841), by the parents within the same house of a child under fifteen (article 843), and by the adopter's parents in certain cases (articles 844, 845). The adoption had to be registered (article 849). Under certain circumstances the adoption could be annulled (articles 851–859). An adoption could be dissolved (rien) by judicial action if there were ill treatment, desertion, or conviction of a crime punished by a year's imprisonment or more, if the adopted child committed an offense which tended to disgrace the family name or endanger the family property, if there had been grave insult to the lineal ascendant of either party, or if after a mukoyōshi-engumi there had been a divorce (article 866). Dissolution could not take place, however, while the adopted child was the head of the house in which he had been adopted (article 874). During the period in which the adoption was valid, the adopted child had the status of a legitimate child of the adoptive parents (article 860) and was a part of their house (article 861).

Adoption thus served a number of desirable purposes within the family system, since it provided for the continuity of the family name, for the continued performance of religious rites, for the orderly descent of property, for the conferring of benefits on promising young members of impecunious branches of the house, and for the provision of suitable husbands for daughters of the family. But it also lent itself to illicit uses, particularly the selling of young girls into prostitution.

The final institution which tended to preserve the family system was the law of testate and intestate succession (*sōzoku*). The rules were divided into two groups, those having to do with succession to headship of the house and those having to do with succession to property. Headship devolved whenever the former head died, retired, lost Japanese nationality, or left the house by virtue of annulment of marriage or adoption or whenever a female head married a *nyūfu* (article 964). In the latter case the *nyūfu* became the head of the house unless there was a declaration of a contrary purpose (articles 736, 788). If the *nyūfu* divorced his spouse, headship again devolved by virtue of article 964 to whoever qualified as the heir under the code. The code provided that the nearest lineal descendant succeeded to the position. If, however, there were several lineal descendants of the ancestor, article 970 laid down the following rules: (1) as between persons of different degrees of relationship (like children and grandchildren) a person of a nearer degree of relationship was preferred; (2) as among persons of the same degree of relationship (like brothers and sisters) males were preferred; (3) as among males or females of the same degree of relationship legitimate children were preferred; (4) as among a legitimate child, a *shoshi*, and an illegitimate child, the legitimate child and the *shoshi*, even though females, were preferred to the illegitimate child; and (5) as among persons not otherwise distinguishable on any of the other grounds, the oldest was preferred. If the presumptive heir had been sentenced for murdering or attempting to murder the ancestor or earlier presumptive heir, had failed to bring formal charges against or inform the authorities about the known murder of the ancestor, had by fraud or duress caused the ancestor to make, revoke, or alter or refrain from making, revoking, or altering a will, or had forged, altered, destroyed, or concealed the ancestor's will relating to the succession, he could not take headship (article 969). During his lifetime the ancestor could also sue at law to have the presumptive heir disqualified if he had ill-treated or grossly insulted the ancestor, if the heir were not physically or mentally qualified to become such, if the heir had been sentenced for an offense tending to disgrace the family name, or if he had been adjudged a spendthrift without hope of reformation (article 975). The ancestor could also disinherit by will (article 976).

Property descended to those of nearest degree or to their lineal descendants if they predeceased the ancestor (articles 994, 995). If there were none in either class, property descended in order to the spouse, to lineal ascendants, or to the head of the house, the lineal ascendants being classified under the same rules applicable to lineal descendants under articles 994 and 995 (article 996). Disabilities similar to those placed on heirs to the headship of the house also operated in cases of descent of property (article 997). Prospective heirs could also be judicially disinherited on the application of the ancestor (article 998) or by having the property devised by will to someone else (article 1064). The heir to either the headship or property succeeded to all the rights of the ancestor (articles 986–991, 1001–1003).

These features of Japan's first "modern" family law are one of the prime illustrations of the manner in which earlier customary practices were perpetuated to blunt the effect of the Meiji legal reforms. Even before 1945 much criticism was directed against these provisions by the progessive elements of the population.

The new Constitution struck directly at a number of these aspects of family law through the language of Article 24:

> 1. Marriage shall be based only on the mutual consent of both sexes and it shall be maintained through mutual cooperation with the equal rights of husband and wife as a basis.
>
> 2. With regard to choice of spouse, property rights, inheritance, choice of domicile, divorce and other matters pertaining to marriage and the family, laws shall be enacted from the standpoint of individual dignity and the essential equality of the sexes.

During the transitional period from the old system to the new there was a special temporary statute adjusting the Civil Code provisions; this special statute was in due course replaced by new Books IV and V of the Civil Code, effective in 1948, and by changes in a number of collateral laws, such as the Family Registration Law and the Penal Code.

Under the present Civil Code consent to marriage is not necessary except in the case of a minor (article 737), minority terminating at the age of eighteen for a male and sixteen for a female (article 731). Under the revised Family Registration Law (*Kosekihō*) the new husband and wife set up their own new registration (article 739), which means that no other member of the family need give approval for the marriage to take effect. Customs change only gradually, particularly in rural areas, however, and there may still be substantial delays between the factual inception of a marriage and its legal inception through registration.[55] Registration of the new family is still done where the old family retained its legal location (*honseki*), but under the new law descendants of the original family can apply to have their new family registrations transferred to the place where they in fact reside (article 108), and a number of persons have taken advantage of the possibility. Though ordinarily a divorced wife returns to her original family register, she may if she wishes apply to have her own registration.

Marriage may still be terminated by either consensual or judicial divorce, but husband and wife are on a legal parity as far as grounds are concerned, and either may divorce the other for acts of unchastity, desertion, continued absence, mental disease, or "any other grave reason for which it is difficult . . . to continue the marriage" (article 770).[56] The creation of the new family courts has also affected somewhat the freedom of divorce, and efforts are made in a number of cases to effect a reconciliation through formal reconciliation proceedings before a family court judge and two conciliation commissioners (*chōtei-iin*). The court will also decide child-custody matters unless the parties are able to agree both to the divorce and to the terms of child custody (article 766). Similar intervention may occur if there is a dispute about property (article 768). The family court may order a division of marital property (*zaisan bun-yo*) but usually sets the amount at a pittance in comparison with a typical American decree.[57] Alimony as such is unknown.

Since the family system is no longer specifically undergirded by the Civil Code, provisions relating to succession cover property only. Under the new articles, particularly articles 887 and 900, primogeniture no longer prevails.

While the postwar code more nearly conforms to practices which appear equitable and reasonable to us, it has not proved entirely workable, in part because it departs too greatly from existing requirements. For instance, the new law of succession and the possibility of partition where a number of children inherit could hardly be strictly enforced.[58] If partition of farm property is made, the resulting parcels may be uneconomical to till; the process carried through a few generations could produce utter fragmentation of real property holdings. If younger children renounce their rights in favor of the elder, they receive nothing from the estate, and if the elder undertakes to buy their shares he may find himself under heavy financial obligation. Apparently in most cases either the other children renounce or else the farm is operated as a unit for the benefit of the whole family, but reconsideration of the problem by the Diet is probably in order.

On the other hand, other provisions are criticized as retaining too much of the older law. There is considerable controversy over article 897, which provides for the devolution of genealogical records, articles of worship, and burial grounds to the person who under earlier practice would have been the head of the house; and over article 750, which provides that the husband or wife assumes the name (*uji*) of the other partner in accordance with prenuptial agreement. Both are attacked as perpetuations of the discredited family system, but both provisions were felt to be consistent with the continuing needs of Japanese society and therefore were retained. Criticism is also levied against the statement of article 730, "Lineal relatives by blood and relatives living together shall mutually cooperate," as an unenforceable moral exhortation which preserves the old family system. Since it has no enforcement provisions, its presence in the code probably does not matter; and the fact that these few articles are all that can be found to argue about is a rather good indication that the new system has found general favor with the Japanese people.

Contracts, Property Interests, and Secured Transactions

Whenever a country's economy moves beyond the barter system, it is likely to develop a rather systematic customary or legal regulation of trade practices. Though Japan was for the most part out of international trade channels during the Tokugawa era, it developed quite sophisticated methods of controlling internal transactions.[59] Records of the seventeenth and eighteenth centuries show the well-established use of bills of exchange, notes and drafts, insurance, negotiable bills of lading, and the like and the existence of such institutions as banks, clearinghouses, and branch business establishments. The broad language of the Civil Code of 1898 did not directly countermand these earlier practices, so that under it legal doctrine developed together with the economy. Because of this flexibility relatively few changes have been made in the code even in the postwar era. Nevertheless, the demands of financing a growing consumer economy have required changes in institutions and experimentation with credit devices, which so far have been accomplished only by experimental departures from commercial custom and by the judicial sanction of these experiments. In several areas there is urgent need for revision of existing legislation, perhaps along the lines of the new Uniform Commercial Code which has been adopted by a number of American states.

The Japanese law of contracts remains substantially unchanged from the prewar era and in form resembles strongly the German code.[60] The only changes were to repeal articles 14–19, which permitted a married woman to enter into contracts only with her husband's consent, and article 120, which permitted a husband to avoid contracts made by his wife. In its inception and tenor the Japanese contract does not differ substantially from the contract in Anglo-American law, except that it need not rest on the consideration[61] which is essential to the validity of a common-law contract. Contracts (*keiyaku*) are agreements of two or more persons which are intended to produce fixed effects under private law among such persons. When the contract becomes binding, both parties are expected to perform. But if substantially changed circumstances make performance impossible, judicial relief will be given against a demand for performance made by the party in whose favor the promise ran, though the nonperforming party will have to make restitution in such a case for whatever he has received of value in the transaction. If the contract relates to the sale of property, risk of loss usually falls on the buyer unless it results from the seller's fault. Contracts may of course be rescinded by mutual agreement, and the aggrieved party may also rescind in case of unexcused nonperformance by the other party.

Apart from possible differences in legal terminology, a Westerner entering into a contract with a Japanese individual or firm will find that a contract is often considered an agreement to enter into a general course of conduct rather than something fixing the precise terms of performance.[62] As a result, there may be basic disagreement over whether or not the agreement has been breached—another indication of how customary practices continue to affect legal interpretation.

The law of checks and bills is based on statutes enacted in 1934 which adopted the Geneva Uniform Laws. There are, therefore, no substantial differences between the rules governing commercial transactions in Japan and those in most other countries; [63] internal and external transfers are readily carried out, subject of course to special laws covering currency control and regulation.[64] The volume of check transactions in Japan is still substantially below that in the United States, and ultimate consumer transactions are mostly on a cash basis. The machinery for processing what correspond to cashier's checks is quite cumbersome, and the office practices of the banks themselves appear inefficient in comparison with those in most large banks in the United States. Acceptance of the use of checks to pay for goods and services and modernization of banking methods, however, will come from changed attitudes on the part of individual citizens, companies, and banks, and formal statutory changes seem for the most part unnecessary.

From the Meiji period on there had been in Japan substantial problems concerning the relationship between landlords, resident and absent, and their agricultural tenants. Moreover, the traditional landlord system was felt to be compatible with totalitarian politics. Consequently, the Occupation instituted reform legislation which restricted the amount of land which landlords could hold and authorized the purchase of surplus holdings at controlled prices by the former tenants or by others who would till the land.[65] Absentee ownership was prohibited absolutely. Administration of these objectives was to be attained through local land committees.

At the expiration of the Occupation, in 1952, a new Agricultural

Land Law was enacted. It retains the same general provisions as the Occupation reform measure. Agricultural and tenanted landholdings cannot exceed 3 *chō* [66] and 1 *chō*, respectively, anywhere except in Hokkaido, where the limits are 12 *chō* and 4 *chō*, respectively. There is no price restriction on the sale and transfer of land, but the transferee must already be a farmer cultivating at least 3 *tan* (2 *chō* in Hokkaido). Individual determinations as to how the law shall be applied are made by agricultural committees (*nōgyō-iinkai*) elected by all adult farming residents in the committee area. Since the law embodies a generally acceptable resolution of an acknowledged problem, it has required no substantial amendment.

The constitutionality of the Agricultural Land Law was attacked in the Supreme Court on the ground that the compensation was so low and its original value so impaired by inflation that it violated Article 29(3) of the Constitution, which requires just compensation for land taken for public use. The Court upheld the measure under Article 29(2), which states that "property rights shall be defined by law, in conformity with the public welfare." Statutes in 1938 and during the war had qualified property rights in farmland to the point that no free market price could develop. The Court disposed of the argument resting on the effect of inflation by stating that increases in the price of rice reflected increased production costs, not the use value of the land, and that in any event prices fixed "in conformity with the public welfare" do not have to match those in a "hypothetical free market." [67]

Criminal Law

The prewar Penal Code was essentially the German law, modified slightly to fit Japanese needs and tradition.[68] There are more numerous provisions covering arson and fire protection and floods and flood control than are usual in Western codes. The old code also provided for increased penalties for crimes against ascendants and a defense or mitigation for crimes arising from efforts to aid or harbor a member of the family who had committed a crime. During the war a few additions to the code were made to facilitate thought control within Japan and to give extraterritorial effect to the Japanese code against both aliens and Japanese subjects.

The present Constitution required certain changes. Since Article 14 requires equality of all persons, articles 73–76 of the Penal Code, giving special protection to the Imperial Family, were repealed, as was article 131, covering trespass on royal palace grounds or premises where the royal family was present. Defamation of the royal family is not specially covered but falls within article 230; here, however, the Prime Minister makes the complaint on behalf of the member of the royal family affected by the statement, an exception to the usual rule that the injured person must make the complaint (article 232).

The chapter covering crimes of foreign aggression was radically revised because of Article 9 of the Constitution. Only conspiracy with a foreign state to use arms against Japan and joining or aiding such a state when it has actually begun an attack (articles 81, 82) and insurrection for the purpose of overthrowing the government or the Constitution (article 77) are punishable. Spying or impairment of war potential is not punishable—the result of the repeal of articles 83–86 of the old code. The jurisdictional provisions (articles 1–4) have been substantially revised; aliens not in Japan at the time of their acts can be punished only for insurrection, levying war against Japan, and various crimes of counterfeiting and forging currency, official documents, public securities, and public seals. A somewhat longer list of crimes may be committed by Japanese outside Japan (article 3), but if either the alien or the Japanese has already been tried, convicted, and punished, the sentence in Japan shall be correspondingly reduced or remitted (article 5).

The requirements of Article 14 of the Constitution also dictated a change in article 183 of the code, which penalized the adulterous wife and her paramour but not the husband and his mistress or partner. The alternatives were the inclusion of the latter parties under the coverage of the law or repeal of the law. After substantial debate the latter course was chosen. Reconsideration was also given to provisions which remitted the punishment when theft had been committed against a member of the family (article 244), when stolen property had been received by a relative (article 257), and when a member of the family had been harbored as a criminal (article 105). The first two provisions were changed to limit the relationship to lineal blood relatives, spouses, relatives living together, and their spouses, and the latter to permit, not require, reduction in the sentence. The Diet left untouched the provisions which aggravated the penalty for killing an ascendant (article 200), inflicting fatal wounds on ascendants (article 205), and abandoning ascendants (articles 218). The provisions of article 205 were attacked as unconstitutional in violation of Article 14 of the Constitution, but the Supreme Court upheld the statute as a reasonable classification based on the character of the offender which was recognized in most countries other than the common-law countries.[69]

The change in postwar mores has brought new legislation dealing with obscenity and prostitution. The punishment for the distribution or display of obscene matter was markedly increased (article 175), and Japanese authorities began a drive to suppress traffic in pornographic matter. There was no greater certainty in Japan than in England or the United States about what line of demarcation could be drawn between smut and literature, and so inevitably a prosecution was brought against the publisher and translator of *Lady Chatterley's Lover*. They were convicted in the district court and appealed on the grounds that the work was not obscene and that the statute violated the guarantees in the Constitution, Article 21, of freedom of speech and press and against censorship. The Supreme Court upheld the conviction.[70] There are some concepts of sexual propriety that change and others that do not. Description of the sex act "is injurious to good moral sense of shame to the extent that one would hesitate reciting it within the family circle or at a public gathering" and "would only serve to excite and stimulate sexual desire and violate the good moral concept concerning sex matters." *Lady Chatterley's Lover* with its descriptive passages was therefore ruled obscene; its literary worth or the subjective intent of the author in writing it was considered immaterial. Article 175 of the code was upheld as a reasonable and traditional limitation on free speech, and specific prosecutions brought under it did not amount to censorship.[71]

Open prostitution was outlawed by the Antiprostitution Law (1956, amended in 1958), which makes criminal prostitution, pandering, maintaining places for the purpose of prostitution, and financing the trade. Special guidance measures for the women were provided by the law and by the Woman's Guidance Home Law (1958). Article 3 of the Antiprostitution Law provides that "no person shall commit prostitution or be the client of a prostitute," but the law carefully fails to provide any penalties for the client.

The provisions of the several statutes covering sentence, probation, parole, prison administration, and rehabilitation of released offenders are enlightened; the various agencies and institutions are well staffed; and, as a result, the recidivism rate is commendably low.

Criminal Procedure

Adequate safeguards surrounding defendants in criminal cases are essential to the fair administration of the criminal law, no matter how enlightened the substantive penal provisions may be. Most Americans are familiar in a general way with the procedural guarantees contained in federal and state constitutions. Since, however, other nations have approached the same basic problems in different ways and expressed their conclusions in different terminology, rather than to offer suggestions based on American experience alone it may be preferable to list the criteria of a fair system developed by the Delhi Conference, because lawyers from a number of legal systems participated in their formulation. The *Conclusions* include the following standards for criminal process under the Rule of Law:

> The application of the Rule of Law involves an acceptance of the principle that an accused person is assumed to be innocent until he has been proved to be guilty. An acceptance of this general principle is not inconsistent with provisions of law which, in particular cases, shift the burden of proof once certain facts creating a contrary presumption have been established. The personal guilt of the accused should be proved in each case.
>
> (1) The power of arrest, whether in flagrante delicto or not, ought to be strictly regulated by law, and should only be exercisable on reasonable suspicion that the person concerned has committed an offense.
>
> (2) On any arrest the arrested person should at once be told the grounds of his arrest.
>
> (3) On any arrest the arrested person should at once and at all times thereafter be entitled to the assistance of a legal adviser of his own choice, and on his arrest should at once be informed of that right in a way which he would clearly understand.
>
> (4) Every arrested person should be brought, within as short a period as possible, fixed by law, before an appropriate judicial authority.
>
> (5) After appearing before such judicial authority, any further detention should not be in the hands of the police. . . .
>
> (1) No person should be deprived of his liberty except in so far as may be required for the purposes of public security or the administration of justice.
>
> (2) Every arrested person should have a right, renewable at reasonably short intervals, to apply for bail to an appropriate judicial authority. He should be entitled to bail on reasonable terms unless either:
>
> > (a) the charge is of an exceptionally serious nature, or
> > (b) the appropriate judicial authority is satisfied that, if bail is granted, the accused is not likely to stand his trial, or
> > (c) the appropriate judicial authority is satisfied that, if bail is granted, the accused is likely to interfere with the evidence, for example with witnesses for the prosecution, or
> > (d) the appropriate judicial authority is satisfied that, if bail is granted, the accused is likely to commit a further criminal offense.
>
> The Rule of Law requires that an accused person should have adequate opportunity to prepare his defence and this involves:
>
> (1) That he should at all times be entitled to the assistance of a legal adviser of his own choice, and to have freedom of communication with him.
>
> (2) That he should be given notice of the charge with sufficient particularity.

(3) That he should have a right to produce witnesses in his defence and to be present when this evidence is taken.

(4) That, at least in serious cases, he should be informed in sufficient time before the trial of the nature of the evidence to be called for by the Prosecution.

(5) That he should be entitled to be present when any evidence for the Prosecution is given and to have the witnesses for the Proscution cross-examined.

No one should be compelled to incriminate himself. No accused person or witness should be subject to physical or psychological pressure (including anything calculated to impair his will or violate his dignity as a human being).

Postal or telephone communications should not be intercepted save in exceptional circumstances provided by law and under an order of an appropriate judicial authority.

A search of the accused's premises without his consent should only be made under an order of an appropriate judicial authority.

Evidence obtained in breach of any of these rights ought not to be admissible against the accused.

The Rule of Law requires that criminal trials should ordinarily take place in public. The proper existence of exceptions to this rule is, however, recognized. The nature of these exceptions should be laid down by law and their application to the particular case should be decided by the Court. . . .

After a final conviction or acquittal no one should be tried again on the same facts, whether or not for the same offense.

Every conviction and sentence and every refusal of bail should be challengeable before at least one higher Court. . . .[72]

Not all these criteria have been realized in any country, including the United States. Some of them were embodied in the prewar procedural code of Japan, but the bulk have come into being only under the new Constitution. The reforms in criminal procedure may in the passage of time prove to be the most significant change which the Occupation made in the Japanese legal system.

Prior to 1945 the Japanese Code of Criminal Procedure was almost identical with the German code and thus provided for an inquisitorial proceeding in which the procurator prepared a bulky file of evidence to be handed on to the judge, who then took primary responsibility for deciding whether a trial would take place and for developing the evidence at the main trial. The role of defense counsel was a passive one. The present Code of Criminal Procedure (1948) and the supplementary rules promulgated by the Supreme Court still retain the general structure of the prewar trial, but the changes and additions made by virtue of the provisions of the present Constitution have made the present-day criminal proceeding a far cry from its predecessor, as the following paragraphs will suggest.

A major concern of Occupation authorities was the arrest powers of the police, for there had been no practicable controls on such powers during the militarist regime. Article 33 of the Constitution prohibits arrests without a warrant except when an offense is actually being committed (the legal term for this is *genkō-han*). The Code of Criminal Procedure was drafted to be consistent with Article 33, but the terms which it embodies have created several problems. The source of one such problem is article 212 of the code, which defines a flagrant offender (*genkō-hannin*) as (1) a person being pursued; (2) a person carrying with him ill-gotten goods, arms, or instruments of crime; (3) a person bearing on his body or clothes visible traces of an offense; or (4) a person who attempts to flee when challenged. None of these alternatives fits literally the constitutional requirement that arrest without warrant be limited to instances in which the offender is caught in the act. When Occupation authorities questioned the inclusion of article 212 in the draft code, the drafting committee explained it on the grounds that the Japanese term *genkō-han* had been derived from a French legal term and incorporated in the prewar code, that the term had been construed to include "quasi-flagrant delict" (*jun-genkō-han*) by both the French and the Japanese courts, and that the word *genkō-han* in Article 33 of the Constitution thus included both concepts. On this assumption the draft was approved by Occupation authorities and submitted to the Diet for passage. The Supreme Court has not yet directly passed on the constitutionality of article 212.

More controversial are the provisions of article 210 of the code which authorize arrest without warrant of persons suspected on sufficient grounds of having committed a serious offense, if there is under the circumstances insufficient time to obtain a judicial arrest warrant—the so-called "emergency arrest" (*kinkyū-taiho*). On the basis of the literal language of the Constitution, Article 33, there would appear to be substantial doubt about the constitutionality of article 210, no matter how obvious the need for such legislation might be and despite the fact that the American arrest law has long recognized equivalent arrest powers in the police. But when the constitutionality of article 210 was attacked, the Supreme Court upheld it as not violative of the "spirit" of Article 33.

Some doubt has also been expressed about the constitutionality of article 2 of the Police Duties Law (1948), which permits a police officer to stop and question anyone whom "he reasonably believes from his attitude or other circumstances has committed or is about to commit a crime or whom he reasonably believes knows something about an offense which has been or is about to be committed." He is also permitted to request the person to accompany him to a police box for questioning, but no force may be used and the citizen is not required to go along. If the citizen refuses, the officer must find authorization for detention under the Code of Criminal Procedure (articles 210, 212). Several high court decisions have upheld the propriety of the law, and it has proved a useful and necessary provision in view of the very restricted arrest powers permitted to the police under present law.[73]

Police officers who make illegal arrests are subject to prosecution, and a number have in fact been prosecuted. They are also personally liable to the injured person in a civil action, though such actions are no more likely in Japan than in the United States to result in actual and adequate compensation to the plaintiff, since the defendants rarely have assets from which recovery can be had. The government can, but need not, by legislation assume responsibility for the acts of its police employees; the present Criminal Compensation Law enacted by the Diet can, however, be invoked only by one who was formally charged as a defendant (*hikokunin*) and subsequently found not guilty; compensation cannot be paid within its terms to one who was the object of an official and formal investigation (suspect, *higisha*) but against whom no formal public charge (indictment) was ever filed. A broadening of the Criminal Compensation Law to permit claims by former suspects who never became defendants has been strongly urged but has not as yet been adopted.[74]

Article 35 of the Constitution protects the citizen against searches and seizures other than as authorized by judicial warrant or under Article 33. Article 21 also guarantees the secrecy of communications (*tsūshin*). There has been some question about how far searches may be carried on incidental to a valid arrest. Though debate still continues, many scholars maintain that article 220 of the code is constitutional when it permits searches without warrant when a valid arrest is made pursuant to warrant (article 199) or without warrant (articles 210 or 212). The Supreme Court has not yet decided the question. Doubt has also been expressed about the constitutionality of article 100, which permits a court to order the seizure and production of mail or telegrams in government custody. The Ministry of Justice's position is that Article 21 of the Constitution is not violated because there is a strong presumption that mail to and from a suspect would contain incriminating matter. This seems questionable, but the Supreme Court has not been asked to rule on the matter. Article 21 is generally felt to preclude wiretapping. Even if evidence is improperly obtained, it will not be excluded, and the injured person must institute civil or criminal proceedings in vindication of his rights.

When a person has been arrested or received by a judicial police officer, he must be delivered to a public procurator within forty-eight hours; the procurator must then produce the individual before a judge within twenty-four hours from that time and obtain a detention order or else release the man (code articles 203–205). The judge may only detain the suspect (*higisha*) when there is reasonable ground to suspect that he has committed a crime *and* either he has no fixed dwelling, there is reason to believe he may destroy evidence, he has previously escaped, or there is reason to believe he will escape. Detention shall not exceed two months in the usual case (article 60). Article 34 of the Constitution requires every arrested or detained person to be informed immediately of the charge against him. The same article prohibits detention without adequate cause and provides that "upon demand of any person such cause must be immediately shown in open court in his presence and the presence of his counsel." The code contains implementing legislation (articles 82–86) and is fairly widely invoked. There is also a Habeas Corpus Law (*Jishinhogohō*, 1948), but the adequate provisions of the Code of Criminal Procedure concerning the review of detention have meant it has not been often invoked.[75] If a suspect has been detained, he is not subject to release on bail, though if the grounds for his detention have terminated, the court will rescind the order of detention (article 87).

After formal charges have been filed, the defendant (*hikokunin*) may become eligible for bail, which is to be granted unless either he is charged with an offense punishable by imprisonment in excess of a year, he has a prior conviction of a serious crime, he is an habitual offender, there is danger that he may destroy evidence or injure the complainant or a witness, or his true name or dwelling is unknown (article 89). This means that in practice most bail is discretionary with the judge. After unreasonably long detention the judge must grant bail (article 91). Bail must be set at a figure sufficient to ensure the presence of the defendant at the appropriate times; in practice bail amounts are set at a reasonable enough figure that the overwhelming majority of those admitted to bail manage to post it, and the default rate is low. Even where bail is not granted or made, the court may suspend the detention by entrusting the accused to the custody of a relative or a protective institution or by restricting his dwelling (article 95). Any release from detention may be rescinded on the motion of the procurator on a showing that the accused has escaped or is about to escape, has failed to appear when summoned, has destroyed or is about to destroy evidence or intimidate the complainant or a witness, or has violated the terms of any restrictions placed on his dwelling by the court or judge at the time of the original order granting bail or rescinding detention.[76]

Investigation of the crime is in the hands of the procurator. He has no power to force persons to give him evidence, and he must warn any person who complies with a request to be interviewed that the latter is under no duty to make a statement (article 198). Under certain circumstances witnesses may be called before a judge and their testimony perpetuated in the presence of the procurator and the accused and his counsel (articles 143–174), but as in the United States the procurator usually relies on what the police bring him or what he determines by his own investigations.

The procurator has almost complete discretion as to whether to file formal charges. When he declines to file charges, he must notify the suspect and the complainant of that fact upon request. In certain crimes involving public officers or subversive activities the complainant may apply to the district court by way of the procurator's office concerned to have public charges instituted. The procurator may reconsider, but if he does not the court may determine that public charges should be instituted, and the resultant court order then serves as the equivalent to an indictment (article 267). In this case a private attorney is appointed to act as prosecuting attorney (article 268). In other cases the aggrieved complainant may appeal to the procurator's inquest (*kensatsu shinsakai*), a postwar innovation. The inquest, which sits in each judicial district, is composed of laymen who investigate complaints of noninstitution of prosecution. If they determine that prosecution should have been instituted, they notify the chief of the district public procurator's office of their findings; he then reviews the matter and may order the institution of prosecution if he wishes. Through 1958 only about 10 per cent of the cases of noninstitution of prosecution were found objectionable by the inquests, and only about half of these resulted in prosecution. Complaints in writing about the activities of procurators are incorporated in their dossiers and may have an adverse effect on promotion and transfer.[77]

After formal charges have been filed, the case is set for trial. The trial itself may be on either inquisitorial or adversary lines. Code and rule provide for examination of the witnesses by the judge unless he permits the parties to conduct it. In practice the judges usually do permit this, and the result is an adversary proceeding more nearly like the Anglo-American proceeding than the German. By Article 37(3) of the Constitution, the defendant has an absolute right to counsel, which accrues at the time he is first brought before the court. If he cannot afford or obtain his own attorney, counsel must be assigned to him. Counsel is given substantial rights under the code to gather and present evidence and is in general on a par with the procurator. The judge must also be unbiased, and to ensure this he does not receive at the time of the indictment anything more than the charge itself; he no longer receives the mass of documents amassed by the procurator during investigation of the case.

Under the Constitution the defendant has a right to a speedy and public trial [Article 37(1)], full opportunity to examine all witnesses and to obtain his own by compulsory process [Article 37(2)], freedom from self-incrimination [Article 38(1)], and the right not to be convicted on his own uncorroborated confession [Article 38(3)]. Coerced confessions or confessions obtained after prolonged arrest or detention are also inadmissible [Article 38(2)]. The proceeding as a whole must follow procedure established by law (Article 31).

After the evidence has been submitted and final argument heard from both sides, the court decides the case. In lesser cases a single judge makes the decision; in more serious cases a three-judge collegiate court decides. The written decision (*hanketsu*) is communicated to the defendant, and when it has become final on waiver of appeal or after completion of appeal, it can then be executed if unfavorable to the defendant. Actual supervision of enforcement is in the hands of the procurator.

Appeal may be taken by either party. There has been some question whether or not Article 39 of the Constitution required a change in prewar practice so as to bar appeal by the procurator. The prewar Japanese terminology covering second prosecutions has not been materially changed in the new Constitution (*mata dōitsu no hanzai ni tsuite kasanete keijijō no sekinin o towarenai*), however, and Article 39 is thus generally deemed to preserve the Roman-civil-law concept of *non bis in idem* rather than to institute the American concept of double jeopardy, and so appeal is permitted the procurator on the same basis as the defendant.[78] *Kōso* appeal is used to raise questions concerning the finding of fact, assessment of sentence, or application of legal rules. *Jōkoku* appeal may be lodged in the Supreme Court on the grounds that a constitutional question is involved or that a position has been taken below contrary to earlier decisions of the Supreme Court or its predecessor.[79] *Kōkoku* appeal lies from certain orders or rulings made prior to final decision where no regular appeal is possible.

Even after a judgment has become final, under certain circumstances the matter can be reexamined in extraordinary proceedings (*hijōkyūsai tetsuzuki*). The most usual remedy is the reopening of the proceedings (*saishin*), which can occur when there is newly discovered evidence indicating innocence or mitigation, proof of forged or perjured evidence at the original trial, or proof that one of the official participants in the original proceedings has been convicted of misconduct (article 435). It may be lodged by the procurator, the defendant, or his legal representative (article 439). At this point, however, the defendant has the protection of the Constitution, Article 39, and therefore the reopening is for his benefit only, and no heavier punishment than that originally inflicted can be assessed (article 452). This proceeding takes place in the original trial court. The other extraordinary proceeding is extraordinary appeal (*hijōjōkoku*), which is lodged by the Procurator-General in the Supreme Court when he believes that the trial or judgment violated the law. It is theoretically brought in the interests of justice, but the original judgment can only be quashed when it was disadvantageous to the accused, a limitation necessary under the Constitution, Article 39. If error in favor of the accused is found, the judgment still stands, though of course there may then be an official holding as to what should have been done which will guide the lower courts in other cases.

Civil Procedure

The procedural law covering civil cases is still substantially the German code. Ordinary civil matters (*tsūjō soshōjiken*) are tried in summary court if they involve small sums and in district court in all other cases. It will be recalled that family-law problems are handled in the family courts. The abolition of the system of administrative courts has also meant that special proceedings against administrative officials and agencies (*gyōsei soshōjiken*) have had to be provided for in the district courts under the Code of Civil Procedure as modified by certain special laws. The Code of Civil Procedure also continues a system of arbitration which the parties may invoke and which will, when applied, be used to work out a mutually acceptable solution.[80] If, however, the solution is rejected, the court has the power to decide the matter as if it had been adversarily litigated from the start. Civil jurisdiction also includes bankruptcy proceedings, creditor process for the enforcement of liquidated claims, and administrative control of land records and corporate registrations.

Regular civil actions begin by the filing of a complaint. Costs or security for costs must be posted, though the court is permitted to subsidize indigent plaintiffs if that seems fair; these costs are subtracted from any judgment which the plaintiff obtains, and assistance is available only when "there is some prospect of his winning the case." Usually the case is brought where the defendant resides. The defendant has the opportunity to answer and to make counterclaims; third persons interested in the matter may also intervene. If a fixed sum of money or specific securities are involved, a summary order can be entered on behalf of the obligee which becomes final unless within two weeks the debtor objects and demands trial. The court in the ordinary trial first conducts oral proceedings between the parties to determine what the underlying issues between them are. Services of counsel are not required, but no person not an attorney can represent a party except in summary court.

After the issues have been determined, the court takes evidence from witnesses who are offered by the parties or whom the court wishes to hear. Today the parties rather than the judge usually examine and cross-examine. In summary courts the judge may summon persons of good reputation and experience to advise him on the matter; this resembles the petit jury in some respects. After all the evidence is in, the court decides the case and enters judgment by a document which must include the reasons. *Kōso* appeal may be filed by either party seeking a retrial, and *jōkoku* appeal may be used to raise questions of law only. There are also special provisions for reopening (*saishin*) on grounds similar to those in the Code of Criminal Procedure.

FOOTNOTES

1. A. V. DICEY, INTRODUCTION TO THE STUDY OF THE LAW OF THE CONSTITUTION 332 (10th ed., London, 1959).
2. *Ibid.* at 198.
3. INTERNATIONAL COMMISSION OF JURISTS, THE RULE OF LAW IN A FREE SOCIETY 197 (Geneva, 1959). (Hereinafter cited as RULE OF LAW.)
4. *Ibid.* at 3.
5. AMERICAN BAR ASSOCIATION SECTION ON INTERNATIONAL AND COMPARATIVE LAW, THE RULE OF LAW IN THE UNITED STATES 29–30 (New York, 1958).
6. It is somewhat difficult to identify exactly what "non-Rule of Law" is, since much of the writing about the Rule of Law uses that term as a laudatory epithet for whatever the author approves. There is also a noticeable tendency toward the use of the term *Rule of Law*, like the terms *peace* and *democracy,* in a substantially contradictory fashion in Communist and non-Communist countries:

> The fact emerges that for the East the 'rule of law' is not a limitation or brake but a dynamic system. The early dreams of a lawless Stateless community are now relegated to some remote future paradise. As the

State runs almost everything under Socialism there is much more law in the East than in the modern West, to say nothing of the old free-enterprise past. The vast realms of commerce and industry and often culture and thought fall within the field of legal regulation. And law is not merely quantitatively greater, it is qualitatively positive, it is the driving force of socialization and change, introducing new rules based on the new ideology in place of the vestiges of the past. . . . Law is the incarnate will of the working class. To violate it is a political blow and to suggest that it is transitory and impermanent is a still greater affront. The whole of life in Eastern Europe is geared to huge economic plans. The planned economy can only operate and function if every obligation which it imposes is strictly observed. . . .

In fact there was some support for the view that the 'rule of law' was older than capitalism, and that there were some more commendable features of it under feudalism, such as the stress on mutuality of rights and obligations. In sweeping away burdensome feudal duties the law reformers of the West had left the enterprising individual too free and with too many rights in proportion to his social obligations. [A. K. R. Kiralfy, *The Rule of Law in Communist Europe*, 8 INT'L & COMP. L. Q. 465, 466, 468 (July, 1959).]

In contrast, Hayek suggests that the economic planning on which the Communist states rely so heavily is the antithesis of the Rule of Law. FRIEDRICH AUGUST VON HAYEK, THE CONSTITUTION OF LIBERTY 231–233 (Chicago, 1960); THE ROAD TO SERFDOM, chap. 6 (Chicago, 1955). Roscoe Pound made somewhat the same objection to administrative law developments under which "there are no laws but only administrative orders" and based on "a theory that law is whatever is done officially and so whatever is done officially is law and beyond criticism by lawyers." *Administrative Procedure Legislation: For the "Minority Report,"* 27 A.B.A.J. 664, 678 (November, 1941).

Sir Adetokumbo A. Ademola, Chief Justice of Nigeria, in his opening address at the African Conference on the Rule of Law, held in Lagos, Nigeria, January 3–7, 1961, endeavored to avoid the East-West conflict thus:

It has been said that the Rule of Law is merely an Anglo-American institution; that the concept of 'Government under Law' and such phrases as the 'Supremacy of Law' and 'the Rule of Law' are all purely Western inventions.

The Communist analysis maintained that everything is legal which is good for the State and the problem of adjusting the legitimate claims of the individual and his society has no place.

The Africans, it was suggested, might find a third legal system which is neither 'the Rule of Law' nor the 'Socialist Legality' propounded by the Communists.

But the Rule of Law is not a Western idea, nor is it linked up with any economic or social system. As soon as you accept that man is governed by Law and not by whims of men, it is the Rule of Law. It may be under different forms from country to country, but it is based on principles; it is not an abstract notion. It exists not only in democratic countries but in every country where the law is supreme, where the dignity of man is respected and provisions made for his legitimate rights. Today, around us we see countries where basic principles are disregarded; where there are cases of arbitrary arrests and detention without trial; cases of denial of individuals to prepare their defence when charged; cases of repression of the opposition in parliamentary government; cases of negation of social and political rights; cases of the Judiciary stifled and paralyzed by fear of dismissal of the judges. When we look around we find some of these encroachments of the Executive on the rights of individuals, which I have mentioned, in countries ostensibly practising parliamentary democracies, but in actual fact the individual is subject to such restrictions which deprive him almost completely of his freedom. [INTERNATIONAL COMMISSION OF JURISTS, AFRICAN CONFERENCE ON THE RULE OF LAW 86 (Geneva, 1961).]

See also SIR WILLIAM IVOR JENNINGS, THE LAW AND THE CONSTITUTION 61 (4th ed., London, 1952):

The test of a free country is to examine the status of the body that corresponds to His Majesty's Opposition.

But these statements also reflect the British tradition and condemn by implication much which the West finds characteristic of Communist societies. Perhaps one can do no more than fall back on Judge Charles E. Wyzanski, Jr.'s statement of the hard core of the Rule of Law:

Indeed all that one seems able to spell out of the rule of law concept, when looked at universally, is first, that the state recognizes a presumption that an individual has the right to have his person or property free from interference by any officer of the government unless that officer can justify his interference by reference to a general law; and second, that the state provides some machinery for the vindication of that right before an independent tribunal in all cases where a crime is charged, and sometimes in other cases involving serious interferences with persons or their property. [ARTHUR E. SUTHERLAND (ed.), GOVERNMENT UNDER LAW 482 (Cambridge, Mass., 1956).]

531

The antithesis of this would, by implication, be the non-Rule of Law.

7. EDWARD A. HOEBEL, THE LAW OF PRIMITIVE MAN 28 (Cambridge, Mass., 1954).

8. *Ibid.* at 275.

9. *Ibid.* at 329.

10. A. S. DIAMOND, PRIMITIVE LAW 344 (London, 1935).

11. The chief laws prior to Tokugawa times were found in the *Jōei shikimoku* of 1232 (the Hōjō Institutes) and the *Kemmu shikimoku* of 1336 (the Ashikaga Code).

12. The following were the principal written laws of the Tokugawa era: *Kuge sho-hatto* (code for Imperial Court nobles) of 1615; *Buke-sho-hatto* (provisions governing the *daimyō*), issued in 1615 and revised substantially in 1635 and 1710; *Shoshi-hatto* (code for samurai) of 1635; *kōsatsu, goningumichō,* and *ofuregaki,* affecting chiefly commoners and issued throughout the period; and *O-sadamegaki* of 1742, which included the famous Code of 100 Articles (*Hyakkajō*).

13. Dan F. Henderson, *Some Aspects of Tokugawa Law,* 27 WASH. L. REV. 85 (1952).

14. The modern Japanese term for "right," *kenri,* was not coined until after the Restoration of 1868. See Takayanagi Kenzō, *The Development of Japanese Law, 1868–1961,* in ARTHUR T. VON MEHREN (ed), LAW IN JAPAN 5, 24 (Cambridge, Mass., 1963). (Hereinafter cited as LAW IN JAPAN.)

15. II JOHN H. WIGMORE, A PANORAMA OF THE WORLD'S LEGAL SYSTEMS 504 (Washington, D.C., 1928).

16. *See* p. 502.

17. Replaced thereafter by the Penal Code of 1907 along German lines.

18. Replaced in 1923 by a code along German lines, which in turn was substantially altered after World War II. See pp. 518–519.

19. On this process *see* Takayanagi, *op. cit. supra* note 14 at 15–17 and 18–21; Abe Haruo, *Criminal Justice in Japan: Its Historical Background and Modern Problems,* 47 A.B.A.J. 555 (1961), and *Self-Incrimination—Japan and the United States,* 46 J. CRIM. L., C. & P.S. 613, 614–616 (1956).

20. *See* Takayanagi, *op. cit. supra* note 14 at 31–32. Parts of the initial code went into effect in 1893 and influenced the Code of 1899. Substantial changes were made before and after World War II.

21. For a fuller account of the history of this dispute, *see* Takayanagi, *op. cit. supra* note 14 at 27–31.

22. Because the language of any code or statute must be relatively broad, there was still room for Japanese traditions governing, for example,

contract and property transactions and interests, to continue to operate. The formal similarity to German, and to a degree French, law has meant, however, that until recent years legal scholars were expected to be as well versed as possible in European law, preferably through study abroad, and this in turn has meant that very often attention was directed at least in form toward European models rather than Japanese traditions.

23. *See* also Nagashima Atsushi, *The Accused and Society: The Administration of Criminal Justice in Japan*, in LAW IN JAPAN 297, 312–313; Takayanagi, *op. cit. supra* note 14 at 22.

24. RULE OF LAW at 13–14, 4–5, 7.

25. *Hyōjōsho* or *rōjū*, as the case might be. The administrative structure is sketched in SIR GEORGE BAILEY SANSOM, A HISTORY OF JAPAN 1615–1867, at 21–24 (Stanford, Calif., 1963).

26. Under the so-called *"Ikeibatsu sokketsurei."* While not formally a part of the judicial system, police command officers exercised judicial powers to punish in a formal way certain petty offenses. *See* HOSOKAWA KAMEICHI, NIHON KINDAI HŌSEISHI (History of the modern Japanese legal system) 158 (1961).

27. The terms are so translated in FUJII SHIN'ICHI, THE ESSENTIALS OF JAPANESE CONSTITUTIONAL LAW 304–306 (Tokyo, 1940). The system is described in KANEKO HAJIME, SAIBANHŌ (Law of the judiciary) 50–55 (1959).

28. There is very little in English describing the court. *See* Hashimoto Kiminobu, *The Rule of Law: Some Aspects of Judicial Review of Administrative Action*, in LAW IN JAPAN 239, 240–241; Fujii, *op. cit. supra* note 27 at 317–325. For a description in Japanese see MINOBE TATSUKICHI, NIPPON GYŌSEIHŌ (Japanese administrative law) 877–891 (1940).

29. These rules, however, supplement the procedural codes rather than lay out the basic system of procedure, as in American federal practice. But it is open to the Court to expand its use of the rule-making power whenever it wishes, since there are no other controls on it than impeachment of the justices or a negative vote against them at the time of a popular referendum.

30. *See* Hattori Takaaki, *The Legal Profession in Japan: Its Historical Development and Present State*, in LAW IN JAPAN 111, 132–134.

31. Self-denunciation may be invoked by the court as a reason for reducing punishment on the authority of Penal Law art. 42.

32. The decision is translated in JOHN M. MAKI, THE SUPREME COURT AND CONSTITUTIONAL REVIEW 362 (1964). (Hereinafter cited as MAKI.)

33. The decision is translated in MAKI at 366.
34. See Itō Masami, *The Rule of Law: Constitutional Development*, in LAW IN JAPAN 207–208, 228–238.
35. RULE OF LAW at 13–14.
36. Kawashima Takeyoshi, *Dispute Resolution in Contemporary Japan*, in LAW IN JAPAN 50–52.
37. The derivation of the term is discussed in R. W. Rabinowitz, *The Historical Development of the Japanese Bar*, 70 HARV. L. REV. 61, 62–64 (1956).
38. See Takigawa Masajirō, Kujiyado no kenkyū (Research on *kujiyado*) (Waseda Daigaku Hikkakuhō Kenkyūsho Kiyō Dai-hachigo, 1959) (Institute of Comparative Law of Waseda University, Publication No. 8, 1959). (In Japanese, summary in English.)
39. Quoted in Rabinowitz, *op. cit. supra* note 37 at 62.
40. On the historical development summarized in the text *see* Hattori, *op. cit. supra* note 30, at 112–138; Rabinowitz, *op. cit. supra* note 37 at 64–78.
41. See Ohira Kaname & George N. Stevens, *Admission to the Bar, Disbarment and Disqualification of Lawyers in Japan and the United States—A Comparative Study*, 38 WASH. L. REV. 22 (1963).
42. See Hattori, *op. cit. supra* note 30 at 146–147; *cf.* Dan F. Henderson, *The Roles of Lawyers in U.S.-Japanese Business Transactions*, 38 WASH. L. REV. 1 (1963).
43. Kawashima, *op. cit. supra* note 36, is an outstanding study of this phenomenon. *See* also Katō Ichirō, *The Treatment of Motor-vehicle Accidents: The Impact of Technological Change on Legal Relations*, in LAW IN JAPAN 399.
44. See Hattori, *op. cit. supra* note 30 at 146–147 and Table 3 at 151. Table 4 at 152 contains lawyer statistics for Japan and selected Western countries that show an extreme underpopulation of lawyers in Japan.
45. See Hattori, *op. cit. supra* note 30 at 145.
46. See Tanabe Kohji, *The Processes of Litigation: An Experiment with the Adversary System*, in LAW IN JAPAN 73, 78.
47. The program and policies of the institute are described in Abe Hakaru, *Education of the Legal Profession in Japan*, in LAW IN JAPAN 155–167.
48. See Hattori, *op. cit. supra* note 30 at 139–145.
49. The so-called "constitution" of Prince Shōtoku cannot be considered a constitution in any modern legal sense. For the text *see* TSUNODA RYUSAKU, THEODORE WILLIAM DE BARY, & DONALD KEENE, SOURCES OF THE JAPANESE TRADITION 49–53 (New York, 1958).

50. On the meaning of the term see Takayanagi, *op. cit. supra* note 14 at 11.
51. Translated in MAKI at 298.
52. *See* p. 499.
53. In general, *see* Itō, *op. cit. supra* note 34. Recently the Supreme Court struck down the forfeiture provisions of Customs Law article 118 as applied to third persons without notice and the opportunity to defend, invoking both Article 31 and Article 29 of the Constitution, the latter of which provides that the right to hold or own property is inviolable. Decision of Nov. 28, 1962, 16 Saikōsai Hanreishū 1577, translated in 7 JAPAN ANN. INT'L L. 104 (1963).
54. *See* Watanabe Yōzō, *The Family and the Law: The Individualistic Premise and Modern Japanese Family Law*, in LAW IN JAPAN 371.
55. *Ibid.* at 381 and Tables 1 & 2, p. 389.
56. *Ibid.* at 382.
57. *Ibid.* at 382–383.
58. *Ibid.* at 385–387.
59. *See* Michida Shinichirō, *The Legal Structure for Economic Enterprise: Some Aspects of Japanese Commercial Law*, in LAW IN JAPAN 507, 508–509.
60. *Ibid.* at 511–514.
61. Usually defined as anything that is of "detriment" to the promisee or of "benefit" to the promisor. GROVER C. GRISMORE, PRINCIPLES OF THE LAW OF CONTRACTS § 55 (Indianapolis, 1947).
62. *Cf.* Henderson, *op. cit. supra* note 42 at 9.
63. Michida, *op. cit. supra* note 59 at 537–544.
64. *See* Carl J. Bradshaw, *Selected Legal Aspects of Business in Japan*, 15 STAN. L. REV. 639, 648–662 (1962), and *Joint Ventures in Japan*, 38 WASH. L. REV. 58, 100–104 (1963).
65. Property is divided into immovables (*fudōsan*) and movables (*dōsan*), corresponding generally to real property and personal property in the Anglo-American system. Ownership (*shoyūken*) means the maximum amount of legally protected interest in either kind of property. Ownership may be held in common, though partition of the estate is possible under certain circumstances. The code provides also for possessory rights (*sen-yūken*) less than ownership, which may continue subservient to the rights of the owner (*shoyūkensha*) or may by the passage of time or other events ripen into ownership. The owner of immovables can create interests less than full ownership. These are divided into superficies (*chijōken*), which permit their holders to own buildings or trees on the land but not the land itself; emphyteuses (*ei-kosakuken*), which authorize farming or graz-

ing the land; and servitudes (*chiekiken*), which create easements of passage, drainage, light and air, etc. In some rural areas there is also the customary *iriaiken*, by virtue of which persons may go into uncultivated areas which they do not own to cut grass, gather firewood, etc.

66. 1 *chō* equals 2.45 acres; 10 *tan* equal 1 *chō*.

67. The decision is translated in MAKI at 228.

68. *See* Hirano Ryūichi, *The Accused and Society: Some Aspects of Japanese Criminal Law* in LAW IN JAPAN 274, at 274–275, and text at note 19 above.

69. The decision is translated in MAKI at 129.

70. The decision is translated in MAKI at 3.

71. Paralleling the "prior-restraint" problems under the First Amendment to the United States Constitution.

72. RULE OF LAW at 9–11 (1959).

73. In general, *see* Abe Haruo, *Police Detention and Arrest Privileges,* 51 J. CRIM. L., C. & P.S. 429, 430–432 (1960).

74. *Ibid.* at 435–437.

75. Judges also are not disposed to make broad use of the writ. *See,* for example, the decision translated in MAKI at 210.

76. In general, *see* Dando Shigemitsu & Tamiya Hiroshi, *Conditional Release of an Accused in Japan,* 108 U. PA. L. REV. 323 (1960).

77. *See* Hattori, *op. cit. supra* note 30 at 135–136.

78. A leading decision is translated in MAKI at 219.

79. These are the only grounds on which an appeal must be heard (article 405). The Court itself may choose to hear any case "which it deems [to] involve an important problem of the construction of law or ordinance" (article 406) and has certain other powers to quash judgments even if no grounds under article 405 exist (article 411). *See* MAKI at xxvi–xxvii.

80. *See* Kawashima, *op. cit. supra* note 36 at 56–57.

JOHN WHITNEY HALL

Aspects of Japanese Economic Development *

ECONOMIC DEVELOPMENT IN JAPAN: THEORY AND PROBLEMS OF PERIODIZATION

The field of economics touches upon a great many subjects which the student of Japanese culture finds most tangibly significant in his effort to comprehend the conditions of life in Japan today. The implicit assumption (now, to be sure, greatly qualified by the economists themselves) that economic man is roughly the same the world over lies at the base of many of the comparative judgments which we as common observers so freely make about a country's standard of living or level of material development. As a professional discipline economics has gone much farther than most of the social sciences in defining the boundaries of its inquiry and in developing a consistent body of theory. Economists, moreover, have been able to integrate Japanese subject matter into their theoretical calculations and have been able to devise relatively exact methods of comparison between specific sets of data in Japan and in other countries. The interests of the economist, of course, are extremely varied, and not all of his inquiries are equally pertinent to the problems of empirical or historical observation which relate to the kind of cultural analysis we have in mind. Consequently it is through the relatively new and inexact branch of economics dealing with growth and development that the economist has contributed most directly to the general study of Japanese culture.

The feature of Japan's modern economy which has most attracted the attention of the economist is its remarkable sustained growth during the past century. This, coupled with the fact that Japan is an Asian country, makes its story of economic growth truly remarkable. Between 1880 and the present, Japan underwent the most rapid economic development of any country in the world. A century ago, Japan was a land bound by a traditional technology, meager resources, and a policy of

* Acknowledgment is due to Robert Spaulding for assistance in writing portions of this chapter. Earlier syllabus materials prepared by Prof. Carl Remer were also relied on. The author is grateful for the critical comments of Prof. Hugh Patrick, from which he profited immensely.

national isolation. Today Japan ranks fifth in production among the advanced industrial nations and has a standard of living comparable with Italy's. These well-known facts define a major problem of interpretation for the economist. While the nonspecialist Western observer is apt to look upon the Japanese achievement as something of a miracle (a rags-to-riches, accomplishment), professional economists have not viewed the Japanese experience in such simplistic terms. To some, Japan has accomplished no more than could be expected of a country which put its mind seriously to improving its economy about one hundred years ago; to others Japan has appeared to lag behind expectations, especially when it came to providing a satisfying and stable way of life for its citizens.

These differences of interpretation are inherent in any major problem of analysis, especially when the subject matter embraces the entire culture and when comparative judgments are called for. Developmental economists are still experimenting with the selection and use of variables and with the standards of comparison which should be adopted for their studies. In the case of Japan some of the basic "facts" are themselves extremely difficult to determine. (For instance, what is Japan's standard of living?) And beyond this the measures of comparison are by no means agreed upon. (Does one judge Japan against European or Asian societies?) The students of economic development, to a greater extent than those of the more theoretical branches of economic analysis, find themselves faced with problems for which the "point of view," the "structure of the problem," or the "selection of variables" can directly affect the final answers. Thus, for example, the American economist may study Japan as an outstanding example of rapid economic growth by an "Asian economy." Yet he should not overlook the evidence that Japan has yet to achieve an equitable balance of economic rewards for its people despite nearly 100 years of modern development. The Japanese economist tends to stress this "failure" of Japan to create a "balanced economy" and to complain about the "unhealthy" conditions of the agricultural sector or the "feudalistic" aspects of industrial management. A trip to the Asian continent would help convince him that Japan has surpassed all Asian societies and has approached the most advanced level of development in many areas of its economy.

What the economist says about the state of the Japanese economy in the developmental (or comparative) sense depends in large part, then, upon what he is looking for and what yardstick of comparison he adopts. The figures which the economist cites are not in themselves absolute statements. And once any figure or set of figures is "interpreted," the economist, to as great a degree as any of the other social scientists, finds himself obliged to deal with observations which range from relatively simplistic economic causal relationships to more complex culturewide phenomena and even psychological and personality traits. He must also deal with the complex problem of the relationship between economic conditions and national or social goals and aspirations. Economic development cannot be separated completely from the political or social environment within which it takes place or the values which it engenders in a society. It is these less measurable factors of the historical and the cultural dimensions of economic development which make the study so important and yet so sensitive to subjective valuations.

In the abstract, three fundamental tasks confront the student of comparative economic development. First, he must devise some scale or spectrum of economic complexity along which economies may be distributed, and he must devise some means of determining at any given moment where an economy stands on such a scale. Second, he must mark upon his scale the points at which significant changes in the nature of the economy or in the process of growth appear to take place. Third, he must attempt to answer the question of causation, of how and why development takes place. The following treatment both of theory in general and of Japanese development in particular will necessarily place its prime emphasis on the first two of these points (periodization and description within a comparative framework). Developmental theory, still in its hypothetical stages, cannot be as satisfactorily dealt with.

Typically, economists have worked with a variety of simplified or aggregated indices of economic development. Perhaps the most universally used measure of this type is the concept of national product per capita. Estimated figures are available for most countries for such composite concepts as "national income" and "gross national product," and these permit simple tabular comparisons between different economies.

Nevertheless, the difficulties which the economist faces in handling these data for comparative or historical purposes are considerable. Standards of calculation for such figures are not necessarily uniform, and, furthermore, there is no hard and fast method of interpreting the significance of the figures once the economist has them in hand. Since societies differ greatly in their internal organization and in the relative stress they place upon particular economic as well as noneconomic factors (for instance, education or medical services), it is most difficult to establish a method of calculating national product which will measure the real economic output of a given society. Moreover, since societies differ according to their necessities (climate can affect the need for fuel or food consumption), a strict reading of the national-product-per-capita figure is not an infallible measure of the level of economic development of a given society.

Another difficulty with the national-product-per-capita measure of economic growth is that it says nothing about the distribution of income or differing patterns of expenditure. An analysis of the range of incomes within a society can reveal a great deal about the structure of its economy. An estimate of economic development should take into consideration, for instance, some factor which is related to the living conditions of the mass of the people. For this reason, developmental economists have from time to time worked with a variety of additional measures, such as distribution of income, composition of production (agriculture, mining, industry, services, etc.), consumption of inanimate energy, savings, distribution of the labor force between agriculture and industry, consumption of calories of food, vital statistics, literacy, readership of newspapers, use of automobiles, radios, telephones, etc. All of these indices, if sets of comparable figures are available, provide checks on the comparative material development of different societies or of the development over time of a single society.

But it must be admitted that these measures are not particularly refined, and their applicability to different societies is not at all uniform. Societies differ in their national or economic goals and so have developed sound reasons for preferences in their economic behavior. A country such as Japan has tended to rate *national* development above individual welfare. In the countries of Scandinavia the reverse may be closer to the truth. These conscious preferences or traditional differences in the pattern of economic behavior loom particularly large in the interpretation of economic development in a country such as Japan. In other words, the "cultural dimension" of Japan's economic development must somehow be taken into account.

At one time it was common to seek an explanation of the cultural factor in Oriental societies through the concept of the "Asiatic economy." Oriental societies such as Japan, it was claimed, differed fundamentally from those of the West in the balance between agriculture and trade and in the nature of their agricultural base. Intensive labor techniques and a heavy use of irrigation made for a particularly static and technologically uninventive economy, creating the conditions which nurtured political absolutism and a marked social stratification between landlords and peasants. This theory, while open to question as a universal means of handling the economies of Asian states, does point up one major feature of the traditional economy of Japan, namely, the heavy reliance on intensive labor for irrigated rice production. The agrarian complex which had as its center the semicooperative life of the village has exerted many obvious and a number of less apparent influences upon the Japanese pattern of economic development. But so also has the traditional pattern of domestic life, domestic architecture, and social intercourse.

Rather than pursue what may well be purely illusory differences between so-called "Eastern" and "Western" styles of economy, students of economic development have suggested various unified theories of growth which make it possible to join the economies of the less advanced societies of the world with those of Europe and the United States in some sort of continuum. It is from these efforts that the concepts of "underdevelopment" and "development," of "traditional" and "modern," have come into the economists' vocabulary. Most developmental economists are agreed that certain tangible criteria characterize a modern as against a premodern or traditional economy and, moreover, that for a traditional economy to become modern certain fundamental and ultimately self-generating changes must take place within the society at large. W. W. Rostow's well-publicized statement of "the stages of economic growth" and particularly his dramatic phrase "takeoff" have popularized the idea that modern economic growth is the result of certain very specific conditions and changes which must take place within a traditional economy (for instance, a 10 per cent investment rate).[1] Rostow's system has been severely criticized for its dogmatism (particularly in its insistence upon a "stage theory" of growth) and for its factual data as well (a 10 per cent investment rate appears not to be an absolute criterion), but it illustrates one kind of effort which developmental economists have made in trying to systematize their thinking on the economic growth process.

Rostow subtitles his book *A Non-Communist Manifesto,* an interesting commentary on how present-day developmental economists regard

[1] W. W. Rostow, *The Stages of Economic Growth,* Cambridge, England, 1960.

the once-prevalent Marxist theory of development. But Marxist theory, which conceives of the process of economic modernization strictly as a transition from feudalism to capitalism, still has its adherents in Japan. A generation ago, the prevalence of Marxist views directed the attention of Japanese scholars almost exclusively to the study of class tensions and class access to the means of production. Since capitalism was assumed to have been carried forward by the bourgeoisie at the expense of the "feudal class," the entire history of the growth of the modern economy in Japan was visualized in terms of the dichotomy between the "penetration of money economy" and the decline of the old village society and of the samurai class. It is important to realize that the developmental economist's conception of "traditional" has little to do with the idea of "feudal" and that the first stages of modern economy cannot be defined simply as "capitalistic." While not neglecting the social and political concomitants to economic modernization (especially when it comes to accounting for the dynamics of the process), scholars of late have attempted to penetrate more deeply into the strictly economic conditions underlying growth.

The works of Simon Kuznets and Alexander Gerschenkron in a theoretical vein or, more specifically with respect to Japan, of Rostow and Henry Rosovsky, while differing on many technical points, nonetheless contain large areas of agreement in their treatment of economic growth as a general phenomenon. They conceive of the existence of an undeveloped or traditional economy in pretty much the terms expressed by Rostow as one "where structure is developed within limited production functions, based on pre-Newtonian science and technology, and on pre-Newtonian attitudes towards the physical world.... The central fact about the traditional society was that a ceiling existed on the level of attainable output per head." [2] (In other words, a slow improvement in basic technology, agriculture, and commerce is not denied, but there are certain quite definite limits to development.) These economists conceive of modern economy in its early stages as being characterized by a syndrome of measurable criteria such as those summarized by Kuznets: (1) the application of scientific thought and technology to industry, transportation, and agriculture; (2) a sustained and rapid rise in real product per capita combined with high rates of population growth; (3) a high rate of transformation of the industrial structure; and (4) the presence of international contacts. And they conceive of at least two major turning points: one which marks the economy's transition from traditional to modern (i.e., takeoff, or breakthrough, characterized in most instances by a high rate of investment), and another which marks

[2] *Ibid.,* p. 4.

the achievement of modern economic growth as a self-sustaining, self-generating phenomenon (i.e., the achievement of a condition in which economic change and growth become the normal expectation of the system itself). Beyond this point most economists differ in their handling of the later phases of economic development; yet there is agreement that measurable structural changes are found between the appearance of "sustained growth" and the consummation of a mature "mass-consumption economy," as Rostow describes it. Changes in structure have been a chief criterion for the differentiation of economies along the continuum of development or for the periodization of the course of a given national development.

As in any problem of historical analysis, periodization is crucial to the telling of the story of Japan's modern economic growth. The organization of the story reveals in most instances the basic intellectual commitment of the economic historian, be it Marxist or strictly empirical. Thus, until recently most Western economic historians (such as G. C. Allen) indulged in a descriptive style of treatment with no strong theoretical framework. Taking their cues from the political historian, such writers tended to fit the economic narrative into the framework of political events, particularly the sequence of wars, or of major changes in political leadership and policy. The result was a form of periodization which placed its emphasis upon the relations between governmental structure (or political mood) and the economy. The typical system of periodization resulting from this approach would be of the following order:

1. 1858 to 1880, an initial period during which the government led the way in creating an environment conducive to modern economic development.

2. 1881 to 1914, the early phase of industrialization, during which growth was stimulated by two wars (against China and Russia), the expansion of the Japanese Empire, and the development of the textile industry.

3. 1914 to 1930, the development of a mature light industry and increased emphasis on heavy industry resulting from the great expansion in the economy brought about by the demands and opportunities created by World War I. But Japan had no sooner become a full-fledged member of the community of advanced economic powers than the world Depression threatened to bring ruin.

4. 1930 to 1937, a period of economic recovery from the Depression and the beginning of heavy industry under increased government planning, military expenditure, and rationalization of the industrial sector.

5. 1937 to 1945, the war years, when the Japanese economy was drained for the war effort and regimented under a totalitarian form of government.

6. 1945 to 1952, recovery under the liberalizing policies of the Allied

Occupation; a period divided between the pre-cold war emphasis on economic reform and the emphasis thereafter on economic recovery and reconstruction.

7. 1953 to the present, the new prosperity.

Such a system of periodization does no great violence to the economic data, but neither does it take its basic form from the economic evidence. The mark of the developmental economist is that he has begun to modify this standard periodization so as to bring out the structure of the process of economic change more forcefully. Such is the advantage of the system of periodization suggested by Ohkawa and Rosovsky in their recent article, "A Century of Growth." [3] The modifications which they make in their system of periodization are primarily three:

1. They place the break between preparation for growth and initial growth at 1885 (i.e., the end of Matsukata Masayoshi's deflation).
2. They consider the twenty years from 1886 to 1905 as the critical period during which Japan achieved modern economic growth.
3. They treat the entire period from 1906 to 1952 as a single phase of economic development characterized by a disequilibrium between the expanding modern sector of the economy and the lagging traditional sector.

The analysis of the modernization of the Japanese economy which follows, while including a good deal of descriptive detail, will attempt to bring out the structural divisions suggested by Ohkawa and Rosovsky. It will emphasize somewhat more than they do the critical disruption caused by World War II and the problem of reconstruction after 1945. It will also incorporate a fourth period, the post-1952 era which William W. Lockwood has called the period of the "new capitalism." [4]

THE TRADITIONAL ECONOMY: PROBLEMS OF EVALUATION

A critical problem in assessing the nature of the early stages of Japan's economic modernization is how to evaluate the base point from which the push toward modernization began. The usual description of Tokugawa Japan as a feudal society with a closed and stagnant economy provides a startling contrast to the burst of activity which took place after 1858. Precisely how much growth there was in the first few decades

[3] Contained in William W. Lockwood (ed.), *The State and Economic Enterprise in Modern Japan,* Princeton, N.J., 1965 (in press).
[4] *Ibid.*

after 1858 and how much institutional change was required to bring this about depend, of course, upon our view of the state of the Tokugawa economy before 1858.

Until recently it was common to picture Japan in the 1850s as a land in a dangerous state of economic stagnation and political decay. This picture has now come under critical revision. The evidences of decay had been drawn from selected data on population stagnation, peasant uprisings, and the financial insolvency of the *daimyō* and shogunate. The assumption that these evidences were direct indices of economic deterioration, however, failed to take into account other aspects of the economy or to consider Japan in the light of comparable societies in the early stages of their economic modernization. More recently it has been possible to cut through some of these earlier limitations and to study the economy of Tokugawa Japan with attention to its obvious weaknesses but also with greater sensitivity to the aspects of the traditional economy which provided a base for eventual economic growth. A fuller appreciation of the complexity of economic change during the Tokugawa era of seclusion has made the rapid expansion of later years more comprehensible without making it less impressive.

Reassessment of the Tokugawa economic base has resulted from two lines of empirical investigation: one into the institutions which provided the structural framework within which the economy operated, and the other into the actual statistics of economic production and the standard of living. The results of these studies have indicated that the Japanese economy in the 1850s, while statistically typical of underdeveloped economies as a whole, nevertheless had numerous potentials for growth. Among the institutional factors, political unity which laid the basis of an economy of national scope was of prime significance. Such unity was not achieved automatically or easily. The Tokugawa hegemony, though often called a military dictatorship, was based less on a preponderance of central power than on a skillful application of the classic principle of divide and rule. The domains of the major *daimyō*, especially those who had been rivals of the Tokugawa before 1600, retained a high degree of autonomy throughout the Tokugawa period, and there was for a long time little economic intercourse between one domain and another. This was partly the result of shogunal policy, which sought to isolate the *daimyō* to prevent dangerous combinations among them, and partly the nature of the economy as such. In the early seventeenth century local economic self-sufficiency was the ideal and the characteristic of most domains; industry was restricted to a few handicrafts, such as textiles, weapons, and ceramics; commerce was considered unproductive and therefore ideologically undesirable.

By the beginning of the eighteenth century, however, these conditions had changed drastically. A commercial economy was encouraged by the new economic requirements of the upper class. The members of the samurai class in nearly all domains had been withdrawn from individual fiefs or villages and congregated in the castle towns of the provinces. Tokugawa policy produced a further and still more artificial concentration of the upper levels of samurai by requiring all *daimyō* to spend half their time in the shogunal capital (Edo) and to leave their immediate families permanently in Edo as hostages to assure their own good behavior.

The financial burden on the *daimyō* from constant travel to and from Edo and from maintaining mansions both in Edo and at home was aggravated by habits of conspicuous consumption (encouraged by nearly all Tokugawa shoguns) and by shogunal levies of large special assessments on the *daimyō* to pay for public works and other undertakings. The problems of financing such costs and the growing separation of the consuming samurai class from the producing peasant class had two major consequences: farming became more specialized, and the number of merchants expanded rapidly. Both developments accelerated the transition from a barter economy to a monetary economy, with the merchant middlemen as the chief beneficiaries of the change. They also meant a steady weakening of the barriers to trade between domains and thus a movement toward an economy of national scope. Cities such as Osaka, Kyoto, and Edo grew to huge proportions and served in various ways as centers of special services, economic exchange, and handicraft production.

Agriculture increased its total output as additional land was brought under cultivation (there was a nearly 80 per cent increase between 1600 and 1850) and as improved technology increased the yield in many parts of the country. Except perhaps in certain highly advanced areas of central Honshu, agriculture did not become primarily commercial until well after the fall of the Tokugawa shogunate. Nonetheless, there was a slow trend toward the concentration of crops in geographically favorable regions and the growing of surpluses for sale. This was a natural outcome of the vast expansion of the urban market (dictated by the concentration of the samurai class) and was made possible by the improvement of transport facilities and the development of monetary exchange and credit systems. Silver and rice certificates circulated in most of the *daimyō* domains, while exchange houses in Osaka and Edo handled exchange transactions between shogunal and *daimyō* territories or between *daimyō* territories.

The same factors encouraged the development in middle and late

547

Tokugawa times of rudimentary forms of manufacturing. Japanese economic historians use the term *manyufakuchua* in the original sense of its English counterpart, to describe the late-Tokugawa innovation of factory-system production of goods by hand, in contrast with the traditional and continuing system of "domestic" or home production. After the reopening of foreign intercourse in 1854, both the shogunate and several domain governments were able to establish Western-style factories to produce iron, armaments, and other products considered militarily essential. These establishments were primitive and isolated, but they indicated the level of technological development achieved (sporadically to be sure) by the middle of the nineteenth century.

While such changes were modifying the nature of the Tokugawa economy, others were at work upon the general institutional structure. Although the state (that is, the shogunate and *daimyō* administrations) never developed adequate means of handling the commercial sector, this was not for lack of making the attempt. Meanwhile, the state managed to perfect a highly effective control over the agricultural sector. A state policy of encouragement of agricultural production together with an extremely efficient system of taxation meant that a high proportion of the national product (between 26 and 29 per cent, as calculated by E. S. Crawcour, or between 20 and 30 per cent, as estimated by James Nakamura) was available to the governments.[5] Moreover, the governments, through borrowing, forced loans, and involvement in partnership arrangements with merchants in monopoly organizations, were considerably involved in commercial affairs and did manage to extract a fair amount from this sector, though never on a systematic basis. Perhaps most important of all was the extremely lively debate which raged during the 1840s and 1850s as government advisers and private critics sought to comprehend the economic crisis of the time and to suggest solutions (usually of a mercantilist nature) to the financial difficulties of the government. The deep concern of government over fiscal and welfare problems showed a turn of mind which was to prove characteristic in the years after 1868.

Of equal significance were changes in the social and economic attitudes of farmers and businessmen in Tokugawa Japan. Indications of the relatively high level of literacy (perhaps 40 to 50 per cent among males) are substantiated by the large number of educational institutions serving the common people and by the volume and complexity of paper work carried on by the village and urban headmen. By the nineteenth century it was apparent that many of the traditional features of rural society were being modified on more rational economic lines. Labor, once performed nearly entirely under conditions of family

5 In *ibid.*

or feudal obligation, had become increasingly an economic commodity paid for in real wages.

How are we to fit such positive evidence into the picture of economic stagnation which was so commonly depicted by scholars of a previous generation? The truth is that it is not inconceivable that both pictures are acceptable within the context of the limited view each offers. Take the question of population during the Tokugawa period by way of explanation. The best estimates we have indicate that after the middle of the eighteenth century population grew very little if at all, remaining at about thirty million. It has long been assumed that population stagnation was a prime index to economic stagnation. But what of the statistics upon which such a judgment is based? Tokugawa population figures leave much to be desired; they lack uniformity of method and date, they exclude untaxed classes, and they seem likely to reflect extensive underreporting or overreporting, depending on the purpose of a particular enumeration. Nor do they provide a good basis for judging the extent of urbanization. Even with the figures we have, it appears that the supposed stability of the population from 1726 to 1852 applies only in the aggregate, with substantial shifts occurring in different parts of the country. Nor is population size necessarily related directly to standards of living and the distribution of wealth. There is much evidence of the increasing wealth of the upper sectors of the commercial and rural landowner class. And the simple interpretation that rural uprisings necessarily reflected worsening conditions rather than heightened expectations has been called in question. Thus, while aggregated figures may lead to one set of conclusions, selected statistics showing differential development or the qualitative improvement of this or that factor can lead to a very different set of conclusions.

Japan's economy in the 1850s, then, literally presents a dual picture. Overall it was typically an underdeveloped (or traditional) economy. Probably some 75 to 80 per cent of the labor force was engaged in agriculture, and this group produced more than 65 per cent of the national product. On the whole, production was not sufficiently high so that the average rural level of living was much above subsistence. While some manufacturing existed, it was heavily preoccupied with textiles and food processing (nearly 70 per cent). Manufacturing was still closely linked to the agricultural village and involved only the most modest outlay of capital. More sophisticated industrial activities were isolated and largely artificially sponsored. The many features of the Tokugawa economy which are cited as evidence of growth and potential receptivity to stimulus toward modern growth were indicative of only the more advanced areas of the country. They do not reveal themselves in the overall figures. Thus in the aggregate, and this is what the economist must eventually work with, the Tokugawa economy showed only those minor trends of growth which one might expect in a traditional economy.

MODERNIZATION OF THE JAPANESE ECONOMY: THE TRANSITION PHASE, 1858–1885

The signing of commercial treaties with the West in 1858 and the political upheaval of 1868 created an entirely new set of economic conditions. Japan was opened to foreign trade and to the knowledge of Western economic theories and new industrial technologies. It was faced both by a challenge to its national (and economic) independence and by an opportunity to profit from the new knowledge and incentives provided by contact with the West. The country reacted to both stimuli.

Whether warranted or not, the initial Western impact upon both the Tokugawa and the new Meiji regimes was to engender fear of conquest by the chief maritime powers of Europe and America. Both regimes concluded that the only way to avert this threat was to remake Japan in the image of the threatening powers, at least in their economic and military aspects. In carrying out this policy, the Tokugawa government had been gravely hampered by its commitment to the existing political, economic, and social system on which its own security depended. The Meiji government, though professing a "return to antiquity," enjoyed in practice the incalculable advantage of being free to repudiate existing institutions and methods in the name of "eliminating feudalism." The resulting political changes were dwarfed by economic and social changes.

In the first years after 1868, the most important development in Japan was the creation of an atmosphere conducive to social change and economic growth. By 1877, the new regime had succeeded in centralizing political authority to a much greater degree than any of its predecessors. It had also removed the most serious inflexibilities of the Tokugawa economic and social structure. The steps which were of greatest economic consequence were the abolition of class distinctions based on occupation, the removal of most controls over freedom of movement and enterprise, the sanctioning of private landownership and free alienation of landholdings, the removal of restrictions on the type of crop planted, the elimination of internal customs barriers, and the drastic revision and systematization of the taxation system.

Such steps, largely permissive, were characteristic of the new government's role in the primary sector of the economy (the so-called "extractive industries"—agriculture, fishing, forestry, and mining). The state also provided such routine services as crop reporting, brought in foreign experts to train Japanese in Western methods of mining, and set up agricultural experiment stations to help adapt foreign crops to Japanese conditions and to develop better methods of farming.

The government took a more direct hand in the other sectors of the economy: the secondary (manufacturing and construction) and the tertiary (transport, communications, trade, finance, etc.). Except in the silk industry, capital and entrepreneurial leadership in these fields came largely from the government in the first decade of the Meiji era. (There was as yet no adequate banking system.) Deriving its revenue, like all previous regimes, chiefly from the land tax, the government built and operated iron foundries, shipyards, machine shops, factories, railways, telegraph lines, and a postal service. It gave technical and financial assistance to private interests in key industries. It hired foreign specialists and imported foreign machinery for new industries and for the mechanization of old ones, such as silk reeling and cotton spinning. Japanese were sent to the United States and Europe to study Western finance, technology, and factory organization. All these innovations were of the utmost significance for the future development of the economy, though their contribution to national output was, of course, still very small.

Historians such as E. Herbert Norman and Japanese economists have been particularly critical of the role of the government in the early stages of Japan's economic modernization. The usual line of attack has been that vested interests working through an authoritarian government squeezed the agrarian sector in order to create a strong state and a war machine capable of imperialistic expansion. More recent studies by Lockwood, Ohkawa, and Rosovsky have shown first of all that the government did not play so dominant an economic role as had been supposed and, second, that agriculture in Japan as elsewhere had the chief responsibility for providing the essential increments of output in the early years of economic development. The features of Japanese economic development hidden by the overemphasis upon the role of the state were the small increments of private economic enterprise demonstrated by the Japanese businessman, the steady improvement in agricultural production, and the remarkable pattern of private saving even at a low standard of living.

What the above signifies is that there was nothing like a planned economy in the early years of the Japanese transition to modern growth. The government was active in the economic sphere, but it was not in full control. Yet, having said this, it is true that the government was deeply involved in creating the conditions which ultimately brought modern economic growth into being. And of all the requisite conditions one of the most crucial, according to Rosovsky, was the creation of a sound financial and monetary base for the modern economy. This was very much the work of the brilliant Minister of Finance Matsukata Masayoshi. Between 1876 and 1881 the government had been obliged to expand its note issue dramatically to cover the expenses of the war in Satsuma and the program of commutation of the samurai stipends. The sharp inflation which followed created a severe budgetary crisis and caused an excess of imports over exports with attendant balance-of-payments problems. The price of agricultural commodities had risen dramatically, yet the government received its main income from the fixed land tax, which meant that its real income had been reduced. In 1881 Matsukata became Finance Minister and immediately instituted a deflationary policy. By drastically increasing government revenue and reducing government expenditure (incidentally selling off government-operated factories and mines) and by reducing the quantity of government paper currency in circulation by some 25 per cent, he put the government on a firm budgetary foundation. Reorganizing the banking system, he established the Bank of Japan in 1882 as the bank of issue. The government was now financially solvent, Japan had achieved a modern currency system, and an adventurous group of entrepreneurs who had weathered the shocks of inflation and deflation and had been able to acquire a wide range of industries by government sale were now poised to carry Japan into a period of rapid economic growth. (The adverse effects upon large groups of ex-samurai, small businessmen, and others who found the pressures of deflation too great have drawn the sympathy of those, notably Norman and Tsuru Shigeto, who object to the "ruthless" manner in which the government created a fiscal base which benefited the more vigorously "capitalistic" elements of the society.)

THE BEGINNING OF INDUSTRIALIZATION, 1886–1905

The real start of modern industrial growth can be placed in the twenty-year period which began at the end of the Matsukata deflation and terminated at the conclusion of the war with Russia. The achievements of the modern sector of the economy during this interval were not dramatic (except perhaps in textiles and railroads), but they were steady and increasingly self-sustaining. Characteristic of this initial phase of industrialization, as one might expect, was the close relationship between the traditional economy (primarily agriculture) and modern development. In fact it was largely through the continuing expansion of the agricultural sector that the investment surpluses which moved modernization ahead were obtained.

Recently the studies of James Nakamura [6] have cast some doubt upon the figures developed by Ohkawa which indicate a growth rate of output in agriculture of 2.6 per cent annually through the period. It is Nakamura's claim that, because of unreported production, the early Meiji base (1878) from which such a rate is calculated was actually much higher than generally assumed, so that the overall growth rate should be scaled down to as low as 0.8 to 1.2 per cent a year. But irrespective of whether growth was large or small in comparative terms, it is certainly true that agriculture contributed a great share in absolute terms to the modernization process. This is apparent most dramatically when we consider that as late as 1882 the land tax accounted for more than 80 per cent of state revenue and that even in 1893 it contributed 45 per cent. It was only after that date that the government diversified its revenue sources chiefly by a continued shift to consumption taxes (excise taxes and state monopolies of tobacco and salt).

How did agriculture manage to sustain such a share of economic growth? There was first of all some expansion in cultivated acreage. The area under rice cultivation, for example, is reported to have increased from 2.5 million *chō* (1 chō equals 2.45 acres) in 1878 to nearly 3 million by 1905. While Nakamura believes some of this increase was due merely to later, more accurate reporting, still it is evident that new irrigation and drainage projects improved the land base in many areas, and also the northern island, Hokkaido, was being opened up to settlement. More important were the advances in farming methods and efficiency. Double-cropping, better fertilizer, the consolidation of farm strips, and other improvements brought a 50 per cent increase in the rice yield per *chō*, from 11.6 *koku* (about 58 bushels) in the 1880s to 17.0 *koku* (about 85 bushels) just before World War I. The net annual production of rice rose from 30,874,000 *koku* at the start of this period to 42,268,000 by 1903. The annual production of grains (barley, naked barley, and wheat) increased in the same period from 11,400,000 to 18,300,000 *koku*. In short, whether some of these advances were in part the result of statistical rather than real changes, agriculture succeeded in supplying nearly all the increased demand for food grains that resulted from the rise in population and per capita consumption.

This is not to say that the agricultural producers improved their living

6 In *ibid.*

standards commensurably. Income from the expanded agricultural production was very unevenly distributed among the producers, and this situation was eventually to lead to considerable distress in the rural areas. Because of high land rents, high interest on farm debts, and high taxes, a large share of farm income went to banks, absentee landlords, and the government. Moreover, there was a sharp rise in tenant farming. In the early years of the Meiji era, about 20 per cent of the cultivated land was farmed by tenants; the percentage had risen to nearly 40 by 1887 and continued to increase thereafter, reaching 45 in 1910. The tenants' rent was paid in kind, and rents ranged as high as 80 per cent of the total crop, with a median of 50 per cent.

Small farmers also suffered from the disruption of secondary enterprises which provided essential supplementary income. After 1887, imports of Indian cotton began to displace domestic cotton, and by the end of the century home production had dwindled to insignificance. The carding, spinning, and weaving of cotton had also been a traditional sideline for farm women, but now it passed to spinning mills. Imports of Chinese lacquer affected the market for farm-produced lacquer ware. Other farm manufactures suffered from competition either with foreign imports or with the greater efficiency of newly mechanized factories.

But fortunately the production of raw silk and the development of the textile industry were to have important consequences for the Japanese farmer. Both silk and cotton were traditionally sources of sideline income for farmers. In the case of silk, farm families grew the mulberry trees, reared the silkworms, and reeled the silk; in some areas they also wove it. The reopening of foreign trade after 1858 had brought a new market into being, and greater numbers of peasants went into the silk business. The foreign requirement for silk of uniform quality soon led to the use of power-driven filatures for reeling, but the hand reel survived as well, mainly in the production of silk for domestic consumption. World demand for silk at this time grew quite rapidly in response to the growth of incomes in the United States and other advanced countries; at the same time, Japan benefited as a new supplier as silk blights from time to time reduced production of silk in Europe. The average annual Japanese output of raw silk had reached more than 15 million pounds during the period from 1899 to 1903. Exporting between two-thirds and three-quarters of its production, Japan had become the world's largest supplier of raw silk.

One of the chief means by which the great expansion in silk production was achieved was the introduction of double-cropping: the addition of a summer-autumn crop of silkworms. For cotton, conditions were considerably different. Once Japan had been opened to world trade, the domestic production of raw cotton became uneconomical. Imports of cheap but finer foreign yarns, chiefly Indian, reduced domestic cotton production to minor importance. But domestic consumption of cotton textiles expanded. A cotton-spinning industry developed first in competition with imports for this domestic market. The mechanization of cotton spinning was rapidly accelerated, and domestic factory yarn soon replaced Indian yarn. Then during the 1890s, especially from 1891 to 1895, Japan moved into the textile-export field. Exports to Korea and China became increasingly important, and the struggle for these two markets had become a major consideration in Japanese foreign policy by the end of the century. For rural Japan, the chief significance of the growth of the textile industry was its employment of large amounts of surplus labor (mainly female) from the villages. Modern industrialization was able to proceed without undue disruption of the traditional social base of the rural areas.

During the first part of the twentieth century, the spinning industry continued to expand, and by 1907, 1,500,000 spindles were producing some 393 million pounds of yarn annually. Weaving was mechanized more slowly and remained primarily a cottage industry despite a steady increase in the size of the largest establishments. By 1913, Japan supplied one-quarter of the world exports of cotton yarn, and Japanese cotton fabrics were giving stiff competition to British and American goods, especially in China. Thus during the initial phase textiles carried the main burden of modern industrialization in Japan.

Other industries, especially those in which state funds had built pilot factories in the first decade after 1868, continued to grow but at a much slower rate than the textile industries. The reasons were much the same as in the experience of other countries in the early stages of industrialization: the higher cost of capital equipment; a smaller degree of adaptability to labor intrusion, small-scale operation, or both; and, particularly, dependence upon prior or parallel development in related areas of the economy. For many such industries, it was not until early in the twentieth century that their growth became self-sustaining.

Japan's deficiency in iron ore and good coking coal retarded the development of the iron and steel industry and induced the government to resume direct investment in this area. The state-owned Yawata Iron Works, opened in 1901, became the nucleus of a modern iron and steel industry, but even by the outbreak of World War I state and private plants combined produced less than one-half of the pig iron and one-third of the steel needed for domestic use. Government subsidies, initiated in 1896, were the key to the development of a shipbuilding industry, but output remained small until the turn of the century. Thereafter, increased subsidies, accumulation of experience, and availability of some kinds of steel and components from domestic sources helped expedite the expansion of the industry. State assistance of one kind or another was also important in the creation of other industries. The foreign-paper industry (as distinguished from the production of the traditional, largely handmade Japanese paper), which was started in 1871, had an annual output of almost 500 million pounds in 1913, dominated by a single massive company (Ōji). After the acquisition of Taiwan from China in 1895, the government subsidized both the production of raw sugar there and the refining of Taiwanese and imported Javanese sugar in Japan. In the last part of the nineteenth century, beer and cement industries grew rapidly from their modest beginnings as state plants that had been sold to private operators in the 1880s. After the turn into the twentieth century the large-scale development of the glass and rubber industries also began.

The emphasis on shipping is understandable, given the country's dependence on trade. Japanese steamship operations in the coastal trade had started shortly after the Meiji Restoration. By 1885, under government pressure, an amalgamation of several existing lines formed the Nippon Yūsen Kaisha (NYK), which was to become one of the world's greatest shipping concerns. The NYK and other firms, notably the second-ranking Ōsaka Shōsen Kaisha (OSK), formed in 1883, began acquiring larger ships and expanding their operations throughout the globe. Before the end of the century, NYK had started its routes to Europe, North America, and Australia, and Japanese shippers were active in Chinese waters after the 1894–1895 war. The importance of the new shipping industry is evident from the growth in the percentage of Japanese trade which it carried. In 1893, only 14 per cent of the ships entering Japanese ports were Japanese-owned, and they carried only 7 per cent of the country's exports and less than 9 per cent of its imports. By 1903, these percentages had risen to 38, 40, and 34, respectively, and ten years later they stood at 51, 52, and 47, making Japan a major maritime power.

Foreign trade in general followed much the same timetable: slow development (as far as the contribution to the aggregate economy was concerned) until the last decade of the nineteenth century and then fast growth to a substantial level by 1905. As the foregoing description of the manufacturing industries suggests, exports were at first dominated by raw materials and the products of traditional industries. In the early 1880s, raw silk, tea, and rice accounted for nearly two-thirds of all exports. Within the next fifteen years, copper and coal had become important exports, but the only major additions from manufacturing were silk piece goods and matches. By 1905, however, exports of cotton yarn and cotton and silk piece goods had begun to overshadow the unprocessed goods. Even more striking changes occurred in the structure of imports. At the beginning of this period, nearly half of Japan's imports were manufactured goods. By 1905, finished manufactures had dropped to less than 25 per cent, while industrial raw materials amounted to one-third of total imports. The stimulus of providing goods for overseas markets had also greatly accelerated the introduction of Western industrial technology into Japan.

The end of the first phase of modern economic growth in Japan is put at 1905 by Rosovsky and Ohkawa not simply because of the advance of the modern sector described above, but because they see evidence of certain important structural changes within the total economy. If at the outset of this period the traditional sector was largely carrying the modern, they claim this was no longer the case by 1905. In fact, by this time the traditional economy began to decline in its growth rate and in its overall contribution to national growth. While, to be sure, the two sectors of the economy remained heavily interdependent, still from this point on the modern economy had begun to serve as its own stimulus, providing from its own resources the investment needed for further growth. Japan, in the opinion of Rosovsky and Ohkawa, had reached the self-sustaining point in its economic development.

The year 1905, of course, is not accepted by all students of the Japanese economy, and 1918 is more often cited as the turning point. Most recently Nakamura has returned to this date on the basis of figures showing a continued growth of agriculture during the World War I years. While we have adopted 1905 in the following paragraphs, some of the uncertainties of periodization may also be evident in the writing.

JAPAN IN THE WORLD ECONOMY: GROWTH AND STRUCTURAL DIFFERENTIATION

To continue in the vein of Rosovsky and Ohkawa, let us assume that the Japanese economy after 1905 was characterized not only by the rapid and autonomous growth of the new industrial sector, but also by certain other features peculiar to Japan, chief among which was the growing differentiation between the traditional and the modern sectors. Before this point those who worked in the traditional sector were approximately in as favorable a position as those who joined the new factories and businesses. Wages were roughly comparable. In fact, throughout the initial stage of industrialization we found many industries divided between their traditional and modern branches: for instance, textiles (domestic versus factory-produced), paper (Japanese versus Western-style), and brewing (sake versus beer). As this industrial complex grew and the demand for labor in the modern sector rose, there came into being a widening gap in both wage and production levels between the two sectors. The result was to create what some economists have called a *dual economy* and what Ohkawa and Rosovsky have termed *differential structure*. Between 1906 and 1930 a large number of factors contributed to the entrenchment of this particular style of economy. Most of these were accentuated by the alternations between boom and depression which agitated the Japanese economy particularly after 1914.

Unlike the other major powers, Japan profited greatly from World War I. The monetary cost of Japanese participation in the war was negligible, and among the 8,538,315 soldiers and sailors killed, only 300 were Japanese. The captured German Pacific islands were not of great economic value, but the acquisition of German interests in Shantung paved the way for the large-scale economic penetration of China proper, beginning with the Twenty-one Demands of 1915.

Of more immediate importance was the unprecedented boom in Japanese production for both domestic and foreign markets. Prewar patterns of international trade were destroyed by submarine warfare and the diversion of resources to the European theater of operations. The Allied governments placed large contracts with Japanese munitions manufacturers, and strong demands arose for Japanese shipping. Neutral markets, particularly in Latin America and East Asia, were vacated by the former chief suppliers, and only Japan was in a position to take them over. During the period 1915–1919, the annual average value of Japanese exports was almost three times as great as in 1910–1914.

Imports also rose in value but not nearly so rapidly. Many former sources of supply were closed to Japan by the war, and industrial expansion was therefore needed to fill a gap in the domestic market. With such a combination of rising demand in home, neutral, and belligerent markets, it is not surprising that the number of workers in factory industry nearly doubled between 1914 and 1919, and the gross value of production more than quintupled.

The wartime boom in Japan (culminating in an 18.8 per cent increase in the gross national product from 1918 to 1919) lasted until March, 1920, or more than a year beyond the cessation of hostilities in Europe. In the spring of 1920, however, there was a sharp collapse of wholesale prices, especially in rice and raw silk. Even so, the Japanese economy rallied more quickly and more completely than the economies of other major powers, and by 1922 most industries were recovering. The conspicuous exceptions were shipbuilding and coal mining, which had undergone unusually drastic wartime expansion. By August, 1923, wholesale prices were rising in Japan while still declining in England and the United States. The disastrous earthquake of September, 1923, brought on a new period of inflation and something of a "reconstruction boom" in the key industrial area of Tokyo and Yokohama.

In 1927 there was another financial crisis, characterized by numerous bank failures and the bankruptcy of many small firms, particularly those which had been set up or expanded during the war. Wholesale prices again declined, though they recovered slightly in 1928 and did not begin their steady drop until the effects of the decision to return to the gold standard were felt along with the advent of the world Depression. Thus, while we shall see that in the aggregate the national product continued to rise steadily and industrialization to expand rather dramatically, particularly in the early 1920s, the cycles of boom and depression were to bring extreme difficulties to certain sectors of the population, especially the agriculturalists.

In Japan proper since 1905, agriculture had apparently reached a point of severely diminishing returns. The production of the principal crop, rice, showed little upward tendency, though there were sharp fluctuations due to climatic conditions. There was a continuing slow increase in the number of acres cultivated (except from 1923 to 1924) and a very slow increase in the yield per acre. The number of farming families remained practically stationary at about 5,500,000, though the total population of Japan proper grew from 46,600,000 to 63,900,000 between 1905 and 1930.

The most important change affecting the agrarian sector was the new competition which was exercised by the colonies. Japanese rice cultivation techniques were introduced on a large scale in two colonial areas, Korea and Taiwan. The result was a notable increase in rice output and a rapid rise in rice exports to Japan proper. Korean rice exports had been negligible at the time of annexation by Japan (1910), but by 1929 Korean rice production had grown by 30 per cent, chiefly because of improved methods of irrigation and cultivation and the increased use of fertilizers. Taiwan's production followed the same pattern on a smaller scale. By 1929, the two colonies were supplying Japan with rice imports equal to about 14 per cent of the production in Japan proper.

Rice prices, meanwhile, were far from stable. On the Tokyo market, the average price per *koku* (about 5 bushels) was ¥16.15 in 1914, or only slightly more than the average for the preceding ten years. During

1915 and 1916, the averages were about 20 per cent lower, at ¥13.06 and ¥13.66, respectively. In the next three years, the price average rose rapidly, to ¥19.80 in 1917, to ¥32.51 in 1918, and to an unprecedented high of ¥45.89 in 1919, a peak not to be reached again until the dark days of 1944. Landowners reaped enormous profits, along with speculators newly rich from wartime profits in industry or commerce.

The most precipitate rise came in the late summer of 1918, when the monthly average climbed from ¥30.39 in July to ¥38.70 in August. Urban discontent erupted in a wave of rice riots all over the country. Troops had to be called out to restore order, the Cabinet resigned, and a new government began generally unsuccessful efforts to stabilize the price of the nation's principal food commodity. The price of rice remained high until September, 1920, and throughout the twenties it was still far above any prewar level, reaching a peak of ¥41.57 in 1925. A large harvest in 1930 caused a sharp decline in price in 1931, but thereafter the trend was consistently upward.

The second-ranking agricultural product, raw silk, had a different history in this period. Production tripled between 1914 and 1929, and the number of producers also rose markedly. By 1929, about 40 per cent of all farming families engaged in cocoon raising as a secondary activity. The additions to the labor force in the reeling mills came largely from the daughters of farm families. Thus, farmers had become steadily more dependent on silk as a major source of cash income, both from the sale of cocoons and from the wages earned by family members working in the reeling mills.

Prices rose very steeply during the war, and in 1920 the average export price was ¥1,191 per 100 *kin* (about 132 pounds). The general collapse of prices in 1920 affected silk only briefly; by 1923, the export price had recovered and even rose, to a figure of ¥2,150 per 100 *kin*. Prices fell after 1925 as the exchange value of the yen rose, but as late as April, 1929, the export price was ¥1,420, comparing favorably with an average of ¥800 or ¥900 before the war. The world Depression, however, played havoc with Japan's chief export market, which was the United States, and by October, 1930, the export price had dropped to ¥540. It continued downward to ¥390 in June, 1932. This sharp break in the market for raw silk coincided with the 1931 break in rice prices. As urban discontent over high rice prices in 1918 had helped to usher in a decade of party governments, so agrarian discontent over low prices for rice and silk contributed to the shift in political power in the thirties. These indicators of the distress of the traditional sector were of great significance.

Throughout these years the industrial sector expanded rapidly in all fields. The silk industry took advantage of continuing improvements in methods of production and in scientific research fostered by the state. The introduction of multiple-thread reeling machines and the extension of the reeling season as a result of the spread of double-cropping in cocoon production brought on a notable expansion of output. With improved equipment and techniques, the reeling mills were able to produce silk more rapidly and in better quality. During this period, the output per reeling basin in the filatures increased by 250 per cent, and reeling became more than ever a factory-system operation. At the end of the period, only 4 per cent of the total output came from hand reels. A similar tendency became apparent in the silk-weaving industry. Mills with more than 50 looms were started in the export branch of the weaving industry, and even in the domestic branch, characterized largely by handloom production, there was some introduction of power looms.

The second great textile industry, cotton, also continued its expansion. Even the destruction of nearly 1,000,000 spindles in the 1923 earthquake did not halt the upward trend in capacity; the number of spindles rose from 1,540,000 in 1907 to 2,415,000 in 1913, to 3,814,000 in 1920, and to 6,650,000 in 1929. At the same time, there was a clear trend toward oligopoly. The average size of the mills increased, and extensive consolidation took place, so that by 1929 seven giant concerns had 56 per cent of the spindles. As in the silk industry, weaving also became more important. There was a growing movement to set up weaving sheds in Japan to use the yarn spun by mills of the same firm, in preference to exporting it. The number of looms owned by the spinning concerns tripled between 1913 and 1929, and the output of cloth quadrupled, in comparison with an output of yarn which did not quite double. Yarn exports to Asia declined, while piece-goods exports expanded. There was also a shift away from concentration on the coarsest types of yarn.

Thus between 1905 and 1929, the textile industries greatly expanded their output and also improved their efficiency by steadily shifting toward more modern and more mechanized methods of production. Moreover, they had as a whole kept their preeminent position in the Japanese industrial system despite the rise of other industries in this period. In 1920 and still in 1930, the textile industries employed about one-fourth of the industrial labor force. In factories employing five or more workers each, textiles accounted for about half of the total number of workers. Within the textile field, 45 per cent of the workers were engaged in silk reeling or silk spinning, 7 per cent in silk weaving, and 31 per cent in cotton spinning and weaving.

The newer industries made rapid progress in this period but were still dwarfed by the textile industries. Of prime importance for later developments was the expansion of iron and steel. Pig iron production multiplied nearly threefold between 1906 and 1929, but the sharp rise in consumption had necessitated increases in imports, and in 1929 Japan still imported 40 per cent of its pig iron. About 90 per cent of the ore for the blast furnaces was imported, chiefly from China and Malaya. The output of finished steel, which totaled only 60,000 tons in 1906, rose to 547,000 tons in 1919 and to more than 2,000,000 tons in 1929. The state-owned Yawata Iron Works continued to dominate the industry, whether in pig iron, ingot steel, or finished steel, but the number of private works was growing, and their scale of operation was expanding.

The absence of foreign competition during World War I caused a rapid growth in domestic production of various types of machinery. Many of the new firms were unable to survive the postwar collapse in prices and the revival of foreign production, but there was continued growth after the war in some fields, notably the output of prime movers, electrical machinery and equipment, textile machinery, bicycles, and scientific instruments. The wartime boom had been especially conspicuous in shipbuilding, as the gross tonnage of merchant ships launched in Japan in 1919 totaled eight times that of 1914. The postwar slump was equally drastic, and recovery was extremely slow in comparison with that of other industries, partly because costs of construction were higher than in other countries. Thus despite the significant growth of the iron and steel industry, at the beginning of the thirties Japanese heavy industry as a whole still lagged behind the development of light industry.

In the twenty years preceding World War I, Japan had experienced an unfavorable balance of foreign trade in every year but three (1895, 1906, 1909). The war brought a temporary but startling reversal of this situation. Since the disruption of normal trade patterns did not begin in earnest until the late summer of 1914, Japan's imports for that year still showed an excess over exports, but it was the smallest excess since 1910. During the next four years, there was a very large annual excess of exports over imports, an excess of unprecedented magnitude. The peak year was 1917, but even in 1919, after the war had ended, Japan's competitive position was still better than in 1913. The average annual value of exports in the period 1914–1919 exceeded that of imports by ¥240 million, or by more than 10 per cent. Largely because the banking system was without experience in dealing with such a huge surplus and lacked the flexibility for rapid adjustment to the situation, Japan did not make use of its windfall profits. Little of the surplus was used to redeem outstanding Japanese obligations, and the large amount invested in foreign countries was put chiefly into short-term securities which were either redeemed or repudiated soon after the war ended. Large amounts also went into political loans to Chinese warlords through whom Japan hoped to exercise control of China; most of these, like the loans to czarist Russia, were never repaid. The rest of the surplus went into the gold reserves of the government and the Bank of Japan, which increased sevenfold between December, 1914, and December, 1920.

By 1920, an import surplus had reappeared; this situation continued through the rest of the period, though the size of the surplus diminished somewhat after 1924. The trend of shifts within the structure of imports and exports followed much the same pattern as in the period after 1886. Finished manufactures became steadily more important among the exports, accounting for 40.9 per cent in 1925–1929. Conversely, industrial raw materials made up 55.6 per cent of the imports in this period.

A prime feature of the economy of the 1920s which illustrated the growing predominance of the industrial sector was the increased trend toward oligopoly in nearly all major industries, whether light or heavy. Even when small-scale workshop production remained important, small producers came to be closely linked to large firms which provided them with capital equipment and materials and bought their products. Both government policy, which tended to encourage bigness, and the postwar boom and depression cycles led to the steady growth and diversification of certain huge combines, the *zaibatsu,* as the Japanese called them.

The *zaibatsu* originated in the early stages of economic development after 1868. (Their ability to buy up businesses and factories during the Matsukata deflation proved an important stimulus.) Concerns such as Mitsui, Mitsubishi, Sumitomo, and Yasuda rode the waves of government support and expanding opportunity to develop into huge companies operating in many different but interrelated fields. The significance of the *zaibatsu* was their bigness, their diversification, and the tightness of the interests controlling them. Most were owned and managed by single families. Hence these combines could operate almost exclusively to their own interest, reinvesting at a high rate in their own expansion. Their size and diversification gave them the strength to weather the uncertainties of the postwar markets and to emerge with an increased share of the national wealth by the end of the 1920s.

No aspect of the economy of the 1920s better illustrates the widening gap between the two sectors into which the Japanese economy had become divided than the contrast between the operations of the *zai-*

batsu on the one hand and village agriculture on the other. That this condition was not healthy for the country was recognized, and yet the condition tended to aggravate itself. The perpetuation of two standards of living, one modern and the other traditional, permitted the modern sector of industry to draw on the almost unlimited supply of labor retained in the traditional sector. Although wages in industry and consumption among urban dwellers increased, declining agricultural prices and hence the real incomes of the rural population blunted the development of the domestic market. The thrust of economic growth continued to be directed outward toward empire and foreign markets. That this situation created severe problems, both internal and external, is indicated primarily in the political sphere, as Japan faced new crises brought on by the dissatisfaction of rural groups and industrial workers. And this dissatisfaction came at a time when Japan encountered new resistance to her expansion in the world market.

MILITARISM, WAR, AND RECONSTRUCTION, 1931–1952

Although the war years are not recognized by Rosovsky and Ohkawa as showing structurally distinguishable economic characteristics, the conditions of life for the Japanese people during these two decades were such that it seems warranted for us to set these years off in our periodization. That the Japanese economy, after a period of relatively slow growth and economic problems during the 1920s, began a surge of growth after 1931 has both political and economic explanations. The political explanation seems obvious, for in that year Japan began a new push toward colonial expansion which was to call for an immediate and rapid building of military forces. From the economic side the explanation is less clear-cut. Economic recovery from the world Depression and the accompanying fundamental changes in the industrial structure are obviously related to the rise of militarism in Japan and the wars of 1931, 1937, and 1941. How and to what degree they were related remains a disputed point. Government deficit spending for military purposes pumped great amounts of aggregate demand into the economy after 1931 and enabled Japan to regain full employment and substantial increases in output. To this must be added, however, the Japanese exchange-rate depreciation, which also stimulated domestic demand and paid for necessary imports. The central question of the 1930s, however, is whether the reorientation of the economy at this time was the cause or the result of a decision to embark on a course of military expansion. The evidence is voluminous but not conclusive.

It is clear that state intervention in the economy was far more extensive and thus far more significant after the Depression than before. Yet the state itself was characterized by a greater diffusion of political power than in the past; and the motives, objectives, and interrelationships of the major groups holding or seeking economic and political power are by no means certain. There has been much disagreement as to the genuineness of the supposed mistrust between the Army and the *zaibatsu* during the thirties and even later. Such questions as this involve an intricate mingling of political, economic, and social factors, and no simple answer can withstand scrutiny.

State intervention in the economy, notably in industry, was common in most modern countries after the economic collapse of 1929. In Japan, as elsewhere, many measures taken in the early stages of this intervention were little more than emergency relief devices to check deflation. Even after the intervention began to take on a more positive character, there was little semblance of any general plan of economic control or programming. This was due in considerable part to disagreement within the government and between government and industrial leaders over what kinds of controls were needed and who was to administer them.

Business, especially big business, preferred "autonomous control" or self-regulation, with which they had had some experience. In the early part of the period, this was generally the line taken by new control legislation and ordinances. During the early thirties, associations or guilds (*kumiai*) were formed or enlarged, under state supervision but private management, to enforce quality controls in exporting; to regulate output, prices, and sales; to establish joint manufacturing facilities for small plants; and to control competition among small commercial enterprises. In 1931, a Major Industries Control Law legalized cartel agreements to limit production, assign production quotas, fix prices, and control distribution. Such agreements were not new; the difference was that they now became legally enforceable. The symbolic linking of the civilian and military objectives into a "trade offensive" was indicative of the attempt to mobilize public opinion behind the national economic effort.

In 1933, a new law gave the Finance Ministry extensive powers over all foreign-exchange transactions, but these were not widely used until 1937. In that year, exports exceeded imports in volume, but import prices rose so much more rapidly that the import surplus exceeded that of any previous year except 1924. Thereafter, a series of new laws imposed strict controls over imports and exports. One device employed was a "link system," by which various categories of export goods were linked (either in volume or in value) with related categories of imported raw materials. This had the effect of sharply curtailing the import of raw materials for domestic consumption, as distinguished from materials imported for processing and export as finished goods. Thus, imports of textiles dropped by two-thirds between 1936 and 1941, while imports of bauxite, nickel, and iron ore rose impressively.

After 1931, Japan like most countries was unable to borrow on long-term credit abroad and had to pay cash for virtually all imports. One consequence was the imposition of government controls over capital and credit, starting in 1937. For example, in 1938 Finance Ministry approval was required for loans or the underwriting of securities in amounts over ¥50,000 (then worth approximately $14,000) and for the establishment or reorganization of companies with a capitalization of ¥500,000 or more (about $140,000). Companies were graded in terms of essentiality to the war effort, and luxury-goods companies were simply forbidden to borrow. Such controls had much to do with the rapid decline of light industries and the rise of heavy industries.

The opening of war with China in 1937 also brought new controls in the production of oil, iron and steel, electric power, machine tools, light metals, aircraft, ships, minerals, textiles, foodstuffs, and fertilizers. The National Mobilization Law of 1938 called for the creation of a national council to plan for the control and allocation of human and natural resources. Price controls and rationing came into general practice, but their effect was felt largely by the consuming population. By 1940, the economy was so complicated by an unsystematic maze of government controls, semiofficial "autonomous controls," and cartel agreements that demands for a "new economic structure" became widespread. Once again, however, the conflict between the Army and business resulted in a compromise. The Key Industries Association Ordinance, effective in September, 1941, established national industrywide control associations (*tōsei kai*) and regional associations of smaller business (*tōsei kumiai*). These associations were under the supervision of various Cabinet ministers but were headed by private businessmen. In general, the men who dominated the cartels also became the presidents of the control associations, with broad powers to plan production and distribution by all member firms. There was still no centralized supervision of the control associations as a group, as the Army desired.

Centralized responsibility for economic planning and mobilization did not emerge until after the Japanese began to suffer serious military reverses, notably in the Guadalcanal campaign at the end of 1942 and the beginning of 1943. Realization that the scale of economic requirements had been underestimated brought an energetic drive to raise overall production and gear it fully to military planning. The key measure was the creation of a Munitions Ministry in November, 1943, after numerous earlier halfway measures. The new ministry superseded the Ministry of Commerce and Industry and the Cabinet Planning Board; it was given wide controls over private companies designated as munitions companies because of their relation to war production. During 1944, 671 such companies were brought under government control. Not all, however, were put under the Munitions Ministry; a major loophole in the planned centralization developed from Army and Navy rivalry over aircraft procurement and the unwillingness of both services to turn the control of aircraft production over to the new agency. The chief advocates of centralized control, the Army and Navy, now showed extreme reluctance to surrender their own control over the production of aircraft, machine tools, and other key products. The desired unification of economic controls was therefore never achieved, and the Munitions Ministry was constantly embroiled in interservice rivalry.

Despite the establishment of numerous government boards and control regulations, the common assumption that the Japanese economy of the 1930s and 1940s was completely government-dominated must be taken with caution. Private interests were never fully submerged under military controls, and opportunities for expansion or entrance into new productive fields, especially in heavy industry, were remarkably varied. Japan's economic success during this period rests in large part therefore upon the activity of private industry. The start of the Depression in Japan is sometimes dated from the 1927 financial crisis, two years before it occurred in the world at large. In any case, the Depression ended earlier in Japan than elsewhere. Recovery began, in fact, in the last quarter of 1931, just as Japan was moving to take over Manchuria and as the nation went off the gold standard. By 1933, the index of industrial production had surpassed pre-Depression indices, and the marked upward trend continued through 1941. It then declined in 1942 and 1943; in 1944 it recovered to the 1941 level, only to drop disastrously in 1945 to a figure lower than that of 1930.

More significant than the overall trend of production was the marked shift within industry. With adjustment for price changes, the statistical record indicates that light industry remained stable between 1930 and 1942, while heavy industry expanded fivefold. In 1930, heavy industry (metals, machinery, tools, shipbuilding, aircraft, ordnance, chemicals, construction materials, etc.) accounted for 38.2 per cent of industrial production; by 1937, its share had risen to 57.8 per cent, and in 1942 it was 72.7 per cent. Since total production nearly tripled in the same period, it is obvious that the expansion of heavy industry was remarkable.

Several of the basic heavy industries had been virtually nonexistent before the thirties. Motor-vehicle production, for example, rose from 500 units in 1930 to 48,000 in 1941. Aircraft production rose from 400 to more than 5,000 planes annually in the same period. Older basic industries also underwent significant expansion. Coal production doubled between 1931 and 1941, and the output of ingot steel almost quadrupled. Electric generating capacity more than doubled, and by 1940 Japan was producing a greater quantity of organic high explosives than the United States. For shipbuilding, the peak year was 1937, when the gross tonnage of merchant-ship production reached 405,195, as compared with 92,093 in 1931. The high year for the construction of naval ships was 1941, when the figure of 231,990 gross tons was attained, as compared with 15,050 tons in 1931. These advances were largely the result of determined governmental stimulation of heavy industries.

Industrial production faltered in 1941 and 1942 because the government seems to have underestimated the cost and duration of the war. By the time it began to rise again, in 1944, the Japanese economy was under severe strain at its most vulnerable point, the importation of raw materials. Japan entered the war with 5,916,000 tons of steel merchant shipping of 500 gross tons or more, and during the war she built, captured, or salvaged another 4,100,000 tons. Of this total some 8,617,000 tons were sunk, and another 927,000 tons were damaged so heavily as to be out of use at the end of the war. This destruction (about 55 per cent from submarine attack, the rest from air attack and mines), coupled with the gradual loss of captured territories, made it impossible to sustain the peak production levels. It is estimated that overall production had dropped by 25 per cent from its earlier high by the first half of the fiscal year 1945 (the Japanese fiscal year begins on April 1).

During this period Japan had also entered a critical phase in the primary sector of its economy. The total population in Japan proper increased steadily throughout the period, though the rate of increase was much lower after 1935 than before. Despite all the official and unofficial propaganda about acquiring new colonies to absorb the surplus population, the number of emigrants each year remained substantially lower than the annual excess of births over deaths. Only in 1944, when the death rate exceeded the birthrate, did emigration result in a net decrease in population.

Nevertheless, the farm labor force was being reduced by two massive developments: large-scale conscription by the armed services and the siphoning of workers into heavy industry. Between 200,000 and 400,000 farm workers moved into factory employment each year from 1937 to 1944. Women were drawn increasingly into farm work and by February, 1944, accounted for 58.4 per cent of the farm labor force, as compared with 45.3 per cent in 1930. An estimated 1,500,000 farm workers were conscripted during the war. Contrary to common belief, however, the incidence of conscription seems to have been much lower in agriculture than in industry. Conscription records were burned in 1945, but after the war Japanese officials estimated that of the total number of men recruited 43 per cent were drawn from industry; 26 per cent from commerce, government, and the professions; 8 per cent from communications and transport; and only 23 per cent from agriculture.

Rice production fluctuated even more wildly than usually, falling or rising by as much as 17 per cent from one year to another. The 1930–1944 average, however, was slightly higher than in 1914–1929, and small harvests in 1931, 1934, and 1941 were offset by large harvests in 1930, 1933, 1936–1939, and 1942. The acreage under rice cultivation increased somewhat in the period 1930–1932, declined in 1933–1934, and rose again from 1935 through 1938. Thereafter, the trend was generally downward, though the total average remained above pre-Depression figures until 1943.

Probably the greatest impacts of the war years on the agrarian sector were the steady deterioration of the quality of labor and technology and the decline in fertility as soil nutrients were not replaced by a sufficient use of fertilizer. As the best manpower was siphoned off and as wartime controls affected the capacity of the farmers to maintain or improve their equipment, agriculture along with depleted and bombed-out industry faced military defeat in a depressed state.

The devastation and disruption of war created massive problems of rehabilitation for the Japanese nation, and it was not until 1952 at the end of the Occupation that the economy again attained its prewar level of production. Yet while figures were comparable on an aggregative basis, it was clear that the Japanese economy was qualitatively quite different in 1952 from what it had been during the 1930s and 1940s. The demands of war, the frantic attempts of the government to tamper with and then patch the economic machinery, the serious dislocations which war brought to the normal pattern of production and consumption, all had had their effect. War accelerated structural change, and this, combined with the revolutionary policies of the Occupation planners, was to create a vastly different style of economy by 1952. It is for this reason that some observers have begun to talk of the year in which the Occupation ended as an economic turning point beyond which Japan entered a new era of stability and consumer consumption. The year

1952 provides us with a convenient point at which to stop for a more analytical assessment of Japan's experience during the first two chapters of her economic development.

JAPAN'S ECONOMIC DEVELOPMENT: SOME EXPLANATORY CONSIDERATIONS

Though the history of Japan's first surge of modern economic development was to end in disastrous military defeat, from the purely economic point of view, that is, in terms of economic growth, industrialization, and the standard of living, the Japanese accomplishment was outstanding. Obviously a "follower nation" in its style of development, Japan had, nevertheless, managed a course of modernization not so unlike that of some of the European nations (economically perhaps most like Sweden, politically like Germany). The most remarkable feature of the achievement was that it had been carried out by a country of non-Western background. Japan was in fact the first of the non-European nations to modernize its economy with any degree of success. Let us briefly recapitulate the high points of this story in statistical terms. For this purpose we adopt the convenient synthesis of Japanese statistical information worked out by William W. Lockwood, using three contrasting five-year periods: 1895–1899, 1910–1914, and 1935–1939. His indices are calculated by using the average for 1910–1914 as 100.

The growth of population in Japan, while considerable, was much more in the pattern of European societies as they passed through the Industrial Revolution. Lockwood provides the following figures:

	Number	Index
1895–1899	42,200,000	83
1910–1914	50,600,000	100
1935–1939	71,200,000	141

The increase of 58 from 83 to 141 is a useful figure to keep in mind for comparative purposes as we consider other aspects of Japanese growth. During a comparable period, the national product rose from slightly above 50 to 100 to 250; thus, national product per capita went from 65 to 100 to 177. Food production between 1910–1914 and 1935–1939 increased from 100 to 161. And since at the same time there was an increase in the production of raw materials from the land, although the increase in cultivated land was only about 6 per cent between 1910 and 1939, it is plain that there was a significant improvement in agricultural production, made possible by better technology, additional double-cropping, and additional and better fertilizers.

Turning to other fields of primary production for which there are useful figures that go back to 1895, we find the following:

	1895–1899	1910–1914	1935–1939
Fishing	41	100	402
Livestock and dairying	50	100	304
Mining	28	100	237

Coal production alone was about eight times as large in 1936 as it had been at the turn of the century. Also, as in other countries, coal was much more effectively used.

In the secondary field of production, particularly in manufacturing, the indices of growth show remarkable increases, as is to be expected. Lockwood's general indices for manufacturing production are 37–100–600. The first figure may be low, since it would seem to discount handicraft production during the 1895–1899 period. But from 1910–1914 to 1935–1939, for which the base data are more reliable, we need have no doubt that a remarkable sixfold growth took place. When this general figure is broken down by industries, the differential pattern of expansion can be appreciated. The indices of the textile industry are, for example, 41–100–416. This industry started early and had more nearly attained maturity by the 1930s than any of the others. The industries that showed the most remarkable growth in the years since 1910 are the following: metals, 100–920; chemicals, 100–1,225; and electricity and gas, 100–1,517.

All these figures take on greater meaning if they are placed alongside comparable figures for other societies. A number of such overall comparisons have been worked out by Lockwood. On the basis of 1913 as 100, he has shown that during the present century to the year 1938 manufacturing activity increased in Japan from 48 to 631, in the United Kingdom from 77 to 122, in the United States from 66 to 167, and in India from 69 to 230. The figures for the same years for the whole world are 67–185.

Another way of looking at Japanese development is to point out that the world's industrial production increased at the rate of 2.8 per cent per year during the thirty years before 1938. League of Nations statisticians estimated an increase of 3.5 per cent per year for the whole world when a comparison was made between the periods 1876–1880 and 1935–1938. It is probable that the rate of growth of manufacturing activity in Japan was about 7.5 per cent per year for the forty years before 1938. This was a remarkable achievement and has probably not been equaled by any large country for so long a period.

Moreover, in Japan the growth of manufacturing production was fully supported by the increased provision of transportation, communications, finance, and other needed services. The figures for railway freight traffic in the years for which Lockwood reports are 24–100–350, and for merchant-ship tonnage 38–100–263.

These figures highlight a picture of impressive economic development during the forty or fifty years before World War II. How was Japan able to accomplish this feat? The answer is still a matter of hypothesis and interpretation of the facts, so that there is no fully agreed-upon view. Though economists have suggested a number of answers, most are still conjectural. The following statements constitute an effort to present these hypotheses in some coherent order.

1. The base provided by Tokugawa economic development must not be discounted: While very few quantifiable data are available on the economy of Tokugawa times, it cannot be doubted that Japan had acquired many of the institutional and structural requirements as well as many of the basic attitudes essential for subsequent economic growth.

2. The time factor was of prime importance: Japan entered upon the world economic stage as a free player quite early in comparison with the other underdeveloped countries of Asia. At the time, it was not placed under the extreme pressures of colonization by any foreign power. Furthermore, the dominant Western economic ideology then favored private development and free trade as well as a strong emphasis on national development. Could Japan have made the same achievement had 1868 been 1911 or 1945 in its timetable?

3. The political leadership which emerged after 1868 provided a crucial element in the early transitional years: Japan demonstrated a remarkable capacity to retain its political stability during the potentially disruptive years of transition from a traditional society. The fact that the leadership was relatively homogeneous and united behind goals of national reform and advancement meant that there was a remarkably purposeful drive toward economic development led by the new government. The fact that the hierarchical sociopolitical system remained basically undisturbed meant that the leadership was able to get the Japanese behind national goals with comparative ease.

4. Early foreign business activity and the early importation of advanced techniques were of importance: It is customary to disregard the early business investments of the foreigners in Japan. This may be correct, but the matter is worth further investigation. As a typical follower nation, Japan was able to rely upon a ready-made system of technology from the more highly advanced countries. This system included not only tools and machinery but the entire complex of production, transportation, marketing, and finance. The whole subject of the intro-

duction of Western technology in Japan needs further study. We know that some 5,000 foreigners were in Japan at one time during the early 1870s, many of them in an advisory capacity in government and business. But the Japanese displaced their foreign advisers as soon as the techniques the latter commanded were mastered. They were not initially dependent on a foreign business community for the conduct of their foreign trade, nor did they become dependent upon the continuous supply of technologically advanced products through contracts with foreign governments or businesses. After 1900 a number of foreign firms became established in Japan but usually in partnership with the Japanese themselves. The operation of such specialized plants as General Motors or Ford reflected the rapidity with which the Japanese created a labor and management base capable of adopting American industrial standards.

5. Foreign capital and foreign investment have been a factor that cannot be disregarded: For the period from the Restoration of 1868 to World War II, Japan on the whole did not rely very heavily on foreign capital, and the greater part of the capital inflow resulted from government borrowing abroad. The Chinese indemnity of ¥360 million (following the Sino-Japanese War) made foreign funds available at a critical time when Japan was in the midst of its first industrial surge. The first foreign borrowing of the Japanese government on any large scale was for essential military imports. The adjustment of this borrowing to the needs of the economy for foreign capital equipment and military goods was particularly important. Moreover, foreign capital when borrowed was most effectively used. Its application was directed by the Japanese themselves, and its effect was felt by the economy directly in certain critical areas of development and in meeting difficulties in the balance of payments.

6. The state played an important role in providing the environment for economic expansion: Lockwood has characterized Japan's economy as a "sponsored capitalism." The activity of the state has been notable for the heavy outlays it made for economic and social overhead (telegraphs, railroads, education, etc.), for arms, and for technological experimentation and improvement. Every effort was made to accomplish these outlays without dependence on foreign capital.

7. The entrepreneur played an important role in Japanese economic development: Prior to World War II most studies of the Japanese economy assumed that economic development, technological change, and effective enterprise organization came chiefly through the state and the *zaibatsu*. Without denying the importance of the contributions of government enterprise and the *zaibatsu*, more recent scholarship (no-

tably beginning with the work by Lockwood) has concluded that the wide and general use of new methods in business came through the efforts of many small businessmen as well as those who developed and managed large enterprises. The state did provide leadership at critical points and made decisions which encouraged new investments and technological change. Government policy also created a favorable milieu for expansion, and the *zaibatsu* pioneered in developing new sources for power and fuel and helped create the transportation system. These developments alone could not have brought about the overall expansion of the Japanese economy, however, had not business and the farms taken advantage of the opportunities given them.

8. Agricultural improvement was effective in maintaining the growth of the largest sector of the economy in the early years: The new land tax system favored adjustment in agriculture on a competitive basis. Meanwhile, the government encouraged scientific research to improve agricultural techniques. The increased availability and use of fertilizers and the spread of irrigation and riparian works (often state-sponsored) added to the productivity of agriculture at the crucial phase in which it occupied the major position in the economy. Or if, as James Nakamura has suggested, agricultural output grew less rapidly than previously thought, there was certainly a substantial margin above subsistence at the outset of the modern growth period which could be channeled into production investment.

9. Capital formation at home was on a fairly large scale or at a fairly rapid rate: The factors that explain the rapidity and the extent of capital formation at home have been carefully analyzed by Henry Rosovsky. It is remarkable that the Japanese of all sectors of the economy have shown a capacity for hard work and a propensity for saving and reinvestment which is relatively high by world standards. The savings rate throughout Japan's early decades of economic development, though perhaps less than 10 per cent of national income, when combined with low rates of increase in consumption and inflation during the same period made for several periods of rather marked economic stability. The climate for investment, though poor at first, improved in the late 1880s, and the status of the businessman was remarkably high from the start.

The capacity of agriculture to provide a surplus for investment was crucial. The place of silk and tea was highly significant in the early acquisition of foreign exchange as a means to pay for needed imports. Moreover, the income accruing from such sales could be used totally for domestic consumption or investment, since production did not require imports as part of the process of production (in obvious contrast with the cotton-textile industry).

The willingness of the Japanese to accept without undue social tension an unequal distribution of income and wealth was also important. This helps to explain the fact that living standards did not rise as fast as national income increased, but it was also true that the rich invested heavily and took economic activities seriously. Conspicuous consumption was discouraged. The fact that the *zaibatsu* owners had little need to share profits, coupled with their own great willingness to save and invest, helped to promote economic development, as did the habit of the Japanese government to use tax revenues for investment and services and the willingness of the state to subsidize and assist industries.

10. Capital formation in Japan was stimulated by what may be called creeping inflation: The banking and financial system provided money and credit in such a way that, despite fluctuations, there tended to be an overall rise in prices over the period. Deficits associated with military and naval expenditures played a part. The financial history of Japan is that of a country that tended to be on the inflationary edge of "sound finance." Such creeping inflation made for profits that could be reinvested and for forced savings on the part of the wage earners and recipients of fixed incomes. Japan also began its growth with a much lower capital-output ratio than comparable European societies, thus favoring a higher rate of growth relative to the rate of new investments.

11. Foreign trade has been a major factor: Lack of domestic supplies of raw materials made foreign trade indispensable. Foreign trade tended to accentuate industrial development, since Japan's comparative advantage soon came to be that of a processing nation, importing raw materials and exporting manufactured goods. The proportion of foreign trade to total output grew steadily from nearly zero in 1858 to roughly one-third in the interwar period. The composition of the trade evolved as the country's comparative advantage in world markets changed over time or as the economy grew.

12. Though there was a rapid rate of industrialization, it did not result in a decline in the actual numbers on the farms or displace traditional farming methods: There were 5,359,000 farms in 1903 and 5,775,000 in 1937. The increased urban labor force, though it came physically in part from the farms, merely kept pace with increases in the total population. This factor tended to keep a downward pressure on wages. The Japanese farmer showed himself willing to accept technological innovation, but he was not able to abandon completely the traditional labor-intensive method of cultivation. Hence a large segment of the population remained tied to a traditional way of life, and this in turn perpetuated a differential economy and wage scale.

13. The urge for economic welfare could be subordinated to national

welfare: The standard of living did improve substantially over time for most Japanese; but it is also undeniable that the improvement, for certain sectors especially, could have been greater or more rapid. Why was this improvement not made more rapidly, or why was there not a greater demand for benefits from the mass of the Japanese people? As far as economic welfare is concerned, throughout modern times Japan has remained densely populated and heavily taxed. A significant portion of government taxes also went into military expenditures. A slower population growth and a greater diversion of tax revenues for welfare purposes would have permitted income per capita to have been higher and more equitably distributed. Why did not the Japanese people demand a greater share of gain in the increase in production? Timing may have been a prime factor in keeping the demand for improved living standards low. The early industrialization took place at a time when the worldwide emphasis on individual welfare was less pronounced than now. The requirements of a strong national development and a strong military posture were more generally accepted, and the vicarious rewards of imperialistic expansion more willingly exchanged for real increases in wages or state outlays on welfare.

14. In the final analysis a dense population was a major resource for economic growth: It has often been claimed that Japan's serious "overpopulation problem" has been a drag on the economy. It is true that the growth of population has tended to delay increases in per capita income. On the other hand, a strongly competitive, abundant, and well-trained labor force was and remains one of the country's main assets. This has been called Japan's *human capital*. Japan's advantage by contrast with other overpopulated, underdeveloped countries lies in the quality of training and the industriousness of the labor force.

15. The "why" of economic development carries us beyond economic analysis into the field of motivation in history: The previous observations are concerned with explanations of how Japan accomplished its rapid economic development. To some extent they provide an explanation of why this development took place. Yet they do not explain the deeper motives which seem to have driven the Japanese toward the goal of modernization. Was it the overwhelming desire of Japan's leaders to defend their country against foreign pressures, to avoid the fate of China, or to emulate the most advanced nations of the world? Perhaps the concept of nationalism is the most serviceable overall explanation. Certainly Japan rose as a nation when international competition was at a high pitch.

Many writers, borrowing Marxist interpretations, see the answer in the workings of class interests and the class struggle. The virus of capitalism, once it affected the Japanese economy, they claim, had to run its course, modified by the particular social and political power structure of the new Japanese state. It is apparent, however, that the major factors upon which the Marxist explanation rests—concepts of class, modes of production, types of government—cannot be simplistically applied to the Japanese experience.

Sociologists have sought reasons for the success of Japanese development in the value system. For instance, the willingness of the Japanese to adhere to patriotic goals and to identify themselves with the state helps to explain why the tremendous national effort to industrialize the country was possible. The goal orientation of the individual Japanese seemed highly practical and politically directed. There can, of course, be no simple answer to the question. Yet we are probably coming closest to the answer in studying social and national values, the individual and collective will of the Japanese themselves. It should be remembered that Japanese society after 1868 was one in which the social and economic rewards for hard work and enterprise were high. The average Japanese could feel confident that work and devotion to goals of advancement would lead to assured success.

16. Japan's pattern of economic development and the course of Japanese imperialism and military expansion are not inevitably related: Many observers, particularly among the Japanese, have claimed that the state policy of imperialist expansion was inevitably related to the particular form of capitalism which the country adopted. While it is undeniable that Japan's modern economy and the course of her political development were closely interrelated, it would be wrong to assume that one was necessarily caused by the other. The economic causes of imperialism as explained by Marxist-Leninist theory or as applied to East Asia by Harold Laski and Parker Moon do not necessarily explain the Japanese example. Much of the drive for military expansion came as a result of the competitive international environment into which the new state was plunged. The economic advantage of expansion often came as the incidental result of prior political or military-defensive decisions. Once Japan had committed itself to the effort to compete among the powers in East Asia, however, the cycle of military buildup and preparation for war was consummated. It would be hard to prove that economic interests were the principal driving force behind Japanese imperialism, but they were closely linked to the outcome.

JAPAN'S POSTWAR RECOVERY: THE "NEW CAPITALISM"

It is estimated that Japan lost approximately 25 per cent of its national wealth as a result of World War II. In 1945 it was a thoroughly defeated nation. Its major cities had been bombed out, its internal transportation was disrupted, and its oceangoing fleet was nonexistent. The former colonial possessions and the overseas investments had been stripped away; the assured sources of raw materials and captive markets were gone, and in their place several million repatriates flocked back to the Japanese homeland. The country's prospects of economic recovery looked black indeed. Yet in less than ten years' time, Japan made an astounding recovery, comparable to that of Britain and Germany. By 1952 the Japanese economy had reached the level of prewar highs. By 1955 the production index of mining and industry was 187, real national income 145, per capita income 111, and consumption 118, compared with the level of 1934–1936. This record of recovery is no less astounding than the rapid achievement of economic modernization in the half-century which preceded the war.

No doubt many of the same factors of industriousness and willingness to suffer privation without complaint, which we noted earlier, help to account for the postwar recovery. We should credit also certain institutional changes brought about by the Occupation reforms, $2 billion of United States aid from 1945 to 1949, and the changed international environment. During the first years after the war, the Japanese economy suffered from the collapse of the wartime economy and the rapid spread of inflation which had been suppressed by governmental controls. The occupying authorities were concerned with immediate problems of relief and with reforms which were designed to alter profoundly the place of the Army and Navy in the life of the country and to destroy Japan's war-making potential. Occupation authorities broke up the major *zaibatsu* combines, carried out a thoroughgoing land reform, enacted anti-monopoly laws, and encouraged the formation of labor unions. By 1948 the Occupation began to shift its main concern from reform to enhancing the recovery of Japan's economy. A stabilization program was undertaken in 1949, and foreign trade, which had begun somewhat earlier, was encouraged. The budget was brought into balance, a uniform foreign-exchange rate of ¥360 to the dollar was introduced, and subsidies were largely eliminated. With the outbreak of the Korean conflict in 1950, Japan found herself in a boom of prosperity resulting from increased demands by the United Nations Forces for her goods and services. The spur to Japan's economy and the foreign-exchange balance built up as a result of this boom have carried over into the present. By 1952 the Japanese economy, as a whole, appeared to be fully recovered from the effects of the war. No longer dependent on special supports from the United States, Japan emerged as a major world economic power, ranking fifth in overall production, sixth in the production and consumption of steel and in the production and export of machinery, and first in the production of ships.

Since 1952 the new Japanese economy has expanded at a rate literally unmatched by that of any other major country: a sustained average rate of growth of more than 9 per cent per year. It is believed by some economists that this new spurt, which shows no immediate signs of abatement, marks the attainment of a new phase of the Japanese economy, a *new capitalism*, as Lockwood has termed it. The new capitalism possesses certain distinctive features which distinguish it from the prewar, and particularly the wartime, economy. Perhaps most apparent to the casual observer is the obvious rise in the general standard of living and level of consumption. The end of military spending has proved a significant factor. The Japanese economy is again substantially directed toward domestic consumption needs. New consumer goods, such as television sets, compact cars, refrigerators, and washing machines, are profusely available for Japanese families in city and village. As the Economic Planning Agency 1964 White Paper put it, Japan had entered a period of "mass consumer spending." With overall living standards approximately the same as those of Italy and with a national income of $520 per capita in 1963, the average Japanese citizen found himself sharing a condition of prosperity beyond anyone's expectations a decade earlier.

More specifically, what are some of the indices of changing economic structure in the decade after 1952? A "growth" economist such as Rosovsky, after citing the high rate of annual increase in the gross national product, points to two related changes which help to account for such growth: a rapid increase in the number of employed workers and an even more marked increase in the productivity workers. This condition is in substantial part due to changes in the industrial sector and the movement of large numbers of the working population from agriculture into industry and the services. (Between 1959 and 1962, for instance, the primary sector lost 2,600,000 workers while the secondary sector gained 4,000,000.) As a consequence of such shifts, the differences in pay scales between modern and traditional sectors of the economy have been drastically reduced. This development has also resulted in a "new look" in agriculture, accompanied by a rapid rate of small-scale mechanization.

Such changes are in turn accounted for, or at least are reflected in, the remarkably high rates of investment. Gross domestic investment rose from an average of 27.3 per cent of the national product during the period 1951–1955 to a fantastic 42.8 per cent in 1961. Moreover, 73 per cent of such investment was made by the private sector. Clearly the new capitalism was based on a vigorous and expanding private economy able to sustain its growth without the artificial supports or distortions which had characterized the period up to the end of the Occupation.

Another factor of extreme importance both for stimulating investment and for making it profitable, as well as for raising the productivity of labor, was the introduction (in large part through patent purchases, joint ventures, etc.) of the most advanced Western (especially American) technology. After a lag of fifteen years caused by the war, Japan was again able to profit by absorbing such technology without the intervening struggle of experimentation or making do with obsolescent equipment.

That the people as a whole are not by any means contented with their economic situation or certain that the economy is safely stabilized is characteristic of the intense drive of the Japanese toward the highest achievement. While acknowledging that domestic consumption is something more than twice that of the average for all Asian countries, they point out that it is still extremely low in comparison with the United States (about one-fifth) or the countries of western Europe. The Japanese estimate that their standard of living is at present not quite one-half that of England, France, or West Germany. And it is this European level to which they currently aspire. To achieve this Japan still faces a number of major problems and the shadows of former problems which still are not easily forgotten. A few of these require our attention.

The "Population Problem"

The Japanese feel that they still have a population problem because of the continuing steady increase in national population (about 750,000 annually). This is actually an extremely low rate of growth compared with the prewar period or with the rate of other countries of the world, but there is still a question as to whether such a continued increase can be cared for at a growing standard of living. Opinions are divided. The Ikeda and Satō governments have had as a major component of their policy the doubling of Japan's national income during the 1960s, a task which would require a steady rate of increase of some 7.2 per cent annually. This prospect requires the continuation of a large number of favorable growth conditions together with the control of population and better labor distribution.

Although no population plateau appears in sight as yet, demographers see signs that in fifteen or twenty years the rate of growth will taper off still further. While Japan's population may reach 100 million by 1971, it may not be more than 108 million by 1990. Such a decline in population growth should eventually take care of the current large supplies of labor in low-productivity uses. Today the Japanese government claims that only 2 per cent of the total labor force of more than 43 million is unemployed. This figure is somewhat misleading, since the government counts as employed anyone who works more than one hour a week, and there is a further complication found in the factor of "disguised unemployment." But these problems have been disappearing in recent years as opportunities for members of farm households to find work in business or industry have improved. In fact, the first voices suggesting that Japan's problem will soon be one of labor *shortage* have been heard.

The Problem of Agriculture

For an industrialized society Japan continues to have a particularly large agricultural population. Some 28 per cent of the total numbers of workers employed in 1963 were engaged in agriculture. Although this is the lowest percentage among Asian countries, it is considerably greater than the percentage for the United States or for the most highly advanced countries of Europe. The agricultural sector is important not only because of its large numbers, but also as a strong force in politics and in the maintenance of traditional social values.

While agricultural technology has improved greatly over the past century and while in recent years the use of farm machinery has increased, nonetheless the basic structure of labor-intensive technology has not changed greatly. In other words, though Japanese agriculture can show some of the highest yields per acre in the world, labor productivity is still relatively low. In Western societies economic modernization has been accompanied by a radical change in the pattern of agricultural production. Farm residents have moved to the cities, while mechanization and growing farm size have increased the per capita efficiency of the remaining farm population. The question of whether Japan can or needs to follow this pattern of large-farm production is very debatable. Such critical factors as the scarcity of land, high rents, the fragmentation of fields, the difficulty of mechanization, and the inertia of village society all inhibit the creation of an agricultural economy similar to that of Western countries. Japan will probably continue for a long time to hold to the small-farm, lightly mechanized but highly scientific style of cultivation. But the limit of increase in per capita income derived from this style of production has not yet been reached in Japan. Furthermore, the Japanese have been highly successful in bringing the industrial and commercial sectors into contact with the rural labor force. The pattern of the future will probably show an increasingly complex interrelationship between city and countryside linked even more closely by the now rapidly spreading road and communications networks.

Industrial Growth and the Problem of Japan's Resources and Trade

To meet the objectives of a reasonable improvement of living standards for a growing population it is estimated that an increase of at least 6.5 per cent a year in total national income must be maintained for the foreseeable future. This increase will require a growth in industrial production of even greater proportions. Since Japanese natural resources are meager, it is estimated that this growth rate can be met only by increasing imports by 10 per cent every year. Coal is expensive to mine, and it is generally of a low grade. Between 80 and 90 per cent of Japan's rubber, zinc, bauxite, and phosphate must be acquired from other countries. Oil, iron ore, and textile raw materials, such as cotton and wool, are almost entirely supplied from abroad. As long as Japan can freely import from such resource-rich countries as the United States, Canada, India, and Malaysia, this condition presents no problems. The improvement of the merchant marine and the many excellent harbors have kept Japan competitive in this respect. But Japan is constantly under pressure to maintain optimum trade relations with a wide variety of countries. After the war she was obliged to modify drastically her pattern of foreign trade from what it had been during the days when her commerce followed her armies and the China market was available under favorable conditions. Moreover, in many parts of the world Japan had to overcome numerous prejudices held by other nations against the Japanese merchant. Because of Japanese pre-World War II practices, such as the direct imitation of competitors' products, dumping, and intense price competition, many countries did little to help Japan enter a free world market. Other nations, primarily those in Southeast Asia, were slow to recover from the hatreds and passions aroused toward the Japanese during the war.

By 1955 the entire trade picture had changed for the better. Until that year Japan was excluded from the General Agreement on Tariffs and Trade (GATT) and thus received none of the advantages of easier trading conditions with other countries. In 1955, however, she was given the rights of the most-favored-nation clause by the majority of the nations signatory to that agreement. Britain, for the most part, continued to be reluctant to give these privileges to Japan in private dealings until 1963. But Japan benefited as the United States accepted increased amounts of Japanese imports.

In looking at present trade patterns, it can be seen that there has been a change not only in the amount of trade but also in its direction. Iron ore and coking coal no longer come from north China and Manchuria. Now coal is obtained from the United States, and iron ore from Malaysia, India, the Philippines, and, again, the United States. Korea and Taiwan are not as important as before World War II, while Thailand and Burma, in line with the new direction of trade, have become important. Today trade faces toward the United States, Latin America, Europe, South Asia, and Africa. The countries of Asia bought less than one-third of Japan's total exports in 1961, as against their purchase of half of her exports in the mid-1930s. The United States now consumes one-quarter rather than one-seventh of Japan's exports. All told, the industrial nations absorbed 53 per cent of Japanese exports in 1961, as against 25 per cent in the 1930s.

The kinds of goods that are imported and exported also have changed. In 1958 food still accounted for about 20 per cent of Japan's total imports; this figure had decreased to 12.6 per cent by 1961. One-fifth or so of the imports are composed of coal, oil, iron ore, and steel scrap; this is approximately double the proportion of these resources imported in the 1930s. Cotton needs have dipped, though textiles still compose one-third of the total exports. Meanwhile, the importance of heavy industry has grown. Exports of steel, other metals, machinery, tools, precision instruments, and, above all, ships, which have grown to form one-half of the total exports, are by now Japan's most important trade items. Their quality has also helped to raise the prestige of Japanese goods abroad.

Japan's economic future rests in large part on her ability continually to develop markets, and this in turn depends upon the commercial and economic conditions of other nations. In her trade relations Japan faces critical problems with the United States (chiefly a matter of the balance of trade and dollar reserves), with the European market (a matter of trade restrictions), and with Southeast Asia (where Japan must export capital goods) and other underdeveloped areas. In each of these areas an unfavorable turn in trade or tariff policy could hurt the Japanese economy directly.

An international problem of great importance arises from the division of the world into Communist and non-Communist blocs. As things stand today, no country can trade extensively on both sides of the Iron Curtain. Yet the memory of Japan's China trade is still strong. Many Japanese appear to think that mainland China would offer Japan a ready market for her goods and would be a reasonable supplier of coal and iron ore, but other economists feel that China as presently politically and economically oriented could not supply more than 10 per cent of Japan's total trade. And in the final analysis, trade with the U.S.S.R. has greater short-term prospects as well as being considerably larger than the China trade today. The issue of greater trade with China creates a constant tension in Japan's domestic politics and international relations, despite the fact that it is clearly with the more advanced industrial states that the country's future lies.

The Problem of Balance in Production Factors

Though what we have called the differential economy has lost some of its sharp distinctions, Japan's industry continues to exhibit extremes between productive systems. At the one pole there are a few large-scale modern enterprises, and at the other there are a large number of small family industries. One-third of the industrial labor force work in small factories, employing 20 or fewer workers. These factories make up 90 per cent of the total number of factories. In contrast, there are a few immense firms hiring more than 1,000 workers. The latter produce a much larger share of the total output with half as much labor. Labor productivity and wages in the capital-intensive enterprises are more than double those for similar jobs in the smaller labor-intensive operations. (The corresponding differential in Europe or the United States is no more than 10 to 15 per cent.) Regional differences in levels of production, wage scales, and standards of living are also quite wide between the major cities and the remote rural areas.

"Dualism" in Japanese industry is still considered a major weakness by many economists, notably the Japanese. It causes discrepancies in the standard of living of workers and accounts for large areas of relatively inefficient production. But this problem is merely one facet of the economic growth pattern which has continued into present-day Japan. And while there are good reasons to desire a more equal distribution and balance of factors, it should be realized that this dualism has played an important role in maintaining a viable balance between economic modernization and social change. Labor-intensive production in both agriculture and industry has served to make less severe the impact of the modern economy on the traditional social fabric. Moreover, Japan has been remarkably successful in combining factors. Big businesses are linked with small family businesses through subcontracting systems, receiving small or half-finished parts at low cost. Yet in the long run Japan must attempt to close the gap between the two extremes of its economy by shifting labor and capital even further to large-scale, efficient production and by sharply increasing the productivity of small-scale enterprises.

The New Role of Government

In the early stages of Japan's economic development government served an important function by providing the services and the freedom of enterprise for rapid business and industrial growth. Since World War II, Japanese central and local government has seriously lagged behind in providing consumer services. While the railroads are well maintained, such services as industrial highways, roads, port facilities, city and town planning, water supply, sewage, housing, and the like have not kept pace with the demand. Japan's cities are today seriously congested and chaotically organized. Automobile and truck volume has increased five-fold over prewar days. Yet of the total road mileage only 47 per cent can carry motor traffic, and of this only 15 per cent is paved. Japan has only recently begun to build on a national scale an automobile highway system which takes into consideration the transportation requirements of the country. On the other hand, government involvement in the economic sphere is still considerable, and many business activities are rather hampered by official red tape.

While government is no longer a dominant factor in the economy, it exerts considerable influence in business planning and decision making through consultation and other indirect pressures. Yet it should be remembered that business exerts a reverse influence on government through its communication with government agencies and through the political parties.

Labor, Management, and Politics

If Japan faces numerous uncertainties in the field of foreign-trade relations, the same is true of the domestic relationships between labor, government, and management. The Japanese labor movement is still young, and management is as yet unused to dealing with unions. Their competitive interests are reflected in domestic politics, where the Socialist Party, gaining its most important support from organized labor, confronts the conservative Liberal Democrats, whose support, other than the rural bloc, is heavily drawn from management. Recent years have seen considerable labor violence. Because of the radically different constituents of the major parties, techniques of consultation, bipartisanship, and compromise are hard to achieve. The continued maintenance of relatively stable political party and labor-management relationships is an important requirement for continued economic development.

This issue, which relates economic health to the political atmosphere, is perhaps the most critical factor in Japan's economic future, especially as we look at it from the United States. Japan today represents a major example of successful economic modernization by an Asian society under a free economy. In a part of the world in which controlled economies are becoming more common and in which the argument that Socialist systems alone provide the means of achieving economic development is becoming louder, the Japanese example stands as an important reminder of what an Asian society can accomplish in another way.

Observers of the political scene in the 1960s are more encouraging over the prospects of continued stability than those who wrote during the 1950s. Certainly, compared with the authoritarian and highly hierarchical political structure of prewar Japan the new capitalism rests on a domestic political base which permits a much wider distribution of political power and a greater volume of mass involvement in the political process. There are still gross imbalances under the so-called "1½-party" system. The political opposition to the dominant Liberal Democratic government still believes that it is deprived of sufficient influence on policy, so that it must contend with a "tyranny of the majority." Yet unquestionably the conservative government incorporates into its plans the welfare objectives pressed by the Socialists. Japanese democracy appears healthy enough to stay alive unless put under unusual or crisis conditions. It appears both to sustain and to be sustained by the affluence of the new capitalism.

General Bibliography

Reference

Borton, Hugh, and others: *A Selected List of Books and Articles on Japan in English, French, and German,* Cambridge, Mass., 1954.

Linton, Howard P. (ed.): "Bibliography of Asian Studies" 1956—, annual issue of *Journal of Asian Studies.* Preceded by "Far Eastern Bibliography" published in *Far Eastern Quarterly,* 1941–1955.

Silberman, Bernard S.: *Japan and Korea: A Critical Bibliography,* Tucson, Ariz., 1962.

An introductory reading list

Allen, G. C.: *Japan's Economic Recovery,* New York, 1958, chaps. 1, 2, and 8–12.

Anderson, Ronald S.: *Japan: Three Epochs of Modern Education,* Washington, D.C., 1959, chaps. 3, 4, and 10.

Beardsley, Richard K., John Whitney Hall, and Robert E. Ward: *Village Japan,* Chicago, 1959, chaps. 4–7 and 11.

Benedict, Ruth: *The Chrysanthemum and the Sword: Patterns of Japanese Culture,* Boston, 1946, chaps. 2, 5–7, and 12.

Bunce, William K. (ed.): *Religions in Japan,* Rutland, Vt., 1955.

Ginsburg, Norton S. (ed.): *The Pattern of Asia,* Englewood Cliffs, N.J., 1958, chaps. 4–6.

Harada, Jirō: *A Glimpse of Japanese Ideals,* Tokyo, 1937, chaps. 1, 2, and 9.

Ike, Nobutaka: *Japanese Politics: An Introductory Survey,* New York, 1957.

Keene, Donald: *Japanese Literature: An Introduction for Western Readers,* Wisdom of the East Series, London, 1953; paperback, New York, 1955.

Kerlinger, Fred: "Behavior and Personality in Japan: Critique of Three Studies of Japanese Personality," *Social Forces,* vol. 31, pp. 250–258, 1953; also available in Bernard S. Silberman (ed.), *Japanese Character and Culture,* Tucson, Ariz., 1962, pp. 400–410.

Lockwood, William W.: *The Economic Development of Japan: Growth and Structural Change, 1868–1939,* Princeton, N.J., 1954, chaps. 1–3.

Nielson, Niels C., Jr.: "Religion and Philosophy in Contemporary Japan," *Rice Institute Pamphlets*, vol. 43, no. 4, 1957.

Reischauer, Edwin O.: *Japan: Past and Present,* rev. ed., New York, 1953.

————: *The United States and Japan,* Cambridge, Mass., 1950, parts II and III.

Sansom, Sir George Bailey: *Japan: A Short Cultural History,* rev. ed., New York, 1943, chaps. 3, 4, 6, 7, 12, 16, 18, 20, 22, and 23.

Scalapino, Robert A., and Masumi Junnosuke: *Parties and Politics in Contemporary Japan,* Berkeley, Calif., 1962, chaps. 1, 2, 4, and 5.

Silberman, Bernard S. (ed.): *Japanese Character and Culture: Selected Readings,* Tucson, Ariz., 1962, pp. 1–35, 101–141, 286–288, 360–399.

Warner, Langdon: *The Enduring Art of Japan,* Cambridge, Mass., 1952.

Select Bibliographies

CHAPTER 1   *A Geographic Profile of Japan* [1]

Ackerman, Edward A.: *Japan's Natural Resources and Their Relations to Japan's Economic Future*, Chicago, 1953.

Cressey, George B.: *Asia's Lands and Peoples*, 3d ed., New York, 1963.

Ginsburg, Norton S. (ed.): *The Pattern of Asia*, Englewood Cliffs, N.J., 1958.

Hall, Robert Burnett: "The Road in Old Japan," in *Studies in the History of Culture, the Disciplines of the Humanities*, Menasha, Wis., 1942, pp. 122–155.

———, and Toshio Noh: *Japanese Geography: A Guide to Japanese Reference and Research Materials*, Ann Arbor, Mich., 1956.

———, and Watanabe Akira: "Landforms of Japan," *Papers of the Michigan Academy of Science, Arts, and Letters*, vol. 18, pp. 157–207, 1932.

Hall, Robert Burnett, Jr.: *Japan: Industrial Power of Asia*, Princeton, N.J., 1963.

Ishida, Ryūjirō (Isida Ryuziro): *Geography of Japan*, Tokyo and Honolulu, 1961.

Japan, Central Meteorological Observatory: *The Climatographic Atlas of Japan*, Tokyo, 1948.

Japan Travel Bureau: *Japan: The Official Guide*, 7th rev. ed., Tokyo, 1959.

K. B. S.: *Bibliography of Standard Reference Books for Japanese Studies with Descriptive Notes*, vol. II, Geography and Travel, Tokyo, 1962.

Ogasawara, Yoshikatsu: "Land Use in Japan," *Bulletin of Geographical Survey Institute*, vol. 11, part 1, pp. 95–119, 1950.

Princeton University Conference: *The New Japan: Prospects and Promise*, Princeton, N.J., 1963. (Note particularly Herbert Passin, "Stability and Instability in Contemporary Japan," pp. 9–19.)

Smith, Guy-Harold, and Dorothy Good: *Japan: A Geographical View*, New York, 1943.

Stamp, Laurence Dudley: *Asia: A Regional and Economic Geography*, 9th ed., New York, 1957.

[1] Works on economic and industrial geography are listed below under "Chapter 12: Aspects of Japanese Economic Development."

Taeuber, Irene B.: *The Population of Japan*, Princeton, N.J., 1958.
Tobata, Seiichi: *An Introduction to Agriculture of Japan*, Tokyo, 1958.
———: *Japan's Agriculture: Farming Population*, Tokyo, 1956.
Trewartha, Glenn: *Japan: A Physical, Cultural, and Regional Geography*, Madison, Wis., 1945.
Tsujimura, Tarō, and Tanaka Kaoru: *Photo-monograph of Japan* (*Shashin chishi Nihon*), Tokyo, 1952. (English captions.)

CHAPTER 2   *Cultural Anthropology: Prehistoric and Contemporary Aspects*

Abegglen, James C.: *The Japanese Factory: Aspects of Its Social Organization*, Glencoe, Ill., 1958.
Ariga, Kizaemon: "The Family in Japan," *Marriage and Family Living*, vol. 16, pp. 362–368, 1954.
Beardsley, Richard K., John Whitney Hall, and Robert E. Ward: *Village Japan*, Chicago, 1959.
Befu, Harumi: "Patrilineal Descent and Personal Kindred in Japan," *American Anthropologist*, vol. 65, pp. 1328–1341, 1963.
Benedict, Ruth: *The Chrysanthemum and the Sword: Patterns of Japanese Culture*, Boston, 1946.
Bennett, John, and Ishino Iwao: *Paternalism in the Japanese Economy: Anthropological Studies of Oyabun-Kobun Patterns*, Minneapolis, 1963.
Cole, Allan B.: *Japanese Society and Politics*, Studies in Political Science, no. 1, Boston, 1956.
Cornell, John B., and Robert J. Smith: *Two Japanese Villages*, Center for Japanese Studies, Occasional Papers, no. 5, Ann Arbor, Mich., 1956.
Dore, Ronald P.: *City Life in Japan: A Study of a Tokyo Ward*, Berkeley, Calif., 1958.
Embree, John F.: *Suye Mura: A Japanese Village*, Chicago, 1939.
Fukutake, Tadashi: *Man and Society in Japan*, Tokyo, 1962.
Ishino, Iwao: "The Oyabun-Kobun: A Japanese Ritual Kinship Institution," *American Anthropologist*, vol. 55, pp. 695–704, 1953.
Kawai, Kazuo: *Japan's American Interlude*, Chicago, 1960.
Kidder, J. Edward: *Japan before Buddhism*, New York, 1959.
Lifton, Robert Jay: "Youth and History: Individual Change in Postwar Japan," *Daedalus*, vol. 91, pp. 172–197, 1962.
Matsumoto, Yoshiharu Scott: *Contemporary Japan: The Individual and the Group*, Philadelphia, 1960.
Nagai, Michio: "Dozoku: A Preliminary Study of the Japanese 'Extended Family' Group and Its Social and Economic Functions," Report no. 7, Project 483, Columbus, Ohio (mimeographed).
Nakano, Takashi: "Recent Studies of Change in the Japanese Family," *International Social Science Journal* (UNESCO), vol. 14, no. 3, pp. 527–538, 1962.

Norbeck, Edward: *Takashima, A Japanese Fishing Community*, Salt Lake City, 1954.

Plath, David W.: *The After Hours: Modern Japan and the Search for Enjoyment*, Berkeley, Calif., 1964.

Reischauer, Edwin O.: *The United States and Japan*, Cambridge, Mass., 1950.

Shibusawa, Keizō (comp. and ed.): *Japanese Life and Culture in the Meiji Era*, Centenary Cultural Council Series, Charles S. Terry (tr.), Tokyo, 1958.

Silberman, Bernard S. (ed.): *Japanese Character and Culture: Selected Readings*, Tucson, Ariz., 1962.

Smith, Robert J., and Richard K. Beardsley (eds.): *Japanese Culture: Its Development and Characteristics*, Chicago, 1962.

Smith, Thomas C.: *The Agrarian Origins of Modern Japan*, Stanford, Calif., 1959.

Vogel, Ezra: "The Go-between in a Developing Society: The Case of the Japanese Marriage Arranger," *Human Organization*, vol. 20, pp. 112–120, 1961.

————: *Japan's New Middle Class: The Salary Man and His Family in a Tokyo Suburb*, Berkeley, Calif., 1963.

Wagatsuma, Sakae: "Democratization of the Family Relations in Japan," *Washington Law Review*, vol. 25, pp. 405–426, 1950.

Yanagida, Kunio (ed.): *Customs and Manners in the Meiji Period*, Centenary Cultural Council Series, Tokyo, 1957.

CHAPTER 3 *The Historical Dimension*

Survey histories, historiography, and bibliographies

Beasley, William G., and E. G. Pulleyblank (eds.): *Historians of China and Japan*, London, 1961.

Fairbank, John K., Edwin O. Reischauer, and Albert M. Craig: *East Asia: The Modern Transformation*, Boston, 1965.

Hall, John Whitney: *Government and Local Power in Japan, 500–1700: A Study Based on Bizen Province*, Princeton, N.J., 1965.

————: "Historiography in Japan," in H. Stuart Hughes (ed.), *Teachers of History*, Ithaca, N.Y., 1954.

————: *Japanese History: A Guide to Japanese Research and Reference Materials*, Ann Arbor, Mich., 1954.

————: *Japanese History: New Dimensions of Approach and Understanding*, Service Center for Teachers of History Publication 34, Washington, D.C., 1961.

Ienaga, Saburō: *History of Japan*, Tourist Library, vol. 15, Tokyo, 1959.

Murdoch, James: *A History of Japan*, Kobe and London, 1902–1926, 3 vols.

Reischauer, Edwin O.: *Japan: Past and Present*, rev. ed., New York, 1953.

————, and John K. Fairbank: *East Asia: The Great Tradition*, Boston, 1960.

Sansom, Sir George Bailey: *A History of Japan to 1334*, Stanford, Calif., 1958.

————: *A History of Japan 1334–1615*, Stanford, Calif., 1960.

————: *A History of Japan 1615–1867*, Stanford, Calif., 1963.

————: *Japan: A Short Cultural History*, rev. ed., New York, 1943.

Smith, Bradley: *Japan: A History in Art*, New York, 1964.

Tsuchiya, Takao: *An Economic History of Japan*, as *Transactions of the Asiatic Society of Japan* (2), vol. 15, 1937.

Tsunoda, Ryūsaku, William Theodore de Bary, and Donald Keene: *Sources of (the) Japanese Tradition*, New York, 1958.

Interpretive works

Akiyama, Kenzō: *The History of Nippon*, Tokyo, 1941.

Benedict, Ruth: *The Chrysanthemum and the Sword: Patterns of Japanese Culture*, Boston, 1946.

Harada, Jirō: *A Glimpse of Japanese Ideals*, Tokyo, 1937.

Haring, Douglas G.: "Japanese National Character: Cultural Anthropology, Psychoanalysis, and History," *Yale Review*, vol. 42, pp. 375–392, 1953.

Hasegawa, Nyozekan: *Educational and Cultural Background of the Japanese People*, Tokyo, 1937.

Maki, John M.: *Japanese Militarism*, New York, 1945.

Okakura, Kakuzō: *The Book of Tea: A Japanese Harmony of Art, Culture, and the Simple Life*, reprinted Rutland, Vt., 1957.

Silberman, Bernard S. (ed.): *Japanese Character and Culture: Selected Readings*, Tucson, Ariz., 1962.

Early history

Asakawa, Kan'ichi: *The Early Institutional Life of the Japanese*, Tokyo, 1903.

Beardsley, Richard K.: "Japan before History," *Far Eastern Quarterly*, vol. 14, no. 3, pp. 317–346, 1955.

Chamberlain, Basil Hall (tr.): *"Ko-ji-ki" or "Records of Ancient Matters,"* 2d ed., Kobe, 1932.

Goodrich, L. C., and Tsunoda Ryūsaku: *Japan in the Chinese Dynastic Histories*, South Pasadena, Calif., 1951.

Groot, Gerard J.: *The Prehistory of Japan*, New York, 1951.

Holtom, Daniel C.: *The Faith of Japan: A Study in Modern Shinto*, London, 1938.

Kidder, J. Edward: *Japan before Buddhism*, New York, 1959.

Satow, Ernest M.: "Ancient Japanese Rituals," *Transactions of the Asiatic Society of Japan*, vol. 7, no. 2, pp. 97–132; vol. 7, no. 4, pp. 409–455, 1879; vol. 9, no. 2, pp. 183–211, 1881; continued by Karl Florenz, vol. 27, pp. 1–112, 1900.

The aristocratic age

Asakawa, Kan'ichi: "The Life of a Monastic Shō in Medieval Japan," *Annual Report of the American Historical Association*, vol. 1, pp. 313–342, 1919.

Crump, James I., Jr.: " 'Borrowed' T'ang Titles and Offices in the Yōrō Code," *University of Michigan Center for Japanese Studies Occasional Papers*, vol. 2, pp. 35–58, 1952.

Joüon des Longrais, Frédéric: *L'Est et l'Ouest: Institutions du Japon et de l'Occident comparées*, Tokyo and Paris, 1958.

Morris, Ivan I.: *The World of the Shining Prince: Court Life in Ancient Japan*, New York, 1964.

Nippon Gakujutsu Shinkōkai (ed.): *The Manyōshū: One Thousand Poems*, Tokyo, 1940. (See especially the introduction, pp. 27–80.)

Reischauer, Robert K.: *Early Japanese History*, Princeton, N.J., 1937, 2 vols.

Sansom, Sir George Bailey: "Early Japanese Law and Administration," *Transactions of the Asiatic Society of Japan* (2), vol. 9, pp. 67–109, 1932; vol. 11, pp. 117–149, 1934.

The feudal age

Asakawa, Kan'ichi: *The Documents of Iriki*, New Haven, Conn., 1929; Tokyo, 1955.

———: "Some Aspects of Japanese Feudal Institutions," *Transactions of the Asiatic Society of Japan*, vol. 46, no. 1, pp. 76–102, 1918.

Boxer, Charles R.: *The Christian Century in Japan, 1549–1650*, Berkeley, Calif., 1951.

Brown, Delmer M.: *Money Economy in Medieval Japan: A Study in the Use of Coins*, Far Eastern Association Monograph, no. 1, New Haven, Conn., 1951.

Hall, John Whitney: "The Castle Town and Japan's Modern Urbanization," *Far Eastern Quarterly*, vol. 15, no. 1, pp. 37–56, 1955.

———: "Foundations of the Modern Japanese Daimyo," *Journal of Asian Studies*, vol. 20, no. 3, pp. 317–329, 1961.

———: "Japanese Feudalism: A Reassessment," *Comparative Studies in Society and History*, vol. 5, pp. 15–57, 1962.

Joüon des Longrais, Frédéric: *L'Est et l'Ouest: Institutions du Japon et de l'Occident comparées*, Tokyo and Paris, 1958.

McCullough, Helen Craig (tr.): *The Taiheiki: A Chronicle of Medieval Japan*, New York, 1959.

Reischauer, Edwin O.: "Japanese Feudalism," in Rushton Coulborn (ed.), *Feudalism in History*, Princeton, N.J., 1956; Stanford, Calif., 1959.

Shinoda, Minoru: *The Founding of the Kamakura Shogunate 1180–1185*, New York, 1960.

Wang, Yi-T'ung: *Official Relations between China and Japan, 1368–1549*, Cambridge, Mass., 1953.

Tokugawa

Bellah, Robert N.: *Tokugawa Religion: The Values of Pre-industrial Japan*, Glencoe, Ill., 1957.

Boxer, Charles R.: *Jan Compagnie in Japan, 1600–1850,* The Hague, 1950.

Dore, Ronald P.: *Education in Tokugawa Japan,* Berkeley, Calif., 1965.

Earl, David M.: *Emperor and Nation in Japan: Political Thinkers of the Tokugawa Period,* Seattle, 1964.

Hall, John Whitney: "The Confucian Teacher in Tokugawa Japan," in David S. Nivison and Arthur F. Wright (eds.), *Confucianism in Action,* Stanford, Calif., 1959.

——: *Tanuma Okitsugu, 1719–1788: Forerunner of Modern Japan,* Cambridge, Mass., 1955.

Keene, Donald: *The Japanese Discovery of Europe,* London, 1950.

Sheldon, Charles D.: *The Rise of the Merchant Class in Tokugawa Japan 1600–1868,* Locust Valley, N.Y., 1958.

Smith, Thomas C.: *The Agrarian Origins of Modern Japan,* Stanford, Calif., 1959.

——: "The Japanese Village in the Seventeenth Century," *Journal of Economic History,* vol. 12, pp. 1–20, 1952.

The modern phase

Beasley, William G.: *The Modern History of Japan,* London, 1963.

——: *Select Documents on Japanese Foreign Policy 1853–1868,* London, 1955.

Beckmann, George M.: *The Making of the Meiji Constitution: The Oligarchs and the Constitutional Development of Japan, 1868–1891,* Lawrence, Kans., 1957.

Blacker, Carmen: *The Japanese Enlightenment: A Study of the Writings of Fukuzawa Yukichi,* New York, 1964.

Borton, Hugh: *Japan's Modern Century,* New York, 1955.

Brown, Delmer M.: *Nationalism in Japan: An Introductory Historical Analysis,* Berkeley, Calif., 1955.

Butow, Robert J. C.: *Japan's Decision to Surrender,* Stanford, Calif., 1954.

——: *Tojo and the Coming of the War,* Princeton, N.J., 1961.

Choi, Kee Il: "Tokugawa Feudalism and the Emergence of the New Leaders of Early Modern Japan," *Explorations in Entrepreneurial History,* vol. 9, pp. 72–84, 1956.

Conroy, Hilary: *The Japanese Seizure of Korea,* Philadelphia, 1960.

Craig, Albert: *Chōshū and the Meiji Restoration 1853–68,* Cambridge, Mass., 1961.

Dore, Ronald P.: *Land Reform in Japan,* London, 1959.

Hall, Robert King (ed.): *Kokutai no Hongi: Cardinal Principles of the National Entity of Japan,* John Owen Gauntlett (tr.), Cambridge, Mass., 1949.

Harrison, John A.: *Japan's Northern Frontier,* Gainesville, Fla., 1953.

Hu Shih: "The Modernization of China and Japan: A Comparative Study in Cultural Conflict," in Caroline F. Ware (ed.), *The Cultural Approach to History,* New York, 1940.

Ike, Nobutaka: *The Beginnings of Political Democracy in Japan,* Baltimore, 1950.

Jansen, Marius B. (ed.): *Changing Japanese Attitudes toward Modernization,* Princeton, N.J., 1965.

————: *The Japanese and Sun Yat-sen,* Cambridge, Mass., 1954.

————: "Ōi Kentarō's Radicalism and Chauvinism," *Far Eastern Quarterly,* vol. 11, no. 3, pp. 305–316, 1952.

————: *Sakamoto Ryōma and the Meiji Restoration,* Princeton, N.J., 1961.

Jones, F. C.: *Japan's New Order in East Asia,* London, 1954.

Kawai, Kazuo: *Japan's American Interlude,* Chicago, 1960.

Kublin, Hyman: *Asian Revolutionary: The Life of Sen Katayama,* Princeton, N.J., 1964.

McLaren, Walter W.: *A Political History of Japan during the Meiji Era, 1867–1912,* London, 1916.

Maruyama, Masao: *Thought and Behavior in Modern Japanese Politics,* London, 1963.

Maxon, Yale Candee: *Control of Japanese Foreign Policy: A Study of Civil-Military Rivalry, 1930–1945,* Berkeley, Calif., 1957.

Morley, James W.: *The Japanese Thrust into Siberia, 1918,* New York, 1957.

Morris, Ivan I.: *Nationalism and the Right Wing in Japan: A Study of Postwar Trends,* London, 1960.

Norman, E. Herbert: *Japan's Emergence as a Modern State: Political and Economic Problems of the Meiji Period,* New York, 1940.

Ōkuma, Shigenobu (comp.): *Fifty Years of New Japan,* 2 vols., London, 1910.

Reischauer, Edwin O.: *The United States and Japan,* Cambridge, Mass., 1950.

Sakata, Yoshio, and John Whitney Hall: "The Motivation of Political Leadership in the Meiji Restoration," *Journal of Asian Studies,* vol. 16, no. 1, pp. 31–50, 1956.

Sansom, Sir George Bailey: *The Western World and Japan,* New York, 1950.

Scalapino, Robert A.: *Democracy and the Party Movement in Prewar Japan: The Failure of the First Attempt,* Berkeley, Calif., 1953.

Smith, Thomas C.: "Japan's Aristocratic Revolution," *Yale Review,* vol. 50, pp. 370–383, 1961.

————: "Old Values and Techniques in the Modernization of Japan," *Far Eastern Quarterly,* vol. 14, pp. 355–365, 1955.

Spinks, C. N.: "The Liberal Myth in Japan," *Pacific Affairs,* vol. 15, pp. 450–456, 1942.

Storry, Richard: *The Double Patriots: A Study of Japanese Nationalism,* Boston, 1957.

————: *A History of Modern Japan,* Baltimore, 1960.

Ward, Robert E., and Dankwart A. Rustow (eds.): *The Political Modernization of Japan and Turkey,* Princeton, N.J., 1964.

Yanaga, Chitoshi: *Japan since Perry,* New York, 1949.

CHAPTER 4 *Language as an Expression of Japanese Culture*

Bloch, Bernard: "Studies in Colloquial Japanese," part I, "Inflection," *Journal of the American Oriental Society,* vol. 66, pp. 97–109, 1946; part II, "Syntax,"

Language, vol. 22, pp. 200–248, 1946; part III, "Derivation of Inflected Words," *Journal of the American Oriental Society*, vol. 66, pp. 304–315, 1946; part IV, "Phonemics," *Language*, vol. 26, pp. 86–125, 1950.

Carroll, John B. (ed.): *Language, Thought, and Reality: Selected Writings of Benjamin Lee Whorf*, Cambridge, Mass., 1956.

Eells, Walter Crosby: "Language Reform in Japan," *Modern Language Journal*, vol. 36, pp. 210–213, 1952.

Gardner, Elizabeth F.: "The Inflections of Modern Literary Japanese," *Language*, vol. 26, Supplement, pp. 5–46, 1950.

——: *An Introduction to Modern Japanese Orthography*, Mirror Series B, no. 1, Yale University, Institute of Far Eastern Languages, New Haven, Conn., 1952.

——, and Samuel E. Martin: *Honorific and Familiar Speech in Japanese*, Mirror Series B, no. 3, Yale University, Institute of Far Eastern Languages, New Haven, Conn., 1952.

Greenberg, Joseph H.: *Universals of Language*, Cambridge, Mass., 1963.

Hattori, Shirō: "Relationship of Japanese to Ryukyu, Korean and Altaic Languages," *Transactions of the Asiatic Society of Japan* (3), vol. 1, pp. 101–133, 1948.

Hoijer, Harry (ed.): *Language in Culture: Conference on the Interrelations of Languages and Other Aspects of Culture*, American Anthropologist Memoir 79, Chicago, 1954.

——: "Linguistic and Cultural Change," *Language*, vol. 24, pp. 335–345, 1948.

——: "The Relation of Language to Culture," in A. L. Kroeber (ed.), *Anthropology Today: An Encyclopedic Inventory*, Chicago, 1953.

Jorden, Eleanor Harz: *The Syntax of Modern Colloquial Japanese*, Baltimore, 1955.

Lehman, Winfred P., and Lloyd Faust: *A Grammar of Former Written Japanese*, Harvard-Yenching Institute Studies, vol. 5, Cambridge, Mass., 1951.

Mandelbaum, David (ed.): *Selected Writings of Edward Sapir in Language, Culture, and Personality*, Berkeley, Calif., 1951.

Martin, Samuel E.: *Essential Japanese: An Introduction to the Standard Colloquial Language*, Tokyo, and Rutland, Vt., 1954.

Miller, Roy Andrew: Review of Eleanor Harz Jorden's *Syntax*, in *Journal of the American Oriental Society*, vol. 76, no. 1, pp. 37–40, 1956.

Nakamura, Hajime.: *Tōyōjin no shii hōhō*, Tokyo, 1948–1949; tr. as *The Ways of Thinking of Eastern Peoples*, Tokyo, 1960.

O'Neill, P. G., and S. Yanada: *An Introduction to Written Japanese*, London, 1959.

Passin, Herbert: "Writer and Journalist in the Transitional Society," in Lucian W. Pye (ed.), *Communications and Political Development*, Princeton, N.J., 1963.

Pike, Kenneth L.: *Language in Relation to a Unified Theory of the Structure of Human Behavior*, Glendale, Calif., 1954, 3 vols.

Rahder, Johannes: "Comparative Treatment of the Japanese Language,"

Monumenta Nipponica, vol. 7, pp. 198–208, 1951; vol. 8, pp. 239–288, 1952; vol. 9, pp. 199–257, 1953; vol. 10, pp. 127–168, 1954.

Sansom, Sir George Bailey: *An Historical Grammar of the Japanese Language,* Oxford, 1928.

Sapir, Edward: *Language,* New York, 1921.

——: "The Status of Linguistics as a Science," *Language,* vol. 5, pp. 207–214, 1929.

Tsunoda, Ryūsaku, William Theodore de Bary, and Donald Keene: *Sources of (the) Japanese Tradition,* New York, 1958.

Whorf, Benjamin Lee: *Four Articles on Metalinguistics,* Department of State, Foreign Service Institute, Washington, D.C., 1949. (Includes "Science and Linguistics," *Technology Review,* vol. 42, no. 6, 1940; "Linguistics as an Exact Science," *Technology Review,* vol. 43, no. 2, 1940; "Language and Logic," *Technology Review,* vol. 43, no. 6, 1941; "The Relation of Habitual Thought and Behavior to Language," in *Sapir Memorial Publication: Language, Culture, and Personality,* Menasha, Wis., pp. 75–93, 1941.) See also John B. Carroll (ed.): *Language, Thought, and Reality: Selected Writings of Benjamin Lee Whorf,* Cambridge, Mass., 1956.

Yamada, Yoshio: *Kambun no kundoku ni yorite tsutaeraretaru gohō* (Word uses transmitted through reading Chinese texts as Japanese), Tokyo, 1935.

Yamagiwa, Joseph K.: "Reforms in the Language and Orthography of Newspapers in Japan," *Journal of the American Oriental Society,* vol. 68, pp. 45–52, 1948.

CHAPTER 5   *Literature and Japanese Culture*

Bibliographies

Bonneau, Georges: "Bibliographie de la littérature japonaise contemporaine," *Bulletin de la Maison Franco-Japonaise,* vol. 9, nos. 1–4, 1938.

Brown, Don: *Japanese Literature in English, 1955–1956,* Tokyo, 1957.

Miner, Earl R.: *The Japanese Tradition in British and American Literature,* Princeton, N.J., 1958.

Numazawa, Tatsuo: *Nihon bungakushi hyōran* (Outlines of the history of Japanese literature), Tokyo, 1934, pp. 1, 178–206.

P.E.N. Club, Japan: *Japanese Literature in European Languages: A Bibliography,* 2d ed., Tokyo, 1961.

Yamagiwa, Joseph K.: *Japanese Literature of the Shōwa Period: A Guide to Japanese Reference and Research Materials,* Ann Arbor, Mich., 1959.

General

Aston, William George: *A History of Japanese Literature,* London and New York, 1889, 1907; London, 1933.

Bonneau, Georges: *Histoire de la littérature japonaise contemporaine, 1868–1938*, Paris, 1940.

Brower, Robert H., and Earl R. Miner: *Japanese Court Poetry*, Stanford, Calif., 1961.

Daniels, F. E. (ed.): *Selections from Japanese Literature (12th to 19th Centuries)*, London, 1959.

Etō, Jun: "An Undercurrent in Modern Japanese Literature," *Journal of Asian Studies*, vol. 23, no. 3, pp. 433–445, 1964.

Feldman, Horace: "The Meiji Political Novel: A Brief Survey," *Far Eastern Quarterly*, vol. 9, no. 3, pp. 245–256, 1950.

Florenz, Karl: *Geschichte der japanischen Litteratur*, Leipzig, 1906.

Hibbett, Howard S.: *The Floating World in Japanese Fiction*, Fair Lawn, N.J., 1959.

K. B. S.: *Introduction to Classic Japanese Literature*, Tokyo, 1948.

————: *Introduction to Contemporary Japanese Literature*, Tokyo, 1939.

————: *Introduction to Contemporary Japanese Literature*, part II, *1936–1955*, Tokyo, 1959.

Keene, Donald (ed.): *Anthology of Japanese Literature from the Earliest Era to the Mid-nineteenth Century*, New York, 1955; Tokyo, 1956.

————: *Japanese Literature: An Introduction for Western Readers*, Wisdom of the East Series, London, 1953.

————: "Literary and Intellectual Currents in Postwar Japan and Their International Implications," in Hugh Borton and others, *Japan between East and West*, New York, 1957.

————: *Modern Japanese Literature*, New York, 1956.

————: *Modern Japanese Poetry*, Ann Arbor, Mich., 1964.

Okazaki, Yoshie: *Japanese Literature in the Meiji Era*, V. H. Viglielmo (tr. and adap.), Tokyo, 1955.

"Problems of Translation from Japanese," papers by Ivan I. Morris, Donald Keene, Howard S. Hibbett, Edwin McClellan, and Edward G. Seidensticker, *Journal–Newsletter of the Association of Teachers of Japanese*, vol. 2, nos. 1, 2, 1964.

Prose

Akutagawa, Ryūnosuke: *Hell Screen ("Jigoku hen") and Other Stories*, W. H. H. Norman (tr.), Tokyo, 1948.

————: *Rashomon and Other Stories*, Kojima Takashi (tr.), New York, Tokyo, and Rutland, Vt., 1952.

————: *Tales Grotesque and Curious*, Glenn W. Shaw (tr.), Tokyo, 1930.

————: *The Three Treasures*, Sasaki Takamasa (tr.), rev. ed., Tokyo, 1951.

Bashō (Matsuo Bashō) *Oku no hosomichi, or the Poetical Journey in Old Japan*, Isobe Yaichirō (tr.), Tokyo, 1933.

Chamberlain, Basil Hall (tr.): *"Ko-ji-ki" or "Records of Ancient Matters,"* 2d ed., Kobe, 1932.

Dazai, Osamu: *No Longer Human,* Donald Keene (tr.), New York, 1958.
———: "Of Women: A Story," Edward G. Seidensticker (tr.), *Atlantic Monthly,* vol. 195, pp. 145–147, 1955.
———: *The Setting Sun,* Donald Keene (tr.), New York, 1956.
Futabatei Shimei: *Mediocrity,* Glenn W. Shaw (tr.), Tokyo, 1927.
Ikku, Jippensha: *Hizakurige or Shank's Mare,* Thomas Satchell (tr.), reprinted Tokyo, and Rutland, Vt., 1960.
Kawabata, Yasunari: *Snow Country,* Edward G. Seidensticker (tr.), New York, 1957.
———: *Thousand Cranes,* Edward G. Seidensticker (tr.), New York, 1959.
Keene, Donald (tr.): "Taketori Monogatari: The Tale of the Bamboo Cutter," *Monumenta Nipponica,* vol. 11 pp. 1–28, 1956.
Kikuchi, Kan: *Victory or Defeat,* Nishi Kiichi (tr.), Tokyo, 1934.
McCullough, Helen Craig (tr.): *The Taiheiki: A Chronicle of Medieval Japan,* New York, 1959.
McKinnon, Richard N. (ed.): *The Heart Is Alone: A Selection of 20th Century Japanese Short Stories,* Tokyo, 1957.
Mishima, Yukio: *Confessions of a Mask,* Meredith Weatherby (tr.), New York, 1958.
———: *The Sound of the Waves,* Meredith Weatherby (tr.), New York and Tokyo, 1956.
———: *The Temple of the Golden Pavilion,* Ivan I. Morris (tr.), New York, 1959.
Mori, Ōgai: *The Wild Geese,* Ochiai Kingo and Sanford Goldstein (trs.), Tokyo, and Rutland, Vt., 1959.
Morris, Ivan I. (ed.): *Twenty-five Stories from Modern Japan,* London and Tokyo, 1961.
Murasaki, Shikibu: *The Tale of Genji,* Arthur Waley (tr.), Boston and London, 1935, 2 vols.
Mushakōji, Saneatsu: *Love and Death,* William F. Marquardt (tr.), New York, 1958.
Natsume, Sōseki: *Kokoro,* Edwin McClellan (tr.), Chicago, 1957.
Ōmori, Annie Shepley, and Kōchi Doi (trs.): *Diaries of Court Ladies of Old Japan,* Tokyo, 1935.
Porter, William N. (tr.): *The Miscellany of a Japanese Priest (Tsurezuregusa),* by Yoshida Kenkō, London, 1914.
——— (tr.): *The Tosa Diary,* London, 1912.
Reischauer, Edwin O., and Joseph K. Yamagiwa (trs.): *Translations from Early Japanese Literature,* Cambridge, Mass., 1951.
Sadler, Arthur Lindsay (tr.): *The Ten Foot Square Hut and Tales of the Heike,* Sydney, Australia, 1928.
——— (tr.): "Heike Monogatari," *Transactions of the Asiatic Society of Japan,* vol. 46 (1918) and vol. 49 (1921).
Saikaku (Ibara or Ihara Saikaku): *Five Women Who Loved Love,* William Theodore de Bary (tr.), Tokyo, and Rutland, Vt., 1956.

————: *The Japanese Family Storehouse, or the Millionaire's Gospel Modernized*, G. W. Sargent (tr., with introduction and commentary), New York, 1959.

Sansom, Sir George Bailey (tr.): "The Tsuredzure Gusa of Yoshida no Kaneyoshi," *Transactions of the Asiatic Society of Japan*, vol. 39, pp. 1–146, 1911.

Sei Shōnagon: *The Pillow-book of Sei Shōnagon*, Arthur Waley (tr.), Boston, 1928.

Seidensticker, Edward G. (tr.): *The "Kagerō Nikki," Journal of a 10th Century Noblewoman*, as *Transactions of the Asiatic Society of Japan* (3), vol. 4, 1955.

Tanizaki, Jun'ichirō: *Ashikari and the Story of Shunkin*, Roy Humpherson and Ōkita Hajime (trs.), Tokyo, 1936.

·————: *The Key*, Howard S. Hibbett (tr.), New York, 1961.

————: *The Makioka Sisters*, Edward G. Seidensticker (tr.), New York, 1957.

————: *Seven Japanese Tales*, Howard S. Hibbett (tr.), New York, 1963.

Vos, Frits: *A Study of the Ise-Monogatari*, The Hague, 1957, 2 vols.

Whitehouse, Wilfrid (tr.): *Ochikubo monogatari, or the Tale of the Lady Ochikubo*, Kobe and London, 1934.

Yoshikawa, Eiji: *The Heike Story*, Uramatsu Fuki Wooyenaka (tr.), New York, 1956.

Drama

Bowers, Faubion: *The Japanese Theatre*, New York, 1952.

Chikamatsu, Monzaemon: *The Battles of Coxinga*, Donald Keene (tr.), Cambridge, Mass., 1951.

————: *The Love Suicide at Amijima*, Donald H. Shively (tr.), Cambridge, Mass., 1963.

————: *The Major Plays of Chikamatsu*, Donald Keene (tr.), New York, 1961.

Ernst, Earle: *The Kabuki Theatre*, London, 1956.

·———— (ed.): *Three Japanese Plays from the Traditional Theatre*, Fair Lawn, N.J., 1959.

Iwasaki Yōzan T., and Glenn Hughes (trs.): *New Plays from Japan*, London, 1930.

———— and ———— (trs.): *Three Modern Japanese Plays*, Cincinnati, 1932.

Kikuchi, Kan: *Tōjūrō's Love and Four Other Plays*, Glenn W. Shaw (tr.), Tokyo, 1925.

Kurata, Hyakuzō: *The Priest and His Disciples*, Glenn W. Shaw (tr.), Tokyo, 1922.

McKinnon, Richard N.: "The Nō and Zeami," *Far Eastern Quarterly*, vol. 11, no. 3, pp. 355–361, 1952.

————: "Zeami on the Art of Training," *Harvard Journal of Asiatic Studies*, vol. 16, pp. 200–225, 1953.

Malm, William P.: *Japanese Music and Musical Instruments*, Tokyo, and Rutland, Vt., 1959.

Mishima, Yukio: *Five Modern Nō Plays*, Donald Keene (tr.), New York, 1958.

Namiki, Gohei: *Kanjinchō: A Japanese Kabuki Play*, Adolph C. Scott (tr.), Tokyo, 1953.
Nippon Gakujutsu Shinkōkai: *Japanese Nō Drama*, Tokyo, 1955.
Sadler, Arthur Lindsay (tr.): *Japanese Plays: Nō-Kyōgen-Kabuki*, Sydney, Australia, 1943.
Sakanishi, Shio: *Kyōgen, Comic Interludes of Japan*, Boston, 1938.
Scott, Adolph C.: *Kabuki Theatre of Japan*, London, 1955.
Waley, Arthur (tr.): *The Nō Plays of Japan*, London, 1921.
Whitehouse, Wilfrid, and Shidehara Michitarō: "Seami jūroku bushū: Seami's Sixteen Treatises," *Monumenta Nipponica*, vol. 4, pp. 530–565, 1941.
Yamamoto, Yūzō: *Three Plays*, Glenn W. Shaw (tr.), Tokyo, 1935.

Poetry

Andō, Ichirō, and others: "Modern Japanese Poems," *Japan Quarterly*, vol. 3, pp. 79–94, 1956.
Benl, Oscar: *Die Entwicklung der japanischen Poetik bis zum 16 Jahrhundert* Hamburg, 1951.
Blyth, R. H. (tr.): *Haiku*, Tokyo, 1949–1952, 4 vols.
———: *Senryū: Japanese Satirical Verses*, Tokyo, 1941.
Brower, Robert H., and Earl R. Miner: "Formative Elements in the Japanese Poetic Tradition," *Journal of Asian Studies*, vol. 16, no. 4, pp. 503–527, 1957.
Henderson, Harold G.: *An Introduction to Haiku*, New York, 1958.
Ishikawa, Takuboku: *A Handful of Sand: From the Works of Takuboku Ishikawa*, Sakanishi Shio (tr.), Boston, 1935.
Itō, Sachio: *Songs of a Cowherd: From the Works of Sachio Itō*, Sakanishi Shio (tr.), Boston, 1936.
Japanese Classics Translation Committee (tr.): *Haikai and Haiku*, Tokyo, 1958.
Kōno, Ichirō, and Rikutarō Fukuda (eds. and trs.): *An Anthology of Modern Japanese Poetry*, Tokyo, 1958.
Ninomiya, Takamichi (tr.): *The Poetry of Living Japan: An Anthology*, Wisdom of the East Series, London, 1957.
Nippon Gakujutsu Shinkōkai: *Haiku*, Tokyo, 1958.
——— (ed.): *The Manyōshū: One Thousand Poems*, Tokyo, 1940.
Pierson, Jan L., Jr. (tr.): *The Manyōshū*, Leiden, 1929–1960, 12 vols.
Waley, Arthur (tr.): *Japanese Poetry: The "Uta,"* London, 1919.
Yasuda, Kenneth (Shōson): *The Japanese Haiku*, Tokyo, and Rutland Vt., 1957.
——— (tr.): *Minase sangin hyakuin: A Poem of One Hundred Links Composed by Three Poets at Minase*, Tokyo, 1956.
——— (tr.): *A Pepper-pod: Classic Japanese Poems Together with Original Haiku*, New York, 1957.
Yosano, Akiko: *Tangled Hair: From the Works of the Poet Akiko Yosano*, Sakanishi Shio (tr.), Boston, 1935.

CHAPTER 6   *The Visual Arts and Japanese Culture*

General

Anesaki, Masaharu: *Buddhist Art in Its Relation to Buddhist Ideals, with Special Reference to Buddhism in Japan,* London, 1916.
Bunot, Jean: *Histoire des arts du Japon.* vol. 1, *Des origines à 1350,* Paris, 1949.
Fenollosa, Ernest: *Epochs of Chinese and Japanese Art,* rev. ed., London, 1921, 2 vols.
Harada, Jirō: *Catalogue of Treasures in the Imperial Repository Shōsōin,* Tokyo, 1932.
————: *History of Japanese Art,* Tokyo, 1913.
Ishida, Mosaku: *The Shōsōin, an Eighth Century Treasure-house,* Harada Jirō (tr.), Tokyo, 1954.
Lee, Sherman E.: *A History of Far Eastern Art,* New York, 1964.
Minamoto, Hōshū: *An Illustrated History of Japanese Art,* Harold G. Henderson (tr.), Kyoto, 1935.
Munsterberg, Hugo: *The Arts of Japan: An Illustrated History,* Tokyo, and Rutland, Vt., 1957.
Paine, Robert T., and Alexander C. Soper: *The Art and Architecture of Japan,* rev. ed., Baltimore, 1960.
Swann, Peter C.: *An Introduction to the Arts of Japan,* New York, 1958.
Terry, Charles S. (comp. and ed.): *Masterworks of Japanese Art,* Tokyo, and Rutland, Vt., 1956.
Tokyo National Museum: *Pageant of Japanese Art,* vol. I, *Painting, 6th–14th Centuries;* vol. II, *Painting, 14th–19th Centuries;* vol. III, *Architecture and Gardens;* vol. IV, *Sculpture;* vol. V, *Ceramics and Metalwork;* vol. VI, *Textiles and Lacquer,* Tokyo, 1952–1954; popular ed. in reduced size but unabridged, Tokyo, 1958.
Warner, Langdon: *The Enduring Art of Japan,* Cambridge, Mass., 1952.
Yashiro, Yukio (ed. in chief), K. B. S.: *Art Treasures of Japan,* Tokyo, 1960, 2 vols.
———— *2,000 Years of Japanese Art,* New York, 1958.

Architecture and gardens

Akiyama, Aisaburō: *Shintō and Its Architecture,* Kyoto, 1936.
Carver, Norman F.: *Form and Space of Japanese Architecture,* Tokyo, 1955.
Drexler, Arthur: *The Architecture of Japan,* New York, 1955.
Futagawa, Yukio: *The Roots of Japanese Architecture,* Tokyo, 1963.
Gropius, Walter, Tange Kenzō, and Ishimoto Yasuhiro: *Katsura: Tradition and Creation in Japanese Architecture,* New Haven, Conn., 1960.

Harada, Jirō: *The Lesson of Japanese Architecture,* rev. ed., Boston, 1954.

House Beautiful: Series of articles by several authors, signed and unsigned, on Japanese architecture and house furnishings, vol. 102, pp. 58–75, 110–145, 1960.

K. B. S.: *Architectural Beauty in Japan,* New York, 1956.

Kishida, Hideto: *Japanese Architecture,* 9th ed., Tokyo, 1960.

Kitao, H. (ed.): *Graphic Architecture,* Tokyo, 1958(?)—. (Series of 120 vols., covering numerous aspects of architecture, furniture, and furnishings and consisting chiefly of photographs with brief captions in English and Japanese. Each volume has a separate title, as well as the series title with the volume number.)

Koike, Shinji: *Contemporary Architecture of Japan,* 2d ed., Tokyo, 1955.

Kuck, L. E.: *The Art of Japanese Gardens,* New York, 1940.

Kultermann, Udo: *New Japanese Architecture,* New York, 1960.

Newson, Samuel: *Japanese Garden Construction,* Tokyo, 1939.

Soper, Alexander C.: *The Evolution of Buddhist Architecture in Japan,* Princeton, N.J., 1942.

Taut, Bruno: *Houses and People of Japan,* rev. ed., Tokyo, 1958.

Yoshida, Tetsurō: *The Japanese House and Garden,* New York, 1955.

Sculpture

Album of Japanese Sculpture, Tokyo, 1952–1953, 6 vols. (Vol. I is entitled simply *Japanese Sculpture;* volumes are arranged by period.)

Kuno, Takeshi (ed.): *A Guide to Japanese Sculpture,* Shigetaka Kaneko (tr.), Tokyo, 1963.

Miki, Fumio: *Haniwa, the Clay Sculpture of Proto-historic Japan,* Roy Andrew Miller (English adap.), Tokyo, and Rutland, Vt., 1960.

Warner, Langdon: *The Craft of the Japanese Sculptor,* New York, 1936.

———: *Japanese Sculpture of the Suiko Period,* New Haven, Conn., 1923.

———: *Japanese Sculpture of the Tempyō Period,* James M. Plumer (ed.), Cambridge, Mass., 1959.

Watson, William: *Sculpture of Japan from the Fifth to the Fifteenth Century,* New York, 1959.

See also entries concerning masks and netsuke in section "Other arts and crafts" below.

Painting

Akiyama, Terukazu: *Japanese Painting,* Basel, 1961.

Binyon, Laurence: *Painting in the Far East: An Introduction to the History of Pictorial Art in Asia, Especially China and Japan,* 4th ed., rev., London, 1934.

Bowie, Henry P.: *On the Laws of Japanese Painting: An Introduction to the Study of the Art of Japan,* San Francisco, 1911; reprinted New York, 1951.

Grey, Basil: *Japanese Screen Painting*, London, 1955.
Grilli, Elise: *Golden Screen Paintings of Japan*, New York, 1960.
————: *Japanese Picture Scrolls*, New York, 1958.
Lemière, Alain: *Japanese Art*, vol. I, *Religious Art*; vol. II, *Handscrolls*; vol. III, *From Sesshu to the Ukiyoye School*; vol. IV, *Colour Prints*, Paris and New York, 1958. (Also numbered as vols. 21–24 in *Petite encyclopédie de l'art*.)
Munsterberg, Hugo: *The Landscape Painting of China and Japan*, Tokyo, 1955.
Naitō, Toichirō: *The Wall-Paintings of Hōryūji*, W. R. B. Acker and Benjamin Rowland, Jr. (trs.), Baltimore, 1943.
Noma, Seiroku (ed.): *Artistry in Ink*, Edward Strong (tr.), New York, 1957. (Treats *sumi-e*, or india-ink paintings.)
Tsuda, Noritake: *Ideals of Japanese Painting*, Osaka, 1940.

Ukiyo-e prints

Binyon, Laurence, and J. J. O'B. Sexton: *Japanese Colour Prints*, London, 1923.
Fujikake, Shizuya: *Japanese Wood-block Prints*, 6th ed., Tokyo, 1959.
Gernsaulier, Helen C.: *The Clarence Buckingham Collection of Japanese Prints*, Chicago, 1955.
Harada, Jirō (ed.): *Japanese Wood-block Printing*, Tokyo, 1939.
Hillier, Jack R.: *Japanese Masters of the Colour Print*, London, 1954.
Hirano, Chie: *Kiyonaga*, Boston, 1939. (Especially good on general techniques of print making.)
Ledoux, Louis V.: *Japanese Prints . . . in the Collection of Louis V. Ledoux*, Princeton, N.J., 1942–1951, 5 vols. (Volume titles vary slightly; arrangement is chronological.)
Michener, James A.: *The Floating World: The Story of Japanese Prints*, New York, 1954.
————: *Japanese Prints from the Early Masters to the Modern*, Tokyo, and Rutland, Vt., 1959.
Statler, Oliver: *Modern Japanese Prints: An Art Reborn*, Tokyo, and Rutland, Vt., 1956.

Calligraphy

See brief discussions in several books listed above, notably Hugo Munsterberg, *The Arts of Japan*; Noma Seiroku (ed.), *Artistry in Ink*; and Peter C. Swann, *An Introduction to the Arts of Japan*. The following books, though referring to Chinese practice, cover in detail the aesthetic considerations and paradigms applying also in Japan.

Chiang, Yee: *Chinese Calligraphy: An Introduction to Its Aesthetic and Technique,* London, 1938.
Driscoll, Lucy, and Toda Kenji: *Chinese Calligraphy,* Chicago, 1935.
Yang Yu-hsun: *La Calligraphie chinoise depuis les Han,* Paris, 1937.

Other arts and crafts

CERAMICS

Koyama, Fujio (ed.): *Japanese Ceramics from Ancient to Modern Times,* commemorative catalog of an exhibition held at the Oakland Art Museum, Oakland, Calif., 1961.
Miller, Roy A.: *Japanese Ceramics,* after Japanese text by Okuda Seuchi and others, Tokyo, 1960.
Mitsuoka, Tadanari: *Ceramic Art of Japan,* 5th ed., Tokyo, 1960.
Okada, Yuzuru, and Kawaguchi Masaaki: *Ceramics and Metalwork,* Pageant of Japanese Art Series, vol. V, Tokyo, and Rutland, Vt., 1958.

LACQUER
Yoshino, Tomio: *Japanese Lacquerware,* Tokyo, 1959.
See also section on "Textiles."

MASKS
Nogami, Toyoichirō: *Masks of Japan,* Tokyo, 1935.

NETSUKE
Meinertzhagen, F.: *The Art of the Netsuke Carver,* London, 1956.
Okada, Yuzuru: *Netsuke: A Miniature Art of Japan,* Tokyo, 1951.
Ryerson, Egerton: *The Netsuke of Japan,* London, 1958.

SWORDS AND SWORD GUARDS
Joly, H. L.: *Japanese Sword Guards,* London, 1910.
Yumoto, John M.: *The Samurai Sword: A Handbook,* Rutland, Vt., 1958.

TEXTILES
Okada, Yuzuru, and Charles S. Terry: *Textiles and Lacquer,* Pageant of Japanese Art Series, vol. VI, Tokyo, and Rutland, Vt., 1958.
Smith, A. D. Howell, and A. Koop: *A Guide to Japanese Textiles,* London, 1919–1920, 2 vols.

FOLK ARTS AND CRAFTS
Munsterberg, Hugo: *The Folk Arts of Japan,* Tokyo, and Rutland, Vt., 1958.
Okada, Yuzuru: *Japanese Handicrafts,* 2d ed., Tokyo, 1959.
Yanagi, Sōetsu: *Folk Crafts in Japan,* Tokyo, 1949.

MISCELLANEOUS
Maeda, Yasuji (Taiji): *Japanese Decorative Design,* Tokyo, 1957.

CHAPTER 7 *Religion and Philosophy*

General

Anesaki, Masaharu: *History of Japanese Religion*, London, 1946.
——: *Religious Life of the Japanese People*, Tokyo, 1938.
Bunce, William K. (ed.): *Religions in Japan*, Rutland, Vt., 1955.
Contemporary Religions in Japan, Tokyo, 1960—, quarterly.
Griffis, William Elliot: *The Religions of Japan*, New York, 1912.
Kishimoto, Hideo (ed.): *Japanese Religion in the Meiji Era*, John F. Howes (tr. and adap.), Tokyo, 1956.
Kosaka, Masaaki (ed.): *Japanese Thought in the Meiji Era*, David Abosch (tr. and adap.), Tokyo, 1958.
Nielsen, Niels C., Jr.: "Religion and Philosophy in Contemporary Japan," *Rice Institute Pamphlets*, vol. 43, no. 4, 1957.
Nishida, Kitarō: *A Study of Good*, V. H. Viglielmo (tr.), Tokyo, 1960.
Tsunoda, Ryūsaku, William Theodore de Bary, and Donald Keene: *Sources of (the) Japanese Tradition*, New York, 1958.

Shinto

Ballou, Robert O.: *Shinto, the Unconquered Enemy*, New York, 1945.
Beardsley, Richard K.: "Shinto Religion and Japanese Cultural Evolution," in Gertrude E. Dole and Robert L. Carneiro (eds.), *Essays in the Science of Culture in Honor of Leslie A. White*, New York, 1960, pp. 63–78.
Holtom, Daniel C.: *Modern Japan and Shinto Nationalism*, rev. ed., Chicago, 1947.
——: *The National Faith of Japan: A Study in Modern Shinto*, London, 1938.
International Congress for the History of Religions, Ninth, Tokyo, 1958, Shinto Committee: *An Outline of Shinto Teachings*, Tokyo, 1958.
International Institute for the Study of Religions: *Directory of the Sectarian Shinto Federation and the Principal Shinto Shrines of Japan*, Tokyo, 1957(?).
Japan, Ministry of Education: *Religion in Japan*, Tokyo, 1959.
Kato, Genchi: *A Study of Shinto, the Religion of the Japanese Nation*, Tokyo, 1926.
Ponsonby-Fane, Richard A. D.: *Studies in Shinto and Shrines*, Kyoto, 1953.
Wheeler, Post: *The Sacred Scriptures of the Japanese*, New York, 1952.

Buddhism

Burtt, E. A. (ed.): *The Teachings of the Compassionate Buddha*, New York, 1955.
Conze, Edward: *Buddhism: Its Essence and Development*, New York, 1951.
—— (ed.): *Buddhist Texts through the Ages*, New York, 1954.

606

Eliot, Sir Charles: *Japanese Buddhism*, London, 1936; reprinted New York, 1960.

Hamilton, Clarence H. (ed.): *Buddhism: A Religion of Infinite Compassion*, New York, 1952.

Humphreys, Christmas: *Zen Buddhism*, London, 1949, 1957.

International Institute for the Study of Religions: *Directory of Buddhist Denominations*, Tokyo, 1957.

Reischauer, August Karl: *Studies in Japanese Buddhism*, New York, 1917.

Saunders, Dale E.: *Buddhism in Japan*, Philadelphia, 1964.

Steinilber-Oberlin, Emile: *The Buddhist Sects of Japan*, London, 1938.

Suzuki, Daisetz T.: *Essays in Zen Buddhism*, London, 1958.

———: *Introduction to Zen Buddhism*, New York, 1949.

Takakusu, Junjirō: *The Essentials of Buddhist Philosophy*, Honolulu, 1957.

———, E. Fromm, and R. De Martino: *Zen Buddhism and Psychoanalysis*, New York, 1960.

Confucianism

Armstrong, Robert Cornell: *Light from the East: Studies in Japanese Confucianism*, Toronto, 1914.

Hall, John Whitney: "The Confucian Teacher in Tokugawa Japan," in David S. Nivison and Arthur F. Wright (eds.), *Confucianism in Action*, Stanford, Calif., 1959, pp. 268–301.

Lin Yu-tang (ed.): *The Wisdom of Confucius*, New York, 1938.

Liu Wu-chi: *A Short History of Confucian Philosophy*, London, 1955.

Shively, Donald H.: "Motoda Eifu: Confucian Lecturer to the Meiji Emperor," in David S. Nivison and Arthur F. Wright (eds.) *Confucianism in Action*, Stanford, Calif., 1959, pp. 302–333.

Smith, Warren W., Jr.: *Confucianism in Modern Japan: A Study of Conservatism in Japanese Intellectual History*, Tokyo, 1959.

Starr, Frederick: *Confucianism: Ethics, Philosophy, Religion*, New York, 1930.

Waley, Arthur (tr.): *The Analects of Confucius*, London, 1938.

Christianity

Boxer, Charles R.: *The Christian Century in Japan, 1549–1650*, Berkeley, Calif., 1951.

Iglehart, Charles W.: *A Century of Protestant Christianity in Japan*, Tokyo, and Rutland, Vt., 1959.

International Institute for the Study of Religions: *Christian Churches and Denominations in Japan*, Tokyo, 1957.

Laures, Johannes: *The Catholic Church in Japan: A Short History*, Rutland, Vt., 1954.

Thomas, Winburn T.: *Protestant Beginnings in Japan: The First Three Decades, 1859–1889*, Tokyo, and Rutland, Vt., 1959.

New religions and others

Bellah, Robert N.: *Tokugawa Religion: The Values of Pre-industrial Japan*, Glencoe, Ill., 1957.

Halpern, C. W.: *The Kurozumi Sect of Shinto*, Tokyo, 1945.

Tenrikyō Church Headquarters: *The Short History of Tenrikyō*, Nara, Japan, 1956.

Tenshō Kōtai Jingū Kyō: *The Prophet of Tabuse*, Tabuse, Yamaguchi Prefecture, Japan, 1954.

Thomsen, Harry: *The New Religions of Japan*, Tokyo, and Rutland, Vt., 1963.

Van Straelen, Henricus: *The Religion of Divine Wisdom: Japan's Most Powerful Religious Movement*, Kyoto, 1957. [Tenrikyō]

CHAPTER 8 *Personality Psychology* [2]

Abe, Maruo: "The Accused and Society: The Growing Emphasis on Therapeutic and Preventive Aspects of Criminal Justice in Japan," in Arthur Taylor von Mehren (ed.), *Law in Japan*, Cambridge, Mass., pp. 324–363, 1963.

Benedict, Ruth: *The Chrysanthemum and the Sword: Patterns of Japanese Culture*, Boston, 1946.

Bennett, J. W., and Nagai Michio: "Echoes: Reactions to American Anthropology—Japanese Critique of the Methodology of Benedict's *Chrysanthemum and the Sword*," *American Anthropologist*, vol. 55, pp. 404–411, 1953.

Buchanan, D. C.: "Japanese Character and Personality as Revealed in Their Culture," in William A. Parker (ed.), *Understanding Other Cultures*, Washington, D.C., 1954.

Caudill, William: "Japanese American Personality and Acculturation," *Genetic Psychology Monographs*, vol. 45, Provincetown, Mass., 1952.

———: "Observations on the Culture Context of Japanese Psychiatry," in M. K. Opler (ed.), *Culture and Mental Health*, New York, 1958.

———: "Similarities and Differences in Psychiatric Illness and Its Treatment in the United States and Japan," *Seishin Eisei* (Mental Hygiene), 61/62, pp. 15–26, Nagoya University, 1959.

———: "Watakushi no pikuchā intabyū gijutsu (The use of a 'picture interview' technique in the study of impulse gratification and restraint)," *Seishin bunsekigaku no susume* (Advancement of psychiatry), vol. 3, pp. 1–13, Yokohama Hiyoshi Byōin, 1959.

———, and George A. DeVos: "Achievement, Culture, and Personality: The

[2] Test items cited in the text are from field data collected in Niiike Buraku, Takamatsu-chō, Okayama Prefecture, under the supervision of Prof. George A. DeVos in collaboration with the Human Relations Research Group, Nagoya University, directed by Prof. Muramatsu Tsuneo.

Case of Japanese-Americans," *American Anthropologist,* vol. 58, pp. 1102–1126, 1956.

DeVos, George A.: "The Relation of Guilt toward Parents to Achievement and Arranged Marriage among the Japanese," *Psychiatry: Journal for the Study of Interpersonal Processes,* vol. 23, no. 3, 1960.

———, and Wagatsuma Hiroshi: "Psychocultural Significance of Concern over Death and Illness among Rural Japanese," *International Journal of Social Psychiatry,* vol. 5, pp. 5–19, 1959.

Doi, Takeo: "Japanese Language as an Expression of Japanese Psychology," *Western Speech,* vol. 20, pp. 90–96, 1956.

———: "Amae: A Key Concept for Understanding Japanese Personality Structure," paper read at the Tenth Pacific Science Congress, Honolulu, August 28, 1961. (Unpublished.)

Durkheim, Emile: *Suicide: A Study in Sociology,* John A. Spaulding and George Simpson (trs.), Glencoe, Ill., 1951.

Goodman, M. E.: "Values, Attitudes, and Social Concepts of Japanese and American Children," *American Anthropologist,* vol. 59, pp. 979–999, 1957.

Gorer, Geoffrey: "Themes in Japanese Culture," *Transactions of the New York Academy of Sciences,* series II, vol. 5, pp. 106–124, 1943.

Haring, Douglas G.: "Aspects of Personal Character in Japan," *Far Eastern Quarterly,* vol. 6, pp. 12–22, 1946.

———: "Japanese National Character: Cultural Anthropology, Psychoanalysis, and History," *Yale Review,* vol. 42, pp. 375–402, 1953.

——— (ed.): *Personal Character and Cultural Milieu,* Syracuse, 1956. (Articles on Japan by D. G. Haring, B. B. Lanham, and E. Norbeck.)

Katō, Hidetoshi (ed. and tr.): *Japanese Popular Culture,* Tokyo, and Rutland, Vt., 1959.

Kerlinger, Fred: "Behavior and Personality in Japan: A Critique of Three Studies of Japanese Personality," *Social Forces,* vol. 31, pp. 250–258, 1953.

LaBarre, Weston: "Some Observations on Character Structure in the Orient: The Japanese," *Psychiatry,* vol. 8, pp. 319–342, 1945.

Lifton, Robert Jay: "Youth and History: Individual Change in Postwar Japan," *Daedalus,* vol. 91, pp. 172–197, 1962.

Moloney, J. C.: *Understanding the Japanese Mind,* New York, 1954.

Nishihara, Kazuyoshi: *Nihonjin no iken* (Japanese opinions), Tokyo, 1963.

Norbeck, Edward, and George DeVos: "Japan," in Frances L. Hsu (ed.), *Psychological Anthropology: Approaches to Culture and Personality,* Homewood, Ill., pp. 19–47, 1961.

Satō, Kōji, and Sonohara Tarō: "A Proposal for an International Study of Suicide," *Psychologia,* vol. 1, pp. 71–73, Kyoto University, 1957.

Seligman, C. G.: "Japanese Temperament and Character," *Transactions and Proceedings of the Japan Society,* vol. 28, pp. 123–142, 1930.

Seward, G. H. (ed.): *Clinical Studies and Cultural Conflict,* New York, 1958. (Articles on Japanese-Americans by C. G. Babcock and W. Caudill, T. E. Bessent, N. L. Farberow and F. S. Schneidman, L. B. Olinger and V. S. Summers, and M. K. Opler.)

609

Sikkema, Mildred: "Observations on Japanese Early Training," *Psychiatry*, vol. 10, pp. 423–432, 1947.

Smith, Robert J., and Richard K. Beardsley (eds.): *Japanese Culture: Its Development and Characteristics*, Chicago, 1962.

Sofue, Takao, and Hiroshi Wagatsuma: *Kokumin no shinri—Nihonjin to Obeijin* (National Character—Japanese, Europeans, and Americans), Tokyo, 1959.

———: "Patterns of the Japanese Personality Indicated by the Rorschach Test," *Japanese Journal of Projective Techniques*, vol. 1, 1954.

Spitzer, H. M.: "Psychoanalytic Approaches to the Japanese Character," in G. Roheim (ed.), *Psychoanalysis and the Social Sciences*, vol. 1, New York, 1947.

Stoetzel, Jean: *Without the Chrysanthemum and the Sword: A Study of the Attitudes of Youth in Postwar Japan*, New York, 1955.

Strong, E. K.: *The Second-generation Japanese Problem*, Stanford, Calif., 1934.

Uematsu, T.: "A Criminological Study on Infanticide," in *Theory and Reality in Criminal Law, Collected Papers in Commemoration of the 64th Birthday of Dr. S. Ono*, Tokyo, 1951.

Wallace, Anthony F. C.: *Culture and Personality*, New York, 1961.

CHAPTER 9 *Education and Modern National Development* [3]

Before 1868

Arai, Hakuseki: " 'Hyo-chu-ori-taku-shiba-no-ki,' Autobiography of Arai Hakuseki," G. W. Knox (tr.), *Transactions of the Asiatic Society of Japan*, vol. 30, no. 2, pp. i–xii, 89–238, 1902.

Bellah, Robert N.: *Tokugawa Religion: The Values of Pre-industrial Japan*, Glencoe, Ill., 1957.

Boxer, Charles R.: *Jan Compagnie in Japan, 1600–1850: An Essay on the Cultural, Artistic, and Scientific Influences Exercised by the Hollanders in Japan from the Seventeenth to the Nineteenth Centuries*, 2d rev. ed., The Hague, 1950.

Dore, Ronald P.: *Education in Tokugawa Japan*, Berkeley, Calif., 1965.

———: "Education: Japan," in Robert E. Ward and Dankwart A. Rustow (eds.). *The Political Modernization of Japan and Turkey*, Princeton, N.J., 1964, pp. 176–204.

———: "Talent and the Social Order in Japan," *Past and Present*, no. 21, pp. 60–72, 1962.

Earl, David M.: *Emperor and Nation in Japan: Political Thinkers of the Tokugawa Period*, Seattle, 1964.

Hall, John Whitney: "The Confusian Teacher in Tokugawa Japan," in David

[3] Works dealing primarily with the period before 1868 or with the period since 1945 are listed separately, but many books in the second and third sections include discussion of earlier periods.

S. Nivison and Arthur F. Wright (eds.), *Confucianism in Action,* Stanford, Calif., 1959, pp. 268–301, 366–369.

Kirkwood, Kenneth P.: *Renaissance in Japan: A Cultural Survey of the Seventeenth Century,* Tokyo, 1938. (See especially chap. 2, pp. 15–61; and chap. 4, pp. 85–140, dealing with the education of the upper and lower classes, respectively.)

Passin, Herbert: *Education and Society in Japan,* New York, 1965. (Has a large section devoted to "Documents on Japanese Education.")

Taeuber, Irene B.: *The Population of Japan,* Princeton, N.J., 1958. (See educational statistics.)

1868–1945

Brown, Delmer M.: *Nationalism in Japan: An Introductory Historical Analysis,* Berkeley, Calif., 1955.

Burton, Margaret: *The Education of Women in Japan,* 2d ed., New York, 1932.

Commission on Christian Education in Japan: *Christian Education in Japan: A Study, Being the Report of a Commission on Christian Education in Japan,* New York, 1932.

Education in Japan: A Series of Letters Addressed by Prominent Americans to Mori Arinori, New York, 1873.

Fukuzawa, Yukichi: *The Autobiography of Fukuzawa Yukichi,* E. Kiyooka (tr.), 2d ed. rev., Tokyo, 1947. (See especially for history of Keiō University, founded by Fukuzawa, and for early Meiji developments in education.)

Hall, Robert King (ed.): *Kokutai no Hongi: Cardinal Principles of the National Entity of Japan,* John Owen Gauntlett (tr.), Cambridge, Mass., 1949.

———: *Shushin: The Ethics of a Defeated Nation,* New York, 1949.

Hasegawa, Nyozekan: *Educational and Cultural Background of the Japanese People,* Tokyo, 1937.

Hita, Gon-ichi: *The Training of Teachers in Japan: A Historical Survey,* Maki Itsu (tr.), Tokyo, 1937.

Holtom, Daniel C.: *Modern Japan and Shinto Nationalism,* rev. ed., Chicago, 1947.

Idditti, Smimasa (Ijichi Sumimasa): *The Life of Marquis Shigenobu Ōkuma, a Maker of New Japan,* Tokyo, 1940. (See especially for history of Waseda University, founded by Ōkuma.)

Japan, Department of Education: *Annual Report of the Minister of State for Education (Abridged),* Eleventh Annual Report (1883) through Fifty-Ninth Annual Report (1931–1932), Tokyo, 1886–1938.

———: *Education in Japan, Prepared for the Panama-Pacific International Exposition, 1915,* Tokyo, 1914.

———: *Education in Japan: Primary Education, Prepared for the Louisiana Purchase Exposition, 1904,* Tokyo, 1904.

———: *Education in Japan under the Department of Education: Administration and Work,* Tokyo, 1937.

611

————: *A General Survey of Education in Japan*, Tokyo, 1938. (Earlier eds., 1930, 1933, 1935, 1937.)

————: *Japanese Code of Education*, Tokyo, 1879.

————: *Japanese Code of Education, Revised (1880)*, Tokyo, 1888.

————: *Ordinances, Notifications, and Instructions Relating to Education*, Tokyo, 1887.

————: *An Outline History of Japanese Education, Prepared for the Philadelphia International Exhibition, 1876*, New York, 1876; reprinted for the Paris Exposition of 1878, Tokyo, 1877.

————: *Outline of Modern Education in Japan*, Tokyo, 1888.

————: *Short History of the Department of Education*, Tokyo, 1887.

Japan, Ministry of Education: *Annual Report*, Tokyo, 1910—, annually.

Keenleyside, Hugh L., and A. F. Thomas: *The History of Japanese Education and Present Educational System*, Tokyo, 1937.

Kikuchi, Dairoku: *Japanese Education: Lectures Delivered in the University of London*, London, 1909.

Lamott, Willis: *Nippon: The Crime and Punishment of Japan*, New York, 1944. (Covers wartime ideological regimentation.)

Masood, Syed Ross: *Japan and Its Educational System: Being a Report Compiled for the Government* [of India], Hyderabad, 1923.

Nitobe, Inazo: *Bushidō, the Soul of Japan: An Exposition of Japanese Thought*, New York, 1905.

————: *Foreign Languages in Japan, Their Use and Study: An Aspect of Intellectual Life in Japanese History*, Osaka, 1929.

———— (ed.): *Western Influences in Modern Japan: A Series of Papers on Cultural Relations*, Chicago, 1931. (See especially papers by Hoshino, "The Education of Women," and Yoshida, "European and American Influences on Japanese Education.")

Okada, Yaichirō (ed.): *Science Education in Japan*, Tokyo, 1937.

Ōkuma, Shigenobu (ed.): *Fifty Years of New Japan*, London, 1909, 2 vols. (See especially vol. II, pp. 113–225, including papers on "Culture and Education in Old Japan," "Educationalists of the Past," "National Education in the Meiji Era," "Commercial Education," and "The Education of Japanese Women.")

Shively, Donald H.: "Motoda Eifu: Confucian Lecturer to the Meiji Emperor," in David S. Nivison and Arthur F. Wright (eds.), *Confucianism in Action*, Stanford, Calif., 1959, pp. 302–333.

Smith, Warren W., Jr.: *Confucianism in Modern Japan: A Study of Conservatism in Japanese Intellectual History*, Tokyo, 1959.

Tokyo Municipal Office: *Education in Tokyo*, Tokyo, 1937.

World Conference Committee of the Japanese Education Association: *Proceedings of the Seventh Biennial Conference of the World Federation of Education Associations, Tokyo, August 2–7, 1937*, Tokyo, 1938, 5 vols. (See especially vols. IV and V, containing papers presented by Japanese delegates; these cover many topics not extensively discussed elsewhere, e.g., adult education, commercial education, preschool and kindergarten education, rural education, and teachers' organizations.)

Yamashita, Tokuji: *Education in Japan*, Tokyo, 1938.
Yoshida, Kumaji, and Kaigo Tokiomi: *Japanese Education*, Tokyo, 1937.

Since 1945

Anderson, Ronald S.: *Japan: Three Epochs of Modern Education*, Washington, D.C., 1959.
Battistini, Lawrence H.: *The Postwar Student Struggle in Japan*, Rutland, Vt., 1956.
Center for Japanese Social and Political Studies: *Journal of Social and Political Ideas in Japan: Education in Japan, 1945–1963*, vol. 1, no. 3, 1963.
Dore, Ronald P.: "The Ethics of the New Japan," *Pacific Affairs*, vol. 25, no. 2, pp. 147–159, 1952.
Eells, Walter Crosby (comp.): *The Literature of Japanese Education, 1945–1954*, Hamden, Conn., 1955.
Finn, Dallas: "Japanese Universities Today," *Yale Review*, vol. 43, pp, 559–573, 1954.
Hall, Robert King: *Education for a New Japan*, New Haven, Conn., 1949.
Hidaka, Daishirō: "Aftermath of Educational Reform," *Annals of the American Academy of Political and Social Science*, vol. 308, pp. 140–155, 1956.
Jansen, Marius B.: "Education, Values, and Politics in Japan," *Foreign Affairs*, vol. 35, pp. 666–678, 1957.
Japan, Ministry of Education: *Bricks without Straw*, Tokyo, 1950.
———: *A Brief History of Institute for Educational Leadership in Japan*, Tokyo, 1953.
———: *Demand and Supply for University Graduates, Japan*, Tokyo, 1958.
———: *Educational Laws and Regulations in Japan*, series 1, *The Constitution [and] The Fundamental Law of Education;* series 2, *School Education Law*, Tokyo, 1955.
———: *Education in Japan: Graphic Presentation, 1957*, Tokyo, 1957.
———: *Education in 1955: Annual Report of the Ministry of Education*, Tokyo, 1957.
———: *Education in 1956: Annual Report of the Ministry of Education*, Tokyo, 1958.
———: *Japan's Growth and Education*, Tokyo, 1963.
———: *Progress of Education Reform in Japan*, Tokyo, 1950.
———: *A Survey of Japanese Education with Statistics*, Tokyo, 1957.
Japanese Education Reform Council: *Education Reform in Japan: The Present Status and the Problems Involved*, Tokyo, 1950.
Japanese National Commission for UNESCO: *Report of a Survey of School Textbooks in Japan, 1954*, Tokyo, 1956.
———: *School Textbooks in Japan, 1957: A Report of a Survey from the Standpoint of Education for International Understanding and Cooperation*, Tokyo, 1958.
Japan Overseas Advertiser: *Japanese Universities and Colleges 1963*, Tokyo, 1963.

Karasawa, Tomitarō: "Changes in Japanese Education as Revealed in Text-books," *Japan Quarterly*, vol. 2, pp. 365–383, 1955.

Lloyd, Wesley P.: *Student Counseling in Japan: A Two-nation Project in Higher Education*, Minneapolis, 1953.

———: *Student Personnel Services in Japan*, Washington, D.C., 1957.

Passin, Herbert: "Writer and Journalist in the Transitional Society," in Lucian W. Pye (ed.), *Communications and Political Development*, Princeton, N.J., 1963.

Reischauer, Edwin O.: "The Broken Dialogue with Japan," *Foreign Affairs*, vol. 39, no. 1, pp. 11–26, 1960.

Report of the Second United States Education Mission to Japan, Washington, D.C., 1950.

Report of the United States Education Mission to Japan, Washington, D.C., and Tokyo, 1946.

SCAP, General Headquarters, Civil Information and Education Section: *Education in Japan*, Tokyo, 1946.

———: *Education in the New Japan*, Tokyo, 1948, 2 vols.

———: *Mission and Accomplishments of the Occupation in the Civil Information and Education Fields*, Tokyo, 1949.

———: *Post-war Developments in Japanese Education*, Tokyo, 1952, 2 vols.

Snyder, Harold E., and Margretta S. Austin (eds.): *Educational Progress in Japan and the Ryukyus*, Washington, D.C., 1950.

CHAPTER 10 *Japan's Political System* [4]

General

Borton, Hugh, and others: *Japan between East and West*, New York, 1957.

Burks, Ardath W.: *The Government of Japan*, New York, 1961.

Cole, Allan B.: *Japanese Society and Politics: The Impact of Social Stratification and Mobility on Politics*, Boston, 1956.

Ike, Nobutaka: "Japan," in George M. Kahin (ed.), *Major Governments of Asia*, Ithaca, N.Y., 1958, pp. 135–240.

———: *Japanese Politics: An Introductory Survey*, New York, 1957.

Jansen, Marius B. (ed.): *Changing Japanese Attitudes toward Modernization*, Princeton, N.J. 1965.

Kai, Miwa, and Philip B. Yampolsky: *Political Chronology of Japan 1885–1957*, New York, 1957.

Linebarger, Paul M. A., Djang Chu, and Ardath W. Burks: *Far Eastern Governments and Politics: China and Japan*, New York, 1954.

Pye, Lucian W.: *Politics, Personality, and Nation Building*, New Haven, Conn., 1962.

[4] The groupings in this section are for convenience only. Many of the books listed contain material pertinent to subheadings other than the one under which they are classified.

Ward, Robert E. (ed.): *Five Studies in Japanese Politics*, University of Michigan Center for Japanese Studies Occasional Paper 7, Ann Arbor, Mich., 1957.

————: *A Guide to Japanese Reference and Research Materials in the Field of Political Science*, University of Michigan Center for Japanese Studies, Bibliographical Series, no. 1, rev. ed., Ann Arbor, Mich., 1961.

————: "Theory and Practice in Recent Studies of Japanese Politics," *World Politics*, vol. 10, no. 3, pp. 449–461, 1958.

———— and Dankwart A. Rustow (eds.): *The Political Modernization of Japan and Turkey*, Princeton, N.J., 1964.

Yanaga, Chitoshi: *Japanese People and Politics*, New York, 1956.

National government and politics, 1868–1945

Amano, Kōroku (comp.): *A Guide to the Imperial Japanese Diet*, Tokyo, 1905.

Beckmann, George M.: *The Making of the Meiji Constitution: The Oligarchs and the Constitutional Development of Japan, 1868–1891*, Lawrence, Kans., 1957.

Brown, Delmer M.: *Nationalism in Japan: An Introductory Historical Analysis*, Berkeley, Calif., 1955.

Butow, Robert J. C.: *Tojo and the Coming of the War*, Princeton, N.J., 1961.

Byas, Hugh: *Government by Assassination*, New York, 1942.

Colegrove, Kenneth W.: "The Japanese Cabinet," *American Political Science Review*, vol. 30, no. 5, pp. 903–923, 1936.

————: "The Japanese Emperor," *American Political Science Review*, vol. 26, no. 4, pp. 642–659; no. 5, pp. 828–845, 1932.

————: "The Japanese Foreign Office," *American Journal of International Law*, vol. 30, no. 4, pp. 585–613, 1936.

————: "The Japanese Privy Council," *American Political Science Review*, vol. 25, no. 3, pp. 589–614; no. 4, pp. 881–905, 1931.

————: *Militarism in Japan*, Boston, 1936.

————: "Powers and Functions of the Japanese Diet," *American Political Science Review*, vol. 27, no. 6, pp. 885–898, 1933; vol. 28, no. 1, pp. 23–39, 1934.

Fahs, Charles B.: *Government in Japan*, New York, 1940.

————: "Political Groups in the Japanese House of Peers," *American Political Science Review*, vol. 24, no. 5, pp. 896–919, 1940.

Hall, Robert King (ed.): *Kokutai no Hongi: Cardinal Principles of the National Entity of Japan*, John Owen Gauntlett (tr.), Cambridge, Mass., 1949.

Ike, Nobutaka: *The Beginnings of Political Democracy in Japan*, Baltimore, 1950.

Itō, Hirobumi: *Commentaries on the Constitution of the Empire of Japan*, Itō Miyoji (tr.), 3d ed., Tokyo, 1931.

Iwasaki, Uichi: *The Working Forces in Japanese Politics: A Brief Account of Political Conflicts, 1867–1920*, New York, 1921.

Iwata, Masakazu: *Ōkubo Toshimichi, the Bismarck of Japan*, Berkeley, 1964.

McLaren, Walter W.: *A Political History of Japan during the Meiji Era, 1867–1912*, London, 1916.

Maxon, Yale Candee: *Control of Japanese Foreign Policy: A Study of Civil-Military Rivalry, 1930–1945*, Berkeley, Calif., 1957.

Nakano, Tomio: *The Ordinance Power of the Japanese Emperor*, Baltimore, 1923.

Norman, E. Herbert: *Japan's Emergence as a Modern State: Political and Economic Problems of the Meiji Period*, New York, 1940.

Reischauer, Robert K.: *Japan: Government—Politics*, New York, 1939.

Scalapino, Robert A.: *Democracy and the Party Movement in Prewar Japan: The Failure of the First Attempt*, Berkeley, Calif., 1953.

Silberman, Bernard S.: *Ministers of Modernization: Elite Mobility in the Meiji Restoration, 1868–1893*, Tucson, Ariz., 1964.

Smith, Warren W., Jr.: *Confucianism in Modern Japan: A Study of Conservatism in Japanese Intellectual History*, Tokyo, 1959.

Storry, Richard: *The Double Patriots: A Study of Japanese Nationalism*, Boston, 1957.

Uyehara, George Etsujiro: *The Political Development of Japan, 1867–1909*, London, 1910.

National government and politics since 1945

Baerwald, Hans H.: *The Purge of Japanese Leaders under the Occupation*, Berkeley, Calif., 1959.

Butow, Robert J. C.: *Japan's Decision to Surrender*, Stanford, Calif., 1954.

Colbert, Evelyn S.: *The Left Wing in Japanese Politics*, New York, 1952.

Cole, Allan B.: *Political Tendencies of Japanese in Small Enterprises, with Special Reference to the Social Democratic Party*, New York, 1959.

Colton, Hattie Kawahara: "The Workings of the Japanese Diet," *Pacific Affairs*, vol. 28, pp. 363–372, 1955.

Colton, Kenneth E.: "Conservative Leadership in Japan," *Far Eastern Survey*, vol. 24, pp. 90–96, 1955.

Dore, Ronald P.: *City Life in Japan: A Study of a Tokyo Ward*, Berkeley, Calif., 1958.

————: *Land Reform in Japan*, London Office of the Prime Minister, 1959.

Japan, Administrative Management Agency: *Fundamental Laws for the Administrative Organization of Japanese Government*, Tokyo, 1958.

————: *Organizational Charts of the Japanese Government, April 1, 1958*, Tokyo, 1958.

Kawai, Kazuo: *Japan's American Interlude*, Chicago, 1960.

Kurzman, Dan: *Kishi and Japan*, New York, 1960.

Levine, Solomon B.: *Industrial Relations in Postwar Japan*, Urbana, Ill., 1958.

Mendel, Douglas H.: *The Japanese People and Foreign Policy*, Berkeley, Calif., 1961.

Morris, Ivan I.: *Nationalism and the Right Wing in Japan: A Study of Postwar Trends*, London, 1960.

Quigley, Harold Scott, and John E. Turner: *The New Japan: Government and Politics*, Minneapolis, 1956.

Scalapino, Robert A., and Masumi Junnosuke: *Parties and Politics in Contemporary Japan*, Berkeley, Calif., 1962.

SCAP, General Headquarters, Government Section: *Political Reorientation of Japan, September 1945 to September 1948*, Washington, D.C., 1949, 2 vols.

Shigemitsu, Mamoru: *Japan and Her Destiny*, New York, 1958.

Swearingen, Rodger, and Paul Langer: *Bibliography on Japanese Communism*, New York, 1950.

——— and ———: *Red Flag in Japan: International Communism in Action, 1919–1951*, Cambridge, Mass., 1952.

Togo, Shigenori: *The Cause of Japan*, New York, 1956.

Uyehara, Cecil H., S. Royama, and S. Ogata: *Comparative Platforms of Japan's Major Parties*, Medford, Mass., 1955.

Ward, Robert E.: "The Constitution and Current Japanese Politics," *Far Eastern Survey*, vol. 25, no. 4, pp. 49–58, 1956.

———: "The Origins of the Present Japanese Constitution," *American Political Science Review*, vol. 50, no. 4, pp. 980–1010, 1956.

Yoshida, Shigeru: *The Yoshida Memoirs*, Boston, 1962.

Prefectural and local governments

Beardsley, Richard K., John Whitney Hall, and Robert E. Ward: *Village Japan*, Chicago, 1959.

Braibanti, Ralph J.: "Administration of Military Government in Japan at the Prefectural Level," *American Political Science Review*, vol. 43, pp. 250–274, 1949.

———: "Executive Power in Japanese Prefectural Government," *Far Eastern Quarterly*, vol. 9, no. 3, pp. 231–245, 1950.

Brett, C. C.: "The Japanese Prefectural Legislature," *Parliamentary Affairs*, vol. 11, pp. 23–38, 1957–1958.

Steiner, Kurt: "The Japanese Village and Its Government," *Far Eastern Quarterly*, vol. 15, no. 2, pp. 185–199, 1956. (See also introduction by Robert E. Ward, pp. 175–183.)

Ulmer, S. Sidney: "Local Autonomy in Japan since the Occupation," *Journal of Politics*, vol. 19, pp. 46–65, 1957.

Ward, Robert E.: "The Socio-political Role of the *Buraku* [hamlet] in Japan," *American Political Science Review*, vol. 45, no. 4, pp. 1025–1040, 1951.

———: "Some Observations on Local Autonomy at the Village Level in Present Day Japan," *Far Eastern Quarterly*, vol. 12, pp. 183–202, 1953.

CHAPTER 11 *Law in Modern Japan*

For anyone who reads Japanese the supply of reference materials is inexhaustible. If one must rely on English, the problems are greater. Code provisions may be found in a number of Japanese government publications, some of which are still current, and in a commercial edition published by Eibun Hōrei Sha. Judicial decisions are more difficult to obtain. JOHN M. MAKI (ed.), COURT AND CONSTITUTION IN JAPAN (Seattle, 1964), gathers a number of leading cases, and many decisions on points of international law are translated in the several volumes of the JAPANESE ANNUAL OF INTERNATIONAL LAW. Otherwise one must rely on summaries in English-language writings on the problem area involved.

For a general understanding of the Japanese legal system, ARTHUR T. VON MEHREN (ed.), LAW IN JAPAN (Cambridge, Mass., 1963), is indispensable. Through it one can enter into most significant materials in Japanese and in Western languages published before 1962. Most law libraries carry the legal periodicals cited in it and in Chapter 11. One may also wish to consult R. W. Rabinowitz, *Materials on Japanese Law in Western Languages*, 4 AM. J. COMP. L. 97 (1955).

CHAPTER 1 2 *Aspects of Japanese Economic Development* [5]

Economic development (general)

Braibanti, Ralph J., and Joseph J. Spengler (eds.): *Tradition, Values, and Socio-economic Development*, Durham, N.C., 1961.
Enke, Stephen, and Virgil Salera: *International Economics*, 3d ed., Englewood Cliffs, N.J., 1957.
Gerschenkron, Alexander: "Economic Backwardness in Historical Perspective," in Bert F. Hoselitz (ed.), *The Progress of Underdeveloped Areas*, Chicago, 1952.
Higgins, Benjamin: *Economic Development*, New York, 1959.
Hirschman, Albert: *The Strategy of Economic Development*, New Haven, Conn., 1958.
Jacobs, Norman: *The Origin of Modern Capitalism and Eastern Asia,* Hong Kong, 1958.
Kuznets, Simon: "Quantitative Aspects of the Economic Growth of Nations: Levels and Variability of Rates of Growth," *Economic Development and Cultural Change,* vol. 5, no. 1, pp. 1–94, 1956; subsequent papers.
Lewis, William A.: "Economic Development with Unlimited Supplies of Labor," *Manchester School,* vol. 22, no. 2, pp. 139–191, 1954; "Unlimited Labor: Further Notes," *Manchester School,* vol. 26, no. 1, pp. 1–32, 1958.
Meier, Gerald M. (ed.): *Leading Issues in Development Economics,* New York, 1964.
———, and Robert E. Baldwin: *Economic Development: Theory, History, Policy,* New York, 1959.

[5] For convenience in use, the major part of this list of selected references is subdivided chronologically. The periodization cannot be more than roughly approximate, however, since many writers either have omitted definition of their period or have included background material on earlier periods. The subdivisions should therefore be construed as general guides and not as inflexible lines of demarcation.

Nurkse, Ragnar: *Problems of Capital Formation in Underdeveloped Countries,* Fair Lawn, N.J., 1957.

Rostow, W. W.: *The Stages of Economic Growth,* Cambridge, England, 1960.

————: "Trends in the Allocation of Resources in Secular Growth," in Léon H. Dupriez (ed.): *Economic Progress,* Louvain, 1955, pp. 367–382.

The traditional economy

Beasley, William G.: "Feudal Revenue in Japan at the Time of the Meiji Restoration," *Journal of Asian Studies,* vol. 19, no. 3, pp. 255–271, 1960.

Bellah, Robert N.: *Tokugawa Religion: The Values of Pre-industrial Japan,* Glencoe, Ill., 1957.

Choi, Kee Il: "Tokugawa Feudalism and the Emergence of the New Leaders of Early Modern Japan," *Explorations in Entrepreneurial History,* vol. 9, pp. 72–90, 1956.

Crawcour, E. S.: "Changes in Japanese Commerce in the Tokugawa Period," *Journal of Asian Studies,* vol. 22, no. 4, pp. 387–400, 1963.

Honjo, Eijiro: *The Social and Economic History of Japan,* Kyoto, 1935.

Norman, E. Herbert: *Japan's Emergence as a Modern State: Political and Economic Problems of the Meiji Period,* New York, 1940. (See chap. 2, "The Background of the Meiji Restoration.")

Sheldon, Charles D.: *The Rise of the Merchant Class in Tokugawa Japan 1600–1868,* Locust Valley, N.Y., 1958.

Smith, Neil Skene (ed.): *Materials on Japanese Social and Economic History: Tokugawa Japan,* London, 1937.

Smith, Thomas C.: *The Agrarian Origins of Modern Japan,* Stanford, Calif., 1959.

————: *Political Change and Industrial Development in Japan: Government Enterprise, 1868–1880,* Stanford, Calif., 1955. (See chap. 1, "The Beginnings of Modern Industry"; chap. 2, "Political Change and Technological Innovation.")

Spencer, Daniel L.: "Japan's Pre-Perry Preparation for Economic Growth," *American Journal of Economics and Sociology,* vol. 17, pp. 195–216, 1958.

Tsuchiya, Takao: *The Development of Economic Life in Japan,* Tokyo, 1937.

————: *An Economic History of Japan,* as *Transactions of the Asiatic Society of Japan* (2), vol. 15, 1937.

Modernization of Japanese economy

Allen, G. C.: *A Short Economic History of Modern Japan,* rev. ed., London, 1963.

————, and Audrey G. Donnithorne: *Western Enterprise in Far Eastern Economic Development: China and Japan,* New York, 1954.

Bronfenbrenner, Martin: "Some Lessons of Japan's Economic Development, 1853–1938," *Pacific Affairs,* vol. 34, pp. 7–28, 1961.

Chenery, Hollis B., S. Shishido, and T. Watanabe: "The Pattern of Japanese Growth, 1914–1954," *Econometrica,* vol. 30, pp. 98–139, 1962.

Dore, Ronald P.: "Agricultural Improvement in Japan: 1870–1900," *Economic Development and Cultural Change*, vol. 9, no. 1, part II, pp. 69–91, 1960.

Emi, Koichi: *Government Fiscal Activity and Economic Growth in Japan 1868–1960*, Tokyo, 1963.

Hagen, Everitt E.: "How Economic Growth Begins: A General Theory Applied to Japan," *Public Opinion Quarterly*, vol. 22, pp. 373–390, 1958.

Hindmarsh, Albert E.: *The Basis of Japanese Foreign Policy*, Cambridge, Mass., 1936. (Despite the title, this deals primarily with economic matters.)

Hirschmeier, Johannes, S. V. D.: *The Origins of Entrepreneurship in Meiji Japan*, Cambridge, Mass., 1964.

Horie, Yasuzo: "Government Industries in the Early Years of the Meiji Era," *Kyoto University Economic Review*, vol. 14, no. 1, pp. 67–87, 1939.

Japan FAO Association: *A Century of Technical Development in Japanese Agriculture*, Tokyo, 1959.

Johnston, Bruce F.: "Agricultural Productivity and Economic Development in Japan," *Journal of Political Economy*, vol 59, pp. 498–513, 1951.

Kojima, Kiyoshi: "Japanese Foreign Trade and Economic Growth," *Annals of Hitotsubashi Academy*, vol. 8, no. 2, pp. 143–168, 1958.

Kuznets, Simon, and others (eds.): *Economic Growth: Brazil, India, Japan*, Durham, N.C., 1955. (See chap. 5, "The Scale of Economic Growth in Japan, 1868–1938," by William W. Lockwood; chap. 6, "Foreign Capital and Domestic Development in Japan," by Edwin P. Reubens; chap. 10, "Population and Labor Force in the Industrialization of Japan, 1850–1950," by Irene B. Taeuber; chap. 17, "Contrasting Factors in the Modernization of China and Japan," by Marion J. Levy, Jr.; chap. 18, "The State and Economic Enterprise in Modern Japan, 1868–1938," by William W. Lockwood.)

Lockwood, William W.: *The Economic Development of Japan: Growth and Structural Change, 1868–1939*, Princeton, N.J., 1954.

——— (ed.): *The State and Economic Enterprise in Modern Japan*, Princeton, N.J., 1965.

Milbank Memorial Fund: *Modernization Programs in Relation to Human Resources and Population Problems*, New York, 1950. (See sec. III, "Japan as a Case Study in Modernization," including three papers: Edwin P. Reubens, "Foreign Capital in Economic Development: A Case Study of Japan"; Irene B. Taeuber, "Population Increase and Manpower Utilization in Imperial Japan"; Warren S. Thompson, "Future Adjustments of Population to Resources in Japan.")

Moulton, Harold G.: *Japan: An Economic and Financial Appraisal*, Washington, D.C., 1931.

Nelson, Richard: "Growth Models and the Escape from the Low-level Equilibrium Trap: The Case of Japan," *Economic Development and Cultural Change*, vol. 8, no. 4, part 1, pp. 378–388, 1960.

Norman, E. Herbert: *Japan's Emergence as a Modern State: Political and Economic Problems of the Meiji Period*, New York, 1940.

Ohkawa, Kazushi: "Economic Fluctuations in Prewar Japan: A Preliminary Analysis of Cycles and Long Swings," *Hitotsubashi Journal of Economics*, vol. 3, no. 3, pp. 10–33, 1962.

————: *The Growth Rate of the Japanese Economy since 1878,* Tokyo, 1957. (The period covered is 1878–1942.)

————: "The Indigenous Components in the Modern Japanese Economy," *Economic Development and Cultural Change,* vol. 9, no. 3, pp. 471–501, 1961.

————, and Henry Rosovsky: "The Role of Agriculture in Modern Japanese Economic Development," *Economic Development and Cultural Change,* vol. 9, no. 1, part 2, pp. 43–67, 1960.

Patrick, H. T.: "Lessons for Underdeveloped Countries from the Japanese Experience of Economic Development," *Indian Economic Journal,* 1961.

Ranis, Gustav: "The Capital-output Ratio in Japanese Economic Devolpment," *Review of Economic Studies,* vol. 26, no. 1, pp. 23–32, 1960.

————: "The Community-centered Entrepreneur in Japanese Development," *Explorations in Entrepreneurial History,* vol. 8, no. 2, pp. 80–98, 1955.

————: "Factor Proportions in Japanese Economic Development," *American Economic Review,* vol. 47, pp. 594–607, 1957.

————: "Financing of Japanese Economic Development," *Economic History Review* (2), vol. 11, pp. 440–454, 1959.

Rosovsky, Henry: *Capital Formation in Japan,* Glencoe, Ill., 1961.

Smith, Thomas C. (ed.): *City and Village in Japan* as *Economic Development and Cultural Change,* vol. 9, no. 1, part II, 1960.

————: "Old Values and New Techniques in the Modernization of Japan," *Far Eastern Quarterly,* vol. 14, pp. 355–363, 1955.

————: *Political Change and Industrial Development in Japan: Government Enterprise, 1868–1880,* Stanford, Calif., 1955.

Taeuber, Irene B.: *The Population of Japan,* Princeton, N.J., 1958.

Takahashi, Chōtarō: "Capital Accumulation in Early Meiji Era," *Asian Affairs,* vol. 1, pp. 130–148, 1956.

Between depression and military defeat, 1930–1945

Bisson, T. A.: *Japan's War Economy,* New York, 1945.

Cohen, Jerome B.: *Japan's Economy in War and Reconstruction,* Minneapolis, 1949.

Schumpeter, E. B. (ed.): *The Industrialization of Japan and Manchukuo 1930–1940: Population, Raw Materials, and Industry,* New York, 1940.

Tsuru, Shigeto: *Essays on Japanese Economy,* Tokyo, 1958.

Postwar recovery and problems of the future

Abegglen, James C.: *The Japanese Factory: Aspects of Its Social Organization,* Glencoe, Ill., 1958.

Allen, G. C.: *Japan's Economic Recovery,* New York, 1958.

Cohen, Jerome B.: "Japan: Reform vs. Recovery," *Far Eastern Survey,* vol. 17, pp. 137–142, 1948.

————: *Japan's Postwar Economy,* Bloomington, Ind., 1958.

Dore, Ronald P.: *Land Reform in Japan,* London, 1959.

The Economist: *Consider Japan,* London, 1962.

Fine, Sherwood M.: *Japan's Post-war Industrial Recovery*, Tokyo, 1953.

Fujioka, M.: "Appraisal of Japan's Plan to Double Income," *International Monetary Fund Staff Papers*, vol. 10, no. 1, pp. 150–185, 1963.

Hunsberger, Warren S.: *Japan in United States Foreign Economic Policy*, U.S. Congress Joint Economic Committee, Subcommittee on Foreign Economic Policy, Washington, D.C., 1961.

Japan, Economic Planning Agency (formerly Board): *Economic Survey of Japan,* Tokyo, 1955–1956, 1956–1957, 1957–1958, 1958–1959, 1959–1960, 1960–1961, 1961–1962, 1962–1963. (Annual vols.)

———: *New Long-range Economic Plan of Japan*, Tokyo, 1957. (Fiscal years 1958–1962.)

———: *New Long-range Economic Plan of Japan 1961–1970*, Tokyo, 1961.

Japan, Ministry of Finance: *General Survey of the Japanese Economy*, Tokyo, 1957.

Kitamura, Hiroshi: "Long-run Projection of the Japanese Economy: A Critical Evaluation," *Kyklos*, vol. 9, fasc. 2, pp. 135–163, 1956.

Kojima, Kiyoshi: "Economic Development and Import Dependence in Japan," *Hitotsubashi Journal of Economics*, vol. 1, no. 1, pp. 29–51, 1960.

Levine, Solomon B.: *Industrial Relations in Postwar Japan*, Urbana, Ill., 1958.

Ohkawa, Kazushi, and Henry Rosovsky: "Recent Japanese Growth in Historical Perspective," *American Economic Review, Papers and Proceedings*, vol. 53, pp. 578–588, 1963.

Okita, Saburō: "Economic Growth of Postwar Japan," *Developing Economies,* preliminary issue 2, Institute of Asian Economic Affairs, 1962.

———: "Japan's Economic Prospects," *Foreign Affairs*, vol. 39, no. 1, pp. 123–131, 1960.

Olson, Lawrence A.: "Four Family Budgets," *American Universities Field Staff LO-1-59*, Feb. 15, 1959.

Patrick, H. T.: *Monetary Policy and Central Banking in Contemporary Japan,* Bombay, 1962.

Taira, K.: "Characteristics of Japanese Labor Markets," *Economic Development and Cultural Change*, vol. 10, no. 2, part 1, pp. 150–168, 1962.

Umemura, M.: "An Analysis of Employment Structure in Japan," *Hitotsubashi Journal of Economics,* vol. 2, no. 2, pp. 16–29, 1962.

Statistical compilations [6]

Bank of Japan, Statistics Department: *Economic Statistics of Japan (Hompō keizai tōkei)*, Tokyo, 1931—, annually.

Ginsburg, Norton S.: *Atlas of Economic Development*, Chicago, 1961.

Japan, Bureau de la Statistique Générale au Cabinet Impérial: *Résumé statistique de l'empire du Japon (Dai XX-kai Nihon teikoku tōkei tekiyo),* Tokyo, 1885–1940, annually.

[6] Publications with bilingual captions in English or French and Japanese are often catalogued under the Japanese titles; these are shown in parentheses.

Japan, Ministry of Welfare: *Vital Statistics (Jinkō dōtai tōkei)*, Tokyo, 1946—, annually.
Japan, Office of the Prime Minister, Bureau of Statistics: *Japan Statistical Yearbook (Nihon tōkei nenkan)*, Tokyo, 1949—, annually.
——: *Monthly Bulletin of Statistics (Tōkei geppō)*, Tokyo, 1949—, monthly.
——: *Statistical Abstract of Japan (Nihon tōkei nenkan tekiyō-han)*, Tokyo, 1950. (This English title has since appeared on the cover of annual editions of *Kokkai tōkei tekiyō* from 1954, but this publication does not carry English captions in the text.)
United Nations, Statistical Office: *Demographic Yearbook*, New York, 1948—, annually.
——: *Statistical Yearbook*, New York, 1948—, annually.

Supplementary bibliographies

A Bibliography on Economic Sciences Published in Post-war Japan in Western Languages, Japan Science Review Economic Series, no. 3, 1956. (Covers period 1945–1955.)
"Bibliography on Economics Published in Japan in Western Languages 1956–1958," *Annals of the Hitotsubashi Academy*, vol. 10, no. 1, pp. 108–139, 1959.
Rosovsky, Henry, and others (comps.): *Quantitative Japanese Economic History: An Annotated Bibliography and a Survey of U.S. Holdings*, Berkeley, Calif., 1961.